SOVIET ECONOMIC STRUCTURE AND PERFORMANCE

SOVIET ECONOMIC STRUCTURE AND PERFORMANCE

THIRD EDITION

Paul R. Gregory
University of Houston

Robert C. Stuart
Rutgers University

1817

HARPER & ROW, PUBLISHERS, New York
Cambridge, Philadelphia, San Francisco,
London, Mexico City, São Paulo, Sydney

Sponsoring Editor: John Greenman
Project Editor: Steven Pisano
Cover Design: ARCON
Text Art: Fineline, Inc.
Production: Debra Forrest
Compositor: ComCom Division of Haddon Craftsmen, Inc.
Printer and Binder: R. R. Donnelley and Sons Company

SOVIET ECONOMIC STRUCTURE AND PERFORMANCE, Third Edition

Library of Congress Cataloging in Publication Data

Gregory, Paul R.
  Soviet economic structure and performance.

  1. Soviet Union—Economic conditions—1918–
2. Soviet Union—Economic policy—1917–
I. Stuart, Robert C., 1938–   . II. Title.
HC335.G723 1986   330.947′0853   85–31740
ISBN 0–06–043507–5

  87 88 89 9 8 7 6 5 4 3

For Annemarie, Andrei, and Mischa;
Beverly, Andrea, and Craig

CONTENTS

5 The Foundation of the Soviet Planned Economy: Planning, Collectivization, and War (1928–1945)   100

6 The Soviet Economy in the Postwar Era (1950–1985)   128

part two
HOW THE SOVIET ECONOMY OPERATES   153

7 How the Soviet Economy Operates: Planning, Pricing, and Markets   155

PREFACE

The first and second editions of this book were written to describe and evaluate the Soviet economy. Their primary focus was on Soviet organizational arrangements for allocating scarce resources and on how well such arrangements have worked over the years. We found, as have most writers on the Soviet economy, that Soviet organizational arrangements have been remarkably resilient to significant change. The founders of the Soviet planning system in the late 1920s and early 1930s would feel quite at home with the contemporary Soviet economic system. This third edition continues to focus on how and how well the Soviet economic system allocates resources among competing ends.

The most intriguing questions addressed by this new edition are: Can (and will) the Soviet leadership finally embark on a path of significant reform of Soviet planning and management institutions? In 1995, will the system's founders find it as easy to recognize the Soviet economic system as in 1985? Will the Soviet leadership opt for significant reform in the near future? Indeed, can the Soviet leadership afford *not* to alter the status quo?

The growth rate of Soviet GNP and productivity, which has not been healthy since the 1960s, appears to be on a long-term downward trend, while the capitalist economies (after ironing out the effects of the business cycle) have experienced rather stable long-term growth. The American economy enters the second half of the 1980s with rapid growth and falling inflation. Conversely, the Soviet satellites in Eastern Europe, with few exceptions, have shared in declining Soviet economic fortunes. The majority of the Eastern European countries have experienced episodes of negative growth in the late 1970s and early 1980s. The Reagan years have seen a marked buildup in real U.S. defense spending, which has placed added strain on the already burdened Soviet economy. There are few signs that the Soviet Union is overcoming its technological backwardness vis-à-vis the Western world; the Soviet Union remains dependent on the capitalist West for innovations and new technology. Soviet agriculture continues to suffer from weather and organizational problems, and Soviet dependence on massive grain purchases in the world market is now taken for granted. Moreover, the Soviets' military and ideological rivals to the East, the Chinese, have experienced rapid economic growth since their own liberalizing reforms of the post-Mao era. Growing Chinese economic power is not a welcome sign to Soviet leaders trying to deal with their own lagging economy. Falling relative oil prices and gold prices in international markets have taken away the significant windfalls that exogenously boosted Soviet economic performance in the 1970s.

Since the death of Brezhnev, the Soviet leadership has changed hands three times. The Andropov and Chernenko interregnums were years of marking time and waiting for sickly, incapacitated leaders to pass from the scene. The appointment of a young and vigorous leader, Mikhail Gorbachev, appears on the surface to present the Soviet Union with an opportunity to address its long-term problems. The problems are apparent; the solutions are obscure. On the one hand, the

Soviets have the liberalizing example of the Hungarians, who are trying to combine their market and their plan without sacrificing party control. On the other hand, the Soviets have the example of the Chinese, who appear to be reintroducing private ownership back into agriculture. Working against significant reforms are the vested interests of the status quo, and it must be recalled that it was the party bureaucracy that elevated Gorbachev to power. Their interests will be hard to ignore.

The second edition of this book, written in the midst of the Brezhnev years, chose to downplay economic reform. It was clear at the time that the cautious reform attempts of the 1960s had been reversed and that there was little prospect for further reform as long as Brezhnev remained in power. At the present time, it is much too early to predict whether there will be meaningful reform of the Soviet economy over the next five to ten years, but it is nevertheless important to set the stage for any reform that might come. It is our own guess that the Soviet leadership, when all is said and done, will settle for the familiar "muddling through" approach of the past, but experience may prove us wrong. Moreover, significant change may come, but on a piecemeal basis rather than as a formal reform program. In any case, the next several years will definitely be an interesting time to study the Soviet economy.

STRUCTURE OF THE THIRD EDITION

The basic organization of this book remains as originally conceived. Part I deals with the economic history of the Soviet Union. This section has been expanded to cover Soviet economic history after World War II. By carrying events up to the present, we provide the reader with a better perspective of the long sweep of Soviet economic history. The presentation of economic history in a self-contained unit allows us to concentrate on how the contemporary Soviet economy works without need for historical digressions in subsequent chapters. The themes of our discussion of Soviet economic history are: the economic base inherited from the tsarist past; the experiments and debates that led to the choice in the early 1930s of the contemporary system of centralized planning and resource allocation; the Soviet development model, with special emphasis on collectivization of agriculture; and economic performance during the various subperiods of Soviet economic history.

Part II describes the workings of the contemporary Soviet economic system. It focuses on planning arrangements, the allocation of materials, the managerial system, the allocation of capital and labor, and the various informal mechanisms used for allocating resources. The major change from the second edition is the deletion of historical discussion and the resulting exclusive emphasis on current institutional arrangements. In dealing with the Soviet economic system, we attempt (largely through the use of Soviet emigré writings and interviews) to present an account of the actual (as opposed to the textbook) workings of Soviet planning and resource allocation.

Part III analyzes Soviet economic performance up to the mid-1980s. It takes a long-run perspective and examines Soviet growth since 1928, but it does deal with growth performance since 1970 as a setting for the reform discussion. We examine Soviet economic performance both in terms of conventional indicators such as GNP growth, productivity growth, changes in living standards, and income distribution, and in less conventional terms such as assessing Soviet military, scientific, and technological performances.

Part IV focuses on economic reform and prospects for the future. It deals with various reforms and experiments that have been attempted in the past, and it looks at ongoing reform discussions and alternatives. The economic reform discussion in this edition is broader than that in past editions because it considers scientific and educational reform in the overall context of economic reform and change.

Our data and information sources remain primarily the writings of Western and Soviet scholars on the Soviet economic system. U.S. government analysts of the Soviet economy continue to supply valuable statistical series on Soviet economic performance. Recent emigrés from the Soviet Union have supplied valuable insights into the actual workings of the Soviet economic system through their own writings and through interviews with American specialists. The results of three major interview projects with former Soviet citizens that are now beginning to be published shed additional light on the routine workings of the Soviet economy.

ACKNOWLEDGEMENTS

The authors would like to acknowledge and thank a large number of scholars for their direct and indirect participation in this project. In the latter category, Abram Bergson and David Granick must be singled out for their guidance during our years of graduate study, and the Harvard University Russian Research Center must be noted as having provided the intellectual stimulation that played an important role in the project's original conception in 1970. In the direct participation category, thanks are due to Carl McMillan, Franklyn D. Holzman, Holland Hunter, Keith Bush, and H. Peter Gray, all of whom kindly commented on some aspect of the first edition of this study. Valuable suggestions for revision of the first edition were supplied by James Millar, Thomas Wolf, Edward Hewett, Earl Brubaker, Vladimir Treml, Gertrude Schroeder Greenslade, Frank Durgin, Anna Kuniansky, and Susan Linz. A number of scholars provided valuable suggestions that improved the third edition. We would like to acknowledge the assistance of Judith Thornton, Gertrude Schroeder Greenslade, Holland Hunter, Susan Linz, Hugh Neary, Ken Gray, Morris Bornstein, Marvin Jackson, and Fyodor Kushnirsky. For the conception, development, and presentation of this work, the authors bear sole responsibility.

PAUL R. GREGORY
ROBERT C. STUART

chapter 1

The Setting of the Soviet Economy

BACKGROUND

This book is about the Soviet economy, how it is organized, how it functions, and with what results. Western interest in the Soviet economy is long-standing and arises for a number of reasons. Economists are interested in the Soviet economy as representative of centrally planned socialism. Comparisons of Soviet-planned socialism to the market capitalist system with which we are more familiar are of both theoretical and practical interest.

The Soviet Union has, over a relatively short span of years, become a major world power. Thus, on pragmatic grounds, we are interested in the strength of the Soviet economy and its ability to finance a major defense establishment, to expand consumer well-being, to engage in foreign trade, and to modify its system of planning and management of industry and agriculture as it pursues modernization. As a major world power and a political adversary, the Soviet Union as a country and as a political and economic system commands our attention.

Russia became a socialist nation (the USSR, or Union of Soviet Socialist Republics) in 1917 after the Bolshevik revolution led by Vladimir Ilich Lenin.[1] However, the Soviet economic system as we know it today dates from the years 1928–1929, when Joseph Stalin moved forcefully to abolish market allocation and to introduce command planning as a means to coordinate economic activity. Stalin also vigorously pursued collectivization of agriculture, a traumatic transformation of the countryside in which private agriculture was replaced by the collective and state farm systems. By the mid-1930s, the "second Soviet revolution" was essentially complete.

1

These changes introduced by the Soviet leadership were, in part, a response to the events prior to 1928. Earlier Soviet experimentation with combined market and command allocation and private and public ownership convinced the Soviet leadership by the late 1920s that command planning and the collectivization of agriculture offered the best future for the Soviet system. As we examine the enduring economic system introduced at the end of the 1920s, we will be concerned with three broad issues. First, in light of the experiences of the 1920s, why did the Soviet leadership decide to pursue such dramatic change so suddenly? Second, was such dramatic change necessary, or were there less dramatic alternatives available that would have yielded similar or superior results? Third, what has been the outcome of the Soviet resource allocation arrangements put in place some 60 years ago? How well have command planning and socialized agriculture served the Soviet Union in the long run?

To understand Soviet economic growth and development, it is necessary to look both backward and forward. Looking backward from the late 1920s, the Soviet Union was, at the time of the Bolshevik revolution in 1917, a relatively primitive country by the standards of Western Europe and the United States. However, the years following the Emancipation Act of 1861, and especially after the 1880s, witnessed significant economic growth of both industry and agriculture. Moreover, the Russian economy was already moving in the typical directions associated with the early stages of economic development. An important, albeit relatively small, industrial base had already been put in place by the outbreak of World War I, not to mention a rail system that compared favorably with those of its more advanced neighbors. Prior to the Bolshevik revolution Russia was the major European exporter of grain. It is important that we understand these early developments if we are to assess the base upon which later socialist policies would build.

Following the Bolshevik revolution of 1917 and prior to the dramatic changes introduced in 1928, the Soviet Union operated under two very different economic regimes. Between 1917 and 1921, the system of War Communism included nationalization of the means of production; a lessening of monetary incentives as a means to motivate workers; and, possibly most important, forced requisitioning of grain from the peasants. This was a period of civil war and sharp retrogression in both industry and agriculture. Nevertheless, the civil war was won by the Red Army organized by Leon Trotsky, and the power of the new regime was consolidated.

The period of War Communism came to an end with the introduction of the NEP, or New Economic Policy, in 1921. Although the so-called "commanding heights" (major sectors) of industry, transportation, and banking remained nationalized, the market mechanism was reintroduced, money incentives returned, and a more or less orderly tax system and state purchases replaced the forced requisitioning of agricultural products. The 1920s was a period of economic relaxation and modernization so that by 1928 the economy had basically recovered from the losses of earlier years.

The NEP period was one of significant economic progress under a system more or less coordinated by the market mechanism. In light of the consolidation of political power and with economic progress at hand, why did Stalin decide to disrupt the status quo in the late 1920s? The 1920s was a battleground of conflicting ideologies and development strategies advanced by different factions within the Communist Party. It was also a period of relatively open discussion and debate. However, despite the fact that the basic problems of economic development—for example, issues of capital formation, the rural sector, and the role of foreign trade—were all discussed in a lively debate, the participants did not foresee the major institutional changes that would be made by Stalin.

The introduction of a socialist planned economy in the late 1920s was the Soviet leadership's response to the perceived need for rapid industrialization. In addition to the creation of state and collective farms to guide economic activity in rural areas, the economic system put in place by Stalin was characterized by public ownership of the means of production (land and capital) and the allocation of resources by means of a national economic plan, not the market. Both of these features, along with manipulation of the income distribution and the centralization of decision-making would become hallmarks of the Soviet (and later other) socialist economic systems.

It is important to stress that the transformations of the 1930s were of major proportions. The largely consumer-oriented economy of the 1920s was transformed into an industry-oriented economy dominated by heavy industry in particular. Moreover, Stalin clearly viewed the peasants, through their production of grain, as holding the key to future Soviet industrialization. However history may judge this period, the Soviet leadership clearly envisioned the new arrangements in agriculture as providing the means to harness grain production to the needs of rapid industrialization.

In historical perspective, Stalin will be remembered for more than the dramatic events of the late 1920s and early 1930s. In particular, he will be remembered for the draconian measures used in the 1930s to achieve a decade of exceedingly rapid economic growth and structural change in the Soviet Union. These transformations were interrupted by the incredible Soviet human and economic losses of World War II. However, the recovery of the late 1940s restored the economy to prewar levels without the introduction of major new initiatives.

The death of Joseph Stalin in 1953 ushered in a new era. While the political and economic system in place since the late 1920s remained intact, Nikita Khrushchev and the post-Khrushchev leadership presided over a period of relative relaxation and reform. Although the post-Khrushchev years have seen less relaxation, nevertheless, incentives have replaced terror in a relative sense. Over the past 30 years, the Soviet Union has increasingly turned away from the Stalinist mode of economic isolation. Having transformed itself from a primarily agricultural country to an industrial and military world power, it is much more concerned with efficiency and modernization in the 1980s.

Looking at the long span of Soviet economic history, one might well judge the post-Stalin era as a relatively long period of "normal" functioning of the socialist planned economy. Evaluations of Soviet economic performance should focus upon the postwar era for this very reason. Most experts, including the

Soviets themselves, would agree that the postwar era can be divided into two periods of different economic performance. The 1950s and 1960s were eras of generally impressive economic performance when judged by the common performance indicators of the growth of output and productivity. The 1970s and 1980s, however, have been characterized by deteriorating economic performance. Thus, the focus of the Soviet leadership is modernization in both industry and agriculture to stem, if not reverse, the recent record of declining performance.

To understand the strengths and weaknesses of the Soviet economy, we must understand the nature of its economic system. A major focus of this study, therefore, will be the theory and practice of planning as it is carried out in the Soviet Union. Since Soviet planning replaces, in substantial measure, the market as a device for resource allocation, we shall pay attention to how resources are allocated in the contemporary Soviet context. Specifically, we want to know how output is determined, not only in aggregate terms, but also for the major sectors of the economy. In addition, we must examine how major inputs are harnessed to achieve these desired results. Our examination of Soviet planning extends to the major sectors of the economy. Different sectors are subject to different problems and are seldom handled in identical fashion by Soviet planners. Thus, in addition to our examination of traditional sectors such as industry, agriculture, and foreign trade, we shall also examine labor markets and investment choice.

Clearly, a major focus of this study must be the long-term performance of the Soviet economy. But it is also important to consider to what degree and for what reasons Soviet economic performance may have varied from one period to another. Moreover, Soviet economic performance can only be judged relative to the performance of other economies. Therefore, our major question is: How well has the Soviet economy performed relative to the capitalist West?

THE SOVIET NATURAL SETTING

The Soviet economic system organizes the economic activity of a very large, wealthy, and diverse nation.[2] While the focus of this book is the economic system, it is important to realize that our analysis and assessment of the economic system cannot be readily isolated from its setting, influenced by national, human, political, ideological, cultural, and historical factors.

In terms of land area, the Soviet Union is almost three times the size of the United States (excluding Alaska and Hawaii), with a land area of approximately 8.6 million square miles. The Soviet Union has a population of over 270 million, 65 percent of whom live in urban areas. This compares to a United States population of over 230 million, 78 percent of whom live in urban areas.

The Soviet Union is a northerly country, with significant regional variations in resources, climate, topography, and population settlement. In the most general terms, the Soviet Union can be divided into three major regions. The bulk of the Soviet population and economic activity (see Fig. 1) is located in the first major

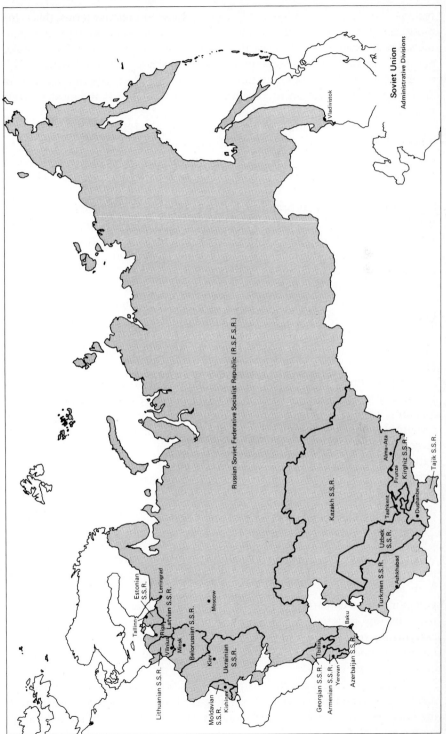

Figure 1 Administrative divisions of the Soviet Union.

region—the plains of the West and European Russia. In relative terms, this is the most densely populated region of the USSR. As one moves east, the Ural mountains, a major source of mineral wealth and hence economic activity, form a major barrier to the vast and sometimes inhospitable expanses of Siberia. Siberia is itself a vast region with substantial natural resources, in effect, the frontier area of Soviet economic development. The area east of the Urals is the most sparsely populated major region of the USSR.

As one moves south, a third major region, Central Asia, is a warm but mostly dry region. This part of the Soviet Union is less developed from an economic standpoint, and it is predominantly Moslem in ethnic composition. It has the most rapidly growing population of the USSR due to its relatively high birthrates.

In terms of natural resources broadly defined, the Soviet Union is a very wealthy nation. Although natural conditions (inadequate warmth, inappropriate moisture, permanently frozen subsoil) constrain Soviet agriculture, the country nevertheless has a substantial endowment of good agricultural land. Possibly the best known agricultural land is the black earth zone in West Central Russia. Although agricultural activity is spread over many areas of the Soviet Union, many parts of the country, while able to grow crops and raise animals, must nevertheless overcome natural disadvantages, thus making agricultural activity in those areas expensive. Whether it is irrigation in the south or drainage in the north, these natural limits are important in assessing Soviet agricultural performance.

Soviet timber reserves are vast, among the best in the world. It is difficult to name a mineral or fuel that the Soviet Union does not have in significant amounts, whether it be coal, iron ore, natural gas, or oil. This extensive natural resource base means that, in practice, the Soviet Union can be (and has been) largely self-sufficient in raw materials. However, as a recent major study of Soviet natural resources concludes, this is only part of the story. Whether judged in terms of domestic needs or, more broadly, with regard to participation in the international economy, the exploitation of Soviet natural resources presents a major challenge. Consider two important dimensions of this challenge. First, the bulk of Soviet natural wealth is located in areas of inhospitable natural conditions. The bulk of new raw materials is located in Siberia with inherent climate and transportation problems. The regional distribution of natural resources plays a major role. Soviet oil from Siberia is a much higher-cost oil than that delivered from the traditional but waning fields of the Caspian Sea. Second, as the Soviet Union increases its participation in international markets, its exports are dominated by raw materials, a pattern more typical of less developed nations and carrying the risks inherent in volatile world raw material markets. Undoubtedly, the Soviet Union would like to modernize its export sector to reduce its reliance on raw material exports.

Natural wealth is an obvious plus for the Soviet Union, and the management of this wealth under socialist planning is a distinct, important, and interesting issue. Has the Soviet planned economy exploited effectively the natural resource wealth of the Soviet Union?

SOVIET REGIONAL DIVERSITY

Our discussion of the Soviet Union of necessity has already touched upon regional differences.[3] Regional differences are a continuous thread in this book. How can we coordinate our thinking about Soviet resource allocation such that the regional dimension is included?

Soviet regional diversity can be characterized in differing ways. Indeed, we have already simplified our overall picture of the Soviet Union by looking at a tripartite regional classification. Possibly the most important classification (especially from the point of view of data availability) is the administrative/political subdivision of the Soviet Union.

The Soviet Union is divided into 15 union republics. Below the level of these republics, the administrative/political units are called provinces (the *oblast'*), and finally, at the lowest level, the districts *(raion)* and/or city *(gorod)*. In fact, the Soviet political/administrative apparatus is somewhat more complex than this simple description suggests. However, if we look briefly at Table 1, the importance of these administrative subdivisions for an understanding of Soviet regional differences is apparent.

Soviet republics vary significantly in many dimensions. An examination of

Table 1   THE SOVIET UNION: SELECTED REGIONAL INDICATORS

	Population			Per capita nominal income (1978: USSR = 100)	Per capita fixed capital (1975: USSR = 100)
	In millions, 1980	Percent urban	Percent Russian		
USSR	264.5	63	52.3	100.0	100
RSFSR	138.4	70	82.5	110.9	115
Ukraine	49.9	62	21.0	95.9	90
Belorussia	9.6	56	11.9	97.9	80
Moldavia	3.9	40	12.8	89.9	69
Kazakhstan	14.8	54	40.8	88.4	102
Transcaucasia					
Georgia	5.0	52	7.4	93.6	75
Azerbaidzhan	6.1	53	7.8	63.6	64
Armenia	3.0	66	2.3	86.7	73
Central Asia					
Uzbekistan	15.7	41	10.8	71.6	54
Kirgizstan	3.5	39	25.8	69.7	60
Tadzhikistan	3.9	35	10.3	59.9	51
Turkmenistan	2.8	48	12.6	75.1	73
Baltic					
Estonia	1.4	70	27.9	126.9	137
Latvia	2.5	69	32.8	113.7	117
Lithuania	3.4	62	8.9	115.1	101

Sources: Population data are from *Narodnoe Khoziaistvo SSSR v 1979 g.* [The national economy of the USSR in 1979] (Moscow: Statistika, 1980), p. 10; *Chislennost' i sostav naseleniia SSSR* [The number and composition of the population of the USSR] (Moscow: Finansy i statistika, 1984), Tables 13–35; per capita income data from G. E. Schroeder, "Regional Living Standards," in I. S. Koropeckyi and G. E. Schroeder, eds., *Economics of Soviet Regions* (New York: Praeger, 1981), p. 120; capital stock data from J. W. Gillula, "The Growth and Structure of Fixed Capital," in I. S. Koropeckyi and G. E. Schroeder, eds., *Economics of Soviet Regions,* p. 160.

population data indicates that they differ greatly in size. The Russian Republic (formally the RSFSR, or Russian Soviet Federated Socialist Republic) is by far the largest, representing just over 52 percent of the total Soviet population according to the 1979 census. The next largest republic by this measure is the Ukraine, representing just over 14 percent of the Soviet population. The remaining republics account for 34 percent of the USSR population and are substantially smaller.

Soviet regional diversity is also reflected in the ethnic composition of the population. While the Russian population accounts for slightly over half of the Soviet population, its share is declining. According to the 1959 Soviet census, the Russian population represented 54.6 percent of the aggregate Soviet population. This number had declined to 52.4 percent in the most recent (1979) census. Moreover, the Russian population is unevenly distributed throughout the country, ranging from over 82 percent of the population in the Russian Republic to a very small 2 percent in Armenia. Although issues relating to the ethnic composition of the Soviet population would take us beyond the central issues of this book, they are nevertheless important to an understanding of the Soviet people as both producers and as consumers.

Urbanization is another important aspect of Soviet regional development.[4] To appreciate the magnitude of the Soviet urban transformation, it is important for the reader to know that in 1926, just before the beginning of the Stalinist industrialization drive, just 18 percent of the Soviet population was classified as urban. By 1979, in the most recent census, fully 62 percent of the population was classified as urban. Through both natural urban growth and migration from rural to urban areas, Soviet urban growth has been rapid over the past half-century. Although the share of population remaining in the countryside remains high for a country that has attained significant economic development, we must treat contemporary Soviet society as an urban-based society, understanding both the problems and the prospects that this raises for the planned socialist economic system.

In our brief discussion of the Soviet natural resource endowment we touched on its widely varied regional distribution, a factor intertwined with the resulting location of economic activity and population centers. It is also evident that the outcome of Soviet economic activity varies regionally.

Although it has long been Soviet policy to decrease regional differentials in the level of living, the evidence in Table 1 suggests that substantial differentials remain. In the late 1970s, per capita nominal income varied from a high of 126.9 in Estonia (USSR average = 100) to a low of 59.9 in Tadzhikistan. Data for the two most populous republics show that RSFSR per capita income is 11 percent above the USSR average and that the Ukraine per capita income was 4 percent below the USSR average. These differences reflect more generally the differences in regional well-being—the Baltic republics are by far the wealthiest, the Central Asian republics are the poorest.

A similar conclusion emerges if we examine the distribution of fixed capital. As the last column of Table 1 indicates, the RSFSR is more abundantly endowed with fixed capital than the Ukraine. The republic richest in fixed capital per person is Estonia, and the poorest republic is Tadzhikistan in Central Asia. The distribution of fixed capital reflects roughly the distribution of economic activity in the USSR.

We turn now to a matter closely related to the nature of the Soviet economic system, namely, the nature of Soviet political and administrative institutions and their impact upon economic policy formulation and execution.

POLITICAL INSTITUTIONS AND CONTROL OF THE ECONOMY[5]

In the Soviet Union, the crucial economic decisions—the allocation of output among consumption, investment, and defense, and the rates of expansion of different sectors—are made administratively, not by the market. Whereas in the United States about one-quarter of the GNP is allocated by administrative decisions through the public sector, in the Soviet Union almost all output is allocated administratively.* In this manner, *planners' preferences* supplant *consumer sovereignty* by taking resource allocation out of the hands of the market and placing it under the control of an administrative apparatus.† In this section, we consider the political apparatus, the planning apparatus, and the intertwining of the two.

Nominally, the Soviet Union is governed by an elected government that is subject to the Soviet constitution. The highest organ of the state is the *Supreme Soviet,* which is comprised of directly elected deputies. Because the Supreme Soviet meets infrequently (and then only to ratify automatically decisions of the party), the *presidium* appointed by the Supreme Soviet carries on the work of the Supreme Soviet between sessions. The *Council of Ministers* is the government bureaucracy of the USSR and is elected by the Supreme Soviet. The Soviet Union is a republic, composed of 15 union republics, and each union republic has a state apparatus that parallels the national apparatus. Beneath the union, republican governments are the provincial *(oblast')* governments, the local *(raion)* governments, and the city *(gorod)* governments.

Parallel to the state apparatus is the Communist Party of the Soviet Union (CPSU).[6] The supreme authority over the party organization is exercised nominally by the Party Congress, made up of delegates from all levels of the party hierarchy. Party congresses are held only at infrequent intervals, and they serve to elect (often perfunctorily) the *Central Committee* of the CPSU, which in turn

---

*This assertion should be interpreted with caution. While the dominant mechanism for Soviet resource allocation is the *plan,* the reader should be aware that the plan cannot be pervasive in all facets of resource allocation. As one considers how the economic system handles less important products and services or local needs, less formal arrangements or even those of the "second economy" can be important.

†By a system of *planners' preferences,* we mean a mechanism for guiding the economic system so that the decisions as to what to produce, how to produce, and who gets the output are made by central planners rather than by the dollar (and political) votes of consumers in the marketplace. Although theoretically under such a system planners may take full account of consumers' wishes, historically this has not typically been the case in the Soviet Union.

appoints the *Politburo*—the most important policy-setting body in the Soviet Union.

At the republican, regional, and local levels, departments of the CPSU duplicate the various state agencies; thus, for each state agency there is a parallel party branch. The CPSU has committees at the province, or *oblast'* level *(obkom)*, the regional, or *raion,* level *(raikom)*, and the city level *(gorkom)*. The first secretary of each of these party committees exercises considerable control in that area. At the enterprise level, a party cell supervises enterprise operations. In large enterprises, the head of the party cell tends to be a full-time party employee. In small enterprises, the job tends to be a part-time activity. Unlike the state apparatus, where lines of authority generally run from the local to the provincial to the republican to the national level, all lines in the party apparatus run directly to Moscow, suggesting a significant centralization of power.

One of the principal functions of all branches of the CPSU is the control and supervision of the economy. This control is exercised in several ways. Many branches of government report directly to the party. The State Planning Committee, for example, reports directly to the Politburo of the CPSU. At lower levels, building projects are first submitted to the party (to the *obkom* or *gorkom,* for example) before being submitted to the appropriate government office. Typically, a party committee will sign off completed construction projects. At the enterprise level, the party organization serves two functions—one, to mobilize the workers to fulfill the plan (often through the enterprise trade union that the party dominates), and the other, to check on the enterprise manager. These are just isolated examples of party supervision.

Perhaps the most potent tool used by the CPSU to influence the economy is the *nomenklatura* system.[7] The *nomenklatura* is a comprehensive list of appointments that are controlled by the party. It is the party that nominates individuals for all important posts in the CPSU, state, industry, and army. At the national level, the Central Committee Cadres Department exercises this function. Party control over *nomenklatura* is crucial insofar as it is party nominees who run for elective office and become enterprise directors and farm managers. It is not surprising to find that while roughly 10 percent of the Soviet population belongs to the CPSU, very few agricultural or industrial managers are not members of the party.

The dominant role of the Communist Party in the Soviet Union is envisioned in Article 6 of the Soviet Constitution:

> The leading and guiding force of Soviet society and the nucleus of its political system, of all state organizations, is the Communist Party of the Soviet Union.[8]

The military also carries out control activities over economic units. In enterprises that produce for the military, an autonomous military representative (the *Voenpred*) is responsible for signing off on military goods. Large enterprises may have a permanent military representative assigned to them. Smaller enterprises are supervised by a military representative responsible for several factories. Enterprises that produce both civilian and military production have their production broken down into a "first department" *(pervy otdel)* and civilian production. The planning and supply of the first department tends to be handled directly by the Ministry of Defense, while the civilian department is handled by the planning apparatus described below.

THE PLANNING APPARATUS

We turn now from party and military control to the state apparatus to consider the planning and organization of the economy. Throughout most of the plan period (1928 to present), the Soviet economy has operated under a ministerial system in which individual enterprises belonging to a particular branch of the economy (aviation, chemicals, metallurgy, etc.) are subordinated to a single ministry. There are three types of ministries: The *all-union ministry* runs the enterprises under its control directly from Moscow, and its enterprises are not answerable to regional authorities. The *union-republican ministry* has offices both in Moscow and in the various republics, and the enterprises under its control are subject to the dual authority of Moscow and the republican Councils of Ministers. The *republican ministry* directs enterprises within the republic and has no direct superior in Moscow. In recent years, republican ministries have been limited primarily to directing enterprises that produce for the local economy. The heads of these ministries are members of the Council of Ministries of the USSR and of the republican Councils of Ministers, respectively.

The ministerial system was introduced in 1932. Initially, three ministries were created—for the heavy, light, and timber industries. Since then, the number has fluctuated from a high of 32 in the late Stalin years, to 11 immediately after Stalin's death, to around 40 in the late 1960s. In 1982, there were 64 ministries, not counting other agencies with ministerial status. The ministries possess considerable power: they control a network of productive enterprises and have tended to develop their own supply and disposal agencies.

A recent organization chart of the Soviet economic-administrative structure is provided in Figures 2 and 3 to illustrate the organization of the Soviet economy according to its ministerial system. The ministries are comprised of summary departments (such as finance and pricing departments) and of chief administrations *(glavks)*. The chief administrations are responsible for enterprises producing specific product lines. For example, one chief administration in the construction materials ministry is in charge of metal pipes; another is in charge of cements, and so on. The functional departments implement general plans (such as the ministry's profit and cost plan or the balance plan for the distribution of equipment) that transcend the boundaries of the functional chief administrations. From the perspective of the enterprise, day-to-day control is carried out by the responsible chief administration.

There are a number of state committees and other agencies whose job it is to coordinate activities among ministries on an economywide basis. The most important state committee is the State Planning Commission, or *Gosplan.* Gosplan, which was established in 1921, is responsible for drawing up national

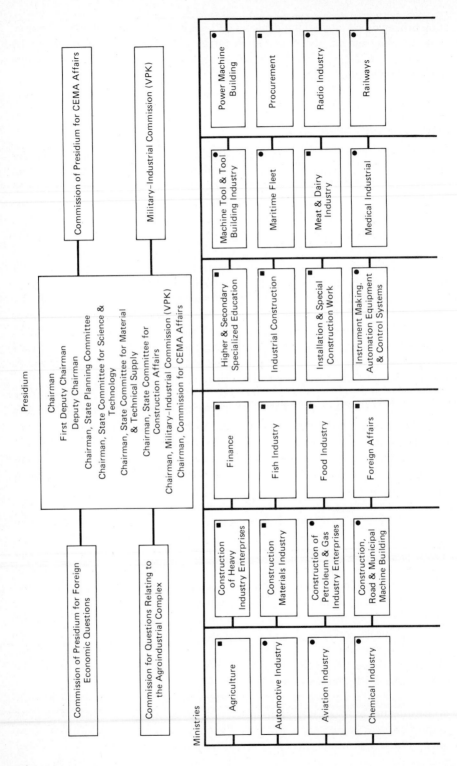

Presidium

Commission of Presidium for Foreign Economic Questions

Commission for Questions Relating to the Agroindustrial Complex

Chairman
First Deputy Chairman
Deputy Chairman
Chairman, State Planning Committee
Chairman, State Committee for Science & Technology
Chairman, State Committee for Material & Technical Supply
Chairman, State Committee for Construction Affairs
Chairman, Military–Industrial Commission (VPK)
Chairman, Commission for CEMA Affairs

Commission of Presidium for CEMA Affairs

Military–Industrial Commission (VPK)

Ministries

Agriculture
Automotive Industry
Aviation Industry
Chemical Industry

Construction of Heavy Industry Enterprises
Construction Materials Industry
Construction of Petroleum & Gas Industry Enterprises
Construction, Road & Municipal Machine Building

Finance
Fish Industry
Food Industry
Foreign Affairs

Higher & Secondary Specialized Education
Industrial Construction
Installation & Special Construction Work
Instrument Making, Automation Equipment & Control Systems

Machine Tool & Tool Building Industry
Maritime Fleet
Meat & Dairy Industry
Medical Industrial

Power Machine Building
Procurement
Radio Industry
Railways

12

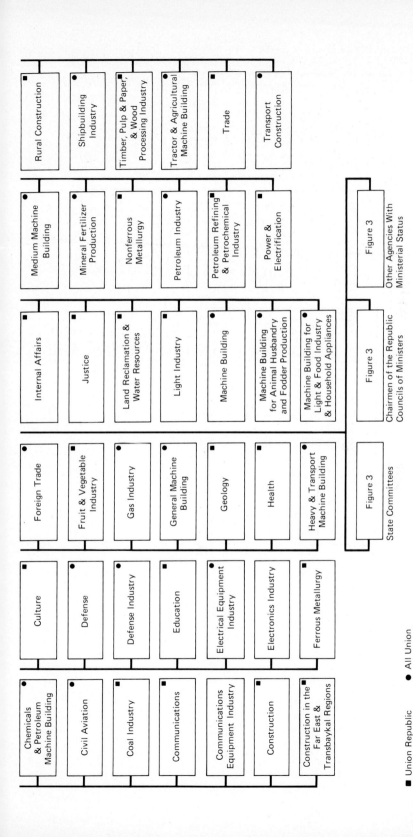

■ Union Republic   ● All Union

Union Republic organizations operate locally through corresponding organizations on the republic level. All union organizations have no such regional counterparts.

Figure 2 The USSR Council of Ministers: Ministries. [*Source:* Paul K. Cook, "The Political Setting," in U.S. Congress Joint Economic Committee, *The Soviet Economy in the 1980s: Problems and Prospects.* (Washington, D.C.: U.S. Government Printing Office, 1982), pp. 19-20.]

13

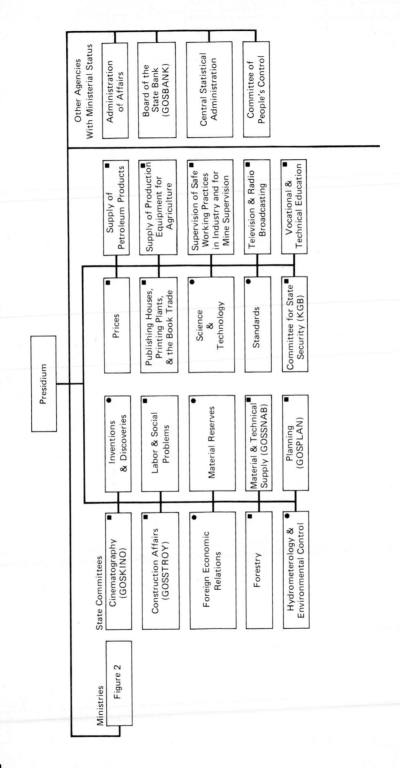

Figure 2

Presidium

Ministries

State Committees

Cinematography (GOSKINO)

Construction Affairs (GOSSTROY)

Foreign Economic Relations

Forestry

Hydrometerology & Environmental Control

Inventions & Discoveries

Labor & Social Problems

Material Reserves

Material & Technical Supply (GOSSNAB)

Planning (GOSPLAN)

Prices

Publishing Houses, Printing Plants, & the Book Trade

Science & Technology

Standards

Committee for State Security (KGB)

Supply of Petroleum Products

Supply of Production Equipment for Agriculture

Supervision of Safe Working Practices in Industry and for Mine Supervision

Television & Radio Broadcasting

Vocational & Technical Education

Other Agencies With Ministerial Status

Administration of Affairs

Board of the State Bank (GOSBANK)

Central Statistical Administration

Committee of People's Control

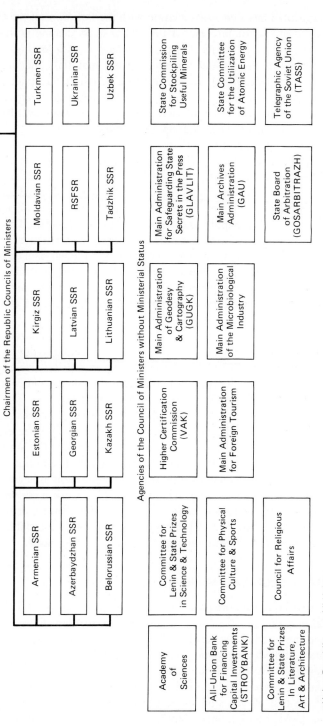

Chairmen of the Republic Councils of Ministers

Armenian SSR	Estonian SSR	Kirgiz SSR	Moldavian SSR	Turkmen SSR
Azerbaydzhan SSR	Georgian SSR	Latvian SSR	RSFSR	Ukrainian SSR
Belorussian SSR	Kazakh SSR	Lithuanian SSR	Tadzhik SSR	Uzbek SSR

Agencies of the Council of Ministers without Ministerial Status

Academy of Sciences	Committee for Lenin & State Prizes in Science & Technology	Higher Certification Commission (VAK)	Main Administration of Geodesy & Cartography (GUGK)	Main Administration for Safeguarding State Secrets in the Press (GLAVLIT)	State Commission for Stockpiling Useful Minerals
All-Union Bank for Financing Capital Investments (STROYBANK)	Committee for Physical Culture & Sports	Main Administration for Foreign Tourism	Main Administration of the Microbiological Industry	Main Archives Administration (GAU)	State Committee for the Utilization of Atomic Energy
Committee for Lenin & State Prizes In Literature, Art & Architecture	Council for Religious Affairs			State Board of Arbitration (GOSARBITRAZH)	Telegraphic Agency of the Soviet Union (TASS)

■ Union Republic   ● All Union

Union Republic organizations operate locally through corresponding organizations on the republic level. All union organizations have no such regional counterparts.

Figure 3 The USSR Council of Ministers: State committees and other agencies. [*Source:* Paul K. Cook, "The Political Setting," in U.S. Congress Joint Economic Committee, *The Soviet Economy in the 1980s: Problems and Prospects* (Washington, D.C.: U.S. Government Printing Office, 1982), p.21.]

economic plans. Gosplan has a close association with the Politburo of the CPSU and is seen as representing the interests of the CPSU in its dealing with other organizations in the Soviet economy. Gosplan is charged with setting output targets for the various ministries and for working out materials and financial balances at the economywide level. In its planning activities, Gosplan works together with the ministries. Gosplan hands down the aggregate targets and approves resource "limits" for the ministries. The ministries work out the finer details of the plan and allocate tasks among enterprises.

There are other state committees that deal with economywide issues. The State Bank *(Gosbank)* monitors enterprise bank accounts and provides working capital credits. The Central Statistical Administration collects economic statistics and monitors plan fulfillment. The State Committee for Material and Technical Supply *(Gossnab)* works out the detailed material supply plans and allocations based upon the more general supply and delivery plans of Gosplan. The State Committee for Construction Affairs *(Gosstroi)* coordinates construction activity for the entire economy. Although the task of coordinating the national economy is shared by a number of state committees and other agencies, it is clear that Gosplan is the dominant planning organ in the Soviet economy. Our later discussion of Soviet economic planning focuses primarily upon the planning activities of Gosplan.

The productive enterprises *(predpriiatie)* occupy the lowest level in the planning hierarchy. They are distinct economic entities operating under an independent accounting system (called *khozrashchet*). Soviet enterprises are supposed to cover their costs from their sales revenue and to earn a planned profit, a portion of which is turned over to the state in the form of a profit tax.

Since 1973, intermediate bodies, called industrial associations (or *obedineniia*), occupy an intermediate managerial position between the enterprises and the ministry. The industrial associations were created through the horizontal or vertical merger of enterprises working in related activities. The notion behind the formation of industrial associations was to improve the economic coordination of the economy by having the ministries and Gosplan work more with the management of industrial associations than with the individual enterprises. Routine operations were to be dealt with by the management of the industrial associations, freeing higher bodies to handle more aggregate planning tasks.

ASSESSING SOVIET ECONOMIC ACHIEVEMENTS

Russia became a socialist economy with the October Revolution of 1917 and instituted central planning in 1928 under the first Five Year Plan. Thus, we have a sufficiently long time period for viewing the Soviet system in perspective. Yet unbiased evaluation of Soviet economic performance is difficult, since many in the West are unsympathetic to the Soviet political system. Nevertheless, amidst a degree of contention, there is substantial agreement concerning the following achievements of the first 65 years of Soviet government.

Possibly the most notable achievement from the Soviet viewpoint is a political one—the expansion of communism. The magnitude of this achievement becomes evident when one compares the tenuous control exercised by the Bolshevik regime over the former Russian Empire in 1918—encircled by unfriendly capitalist countries and plagued by civil war, foreign intervention, and a shaky economy—with the current situation in which roughly one-third of the world's population lives under some form of communism. The Soviet Union is no longer encircled by unfriendly capitalist countries; rather, it has fashioned a bloc of (sometimes reluctant) socialist allies in Eastern Europe to act as buffers between itself and the capitalist world. The limits to the expansion of the communist system remain to be determined and will depend upon the course of Eurocommunism in Western Europe, the Soviets' willingness to use military force in the Third World, and the attraction of the communist system to developing countries. Ironically, a major political threat to the Soviet Union—The People's Republic of China—comes from within the socialist world.

Second, the Soviet command economy has failed to succumb to alleged internal contradictions after more than a half-century of operation, though at one time some prominent Western economists saw such a result as inevitable. We use the term "command economy" to indicate that resource allocation basically proceeds according to administrative orders rather than to market signals. The long-run ability of the Soviet system to function without private ownership of the factors of production and without profit motivation is no longer seriously questioned. The Soviet Union has established itself as the world's second largest economic power (the magnitude of which Table 2 readily demonstrates), and it would now be foolish to question its economic viability. Instead, the performance of the Soviet command economy relative to market economies is now the subject of contention, surely a lesser question than whether the system can operate at all.

Third, the speed with which the Soviet Union transformed itself from relative economic backwardness into industrial and military strength must be listed as a major achievement. Russia in 1917 was predominantly agricultural, with high mortality rates, especially among infants. Nearly 60 percent of the population was illiterate. The industrial sector's shares of output and labor force were quite small, and the domestic machinery sector was poorly developed, requiring heavy dependence upon the capitalist world for capital equipment. By 1937, most of the indicators had been reversed; the USSR had been transformed into an industrial economy without reliance upon foreign aid or extensive imports from the West (with the exception of industrial technology). Both during and after the period of rapid industrialization, Soviet GNP grew at high rates by international standards, all but declining in recent years. Commenting on the speed of Soviet industrialization in the 1930s, Simon Kuznets, a Nobel laureate scholar of modern economic growth, writes:

> As in all countries, economic growth in the USSR meant a decline in the shares of national product originating in, and labor force attached to, the A [agriculture] sector. But the rapidity of this shift was far greater in the USSR than in the other

Table 2 ECONOMIC INDICATORS—USSR AND USA COMPARISONS, 1983

	USSR	USA
GNP (billion 1983 U.S. $)	1,843	3,311
Population, midyear (million persons)	273	235
Per capita GNP (1983 U.S. $)	6,765	14,120
Grains (million metric tons)	195	208.5
Milk (million metric tons)	96.4	63.5
Potatoes (million metric tons)	83	14.8
Meat (million metric tons)	16	25
Crude oil (thousand barrels per day)	11,864	8,680
Natural gas (trillion cubic feet)	18.9	16.6
Electric power (billion kilowatt-hours)	1,416.4	2,459.2
Coal (million metric tons)	486	658.9
Primary energy production (million barrels per day of oil equivalent)	29.2	30.8
Crude steel (million metric tons)	153	75.6
Cement (million metric tons)	128	63.9
Aluminum (thousand metric tons)	2,795	3,353
Refined copper (thousand metric tons)	1,540	1,613
Iron ore (million metric tons)	245	38.6
Plastics (million metric tons)	4.4	14
Bauxite (thousand metric tons)	8,900	662
Tractors (thousands)	564	91.6
Automobiles (million units)	1.3	6.7
Trucks, including buses (million units)	0.9	3.7
Refrigerators in use (per thousand persons)[a]	268	349
Washing machines in use (per thousand persons)	205	260
Gold production (million troy ounces)	10.7	1.6

Source: National Foreign Assessment Center, *Handbook of Economic Statistics,* 1984, CPAS84-10002, U.S. Government Printing Office, September 1984.
[a] 1982

developed countries . . . the shift of labor force out of agriculture of the magnitude that occurred in the USSR in the 12 years from 1928 to 1940 took from 30 to 50 years in other countries . . . and the same was true of the decline in the share of the A sector in national product. A comparable shift took from 50 to 60 years in most other countries.[9]

Fourth, by devoting a larger share of resources to defense than do the United States and Western Europe, the Soviets have produced a defense capability equivalent or superior to that of the United States. Over the past decade, the Soviet Union has outspent the United States by substantial amounts both in the aggregate and in the important areas of strategic and general-purpose forces.[10] Thus, the Soviets have been able to achieve military parity (or even superiority) vis-à-vis the United States and Western Europe, utilizing an economic base 55 percent that of the United States and 33 percent that of the North Atlantic Treaty Organization (NATO) countries combined.[11]

On the other hand, the weaknesses exhibited by the Soviet economic system are equally well-known and are not seriously contested: the Soviet economy's inability to provide consistent increases in living standards, especially during the initial Five Year Plan periods, and its inability to produce an assortment of consumer items corresponding to the demands of the population for quantity and quality are serious problems. Second, in terms of absolute economic efficiency, the Soviets have tended to generate less output per unit of input, by their own admission, than the American and most Western European economies. This relative economic inefficiency has become more bothersome with the slackening pace of population and labor force growth, rising defense spending, and the growing reluctance of Soviet consumers to accept low-quality merchandise. Various attempts to solve the problems of consumer supply and industrial inefficiency through experiments and reform have not proved successful. Third, Soviet economic successes have often been achieved at the cost of human life, political freedom, and material deprivation, making an overall evaluation of the system extremely difficult. The most immediate cost of rapid industrialization was the establishment of dictatorial control over the population in order to implement the extreme austerity of the first Five Year Plan.

Also, the agricultural sector has thus far failed to be an adequate and reliable supplier of meat and vegetable products. In addition, the output of the major grain crops is still subject to large annual fluctuations, and the regime has been forced to negotiate long-term agreements to import substantial amounts of grain from the West. While these imports do not necessarily prove the failure of Soviet agriculture (most industrialized countries import food products), they are nevertheless a disappointment to a Soviet leadership that has devoted considerable resources to improve agricultural performance. The increased reliance on the West for basic food supplies and the periodic shortages of food staples in a large country with a high concentration of employment in agriculture point dramatically to the Soviet Union's unresolved agricultural problem.

The inability of the Soviet economy to reverse the decline in the rate of economic growth that became evident in the early 1960s must be cited as a final weakness. Although Soviet growth remains respectable by international standards, it has fallen below that of some fast-growing capitalist countries (Japan, West Germany) in the postwar era. (In the 1980s, Soviet economic growth has been near the average growth rate of the major capitalist countries.) To a country that has long cited rapid growth as a sign of the superiority of the communist system, the lagging rate of growth must be a serious disappointment.

THE ROLE OF VALUE JUDGMENTS

Discussions about the Soviet economy inevitably turn to value considerations: Is a predominately private enterprise economy, such as we have in the United States and much of Western Europe, somehow superior or inferior to the Soviet economy? Although the question is legitimate, we maintain that the answer must ultimately reflect subjective individual biases (personal value judgments) and cannot rest on objective grounds.

The question of the ends or goals of a society serves as an illustration. It is generally assumed that the economic goal of a private enterprise society is the satisfaction of consumer wants concerning the production and distribution of goods and services. In other words, consumer satisfaction is the end of such an economy, and *consumer sovereignty* is said to prevail. As a general rule, if the demand for a particular product increases, more of that commodity will be produced, probably at a slightly higher price. The important point is that consumers (assuming a given set of supply relationships) determine the output mix of the economy by exerting effective demand in the marketplace. This pure case must be modified, however, to be applied to real market economies. Governments, through their monetary and fiscal powers, can alter both the current output mix and the distribution of present output between current consumption and investment, just as advertising can, to some extent, mold consumer preferences directly.

The ends of society in a centrally planned socialist economy are generally pictured quite differently. The goal of such a society is said to be the satisfaction of *planners' preferences.* A central plan, which administratively determines the current output mix and then distributes it between current consumption and investment, substitutes planners' preferences for consumers' preferences. This does not necessarily mean that consumer desires will be wholly neglected. In fact, it is theoretically possible for the planning agency to plan output to fit consumers' preferences by employing a complex market research network. In practice, however, there generally has been a dichotomy between consumers' and planners' preferences. In fact, a basic rationale for the planners' preferences system is that it enables the planners to do as they, not the consumers, see fit.

Can we judge the superiority of one economic system over the other on the basis of the goals of the two societies? The answer, we think, is no—for to do so would require a weighting system that could gauge the relative importance of the goals of each so that the aggregate achievement of one society could be compared with that of the other society. Pure objectivity in either direction is impossible, because the weighting itself implies an existing preference for one set of goals over the other. Insofar as value judgments differ among individuals, there is no scientific or objective basis for such a conclusion.

Using strictly economic criteria, the superiority of one economic system over another can only be demonstrated when one or more individuals feel themselves "better off" and no one feels "worse off" under the one system relative to their perceptions of their own welfare under the other system. But such cases are not likely to be found in the real world.[12] One might argue that the Soviet system involves a reduction in current welfare since Soviet planners have generally opted for high investment and low consumption ratios; therefore, the private enterprise system provides higher levels of welfare and is thus superior. The Soviets could reply to this contention that the welfare of future generations has been enhanced as a result of their investment policy and that their system is superior. The whole argument would then hinge on whose welfare should be valued more highly: the welfare of the present generation or of future generations—which again would involve a value judgment.

An alternative approach would be to evaluate economies according to whether they derive maximum output from their limited resources. To do so would be to judge an economic system solely on the basis of its *technical efficiency*—with the goals of the society accepted as givens.* Even this criterion can be objected to on the grounds that a technically efficient economy producing that mix of output designated either by planners or consumers can have an extremely "poor" distribution of income among the members of society and is therefore "inferior" to a less efficient economy having a "better" distribution of income. This, of course, brings us back to close the circle—in that "better" or "inferior" distributions of income can only be determined by specific value judgments.

We are not suggesting that value judgments should not be made in comparing economic systems; rather, we are pointing out that such judgments must be made with the explicit understanding that they *are* value judgments and should be treated as such. For example, the substitution of planners' for consumers' preferences in the USSR was accomplished by imposing a dictatorship that subjected the Soviet population to considerable suffering and discomfort during the 1930s. Moreover, democratic political principles—defined in the Western sense of the word—remain foreign to the modern Soviet system. Any reader might find these facts personally objectionable. Nevertheless, such an objection rests upon personal value judgments, and it should be recognized that others (Soviet planners, for example) may subjectively argue that dictatorship (the "dictatorship of the proletariat") and deprivation were the necessary price of building a socialist society.[13] It is difficult to prove one viewpoint right or wrong on purely objective grounds.[14] Some might find this proposition difficult to accept in view of what they consider to be obvious deficiencies of the Soviet economic and political system.

*The matter of economic priorities can be illustrated using the familiar Production Possibilities Schedule (PPS). The graph below pictures a hypothetical economy that produces two types of goods: (1) producer and defense goods, and (2) consumer goods:

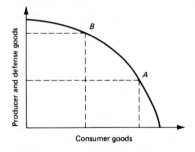

This economy is endowed with a fixed stock of land, labor, and capital, which producers employing the available technology convert into output. Insofar as total resources are limited, the economy cannot produce unlimited quantities of output; instead, it must choose among a large number of maximum combinations of goods that the economy can produce. A technically efficient economy, which generates a maximum amount of output from its stock of inputs, is said to be operating on its Production Possibility Schedule. Let us say that a consumer-oriented economy would choose point *A* and a planned socialist economy would choose point *B* on the PPS. One cannot say that *A* is superior to *B* or that *B* is superior to *A* because both statements would be personal value judgments, which vary according to individual preferences and prejudices.

PURPOSE AND SCOPE OF THIS BOOK

The present work on Soviet planned socialism is designed to serve as a basis for introductory courses in Soviet economics, comparative economic systems, and the economics of socialism. In the latter two courses, it would be combined with readings on other models of socialism.

We assume a level of sophistication generally acquired in a one-year introductory economics course. We emphasize the broad issues in the operation of the Soviet planned economy without lingering over its institutional aspects, which are quite complex and which change rather frequently. A basic understanding of the working arrangements of the Soviet economy is deemed more important: In what manner and how effectively are resources allocated by the Soviet command economy? This question can be answered only by relying extensively upon theoretical abstraction. Thus, central tendencies are described without concentrating on the numerous deviations from these tendencies. This is the only way to develop an ordered framework to view the economy of the Soviet Union in its entirety.

The book consists of four parts. Part I, entitled "Origins of the Soviet Economy," focuses on the economic history of the Soviet Union from the Tsarist period to the mid-1980s. Chapter 2 recounts the nature and extent of Russian economic development prior to the Revolution of 1917. The objectives of this chapter are to determine the nature of the economic base inherited from the Tsars, to facilitate an evaluation of the achievements of the Soviet period, and to allow comparisons with the developing countries.

Chapter 3 deals with the period from 1918 to 1928, that is, War Communism and the New Economic Policy. This chapter examines the two Soviet economic organizations of this period and their roles in the evolution of the Soviet planned economy.

Chapter 4 describes the Soviet Industrialization Debate that preceded the adoption of the first Five Year Plan in 1928. The outcome of the debate is evinced by a discussion of the vast institutional and structural changes that occurred during the 1930s once the all-out industrialization decision had been made.

Chapter 5 deals with the foundations of the Soviet planned economy by considering the evolution of central planning in the Soviet Union during the late 1920s and early 1930s and the introduction of collective agriculture into the Soviet countryside. It recounts the formation of the ministerial system and the role of Gosplan in economic planning. The most important topic of this chapter is the Soviet development model, the most conspicuous feature of which was the forced collectivization of agriculture. The effects of collectivization on short-run and long-run economic performance are considered. Chapter 5 ends with a brief discussion of the Soviet economy during World War II.

Chapter 6 highlights the major events of the postwar era from the end of World War II to the mid-1980s. It begins with the transition to a peacetime economy—an event accompanied by the change from the Stalin dictatorship to the Khrushchev years. Economic performance during the Khrushchev years is discussed along with the organizational changes and experiments in both agriculture and industry initiated by Khrushchev. Soviet economic performance in the Brezhnev and post-Brezhnev years is the focus of the remainder of the chapter.

Part II, "How the Soviet Economy Operates," focuses on the process of resource allocation in the Soviet command economy. Chapter 7 deals with the functioning of the Soviet economy in terms of institutions, industrial planning, and price setting. The informal "second economy" is also discussed. Chapter 8 continues this topic in a discussion of decision-making by the Soviet manager, of labor allocation, and of the investment decision.

Chapter 9 discusses resource allocation in Soviet agriculture. The characteristics of Soviet collectivized agriculture are considered. The Soviet search for long-run solutions to agricultural problems is the main focus of this chapter.

In Chapter 10, attention is drawn to the Soviet foreign trade sector. The institutional planning and operation of foreign trade is first considered both in terms of the Soviet foreign trade monopoly and of the Council for Mutual Economic Assistance (COMECON) organization. The results of the Soviet foreign trade sector are then examined, especially as they bear upon the important question of the role of foreign trade in the course of Soviet industrialization and its impact upon economic integration within the Soviet bloc.

Part III deals with Soviet economic performance. Chapter 11 considers Soviet economic performance in terms of a series of performance indicators: economic growth, dynamic efficiency, static efficiency, income distribution, consumer welfare, and economic stability. Chapter 12 continues the evaluation of Soviet performance by considering further indicators: military power, technological performance, and environmental quality.

Part IV analyzes Soviet economic reform and future prospects. Past attempts at economic reform are considered, and current reform discussions are evaluated in Chapter 13. The prospects for the improvement of Soviet economic performance are also considered.

REFERENCES

1. For a survey of economic issues, see A. Nove, *An Economic History of the USSR* (New York: Penguin, 1969).
2. R. G. Jensen, T. Shabad, and A. W. Wright, eds., *Soviet Natural Resources in the World Economy* (Chicago: University of Chicago Press, 1983).
3. There is a large body of literature devoted to regional aspects of the Soviet economy. See, for example, V. N. Bandera and Z. L. Melnyk, eds., *The Soviet Economy in Regional Perspective* (New York: Praeger, 1973); I. S. Koropeckyj and G. E. Schroeder, eds., *Economics of Soviet Regions* (New York: Praeger, 1981); and NATO, *Regional Development in the USSR: Trends and Prospects* (Newtonville, Mass.: Oriental Research Partners, 1977).
4. For a survey of basic issues, see H. W. Morton and R. C. Stuart, eds., *The Contemporary Soviet City* (Armonk, N.Y.: M. E. Sharpe, 1984).
5. Our discussion relates to institutions in the postwar period. It is based upon J. F. Hough and M. Fainsod, *How the Soviet Union Is Governed* (Cambridge, Mass.: Harvard University Press, 1979); A. Bergson, *The Economics of Soviet Planning* (New Haven, Conn.: Yale University Press, 1964), chap. 3; P. Cook, "The Political Setting,"

in Joint Economic Committee, *Soviet Economy in a Time of Change* (Washington, D.C.: U.S. Government Printing Office, 1979), vol. 1, pp. 38–50; A. Nove, *The Soviet Economy,* rev. ed. (New York: Praeger, 1969); A. Nove, *The Soviet Economic System* (London: Allen & Unwin, 1977); F. Kushnirsky, *Soviet Economic Planning, 1965–1980* (Boulder, Colo.: Westview Press, 1982); W. J. Conyngham, *The Modernization of Soviet Industrial Management* (New York; Cambridge University Press, 1982); G. E. Schroeder, "Soviet Economic 'Reform' Decrees: More Steps on the Treadmill," in U.S. Congress, Joint Economic Committee, *Soviet Economy In the 1980's: Problems and Prospects,* part I (Washington, D.C.: U.S. Government Printing Office, 1982), pp. 65–88; M. Bornstein, "Improving the Soviet Economic Mechanism," *Soviet Studies,* vol. XXXVII, no. 7 (January 1985), 1–30.

6. The Communist Party is, of course, a crucial mechanism in Soviet society. For a detailed treatment of party structure and functions, see L. Shapiro, *The Communist Party of the Soviet Union* (New York: Random House, 1971); and T. H. Rigby, *Communist Party Membership in the U.S.S.R., 1917–1967* (Princeton, N.J.: Princeton University Press, 1968). For the official Soviet view (subject to change in different editions), see *History of the Communist Party of the Soviet Union* (Moscow: Foreign Languages Publishing House, 1960). For recent evidence, see T. H. Rigby, "Soviet Communist Party Membership Under Brezhnev," *Soviet Studies,* vol. 28, no. 3 (July 1976), 317–337; T. H. Rigby, "Addendum to Dr. Rigby's Article on CPSU Membership," *Soviet Studies,* vol. 28, no. 4 (October 1976), 613; A. L. Unger, "Soviet Communist Party Membership Under Brezhnev: A Comment," *Soviet Studies,* vol. 29, no. 2 (April 1977), 306–316. For a discussion of the more general question of political participation, see J. F. Hough, "Political Participation in the Soviet Union," *Soviet Studies,* vol. 28, no. 1 (January 1976), 3–20.

7. For more detail on the *nomenklatura* system, see B. Harasymiw, "Nomenklatura: The Soviet Communist Party's Leadership Recruitment System," *Canadian Journal of Political Science,* vol. 2, no. 4 (December 1969), 493–512; J. F. Hough, *The Soviet Prefects* (Cambridge, Mass.: Harvard University Press, 1969), pp. 114–116, 150–170.

8. *Constitution (Fundamental Law) of the Union of Soviet Socialist Republics* (Moscow: Novosti Press Agency Publishing House, 1978), p. 21.

9. S. Kuznets, "A Comparative Appraisal," in A. Bergson and S. Kuznets, eds., *Economic Trends in the Soviet Union* (Cambridge, Mass.: Harvard University Press, 1963), pp. 345, 347.

10. Soviet Defense Trends, A Staff Study Prepared for the Use of the Subcommittee on International Trade, Finance, and Security Economics of the Joint Economic Committee of Congress, Washington, D.C., U.S. Government Printing Office, September 1983.

11. National Foreign Assessment Center, *Handbook of Economic Statistics,* 1984, CPAS84-10002, Washington, D.C., U.S. Government Printing Office, September 1984, pp. 22 and 23.

12. For a discussion of welfare criteria and their applicability to comparing economic systems, see, for example, A. Bergson, "Market Socialism Revisited," *Journal of Political Economy,* vol. 75, no. 5 (October 1967), 655–672; and M. Dobb, *Welfare Economics and the Economics of Socialism* (Cambridge: Cambridge University Press, 1969).

13. For instance, the official Soviet text, *Political Economy,* argues that such suffering and sacrifice were required to overcome the economic backwardness of Russia. *Political Economy: A Textbook,* 4th ed. (East Berlin: Dietz Verlag, 1964), p. 383.

14. For a discussion of criteria for comparing economic systems, see B. A. Belassa,

"Success Criteria for Economic Systems," in M. Bornstein, ed., *Comparative Economic Systems, Models and Cases,* rev. ed. (Homewood, Ill.: Irwin, 1969), pp. 2–18; for more detailed treatments, see A. Eckstein, ed., *Comparison of Economic Systems* (Berkeley: University of California Press, 1971), pp. 25–240; M. Bornstein, "Comparing Economic Systems," in M. Bornstein, ed., *Comparative Economic Systems, Models and Cases,* 4th ed. (Homewood, Ill.: Irwin, 1979), pp. 3–18; and J. M. Montias, *The Structure of Economic Systems* (New Haven and London: Yale University Press, 1976), chap. 4.

one

ORIGINS OF THE SOVIET ECONOMY

chapter *2*

Economic History of Russia to 1917

The economic record of the Soviet period cannot be evaluated in proper perspective without knowing the economic base the Bolsheviks inherited from the tsars. If economic development during the tsarist period had been extensive, then the rapid industrialization of the 1930s would be merely a continuation of past development. If, on the other hand, the Bolsheviks inherited a backward and stagnant economy, then their achievements must be gauged differently.

Both the rate and the level of Russian economic development prior to 1917 are matters of some controversy. Lenin proclaimed the backward tsarist economy, with its isolated pockets of modernity, as the "weakest link" in the capitalist chain; official Soviet ideology argues that the economic backwardness inherited from the tsarist period made the sacrifices of the 1930s necessary. Were it not for the dramatic restructuring of the economic system in the 1930s, today's Soviet economy would not be as far advanced as it is. Western economic historians (such as Alexander Gerschenkron and W. W. Rostow) have tended to focus on the rapid industrial growth achieved after 1880 while emphasizing the feudal problems of Russian agriculture.[1] Other Western economic historians have tended to view tsarist agriculture in a more favorable light.

Our approach to the question of Russian economic development is to first consider the development of industry and agriculture during the last half-century of tsarist rule, and then turn to other factors, such as growth of per capita GNP, changes of industrial structure, and demographic characteristics, suggested by Simon Kuznets as being indicators of "modern economic growth."[2]

INDUSTRIAL GROWTH UNDER THE TSARS

Although it is usually difficult to trace the development of the industrial sector in a country as ancient as Russia, the reign of Peter the Great (1698–1725), an important turning point in Russian economic history, provides us with a convenient place to begin.

Peter the Great, impressed by the technology and industrial expertise he observed during his extensive early travels in Western Europe, determined to industrialize Russia by importing Western technology and technicians en masse. Military considerations played an important role in this decision. Peter the Great provided the initial impetus to move the backward Russian economy toward the development of an increasingly modern industrial sector, by eighteenth-century standards. As a result, eighteenth-century Russia acquired a nascent industrial capacity that, when combined with its vast natural and manpower resources, enabled it to compete militarily with the West for nearly two centuries despite a succession of less vigorous Russian tsars. After Peter the Great, however, a gap began to widen between the Russian economy and its industrializing Western European competitors, especially during the nineteenth century.[3] In fact, during this two-century period, industrialization came to be regarded in Russia as a threat to the autocracy. Tsarist authorities feared that railroads would spread egalitarianism and that the growth of factory towns would spawn a rebellious proletariat.[4] One of history's great ironies was the firm entrenchment during the reign of Peter the Great of feudalism—a retrogressive social institution that later was to become a great obstacle to long-term economic development. Serfdom was used by Peter the Great to finance his military ventures; and, indeed, he staffed his new factories, mines, and postal system with serf labor to implement his progressive industrial policies.

The Crimean War (1854–1856) forced Russian leaders to realize the relative industrial backwardness of Russia vis-à-vis the industrializing Western powers. The potential dangers of this gap were painfully obvious, especially to an empire-conscious country accustomed to respect as a formidable military power. As a result, the Russian government began to promote industrialization in a reversal of its earlier anti-industrialization stance, especially under the forceful leadership of Count Sergei Witte, the Minister of Finance from 1892 to 1903. Industrial development was fostered by the government in a variety of ways. The state sponsored massive railroad construction, spurred by the obvious military importance of railway transport in a land as massive as the Russian Empire. In 1860, the Russian rail network consisted of 1,600 kilometers of track. By 1917, 81,000 kilometers had been built.[5] This new transportation network opened up the iron and coal resources of the Ukraine, which soon overtook the Ural region as the metallurgical center of the Russian Empire. In addition, it opened up world markets for Russian wheat. Russian exports of wheat products increased five times between the 1860s and 1900, competing with North American wheat, which had also been made available to the world market by the railroads.[6] The state acted as guarantor of bonds, thereby promoting the widespread participation of foreign capital in industrial development. A succession of finance ministers pursued a conservative monetary policy, which stabilized the ruble exchange rate and allowed Russia to join the international gold standard in 1897. Domestic heavy industry was promoted by a series of measures such as high protective tariffs, profit guarantees, tax reductions and exemptions, police help in labor disputes, and government orders at high prices to ensure adequate demand for domestic production. In addition, the state actively recruited foreign entrepreneurs for Russian industry. The military objectives of the state are seen in the Ministry of Finance's promotion of heavy industry over the small-scale light industry during this period.[7]

A modern entrepreneurial class began to form in nineteenth-century Russia. Russian entrepreneurs were drawn from the civil service and nobiltiy as well as the ranks of Jewish merchants and Old Believer sects.[8] Russian entrepreneurs, like the Western entrepreneurs working in Russia, operated in a legal setting that was ambivalent toward private enterprise. The tsar's signature was required on the charter of every joint-stock company, placing the tsarist bureaucracy in a position to determine who would be allowed to form limited liability corporations. Russian industrialists often got their start in business through state subsidies, tariffs, or preferential state orders. Corrupt practices were common, with industrialists purchasing state favors with bribes. Bribery appeared to be one of the ordinary costs of conducting business in bureaucratic Russia. For its part, the Russian economic bureaucracy, under the leadership of the finance ministry, was ambivalent in its attitude toward modern capitalist institutions. On the one hand, the succession of able finance ministers understood the importance of promoting private initiative and attempted by and large to recruit entrepreneurs on the basis of talent rather than family connections. On the other hand, the Russian state feared the consequences of unbridled capitalism. Russian industrialists, who banded into lobbying organizations such as the Association of Industry and Trade, shared this ambivalence. They argued for fewer restrictions on their activities while at the same time continuing to rely on state protection, subsidies, and state credits.

The Russian legal and state system at the turn of the twentieth century was not unusual for a relatively backward country with great economic potential and a firmly entrenched state bureaucracy. The economic potential was sufficiently great to bring in foreign capital from abroad, attracted primarily by the higher rates of return in Russia. The profit potential was sufficiently great to cause the emergence of a class of home-grown entrepreneurs, while at the same time promoting bureaucratic corruption that added to the business costs of Russian industrialists. The entrenched Russian bureaucracy, unlike the less well-entrenched British bureaucracy, found it difficult to sit on the sidelines. As a result, there was more active bureaucratic meddling in economic affairs.

In the 1880s, an acceleration in the rate of growth of industrial output took place. There has been considerable debate about the causes of this acceleration. Some economic historians, such as Arcadius Kahan, have argued that the upturn in industrial growth was a consequence of natural market forces, spurred by the enormous profit potential of the resource-rich Russian empire.[9] Kahan and others maintain that state activities either hampered (or did not contribute to in a significant way) industrial growth, and they cite the fact that state subsidies to industry were actually quite modest during this period. Others have argued that the acceleration (or "spurt") in industrial growth was the direct result of state intervention.

A prominent scholar of Russian economic history, Alexander Gerschenkron, has proposed the relative backwardness hypothesis to explain this spurt.[10] He suggests that whenever the gap between economic potential and economic actuality of a nation becomes too great, that is, whenever a nation with great economic promise as measured by its total resource endowment becomes backward relative to other countries (as Russia was around 1860), tension is created, new institutions are substituted for missing preconditions, and a spurt of industrial growth occurs. In the case of Russia, the tension was great, the resulting industrial spurt was significant, and the Russian state, which acted as a substitute for missing entrepreneurial resources and deficient demand, was the instigator of industrialization.

Between 1880 and 1900, industrial production more than tripled, accelerating again between 1906 and 1914 after the depression at the turn of the century and the political instability of the 1905 revolution.[11] The extent of Russian industrial progress between 1861 and 1913 is shown in Table 3 (pp. 34–35), which indicates that by 1913, Russia had risen to become the world's fifth largest industrial power, behind the United States, England, Germany, and France, and had succeeded in narrowing the gap between itself and the leading producers of key industrial products.

These aggregate figures mask the low per capita output of Russian industry, which can be inferred from the population and output figures in Table 3. Despite the considerable growth of industrial output, Russia on the eve of World War I belonged to the group of poor Western European countries (Spain, Italy, and Austria-Hungary) in terms of industrial output per capita.

Russian industrial growth between 1880 and 1913 was rapid, and the industrial gap between Russia and the more advanced industrialized countries, although it remained significant, was narrowed. For this reason, economic historians who have concentrated on Russian industrial development prior to 1917 have traditionally taken a fairly sanguine view of Russian economic development during the last three decades of tsarist rule.

Is this conclusion justified? While significant industrial development is a necessary condition, it is not sufficient in itself to produce overall economic development. Insofar as the growth of GNP (industry, agriculture, services) and per capita GNP—not industrial growth alone—are the most generally accepted indicators of the rate of economic development, we must focus upon the performance of the second major sector, agriculture, during this period of rapid industrialization before a balanced picture of Russian economic development can be obtained.

RUSSIAN AGRICULTURE UNDER THE TSARS

The agricultural revolutions that accompanied the industrialization of Western Europe and England were generally preceded by the breakdown of feudalism, which prepared the way for a modern agriculture unfettered by traditional culti-vation methods and restrictions. Feudalism developed rather late in Russia, at a time when this institution was declining or extinct in the more advanced Western nations. Perhaps as a result of its late emergence, feudalism in Russia embodied particularly odious forms of servitude in which serfs were bound to the soil, could be deported to Siberia, were conscripted virtually for life into the army, and sold on the open market by their masters. Depending upon the region of the country, Russian serfs were either required to provide labor services on the landlord's land *(barshchina)* or to make payments in kind from their crops (later money) for the use of their allotted land *(obrok)*. In addition, peasant land was held communally and was periodically redistributed by the village elders, who constituted a form of village self-government.

Russian feudal agriculture provided little incentive for the individual peas-ant. Serf labor was so inefficient that it became customary to call *barshchina* "all that is done slowly, incorrectly, and without incentive."[12] Mobility from the countryside to the town was limited. A peasant working in the town not only had to pay a large portion of his earnings to his master but also had to return to his village if so ordered, unlike the earlier Western European practice whereby serfs could gain their freedom by living in the town.

The Emancipation Act of 1861, which freed the serfs and divided the land holdings of the landed aristocracy (the gentry) between the peasant and the gentry, was a significant watershed, for it provided a unique opportunity to establish the foundations for a modern Russian agriculture. However, the pri-mary objective of the Russian emancipation, initiated by the tsar himself, was not to promote economic development, but to prevent further peasant revolts and preserve the autocracy while retaining a form of agriculture that could still be controlled. The vested land interests were favored. While the peasants received their juridical freedom, they were allotted plots of gentry land to be "redeemed" by the holder. The remaining gentry land (well over 50 percent) was retained by its original owners. The peasants were generally dissatisfied with the size of their plots; many were too small to provide earnings for the redemption payments due to the state (which had purchased the land from the gentry).

Some peasants accepted "beggar's allotments"—small plots of land free from all obligations—and became small freeholders. The state peasants received land as well, under more generous terms; but as late as 1877, the crown and the state treasury still owned almost 50 percent of the land in European Russia.

Let us now consider the principal features of the Emancipation Act of 1861 from the viewpoint of economic efficiency.[13] While the reform did contain positive elements—an increase in the large estates that created export surpluses, the introduction of a money economy into the countryside via redemption payments, and the psychological impact of emancipation—it placed serious constraints upon agricultural development. Communal agriculture was retained, as a means of control over the rural population in the institution of the *mir* or *obshchina* (the village communal organizations). The agricultural communes were held responsi-ble for the debts of their individual members; therefore, the more prosperous commune members were liable for the defaults of the poorer. With this feature, there was reduced incentive to accumulate wealth within the commune.[14] The

Table 3 SELECTED ECONOMIC AND SOCIAL INDICATORS, RUSSIA AND OTHER COUNTRIES, 1861 AND 1913

	Population (millions)	National income, 1913 rubles (million)	Per capita national income	Grain output (100 metric tons)	Coal output (million metric tons)
1861					
Russia	74	5,269	71	41,500	0.38
United Kingdom	20	6,469	323	n.a.	85.0
France	37	5,554	150	26,220	9.4
Germany	36	6,313	175	28,706	18.7
United States	32	14,405	450	39,318	13.3
Netherlands	3	n.a.	n.a.	1,292	n.a.
Norway	2	331	166	802	n.a.
Sweden	4	449	112	1,265	0.03
Italy	25	4,570	183	6,455	0.03
Spain	16	n.a.	n.a.	n.a.	0.35
Austria-Hungary	35	n.a.	n.a.	20,745	2.5
1913					
Russia	171	20,266	119	123,000	36.1
United Kingdom	36	20,869	580	8,948	292.0
France	39	11,816	303	30,870	40.8
Germany	65	24,280	374	85,445	277.3
United States	93	96,030	1,033	146,100	517.0
Netherlands	6	2,195	366	3,686	1.9
Norway	2	918	659	1,076	n.a.
Sweden	6	2,040	340	4,979	0.36
Italy	35	9,140	261	13,128	0.7
Spain	20	3,975	199	9,025	3.9
Austria-Hungary	50	9,500	190	38,953	54.2

	Pig iron (1000 metric tons)	Crude steel[a] (1000 metric tons)	Raw cotton (1000 meters)	Rail network (1000 km)	Infant mortality (per 1000)
1861					
Russia	320	7	43.0	2.2	239[b]
United Kingdom	3,772	334	457.0	14.6	148
France	967	84	110.0	9.6	190
Germany	592	143	74.0	11.5	260
United States	830	12	213.0	50.3	n.a.
Netherlands	n.a.	n.a.	3.6	0.34	196
Norway	0	n.a.	n.a.	0.07	113
Sweden	170	9	7.7	0.57	124
Italy	27	0	12.0	2.8	232
Spain	67	n.a.	27.0	2.9	174
Austria-Hungary	315	22	44.0	3.2	264
1913					
Russia	4,641	4,918	424	70.2	237
United Kingdom	10,425	7,787	988	32.6	108
France	5,207	4,687	271	40.7	112
Germany	16,761	17,609	478	63.4	151
United States	34,700	31,800	1,458	400.0	115
Netherlands	n.a.	n.a.	36	3.2	91
Norway	n.a.	0	n.a.	3.1	64
Sweden	730	591	22	14.3	70
Italy	427	934	202	18.9	138
Spain	425	242	88	15.1	155
Austria-Hungary	2,381	2,611	210	23.0	190

Source: P.R. Gregory, Russian National Income, 1885–1913, (Cambridge: Cambridge University Press, 1982), pp. 155–156; n.a. denotes figure not available.
[a] 1871.
[b] Average 1867–1869.

peasant family could not officially withdraw its land from the commune until all debts on the land were met and then only with a two-thirds vote of the membership. Nor could the peasant leave agriculture permanently for the city until his land was free of obligations—the rigid internal passport system was supposed to ensure peasant compliance. In addition, the land was to be redistributed periodically within the commune, thereby reducing incentives to improve a particular plot. In short, the Emancipation Act made it difficult for the peasant to develop both a sense of private property and an interest in long-term productivity improvements, factors that had proved crucial in the agricultural revolutions of other countries.

According to Gerschenkron, the guiding principles of the Russian agrarian program between 1861 and 1906 were:

> To preserve the *obshchina* until the liquidation of the redemption debt, to prolong the amortization of that debt so as to protect the *obshchina,* and at the same time to continue to hold the peasantry in the vise of ruinous aggregate taxation.[15]

Gerschenkron has argued (along with Lenin and Soviet scholars) that massive peasant dissatisfaction with the Emancipation Act was a significant cause of the Revolution of 1905. Peasant unrest during this period bordered on spontaneous armed rebellion in the countryside, which prompted the state to enact measures to improve the lot of the peasant: joint responsibility was abolished in 1903, and 50 percent of peasant indebtedness was forgiven in 1906 and finally canceled fully in 1907. From the point of view of long-run economic development, the Stolypin Reforms of 1906 and 1910 were significant government measures because they sought to weaken communal agriculture and to create a class of small peasant proprietors. Their principal provision made it easier for individual peasants to withdraw from the commune, which—combined with the reduced indebtedness of the peasantry—opened the way for private agriculture in Russia. Heads of households could demand their portion of commune land and withdraw from the commune. They could further demand consolidation of their land into a single area.

It is difficult to predict what impact the Stolypin Reforms would have had on the Russian economy had they been given sufficient time to take effect. Most authorities agree that they would have strengthened Russian agriculture. Western authorities (Gerschenkron, Lazar Volin, Jerome Blum, and G. T. Robinson) have joined tsarist and Soviet scholars in emphasizing the poor performance of Russian agriculture after 1861. These authorities point to a possible decline in per capita grain availability between 1870 and the 1890s, accounts of appalling poverty in the Russian village,[16] rising peasant tax arrears, and the increasing number of mortgaged estates as evidence of an "agrarian crisis." Moreover, the existence of an agrarian crisis provides a convenient explanation for the revolution of 1905 and support for the Gerschenkron proposition that the burden of industrialization was borne by the Russian peasant.

This entirely pessimistic picture of Russian agriculture has been questioned by a number of scholars. Internal passport data have been analyzed to demonstrate that the Russian peasant was relatively free to go to the city or to outlying provinces, despite official restrictions on such movements. Analyses of peasant taxes reveal that the growing arrears may not be indicative of the exhaustion of the tax-paying capacity of the Russian village. In fact, Russian peasants may have adjusted their tax payments automatically according to their sense of social justice.[17] Most importantly, recent studies demonstrate that the output and marketing performance of Russian agriculture was much better than the earlier literature had suggested.

Basically, the more recent studies of Russian agricultural output and peasant living standards find that, on average, Russian peasants were experiencing rising living standards (alongside urban workers) during the period of rapid industrialization. Over the 1885–1913 period, there does not appear to have been a noticeable shift in the distribution of consumption expenditures between the city and countryside. The growth rates of agricultural output and of output per capita were quite respectable by Western European standards, lagging only slightly behind the growth rate of total output. There was positive growth of agricultural labor productivity, at perhaps two-thirds the rate in industry.[18] The aggregate figures point to rising peasant living standards, rising agricultural productivity, and to rising per capita agricultural output. Agricultural progress was, however, quite uneven. The Russian grain market was not integrated (there was substantial regional variation in agricultural prices); the regional distribution of transportation services was uneven; and significant resources continued to be devoted to agriculture in grain deficit regions ill-suited by climate and soil conditions to agricultural pursuits.[19] A generally rising trend in agriculture is quite consistent with the accounts of regional and individual poverty that abound in the Russian and Soviet literatures (see reference 16, for example).

The conclusion that Russian agriculture performed reasonably well despite the strictures placed upon it by the 1861 emancipation is not surprising. In a country as vast as Russia, it would have been difficult for the bureaucracy to restrain peasant mobility (as the passport data demonstrate). An artificial separation of the economy into a prosperous and growing industrial sector and a backward and stagnant agricultural sector would be an unexpected economic result. Unless the agrarian population could be rendered immobile, the natural tendency would be for labor to seek out its highest return, and this tendency would lead to a rough equalization of real wages between the city and countryside in the long run. It would also be difficult to keep Russian agriculture, with its close ties to world markets, isolated from the agricultural revolutions of Western Europe, North America, and Australia. It should also be remembered that Russian agriculture was expanding extensively during the late nineteenth century into new areas not subject to the restrictions of the peasant emancipation.

ECONOMIC GROWTH UNDER THE TSARS

Russian industrial growth was more rapid than that of her European neighbors after 1880. Russian agricultural performance, according to recent evidence, was better during the industrialization era than had been thought by earlier historians. To provide some perspective on the issue of modern economic growth in Russia, an assessment of Russian economic performance relative to that of the industrialized countries is required. In such an assessment, the position of the Russian Empire at the beginning of the "modern era" (1861) and on the eve of World War I must be established, and the Russian record of economic growth and structural change must be considered.

Data on population, national income, and various output series have been assembled (see Table 3) for Russia and other countries for the years 1861 and 1913. These figures allow one to draw a general picture of the Russian economy at the end of the tsarist era and to trace its progress from the emancipation to the eve of World War I.

On the eve of the war, Russia was one of the world's major economic powers, but the dichotomy between the country's aggregate economic power, as dictated by the magnitude of the Russian Empire, and its relative poverty on a per capita basis is striking. Russia began its modern era with a population twice as large as its next most populous neighbor (France) and ended the era three times as large as its largest European neighbor (Germany). This increase indicates the more rapid growth of population in Russia than in Europe.*

With such a large population, exceptionally low per capita output levels would be required to prevent Russia from being one of the world's major economic powers. This point is confirmed by the national income rankings. By 1913, Russia's national output was above France's, equal to England's, 80 percent that of Germany, and twice that of Austria-Hungary. In relative terms, the only decline between 1861 and 1913 was vis-à-vis the United States, a country that experienced a rapid growth of population and national output during this period.

Russia's economic power was concentrated in agriculture. In 1861, Russia produced more grain than any other country and was surpassed only by the United States in 1913. On a per capita basis, however, Russia ranked well behind the more advanced grain-producing countries, such as the United States and Germany, but was roughly on a par with countries such as France and Austria-Hungary. Russia's position as a major industrial power was less well-established. In 1861, Russia was a minor producer of major industrial commodities (coal, iron, and steel) and had only a rudimentary transportation system, despite its vast territory. By 1913, Russia's relative position had improved somewhat, especially relative to France and Austria-Hungary, but Russia still lagged seriously behind the major industrial powers. It was only in textiles that Russia occupied a position roughly equivalent to that of Germany, the continent's largest industrial producer.

The relative backwardness of the Russian economy is masked by aggregate figures but is evident from per capita comparisons. Russia began its modern era with a per capita income one-half France's and Germany's, one-fifth England's,

---

*Russian population growth was much like that in the European offshoots, Australia and North America, with a crucial difference. Russia's rapid population growth was due entirely to high rates of natural increase, while immigration played an important role in North America and Australia.

and 15 percent that of the United States. By 1913, Russia's relative position had declined, due primarily to rapid population growth and slow output growth until the 1880s. Russia's 1913 per capita income was less than 40 percent that of France and 33 percent that of Germany, still one-fifth England's, and one-tenth that of the United States. On a per capita income basis, 1913 Russia was a poor European country, ranking well below Spain, Italy, and Austria-Hungary.

Russia's most important relative achievement was the development of a rail network that was Europe's largest by 1913 and was comparable on a per capita basis to countries like Italy and Austria-Hungary. The one social indicator in Table 3, infant mortality, shows that the advances in public health experienced in other countries were not shared by the masses in the Russian village. Russia entered its modern era in 1861 with a rate of infant mortality not much different from that of Western Europe. Yet 50 years later, infant mortality was virtually unchanged in Russia, while in other countries it had declined significantly.

Growth of Per Capita NNP

A distinctive feature of modern economic growth (MEG) is accelerated and sustained growth of per capita output. This rapid growth contrasts with the secular stagnation of the premodern period. Annual rates of growth of Russian net national product (NNP), population, and per capita NNP are given in Table 4. These figures suffer from several weaknesses, yet they should be accurate within a reasonable margin of error.

The growth of Russian NNP was relatively slow from the emancipation to the early 1880s, but this was prior to the establishment of a modern transportation system. Between 1861 and 1883, the growth rate of per capita income was negligible, and labor productivity apparently failed to increase. However, in assessing tsarist economic growth, one should focus on the "industrialization era" from the mid-1880s and compare Russian growth performance with that of the industrialized countries.

During Russia's industrailization era, the growth of Russian national income was above average when compared to other countries during the same period. The Russian growth rate of 3.3 percent per annum was equaled or

Table 4 PATTERNS OF RUSSIAN GROWTH (PERCENT PER ANNUM)

	NNP	Population	Per capita NNP	Labor force	NNP per worker (1–4)
1861–1863 to 1881–1883	1.8	1.1	0.7	1.9	0.1
1883–1887 to 1909–1913	3.3	1.6	1.7	1.7	1.6

Sources: The 1861–1883 figures are for the 50 European provinces and are from P. R. Gregory, "Economic Growth and Structural Change in Tsarist Russia: A Case of Modern Economic Growth?" *Soviet Studies,* vol. 23, no. 1 (January 1972), 422. The 1883–1913 figures are for the Russian Empire and are from P. R. Gregory, "Economic Growth and Structural Change in Tsarist Russia and the Soviet Union: A Long-Term Comparison," in S. Rosefielde, ed., *Economic Welfare and the Economics of Soviet Socialism* (Cambridge: Cambridge University Press, 1981).

surpassed by only four countries and exceeded the growth rate of the two other "follower" countries, Italy and Japan.[20] Russian growth was similar to that of the European offshoots in North America and Australia, which also experienced rapid population growth.

On a per capita and per worker basis, Russian output growth was average relative to the industrialized countries. Thus, Russia's above-average output growth was largely the consequence of relatively rapid population and labor force growth. Russian economic growth was, therefore, of a largely "extensive" character, that is, was caused principally by the growth of inputs rather than the growth of output per unit of input. The less reliable evidence on tsarist capital stock suggests that roughly two-thirds of Russian output growth was accounted for by the growth of conventional labor and capital inputs.[21] Again, the Russian experience is similar to that of the European offshoots, which also grew "extensively" during this period.

The conclusion follows from this evidence that after 1885, the Russian Empire grew at total, per capita, and per worker rates that were at least average relative to those of the industrialized countries. Although Russian growth over the entire 1861 to 1913 period was indeed relatively slow,[22] this was due to the slow growth until the 1880s. During the industrialization era, Russian growth appears to have taken on the classical features of modern economic growth.

Structural Change

Another means of establishing whether Russia was indeed undergoing the initial stages of MEG after the mid-1880s is to compare Russian structural change with that of the industrialized countries during the early phases of MEG. In Table 5, shifts in the structure of Russian national income both by producing sector and by final use are shown. These shifts reveal the expected MEG pattern of structural change—rising shares of industry, falling shares of agriculture, rising shares of net investment, and falling shares of personal consumption.

One way to assess these changes is to compare them with the structural shifts experienced by the industrialized countries during their first 30 years of MEG. Utilizing data from Kuznets,[23] one finds that the amount of structural change experienced in Russia during its industrialization era was about average (or perhaps slightly below average) for a country undergoing the initial stages of MEG. Thus, the evidence on structural change supports the proposition that Russia was in the process of embarking upon a path of MEG during its industrialization era.

Investment in Human Capital

Between the emancipation and the 1880s, labor productivity failed to increase; thereafter, it grew at an average rate relative to that of the industrialized countries. One possible explanation for the initiation of productivity growth is the increased public and private investment in human capital after 1880. There is little firm evidence on literacy rates prior to 1897, but data on the literacy rates

Table 5   RUSSIAN ECONOMIC STRUCTURE DURING THE INDUSTRIALIZATION ERA

	Shares in National Product by Producing Sector (Percentages)		
	Agriculture	Industry, construction, transportation, and communication	Trade and services
1883–1887	57.5	23.5	19.0
1909–1913	51.0	32.0	17.0

	Shares in National Product by Final Use (Percentages)			
	Personal consumption	Government	Net domestic investment	Net foreign investment
1885–1889	83.5	8.1	8.1	0.3
1909–1913	79.6	9.7	12.1	−1.5

Source: P. R. Gregory, "Economic Growth and Structural Change in Tsarist Russia and the Soviet Union: A Long-Term Comparison," in S. Rosefielde, ed., *Economic Welfare and the Economics of Soviet Socialism* (Cambridge: Cambridge University Press, 1981).

of military recruits and in St. Petersburg and Moscow show that the increase in literacy was barely perceptible prior to the early 1880s.[24] From the mid-1880s on, however, the growth of literacy rates accelerated. Between 1884 and 1904, the literacy rates of military recruits more than doubled, from 26 percent to 56 percent. For the country as a whole, the 1897 illiteracy rate was 72 percent (see Table 6), with urban literacy almost three times rural literacy. Between 1897 and 1913, further progress was made in providing education to the population, and a rough estimate places Russian illiteracy in 1913 at 60 percent of the over-10-year-old population. For comparison, we note that U.S. illiteracy in 1900 was only 11 percent of the over-10 population.

The low literacy rates of the Russian population prior to the revolution is a fairly convincing indicator of the social backwardness of the economy. As studies of the development process have demonstrated, there is a close link between the quality of the labor force (as measured by educational achievement) and the level of economic development.[25] In the Russian case, the limited pool of educated workers constrained overall industrialization and may have forced Russian industry to adopt capital intensive production techniques to utilize more efficiently the limited supply of skilled industrial laborers (some of whom were

Table 6   ILLITERACY RATES: RUSSIA IN 1897 AND 1913—UNITED STATES IN 1900 (PERCENT OF TOTAL POPULATION OVER 10 YEARS OF AGE)

		Urban	Rural	Total
Russia	1897	55[a]	83[a]	72
	1913	—	—	60
United States	1900	—	—	11

Source: A. G. Rashin, *Formirovanie rabochego klassa v Rossii* [The formation of the working class in Russia] (Moscow: 1958), pp. 579–581.
[a] Percent of entire population.

imported from abroad).[26] The extremely low rural literacy rates show that while
the pool of rural labor was substantial, it was not perhaps suited for employment
under modern factory conditions without considerable training.

Demographic Patterns

MEG has characteristic demographic patterns as well. As Kuznets[27] notes, the
dominant MEG trend in birthrates is downward throughout the modern period,
although changes in premodern institutional practices may create initial increases
in birthrates. The death rate declines rapidly during MEG, being the principal
factor behind the acceleration of population growth. The most conspicuous bene-
factors of the declining death rate are the younger age groups, owing to increased
control over infant mortality. Comparing premodern and modern rates, Kuznets
notes that premodern birthrates varied substantially among countries, ranging
from highs of 55 per 1000 to lows of 31 per 1000. The average premodern death
rate was around 30 per 1000 in Western Europe and somewhat lower in the areas
of European settlement in North America and Australia. From these initial levels,
birth and death rates declined, the death rate approaching a lower limit of around
10 per 1000 in recent times.

Russia began the postemancipation development in 1861 with a demographic base like that of Western Europe and North America some 75 to 100
years earlier (see Table 7). The Russian birthrates of the early 1860s were exceeded only by the U.S. rates of the 1790–1800 period. The Russian 1861 death
rate was well above the eighteenth-century Western Europe average of approximately 30 per 1000. The Russian death rate began to decline steadily during the
late 1890s but remained high relative to Western European standards. The 1913
Russian death rate of 27 per 1000 was still more than double the Western
European average of 13 per 1000 for that same year.

Table 7   BIRTHRATES, DEATH RATES, AND RATES OF NATURAL
          INCREASE: 50 EUROPEAN RUSSIAN PROVINCES, 1861–1913
          (PER 1000)

	Birthrate	Death rate	Rate of natural increase
1861–1865	51	37	14
1866–1870	50	37	12
1871–1875	51	37	14
1876–1880	50	36	14
1881–1885	51	36	14
1886–1890	50	35	16
1891–1895	49	36	13
1896–1900	50	32	17
1901–1905	48	31	17
1906–1910	46	30	16
1910–1913	44	27	17

Source: A. G. Rashin, *Naselenie Rossii za 100 let* [The population of Russia for 100 years]
(Moscow: Sotzekizdat, 1956), p. 155.

The high Russian death rate can be explained by the high rate of infant mortality—27 deaths per 100 during the 1867–1871 period and 24 deaths per 100 in 1911. This limited decline over a 40-year period indicates the meager success that tsarist Russia had in reducing infant mortality.[28]

The Russian birthrate hovered around 50 per 1000 from 1860 to 1900, after which it declined steadily; but in 1913, it was still twice the Western European average of the same year. Thus, although Russian birth and death rates began to conform to MEG patterns around the turn of the century, they still roughly corresponded to premodern levels at the time of the Revolution.

RUSSIA'S DEPENDENCE ON THE WEST

Tsarist Russia's economic dependence on the West was a topic of considerable importance during the Soviet industrialization debates of the 1920s (Chapter 3). Russia's dependence on foreign capital goods bears on our discussion of Russia's economic development because heavy dependence is accepted as an indicator of underdevelopment.[29] As an economy develops, it becomes able to produce domestically the capital equipment that it had been required to import earlier (import substitution) and thus to reduce its dependence on foreign capital.

To determine Russia's dependence on foreign technology, one must first consider its domestic production of capital equipment. A possible rough indicator of Russia's domestic machinery-producing capacity was the relative importance of metal products (engineering) in the tsarist Russian economy. In 1913, metal products accounted for 10 and 12 percent of manufacturing net output and labor force, respectively. During that same period, the average manufacturing product share of engineering in England, the United States, and Germany was 21 percent.[30] Russia in 1913 devoted less than half as much of its manufacturing resources to machinery as did the major industrial powers of the West. Inasmuch as Russia in 1913 devoted a much smaller proportion of total resources to manufacturing than the three major industrial powers, the share of total resources devoted to the production of capital equipment was even smaller.

The relatively small portion of resources devoted to capital goods is perhaps surprising in view of the apparent zeal with which the Russian state one-sidedly promoted the investment goods industries at the expense of consumer goods industries during the 1890s, which, according to Gerschenkron, resulted "in the relative top-heaviness of the Russian industrial structure as well as its relative concentration upon producer goods."[31]

It is clear that the development of the tsarist economy was dependent upon the transfer of foreign technology and equipment. The data also show that Russian development was aided by the receipt of saving from abroad to finance domestic capital formation. Russia was, in fact, a large debtor country during the 1880–1913 period, receiving significant capital inflows from France, England, and Belgium. Foreign capital probably accounted for 40 percent of industrial investment, 15 to 20 percent of total investment, and about 2 percent of NNP at the end of the tsarist era.[32]

As a frame of reference, one might compare the Russian foreign debt experience with that of two other large countries, the United States and Japan, both of which were debtor countries at early stages of their economic development. Foreign capital accounted for about 1 percent of U.S. GNP and 10 percent of investment during the mid-1880s, when U.S. dependence on foreign capital was at its peak. It accounted for 0.2 percent of Japanese GNP between 1887 and 1896, rising briefly to a high of 4 percent between 1897 and 1906, after which Japan became a capital exporter.[33] This comparison suggests that tsarist Russia was more dependent upon foreign capital in both magnitude and duration than were either the United States or Japan during their dependence periods. The inability of the domestic economy to meet the needs of industrialization and the resulting extensive dependence on foreign capital left a deep impression on the Bolshevik leaders and played an important role in Stalin's industrialization and collectivization decisions of 1928 and 1929 (Chapter 4).

WAS RUSSIA UNDERDEVELOPED IN 1914?

Imperial Russia began the initial phases of modern economic growth during the industrialization era after the early 1880s. Prior to 1880, the rate of growth of national output was quite slow in aggregate and per capita terms, and labor productivity was not increasing. During the industrialization era, the growth of national output was rapid relative to the industrialized countries, while per capita and per worker growth rates were average vis-à-vis the industrialized countries. Suggested causes of the improvement in Russian growth performance are the creation of a modern transportation network and the growing investment in human capital. In addition to the acceleration in growth rates and efficiency characteristic of modern economic growth, Russia experienced between the 1880s and 1913 the structural shifts typical of MEG. The Russian economy was well-integrated into the world economy by the 1880s. Russia and the United States were the major suppliers in world wheat markets, a relatively modern rail and shipping network linked Russia with world markets, and the Russian economy participated in the booms and busts of the European business cycle.

Despite this sustained progress over a 30-year period, the tsarist economy was still relatively backward on the eve of World War I. Russia's per capita income ranking placed her among the poorest countries of Europe. The sheer size of the Russian Empire and the magnitude of Russian agricultural output masked the per capita weakness of industrial outputs. The peasant, not the industrial worker, was still the dominant figure in the Russian economy. A minority of the population—and therefore the labor force—was literate, indicating poorly developed human capital; illiteracy was nearly complete among the vast, underemployed peasant population. Russia's demographic pattern was still roughly comparable to that of the developed countries during their premodern periods. Birthrates, death rates, and, especially, rates of infant mortality remained stubbornly high. Industrialization remained dependent upon foreign capital. It is not clear whether the most highly organized institution, the tsarist bureaucracy, was a help or hindrance to economic development.

The formidable task of creating a modern industrialized economy still lay ahead when the Bolsheviks came to power in 1917. The Soviets directed them-selves to their task in 1928, after recovery from the ravages of World War I and the civil war (1917 to 1920), and came to grips with the universal economic and political problems of economic development that the developed countries had faced before them. The Soviet response to this task was distinctive in that the Soviets chose to combine nonmarket forces with political dictatorship to generate rapid development, whereas other countries chose to rely primarily upon market forces and some form of political representation. We shall call this response the "Soviet development model." It serves as a recurring theme throughout this book.

The assessment of economic performance during the late tsarist era is important for two reasons. The first is that it permits us to evaluate economic performance during the Soviet era. Without knowing the economic base and the growth tradition inherited by the Soviet leadership, one cannot judge properly the achievements of the Soviet peirod. For this reason, we shall return to the tsarist period base in our assessment of Soviet economic performance. The second reason is that one cannot judge the relevance of the Soviet development model for use by contemporary less-developed countries (LDCs) without knowing the starting point of the Soviet experiment. Did the Soviet leadership launch its industrializa-tion drive in 1928 from an economic base superior to that of today's LDCs?

In many respects, the similarities between the Russian economy in 1914 and the contemporary LDCs are striking: the low literacy rates, the high rates of birth and infant mortality, the concentration of the labor force in agriculture, and the dependence on foreign capital. Yet despite these features of relative backward-ness, the evidence suggests that the Russian economy did have a substantial head start when compared to that of today's LDCs.

First, Russia in 1914 was a much richer country on a per capita income basis than most LDCs today. In 1914, Russian per capita income was some 33 to 40 percent that of its richest European neighbors, whereas per capita incomes in contemporary LDCs are only a small fraction of those in the industrialized countries. Although one cannot compare income levels of countries 65 years apart, it is nevertheless informative to note that 1913 Russian per capita income in 1985 U.S. dollars was in the range of $695 to $1235,[34] figures that would place it in the middle range of contemporary LDCs. Moreover, 1913 Russian per capita income was not notoriously high or low compared with the MEG starting points in Europe and North America.[35]

A second advantage vis-à-vis the contemporary LDCs relates to agricul-tural marketings. During the industrialization era, Russian agriculture tended to market a fairly substantial portion of its output outside of villages. For grain, the marketed portion averaged a fairly steady 25 percent from the 1880s to 1913.[36] Thus, Russian agriculture was able to produce a marketed surplus available for export and industrial raw materials, and was able to feed the urban population —a crucial requirement for successful economic development. In the poorer LDCs, agriculture tends to operate closer to peasant subsistence levels and is unable to provide the margin so crucial to industrial development.

A third advantage inherited by the Soviet regime was the Russian experi-ence with rapid industrial growth and infrastructure investment, especially after

1880. In fact, we have argued that the beginnings of modern economic growth can be discerned during this period. This industrialization provided the nucleus of a factory labor force and management personnel, and the rail network served as a valuable asset for an industrializing country. Few LDCs can launch industrialization from such a favorable base.[37]

REFERENCES

1. A. Gerschenkron, *Economic Backwardness in Historical Perspective* (Cambridge, Mass.: Harvard University Press, 1962), chap. 1; W. W. Rostow, *The Stages of Economic Growth* (Cambridge: Cambridge University Press, 1965), p. 67; W. W. Rostow, *The World Economy: History and Prospect* (Austin and London: University of Texas Press, 1978), pp. 426–429; M. E. Falkus, *The Industrialization of Russia, 1700–1914* (London and Basingstoke: MacMillan, 1972), pp. 1–25; and V. I. Lenin, *The Development of Capitalism in Russia* (Moscow: Progress Publishers, 1977).

2. S. Kuznets, *Modern Economic Growth* (New Haven, Conn.: Yale University Press, 1966), chap. 1.

3. A. Kahan, "Continuity in Economic Activity and Policy During the Post-Petrine Period in Russia," in W. L. Blackwell, ed., *Russian Economic Development from Peter the Great to Stalin* (New York: New Viewpoints, 1974), pp. 51–70.

4. A. Gerschenkron, "Russian Agrarian Policies and Industrialization, 1861–1917," in *Continuity in History and Other Essays* (Cambridge, Mass.: Harvard University Press, 1968), pp. 144–147.

5. P. A. Khromov, *Ekonomicheskoe razvitie Rossii* [The economic development of Russia] (Moscow: 1967), p. 280.

6. *Ibid.*, pp. 361–362; M. E. Falkus, "Russia and the International Wheat Trade, 1861–1914," *Economica,* vol. 33, no. 132 (November 1966), 416–429; and J. Metzer, "Railroad Development and Market Integration: The Case of Tsarist Russia," *Journal of Economic History,* vol. 34, no. 3 (September 1974), 529–550.

7. A. Gerschenkron, "The Early Phases of Industrialization in Russia: Afterthoughts and Counterthoughts," in W. W. Rostow, ed., *The Economics of Takeoff into Sustained Growth* (New York: St. Martin's Press, 1963), pp. 152–154; and J. P. McKay, *Pioneers for Profit: Foreign Entrepreneurship and Russian Industrialization, 1885–1913* (Chicago: University of Chicago Press, 1970).

8. For a collection of authoritative studies of Russian entrepreneurship, see G. Guroff and F. V. Carstensen (eds.), *Entrepreneurship in Imperial Russian and the Soviet Union* (Princeton, N.J.: Princeton University Press, 1983). In particular, see the studies by Thomas Owen, Arcadius Kahan, Boris Anan'ich, Fred Carstensen, and Ruth Amende Roosa.

9. Arcadius Kahan has examined the pattern of state expenditures during the period of rapid industrialization and found that only a very small portion of the imperial budget was devoted to promoting industrialization. It is primarily for this reason that Kahan has disputed the fact that the Russian state played a crucial role in promoting Russian industrialization. For further information, see A. Kahan, "Government Policies and the Industrialization of Russia," *Journal of Economic History,* vol. 27, no. 4 (December 1967).

10. Gerschenkron, *Economic Backwardness,* chap. 1.

11. R. Goldsmith, "The Economic Growth in Tsarist Russia, 1860–1913," *Economic Development and Cultural Change,* vol. 9, no. 3 (April 1961), 462–463; and A.

Gerschenkron, "The Rate of Growth in Russia Since 1885," *Journal of Economic History* (supplement), vol. 7 (1947), 144–174.

12. M. V. Dovnar-Zapol'skii, *Na zare krestianskoi svobody* [At the daybreak of peasant emancipation] (Kiev: 1911), p. 179.

13. The following discussion is based primarily upon Gerschenkron, "Russian Agrarian Policies," pp. 140–256, and Lazar Volin, *A Century of Russian Agriculture From Alexander II to Khrushchev* (Cambridge, Mass.: Harvard University Press, 1970), Part I.

14. Olga Crisp argues that this provision served to introduce a form of income tax, graduated according to ability to pay within the commune: O. Crisp, *Studies in the Russian Economy Before 1914* (London and Basingstoke: Macmillan, 1976), essay 3.

15. Gerschenkron, "Russian Agrarian Policies."

16. We relate a couple examples of rural poverty in Russia during the 1870s and 1880s. In the Kazan province, it was estimated that the yield per *desiatin* on fertile land was about 1.9 rubles. Obligations (taxes, redemption payments, etc.) per *desiatin,* however, were 2.8 rubles, which means that the peasant had to make up the difference by gainful employment either in industry or as a hired hand: Yu. Yanson, *Opyt statisticheskogo isledovaniia o krestianskikh nadelakh i platezhakh* [Experience of statistical investigations of peasant plots and payments] (St. Petersburg: 1877), pp. 75–85. A study of the Novgorod province revealed that total peasant income was 8.8 million rubles, of which 70 percent was earned outside agriculture. Bread purchases, taxes, and other obligations came to 6.3 million rubles, leaving a remainder of 2.6 million rubles, or 12 rubles per household for other consumption items: A. A. Kornilov, *Krestianskaia reforma* [The peasant reform] (St. Petersburg: 1905), pp. 194–195.

17. Crisp, *Studies in the Russian Economy,* essays 1 and 3; and J. Simms, "The Crisis in Russian Agriculture at the End of the 19th Century," *Slavic Review,* vol. 36, no. 3 (September 1977), 377–398. For more on this point, see the discussion between J. Sanders and J. Simms in "Once More Into the Breach, Dear Friends: A Closer Look at Indirect Tax Receipts and the Condition of the Russian Peasantry, 1881–1899," *Slavic Review,* vol. 43, no. 4 (Winter 1984), pp. 657–671.

18. The available studies of Russian national income point to agricultural output rising more rapidly than the rural population. Studies of Russian capital stock find that agricultural capital stock (livestock, structures, and equipment) was rising on a per capita basis. Available statistics also point to agricultural exports rising more rapidly than agricultural output. A study of Russian peasant living standards points to rising per capita consumption of the Russian agrarian population. On these points, see A. Kahan, "Capital Formation During the Period of Early Industrialization in Russia 1890–1913," *Cambridge Economic History of Europe,* vol. VII, part II (Cambridge: Cambridge University Press, 1982), appendices 8 and 9; Goldsmith, "Economic Growth in Tsarist Russia"; P. Gregory, "Grain Marketings and Peasant Consumption, Russia, 1885–1913, *Explorations in Economic History,* vol. 17, no. 2, (April 1980) 135–164; and Gregory, *Russian National Income,* chap. 6. Curiously, statistical studies conducted by Russian economists in the early twentieth century generally find rising per capita output in agriculture. For the most authoritative sources, see P. I. Liashchenko, *Ocherki agrarnoi evoliutsii Rossii* [Studies of the agrarian evolution in Russia] (Petersburg: No publisher given, 1908) and S. N. Prokopovich, *Opyt ischisleniia narodnogo dokhoda 50 gubernii Evropeiskoi Rossii v. 1900–1913 gg.* [An attempt to estimate the national income of the 50 European Russian provinces in the years 1900 and 1913] (Moscow: Soviet Vserossiiskikh Kooperativnykh Siezdov, 1918).

19. For authoritative studies of regional aspects of Russian agricultural production, see A. I. Chuprov and A. S. Posnikov, eds., *Vliianie orozhaev i khlebnykh tsen na nekoto-ryie storony russkago narodnago khoziaistva* [Influence of harvests and grain prices on several aspects of the Russian national economy] (Petersburg: Kirshbaum, 1897) and I. D. Koval'chenko and L. V. Milov, *Vserossiisky agrarny rynok XVIII–nachalo XX veka* [The all-Russian agrarian market from the eighteenth to the beginning of the twentieth century] (Moscow: Nauka, 1974).

20. P. R. Gregory, "Economic Growth and Structural Change in Tsarist Russia and the Soviet Union: A Long-Term Comparison," in S. Rosefielde, ed., *Economic Welfare and the Economics of Soviet Socialism* (Cambridge: Cambridge University Press, 1981).

21. *Ibid.*

22. Goldsmith, "The Rate of Growth in Tsarist Russia," 441–443.

23. These results are reported in Gregory, "Economic Growth and Structural Change in Tsarist Russia and the Soviet Union: A Long-Term Comparison."

24. Data on investment in schooling in Russia are summarized in O. Crisp, "Labor and Industrialization in Russia," *Cambridge Economic History of Europe,* (Cambridge: Cambridge University Press, 1978), vol. 7, part 2, pp. 387–399; and in A. Kahan, "Capital Formation During the Period of Early Industrialization in Russia," in the same volume, pp. 293–295.

25. F. Harbison and C. Myers, *Education, Manpower and Economic Growth* (New York: McGraw-Hill, 1964), chaps. 1 and 2.

26. Gerschenkron writes, "[the] labor supply to Russian industry was inadequate in quantity and inferior in quality. . . . Therein lies the explanation for the paradoxical situation that a country, so poor in capital and holding much of its accumulated wealth in hands that would not make it available for industrial venture, contrived to build up . . . a modern industrial structure . . . [which] compared favorably with those of economically advanced countries." In Gerschenkron, "Russian Agrarian Policies," pp. 210–211. For a contrary interpretation, see P. Gregory, "Some Empirical Comments on the Theory of Relative Backwardness: The Russian Case," *Economic Development and Cultural Change,* vol. 22, no. 4 (July 1974), 654–665.

27. Kuznets, *Modern Economic Growth,* pp. 40–51.

28. In 1886, the average life span was 29 years for males and 32 for females, which shows the marked effect of the high rate of infant mortality on age structure. See A. G. Rashin, *Naselenie Rossii za 100 let* [The population of Russia for 100 years] (Moscow: Sotzekizdat, 1956), p. 205.

29. See in particular H. Chenery, "Patterns of Industrial Growth," *American Economic Review,* vol. 50, no. 4 (September 1960), 624–653.

30. P. Gregory, *Socialist and Nonsocialist Industrialization Patterns* (New York: Praeger, 1970), pp. 28–29, 34, 171–174.

31. Gerschenkron, "The Early Phases of Industrialization in Russia," pp. 152–154. For a study that seeks to demonstrate that Russian industry was not top heavy in heavy industry, see Gregory, "Some Empirical Comments."

32. These figures are from B. Bonwetsch, "Das ausländische Kapital in Russland" [Foreign capital in Russia], *Jahrbücher für die Geschichte Osteuropas* [Yearbooks for the History of Eastern Europe], Band 22, Heft 3, 1974, pp. 416–418; and P. Gregory, "The Russian Balance of Payments, the Gold Standard, and Monetary Policy," *Journal of Economic History,* vol. 39, no. 2 (June 1979), 379–399.

33. Kuznets, *Modern Economic Growth,* pp. 332–334.

34. S. Cohn, *Economic Development in the Soviet Union* (Lexington, Mass.: Heath, 1970),

p. 111; National Foreign Assessment Center, *Handbook of Economic Statistics 1979,* ER 79–10274, Washington, D.C., U.S. Government Printing Office, August 1979, pp. xi, 27.
35. S. Kuznets, *Economic Growth of Nations* (Cambridge, Mass.: Harvard University Press, 1971), p. 24.
36. S. G. Wheatcroft, "The Reliability of Russian Prewar Grain Output Statistics," *Soviet Studies,* vol. 26, no. 2 (April 1974), pp. 157, 180; Gregory, "Grain Marketings and Peasant Consumption."
37. C. Wilber, *The Soviet Model and the Underdeveloped Countries* (Chapel Hill: University of North Carolina Press, 1969), disagrees with this assessment. He argues that the combined populations of LDCs with economic bases at least equal to the Soviet Union's 1928 base number more than 900 million. This conclusion is based upon physical indicators—literacy, wheat yields, energy consumption, and so on.

SELECTED BIBLIOGRAPHY

Non-Soviet Sources

A. N. Antisiferov, *Russian Agriculture During the War* (New York: Greenwood Press, 1930).

W. Blackwell, ed., *Russian Economic Development from Peter the Great to Stalin* (New York: New Viewpoints, 1974).

J. Blum, *Lord and Peasant in Russia* (New York: Atheneum, 1965).

O. Crisp, *Studies in the Russian Economy Before 1914* (London and Basingstoke: Macmillan, 1976).

M. E. Falkus, *The Industrialization of Russia, 1700–1914* (London and Basingstoke: Macmillan, 1972).

A. Gerschenkron, "Russian Agrarian Policies and Industrialization, 1861–1917," *The Cambridge Economic History of Europe,* vol. 6 (Cambridge: Cambridge University Press, 1965), pp. 706–800.

———, "The Early Phases of Industrialization in Russia: Afterthoughts and Counterthoughts," in W. W. Rostow, ed., *The Economics of Takeoff into Sustained Growth* (New York: St. Martin's Press, 1963).

———, "The Rate of Growth in Russia Since 1885," *Journal of Economic History* (supplement), vol. 7 (1947), 144–174.

D. Geyer, ed., *Wirtschaft und Gesellschaft in vorrevolutionären Russland* [Economy and society in prerevolutionary Russia] (Cologne: Kiepenheuer & Witsch, 1975).

R. Goldsmith, "The Economic Growth of Tsarist Russia, 1860–1913," *Economic Development and Cultural Change,* vol. 9, no. 3 (April 1961), 441–476.

P. R. Gregory, *Russian National Income, 1885–1913* (Cambridge: Cambridge University Press, 1982).

G. Guroff and F. V. Carstensen, *Entrepreneurship in Imperial Russia and the Soviet Union* (Princeton, N.J.: Princeton University Press, 1983).

J. P. McKay, *Pioneers for Profit: Foreign Entrepreneurship and Russian Industrialization, 1885–1913* (Chicago: University of Chicago Press, 1970).

R. Munting, *The Economic Development of the USSR* (London: Croom Helm, 1982), chap. 1.

J. Nötzold, *Wirtschaftspolitische Alternativen der Entwicklung in der Ära Witte und Stolypin* [Economic political alternatives in the era of Witte and Stolypin] (Berlin: Duncker & Humblot, 1966).

T. C. Owen, *Capitalism and Politics in Russia: A Social History of the Moscow Merchants* (Cambridge: Cambridge University Press, 1981).

R. Portal, "The Industrialization of Russia, *The Cambridge Economic History of Europe,* vol. 6 (Cambridge: Cambridge University Press, 1965), pp. 801–872.

M. M. Postan and Peter Mathias, eds., *The Cambridge Economic History of Europe,* vol. 7, part 2 (Cambridge: Cambridge University Press, 1978), section on Russia.

G. T. Robinson, *Russia Under the Old Regime* (New York: Macmillan, 1949).

M. I. Tugan-Baranovsky, *The Russian Factory in the 19th Century,* translated by A. and C. Levin (Homewood, Ill.: Irwin, 1970).

L. Volin, *A Century of Russian Agriculture* (Cambridge, Mass.: Harvard University Press, 1970).

T. von Laue, *Sergei Witte and the Industrialization of Russia* (New York: Columbia University Press, 1963).

Soviet Sources

V. I. Bovykin, *Formirovanie finansogo Kapitala v Rossii* (Moscow: Nauka, 1984).

P. A. Khromov, *Ekonomicheskoe razvitie Rossii* [The economic development of Russia] (Moscow: 1967).

———, *Ekonomicheskoe razvitie Rossii v 19. i 20. vekakh* [The economic development of Russia in the 19th and 20th centuries] (Moscow: Gospolitizdat, 1950).

V. I. Lenin, *Development of Capitalism in Russia* (Moscow: Progress 1977).

P. I. Lyaschenko, *History of the National Economy of Russia to the 1917 Revolution* (New York: Macmillan, 1949).

A. G. Rashin, *Formirovanie rabochego klassa v Rossii* [The formation of the working class in Russia] (Moscow: Sotseklitizdat 1958).

———, *Naselenie Rossii za 100 let* [The population of Russia for 100 years] (Moscow: Sotzeklitizdat 1956).

chapter *3*

The Economic Precedents of the Twenties

The Soviet Economy Under War Communism and the New Economic Policy (1918–1928)

This chapter considers the events of the period from 1918 to 1928 and their impact upon later Soviet economic policies. During this period, the economy operated under two quite different administrative regimes—War Communism and the New Economic Policy (NEP)—which provided experience to assist in making the final choice of comprehensive central planning (1928) and collectivization of agriculture (1929).

The lessons of War Communism and the New Economic Policy provide insights into the evolution of the Soviet economic system. The Soviet planning system did not appear from a vacuum; rather, it emerged gradually as a response to the practical economic problems of earlier periods. Our emphasis of the precedents of the 1920s is not meant to deny the important impact of the early Five Year Plan period (the 1930s) and World War II upon the evolution of the current system. These topics are dealt with in Chapter 5.

WAR COMMUNISM (1918–1921)[1]

In general terms, War Communism was an abortive attempt on the part of the inexperienced Bolshevik leadership to attain full communism directly without going through any preparatory intermediate stages: the use of money was virtually eliminated, private trade was abolished, workers were militarized and paid virtually equal wages in kind, and farm output was requisitioned. Were these war measures the product of the ideological intent of the Bolshevik leadership to establish full communism directly, or were they forced responses to the civil war? The most generally accepted view, as postulated by the well-known British authorities on War Communism, Maurice Dobb and E. H. Carr,[2] is that War Communism was forced upon the Bolshevik leadership by the Russian civil war and that the various theoretical arguments posited by the Bolshevik leadership in support of War Communism were "no more than flights of leftist fancy." In fact, Lenin—and Leon Trotsky—often referred to War Communism as the measures of a "besieged fortress." The opposite view, postulated by Paul Craig Roberts,[3] argues that Lenin originally conceived War Communism, with its elimination of market institutions and its introduction of administrative controls, as a necessary step in the socialist revolution. In Roberts's view, War Communism was adopted for ideological reasons as a product of Marxian ideas (as interpreted by Lenin), not as a forced response to the wartime emergency. We can provide no final answer to this controversy; instead, we shall attempt to outline as objectively as possible the basic features of War Communism.

The roots of War Communism can be traced to the October Revolution. One of the first actions of the fledgling Bolshevik regime was to nationalize the remaining large estates (the Land Decree of November 8, 1917) and to sanction the distribution of this land among the peasants. This action legalized in part the spontaneous appropriation of land by the peasantry, a process that had already taken place to a large degree. Irrespective of its causes, this change in land tenure was to have a far-reaching impact upon economic policy throughout the 1920s. In their enhanced capacity as full proprietors, the peasants were no longer obligated to deliver a prescribed portion of their output either to the landlord (as a rental payment) or to the state (as a tax or principal payment). Now they, not the state or landlord, made the basic decisions about how much to produce and what portion of this output would be sold. Thus, the total agricultural output and the *marketed portion* thereof became dependent for the first time upon the Russian peasant. Moreover, the 1917 revolution essentially did away with large farm production units. Before the revolution, 4 percent of the farm households farmed more than 13 *desiatins* of land, and another 13 percent were landless. By 1922, virtually no farm families had land holdings of more than 13 desiatins, and only 5 percent were without land.[4]

There was a revival of the *mir* during and after the Revolution. The mir was the institution that had confiscated and redistributed the land of the gentry, and it remained the principal voice of legal and administrative authority within the village during the early years of Soviet rule. The village assembly settled most of the questions of interest to the peasants and was able to steer a course independent of the *selsovet,* the local administrative arm of the Bolshevik government. However, as M. Lewin writes, one should not overemphasize the socialist instincts of the peasants.[5] The peasants remained attached to their village communities, and in their eyes, the purpose of the Revolution was to give them their own farms. That the land was nationalized and belonged to the mir did not detract from the peasants' conviction that the land was theirs to farm and manage as they saw fit.

The initial Bolshevik attitude toward private industry was cautious and restrained, since an uneasy truce between Bolshevik and capitalist was required to prevent a drop in industrial output. Workers' Committees in privately owned enterprises were given the right to supervise management, but, at the same time, the proprietor received the executive right to give orders that could not be countermanded by the Workers' Committees. Also, the Workers' Committees were denied the right to take over enterprises without the permission of higher authorities. Only enterprises of key importance—such as banking, grain purchasing and storage, transportation, oil, and war industries—were nationalized, establishing a form of state capitalism based upon state control of key positions in the economy, mixed management of enterprises, and private ownership of agriculture, retail trade, and small-scale industry.

The uneasy truce between the Bolsheviks and the capitalists and the peasants did not last long. By 1918, the Bolsheviks were locked in a struggle for survival with the White Russian forces supported in part by foreign powers. The Germans were in possession of the Ukraine, while the White Russian armies occupied the Urals, Siberia, North Caucasus, and other economically important regions. Poland invaded in May of 1920. At one time, the Bolsheviks retained only 10 percent of the coal supplies, 25 percent of the iron foundries, less than 50 percent of the grain area, and less than 10 percent of the sugar beet sources of the former Russian Empire.[6] At one point, three-quarters of USSR territory was occupied by opponents of Soviet authority.

To divert industrial and agricultural resources from private into military uses, the Bolsheviks, lacking a domestic tax base and access to foreign aid, resorted to printing money. This expansion of the money supply combined with shrinking supplies of consumer goods created hyperinflation. On November 1, 1917, the amount of money in circulation was 20 billion rubles. The rate of monetary emission accelerated thereafter, and by July 1, 1921, 2.5 trillion rubles were in circulation. Supplies of consumer goods offered for sale dwindled as materials were diverted to military uses, and prices rose more rapidly than the rate of growth of the money supply. Between 1917 and 1921, prices increased 8000-fold.[7]

The hyperinflation resulted in the near destruction of the market exchange economy. Peasants were reluctant to exchange their products for depreciating money, as were manufacturers and artisans. The economy increasingly employed barter to effect transactions, and this led to what the Soviets call the "naturalization" (demonetization) of the economy. This naturalization process was welcomed by the left wing of the Bolshevik party, which termed the government printing press "that machine gun which attacked the bourgeois regime in its rear, namely, through its monetary system."[8] The naturalization of the economy created, however, an immediate crisis for the Soviet leadership. The central government found itself powerless to obtain through the market those goods, food supplies in particular, that it needed to fight the war.

War Communism Policies

The Bolshevik leadership under Lenin responded by introducing War Communism, a system by which the leaders attempted to substitute administrative for market allocation to marshal resources for the war. The crux of War Communism was its policy of forcibly requisitioning agricultural surpluses. Police (the *Cheka*) and party activists were sent into the countryside to collect the "surpluses" of the rich and middle peasantry—a policy that severed the existing market link between industry and agriculture. In theory at least, the link was to be maintained by state allocation of manufactured products to the peasants and barter transactions for the remaining agricultural output. In fact, the peasants received only from 12 to 15 percent of prewar supplies of manufactured goods.[9] Initially, the regime had hoped to preserve the market link with agriculture by setting aside manufactured commodities to promote exchange with the countryside, but the peasants failed to respond. On May 9, 1918, the system of requisitioning (called the *prodrazverstka*) was initiated, and the commissar for food was invested with extraordinary powers to confiscate food products from the farm population. Thus, a "food dictatorship" was established, and the Bolshevik government took over the task of collecting and distributing agricultural products.

Nationalization of the economy was the second major policy of War Communism. The sugar industry was the first to be nationalized in the spring of 1918, and by the autumn of 1920, a total of 37,000 enterprises had been nationalized, of which roughly half were small-scale businesses that did not use mechanical power. This pervasive nationalization of industry may be regarded in part as a crisis response, for a large number of former industrial proprietors had gone over to the White Russian side, and there was widespread fear of German takeovers of German-owned enterprises. Also, nationalization from below by workers had been proceeding at a rapid pace despite government attempts to control unauthorized worker takeovers. On the other hand, the excessive nationalization from above down to enterprises employing only one worker may perhaps be regarded as an ideological response not to be justified by the crisis situation. Nominally, the nationalized enterprises were subject to central direction by the state budget and national industrial boards. In actual practice, centralized coordination was generally lacking.

The abolition of private trade was the third cornerstone of War Communism policy. Private trade was regarded as incompatible with the War Communism system of centralized requisitioning and allocation. Government trade monopolies and monopsonies (mainly the Commissariat of Supply and the Commissariat of Agriculture) were set up to replace private organizations and concentrate commodity distribution in the hands of the state. In November 1918, all private internal trade was abolished, and the state ostensibly became the sole supplier of consumer goods to the population. In fact, the black market continued to supply a significant portion of total consumption goods and was unofficially tolerated by the authorities.[10] In the most critical moments of 1918, the Soviet government made it legal for workers to purchase up to 20 kilograms of grain directly from peasants, but this provision was quickly rescinded when it threatened to disrupt government requisitioning.[11]

Semimilitary controls over industrial workers became a major means of labor allocation. The movement of industrial workers was restricted, and they could be mobilized for special work. In some cases, army personnel were used for special projects. Labor deserters received severe penalties according to a decree of November 28, 1919, which placed the employees of state enterprises under military discipline.

The mobilization of labor was managed in large part by Leon Trotsky, the organizer of the Red Army. Trotsky's intention was to create a system of universal labor mobilization, and by the end of 1918, his mobilization plans were being put into effect. Labor was decreed to be compulsory for all able-bodied persons, compulsory labor service was declared for the peasantry, labor armies (one under the leadership of Stalin in the Ukraine) were created by delaying demobilization, and the Commission for Universal Labor Service was created with Trotsky at its head.[12] In 1920, railway workers, firemen, miners, construction workers, metal workers, and shipbuilders were mobilized. The Siberian labor army was engaged in coal mining, forestry, and rail construction; and the Caucasian labor army was charged with rail construction and crude oil extraction.[13]

The War Communism system of distribution attempted to apply class and social principles to distribution. Under the "class ration," introduced in 1918, wages were to be based upon the type of work being done. Since money wages had lost most of their meaning as a consequence of hyperinflation, the highest ration (wage) would go to workers performing heavy work under dangerous conditions; the lowest, to the free professions and the unemployed. The highest category was to receive a ration four times that of the lowest category. The wartime chaos of the period made it difficult for the state to adhere to these class ration principles because in most regions state supply agencies were doing well to keep the population above subsistence. Special rations were used, however, to supply the workers of priority industries, and in 1919, 30 categories of workers were placed on preferential rations.[14]

The final feature of War Communism was the naturalization of economic life. The procurement of agricultural products through requisitioning and confiscation replaced the market link between the city and countryside. Every citizen had to be registered with a state or cooperative shop to obtain legal rations. Settlements among state enterprises were made via bookkeeping transactions that had little real meaning. In 1920, postal services, housing, gas, electricity, and public transportation were made available free of charge, and it was decided that foodstuffs supplied through the Food Commissariat should also be free of charge.[15]

An Evaluation of War Communism

Any evaluation of War Communism must emphasize a frequently neglected point made by the Soviet literature: War Communism did enable the Bolsheviks to muster sufficient resources to win the civil war. In this sense, War Communism may be viewed as an important political and military success. It is easy to overlook this basic point and to concentrate instead on the system's many weaknesses. We seek rather to evaluate War Communism in terms of the question: Was War Communism a viable economic system for coping with the long-term problems of economic growth and development facing the Soviet regime during the 1920s?[16]

As one might expect, War Communism's replacement of market exchange by administrative resource allocation created several serious problems. First, there was a sharp decline in both agricultural output and marketings to the state during the 1918 to 1921 period, even after adjustment for war devastation. Peasants were holding back grain in storage, were planting less, and were selling to private traders. The area of Siberia sown in wheat was halved and in the Volga and Caucasus regions was reduced to as little as one-quarter of previous levels. Actual sowing concealed from authorities was reported to be as high as 20 percent of the sown area in some regions.[17] Since agricultural surpluses in excess of family subsistence were requisitioned, there was no incentive to produce a surplus. Instead, the peasants, if they could not conceal their surplus from the authorities, restricted output to the subsistence needs of their family. Thus, War Communism's agrarian policy estranged Russian peasants from the Bolshevik regime and encouraged them to engage in dysfunctional behavior, such as restricting output and hoarding or concealing surpluses during a period of agricultural shortages.

Soviet industry was also faced with serious problems. Almost all enterprises, with the exception of certain small-scale handicraft shops, had been nationalized without first establishing a suitable administrative structure to coordinate their activities. The industrial census of 1920 showed over 5,000 nationalized enterprises employing only one worker.[18] The abolition of private trade, which was to be superseded by state rationing, removed the existing market link between consumer and producer. Producers, except those selling to the black market, therefore, were no longer directed by the market in their production decisions.

Ostensibly, large-scale industry was to be coordinated by the Supreme Council of the National Economy (VSNKh), which was broken up into departments *(Glavki),* each of which was to direct a particular industry. The *Glavki* were usually grouped into trusts. For example, the mining trust contained six *Glavki.* By 1920, there were over 50 *Glavki* charged with controlling production and distribution.[19] In addition, the provincial economic councils *(Gubsovnarkhozy)* were the local organs of VSNKh. This arrangement bordered on chaos. In 1920, there were over 37,000 nationalized enterprises. The *Glavki* possessed insufficient information about local enterprises to direct them effectively—to such a degree that an investigative committee of 1920 found that many *Glavki* not only "do not know what goods and in what amounts are kept in warehouses under their control, but are actually ignorant even of the numbers of such warehouses."[20] As a result, the directives that the *Glavki* issued to the local authorities rarely corresponded to local capacities and requirements, causing a prolonged struggle between central and local administrations. Often, local authorities merely gave formal compliance to directives from above and then countermanded them, knowing they could do so with impunity.

VSNKh was the principal champion of centralized control during War Communism, and under its influential chairman, Aleksei Rykov, it fought against the "Left Communist" contingent, which favored workers' control of factories. Rykov also attacked the concept of trade union control of enterprises, citing Lenin's opposition to workers' control and Lenin's support of rational one-man management. Nevertheless, VSNKh's success in establishing centralized control was modest. Individual industries were being run independently by the *Glavki* and local authorities with virtually no centralized coordination. Various national and local organizations had overlapping and conflicting responsibilities concerning the distribution of consumer and producer goods. Primitive plans were drawn up for particular industries, but these plans were not presented in the form of a national plan to be approved by government. The first effort at national economic planning was the general electrification plan (GOELRO), completed in December of 1920.

In sum, War Communism industry operated essentially without direction, either from the market or from planners. Bottlenecks were eliminated by employing "shock" *(udarny)* methods, which meant that whenever congestion in a particular sector became alarming, it would receive top priority in the form of adequate supplies of fuels, materials, and rations. The shock system provided a means of establishing priorities and was beneficial in this sense. However, while the concentration of resources in the shock industries allowed them to surge ahead and overcome the original bottleneck, the nonshock industries had in the process fallen behind and had created new bottlenecks, which would then be attacked by additional shock methods. In this manner, some weak sense of general direction was supplied to the economy to replace total chaos. The shock system was somewhat effective as long as it remained undiluted, which meant that the number of shock industries at one time had to be limited. As time went by, the agitation for widening the shock categories became so intense that eventually even the manufacture of pens and pencils was included, thus destroying the whole purpose of the shock method—to set up a system of priorities.

Finally, the lack of an adequate system of incentive wages led to industrial labor supply problems. The government controlled the legal distribution of consumer commodities among members of the industrial labor force, thereby controlling a significant portion of real industrial wages. The Bolshevik Party never officially subscribed to a utopian view of income distribution according to need; instead, it was realized that wage differentials were important in attracting labor in skilled and/or arduous jobs. For example, the Ninth Congress of the Communist Party in 1920 resolved that the food supply system should give preference to the industrious worker, and the Third Trade Union Conference of the same year proposed incentive premiums in kind to be paid to diligent workers.

The result, however, contradicted the intention and was one reason Trotsky referred to War Communism wage policy as the measure of a "beseiged fortress." In fact, wages were rationed out to industrial workers on a fairly equal basis because, first, shortages were so severe that local supply authorities were content to keep the working force at subsistence and, second, it proved too complex to devise a system of incentive wages to be paid in kind.

The result of this egalitarianism was an insufficient pool of qualified labor in industry. Instead of being drawn into factories, labor was flowing out of them during War Communism. The number of townspeople declined from 2.6 million in 1917 to 1.2 million in 1920.[21] Morale was poor, worker sabotage was rampant, absenteeism was high, and the tenuous loyalty of specialists was slipping. These developments were especially ominous in view of the dearth of skilled industrial

Table 8   PRODUCTION AND TRADE INDEXES, USSR: 1913 AND 1920 (1913 = 100)

	Industry	Agri-culture	Trans-portation	Exports	Imports
1913[a]	100	100	100	100.0	100.0
1920	20	64	22	0.1	2.1

Sources: G. W. Nutter, "The Soviet Economy: Retrospect and Prospect," in D. Abshire and R. V. Allen, eds., *National Security: Political, Military, and Economic Strategies in the Decade Ahead* (New York: Praeger, 1963), p. 165; M. Kaser, "A Volume Index of Soviet Foreign Trade," *Soviet Studies,* vol. 20, no. 4 (April 1969), 523–526.
[a]The 1913 figures refer to interwar territory of the USSR.

laborers during this early period. Strikes became quite common during the latter part of 1920.

The Soviet regime had succeeded in solidifying its position by the end of 1920. A peace treaty had been signed with Poland, and the White Russian army had been driven out of the crucial industrial and agricultural regions that it had occupied earlier. The crisis under which War Communism had come into existence had been overcome, and the dangers of continuing that economic policy were growing more apparent. The still powerful trade unions were revolting against the crippling centralization of industry and the conscription of labor. The alienated peasant population called for abolition of the state grain monopoly. Industrial workers were restive, the military was in a rebellious mood, and the Soviet regime was in danger of falling victim to internal discontent. Factory output had fallen to less than 15 percent of its prewar level.[22] Table 8 shows the extent of the drops in industrial and agricultural output, the decline in transportation services, and the USSR's virtual withdrawal from export and import markets. At the end of 1920 and the beginning of 1921, there were peasant uprisings in the countryside against the continuation of requisitioning after the end of hostilities. The final blow was the Kronstadt Uprising of March 1921, when the sailors of the Kronstadt naval base revolted in support of the Petrograd workers. The Soviet leadership moved quickly to dispel this discontent by replacing War Communism with the New Economic Policy (NEP) in March of 1921.

THE NEW ECONOMIC POLICY (1921–1928)

Just as War Communism may have been thrust upon the Soviet regime by the civil war in 1918, the New Economic Policy was forced upon the Soviet leadership by the excesses of War Communism. For whatever its reasons, the Soviet leadership at the time took pains to stress the temporary nature of both periods. Lenin declared that "War Communism was thrust upon us by war and ruin. It was not, nor could it be, a policy that corresponded to the economic tasks of the proletariat. It was a temporary measure."[23] In the same vein, Lenin described NEP as a temporary step backward (away from socialism) in order later to take two steps forward. From the viewpoint of the Bolshevik leadership, NEP was a transitional step backward because of the important roles that "antisocialist" institutions, such as private ownership, private initiative, and capitalist markets, were allowed to play during this period.

The most striking feature of NEP was its attempt to combine market and socialism: agriculture remained in the hands of the peasant, the management of industry (with the exception of the "commanding heights") was decentralized. Market links between industry and agriculture and between industry and consumer replaced state control of production and distribution. Most industrial enterprises were denationalized. But many of the largest enterprises—the so-called commanding heights—remained nationalized and encompassed about three-quarters of industrial output. In this manner, it was thought that the state could provide general guidance by retaining direct control of the commanding heights of the economy—heavy industry, transportation, banking, and foreign trade—while allowing the remainder of the economy to make its own decisions.

The political basis of NEP was the *Smychka,* or alliance, between the Soviet regime (supposedly representing the urban proletariat) and the peasant. An important political objective of NEP was to regain the political and economic support of the peasant. Thus, the War Communism policy of requisitioning agricultural surpluses had to be abandoned, for the peasants would never ally themselves with a regime that confiscated their surpluses. Market agriculture had to be reestablished in its place, freeing the peasant both to sell surpluses freely and to buy industrial products freely.

The *Smychka* strategy represented a significant concession from the Bolshevik leaders, whose freedom of action was accordingly severely restricted because they were limited to policies that would not alienate the peasant. This at times placed them in the tenuous position of having to choose between the support of the peasantry and the attainment of basic party objectives. However, there was even a more fundamental contradiction. The reestablishment of market agriculture would serve to create a commercially minded peasantry and an environment that would reward success and penalize failure. The very success of NEP would require increasing economic differentiation among the agricultural population and the emergence of a class of relatively prosperous peasants, who would produce the critical market surpluses. Marx had condemned the wealthy and middle peasant as adamant opponents of socialism, but NEP would serve to promote this class. Thus, the ideological concession underlying NEP was apparently very great.[24]

NEP Policies

The cornerstone of NEP was the proportional agricultural tax (the *prodnalog*) introduced in March of 1921 to replace the War Communism system of requisitions. First paid in kind, and by 1924 in money, it was a single tax, based upon a *fixed proportion* of each peasant's *net produce.* The state now took a fixed proprortion production, and the peasant again had an incentive to aim for as a large a surplus as possible. The *prodnalog* was differentiated according to income level (as dictated by the size of the landholding and farm animals) and by family size. In 1923, for example, the *prodnalog* varied from 5 percent (landholdings less than one-quarter hectare) to 17 percent (more than three hectares) of annual income. Throughout the NEP period, the burden of the *prodnalog* was shifted increasingly to the middle and upper peasants, and it accounted for some one-quarter of state revenues during NEP. According to studies conducted in the mid-1920s the tax burden on peasants was lower during NEP than in 1913. In 1913, approximately 14 percent of peasant income went to pay various taxes. In the mid-1920s, this percentage was below 10 percent. More recent studies by Western historians find that the tax burden during NEP was about the same as in 1913 when all forms are considered.[25]

The agriculture tax was the first step in reestablishing a market economy; it, in turn, necessitated further measures. Unless the peasants could dispose profitably of their after-tax surplus, they would have little incentive to produce above subsistence. Therefore, the state granted the peasants commercial autonomy to sell their output to the buyer of their choice, be it the state, a cooperative, or a private dealer. This measure required the legalization of private trade, which was again permitted to compete with state and cooperative trade organizations. Now the peasants could market their after-tax surplus at terms dictated by market forces, not by a state monopoly. The resurgence of private trade provided a further incentive for peasants to market their surplus, for they no longer faced a state supply monopoly, rationing out industrial products to them. Finally, peasants were allowed to lease land and to hire farm laborers, both of which had been forbidden under War Communism.

Within one year, private activity dominated Soviet retail trade and restored the market link between consumer and producer. By the end of 1922, nine-tenths of all retail trading outlets were private, and they handled about three-quarters of the value of all retail trade turnover, with state and cooperative outlets handling the balance.[26] The private trader, or *Nepman* as he was called, was less strongly entrenched in wholesale trade, which remained dominated by state and cooperative organizations.

NEP also brought about significant changes in Soviet industry. The majority of industrial enterprises were permitted to make their own contracts for the purchase of raw materials and supplies and for the sale of their output; during War Communism, the state had performed these functions. Small enterprises employing 20 persons or less were denationalized, and a small number of them were returned to their former owners. Others were leased to new entrepreneurs, thereby re-creating a class of small-scale capitalists. The Bolsheviks even granted a limited number of foreign concessions. (The lessee typically signed a contract of six year's duration obligating the enterprise to sell a prescribed portion of its output to the state.) Denationalization was limited to small-scale enterprises, and the overwhelming portion of industrial production during NEP was turned out by nationalized enterprises. The industrial census of 1923 showed that private enterprises accounted for only 12.5 percent of total employment in "census" establishments.[27] In addition, only 2 percent of the output of large-scale industry was produced by the private sector in 1924–1925.[28]

While much of large-scale industry remained nationalized, decision-making throughout industry was decentralized to a great extent. Nationalized enterprises were divided into two categories: the commanding heights of the economy—fuel, metallurgy, war industries, transportation, banking, and foreign trade—were not

separated from the state budget and remained dependent upon centralized allocations of state supplies. The remaining nationalized enterprises were granted substantial financial and commercial autonomy from the state budget. The latter
enterprises were instructed to operate commercially, that is, to maximize profits
and to sell to the highest bidder, be it state or private trade. Most important, they
were not obligated to deliver output according to production quotas to the state,
as under War Communism.

The nationalized enterprises of this second category were allowed to feder-
ate into trusts, which soon became the dominant form of industrial organization
during NEP. By 1923, the 478 chartered trusts accounted for 75 percent of all
workers employed in nationalized industry.[29] These trusts were given the legal
authority to enter into independent contracts. They were to be supervised loosely
either by VSNKh or by the *Sovnarkhozy* (the regional economic councils), but
their commercial independence was protected in that the state was not allowed
to acquire the property or products of a trust except by contractual agreement.
The most powerful trusts remained under the direct administration of VSNKh.
About 25 percent of industrial production (mainly light industry) remained under
Sovnarkhoz supervision. In light industry, the trusts were largely independent of
state control other than the usual forms of fiscal and monetary intervention. In
some key sectors of heavy industry, VSNKh exercised much stricter controls over
trusts in the form of specific production and delivery targets. The profits of trusts
were subject to property and income taxation in the same manner as private
enterprises. The monopoly State Bank controlled trust commercial credit. Although the commanding heights enterprises remained within the state budget,
they also were instructed to operate as profitably as possible to eliminate reliance
on subsidies. Emphasis on capitalist-type cost accounting was the order of the
day.

NEP was not a command economy. Planning authorities generally provided trusts with "control figures," which were to be used as forecasts and guides
for investment decisions. Mandatory output plans were drawn up only in the case
of a few key sectors in heavy industry. The limited physical planning and distribution was carried out through the Committee of State Orders (representing the
commissariats), which placed orders through VSNKh, which in turn negotiated
the order with the producer trusts. During the major part of NEP, the most
important force of economic control and regulation was the Peoples Commissariat of Finance *(Narkomfin),* which exerted its influence through the budget
and credit system (the so-called dictatorship of finance). Planning during the
NEP period was carried out by a variety of organizations—VSNKh, the State
Planning Committee *(Gosplan,* established in 1921), the commissariats, and local
authorities. Until the late 1920s, planners limited themselves primarily to fore-
casting trends as dictated by market conditions. Also, there was a notable lack
of coordination among the various planning agencies until Gosplan established
itself as the dominant coordinating planning body after 1927.[30]

One basic notion of a way to guide the economy during NEP was to
amalgamate producing enterprises in order to simplify control and coordination.
An important phenomenon was the amalgamation of trusts into syndicates,

initially for the purpose of coordinating industry sales. In addition to easing the planning burden, trusts and syndicates were favored by the Soviet leadership's ideological preference for large-scale industry.[31] By the late NEP period, the syndicates came to dominate the sales of state industry, accounting for 82 percent of state industry sales in 1927–1928 and for all sales of ferrous metal.[32] The trusts and syndicates acquired considerable commercial autonomy. Syndicates were allowed to enter directly into foreign trade agreements (without permission of the state foreign trade monopoly) and had the right to receive credit from credit institutions located in the Soviet Union and in some instances from foreign banks. The growing autonomy of trusts and syndicates had its disadvantages for the Soviet leadership, particularly when the trusts attempted to charge monopoly prices for their products, as we shall discuss below.

Use of money had been virtually eliminated during War Communism as a result of hyperinflation and had been replaced by a system of barter and physical allocation. Such a system, however, would have been too clumsy for the new market system of NEP. To avoid this obstacle, the Soviets reintroduced the use of money with the reopening of the State Bank in 1921 for the expressed purpose of aiding the development of the economy. Both public and private enterprises were encouraged to deposit their savings in the State Bank; limitations on private bank deposits were removed and safeguards were established to protect such deposits from state confiscation. A new stabilized currency, the *chervonets,* was issued by the State Bank in 1921, a balanced budget was achieved in 1923–1924, a surplus in 1924–1925, and the old depreciated paper ruble was withdrawn from circulation in the currency reform of May 1924. Thereby a relatively stable Soviet currency was created, which for a time was even quoted on international exchanges. Money transactions between state enterprises replaced earlier barter transactions.

NEP also witnessed an attempt to reestablish relatively normal trading relations with the outside world.[33] A state monopoly over foreign trade had been established shortly after the Bolshevik takeover, and foreign trade virtually disappeared during the civil war. During NEP, the Soviet leadership was reluctant to become dependent upon capitalist markets, which they believed would suffer from increasingly severe crises. Rather, the NEP strategy of trade was enunciated in Lenin's dictum of "learning from the enemy as quickly as possible." Thus, the trading monopoly aimed at the importation of capitalist technology (and foreign experts) and of equipment that could not be produced at home. With this strategy in mind, foreign concessions were granted and credits from the capitalist world were sought. It was thought that in their scramble for Russian markets, the capitalist countries would mute their political hostility to the Soviet regime, which had repudiated tsarist Russia's foreign debt.

The volume of foreign trade grew rapidly during NEP, from 8 percent of the prewar level in 1921 to 44 percent in 1928.[34] Yet unlike the production figures, which showed a recovery to prewar levels, the volume of foreign trade throughout NEP remained well below half that of the prewar level. Credits from the capitalist nations were not forthcoming and foreign policy failures made them even less likely. The concessions program never got off the ground; at the end of NEP, there were only 59 foreign concessions, accounting for less than one percent of the output of state industry.

The Economic Recovery of NEP

Just as War Communism provided the means for waging the civil war, NEP provided the means for recovery from the war, and, in this sense, it was an important strategic success for the Soviet leadership. The economic recovery during NEP was impressive (see Table 9).

In 1920, production statistics (Table 8) indicated the low level of economic activity that existed at the end of War Communism. Industrial production and transportation were both only one-fifth of the prewar level. The shortage of fuel threatened to paralyze industry and transportation, and industry was living on dwindling reserves of pig iron. The food shortage led to the exhaustion and demoralization of the labor force. Agricultural production was 64 percent of the prewar level. Foreign trade had virtually disappeared.

In 1928—on the eve of the first Five Year Plan and at the end of NEP— the official statistics provide a striking contrast: both industry and agriculture had surpassed their prewar levels. Foreign trade remained well below prewar levels but had recovered substantially from the negligible War Communism volumes.

More recent calculations suggest that official Soviet figures may have over-stated the extent of recovery during NEP and that Soviet national income in 1928 was still below 1913 levels. Surprisingly, this position appears to be supported by A. L. Vainshtein, the noted Soviet authority of Soviet national income.[35] Subse-quent research may be able to determine more precisely the extent of the eco-nomic recovery during the NEP period. The recovery from the economic devasta-tion shown by the figures for 1920 was impressive irrespective of which set of statistics one chooses to use. Although the NEP recovery was impressive, particu-larly as judged by official statistics, one should note that high rates of growth during recovery periods are to be expected once a suitable economic environment is established. NEP policies provided this suitable framework for recovery.

The End of NEP

According to Soviet statistics, the highest level of NEP is usually dated to 1926, when prewar production levels were generally surpassed. The absolute growth of the nonagricultural private sector stopped in 1926.[36] At that time, all seemed to be going well; yet two years later, NEP was abandoned in favor of the radically different system of state central planning, collectivization of agriculture, and nationalization of industry and trade. This radical turn of events seems puzzling in view of the impressive NEP successes. Why was NEP abandoned? Several considerations stimulated the decision.

First, a large number of party members viewed NEP as a temporary and unwelcome compromise with class enemies. Now that the state was stronger, they argued, the offensive against class enemies could be resumed.[37] Second, the Soviet

Table 9   **SELECTED INDICATORS OF SOVIET OUTPUT LEVELS IN 1928**
              RELATIVE TO 1913 (1913 = 100)

National income		Selected physical production series	
1913 prices	117	Grain production	87
1926/27 prices	119	Pig iron	79
		Steel	102
		Coal	122
Industrial production		Cotton cloth	104
1913 prices	129	Freight turnover	104
1926/27 prices	134–139	Electric power	203
		Foreign trade	
Agricultural production		Exports	38
1926/27 prices	111	Imports	49

Sources: A. L. Vainshtein, *Narodny dokhod Rossii i SSSR* (Moscow: Nauka, 1969), p. 102; Gosplan SSSR, *Kontrol'nye tsifry narodnogo khoziaistva SSSR na 1928/29 g.* (Moscow: Izdatel'stvo Planovoe Khoziaistvo, 1929, p. 68; R. W. Davies, "Soviet Industrial Production, 1928–1937: The Rival Estimates," *Centre for Russian and East European Studies Discussion Papers,* no. 18 (University of Birmingham, 1978), p. 63; S. G. Wheatcroft, "Grain Production Statistics in the USSR in the 1920s and 1930s," *Centre for Russian and East European Studies Discussion Papers,* no. 13 (University of Birmingham, 1977), p. 23; Wheatcroft, "Soviet Agricultural Production, 1913–1940" (mimeographed, 1979); A. Bergson, *The Real National Income of Soviet Russia Since 1928* (Cambridge: Harvard University Press, 1961), p. 7; M. Kaser, "A Volume Index of Soviet Foreign Trade," *Soviet Studies,* vol. 20, no. 4 (April 1969), pp. 523–26.

authorities feared that economic policy might become dominated by the growing numbers of prosperous peasants and *Nepmen.* Increasingly, policies were being dictated to suit the needs of the peasants, not the objectives of the state. A prime example of this was the "Scissors Crisis" of 1923, which forced the Soviet regime into the paradoxical stance of favoring private agriculture over socialist industry. The Scissors Crisis merits a slight digression at this point.

According to Soviet figures, the total marketed surplus of agriculture in 1923 was 60 percent of the prewar level, with grain marketings falling even below this figure. On the other hand, industrial production was only 35 percent of the prewar level.[38] The more rapid recovery of agriculture placed upward pressure on industrial prices relative to agricultural prices. The different sectoral recovery rates were not the sole determinants of relative price movements. A portion of the already limited output of industry was being withheld from the market by the industrial trust and syndicates, who were using their monopoly power to restrict trust sales to raise prices. The net result was an even more rapid rise of industrial prices relative to agricultural prices. The relative price movements between early 1922 and late 1923 (Fig. 4) take on the shape of an open pair of scissors, from whence came the term "Scissors Crisis."

The Soviet authorities viewed the opening price scissors with alarm, for they expected the peasants to react by refusing to market their surpluses as their terms of trade with the city fell. Moreover, Soviet authorities were very sensitive to signs of peasant unrest. In 1924, there were a number of disturbing developments. In August, there was an uprising of Georgian peasants. There was also a ground swell to form a peasant association that would represent peasant interests against the party, and in the elections to the Soviets in fall of 1924, the peasant turnout was under 30 percent (despite party efforts to have mass peasant participation).[39]

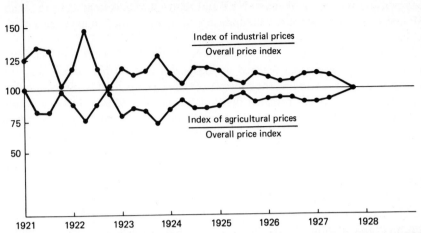

Figure 4 The Scissors Crisis. (*Source:* A. L. Vainshtein, *Tseny i tsenoobrazovanie v SSSR v vosstanovitel'ny period* [Prices and price formation in the USSR in the transition period] (Moscow: Nauka, 1972), pp. 158–167.)

During the prewar period, Russian peasants marketed (outside of the village) on the average 30 percent of their output. In early 1923, before the price scissors had opened sharply, they marketed about 25 percent, and Soviet authorities feared a further drop. It is uncertain what did happen to peasant marketings as the scissors opened, since statistics for this early period are difficult to find. A student of the scissors crisis, James Millar, suggests that the Bolsheviks mistakenly *expected* peasant marketings to decline as agricultural prices fell in relative terms.[40] In fact, Millar argues, the peasants had traditionally responded to a decline in the terms of trade with the city by selling more to the city in order to maintain their standard of living. The Millar argument is supported by evidence showing that prewar grain marketings were not significantly affected by the terms of trade.[41] Grain marketing statistics for the Ukraine do, however, suggest a reduction in peasant marketings between 1923 and 1925, but such evidence is quite fragmentary,[42] and it is difficult to determine whether Millar's or the Soviets' perception of peasant behavior is correct.

Rightly or wrongly, the Soviet government viewed this development as a threat to the NEP recovery, for the industrial worker had to be fed and light industry required agricultural raw materials. The regime's reaction to a similar problem in 1918 had been to requisition agricultural surpluses, which resulted in a costly reduction of agricultural output; a return to requisitioning would jeopardize the progress made by NEP between 1920 and 1923. Further, influential party officials, particularly Nikolai Bukharin, feared (probably irrationally) an insufficient aggregate demand if the Scissors Crisis continued: if the peasants refused to market their output, peasant demand for industrial commodities would shrink, thereby causing an eventual glut of industrial commodities, which would also threaten the industrial recovery.

In essence, the Scissors Crisis forced the Soviet leadership to choose between two alternatives: to abandon NEP and return to requisitioning, or to retain NEP and to favor agriculture over industry to preserve the tenuous peace with the peasantry.

A third source of dissatisfaction with NEP was the conviction at that time that economic recovery had reached its limits and that further advances could be achieved only by expanding the capacity of the economy, that is, by accumulating capital. NEP statistics revealed that much capacity had been lost as a result of World War I and the civil war: the capital stock of heavy industry as of 1924 was estimated to be 23 percent below its 1917 peak, and this capital equipment was on the whole old and outmoded. In 1924, the output of steel, a principal component of investment equipment, was 23 percent of 1913 output. Thus, industrial capacity had been lost between 1917 and 1924 and little had been done to replace it, although the building of socialism in the Soviet Union and expansion of military capacity were priority objectives of the Soviet state. After eight years of Soviet rule, investment and military commodities accounted for the same proportion of industrial output as they had prior to the revolution. For example, 28 percent of manufacturing net output was devoted to heavy industry in 1912, and this share had only risen to 29 percent by 1926.[43] To a regime already committed to the ideological primacy of large-scale heavy industry, this was an unacceptable outcome.

In spite of their dissatisfaction with the course of industrial development during the 1920s, the Soviet leadership viewed its hands as tied as long as NEP was retained. They feared that a drive to increase industrial capacity—that is, to increase the share of heavy industry—would reduce the availability, and consequently raise the prices, of manufactured goods in the short run and would further turn the terms of trade against agriculture, thus creating an additional agricultural supply crisis that would impede industrialization.

Moreover, the NEP period demonstrated to the Soviet leadership its inability to make policy in a market environment. First, the Soviet authorities failed to understand normal speculative behavior in a world of fluctuating prices. Particularly in agriculture, products will be withheld from the market when producers believe that prices are temporarily low. Thus, when Soviet pricing authorities would set low agricultural prices, grain producers would withhold their products from the market in expectation that the lower prices would not hold. It was primarily the more affluent agricultural producers who could afford to withhold grain from the market (to wait for better prices); therefore, most speculative grain stockpiling would naturally be done by the upper peasants. Second, Soviet authorities failed to appreciate fully the general inflationary pressures of the mid-1920s. Between 1924 and 1927, the money supply rose by 2,665 percent, which meant that there were strong inflationary pressures both in industry and in agriculture. Many of the Soviet pricing policies (both in agriculture and in industry) were simply undertaken to hold down the rate of inflation. However, economic history tells us that, whenever price controls are introduced in tandem with excessive monetary growth, economic distortions of all sorts are bound to emerge. Third, Soviet authorities failed to understand common notions of opportunity costs. There were a number of instances in the mid-1920s when the state prices for grains were set below the opportunity costs of producing the grains. It is not unexpected that peasants would reduce their production and marketings of grains with prices below opportunity costs. Fourth, Soviet authorities appeared to be much more interested in grain collected by the state than in the total amount of grain offered to the market. Soviet authorities throughout the 1920s were much more interested in how much grain they were able to obtain from the peasants than in total grain marketings (both to the state and to the population).[44]

The handling of the Scissors Crisis described above is a classic case of these points. Although the scissors probably would have closed by themselves when (and if) the peasants reduced their marketings, the Soviet government intervened directly to improve the peasants' terms of trade. First, maximum selling prices were set for industrial products and price cuts for selected products were ordered. Second, imports of cheaper industrial commodities were allowed to enter the country. Third, the State Bank restricted the credit of the industrial trusts to force them to unload excess stocks. VSNKh even began to use quasi-antitrust measures against the syndicates, and some were abolished.[45] The substantial closing of the scissors (Fig. 4) by mid-1925 indicates the apparent success of these measures.

However, the setting of maximum industrial selling prices in a period of rising wage and price inflation had an important side effect: an excess demand for industrial products was soon created, which could not be eliminated through price increases, as ceilings had been set. Despite this excess demand and its resulting shortages, no formal rationing system was in effect, which meant that lucrative profits could be made by the *Nepmen* by selling at prices in excess of ceiling prices. This general shortage of industrial commodities has been called the "goods famine," and the peasants—because of their isolation from the market—were hit especially hard.[46] Despite the efforts of the Peoples' Commissariat for Trade to sell in the village at the established ceiling prices, the peasants had to buy primarily from the *Nepman,* who sold at much higher prices. Thus the peasants, despite the nominal closing of the scissors, still lacked incentive to market their surplus. In fact, there is some evidence to suggest that grain marketings were falling as the scissors were closing.[47] The *net* marketings of grain in 1926–1927 were between 50 and 57 percent of prewar levels, although grain output was close to the prewar level.[48]

The state's pricing policy had another serious side effect that eventually destroyed the market orientation of NEP. Initially, two sets of industrial and agricultural prices coexisted side by side: the higher prices of the *Nepmen,* who sold to a great extent in the villages, and the official state ceiling price. In 1927, prices in private stores were 30 percent higher than in state stores. By the end of 1928, they were 63 percent above official state prices.[49] The *Nepman* soon came to be regarded as a black marketeer and an enemy of the state. Beginning in late 1923, policies were adopted to systematically drive out the *Nepmen* and widen the state's control over trade. This objective was pursued through the control of industrial raw materials and goods produced by state industry, surcharges on the rail transport of private goods, and taxes on profits of *Nepmen.* In 1926, it became a crime punishable by imprisonment and confiscation of property to make "evil intentioned" increases in prices through speculation. Finally, in 1930, private trade was declared a crime of speculation.

Similar phenomena can be noted in agriculture. After 1926–1927, the state lowered grain procurement prices (which eventually caused peasants to divert production to higher priced crops and livestock), and a larger gap between state procurement prices and private purchase prices developed. Statistical studies undertaken during this period show that state procurement prices for the four major grains were below production costs in 1926 and 1927. Due to the higher production costs of small and middle peasants, the losses on sales to the state were highest for small and middle peasants.[50] The peasants responded by refusing to market their grain to state procurement agencies, creating the "grain procurement crisis" discussed in Chapter 4. Again, the private purchaser was systematically forced out of the agricultural market by the state. This trend culminated in 1929, when compulsory delivery quotas replaced the agricultural market system.

Such actions effectively signaled the end of NEP, for the market upon which NEP primarily depended was no longer functioning. Prices were set by the state, acting through the *Glavki,* trusts, and syndicates, and they no longer reflected supply and demand. The economy was without direction either from market or plan—a situation that was not to be tolerated long.

The high unemployment rate of the mid— and late 1920s was yet another reason for official dissatisfaction with NEP. Rising unemployment was supposed to be a problem that troubled only capitalist societies; yet rural underemployment was estimated to be between 8 and 9 million, and there were well over a million unemployed in the cities.[51] The existence of such high unemployment was not only ideologically embarrassing to the Soviet leadership, but the social unrest it engendered represented a real political threat to the regime.

A final source of dissatisfaction with NEP relates to national security problems. The fear of imperialist conspiracies, England's breaking off of diplomatic relations in 1927, and concern over Japanese activities in the Far East, prompted the Soviet leaders to realize that rapid industrialization would be required to meet the security needs of the Soviet Union and that NEP was not well-suited to generate such rapid industrialization. The Soviet leadership in 1927 expected a war with the capitalist West, and panic purchases by the population worsened the supply situation.[52]

THE PRECEDENTS OF THE 1920s

During the 1920s, the economic problem of resource allocation was dealt with by using two radially different economic systems. The first—War Communism —relied heavily upon command elements, whereas the second—NEP—attempted to combine market and command methods. The experiences of this early period tended to establish precedents that had a visible and lasting impact upon the eventual organizational structure of the Soviet planned economy. These precedents are introduced at this point as recurring themes throughout the ensuing chapters.

First, we emphasize the Soviet experiences with central planning during the 1920s. War Communism indicated that the market cannot be eliminated by fiat, for unless an enforceable plan is introduced in its place, the economy will be without direction other than that provided by the "sleepless, leather-jacketed commissars working around the clock in vain effort to replace the market."[53] To use Trotsky's apt description: "Each factory resembled a telephone whose wires had been cut."[54] The "paper" planning of War Communism was shown to be virtually no plan at all, and unless planners have detailed and coordinated information from the enterprise level and up and the political and economic muscle to ensure compliance, planning will be ineffective. A further precedent in the area of planning was the importance of shock tactics in a world of deficient information and imperfect control. Thus, the concentration of resources on priority projects to eliminate bottlenecks was seen as a way to give guidance to the planned economy in accordance with politically determined priorities. It was also noted that the success of shock tactics depended upon their limited application. This precedent can be seen in the "storming" tactics and the practice of singling out a few key branches for preferential treatment that persist until today. The 1920s also introduced the issue of central versus regional direction, which was to become a recurring theme throughout later periods. The friction between central and regional planning authorities (the *Glavki,* the *Sovnarkhozy,* and local authorities) throughout the 1920s revealed an imperfect harmony of national and regional interests that persists to the present period. Thus, the vacillation between ministerial and regional planning, a particularly important issue during the Khrushchev years, had its roots in the 1920s. The NEP period also witnessed the growing reliance on amalgamations of state enterprises into trusts and syndicates. These amalgamations, forerunners of the modern Soviet industrial associations, served as a link between the central administrators and the producing enterprises and thus eased the burden on the administrators.

Second, the Soviet leadership's experiences with peasant agriculture during the 1920s also set important precedents. It was widely feared that peasant agriculture could be a thorn in the side of rapid industrialization, for the success of industrialization was seen as being dependent upon peasant marketings to the state. It was thought that attempts on the part of the state to extract surpluses from the peasantry without offering economic incentives in return would be met by reductions in agricultural output and/or marketings. The Soviet leaders' apprehension was the impetus for the introduction of force into the countryside with the collectivization of agriculture in 1929 and provides an explanation for the continuing reluctance of the leadership to reinstate individual peasant farming (other than the small household plot), despite the often disappointing performance of collective agriculture.

The third important precedent of this early period was the development of an ingrained mistrust of the market that persists to the present. Most of the experiences with the market during the late NEP period were negative. The predominant trusts utilized their monopoly power to restrict output and withhold stocks. The *Nepmen* sold at high market prices despite the efforts of state pricing authorities to set limits on industrial prices. The peasants withheld their output whenever they deemed market incentives insufficient. For these and other reasons, the market was virtually abolished after 1929, with only such minor exceptions as the collective farm market, the "second economy," and, in part, the labor market. It is in this context that one can better understand the Soviet leadership's inbred opposition to fluctuating prices, output and input decisions based on profit maximization, and other market phenomena that persists to the present. Yet both War Communism and NEP convinced the Soviet leadership of the inevitability of an uneasy truce between the market and the central authorities. Throughout the transition period, the bulk of consumer goods continued to be supplied by private markets, even during periods when market transactions of this type were proscribed. During War Communism, the Soviet state continued to print money, whose use was proscribed in legal transactions, knowing full well that it was destined for illegal private markets. During NEP, the *Nepmen* were tolerated because the state knew that it would be unable to supply populations living in remote areas.

Viewing this antimarket bias in perspective, one could perhaps argue that it was irrational and stemmed from an insufficient understanding of the forces of supply and demand. On the other hand, the bias might be viewed as a rather keen perception of a development problem not always realized: Often, during periods of rapid industrialization, the interests of the state may conflict with the interests of individual consumers and producers—especially if the state lacks the means and expertise to manipulate the market; the individual wishes to consume, while the state wishes to save, for example. Could not one then argue that the most rational course of action is to eliminate or, at the minimum, substantially modify the market during early phases of development?

A fourth precedent, which can be related directly to the experiences of War Communism labor policies, was the evident necessity of freedom to choose occupations. If workers are to be productive, they must be allowed to choose their occupation on the basis of economic incentives. The militarization of labor that was attempted under War Communism proved to be an ineffective tool for allocating labor. Not only must wages be differentiated, but the resultant money income must have meaning in terms of real purchasing power, that is, a consumer goods market must exist. The labor experiences of War Communism set an important precedent in favor of free occupational choice—a precedent followed in subsequent periods except when temporarily abandoned during the late 1930s and 1940s in response to the tremendous turnover of the inexperienced factory labor force and wartime emergency.

A final precedent was the need to establish state control over the trade unions and other worker groups. During both War Communism and NEP, powerful forces within the party favored worker or trade union control over enterprises and trade union protection of worker interests. Opponents of these positions argued for the "statization" of the trade unions, for example, that the trade union should be the representative of state interests and that there should be "one-man management" in the enterprise. By the end of NEP, the statization of the trade unions was virtually complete and the doctrine of one-man management was firmly entrenched. The reasons for party distrust of independent trade unions and worker councils are clear. Immediately after the revolution, the central authorities had been unable to restrain wildcat nationalizations and worker takeovers. Moreover, in the absence of a coordinated central planning system, worker-dominated enterprises were operated in the interests of local workers, not in the interests of the party.

The year 1928 found the Soviet Union on the eve of the Five Year Plan period—about to embark on an ambitious program of forced industrialization. It was during this period that the Soviet command system evolved in large part into its present form. The period that we have just discussed—from the revolution to the first Five Year Plan—is important because of its impact on this command system. One might in fact argue that War Communism and NEP represented a practical learning experience for the Soviet leadership. The next chapter describes another (more theoretical) learning experience that also had a significant impact on the evolution of the Soviet command system: the Soviet Industrialization Debate.

REFERENCES

1. The discussions of War Communism and NEP are largely based upon the following sources: A. Nove, *An Economic History of the USSR* (London: Penguin, 1969), chaps. 3 and 4; E. Zaleski, *Planning for Economic Growth in the Soviet Union, 1918–1932* (Chapel Hill: University of North Carolina Press, 1971), chap. 2; M. Dobb, *Soviet Economic Development Since 1917,* 5th ed. (London: Routledge & Kegan Paul, 1960), chaps. 4–9; E. H. Carr and R. W. Davies, *Foundations of a Planned Economy, 1926–1929,* vol. 1, part 2 (London: Macmillan, 1969), chaps. 33–35. M. Lewin, *Russian Peasants and Soviet Power* (London: Allen & Unwin, 1968), chaps. 1–15; Y. Avdakov and V. Borodin, *USSR State Industry During the Transition Period* (Moscow: Progress Publishers, 1977); L. Szamuely, *First Models of the Socialist Economic Systems* (Budapest: Akademiai Kiado, 1974); V. A. Vinogradov et al., eds., *Istoriia sotsialisticheskoi ekonomiki SSSR* [History of the socialist economy of the USSR] (Moscow: Nauka, 1976), vols. 1 and 2; V. P. Diachenko, *Istoriia finansov SSSR* [History of USSR finance] (Moscow: Nauka, 1978), chaps. 2–4; S. Merl, *Der Agrarmarkt und die Neue Ökonomische Politik* (Munich: Oldenbourg Verlag, 1981).
2. Dobb, *Soviet Economic Development,* chaps. 4–9.
3. P. C. Roberts, *Alienation and the Soviet Economy* (Albuquerque: University of New Mexico Press, 1971), chap. 2. The position that Lenin adopted War Communism for ideological reasons is also supported by the Hungarian authority Szamuely, *First Models of the Socialist Economic Systems,* pp. 7–62. This interpretation is bitterly opposed by current Soviet ideology. For a typical attack on "bourgeois falsifications," see Vinogradov et al., *Istoriia sotsialisticheskoi ekonomiki SSSR,* vol. 1, pp. 251–252.
4. Merl, *Der Agrarmarkt,* p. 411.
5. Lewin, *Russian Peasants and Soviet Power,* pp. 26–28.
6. Dobb, *Soviet Economic Development,* p. 98; Vinogradov et al., *Istoriia sotsialisticheskoi ekonomiki SSSR,* vol. I, p. 236.
7. Szamuely, *First Models of the Socialist Economic Systems,* p. 21; Diachenko, *Istoriia finansov SSSR,* pp. 54–55.

8. A statement of E. Preobrazhensky quoted in Zaleski, *Planning for Economic Growth,* p. 20.

9. Dobb, *Soviet Economic Development,* p. 117.

10. Nove, *An Economic History of the USSR,* p. 62. Estimates of the period suggest that in the large towns only 31 percent of all food came through official channels (1919). Szamuely, *First Models of the Socialist Economic Systems,* p. 18, supplies similar estimates showing that most consumption requirements were satisfied in the free (black) market.

11. Vinogradov et al., *Istoriia sotsialisticheskoi ekonomiki SSSR,* vol. I, p. 374.

12. R. Day, *Leon Trotsky and the Politics of Economic Isolation* (Cambridge: At the University Press, 1973), chap. 2.

13. Szamuely, *First Models of the Socialist Economic Systems,* pp. 12–14.

14. *Ibid.,* pp. 14–17.

15. *Ibid.,* pp. 17–18.

16. Soviet doctrine depicts War Communism as a genial tactical victory by Lenin to win the civil war, while conceding that the USSR was not yet prepared for the elimination of capitalist vestiges. On this, see Vinogradov et al., *Istoriia sotsialisticheskoi ekonomiki SSSR,* vol. I, pp. 244–246.

17. Dobb, *Soviet Economic Development,* p. 117.

18. Nove, *An Economic History of the USSR,* p. 70.

19. For accounts of the organization of the War Communism economy, see Zaleski, *Planning for Economic Growth,* pp. 27–29; and S. Oppenheim, "The Supreme Economic Council, 1917–21," *Soviet Studies,* vol. 2, no. 1 (July 1973), 3–27.

20. Dobb, *Soviet Economic Development,* p. 112.

21. Nove, *An Economic History of the USSR,* pp. 66–67.

22. *Ibid.,* p. 94.

23. Quoted in Dobb, *Soviet Economic Development,* p. 130. According to Roberts, *Alienation and the Soviet Economy,* pp. 36–41, this quote is not reflective of Lenin's true position during War Communism. Instead, Lenin tended to view War Communism as a basically correct movement in the direction of revolutionary socialism, which he was forced to back away from by the strikes and civil unrest of 1920. Roberts points out the pains taken by Lenin during this period to justify the abandonment of War Communism on ideological grounds, which would have been unnecessary if War Communism had simply been a temporary wartime measure.

24. A quote from Stalin on this point (from the late 1920s, after he adopted his antipeasant stance): "What is meant by not hindering *kulak* farming? [The term *kulak* refers to the prosperous peasant.] It means setting the *kulak* free. And what is meant by setting the *kulak* free? It means giving him power." I. V. Stalin, *Sochinenia* [Collected works] (Moscow: 1946–1951), vol. XI, p. 275. Quoted in A. Erlich, *The Soviet Industrialization Debate, 1924–1928* (Cambridge, Mass.: Harvard University Press, 1960), pp. 172–173.

25. Vinogradov et al., *Istoriia sotsialisticheskoi ekonomiki SSSR,* vol. 2, pp. 37–38; S. Merl, *Der Agrarmarkt und die Neue Ökonomische Politik* (Munich: Oldenbourg Verlag, 1981), pp. 303–308.

26. Dobb, *Soviet Economic Development,* p. 143; and Merl, *Der Agrarmarkt,* p. 56.

27. Dobb, *Soviet Economic Development,* p. 142. Census establishments were those employing 16 or more persons along with mechanical power or 30 or more without it. G. W. Nutter, *The Growth of Industrial Production in the Soviet Union* (Princeton, N.J.: Princeton University Press, 1962), pp. 187–188.

28. Nove, *An Economic History of the USSR,* p. 104.

29. Dobb, *Soviet Economic Development,* p. 135. Also see W. Conyngham, *Industrial Management in the Soviet Union* (Stanford: Hoover Institution Press, 1973), pp. 17–24.

30. Carr and Davies, *Foundations of a Planned Economy,* pp. 787–836.

31. Avdakov and Borodin, *USSR State Industry,* chaps. 3 and 4.

32. *Ibid.,* p. 339.

33. For discussions of NEP trade policy, see M. R. Dohan, *Soviet Foreign Trade in the NEP Economy and Soviet Industrialization Strategy,* unpublished doctoral dissertation, Massachusetts Institute of Technology, 1969; L. M. Herman, "The Promise of Economic Self-Sufficiency under Soviet Socialism," in M. Bornstein and D. Fusfeld, *The Soviet Economy: A Book of Readings,* 3rd ed. (Homewood, Ill.: Irwin, 1970), pp. 260–290; W. Beitel and J. Nötzold, *Deutsch-Sowjetische Wirtschaftsbeziehungen in der Zeit der Weimarer Republik* [German-Soviet economic relations in the time of the Weimar Republic] (Ebenhausen: Stiftung Wissenschaft und Politik, 1977).

34. M. Kaser, "A Volume Index of Soviet Foreign Trade," *Soviet Studies,* vol. 20, no. 4 (April 1969), 523–526.

35. See on this M. E. Falkus, "Russia's National Income, 1913: A Revaluation," *Economica,* vol. 35, no. 137 (February 1968), 61. This position is also supported in P. R. Gregory, *Russian National Income, 1885–1913* (Cambridge: Cambridge University Press, 1982), chap. 5. For Vainshtein's position, see A. L. Vainsktein, *Narodny dokhod Rossii i SSSR* [National Income of Russia and the USSR] (Moscow: Nauka, 1969), p. 106.

36. Nove, *An Economic History of the USSR,* p. 137.

37. *Ibid.,* p. 138.

38. Cited in Dobb, *Soviet Economic Development,* pp. 161–162.

39. Merl, *Der Agrarmarkt,* pp. 40–43.

40. J. R. Millar, "A Reformulation of A. V. Chayanov's Theory of Peasant Economy," *Economic Development and Cultural Change,* vol. 18, no. 2 (January 1970), 225–227.

41. P. R. Gregory, "Grain Marketings and Peasant Consumption, Russia, 1885–1913," *Explorations in Economic History,* vol. 17, no. 2 (April 1980), 135–164.

42. J. F. Karcz, "Thoughts on the Grain Problem," *Soviet Studies,* vol. 18, no. 4 (April 1967), 407. Unfortunately, the one effort to test Russian peasant behavior in response to changing relative prices using modern econometries, failed to yield decisive answers. On this, see R. M. Harrison," Soviet Peasants and Soviet Price Policy in the 1920s," *CREES Discussion Papers, SIPS,* no. 10, University of Birmingham, 1977.

43. Erlich, *The Soviet Industrialization Debate,* pp. 105–106; P. R. Gregory, *Socialist and Nonsocialist Industrialization Patterns* (New York: Praeger, 1970), p. 28.

44. For an account of the thinking of Soviet authorities on these points see Merl, *Der Agrarmarkt,* pp. 50–140. The monetary growth figures cited above are from *Statisticheski spravochnik SSSR za 28 1928* [The USSR Statistical Handbook 1928] (Moscow: Ts.S. U., 1929), p. 600.

45. Avdakov and Borodin, *USSR State Industry,* pp. 196–198.

46. Karcz, "Thoughts on the Grain Problem," 419.

47. The marketed share of grain for the Ukraine between 1923 and 1926 was: 1923–1924, 26%; 1924–1925, 15%; 1925–1926, 21%.

48. R. W. Davies, "A Note on Grain Statistics," *Soviet Studies,* vol. 21, no. 3 (January 1970), 328. The controversy over grain marketings during the late 1920s will be discussed in Chapter 4.

49. *Statisticheski spravochnik SSSR za 1928* [The USSR Statistical handbook 1928] (Moscow: Ts.S.U, 1929), p. 727.

50. These studies are cited by Merl, *Der Agrarmarkt,* p. 104.
51. L. M. Danilov and I. I. Matrozova, "Trudovye resursy i ikh ispol'zovanie" [Labor resources and their utilization], in A. P. Volkova et al., eds., *Trud i zarabotnaia plata v SSSR* [Labor and wages in the USSR] (Moscow: Nauka, 1968), pp. 245–248.
52. M. Reiman, *Die Geburt des Stalinismus* [The birth of Stalinism] (Frankfurt/Main: EVA, 1979), chap. 2.
53. Nove, *An Economic History of the USSR,* p. 74.
54. Quoted in Szamuely, *First Models of the Socialist Economic Systems,* p. 97.

SELECTED BIBLIOGRAPHY

Non-Soviet Sources

W. Beitel and J. Nötzold, *Deutsch-Sowjetische Wirtschaftsbeziehungen in der Zeit der Weimarer Republik* [German-Soviet Economic Relations in the Time of the Weimar Republic] (Ebenhausen: Stiftung Wissenschaft und Politik, 1977).

E. H. Carr and R. W. Davies, *Foundations of a Planned Economy, 1926–1929,* vol. 1, parts 1, 2 (London: Macmillan, 1969).

R. W. Davies, "Soviet Industrial Production, 1928–1937: The Rival Estimates," *CREES Discussion Papers, SIPS,* no. 18, University of Birmingham, 1978.

R. Day, *Leon Trotsky and the Politics of Economic Isolation* (Cambridge: At the University Press, 1973).

M. Dobb, *Soviet Economic Development Since 1917,* 5th ed. (London: Routledge & Kegan Paul, 1960), chaps. 4–9.

A. Erlich, *The Soviet Industrialization Debate, 1924–1928* (Cambridge, Mass.: Harvard University Press, 1969).

M. Harrison, "Why Was NEP Abandoned?" in R. Stuart, ed., *The Soviet Rural Economy* (Totowa, N.J.: Rowman & Allanheld, 1984), pp. 63–78.

M. Lewin, *Russian Peasants and Soviet Power* (London: Allen & Unwin, 1968).

S. Merl, *Der Agrarmarkt und die neue Ökonomische Politik* [The Agrariam Market and the New Economic Policy] (Munich: Oldenbourg Verlag, 1981).

A. Nove, *An Economic History of the USSR* (London: Penguin, 1969), chaps. 3–6.

S. Oppenheim, "The Supreme Economic Council, 1917–21," *Soviet Studies,* vol. 25, no. 1 (July 1973), 3–27.

M. Reiman, *Die Geburt des Stalinismus* [The birth of Stalinism] (Frankfurt/Main: EVA, 1979).

P. C. Roberts, *Alienation and the Soviet Economy* (Albuquerque: University of New Mexico Press, 1971).

L. Szamuely, *First Models of the Socialist Economic Systems* (Budapest: Akademiai Kiado, 1974).

S. G. Wheatcroft "A Reevaluation of Soviet Agricultural Production in the 1920s and 1930s," in Robert Stuart, ed., *The Soviet Rural Economy* (Totowa, N.J.: Rowman Allanheld, 1984), pp. 32–62.

E. Zaleski, *Planning for Economic Growth in the Soviet Union, 1918–1932* (Chapel Hill: University of North Carolina Press, 1971), chaps. 1 and 2.

S. Male, *The Economic Organization of War Communism, 1918–1921* (New York: Cambridge University Press, 1985).

S. G. Wheatcroft and R. W. Davies, eds. *Materials for a Balance of the National Economy, 1928–1930* (New York: Cambridge University Press, 1985).

Soviet Sources

Y. Avdakov and V. Borodin, *USSR State Industry During the Transition Period* (Moscow: Progress Publishers, 1977).

V. P. Diachenko, *Istoriia finansov SSSR* [History of USSR finance] (Moscow: Nauka, 1978).

E. G. Gimpel'son, *Veliki Oktiabr i stanovlenie sovetskoi sistemy upravleniia narodnym khoziastvom* [The great October and the creation of the Soviet system of regulation of the national economy] (Moscow: Nauka, 1977).

S. G. Strumilin, *Na planovom fronte* [On the planning front] (Moscow: Nauka, 1963).

A. L. Vainshtein, *Narodny dokhod Rossii i SSSR* [National income of Russia and the USSR] (Moscow: Nauka, 1969).

V. A. Vinogradov et al., eds., *Istoriia sotsialisticheskoi ekonomiki SSSR* [History of the socialist economy of the USSR], vols. 1–3 (Moscow: Nauka, 1976).

chapter 4

The Soviet Industrialization Debate (1924–1928)

An extraordinary debate on how to initiate economic development took place in the Soviet Union between 1924 and 1928[1] that anticipated Western discussion on the same topic by some 25 years. Its participants ranged from leading party theoreticians to nonparty economists, and its audience included almost everyone of political and intellectual importance in the Soviet Union. The most remarkable feature of this debate was that it raised a multitude of questions concerning development strategy—issues of balanced growth versus unbalanced growth, agricultural savings, the proper scope of planning, taxation, and inflation to promote development—that are still widely debated among Western students of economic development. The debate focused upon the alternative development strategies open to the Soviet economy in the late 1920s. An important point to note is that Stalin, who actually made the eventual choices of central planning and collectivization in 1928 and 1929, respectively, was an observer of and a participant in this debate.

In the present chapter, we consider the major issues of the Soviet Industrialization Debate, without undue emphasis on details and biographical information. The Marxist–Leninist legacy provides the ideological foundation of the debate and is discussed first. We limit ourselves to the views of spokesmen for three important factions: Lev Shanin and N. I. Bukharin representing different views within the right wing of the Bolshevik party, and E. A. Preobrazhensky, the economic spokesman of the left wing of the party. We omit mention of significant contributors such as Bazarov, Rykov, Groman, Sokolnikov, and many others, not because they are unimportant but because of space limitations and because the three views presented cover a broad spectrum of the debate, subsuming many of the ideas of other participants.

THE SETTING OF THE SOVIET INDUSTRIALIZATION DEBATE

The rate of economic recovery of NEP probably reached its peak in 1926, but the industrial capacity lost during World War I had not been replaced by the limited industrial investment during NEP. Therefore, industrial capacity during the late 1920s was probably below prewar levels. The investment rate in 1928 was likely near that of 1913. Depending on the prices used, 1928 investment proportions were either slightly above or slightly below those of 1913.[2] The economic instability of the 1920s—the Scissors Crisis and the goods famine, the desire for rapid industrialization, and concern with defense—pointed to the need for massive capital accumulation in industry.[3] Yet could this capital accumulation occur without ruinous inflation? This was the inflationary imbalance dilemma that initially sparked the Soviet Industrialization Debate.

The Soviet inflationary imbalance of the 1920s can be described in terms of some elementary macroeconomic concepts: the rapid NEP recovery had brought aggregate demand back close to the capacity limits of the economy. In fact, given the loss of industrial capital stock and the limited net investment of the 1920s, the fact that industrial output had regained prewar levels indicates that industrial capacity was probably already being overtaxed by the recovery of the mid-1920s. If, in this situation, considerable industrial investment was undertaken to raise industrial capacity, additional income would be created through the investment multiplier, thereby generating severe inflationary pressures. This was the Soviet inflationary imbalance in a nutshell: industrial investment was required to raise industrial capacity, yet the capacity-creating effect of investment would be felt only after a period of time. The income-generating effect of investment, however, would be felt almost immediately, thus creating an inflationary problem.

If this inflation were to occur, the peasant would again be alienated by the increasing prices of manufactured goods, which would rise rapidly as capacity was diverted to producing investment goods. The terms of trade would again move against agriculture and another Scissors Crisis would ensue. It was felt that an industrialization drive would redistribute wealth away from the peasant (through declining terms of trade) and that such a redistribution could have disastrous effects on political stability and grain marketings. The *Smychka* basis of NEP would be jeopardized, and some alternative system would have to be substituted to feed the industrial workers.

The second alternative, a slow rate of capital accumulation, would avoid excessive inflation and preserve the alliance with the peasant. On the other hand, the basic problem—the low capacity of the economy—would not be met, thereby keeping the economy on the brink of inflation without achieving long-run objectives.

This inflationary imbalance dilemma was the spark that ignited the Soviet Industrialization Debate in 1924. The scope of the debate then broadened to include far-reaching discussions of the long-run development alternatives available to a growing economy. The fact that the relevance of the issues raised by the Soviet Industrialization Debate is not limited to the Soviet Union of the 1920s strengthens our conviction that the problems facing developing economies are similar, irrespective of the nature of the economic system utilized during the development process.

The political background of the debate should be outlined as well.[4] After Lenin's death in January of 1924, the leadership of the Communist Party was split by a bitter factional debate. The "united opposition" of the left, led by Leon Trotsky, Grigory Zinoviev, and Lev Kamenev, opposed the NEP concessions to the peasant and to private trade and was a persistent critic of the foreign policies of the party leadership. The left opposition advocated "superindustrialization" and harsh discriminatory measures against the more prosperous peasants, and resisted the notion of "building socialism in one country."* The party leadership consisted of a coalition between the Bolshevik "moderates"—Nikolai Bukharin, the editor of *Pravda,* who was a recognized Marxist theoretician and a popular revolutionary figure; Mikhail Tomsky, the trade union leader; and Aleksei Rykov, the head of the government bureaucracy—and Joseph Stalin, the general secretary of the Communist Party. This ruling coalition favored the continuation of NEP, the avoidance of a superindustrialization drive, the preservation of the *Smychka,* and efforts toward rapprochement with the capitalist world.

Thus, the leadership coalition had a vested interest in the success of the NEP experiment and the policy of rapprochement with the West. The latter policy was important because through it they hoped to attract foreign credits to bolster the NEP recovery. Serious setbacks occurred on both fronts in 1927: voluntary grain marketings fell well below government targets, and the government suffered serious foreign policy setbacks—the British broke off diplomatic relations, there were troubles in Poland, and Chiang Kai-shek turned on the Chinese communists. The Soviet Union was gripped by a war scare, and it was felt that a major war with the capitalist West was imminent. Sensing a weakening in the political base of the ruling coalition, Trotsky and the left opposition chose to challenge the leadership, a challenge that was successfully repulsed and resulted in the expulsion of Trotsky from the party in December of 1927.

This recitation of the political setting of the mid-1920s is relevant to a discussion of the Industrialization Debate because it shows that the debated issues were the very ones that divided the leadership of the Communist Party. Thus, the debate was much more than an abstract theoretical discussion concerning development alternatives. Rather, it was a debate that dealt with the most pressing political issues of the day.

THE MARXIST–LENINIST LEGACY

The participants in the Soviet Industrialization Debate addressed themselves to the proper way to industrialize the Soviet economy. The debate centered to a great extent on sectoral growth strategies, that is, on whether industry (the "state sector") or agriculture (the "private sector") should be favored or whether sec-

---

*The debate over "socialism in one country" refers to the issue of whether socialism could be achieved in an isolated socialist country (the Soviet Union) or whether a world socialist revolution would first be required. This issue is discussed in the next section.

toral growth should be balanced.* This same question has been widely discussed by Western economists in the postwar period and has been called the "balanced versus unbalanced growth controversy."

The Soviet Industrialization Debate of the mid-1920s drew heavily upon the theoretical legacies of Marx and Lenin. All participants in the debate had as their goal the "building of socialism," all agreed the state (society) should own the means of production at least in industry, and all used appropriate quotations from Marx and Lenin to support their programs.

Marx

The Marxist legacy consists of Marx's (and Friedrich Engel's) limited instructions concerning the shape of the future socialist society and of Marx's model of expanded reproduction, a model that states the conditions for a growing economy.[5] Marx's expanded reproduction scheme is of direct relevance to the Industrialization Debate, for it provided a conceptual model for determining sectoral priorities. A further Marxist legacy that was to achieve considerable prominence in the debate was Marx's notion of primitive capitalist accumulation, the process by which capital initially came to be controlled by the capitalist class. The primitive capitalist accumulation notion was important to the debate insofar as Soviet socialist thinkers sought after Socialist parallels to primitive capitalist accumulation.

Let us begin with Marx's instructions concerning the shape of future socialist societies. They are quite brief because Marx believed that the details of the future communist society were unforeseeable. According to the Marxian dialectic, societies must inevitably evolve into higher-order economic systems. Feudalism must inevitably replace slavery, capitalism must inevitably replace feudalism, and socialism must inevitably replace capitalism, for each system possesses internal contradictions that eventually explode into qualitative changes, that is, the rapid transition from one economic system to the other. The basic contradiction of capitalism, the class struggle between the worker and the capitalist, would inevitably lead to the violent overthrow of capitalism and the establishment of a socialist society. The first phase of the new socialist society would consist of a transition period that would vary from society to society depending upon the legacy of the preceding stage of capitalism. Only when communism, the final stage of social evolution, had been reached would differences among societies be eliminated. Thus, Marx had remarkably little to say about the critical period of transition from capitalism to communism.

Marx believed that the socialist revolution would occur in the advanced capitalist countries, in societies that had already developed a powerful productive apparatus. The new socialist government could, therefore, take charge of this

---

*The discussion of sectoral priorities can be cast in terms of either industry and agriculture or the state sector and the private sector. During the debate, industry (in particular, heavy industry) was owned primarily by the state and agriculture had private owners. It may be more accurate to picture the debate over priorities as a battle between the state-owned and the private sectors. On this, see Millar, "A Note on Primitive Accumulation," pp. 387–392.

productive apparatus and free it from the wastes of capitalist crises and costly imperialist competition. Thus, the period of transition to communism, the stage of abundance where members of society can be rewarded according to wants and needs, would not be too long in duration. In the meantime, the transition period would be characterized by the distribution of goods to individuals according to their contribution to the productive process. Those who contribute more in terms of labor services should receive more back from society. A planning system would replace the market; workers would receive vouchers from society indicating the amount of work they had performed. The workers would then be entitled to withdraw from society's production a value of goods (after deductions for investment, depreciation, etc.) equivalent to their contribution to society's output. The distribution of income would, therefore, remain unequal during the transition period, a defect inevitable during the first phase of communist society, but this system is fair in that it involves an exchange of equivalent values (labor for labor).[6]

During the transition period, the objective of socialist planners should be to accelerate the rate of economic growth and thus shorten the waiting time for the abundant communist society. In his model of expanded reproduction, Marx described the necessary relationship among economic sectors required to bring about economic growth. It might be noted that these are physical relationships, independent of the society's economic system; therefore, they would hold in socialist as well as capitalist societies. The condition for economic growth (expanded reproduction) can be illustrated by beginning with a stationary economy that is not growing (simple reproduction).[7]

Marx divided the economy into two broad sectors: Sector I, in which the means of production are produced, and Sector II, in which consumer goods are produced. For our purposes, we equate Sector I with heavy industry and Sector II with agriculture and light industry. Using Marx's labor theory of value, which states that the value of output will equal the value of direct and indirect labor inputs plus surplus value (profits), the value of each sector's output can be written as

$$V_1 = c_1 + v_1 + s_1$$

$$(1)$$

$$V_2 = c_2 + v_2 + s_2$$

where V denotes the value of sector output; c denotes fixed capital costs and depreciation; v refers to the variable costs, primarily labor costs; and s denotes the surplus value (or profits) of each sector. The subscripts 1 and 2 refer to Sector I and Sector II, respectively.

In a stationary economy, the output of Sector I (investment goods) equals the depreciation requirements of Sectors I and II, or

$$V_1 = c_1 + c_2 \qquad (2)$$

and this is Marx's condition of simple reproduction. On the other hand, the economy will grow if the net capital stock of the economy expands, and this occurs when the output of Sector I exceeds the depreciation expenses of I and II, or

$$V_1 > c_1 + c_2 \tag{3}$$

This is Marx's condition of expanded reproduction.

For the economy to be in equilibrium (an equilibrium of supply and demand for the output of Sector I), capital accumulation (saving) equal to $V_1 - c_1 - c_2$ must take place. In capitalist societies, Marx assumed that workers (the recipients of v) would be at subsistence and would thus not be a source of capital accumulation. The capitalists, the recipients of surplus value s, would, therefore, be the source of capital accumulation. Marx did not expand upon the sources of capital accumulation during the transition period—a topic of heated controversy during the Industrialization Debate, but he did describe the process of capital accumulation during the early phases of capitalism, called "primitive capitalist accumulation."[8]

In the Marxian schema, the notion of primitive capitalist accumulation is used to explain how capital came to be controlled by a capitalist class in the first place. Marx rejected the argument that capitalists acquired capital through their own (or their ancestors') abstinence from consumption. Instead, he argued that this process occurred primarily through expropriation of the property of the weak (the serfs, the urban workers, etc.) by the strong (the state, the church, robber barons, the merchants). In this manner, the poorer segments of society were divorced from the means of production and were forced to offer their labor to the capitalist class.

What directions could the new Soviet leadership draw from the Marxist legacy in preparing their blueprints for the new socialist society? The first directive is that during the period of transition to communism, distribution should be according to one's contribution to production. The second is that some form of planning should replace the anarchy of capitalist markets. The third instruction follows from Marx's model of expanded reproduction, namely, that growth can be accelerated by giving priority to the investment goods sector over the consumer goods sector. One may care to read a final directive into Marx concerning the initial stages of capital accumulation in a new socialist state. Insofar as capitalists initially gained control of capital by expropriation (primitive capitalist accumulation), the socialist state may adopt the same method to expropriate capital from the remaining capitalists (primitive socialist accumulation).

Lenin

Lenin, in his theoretical writings, had to reconcile the socialist revolution in Russia with Marx's clear prediction that it would occur in the advanced capitalist countries. Lenin's explanation represents a basic revision of Marxism in that he argued that the socialist revolution would occur, for a variety of reasons, in the "weakest link" in the capitalist chain and that Russia was that weakest link.[9] Russia's economic backwardness presented further theoretical problems for Lenin, for Marx felt that the task of making the transition from capitalism to communism would be eased by the inheritance of an advanced industrialized economy. This was not the case of Russia in 1917.

Lenin's writings on the strategy of the transition period represent an important contribution to Marxist–Leninist doctrine, although they are of less immediate relevance to the Industrialization Debate.[10] Lenin argued that the backward nature of the Russian economy required a transition period between capitalism and socialism, which he called state capitalism. In Lenin's view, a strong Soviet state would be required to capture the commanding heights of the economy. By having the state nationalize and control banking, transportation, utilities, and heavy industry, the Soviet state would be in a position to exercise control over the nonstate sector (light industry and agriculture), which would remain temporarily in private hands. With this strategy, the Soviet government would obtain the many benefits that capitalism had to offer (the services of specialists, foreign concessions, private trade) while exercising grand control over economic affairs. Lenin, in justifying why the socialist revolution would start in Russia, put a great deal of effort into demonstrating the advanced nature of Russia's commanding heights industries. Lenin pointed to the high concentration ratios of Russia's heavy industries and emphasized the role of foreign capital in promoting this concentration. Thus, in Russia, the Bolshevik state inherited pockets of advanced capitalism when they took over the country. These pockets of advanced capitalism, which would spawn the revolutionary proletariat, would provide the heavy industry base for building socialism. The enormous productive potential of capitalism, admired by Marx, would thus be put to the benefit of the working classes. In advocating state capitalism, Lenin was opposed by Nikolai Bukharin, who argued that the state should be "smashed," for Bukharin feared that a strong state might lead to the restoration of capitalism.

Although the state would control the commanding heights, light manufacturing and handicraft could remain (at least temporarily) in private hands. In agriculture, farming could remain in the hands of private peasants. Over time, however, peasants would recognize the advantages of large-scale mechanized farming, and they would voluntarily join large collective farms.

The failure of the Russian socialist revolution to spark the world revolution predicted by Marx presented Lenin with further doctrinal difficulties.[11] Was it possible to "build socialism in one country" (in relatively backward Russia), or would socialism in Russia have to wait on a successful socialist revolution in the advanced capitalist countries? This was a doctrinal issue that split the Bolshevik leadership. On the one side, Leon Trotsky argued for a "permanent revolution," maintaining that Russia could not hope to build socialism successfully without the assistance of more advanced socialist nations. Nikolai Bukharin (and later Stalin) opposed Trotsky by arguing that the Soviet Union's resource base and potential economic power were sufficiently strong to build socialism in Russia, isolated from the outside capitalist world. Lenin failed to make a definitive statement in this controversy, although he appeared to believe that the success of the Soviet experiment would eventually depend upon the spread of the revolution to the advanced nations. He did, however, argue that "breathing spells" would be required to allow consolidation of revolutionary gains before the permanent revolution could continue. Thus, contrary to Trotsky, Lenin did not believe that the world socialist revolution would be a continuous process.

Defining Lenin's legacy to the participants in the Industrialization Debate is difficult because Lenin, as a practical politician, was forced to justify Marxist theory to a wide range of conflicting policies. In the early months after the Revolution, Lenin laid out his blueprints for the fledgling Soviet regime (the "April theses"), in which the basic features of state capitalism were outlined. Shortly thereafter, he was obliged to justify War Communism and then, three years later, to explain the advent of NEP. For this reason, the participants in the debate found it possible to cite Lenin in support of their own programs by referring to different periods of Lenin's writings.

Having dealt with the Marxist–Leninist legacy, we now turn to the Soviet Industrialization Debate, a debate that began in earnest shortly after the death of Lenin. To a great extent, the debate was about the type of economic system —NEP or a War Communism-like system—that would be best suited to building socialism. Thus, when NEP was abandoned in 1928, the outcome of the debate was clear.

PREOBRAZHENSKY—UNBALANCED GROWTH OF INDUSTRY

E. A. Preobrazhensky, the vocal spokesman of the left wing of the Bolshevik Party, took up where Marxian expanded reproduction left off and argued that a discontinuous spurt in the output of investment goods was required to attain rapid industrialization.[12] Preobrazhensky envisioned two possible courses of action at the end of the 1920s: the Soviet economy could either continue to stagnate or even retrogress to lower levels of capacity, or a "big push" to expand capacity could be undertaken. In taking this latter step, which he supported, halfway measures would not be advisable for a spurt below the crucial minimum effort of investment would be self-defeating.

Preobrazhensky based this conclusion upon several factors. It was his opinion that the inflationary imbalance had two causes: the low capacity of the industrial sector, and a loss of saving ability—the latter being a consequence of institutional change in agriculture. Prior to the revolution, the peasants had been forced to "save" in real terms a substantial portion of their output, which was delivered either to the state or to the landlord.* This saving limited their capacity to purchase industrial products. The revolution, however, established them as free proprietors. Rent payments were eliminated and agricultural taxes (in 1924–1925) were less than one-third of prewar obligations.[13] The peasants became accustomed to receiving industrial commodities in return for the sale of their agricultural surplus. According to Preobrazhensky, this caused a "drastic disturbance of the equilibrium between the effective demand of the village and the marketable output of the town."[14] That is, the effective demand of the peasant had increased substantially without a substantial increase in industrial capacity—thus creating an inflationary gap.

---

*This view is supported by Alexander Gerschenkron's analysis of the objectives of the 1861 Emancipation Act (see Chapter 1).

Preobrazhensky suggested that net investment in industry must be raised significantly to close the gap between effective demand and capacity and that the inflationary effects of this action must be neutralized by altering the structure of demand significantly away from consumption and toward saving. Once the new industrial capacity had been created, private consumption could again be free to approach its previous position.

As far as the sectoral allocation of this net investment was concerned, Preobrazhensky argued for unbalanced growth to favor industry in general and heavy industry in particular on the grounds that the short-run benefits of investment in agriculture and light industry would be well outweighed by the long-run benefits of investment in capacity-expanding heavy industry. Thus, he emphasized that investment goods and consumer goods industries must be arranged in "marching combat order," in keeping with the Marxian theory of economic dynamics.*

*This conclusion follows the Fel'dman growth model of 1928. Employing Marxian definitions and accepting Marx's division into an investment goods sector (Department A) and a consumption goods sector (Department B), G. A. Fel'dman developed a mathematical model for the USSR State Planning Commission that made a stronger case for unbalanced growth in favor of Department A than the original Marxian model of expanded reproduction outlined above. Fel'dman made several implicit and explicit assumptions in deriving his model: (1) that the state had the power to control the division of total investment between Department A and Department B; (2) that once investment had been made in one sector, this capital could not be shifted later for use in the other sector; (3) that the economy was closed to trade with the outside world; (4) (implicitly) that the state controlled aggregate consumption and saving rather than individuals (given a particular aggregate investment goal, the state could make saving equal that amount); and (5) that capital was the sole limiting factor of production and that labor was overabundant.

Given these assumptions, Fel'dman concluded that the rate of growth of GNP in the long run depends upon the proportion of output of the investment goods sector that is ploughed back into that sector. If a substantial portion of the Department A output goes into the consumer goods sector, then the rate of growth of total output will be small. The long-term rate of growth of consumption also depends upon reinvestment in the investment goods sector. A high reinvestment ratio will yield high rates of growth of consumption in the long run, whereas a low reinvestment ratio will yield a relatively high short-term rate and a relatively low long-term rate of growth of consumption. That is, current consumption must be sacrificed in order to obtain a maximum rate of growth of both output and consumption in the long run. In sum, Fel'dman's model concludes that the bulk of investment must flow into the capital goods sector at the expense of consumer goods sectors if the growth rate of consumption and GNP is to be maximized in the long run. The partial derivation of the Fel'dman model is given below:

$$I_t^1 = \alpha I_t \tag{1}$$

$$I_t - I_{t-1} = \frac{\alpha I_{t-1}}{V_1} \tag{2}$$

$$I_t = \left(1 + \frac{\alpha}{V_1}\right) I_{t-1} \tag{3}$$

$$= I_0 \left(1 + \frac{\alpha}{V_1}\right)^{t-1} \tag{4}$$

$$C_t - C_{t-1} = \frac{(1 - \alpha)I_{t-1}}{V_2} \tag{5}$$

In arguing in favor of a big push, Preobrazhensky stressed that moderate increases in the capacity of the capital goods sector would be self-defeating: the technological gap between the USSR and the advanced capitalist powers had become so wide that it was now impossible to adopt advanced technology gradually. Second, he echoed a view widely held at the time that the replacement requirements of the Soviet economy had become so immense that a significant increase in investment was required just to keep industrial capacity from falling.

According to Preobrazhensky, foreign trade could, to some extent, act as a substitute for domestic capital production by importing foreign capital. However, the Soviets' capacity to import was limited by the lack of foreign credits (which would probably not be offered by the capitalist foes of the USSR) and by the small size of the exportable agricultural surplus. However feasible, he argued that a foreign trade monopoly would be essential to ensure that machinery and not luxuries would be imported. In any case, considering the massive capital requirements of the Soviet economy in the 1920s, Preobrazhensky felt that the foreign sector could only play a limited role in the Soviet capacity buildup.*

The long-run payoff of Preobrazhensky's policy of one-sided reinvestment in the capital goods sector would be an enhanced capacity to produce manufactured consumer goods and industrial farm machinery. Yet he recognized that it would take years for this to happen:

> ... a discontinuous reconstruction of fixed capital involves a shift of so much means of production toward the production of means of production, which will yield output only after a few years, that thereby the increase of the consumption funds of the society will be stopped.[15]

$$C_t - C_{t-1} = \frac{I_0(1 - \alpha) [1 + (\alpha/V_1)]^{t-2}}{V_2} \tag{6}$$

Where I = total investment
          I^1 = investment allocated to A
          C = total consumption
          α = portion of I allocated to A
          V_1 = capital coefficient of A
          V_2 = capital coefficient of B
          t = time subscript

See E. Domar, "A Soviet Model of Growth," *Essay in the Theory of Economic Growth* (New York: Oxford University Press, 1957), pp. 223–261.

*Apparently, Preobrazhensky's view of the role of foreign trade did not coincide with the views of the political leader of the left wing, Trotsky. Trotsky's belief in the inability of the Soviet Union to build socialism on its own forced him to argue that the USSR remain integrated in the world economy. He felt that economic and political events would be dictated by events in the outside world and that Russia's economic weakness could be ameliorated by exchange with the more advanced world, especially when capitalist crises forced the advanced capitalist countries to compete for the Russian market. For these reasons, Trotsky attacked the trade policies of the ruling coalition as being too autarkic. Preobrazhensky may have agreed with Tortsky on these points, but he felt that a major capitalist crisis was imminent and that this crisis would destroy the Soviet industrialization drive if the USSR were integrated into the world economy. For discussions of Trotsky's views on economic integration, see Day, *Leon Trotsky and the Politics of Economic Isolation,* part 2; and Nove, "A Note on Trotsky," pp. 582–584.

To dampen the interim inflationary pressures, Preobrazhensky proposed the system of primitive socialist accumulation, which was to replace the market so as to force the economy to save more for capital investment than it would have had the market prevailed. Instead of the market, state trade monopolies would set prices. By purchasing at low delivery prices and then selling at higher retail prices, the state would be able to generate a form of profit or forced saving (effecting a downward shift in the consumption function in real terms) that would reduce inflationary pressures. Preobrazhensky further suggested that during the period of primitive socialist accumulation, the main burden of industrialization should be placed on the peasantry in the form of low state purchase prices and high manufactured consumer goods prices, thereby extracting forced saving through a reduced peasant living standard.

In addition to his ideological preference for state industry, Preobrazhensky chose to burden the peasants because of the high potential of their saving capacity as exhibited prior to the Revolution and because of peasant agriculture's ability to be independent of industry. The overall purpose of primitive socialist accumulation was to let the state, not private individuals, decide how much would be saved. In doing so, the state would try to equate real saving (composed of both voluntary and involuntary savings) with the output of the capital goods sector (real investment).

Preobrazhensky's notion of primitive socialist accumulation contained ideological as well as economic motives. On the ideological front, the battle would be waged between the state sector (nationalized heavy industry) and the private sector (agriculture and handicraft manufacturing), and Preobrazhensky believed that the state must ensure the victory of the socialist sector. Primitive socialist accumulation would transfer resources out of the private sector (primarily agriculture) and into the state sector by imposing "nonequivalent exchanges" between the city and countryside. The exchange of industrial and agricultural commodities would be nonequivalent because of the state's manipulation of agricultural prices. Once the state had eliminated the private sector as a viable threat, the socialized sector would become the source of capital accumulation.[16]

Preobrazhensky clearly recognized the dangers inherent in primitive socialist accumulation. Given the large volume of savings that had to be extracted from agriculture, extremely low agricultural purchase prices would have to be set. The peasant would again be faced with deteriorating terms of trade and would withdraw from the market, alienated from the Soviet regime. In Bukharin's words, primitive socialist accumulation would "kill the goose [agriculture] that laid the golden eggs." This was the weakest point of his program and proved the focus for strong attacks by his opponents. How was the industrialization drive to be sustained if agricultural supplies were not available? The platform of the left wing did call for increased emphasis on collective and state farming, but the development of socialized agriculture would be a slow evolutionary process.[17]

SHANIN—UNBALANCED GROWTH OF AGRICULTURE

Lev Shanin, a representative of the extreme right wing of the Bolshevik Party, favored a program of unbalanced growth of agriculture within an essentially free market environment. The inflationary imbalance of the mid-1920s also provided the point of departure for Shanin. In view of this imbalance, Shanin thought that the Soviet economy should adopt a short-term horizon in planning policy. If massive investments were made in heavy industry with its long gestation periods, demand-creating income would be released without a parallel increase in capacity except in the long run, and by that time it would be too late. Thus, Shanin emphasized the income-generating side of capital investment, whereas Preobrazhensky emphasized its capacity-creating aspect.

The difficult transition from NEP recovery to new construction of capacity could be smoothed, according to Shanin, by adopting an agriculture-first policy. There were several reasons for this conclusion.

First, Shanin argued that the short-term increment in real output to be derived from an additional ruble of investment (the marginal output-capital ratio) in agriculture far exceeded that of industry, especially in view of agriculture's surplus population and its low capital intensity.[18]

Second, Shanin believed that there was a higher propensity to save in agriculture than in industry. According to this assumption, aggregate saving (a crucial factor in an inflation prone economy) would be enhanced by a redistribution of money income in favor of agriculture.[19] Using these two assumptions, Shanin derived his agriculture-first policy.

Shanin presented his arguments by contrasting two alternative investment programs: one channeling investment into industry, the other channeling investment into agriculture. By investing a given amount in agriculture, a relatively large increase in capacity would be generated because of agriculture's low marginal capital-output ratio. In addition, the increased investment in agriculture would increase agricultural incomes, and because of the high marginal propensity to save in agriculture, this increase in income would create a relatively large amount of incremental saving and inflationary pressures would be reduced. On the other hand, an equivalent amount of investment in industry would not only generate a smaller increase in capacity but would also fail to create as large an increase in saving because of the high marginal propensity to consume of the industrial worker.

Figure 5 illustrates Shanin's argument: Part A shows the consumption function of industrial workers (C_I), with a high marginal and average propensity to consume out of personal income. Industrial personal income in the mid-1920s is represented by IY^0, which yields a consumption level of IC^0 for industry. The consumption function of agriculture (C_A) in Part B is drawn to have a low marginal but high average propensity to consume at the initial agricultural income level (AY^0) of the mid-1920s. The agricultural consumption level is AC^0. The aggregate personal income of the economy in the mid-1920s is Y^0 (in Part C), which is the sum of IY^0 and AY^0 (from Parts A and B). Aggregate consumption is C^0, which is the sum of IC^0 and AC^0 (from Parts A and B). This consumption level is assumed to equal the real output of consumer goods of the two sectors operating at full capacity, which is denoted by K^0.

The graphs (Fig. 5) can be used to support Shanin's invest-in-agriculture policy: because of agriculture's smaller marginal capital-output ratio, agricultural investment would tend to raise capacity (K) more than would industrial

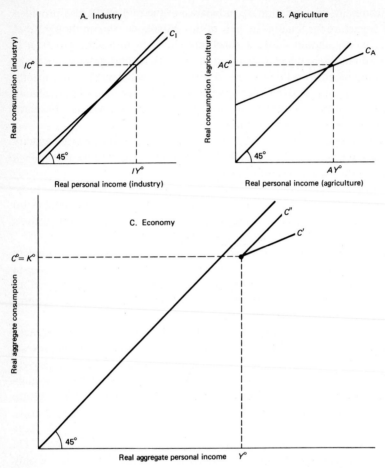

Figure 5

investment. In this manner, inflationary pressures in the consumption goods sector would be eased, for the additional investment would raise personal income and consequently consumption—hence the necessity to raise capacity. Second, because of the lower marginal propensity to consume within the agricultural sector, more savings could be generated by investing in agriculture, thereby raising agricultural income. As agricultural income rose, the economy would expand along the C' consumption function (which tends toward agriculture's marginal propensity to consume). If investment were made in industry, the economy would expand along C'', which tends toward industry's higher marginal propensity to consume. In this manner, Shanin's invest-in-agriculture policies would allow the economy to expand through additional investment and without inflation.

According to Shanin, two benefits would be derived from investment in agriculture. First, the capacity of the economy would be increased by a larger amount and in a shorter period of time, thereby ameliorating the short-term inflationary imbalance. Second, the creation of additional income in agriculture would generate a larger amount of incremental saving that could be used to finance additional investment without inflation.

Finally, Shanin emphasized the benefits to be gained from foreign trade. By trading according to its comparative advantage in agriculture, the Soviet Union could exchange agricultural products for industrial capital equipment, thereby building up the capital stock of industry while at the same time avoiding the inflation that would have occurred had the investment initially been in industry.[20]

Shanin envisioned that his policies would have to be carried out within an essentially free market environment to ensure the support of the peasantry and thereby the efficient utilization of investment in agriculture. He was sufficiently realistic to see that his proposals would have to be altered in the case of an imminent military threat, which would require the short-run enhancement of industrial capacity irrespective of the economic consequences. He also saw that certain industrial investments, such as in transportation, would be required to carry out his agricultural programs.[21] Therefore, industrial investment could not be neglected entirely. Another circumstance mitigating against the full-scale adoption of his agriculture-first program would be the exhaustion of foreign markets for Soviet agricultural products. Nevertheless, he minimized the importance of these exceptions and did not allow them to materially alter his main conclusions.

In the long run, after the initial inflationary imbalance had been eliminated, Shanin proposed a shift in emphasis toward industry, a shift toward reinvesting in capital goods which could be now accomplished free of inflationary pressures. At this time, the building of socialism could begin in earnest, unhindered by short-term inflationary problems.

BUKHARIN—BALANCED GROWTH

Nikolai Bukharin was the official spokesman of the right wing of the Bolshevik Party. A close personal associate of Lenin and possessing credentials as a leading Marxist theoretician, Bukharin remained a potent individual force in Soviet politics until the Stalin purges of the 1930s.[22] Prior to NEP, Bukharin's ideas were closely attuned to those of the left wing of the party, and he even co-authored a standard textbook on communism with Preobrazhensky. But NEP brought about a significant change in Bukharin's thinking. Throughout the NEP period, he remained an influential supporter of the NEP economic system and acted as its advocate in the face of attacks from the left wing.

Whereas Preobrazhensky felt that the victory of socialist ownership over private property had to be engineered by the state through unequal exchanges between the city and countryside, Bukharin felt that this outcome would be ensured by the natural superiority of socialist ownership.[23] The proletariat was in a position to exercise political control over the country and would thus be able to contain the antisocialist tendencies of the peasant, but market relations between the city and countryside would ensure that harmony between the peasant and the industrial worker (the *Smychka*) would be maintained. Any effort to introduce nonequivalent exchanges would destroy the foundation of economic development.

Unlike the left wing, Bukharin and his followers felt that socialized industry did not require discriminatory government action to assert its superiority. Rather, state industry would naturally grow more rapidly than the rest of the economy, and its share would inevitably increase. In this manner, the superiority of socialist ownership would be demonstrated to those outside the state sector, and they would gradually be attracted to join the state sector on a voluntary basis. The peasants would increasingly join consumer and producer cooperatives, and the state would encourage agricultural cooperation through favorable credit terms granted by the State Bank. Eventually, the peasants would join collective farms voluntarily. This action, however, would have to be noncoercive, for it would be counterproductive to impose collectivization on the peasantry before the peasants themselves were convinced of the superiority of the socialist form.

So much for the political side of the Bukharin program. On strictly economic grounds, he argued in favor of the balanced growth of industry and agriculture, granting that socialized industry would grow more rapidly than the economy as a whole. According to Bukharin, any investment policy that one-sidedly favors agriculture over industry or vice versa, or one branch of industry over another, will fail because of the interdependence of economic sectors.[24] First, industry cannot function successfully without agricultural supplies: the productivity of the industrial worker depends upon the availability of marketed agricultural foodstuffs. Further, industrial capacity will be reduced greatly if agricultural raw materials are not available for sale. Industry requires sophisticated capital equipment, which it initially cannot produce domestically and which cannot be purchased abroad if agricultural surpluses are not exported to finance such imports. Agricultural producers, on the other hand, depend upon industry for hand tools, agricultural machinery, and manufactured consumer goods. If these goods are not forthcoming, the peasants will retaliate by not supplying agricultural products for industry.

Bukharin recognized the need for capital accumulation but argued that it should be kept within manageable proportions. The overextension of one sector or subsector of the economy at the expense of other sectors would create critical bottlenecks—steel shortages, deficits of vital agricultural raw materials, insufficient foreign exchange earnings—that would inevitably retard overall economic development. According to Bukharin, any formula calling for maximum investment in heavy industry without a corresponding expansion of light industry would not only aggravate the goods famine, owing to the channeling of investment resources into time-consuming capital goods industries, but would also threaten to undermine the NEP recovery.

Because he emphasized economic interrelationships, Bukharin's program called for the gradual expansion of all sectors simultaneously. The critical link between agriculture and industry would be maintained by creating a favorable atmosphere for peasant agriculture. Instead of setting low agricultural delivery prices and high industrial prices, the state should do the opposite: first, to provide an incentive for the peasant to produce and market a larger output, and second, to pressure state enterprises to lower costs. It would not be necessary to force saving from agriculture as Preobrazhensky proposed; instead, only a stable economic environment free of the uncertainties of War Communism and NEP would be needed. In such a situation, the peasants would return to their traditional frugality, creating the savings to finance further expansion of capacity. Bukharin's advice to the peasant was to "get rich," a slogan from which Stalin carefully disassociated himself.[25]

To resolve the incongruence between limited industrial capacity and his call for moderate capital investment to be spread evenly among economic sectors, Bukharin proposed a series of measures to economize and utilize the available capital more fully. Small-scale manufacturing and handicrafts were to undergo a technological "rationalization" and be transformed into supposedly more efficient producers' cooperatives. Large-scale investment projects were to be made more efficient by better planning and more efficient construction work. Maximum attention was to be accorded to the speedy completion of investment projects. The available capital equipment was to be used more exhaustively by employing multiple shifts. Attention was to be given to appropriate factor proportions, that is, capital was not to be invested in areas where labor could do the job as efficiently. The state pricing policy should stimulate cost economies and more efficient use of available resources by eliminating monopoly profits.[26] Nevertheless, Bukharin was forced to admit that balanced growth meant steady but slow progress toward socialism. His own expression was "progress at a snail's pace," a phrase that was used against him in his struggles against the left wing and then later with Stalin.[27]

Although Trotsky had criticized the foreign trade strategy of the right wing as too autarkic, the trade policies advocated by Bukharin and his associates recognized the Soviet Union's initial dependence upon the advanced capitalist powers.[28] Bukharin argued that during the early stages of industrialization, the USSR must import large quantities of industrial equipment from abroad and pay for those commodities with agricultural exports. Yet the long-term goal must be independence from the capitalist world and the "building of socialism in one country." Thus, the Soviet Union's dependence upon foreign imports should be of limited duration, lasting only until domestic industry would be capable of producing the necessary capital equipment at home.

In sum, Bukharin favored the balanced expansion of both industry and agriculture under a general policy of moderate capital accumulation financed by the voluntary saving of the peasantry. This balanced growth was to be fostered by an environment that would encourage the peasantry to produce and sell their surplus to the city. State pricing policy would be used to gain the favor of the peasants by setting low industrial and high agricultural prices. By fostering methods to increase the efficiency of capital utilization, a return to the goods famine of the 1920s could be avoided without resorting to the massive industrialization drive favored by the superindustrialists of the left wing. The foreign sector would play an important role in that it would provide the foreign machinery to sustain the growing capacity of industry.

STALIN'S CONSOLIDATION OF POWER

In a series of adroit political maneuvers, Stalin consolidated his power within a rather brief period of time after Lenin's death in 1924. First, he allied himself with the right wing of the party (Bukharin, Rykov, and Tomsky) to purge the leftist opposition led by Trotsky from positions of power—a phase completed in late 1927. Then, Stalin turned his attention to the "right deviationist" Bukharinites, who were denounced by the Central Committee of the Communist Party in November of 1928. This occurred just one month after Stalin's adoption of the more ambitious alternative draft of the first Five Year Plan, which was supportive of the original left-wing industrialization program.[29]

The variant of the first Five Year Plan adopted in 1928 and formally approved in April 1929 staggered the imagination of even the superindustrialists. The low capacity of the Soviet industrial sector was to be subjected to an all-out attack: the Soviet fixed capital stock was to double within five years to provide the industrial base for building socialism. The first Five Year Plan also called for a 70 percent expansion of light industry, which was quite unrealistic in view of the limited industrial capacity in 1928.[30]

Stalin's changeover from his alliance with the Bukharinites and their pro-NEP policies to an acceptance of the program of the already purged left wing should be described.[31] During the Industrialization Debate, Stalin was clearly aligned with the Bukharin position. Stalin emphasized the achievements of NEP and ridiculed the left's superindustrialization proposals and the left's demand that "tribute" (primitive socialist accumulation) be paid by the peasants. Although Stalin underscored the advantages of large-scale farming, he made it clear that any movement in the direction of collective farming would be gradual and voluntary. Throughout the Industrialization Debate, Stalin refrained from making independent contributions that could later be attributed to him alone, and even the doctrine that socialism could be built in one country that is generally credited to Stalin was in reality Bukharin's contribution.

The foreign policy setbacks and the grain collection problem of 1927 emboldened Trotsky and the left opposition to challenge the ruling coalition. Stalin, allied with the moderates, was able to repulse the attack, but he came to believe that the left had correctly foreseen the crises encountered in 1927, in particular the problem of state grain collections from a reluctant peasantry. To increase grain collections, Stalin came to rely more and more on coercion and emergency measures, personally directing state grain collections in Siberia. The coalition with Bukharin was kept intact by carefully timed concessions to the right wing concerning the lifting of force in the countryside. Stalin came away from his experiences in 1927 with the conviction that force was the answer to the agrarian problem, for primitive socialist accumulation without the power to force peasant deliveries would not work. From this point on, Stalin ceased to serve as defender of the NEP system and began instead to criticize lagging NEP performance and to call for a superindustrialization drive. Moreover, he began to reiterate Trotsky's call for tribute from the peasants and to warn of *kulak* sabotage of grain collections. Encouraged by Stalin's move to the left, former Trotskyites such as Preobrazhensky returned to the party fold, only to perish later in the purges.

The first Five Year Plan was adopted in October of 1928, amidst a new grain collection crisis that was to have a crucial impact upon subsequent events. According to Stalin, the success of the industrialization program was clearly jeopardized, for it was dependent upon an increasing supply of food products and agricultural raw materials from the countryside. As long as the peasants refused to turn over such deliveries to the city, they held the power to halt the entire industrialization program.[32] The peasants' reluctance to sell their output to the state was understandable in light of the low purchase prices paid by the state and the increasing use of coercion to collect grain.

Stalin's answer to the crisis he perceived was to mount a counteroffensive designed to break once and for all the peasants' hold over the pace of industrialization. In the autumn of 1929, he ordered the wholesale collectivization of agriculture. Peasant landholdings and livestock were forcibly amalgamated into collective farms, which were obligated to deliver to the state planned quotas of farm products at terms dictated by the state.

The ensuing turmoil was great not only in the countryside, which burst into open rebellion, but also in Soviet cities, which received a vast influx of workers from the countryside and saw a significant redistribution of labor among industrial branches as enterprises attempted to fulfill their taut production targets.

THE OUTCOME OF THE SOVIET INDUSTRIALIZATION DEBATE

The actual Soviet industrialization pattern that emerged after 1928 (A, B, and C, Table 10) bears a close resemblance to Preobrazhensky's industrialization program: Soviet economic growth between 1928 and 1940 was heavily biased in favor of industry in general and of heavy industry in particular. Industrial production grew at an annual rate of 11 percent, whereas agricultural production grew at an annual rate of only one percent between 1928 and 1937 (C 3 and 4). The negative rate of growth of livestock graphically indicates the impact of collectivization upon agricultural performance. The same trends are apparent in the differential rates of growth of the agricultural and nonagricultural labor forces between 1928 and 1937 (C 2): the former declined, while the latter expanded rapidly at an annual rate of almost 9 percent.

The structural transformations resulting from these differential sector growth rates are impressive (B). Agriculture's shares of net national product and labor force declined from 49 percent and 71 percent, respectively, in 1928 to 29 and 51 percent, respectively, in 1940, whereas the increase in industry's product and labor force shares was from 28 and 18 percent, respectively, to 45 and 29 percent, respectively, during the same period.

The most remarkable feature of the 1930s was the extent to which the pro-heavy-industry bias asserted itself (as Preobrazhensky said it should). Between 1928 and 1937, heavy manufacturing's net product share of total manufacturing more than doubled, from 31 percent to 63 percent, whereas light manufacturing's product share fell from 68 percent to 36 percent.

The impact of this production program upon real consumption levels in the absence of significant foreign trade (the ratio of imports plus exports to GNP sank to one percent by 1937, E) had already been foreseen by Preobrazhensky. Between 1928 and 1937, household consumption scarcely grew (at an annual rate of 0.8 percent), and the share of consumption in GNP (in 1937 prices) declined

Table 10 OUTCOME OF THE SOVIET INDUSTRIALIZATION DEBATE: THE INDUSTRIALIZATION DRIVE OF 1928–1940

	1928	1933	1937	1940
A. Changes in manufacturing				
1. Heavy manufacturing ÷ overall manufacturing				
Net product share (1928 prices)	31	51	63	—
Labor force share	28	43	—	—
2. Light manufacturing ÷ overall manufacturing				
Net product share (1928 prices)	68	47	36	—
Labor force share	71	56	—	—
B. Changes in major economic sectors, structure of output				
1. Share in net national product (1937 prices)				
Agriculture	49	—	31	29
Industry	28	—	45	45
Services	23	—	24	26
2. Share in labor force				
Agriculture	71	—	—	51
Industry	18	—	—	29
Services	12	—	—	20
C. Rates of growth (1928–1937)				
1. GNP (1937 prices) (%)			4.8	
2. Labor force				
Nonagricultural (%)			8.7	
Agricultural (%)			−2.5	
3. Industrial production (1937 prices) (%)			11.3	
4. Agricultural production (1958 prices) (%)			1.1	
Livestock (%)			1.2	
5. Gross industrial capital stock (1937 prices) (billion rubles)	34.8	75.7	119	170
D. Changes in the structure of GNP by end use (1937 prices)				
1. Household consumption ÷ GNP	80	—	53	49
Annual growth rate (1928–1937) (%)			0.8	
2. Communal services ÷ GNP	5	—	11	10
Annual growth rate (1928–1937) (%)			15.7	
3. Government administration and defense ÷ GNP	3	—	11	21
Annual growth rate (1928–1937) (%)			15.6	
4. Gross capital investment ÷ GNP	13	—	26	19
Annual growth rate (1928–1937) (%)			14.4	
E. Foreign trade proportions				
1. Exports + imports ÷ GNP (%)	6[a]	4	1	—
F. Shares of the socialist sector in				
1. Capital stock (%)	65.7	—	99.6	—
2. Gross production of industry (%)	82.4	—	99.8	—
3. Gross production of agriculture (%)	3.3	—	98.5	—
4. Value of trade turnover (%)	76.4	—	100.0	—
G. Prices				
1. Consumer goods prices (state and cooperative stores, 1928 = 100)	100	400	700	1000
2. Average realized prices of farm products (1928 = 100)	100	—	539	—

Sources: A: P. R. Gregory, *Socialist and Nonsocialist Industrialization Patterns* (New York: Praeger, 1970), pp. 28–29, 36. Heavy manufacturing is defined according to the International System of Industrial Classification as ISIC 30–38. Light manufacturing is defined as ISIC 20–29. B: S. Kuznets, "A Comparative Appraisal," in A. Bergson and S. Kuznets, eds., *Economic Trends in the Soviet Union* (Cambridge, Mass.: Harvard University Press, 1963), pp. 342–360. C: Bergson and Kuznets, *Economic Trends,* pp. 36, 77, 187, 190, 209. D: A. Bergson, *Real Soviet National Income and Product Since 1928* (Cambridge, Mass.: Harvard University Press, 1961), pp. 217, 237. E: Bergson and Kuznets, *Economic Trends,* pp. 288–290. F: *Narodnoe khoziaistvo SSSR v 1958 g.* [The national economy of the USSR in 1958], p. 57. G: F. D. Holzman, "Soviet Inflationary Pressures, 1928–1957: Causes and Cures," *Quarterly Journal of Economics,* vol. 74, no. 2 (May 1960), 168–169.
[a]1929.

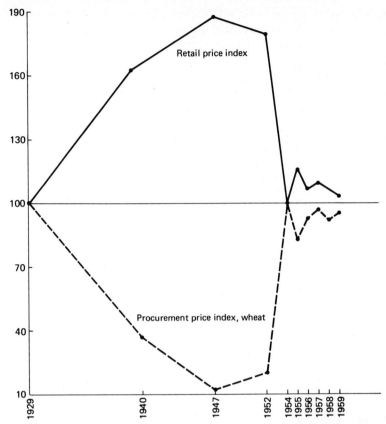

Figure 6   Correlation of state wholesale prices for objects of mass consumption and purchase price of wheat (USSR 1929 = 100). (*Source:* A. N. Malafeev, *Istoriia tsenoobrazovaniia v SSSR* [The history of price formation in the USSR] (Moscow: 1964), p. 286. These figures are not directly comparable to those in Figure 4, which relate an index of agricultural prices to an index of all prices, because of the vast change in agricultural prices after 1929, when procurement prices began to diverge significantly from the retail prices of agricultural commodities, and because Figure 6 refers only to wheat prices, not to a more general farm price index.

markedly, from 80 percent to 53 percent. During the same period, gross capital investment grew at an annual rate of 14 percent, and the ratio of gross investment to GNP doubled, from 13 percent to 26 percent. If we define total consumption expenditures to include both private consumption and communal services, and nonconsumption expenditures to include investment, government administration, and defense, then total consumption fell between 1928 and 1937 from 85 percent of GNP to 64 percent of GNP (D).

The changing institutional setting within which these transformations were occurring should also be noted (Table 10, F): between 1928 and 1937, the socialist sector share of total capital stock, industry, agriculture, and trade expanded sharply, so that by 1937 the socialist sector totally dominated all economic activity.

Part G in Table 10 has special relevance to the outcome of the industrialization debate. Consumer prices rose by 700 percent between 1928 and 1937 and probably would have risen even faster without the extensive formal and informal rationing of the period. Average realized prices of farm products, which are weighted averages of the extremely low state procurement prices, the above-quota state delivery prices, and collective farm market prices, on the other hand, rose by 539 percent, which indicates a reopening of the price scissors against agriculture between 1928 and 1937. An examination of some partial data (Fig. 6) suggests that, in fact, the scissors did reopen and were not closed again until the mid-1950s, with a resultant squeeze upon the agricultural sector in terms of low procurement prices.

In sum, the left opposition program was apparently the model for the Soviet industrialization drive. The pro-industry and pro-heavy industry bias of the first two Five Year Plans is clearly shown in Table 10 and was implemented at the expense of the agricultural sector and the consumer. The expected deterioration in the agricultural terms of trade occurred, but it did not halt the industrialization drive, possibly owing to the forced collectivization of agriculture.

In retrospect, the Soviet industrialization drive must be seen as a remarkable and rapid shift of the Soviet economic structure. Economic growth was rapid, especially growth of industry and industrial capital stock. On the negative side, growth of agriculture and consumption were slow (and even negative in some periods). As we examine this process in greater detail, it will become even more apparent that like any approach to economic development, the "Soviet development model" is not without cost. Thus, the costs and benefits of alternative development models must always be carefully considered. We shall return to this issue in Chapter 5.

REFERENCES

1. Our discussion of the Soviet Industrialization Debate is drawn primarily from the following sources: A. Erlich, *The Soviet Industrialization Debate, 1924–1928* (Cambridge, Mass.: Harvard University Press, 1960); N. Spulber, *Soviet Strategy for Economic Growth* (Bloomington: Indiana University Press, 1964); N. Spulber, ed., *Foundations of Soviet Strategy for Economic Growth* (Bloomington: Indiana University Press, 1964); A. Erlich, "Stalin's Views on Economic Development" in E. Simmons, ed., *Continuity and Change in Russian and Soviet Thought* (Cambridge, Mass.: Harvard University Press, 1955), pp. 81–99; M. Lewin, *Russian Peasants and Soviet Power* (London: Allen & Unwin, 1968), chaps. 6–9; S. F. Cohen, *Bukharin and the Bolshevik Revolution* (New York: Knopf, 1973); M. Reiman, *Die Geburt des Stalinismus* [The birth of Stalinism] (Frankfurt/Main: EVA, 1979); A. Nove, "A Note on Trotsky and the 'Left Opposition,' 1929–31," *Soviet Studies,* vol. 29, no. 4 (October 1977), 576–589; J. R. Millar, "A Note on Primitive Accumulation in Marx and Preobrazhensky," *Soviet Studies,* vol. 30, no. 3 (July 1978), 384–393; R. Day, "Preobrazhensky and the Theory of the Transition Period," *Soviet Studies,* vol. 27, no. 2 (April 1975), pp. 196–219.

2. P. Gregory, *Russian National Income, 1885–1913* (Cambridge: Cambridge University Press, 1982), pp. 185–186.

3. The growth models developed during this period by V. A. Bazarov and V. G. Groman predicted a declining growth rate as the Soviet economy approached its prewar equi-

librium. For a discussion of these models, see L. Smolinski, "The Origins of Soviet Mathematical Economics," in H. Raupach et al., eds., *Yearbook of East-European Economics,* Band 2 (Munich: Gunter Olzog Verlag, 1971), p. 144.

4. For discussions of the political setting, see Cohen, *Bukharin and the Bolshevik Revolution,* chaps. 7–9; Reiman, *Die Geburt des Stalinismus,* chaps. 1–6; Lewin, *Russian Peasants and Soviet Power,* chaps. 6–12.

5. This discussion is based upon P. M. Sweezy, *The Theory of Capitalist Development* (New York: Modern Reader Paperbacks, 1968), chaps. 5 and 10; Day, "Preobrazhensky and the Theory of the Transition Period," pp. 196–199; F. Engels, *Anti-Dühring* (Moscow: Progress Publishers, 1975).

6. The reader is referred to Marx's own discussion of these matters in Karl Marx, *Critique of the Gotha Program* (Moscow: Progress Publishers, 1971), pp. 9–21.

7. Sweezy, *The Theory of Capitalist Development,* pp. 75–95, 162–169.

8. This discussion of primitive capitalist accumulation is based primarily upon Millar, "A Note on Primitive Accumulation," pp. 384–392.

9. For a discussion of Lenin's revision of Marx in light of the Russian experience, see P. R. Gregory and R. C. Stuart, *Comparative Economic Systems,* 2nd ed. (Boston: Houghton Mifflin, 1985), chap. 4.

10. In addition to the references already cited in this chapter, see H. Ray Buchanan, "Lenin and Bukharin on the Transition from Capitalism to Socialism: The Meshchersky Controversy, 1918," *Soviet Studies,* vol. 28, no. 1 (January 1976), 66–82. For a modern study of industrial concentration in Russia prior to the revolution by a Soviet author, see V. I. Bovykin, *Formirovanie finansovo kapitala v Rossii* [Formation of financial capital in Russia] (Moscow: Nauka, 1984).

11. For a most detailed discussion of this controversy, see R. Day, *Leon Trotsky and the Politics of Economic Isolation* (Cambridge: At the University Press, 1973).

12. Preobrazhensky's views are outlined in his famous work, *Novaia ekonomika* [The new economics], which is available in English translation. See E. A. Preobrazhensky, *The New Economics,* B. Pierce, trans. (Oxford: Oxford University Press, 1964).

13. Erlich, *The Soviet Industrialization Debate,* p. 35.

14. *Ibid.,* p. 35.

15. Quoted in Erlich, *The Soviet Industrialization Debate,* pp. 56–57.

16. Lewin, *Russian Peasants and Soviet Power,* pp. 146–152; Millar, "A Note on Primitive Accumulation," pp. 387–393.

17. Stalin's solution to this dilemma—collectivization of the peasantry, which eliminated the peasant's freedom to dispose of surpluses—did not occur to Preobrazhensky. Several years after the collectivization decision, Preobrazhensky declared in a speech: "Collectivization—this is the crux of the matter! Did I have this prognosis of the collectivization? I did not." Quoted in Erlich, *The Soviet Industrialization Debate,* p. 177. Erlich adds to this: "He [Preobrazhensky] was careful not to add that neither did Stalin at the time when the industrialization debate was in full swing. And he was wise not to point out that the decision to collectivize hinged not on superior intellectual perspicacity but on the incomparably higher degree of resolve to crush the opponent. . . ."

18. L. Shanin, "Questions of the Economic Course," in N. Spulber, ed., *Foundations of Soviet Strategy for Economic Growth* (Bloomington: Indiana University Press, 1964), p. 219.

19. *Ibid.*

20. Erlich, *The Soviet Industrialization Debate,* pp. 140–141.

21. *Ibid.,* p. 132.

22. Cohen, *Bukharin and the Bolshevik Revolution.*

23. Lewin, *Russian Peasants and Soviet Power,* pp. 132–142.

24. Erlich, *The Soviet Industrialization Debate,* pp. 82–83.

25. *Ibid.,* pp. 86–87.

26. *Ibid.,* pp. 84–86.

27. Lewin, *Russian Peasants and Soviet Power,* p. 139.

28. Day, *Leon Trotsky and the Politics of Economic Isolation,* chap. 7.

29. *Ibid.,* chap. 9. It was not until the Stalin purges in the late 1930s that this political process was complete. Preobrazhensky, Shanin, and Bukharin all lost their lives in the purges.

30. *Ibid.,* p. 166.

31. Accounts of Stalin's move to the left are found in Erlich, "Stalin's Views on Economic Development," pp. 81–99; Reiman, *Die Geburt des Stalinismus,* chaps. 5–8; Lewin, *Russian Peasants and Soviet Power,* chaps. 9–17.

32. According to Jerzy Karcz, there was no real agricultural crisis during this period. The grain collection "crisis" was precipitated by the lowering of state grain procurement prices in 1926–1927, while procurement prices for animal products were raised. Peasants shifted their attention to animal products, fed grain to livestock, and held grain in stock, waiting for grain prices to be increased. Total agricultural sales did not fall during this period. Thus the "crisis" was caused not by the weakness of peasant agriculture but by the ineptitude of state pricing policy. In addition, Karcz raises the question of deliberate falsification of grain statistics by Stalin to gain support for collectivization. J. F. Karcz, "Thoughts on the Grain Problem," *Soviet Studies,* vol. 18, no. 4 (April 1967), 399–434. For a different view, see R. W. Davies, "A Note on Grain Statistics," *Soviet Studies,* vol. 21, no. 3 (January 1970), 314–329. This controversy will be discussed in detail in Chapter 5.

SELECTED BIBLIOGRAPHY

N. Bukharin, *The Politics and Economics of the Transition Period,* Kenneth Tarbuck, ed., (London: Routledge & Kegan Paul, 1979).

S. F. Cohen, *Bukharin and the Bolshevik Revolution* (New York: Knopf, 1973).

R. Day, *Leon Trotsky and the Politics of Economic Isolation* (Cambridge: At the University Press, 1973).

M. Dobb, *Soviet Economic Development Since 1917,* 5th ed. (London: Routledge & Kegan Paul, 1960), chap. 8.

F. Engels, *Anti-Dühring* (Moscow: Progress Publishers, 1975).

A. Erlich, "Stalin's Views on Soviet Economic Development," in Ernest Simmons, ed., *Continuity and Change in Russian and Soviet Thought* (Cambridge, Mass.: Harvard University Press, 1955), pp. 81–99.

———, *The Soviet Industrialization Debate, 1924–1928* (Cambridge, Mass.: Harvard University Press, 1960).

N. Jasny, *Soviet Economists of the Twenties: Names to be Remembered* (Cambridge: At the University Press, 1972).

V. I. Lenin, *Imperialism, the Highest Stage of Capitalism* (Moscow: Progress Publishers, 1970).

M. Lewin, *Russian Peasants and Soviet Power* (London: Allen & Unwin, 1968), chaps. 6–9.

K. Marx, *Critique of the Gotha Program* (Moscow: Progress Publishers, 1971).

J. R. Millar, "A Note on Primitive Accumulation in Marx and Preobrazhensky," *Soviet Studies,* vol. 30, no. 3 (July 1978), 384–393.

A. Nove, "A Note on Trotsky and the 'Left Opposition,' 1929–31," *Soviet Studies,* vol. 29, no. 4 (October 1977), 576–589.

———, *An Economic History of the USSR* (London: Penguin, 1969), chap. 5.

M. Reiman, *Die Geburt des Stalinismus* [The birth of Stalinism] (Frankfurt/Main: EVA, 1979), chaps. 3–9.

N. Spulber, ed., *Foundations of Soviet Strategy for Economic Growth* (Bloomington: Indiana University Press, 1964).

———, *Soviet Strategy for Economic Growth* (Bloomington: Indiana University Press, 1964), chaps. 1–4.

P. M. Sweezy, *The Theory of Capitalist Development* (New York: Modern Reader Paperbacks, 1968).

R. C. Tucker, ed., *The Lenin Anthology* (New York: Norton, 1975).

chapter 5

The Foundation of the Soviet Planned Economy: Planning, Collectivization, and War (1928–1945)

We have already described the precedents of the 1920s and the impact of the Soviet Industrialization Debate upon the course of Soviet industrialization during the 1930s. Our attention now turns to the historical evolution of the Soviet command economic system during the early plan era, specifically to the development of a coordinated central planning apparatus and to the introduction of forced collectivization into the countryside. World War II provided a stern test of the command economy put in place in the 1930s. The war imposed enormous costs on the Soviet Union and also caused some changes in the resource allocation system.

The 1920s witnessed two significant struggles over the nature of economic planning in the Soviet Union. The first was the debate over the theory of planning in a socialist economy—the debate between the so-called *genetic* and *teleological* schools of planning. The second was the struggle among the various planning bodies in existence during the 1920s for ascendancy in the planning hierarchy—a battle eventually won by *Gosplan* (the State Planning Committee). Let us first turn to the planning debate.

THE PLANNING DEBATE: THE GENETICISTS VERSUS THE TELEOLOGISTS[1]

During NEP, an important controversy arose concerning the proper role of economic planning in the Soviet Union. The debate centered largely around the issue of whether planning was to be directed (and limited) by market forces or molded by the will of planners, unconstrained by market forces and limited only by the physical constraints of the economy. The so-called *geneticists* advocated the first approach to planning, the most notable being N. D. Kondratiev (the prominent Russian authority on business cycles), V. A. Bazarov, and V. G. Groman, the latter two being *Gosplan* economists. The geneticists basically argued that economic planning should be directed by consumer demand, which would dictate to planners the needed direction of change in the economy. Thus, the principal function of the planner would be to forecast and project market trends to aid central and local administrators in their decision-making, that is, the geneticists envisioned a form of *indicative* planning, as it is called today. In drawing up such plans, authorities should always make sure of their internal consistency, for the geneticists viewed the economy as a vast complex of interrelated sectors (a general equilibrium system), the balance of which would be severely disturbed if planners neglected sectoral interrelationships. For example, to expand the heavy industry sector without concern for the resulting impact on the equilibrium of other interrelated sectors would create serious disproportions that would impede overall development. Thus, the geneticists advocated a form of planning that was largely consistent with the precepts of NEP, in view of the dominant role that market forces would be allowed to play in the planning process. The advocates of genetic planning, therefore, were supportive of NEP and were associated with the party's right wing.

The *teleological* approach to planning, as advocated by S. Strumilin, G. L. Pyatakov, V. V. Kuibyshev, and P. A. Fel'dman, stated that the economic plan should be consciously formulated by social engineers and shaped by national goals established by the state. Such planning should seek to *overcome* market forces, rather than be directed by them as the geneticists argued. The market and finance, according to the teleologists, should *follow* the plan rather than dictate the plan. Planning should begin only after national economic goals have been set by the political authorities. Then, the planners should form economic strategy, largely in terms of binding targets for basic industries, limited only by the availability of investment, and such investment should be allocated to meet the needs of industry independently of market forces.

In drawing up output and investment plans, the teleologists argued that planners need not be constrained by the need to preserve the general equilibrium of the economy, for to do so would be to subject the growth of the economy to the spontaneous forces of the market. Instead, the concept of equilibrium should be denounced as an unnecessarily severe constraint on the flexibility of planners. As stated by one teleologist, to accept the direction of the market meant acceptance of the "genetic inheritance" of 300 years of tsarism.[2]

According to the teleologists, the actual process of plan construction should proceed according to a system of "successive approximations." That is, first, plans for the leading branches (namely, heavy industry) were to be drawn up; then, the plans for other sectors (light industry, agriculture, trade, etc.) would be molded into the framework of the first set of plans. In this manner, the plans of lower-priority sectors would be predetermined by the plan for heavy industry, not by the market.

The late 1920s witnessed the conclusive victory of the teleological viewpoint. As the NEP system was gradually abandoned, the advocates of the genetic approach, tied as it was to a market-directed system of planning, saw their support within the party deteriorate. From the summer of 1927, actual planning paid little attention to market equilibrium and financial stability as advocated by the geneticists. Instead, attention turned to physical planning involving a "ferocious straining of effort," the outcome of which would be "decided by struggle."[3] The teleological approach to planning is obviously consistent with the super-industrialization notions of the left adopted by Stalin in 1928. Eventually, the geneticists came to be accused of counterrevolution and right-wing Menshevism. The advocates of the teleological approach, namely, Strumilin, Krzhizhanovsky, and others, remained prominent in the *Gosplan* apparatus during the 1930s and played a guiding role in the planning for rapid industrialization.

THE EVOLUTION OF THE PLANNING STRUCTURE[4]

A variety of agencies dealt with planning problems throughout the 1920s— VSNKh (the Supreme Council of the National Economy), the People's Commissariat of Finance, the People's Commissariat of Transportation, *Gosplan* USSR (State Planning Committee of the USSR), the regional *Gosplans,* the *Sovnarkhozy,* local authorities, and many others. However, of these agencies, only *Gosplan* was explicitly and exclusively concerned with economic planning. *Gosplan's* duties (according to a 1922 decree) were "the preparation not only of a long-range plan but also of an operational plan for the current year."[5]

From modest beginnings in February of 1921 (in 1925, *Gosplan* employed only around 50 economists and statisticians[6]), *Gosplan* gradually came to be accepted by the late 1920s as the planning agency in charge of coordinating economic planning for the entire economy. Much of this recognition emerged as a consequence of *Gosplan's* work on the annual *control figures,* or tentative output targets, for the various branches of the economy. The first control figures were prepared covering the year 1925–1926, and while they did not initially prove important in directing economic activity, the figures were used to establish the principle that economic policy should be guided on an annual basis by control figures prepared by *Gosplan.* In this manner, *Gosplan* came to play a supervisory role in the preparation of plans by other administrative bodies. The early control figures had a definite geneticist flavor, as they were designed to forecast rather than manipulate. The growing importance of *Gosplan's* control figures is clear: by 1926, the control figures were the first order of business of the Central Committee meeting of the party. In 1927, the party gave full compulsory status to the 1927–1928 control figures, which had taken on a strong teleological character.

While *Gosplan's* role as the coordinator of all planning was developing, it had little to do with the actual operational planning of the economy, especially at the enterprise and trust levels. Such work was primarily performed by the central planning staff of VSNKh and by the *Glavki* planning offices of VSNKh. In this manner, annual plans, including production and financial targets known as *promfinplans,* were drawn up. The major problem with the *promfinplans* was that they tended to be compiled on a sector-by-sector basis, with little attention given to the overall result when these plans were combined. *Gosplan,* which was charged with overall planning, complained that it received the *promfinplans* too late to coordinate them with the overall control figures. All *Gosplan* could do was to accept the *promfinplans* as an accomplished fact. Gradually, the *promfinplans* drawn up by VSNKh were merged into the control figures compiled by *Gosplan.* Beginning in 1925, VSNKh was instructed to prepare its *promfinplans* on the basis of *Gosplan's* 1925–1926 control figures. By 1926–1927, VSNKh was in the habit of compiling a comprehensive *promfinplan* for all industry, to be scrutinized by *Gosplan* and the Peoples Commissariat of Finance, and it was established that the *promfinplan* was clearly dependent upon the control figures.

During this period, the machinery for physical planning was also being developed—the system of *material balances.* As certain basic industrial commodities grew scarce as early as 1925 and the administrative allocation of commodities increased, planning bodies began compiling balances for critical industrial materials. In 1925, a balance for the production and uses of iron and steel was compiled; and in 1927, an energy balance of fuel and power consumption was drawn up. The balance system was extended to building materials in 1928.[7] In charge of coordinating these balances through the *promfinplan* and control figure system were VSNKh and *Gosplan,* but initially this coordination proved too complex in the absence of detailed statistical information, and most of these early material balances were poorly prepared.

Thus, the plan period began with the adoption of the first Five Year Plan in 1928, with the following planning principles established: First, *Gosplan* was to be the central coordinating planning body to which all other planning bodies were to submit their proposals. Second, the annual control figures prepared by *Gosplan* were to provide the general direction for the economy on an annual basis. Third, the actual detailed operational plans for industries and for enterprises (the *promfinplans*) were to conform to the control figures prepared by *Gosplan.* Fourth, materials were to be allocated through a system of balances, compiled from the control figures and *promfinplans,* which would elaborate the supplies and uses of basic industrial materials.

Gosplan's elevation to full planning authority came in 1932 with the development of the ministerial system. Between 1928 and 1932, the functions of VSNKh had grown increasingly complex and confused; and in 1932, VSNKh was, in effect, dissolved as a central coordinating agency for industry. Its chief departments, the *Glavki,* which later became ministries, were allowed to take direct power over planning and administering their enterprises. Earlier, VSNKh had served to coordinate the activities of the industrial departments—a role that *Gosplan* now inherited. VSNKh itself became three separate ministries (Commisariats): heavy industry, light industry, and wood-working. During the late 1920s and early 1930s, party control over economic affairs was expanded. Major economic powers resided in the Politburo under Stalin. Direct central committee control was applied to major construction and industrial projects. Stalin immersed himself in overseeing even minor economic details. The party cadres department handled the task of providing nominations for important positions in the economy. In general, the party came to serve, at all levels, as a general troubleshooter to deal with bottlenecks. Local party officials were charged with mobilizing the masses to plan fulfillment.

Soviet authorities recognized the need for long-range planning to serve as a guide for annual plans.[8] After some experimentation with long-range sectoral plans (for metals, industrial branches, transportation, and agriculture), *Gosplan* assumed responsibility in 1925 for drawing up Five Year Plans for the national economy. The five-year period was chosen because major construction projects in industry, transportation, and construction were felt to have a five-year gestation period and because annual fluctuations in agriculture could be smoothed out over this time interval. After some experimental efforts at five-year planning, *Gosplan* initiated the practise of developing the long-range plan in two variants: a minimum variant based upon cautious assumptions, and a bold maximum variant.

The maximal variant of the plan for 1928–1933 (the first Five Year Plan) was formally adopted by the party in April of 1929 and reflected the teleological thinking of Stalin. It was a 2000-page document, authored by the leading proponents of the teleological approach, G. M. Krzhizhanovsky and S. Strumilin, and it called for the industrialization of the country at a maximum pace as was discussed in the previous chapter.

The manner in which Five Year Plans were to be broken down into annual operational segments and the enforcement and implementation of economic plans were resolved as well during the early Five Year Plan era. One lesson that was learned early on was that Five Year Plans cannot be written in stone, for circumstances change over a five-year period. Thus, the Five Year Plans could not be neatly divided into five annual plans. Instead, the Five Year Plan had to be constantly revised, so that the end result often bore little resemblance to the original targets. As Eugene Zaleski describes it, the Five Year Plan represented "a vision of growth, itself at the service of development strategy."[9] As the objectives of the long-range and annual plans were not necessarily compatible, it was decided that the state agencies controlling material supplies and credits were the ones to determine what parts of the "vision" were to be realized. For example, the first Five Year Plan (maximum variant) called for a quadrupling of investment in state industry, an 85 percent increase in consumption expenditures, a 70 percent increase in real wages, and a 30 percent increase in peasant incomes. These targets represented the planners' vision, but it was the responsibility of the economic administrators in charge of material allocations to ensure that priority targets (industrial investment) were fulfilled.

This period also witnessed the evolution of a centralized administration for the setting of prices. Extensive centralized price setting and regulation, introduced during the early plan era, proved to be a complex task involving issues well beyond the setting of prices per se and requiring the expansion of administrative arrangements.[10] Although the setting of prices was largely decentralized during the NEP period (typically reflecting cost-price relationships of the pre-Soviet period), the Commission for Internal Trade and VSNKh gained increasing authority toward the end of NEP. This tendency toward the centralization of price formation and related functions was greatly enhanced after the introduction of comprehensive central planning in 1928. Not only were internal prices subsequently shielded from world prices through the creation of a state monopoly in foreign trade, but also a series of decrees in the late 1920s and early 1930s harnessed the price system toward the achievement of state goals. Price discrimination in state purchases (buying the same product at different prices—determined by factory costs of production—and then selling at one set price) was introduced, as were multiple pricing (charging different retail prices for the same product), profit margin controls, and differentiated sales taxes (the so-called turnover tax), the latter serving as a primary mechanism for generating state revenues.

The early 1930s witnessed the significant expansion of the number of administrative organs concerned directly or indirectly with price formation, although during the 1930s there was a measure of consolidation with VSNKh and later with the ministries that became the main price-setting bodies.[11] This period also witnessed the tightening of financial controls over enterprises. Commercial credits between enterprises were forbidden, and Gosbank (the state bank) and various specialized banks controlled all credit operations. Moreover, direct grants from the state budget became a major source of investment finance.

ORGANIZING THE SOCIALIST ECONOMY: THE 1930s

Thus far, we have described the creation of the Soviet planning apparatus in the late 1920s and early 1930s. From this discussion, one might view the Soviet economy as being thoroughly under the control of the planning mechanism. In fact, this was not the case. It would soon become evident that the Soviet economy was more of a managed than a planned economy.[12] Let us review the evidence.

There were three major Five Year Plans between 1928 and 1942, the first from 1928 through 1933, the second from 1934 through 1937, and the third from 1938 through 1942. Although the implementation of planning in this period necessarily captures much of our attention, in fact, the planning system was rather less than a full-blown administrative and managerial system. Indeed, the plan periods themselves were less than firm; the first Five Year Plan ended early largely due to pressure for overfulfillment. The second plan was late being developed, as pressure mounted for ever-increasing levels of achievement. The third plan was disrupted by military preparations and, ultimately, the beginning of World War II.

During this period, economic policy and thus the directives for the development of the Soviet economy were part of the Five Year Plans. However, as Eugene Zaleski has emphasized, conditions of extreme austerity existed.[13] Thus, planning in these years, and perhaps to some degree also in later years, incorporated much beyond simply economic aspects, most notably political and ideological aspects of change. Plans were to serve as a device to motivate the population.

Cast in this perspective, it is difficult to assess the performance of the Soviet economy in the 1930s simply by looking at plan targets and plan results. In some cases, data are simply not available; but, most important, multiple plan variants were prepared, and changes were made through time based upon year-to-year

Table 11   SOVIET PLAN FULFILLMENT IN THE 1930s (PERCENT FULFILLMENT)

Objective	First Five Year Plan (1928–1932)	Second Five Year Plan (1933–1937)
National income		
Official estimate	92	96
Western estimate	70	67
Industrial output		
Official estimate	101	103
Western estimate	60–70	76–93
Producer goods		
Official estimate	128	121
Western estimate	72	97
Consumer goods		
Official estimate	81	85
Western estimate	46	68
Agricultural production		
Official estimate	58	63–77
Western estimate	50–52	66–78
Labor productivity		
Official estimate	65	
Western estimate	36–42	86
Retail trade		
Official estimates		
Western estimates	39	54

Sources: N. Jasny, *Essays on The Soviet Economy* (New York: Praeger, 1962), p. 266; E. Zaleski, *Stalinist Planning For Economic Growth: 1933–1952* (Chapel Hill: University of North Carolina Press, 1980), p. 503; A. Nove, *An Economic History of the USSR* (London: Penguin, 1969), p. 353.

actual performance. In general, plans were unrealistic. Plan fulfillment varied markedly from one sector to another and from one product to another within a sector.[14] A general picture of plan fulfillment is presented in Table 11.

Also, the planning apparatus did not, in these early years, manage the entire economy, though it certainly did cover the key sectors. In this sense, there was a degree of decentralization in that some functions in some sectors, for example, materials allocation, might be largely local in character.

Most observers would probably agree that the first Five Year Plan was, including revisions, very ambitious, indeed. It did result in substantial achievements, though with considerable variability from one sector to another. However, by 1933 (a bad year), the initial euphoria had diminished. Labor discipline was a problem, with turnover high and training inadequate. Although money wages were increasing, inflation and rationing of consumer goods constrained or eliminated any increases in real levels of living in the early 1930s.

The purges began in 1934, ironically also the beginning of three years of good, steady growth. However, progress was tempered in 1937 (another bad year), after which preparations for war and the onset of war changed the character of the Soviet economy.

THE DECISION TO COLLECTIVIZE

Developments in the agricultural sector during the late 1920s were as significant in the evolution of the Soviet planned economy as was the formation of the centralized planning structure. Our examination of War Communism and NEP pointed, above all, to the crucial nature of the relationship between the peasant and the state. This relationship, the subject of continuing discussion in the 1920s, was abruptly formalized by the Communist Party under Stalin's leadership when the historic collectivization movement (the forcing of the collective farm, the *kolkhoz,* on the countryside) was begun in 1929.

Our purpose here is to examine the decision to collectivize (i.e., the decision to introduce a significant command element into the Soviet countryside) and in particular to understand the reasons for collectivization as perceived by the Soviet leadership at that time. In addition, it is important that we examine the process of collectivization as it was, in fact, carried out and, finally, the impact of this process upon both immediate postcollectivization agricultural performance, and long-term Soviet agricultural development.[15]

Underpinnings of the Collectivization Decision

The focus of the Soviet Industrialization Debate of the 1920s was the strategy of industrialization; the desire to industrialize was not a matter of contention among the participants. From this discussion and the fact that the Soviet Union was in the 1920s primarily an agricultural economy, it is not surprising that alternative roles for the agricultural sector in the development process would be a point of focus for the participants.

Recall that Preobrazhensky had argued that the rate of saving had to be increased as industrial investment rose. The peasant, according to Preobrazhensky, should bear the burden of this increase in the savings rate through the system of primitive socialist accumulation, whereby savings would be extracted from the countryside by setting low agricultural prices. How to ensure the critically needed peasant marketings under such a system was a question that Preobrazhensky was unable to answer. Bukharin, on the other hand, argued that any system designed to extract involuntary savings from the peasants would destroy any positive relationship between peasant and state and lead to active peasant resistance in the form of reduced peasant marketings. Instead, Bukharin argued, it would be better to adopt a slower rate of economic growth and set prices to favor the peasant. The perceived behavior of the peasants during the Scissors Crisis was thought to underscore this view—that is, the falling trend in peasant marketings as relative agricultural prices dropped.*

Against this background, it should be pointed out that Lenin had long stressed the need to take advantage of economies of scale in agricultural production. Although there was experimentation with various forms of agricultural collectives in the 1920s, these were largely unsuccessful.[16] It was evident that the peasants would not join collective farms voluntarily in the short run. Although both wings of the party favored the growth of agricultural collectives, leading party officials realized that voluntary collectivization would be at best a slow and

---

*As was pointed out in Chapter 2, there is some controversy surrounding the Scissors Crisis and the traditional interpretation of the Russian peasant's response to falling agricultural prices.

evolutionary process. The right wing of the party was not distressed by the fact that the regime would have to rely on peasant farming in the near term, for it was felt that a workable alliance *(Smychka)* with the peasant could be maintained. The left wing, on the contrary, was alarmed by the growing reliance upon peasant farming, especially upon the prosperous *kulak,* who was regarded as a dangerous counter-revolutionary threat.[17] Thus, in 1928, collectivization was regarded by the different party factions as a desirable long-term solution to the agrarian problem, but few could have foreseen (or would have supported) the forced collectivization drive that was to follow shortly.

To what extent Stalin was personally responsible for the collectivization decision and all its ramifications is unclear.[18] He did, however, use as a major justification for instigating collectivization the *grain procurement crisis* of 1928, a matter that merits further attention. According to the best evidence available (see Table 12), the output of key agricultural products, for example, grain, was significantly below the 1913 levels in the early 1920s.[19] However, the indices of both gross agricultural production and livestock production were higher (though not by much) in 1928 than in 1913.

Stalin, however, in a now famous presentation made in May 1928, put forward data to suggest that *grain* output (considered a critical indicator by the Soviet leadership) had declined between 1913 and 1926–1927, but, most important, that the *marketed share* of grain had declined much more rapidly.[20] According to Stalin's data, between 1913 and 1926–1927, gross output of grain declined slightly, but the marketed share declined by roughly 50 percent. In addition, while grain production and marketings by the *kulaks* fell sharply (both had declined to less than one-third of prewar levels), output and marketings of the middle and poor peasants had expanded. For Stalin, this was evidence of the need to move against the *kulaks.* The talk of moving against the *kulaks* made for good window dressing, but Stalin was well aware that the bulk of grain supplies was in the hands of the middle peasants. In the turmoil that followed, it was, therefore, necessary to blur the distinction between the *kulak* and the middle peasant (the *seredniak*). In fact, in the heat of the collectivization campaign, a *kulak* became any peasant who resisted collectivization.

There are, however, two important reservations to Stalin's data. First, as Jerzy Karcz has pointed out, Stalin's grain data were "... completely misleading and presents an exceedingly distorted picture of the relation between 1913 and 1926–1927 grain marketings."[21] According to Karcz, these data, when appropriately reconstructed as grain balances for these years, show that, in fact, gross grain output had, by 1928, all but recovered to prewar levels and that the problem was the definition of marketings. Thus, in the data brought forth by Stalin, *gross marketings* were presented for 1913 while *net marketings* were given for 1926–1927.[22] With two sets of data, quite incomparable, Stalin's case for collectivization as the answer to the marketing problem appeared to be strong.

A second and related factor, according to Karcz, was the role of government policy in bringing about the grain procurement "crisis." In a few years immediately preceding collectivization, net grain marketings did decline precisely because the state lowered grain procurement prices in 1926–1927, naturally

Table 12 SOVIET AGRICULTURAL PRODUCTION: 1913–1938[a]

Year	(1) Gross agricultural production (1928 = 100)	Grain Variants[b] High	Grain Variants[b] Low	Cotton	Sugar Beets	Potatoes	Meat	Milk	Eggs	(2) Livestock Production (1928 = 100)
1913	96	92.7	79	0.5	10.8	29.9	4.0	25.1	10.2	87
1924	—	51.4	44	n.a.	3.5	35.3	3.3	26.3	n.a.	—
1925	—	72.5	62	0.6	9.1	38.4	3.7	28.2	9.6	—
1926	—	76.6	66	0.6	6.4	42.8	4.1	30.5	10.5	—
1927	—	71.7	62	0.7	10.4	42.5	4.3	30.6	10.5	—
1928	100	73.3	63	0.8	10.1	45.2	4.9	31.0	10.8	100
1929	93	71.7	62	0.9	6.3	45.1	5.8	29.8	10.1	87
1930	88	78.0	67	1.1	14.0	44.6	4.3	27.0	8.0	65
1931	84	68.0	62	1.3	12.1	40.6	3.9	23.4	6.7	57
1932	76	68.0	62	1.3	6.6	37.2	2.8	20.6	4.4	48
1933	82	74.0	68	1.3	9.0	44.0	2.3	19.2	3.5	51
1934	86	75.0	68	1.2	11.4	44.2	2.0	20.8	4.2	52
1935	99	80.0	75	1.7	16.2	53.8	2.3	21.4	5.8	74
1936	93	66.0	60	2.4	16.8	44.7	3.7	23.5	7.4	76
1937	116	100.0	95	2.6	21.9	58.8	3.0	26.1	8.2	83
1938	107	76.0	70	2.6	16.7	37.5	4.5	29.0	10.5	100

Source: From S. G. Wheatcroft, "A Reevaluation of Soviet Agricultural Production in the 1920s and 1930s," in R. C. Stuart, ed., *The Soviet Rural Economy* (Totowa, N.J.: Rowman & Allanheld, 1984), 11. 42–3, 49. n.a. = not available.

[a]All data are million tons, except eggs, which are billions; and agricultural production and livestock production, which are constant price indexes.

[b]The grain variants are based upon differing views in the comparability of pre and post collectivization series. The high variant has been adjusted, the low variant has not been adjusted.

encouraging peasants to market their grain through other than state channels—
that is, where prices were more attractive—and to hold back their grain in
anticipation of higher prices. In the previous chapter, we noted that state grain
procurement prices were below the production costs of small and middle peasants. At the same time, peasant taxes were lowered, as were the prices of manufactured goods, thus stimulating peasant demand. Also, in the face of lower state
grain procurement prices, peasants were encouraged to shift into the production
of meat and related products, the prices of which were generally rising. Thus,
although peasant marketings of grain were falling, the output and marketings of
other farm products were rising in response to more favorable prices and were
offsetting the declining grain marketings.

The immediate justification for collectivization may, therefore, have been
based upon inadequate statistical information and the will to impose adverse state
policy on the peasants, in addition to ideological underpinnings and the drive for
large-scale production units.[23] As S. G. Wheatcroft has shown, comparisons of
output and marketings of the twenties with prewar figures will be subject to wide
margins of error; so the controversy over Stalin's statistics will probably never
be resolved. However, from the vantage point of the state, the grain crisis was
real. State grain collections from the peasants *(zagotovki)* were alarmingly low
(the peasants were selling on the private market), and the government had to
undergo the humiliating experience of importing grain.[24] Even Bukharin became
convinced that harsher methods were necessary. At this time, Stalin unleashed
an emergency campaign to increase state grain collections, dispatching trusted
party officials to supervise the campaign. Grain supplies were confiscated, road
blocks were set up, and peasants holding grain were charged as speculators. Stalin
suspended these emergency measures in 1928 to quiet down the alarmed Bukharinites, but he came away from the experience convinced that force and coercion
could be applied successfully in the countryside once the Bukharinites were
destroyed.

The Collectivization Process

While the discussion of collectivization and Stalin's arguments on its behalf were
well under way in 1928, it was not until mid-1929 that central control over
existing cooperatives was substantially strengthened and the system of grain
procurements changed—in short, the beginning of the process of mass collectivization.[25] By the latter part of 1929, an all-out drive for collectivization had been
initiated by the Communist Party, becoming in large measure an organized
movement against the *kulaks* and the middle peasants. Lacking strength in the
countryside (less than one percent of the farm population belonged to the party
or *komsomol*), the party sent 25,000 representatives, drawn largely from the
ranks of industrial workers, to oversee collectivization. The most burning issue,
once the all-out collectivization decision had been made, was whether or not to
admit kulaks to the collectives. In a speech before the November party plenum,
Stalin spoke for the first time of eliminating the kulak.

There were significant regional differences in the speed of collectivization and also a continuing debate over the precise organizational form to be utilized. The data in Table 13 suggest, however, that the overall speed of collectivization was rapid. Between July 1, 1929, and March 1, 1930, for example, the proportion of peasant households in collective farms increased from 4 percent to 56 percent.[26] In effect, the collective farm had supplanted the centuries-old *mir* form of village government within a year's time.

Although the fiction was maintained that the collectivization movement was a spontaneous action on the part of the peasantry, resisted only by the *"kulak* saboteurs,"* there can be little doubt that collectivization was imposed on an unwilling peasantry by brutal force. Vague definitions of what constituted a *kulak* household were employed to permit the arrest and deportation of peasants resisting collectivization. Militia and the secret police (then called the GPU) were sent into the countryside to force peasants into collectives along with thousands of armed party faithful from the city. The "dekulakization" drive resulted in the flight, execution, deportation, and resettlement of millions of peasants and provided the initial manpower for a vast army of penal labor. According to one estimate, 3.5 million peasants became a part of the *gulag* penal labor force, 3.5 million were resettled, and another 3.5 million died during forced collectivization.[27] There is considerable controversy over the number of victims of collectivization, but there is little doubt that it numbered in the millions.

Although Stalin, in a famous speech in March 1930, warned against proceeding too rapidly and blamed local party leaders for the excesses that had occurred, in fact, the pace of collectivization remained rapid, and by the mid-1930s the process was basically completed.[28] The role of the Communist Party in the countryside was formally strengthened when in 1933 political departments *(Politotdely)* were established in the machine tractor stations. The machine tractor stations (MTS) had themselves been established in 1930; and, in addition to serving as a mechanism for supplying machinery and equipment to the collective farms (for which payment in kind would be made to the state), they were to play a significant role in the management of collective farms.[29] Informal party control in the countryside had also been strengthened considerably by collectivization,

Table 13 **EXPANSION OF THE COLLECTIVE FARM SECTOR, 1918–1938 (SELECTED YEARS)**

Year	Collective farms (in thousands)	Households in collectives (in thousands)	Peasant households collectivized (percentage)
1918	1.6	16.4	0.1
1928	33.3	416.7	1.7
1929	57.0	1,007.7	3.9
1930	85.9	5,998.1	23.6
1931	211.1	13,033.2	52.7
1932	211.1	14,918.7	61.5
1935	245.4	17,334.9	83.2
1938	242.4	18,847.6	93.5

Source: Volin, *A Century of Russian Agriculture* (Cambridge, Mass.: Harvard University Press, 1970), p. 211.

through the party's placing of "reliable" men in the posts of collective farm chairman.

THE IMMEDIATE IMPACT OF COLLECTIVIZATION

The most immediate result of collectivization was a decline in agricultural output. Although there were year-to-year fluctuations, the general decline is unmistakable (see Table 12). The index of gross agricultural production (1928 = 100) declined from a precollectivization high in 1928 to an immediate postcollectivization low of 76 in 1932.[30] In large part this can be accounted for by a sharp decline in gross production of livestock products to 48 in 1933.[31] In general, the decline in meat, dairy, and egg production was more severe than the decline in cultivated crops. Although grain output declined in the initial years of collectivization (1928 through 1932, with the exception of 1930), both gross and net marketings of grain increased between 1928–1929 and 1931–1932, due to some extent to a sharp decline in the number of cattle for which grains for fodder were now not necessary.[32] The worsening of agricultural performance during the first Five Year Plan (1928–1932) plus the losses from state reserves were major factors contributing to the famine that reached a peak in 1932–1933.

The loss of lives (especially severe in grain-producing regions) from both the collectivization process *per se* and the famine thereafter (the famine being the major factor) has been the subject of considerable discussion, but very little hard data are available by which to assess its severity. The most frequently quoted estimate of lives lost is five million, although the reader should be cautioned that other estimates vary from one to ten million.[33]

In addition to the loss of life and the decline in agricultural production, there was a sharp decline in agricultural capital stock, most notably caused by the mass destruction of animal herds as the peasants vented their hostility toward the collectivization process by slaughtering their livestock rather than bringing them into the collective farms. The impact of this development can be observed in Table 14. In addition, Naum Jasny, one of the research pioneers in this area, has indicated that other forms of capital stock—notably buildings and machinery

Table 14   NUMBERS OF LIVESTOCK IN THE SOVIET UNION, 1928–1935
            (IN MILLIONS OF HEAD)

Year	Cattle (total)	Cows	Pigs	Sheep	Goats	Horses
1928[a]	60.1	29.3	22.0	97.3	9.7	32.1
1929	58.2	29.2	19.4	97.4	9.7	32.6
1930	50.6	28.5	14.2	85.5	7.8	31.0
1931	42.5	24.5	11.7	62.5	5.6	27.0
1932	38.3	22.3	10.9	43.8	3.8	21.7
1933	33.5	19.4	9.9	34.0	3.3	17.3
1934	33.5	19.0	11.5	32.9	3.6	15.4
1935	38.9	19.0	17.1	36.4	4.4	14.9

Source: E. Strauss, *Soviet Agriculture in Perspective* (London: Allen & Unwin, 1969), p. 307.
[a]Borders of the Soviet Union as of 1939.

—simply disappeared during the turmoil of collectivization.[34] The impact of collectivization upon per capita incomes of the farm population was predictable: they fell sharply to perhaps one-half the 1928 level.[35]

COLLECTIVIZATION AND ECONOMIC DEVELOPMENT

Thus far, we have focused upon the immediate response of the peasants to the collectivization drive of the 1930s. To be sure, there were substantial initial social costs in the form of falling agricultural production. But to what extent were these initial costs offset by benefits? Put another way, was collectivization the mechanism that harnessed the rural economy to the industrialization drive of the 1930s and "solved" the problem of the peasants?

To examine these broader issues, we turn to the literature on economic development. In a simple two-sector economy consisting of agriculture and industry, low levels of economic development are generally associated with a dominant role for the agricultural sector as measured in terms of product shares, factors shares, population distribution, and the like.[36] In the couse of development, agriculture acts as a contributor to the development process by supplying labor and capital resources to the rest of the economy. In such a model, agriculture performs the following supportive functions:

1. Provision of manpower for industry.
2. Expansion of output and marketings to supply foodstuffs for the expanding nonagricultural sector and raw materials for industry.
3. Provision of agricultural products for export to earn foreign exchange to pay for importation of machinery and equipment.
4. Assistance to capital accumulation in the industrial sector by the transfer of savings from the rural to the industrial sector.

As far as the first supportive role is concerned, Soviet agriculture did without a doubt provide a vast amount of manpower to industry within a relatively brief amount of time. Between 1926 and 1939 alone, the urban population increased from 26.3 million to 56.1 million—a net gain of some 30 million—and by 1959, this figure had increased to 100 million—a net overall increase of over 73 million, of which 43.4 million (well over one-half) can be accounted for by migration from rural to urban areas.[37] This internal migration, along with the increasing participation rates of the urban population, sustained an average annual rate of growth of the nonagricultural labor force of 8.7 percent between 1928 and 1937, while the agricultural labor force declined at an annual rate of 2.5 percent during the same period. This vast transformation was effected by both market and nonmarket forces: First, a substantial gap between urban and rural incomes was created, thereby promoting movement out of agriculture. Second, massive recruitment campaigns were carried on in the countryside to facilitate the transfer.

Most experts would agree that collectivization was at least in part responsible for the flow of labor from rural areas to industry in the 1930s. In effect, collectivization "pushed" labor out of agriculture, rather than the more common case of industrial prosperity "pulling" labor from the countryside. The contemporary debate over the merits of Soviet collectivization focuses on whether collectivization was necessary to promote this outflow or, if not necessary, whether it was the most efficient mechanism to facilitate the labor outflow from the rural areas.

In this debate, Michael Ellman has argued that collectivization was necessary to generate sufficient supplies of urban (industrial) labor. Given the vast manpower needs of Soviet industry, sufficient labor would not have been available without collectivization. James Millar, on the other hand, maintains that in this respect collectivization was both unnecessary and undesirable. Millar maintains that flows of labor from rural to urban areas have always been adequate (in fact, frequently more than adequate) in countries experiencing development. Moreover, the urban unemployed or underemployed could have been mobilized to meet additional industrial manpower needs if the influx from agriculture had not been sufficient.[38]

In sum, while collectivization, combined with a fair measure of state control, led to an outflow of labor from rural areas in the 1930s, the necessity and effectiveness of the use of forced collectivization for this purpose is still under debate. Although labor flows voluntarily into industry during economic development, the Soviet process is distinguished by the great speed of this flow.

How well Soviet agriculture performed the second supportive function during the crucial early years of industrialization is also the subject of controversy. The figures on grain marketings (Table 15) provide valuable insights.

The evidence presented in Table 15 supports the view that in spite of

Table 15 SOVIET GRAIN PRODUCTION AND PROCUREMENT, 1929–1938[a]

Year	Grain[b] production (million metric tons)	Grain procurement[c] (million metric tons)	Procurement ÷ Production
1929	66.8	10.8	16.2
1930	71.0	16.0	22.5
1931	65.0	22.1	34.0
1932	65.0	23.7	36.5
1933	71.0	23.3	32.8
1934	71.5	26.0	36.4
1935	77.5	28.4	36.6
1936	63.0	25.7	40.8
1937	97.5	31.8	32.6
1938	73.0	31.5	43.1

Sources: Grain production data from S. G. Wheatcroft, "A Reevaluation of Soviet Agricultural Production in the 1920s and 1930s," 42–43; Procurement data 1929–1932 from R. W. Davies, *The Industrialization of Russia* vol. 1, Table 8; Procurement data for 1932 from J. F. Karcz, "Khrushchev's Agricultural Policies," in M. Bornstein and D. F. Fusfeld, eds., *The Soviet Economy: A Book of Readings,* 3rd ed. (Homewood, Illinois: Richard D. Irwin, 1970), p. 44; Procurement data 1933–1938 from E. Zaleski, *Stalinist Planning For Economic Growth,* Statistical Appendix.

[a]These data should be interpreted with caution as representing general trends. There are important and controversial issues of definition and measurement.

[b]Simple average of the high and low variants from Table 12.

[c]Procurements (actually grain collections) 1929–1931 are for the agricultural year (i.e., 1929 = 1928–1929), while procurements for 1932–1938 are for plan (calendar) years.

fluctuations, from the late 1920s through the late 1930s, grain procurements generally increased more rapidly than grain production. Thus, grain procurements increased from a low of roughly 16 percent in 1929 to a high of roughly 43 percent in 1938.

Jerzy Karcz has attempted to show that the entire increase in gross grain marketings between 1928 and 1933 can be accounted for not by the ability of the state to gather additional grain per se from *kolkhozy,* but by the reduction in animal herds—which would otherwise consume grains—that took place during collectivization.[39] However, one may question this conclusion in the light of the large state exactions during poor harvest years that exacerbated the famine of 1932–1934. Also, the drastic decline in peasant living standards during the 1930s might be cited as counterevidence to Karcz's conclusions.

As far as the third function is concerned, Soviet agriculture did contribute to overall economic development during the first Five Year Plan by earning crucial foreign exchange to pay for machinery imports from the West. Between 1929 and 1931, Soviet imports increased by over 60 percent (in volume terms) despite the worsening terms of trade resulting from the collapse of agricultural prices in the world market during this period. In fact, Soviet imports were severely limited by balance-of-payments constraints—given the Western countries' unwillingness to grant long-term credits to the fledgling communist regime. The Soviet government's sole recourse, therefore, was to continue to market abroad the traditional Soviet export commodities—grain and wheat, timber, and petroleum. Between 1929 and 1931, Soviet exports expanded somewhat less than 50 percent, and this expansion was spearheaded by an increase in the proportion of the total domestic output of agricultural products exported. In 1928, for example, less than one percent of the domestic output of grain, wheat, and corn was exported; yet by 1931, 14 percent of the output of grain, 18 percent of wheat, and 2 percent of corn was exported. In this manner, agricultural exports were used to finance machinery and ferrous metals imports, which rose from one-third of total Soviet imports in 1928 to almost three-quarters by the end of the first Five Year Plan.[40] The costs of maintaining agricultural exports were considerable, for they worsened the famine of 1932–1934. As one student of this famine writes[41]:

> The immediate cause was not poor harvests but the requisitioning of grain from moderate harvests in such quantities that not enough was left for the peasants themselves. The main reasons for this drastic policy appear to have been, first the attempt to maintain exports of agricultural produce and hence imports of machinery. . . .

The most controversial rule of Soviet agriculture in economic development relates to the fourth function, namely, the transfer of savings from the countryside to the city. On the surface, it would appear that the Preobrazhensky model of primitive socialist accumulation was indeed used successfully in forcing savings from the rural population during the early years of industrialization. While estimates of the extent of decline must be quite crude, Naum Jasny has estimated that per capita income of the farm population had fallen to 53 percent of the 1928 level by 1932–1933, which perhaps is not too unrealistic in view of the fact that the peasants' standard of living during the best prewar year for the Russian peasantry (1937) was still only 81 percent that of 1928.[42] Although it would appear from such figures that Soviet agrarian policies succeeded in marshaling forced savings from the rural sector, such a judgment may be premature for reasons discussed below. In any case, the burden of industrialization was also borne by the urban sector. Mindful of the significant decline in urban living standards during the 1930s, Abram Bergson notes the following[43]:

> Contrary to a common supposition, the industrial worker fared no better than the peasants under Stalin's five year plans. Indeed, he seemingly fared worse, although I believe he was able to maintain in some degree the margin he enjoyed initially in respect to consumption per capita.

It may be as well that the decline in both urban and rural standards during the first Five Year Plan has been underestimated, so that the savings "forced" from the Soviet population were indeed quite significant.[44]

However, the fundamental issue here is the role of collectivization in the extraction of a surplus from the countryside to form the basis of the industrial expansion of the Soviet economy in the 1930s and thereafter. That savings were forced via reductions in living standards is not at issue, for investment rates (saving rates) did explode during the early 1930s as a consequence of transferring income from individuals to the state. The issue instead is: Was the collective farm responsible? Although the Western assessment of collectivization has generally been negative, especially in a long-run perspective, the *kolkhoz* has been credited by some as being the mechanism that served to extract a surplus from the countryside and hence played a crucial role in the accumulation process.[45]

Although it has proved difficult to achieve precision in defining and measuring an agricultural surplus, evidence provided by the Soviet economist A. A. Barsov and analyzed by James Millar appears to demonstrate that during the crucial period of the first Five Year Plan, Soviet agriculture was a net *recipient* of resources.[46] For surpluses to be transferred from agriculture to industry, the flow of deliveries from agriculture to industry must exceed the flow of deliveries from industry to agriculture (grain for tractors, if you will). As these are flows of physical commodities, the outcome will depend upon the prices applied. Millar uses the prices of 1928 (which place a low relative valuation on agriculture) and finds an inflow to agriculture on a net basis. Michael Ellman uses modified 1913 prices (which place a higher relative valuation on agriculture prices) and obtains a net outflow. But the crucial point is that both Millar and Ellman find that the advent of collectivization failed to alter the magnitude of the surplus, however it is measured. Thus, one cannot argue that collectivization was responsible for any significant change in the surplus. Millar summarizes his view as follows[47]:

> Ultimately, therefore, although the state did succeed in raising real resources from the peasantry for investment purposes, the destruction occasioned by resistance to collectivization obliged it to turn around and use those resources

for replacement investment in agriculture. This inflow, together with the net inflow to the private sector that was financed by the favorable change in the terms of trade with the nonrural population, caused the agricultural sector taken as a whole to become a net recipient of resources during the first Five Year Plan. Whatever its merits may have been on other grounds, mass collectivization of Soviet agriculture must be reckoned as an unmitigated economic policy disaster.

COLLECTIVIZATION: AN ASSESSMENT

Collectivization ranks among the most controversial events in contemporary Soviet economic history. From an economic viewpoint, the usual Western literature on collectivization focuses upon two major themes. First, as we have noted above, collectivization is viewed as having been a major disaster, inflicting major costs, both short-term and long-term, upon the Soviet peasant population and the economy as a whole.

Second, and beyond the issue of costs, collectivization is viewed as introducing a unique if cruel mechanism for harnessing the agricultural surplus (and the rural population) to the service of the industrial sector. As noted above, some specialists argue that collectivization was the means for providing the surplus necessary for industrialization.

Since Millar's presentation of the Barsov evidence, it would seem that, for the period under study, and defined in terms of net sectoral flows, agriculture did not provide a significant surplus. Indeed, even with varying price weights used to aggregate the intersectoral flows, agriculture at best provided a very small net positive flow, one which changed little, if at all, during the collectivization drive.

Surely, if we accept this evidence at face value, it must change the traditional view of collectivization, specifically the view of agriculture as a contributor of a large net surplus to the industrialization drive. There is little dispute that collectivization lowered Soviet agricultural productivity in both the short and long run. Moreover, if sufficient labor would have migrated voluntarily to the cities anyway, collectivization would not have been necessary to meet the manpower needs of industry. If these points are correct, the major lasting benefit the Soviet regime obtained from collectivization was the imposition of political control over the countryside. The political benefits to a Stalin of bringing a potentially unruly and unfriendly segment of the population under control were considerable.

Prior to the Barsov–Millar hypothesis, Western economists argued that, because a surplus was extracted from agriculture, it was the agricultural sector that bore a major burden of the industrialization drive. The peasants gave up the grain which they would have eaten and/or converted into consumer goods. The revisionist view of the surplus does not really alter the question of burden to any appreciable degree. To the extent that offsetting flows from nonagriculture to agriculture were agricultural inputs, they would do little for the immediate peasant standard of living, particularly given state exactions at low prices. In this sense, the peasants must have borne a burden even though the newly supplied inputs to agriculture may have improved the long-term prospects for improved agricultural production.

The Soviet investment rate doubled between 1928 and 1937 (Table 10). The industrial capital stock almost quadrupled over the same period. The investment rate in 1913 was likely not much below that of 1928.[48] Thus, it is clear that massive capital accumulation, concentrated primarily in industry, took place in the 1930s. The agricultural surplus controversy does not dispute this basic point. At issue rather is whether the agricultural population bore a disproportionate share of this accumulation burden. The evidence presented in Table 10 suggests that, despite rapid economic growth, both urban and rural living standards stagnated, the agricultural more than the urban one. The burden was heavy, and both urban and rural workers shared the forced savings that made this rapid capital accumulation possible.

STRUCTURAL CHANGE IN THE 1930s

Before we turn to a discussion of the Soviet economy during the war years, it is useful to reflect upon the tumultous decade of the 1930s. Assessment of the achievements of this period is difficult. Unquestionably, there were substantial gains, though these gains were uneven and undoubtedly achieved at major cost. Moreover, if we assess economic growth in terms of value aggregates (as we generally must do), the problems of valuation in a period of such rapid change are great. Even the assessment of plan achievement is, as we have emphasized, difficult since plan targets were changed so often. The evidence presented in Table 11 suggests much variability of early plan fulfillment. Moreover, Western and official Soviet interpretations of this record differ substantially. However, as we assess the long-term record of Soviet aggregate economic growth, it will be apparent that judged by world historical standards, Soviet economic growth in the 1930s was rapid.

Possibly the most effective way to appreciate the rapidity and the magnitude of change in the Soviet economy in the 1930s is to look again at the structural changes that took place. Some figures are presented in Table 16.

The reader might recall that our earlier assessment of structural change for the immediate prerevolutionary years noted that, while there had been only limited change, it was directionally consistent with modern economic growth. In contrast, it is clear that there was a sharp structural change in the 1930s. In particular, the share of industry increased significantly, while that of agriculture declined. The importance of consumption also declined sharply, although part of this decline may have been offset by increases in communal consumption within the government share of NNP. The share of net domestic investment more than doubled. The importance of trade declined sharply, a matter to which we shall return in Chapter 10. Finally, as we have noted, although there are severe difficulties in assessing Soviet economic growth in the 1930s (about which more in Chapter 11), nevertheless, by world historical standards, economic growth is generally thought to have been rapid during these years.

Table 16   STRUCTURAL CHANGE OF SOVIET ECONOMY IN THE 1930s

	1928	1937
Sector shares of NNP (%)		
Agriculture	49	31
Industry	28	45
Services	23	24
End use shares of NNP (%)		
Consumption	82	55
Government	8	22
Net domestic investment	10	23
Foreign trade		
Exports + Imports/NNP	6.2	1
Economic growth (average annual %)		
Total product: 1928–1940	5.1	
Per capita product: 1928–1940	3.9	

Source: P. R. Gregory, "Economic Growth and Structural Change in Czarist Russia and the Soviet Union: A Long-Term Comparison," in S. Rosefielde, ed., *Economic Welfare and The Economics of Soviet Socialism* (New York: Cambridge University Press, 1981), p. 39.

The 1930s was an unusual decade in the contemporary Soviet experience. Indeed, it is unusual when compared to the early development experiences elsewhere, not so much in direction of change but rather in terms of the speed of change and the mechanisms used to promote these changes.[49] It was, however, interrupted by war, another event having a major impact upon the Soviet economy.

THE SOVIET ECONOMY DURING WORLD WAR II

The impact of World War II upon the Soviet Union in general and the Soviet economy in particular[50] is a subject that has been receiving increasing attention from both Soviet and Western scholars. The subject is of immense contemporary interest in the Soviet Union, where the war achievements are viewed in the broadest terms as demonstrating the viability of the Soviet social and economic system even under the most extreme conditions.

Our interest in World War II centers not only upon the costs of the war to the Soviet system, but also on the short- and long-term adjustments that resulted and the resiliency of the planned socialist economy under new and very different conditions from those prevailing earlier.

The impact of World War II on the Soviet economy was immense. For example, in terms of loss of life, Soviet authors frequently cite a figure of 20 million, or approximately 10 percent of the 1940 Soviet population, of which roughly one-half was from military action. However, if one were to count indirect losses, for example, early deaths from war-related injuries, prisoners of war who chose not to be repatriated, and those entering the gulag camps, the figure for loss of life would undoubtedly be much higher. In a recent survey of the impact of World War II on the Soviet economy, James Millar has suggested a figure of 30 million, or approximately 15 percent of the Soviet population as of 1940.[51] As we shall see shortly, much more than loss of life was involved.

In addition to population loss of the sort noted above, the war losses imposed major and long-standing demographic changes on the Soviet population. Specifically, war losses resulted in a substantial male deficit (much greater than would be anticipated under more normal conditions), leading to other important changes, for example, in marriage rates and birthrates and hence population growth. Moreover, as Barbara Anderson and Brian Silver note in a recent study, the war-related male deficit resulted in a substantial increase in russification through intermarriage.[52] These and related demographic trends would persist long after the end of the war.

Germany invaded the Soviet Union in June of 1941. Soviet territorial losses resulting from this invasion were sudden and large. In a recent study of the economic impact of World War II on the Soviet economy, Susan Linz indicates that between July and November of 1981, 1,523 major industrial enterprises were moved eastward along with 6 million people. While this eastward movement facilitated later production, it resulted in immediate disruption. The Soviet economy, after the German invasion, did not recover production levels of 1940 until 1942; and by the end of the war, output levels were 20 percent below those of the prewar period, not to mention an estimated 30 percent destruction of the Soviet capital stock.[53]

The aggregate cost of the war to the Soviet economy has been estimated in a number of different ways. The official Soviet claim is that the war cost the USSR "two Five Year Plans," not including the loss of life noted above. Recent Western estimates confirm this sort of magnitude. Linz and Millar find that losses range from four to ten years of effort by the labor force available in 1940 or 1945. Summarizing the issue of war losses, Millar notes: "Put differently, the economic cost of the war was equal to, and possibly even greater than, the total wealth created during the industrialization drive of the 1930s."[54]

How was this war effort financed by the Soviet Union? Again, Millar notes that ". . . the population as a whole increased its work effort and reduced its claim on current output during the war years."[55] Specifically, a number of important changes were made. First, resource allocation priorities were obviously changed. The share of national income devoted to the war effort increased sharply, from about 10 percent in 1940 to slightly under 50 percent by 1943.[56] This change was in part facilitated by the nature of the Soviet economic system and the extraordinary mechanisms (about which more later) put in place during the war years. In general, there was a major shift of resources away from traditional uses (especially consumption and investment) toward war uses.

Second, consumer demand was effectively constrained in a number of ways, although not all efforts in this area worked smoothly and effectively. Rationing of consumer goods was introduced in July 1941 in successive stages. In addition, the distribution of key consumer goods was centralized. However, Soviet efforts to control wages were not always effective. This fact, in combination with the existence of various retail markets under differing degrees of control, meant that, in fact, multiple prices existed for the same goods. For example, the prices in collective farm markets in 1943 were higher than state ration prices by a factor of 14.[57]

Third, labor allocation procedures were changed. While we shall leave the general issue of labor allocation for a subsequent chapter, suffice it to say here that the importance of administrative controls in the labor allocation process increased significantly. Direct mobilization of labor was introduced in December 1941, with strong disciplinary measures enforced. These measures were in large part a response to severe labor shortages imposed by the war effort. For example, the magnitude of the Soviet civilian labor force decreased from 31 million in 1941 to 18 million in 1942.[58] This labor shortage had serious repercussions on the economy, not the least important of which was a tendency for wage inflation, which necessitated offsetting tax increases.

How was the Soviet economy administered during the war? Western observers have noted that, while there were important wartime changes in the administrative structure of the Soviet economy, these changes were for the most part superimposed on top of existing arrangements and were derived from previous experience, for example, the civil war period.[59] A series of new agencies was created, effectively centralizing power and facilitating rapid shifts of resources. For example, the overall war effort was directed by the State Committee for Defense headed by Stalin. Regional shifts were directed by the Evacuation Committee. Moreover, while the planning and materials allocation system put together in the 1930s remained intact, Zaleski has pointed out that, in fact, much less attention was paid to national plans, and much more attention was paid to specific plans for war-related activities. The more limited number of specific, defense-related plans allowed the planners to control defense production more closely. The remainder of the economy was guided not only by general plans but was also regulated by the state budget and the use of newly imposed rationing powers.

Gosplan and the war-related ministries and commissions gained power through the increased importance of the material balances. Thus, at the height of the war effort, central plans were being drawn up for 30,000 materials and supplies to be allocated to 120 large users.

The administrative response to the war was quick and effective using previously demonstrated strengths (for example, the priority principle) to shift resources into the war effort.

Thus far, we have focused on the costs of the war and the manner in which the economic system was altered to handle the war effort. But how were these costs borne by the Soviet people? In contrast to market economies where the concern focuses on market methods to maintain labor discipline in the face of limited growth of rewards, Soviet leaders resorted to strict administrative methods to enforce labor discipline.[60] At the same time, taxes were increased as a means of restricting consumer demand and financing the war effort. Both direct and indirect taxes were increased. In addition to the increase in the rates for existing taxes, new taxes (notably the war tax) were introduced along with other exactions through bond purchases, multiple levels of distribution in retail trade, and the like. Deficit financing was used, as the government printed money to pay for the war effort. In a sense, Soviet financing of the war effort was based on the use of familiar tools, though possibly with greater emphasis on direct taxation than that generally found in market systems.

In sum, World War II imposed a tremendous burden on the Soviet Union. The economic system was effectively transposed to handle that burden by shifting resources into the successful war effort. All sectors of Soviet society, whether the ministries, the Communist Party, or transportation, were geared to the war effort. While we will pursue postwar economic development in the following chapter, it is useful to note here that the Soviet postwar transition to a peacetime economy was not easy, nor was it the same as transitions in other war-ravaged economies.

While controls were relaxed, other controls were implemented, and the Stalinist mode of operation would remain in effect until the Khrushchev era of the 1950s. The problem of pent-up demand, which served as a stimulus to the postwar growth of consumption (and hence consumer goods production) in market systems, was effectively curtailed in the Soviet Union. While rationing and other such direct controls were relaxed and removed, the currency reform of 1947 proved to be a more direct means to extract currency from the population.[61] Thus, one new ruble was given for each old ruble in a generally complicated currency reform. In addition, the prewar priorities were generally reasserted, such that the Soviet consumer would have to wait for the anticipated postwar relaxation.

THE SOVIET ECONOMY THROUGH WORLD WAR II: A SUMMARY

The contemporary Soviet economy as we presently know it dates from the very end of the 1920s. In this period, as the NEP system came to an abrupt end, Stalin, firmly in command, introduced two major changes into the Soviet economy: national economic planning and collectivization. Both would be cornerstones of an economic system vastly different from that prevailing earlier, a system that, with changes over the years, exists to the present day.

In this chapter, we have examined the underpinnings of both the planning decision and the collectivization decision. We have emphasized that planning was introduced as a means to control both the pace and the directions of economic development. At the same time, collectivization was introduced as a means to harness the peasants, indeed the rural sector, to the industrialization drive, although, as we have seen, collectivization and its use as a mechanism to finance the development process have been called into question in recent years.

In addition to our examination of these two major decisions, we have examined the Soviet economic system in its formative years, the 1930s and thereafter in the tumultuous years of World War II. By most standards, the 1930s well earned their reputation as a period of unprecedented economic growth and structural change in the Soviet Union—forced draft industrialization, to be sure.

The costs were high, yet the achievements were, by most standards, great. Indeed, a severe test of these achievements came when the Germans invaded the Soviet Union in 1941. This event, which would foreshadow a conflict of immense proportions, placed a large burden upon the Soviet Union and the Soviet economic system; and yet, as we have seen, the system proved capable to the challenge. Although the losses were great and the postwar conversion slow, nevertheless, the 1950s ushered in a new era, particularly after the death of Joseph Stalin in 1953. We now turn our attention to the development of the Soviet economy in the postwar era.

REFERENCES

1. Our discussion of the planning debate of the 1920s is based on the following sources: E. H. Carr and R. W. Davies, *Foundations of a Planned Economy, 1926–1929,* vol. 1, part 2 (London: Macmillan, 1969), pp. 787–801; N. Spulber, *Soviet Strategy for Economic Growth* (Bloomington: Indiana University Press, 1964), pp. 101–111.
2. Statement of P. Vaisburg in *Planovoe khoziaistvo* [The planned economy], no. 4 (1928), 167. Quoted in Carr and Davies, *Foundations of a Planned Economy,* p. 793.
3. *Pravda,* September 14, 1927. Quoted in Carr and Davies, *Foundations of a Planned Economy,* p. 818.
4. Our discussion is based on the following sources: Carr and Davies, *Foundations of a Planned Economy,* chaps. 33–35; A. Nove, *An Economic History of the USSR* (London: Penguin, 1969), pp. 212–215, 263–267; M. Dobb, *Soviet Economic Development Since 1917,* 5th ed. (London: Routledge & Kegan Paul, 1960), chap. 13; E. Zaleski, *Planning for Economic Growth in the Soviet Union, 1918–1932* (Chapel Hill: University of North Carolina Press, 1971), pp. 40–73; Y. Avdakov and V. Borodin, *USSR State Industry During the Transition Period* (Moscow: Progress Publishers, 1977); W. Conyngham, *Industrial Management in the Soviet Union* (Stanford, CA: Hoover Institution Press, 1973), pp. 34–42.
5. Zaleski, *Planning for Economic Growth,* p. 41.
6. Carr and Davies, *Foundations of a Planned Economy,* p. 802.
7. Carr and Davies, *Foundations of a Planned Economy,* pp. 830–831. Also see Z. K. Zvezdin, *Ot Goelro k planu pervoi piatiletki* [From Goelro to the first Five Year Plan] (Moscow: Nauka, 1979).
8. Zaleski, *Planning for Economic Growth,* pp. 29–73.
9. E. Zaleski, *Stalinist Planning for Economic Growth, 1933–1952* (Chapel Hill: University of North Carolina Press, 1980), p. 483.
10. The discussion here is based upon R. Hutchings, "The Origin of the Soviet Industrial Price System," *Soviet Studies,* vol. 13, no. 1 (July 1961), 1–22.
11. For details of the organizational arrangements, see Hutchings, "The Origin of the Soviet Industrial Price System," 13–14.
12. In this section, we rely upon Zaleski, *Planning for Economic Growth;* and Nove, *An Economic History of the USSR.*
13. Zaleski, *Planning for Economic Growth,* chap. 19.
14. For details of plan fulfillment in the 1930s, see Zaleski, Statistical Appendices.
15. In the present section, we rely heavily upon the following sources: J. F. Karcz, "From Stalin to Brezhnev: Soviet Agricultural Policy in Historical Perspective," in J. R. Millar, ed., *The Soviet Rural Community* (Urbana: University of Illinois Press, 1971), pp. 36–70; J. F. Karcz, "Thoughts on the Grain Problem," *Soviet Studies,* vol. 18, no. 4 (April 1967), 399–434; M. Lewin, *Russian Peasants and Soviet Power* (London: Allen & Unwin, 1968); J. R. Millar and C. A. Guntzel, "The Economics and Politics of Mass Collectivization Reconsidered: A Review Article," *Explorations in Economic History,* vol. 8, no. 1 (Fall 1970), 103–116; A. Nove, "The Decision to Collectivize," in W. A. D. Jackson, ed., *Agrarian Policies and Problems in Communist and Non-Communist Countries* (Seattle: University of Washington Press, 1971), pp. 69–97; E. Strauss, *Soviet Agriculture in Perspective* (London: Allen & Unwin, 1969), chaps. 5–6;

L. Volin, *A Century of Russian Agriculture* (Cambridge, Mass.: Harvard University Press, 1970), chaps. 10–11; R. W. Davies, "A Note on Grain Statistics," *Soviet Studies,* vol. 21, no. 3 (January 1970), 314–329; S. G. Wheatcroft, "The Reliability of Russian Prewar Grain Output Statistics," *Soviet Studies,* vol. 26, no. 2 (April 1974), 157–180; A. Vyas, "Primary Accumulation in the USSR Revisited," *Cambridge Journal of Economics,* vol. 3 (1979), 119–130; R. W. Davies, *The Industrialization of Soviet Russia,* vols. 1 and 2 (Cambridge: Harvard University Press, 1980).

16. The reader interested in the agricultural collectives of the 1920s should consult D. J. Male, *Russian Peasant Organization Before Collectivization* (Cambridge: Cambridge University Press, 1971); R. F. Miller, "Soviet Agricultural Policy in the Twenties: The Failure of Cooperation," *Soviet Studies,* vol. 27, no. 2 (April 1975), 220–244; S. Merl, *Der Agrarmarkt und die Neue Ökonomische Politik* (Munich: Oldenbourg Verlag, 1981), chap. 5. and R. G. Wesson, *Soviet Communes* (New Brunswick, N.J.: Rutgers University Press, 1963).

17. Class stratification played an important role in the thinking about collectivization and its actual implementation. Although census data from the 1920s suggest that the wealthy peasants *(kulaks)* were a very small proportion of the total peasant population, they were nevertheless seen as politically unreliable at best and enemies of the Soviet industrialization program at worst. For a detailed discussion of the problems of class stratification in this case, see Lewin, *Russian Peasants and Soviet Power,* chaps. 2 and 3.

18. Millar and Guntzel, "Economics and Politics of Mass Collectivization," 112.

19. For a discussion of various output series, see S. G. Wheatcroft, "A Reevaluation of Soviet Agricultural Production in the 1920s and 1930s," in R. C. Stuart, ed., *The Soviet Rural Economy* (Totowa, N.J.: Rowman and Allanheld, 1984), pp. 32–62.

20. For details of Stalin's argument and related data, see Karcz, "Thoughts on the Grain Problem," 399–402.

21. Karcz, "Thoughts on the Grain Problem," 403.

22. *Ibid.,* 403–409. Gross marketings include sales to other peasants within the village. Net marketings include only sales outside of agriculture.

23. Karcz's analysis of grain marketings and agricultural performance during the late 1920s has been disputed by R. W. Davies. Thus, we cannot know for sure whether Stalin's analysis of the agricultural "crisis" was erroneous. For example, Davies estimates that the 1926–1927 net grain marketings were slightly more than one half of prewar marketings—a figure close to Stalin's. See Davies, "A Note on Grain Statistics," 328; also S. G. Wheatcroft, "A Reevaluation of Soviet Agricultural Production in the 1920s and 1930s."

24. Lewin, *Russian Peasants and Soviet Power,* pp. 214–244.

25. *Ibid.,* p. 409.

26. Volin, *A Century of Russian Agriculture,* p. 222.

27. S. Swianiewicz, *Forced Labor and Economic Development* (London: Oxford University Press), p. 123.

28. Volin, *A Century of Russian Agriculture,* pp. 228–229.

29. For a detailed account of the history and functions of the MTS, see R. F. Miller, *One Hundred Thousand Tractors* (Cambridge, Mass.: Harvard University Press, 1970), especially chap. 2.

30. Wheatcroft gives a high and low variant calculation. The difference between the two is minimal. Wheatcroft, "A Reevaluation of Soviet Agricultural Production in the 1920s and 1930s."

31. For an alternate livestock index, see Strauss, *Soviet Agriculture,* p. 303.

32. Karcz, "From Stalin to Brezhnev," 42.
33. For detailed discussion of various estimates, see D. G. Dalrymple, "The Soviet Famine of 1932–1934," *Soviet Studies,* vol. 15, no. 3 (January 1964), 250–284.
34. N. Jasny, *The Socialized Agriculture of the USSR* (Stanford, Calif.: Food Research Institute, 1949), p. 323.
35. N. Jasny, *Essays on the Soviet Economy* (New York: Praeger, 1962), p. 107. Jasny's figures on per capita income of the Soviet farm population in constant prices reveal the following picture: 1928, 100; 1932–33, 53; 1936, 60; 1937, 81; 1938, 63.
36. For a detailed discussion of the role of agriculture in economic development, the reader is referred to J. W. Mellor, *The Economics of Agricultural Production* (Ithaca, N.Y.: Cornell University Press, 1966).
37. W. Eason, "Labor Force," in A. Bergson and S. Kuznets, eds., *Economic Trends in the Soviet Union* (Cambridge: Harvard University Press, 1963), pp. 72–73.
38. See J. R. Millar, "Views on the Economics of Soviet Collectivization: The State of the Revisionist Debate," in R. C. Stuart, ed., *The Soviet Rural Economy,* pp. 109–117.
39. J. F. Karcz, "From Stalin to Brezhnev: Soviet Agricultural Policy in Historical Perspective," in J. R. Millar, ed., *The Soviet Rural Community* (Urbana: University of Illinois Press, 1971), p. 42.
40. F. D. Holzman, "Foreign Trade," in A. Bergson and S. Kuznets, eds., *Economic Trends in the Soviet Union* (Cambridge, Mass.: Harvard University Press, 1963), pp. 294–295.
41. P. Hanson, *The Consumer Sector in the Soviet Economy* (Evanston, Ill.: Northwestern University Press, 1968), p. 36.
42. N. Jasny, *The Soviet Economy During the Plan Era* (Stanford, Calif.: Food Research Institute, 1951), p. 107.
43. A. Bergson, *The Real National Income of Soviet Russia Since 1928* (Cambridge, Mass.: Harvard University Press, 1961), p. 257.
44. S. Rosefielde, "The First Greap Leap Forward Reconsidered: The Lessons of Solzhenitsyn's Gulag Archipelago," *Slavic Review,* vol. 39, no. 4 (December 1980), pp. 559–587. See also comments by H. Hunter, R. W. Davies, and S. Wheatcroft, Igor Birman, and P. Gregory on this subject in the same issue.
45. In addition to earlier writings by Maurice Dobb, another exposition of this viewpoint is: M. Ellman, "Did the Agricultural Surplus Provide the Resources for the Increase in Investment in the USSR During the First Five Year Plan?" *Economic Journal,* vol. 85, no. 4 (December 1975).
46. For a summary of the evidence and appropriate references, see J. R. Millar, "Mass Collectivization and the Contribution of Soviet Agriculture to the First Five Year Plan: A Review Article," *Slavic Review,* vol. 33, no. 4 (December 1974), 750–766; J. R. Millar, "Soviet Rapid Development and the Agricultural Surplus Hypothesis," *Soviet Studies,* vol. 22, no. 1 (July 1970). For the original data and discussion, see A. A. Barsov, *Balans stoimostnykh obmenov mezhdu gorodom i derevnei* [Balance of the value of the exchange between the city and the country] (Moscow: Nauka, 1969); A. Vyas, "Primary Accumulation in the USSR Revisited," *Cambridge Journal of Economics,* vol. 3, no. 3 (1979), 119–130; J. Millar, "Views on the Economics of Soviet Collectivization of Agriculture: The State of the Revisionist Debate," in R. C. Stuart, ed., *The Soviet Rural Economy,* pp. 109–117.
47. Millar, "Mass Collectivization," 764.
48. P. Gregory, *Russian National Income 1885–1913* (Cambridge: Cambridge University Press, 1982), pp. 185–186.
49. For a discussion of modeling alternative scenarios, see H. Hunter, T. F. Bresnahan,

and E. J. Rutan, III, "Modelling Structural Change Using Early Soviet Data," *Journal of Development Economics,* vol. 9 (August, 1981), 65–87.

50. This discussion of World War II is based largely on the following sources: Nove, *An Economic History of the USSR,* chap. 10; Zaleski, *Stalinist Planning for Economic Growth,* chaps. 14 and 15; J. R. Millar, "Financing the Soviet Effort in World War II," *Soviet Studies,* vol. 32, no. 1 (January 1980); J. R. Millar and S. J. Linz, "The Cost of World War II to the Soviet People," *Journal of Economic History,* vol. 38, no. 4 (December 1978), 959–962; N. A. Voznesensky, *Soviet Economy During the Second World War* (New York: International Publishers, 1949), translated from the Russian; S. J. Linz, ed., *The Impact of World War II on the Soviet Union* (Totowa, N.J.: Rowman & Allanheld, 1985); T. Dunmore, *The Stalinist Command Economy* (New York: St. Martins Press, 1980).

51. J. R. Millar, "Conclusion: Impact and Aftermath of World War II," in S. J. Linz, ed., *The Impact of World War II on the Soviet Union,* p. 292.

52. S. J. Linz, "World War II and Soviet Economic Growth, 1940–1953" in S. J. Linz, ed., *The Impact of World War II,* pp. 11–34.

53. B. A. Anderson and B. D. Silver, "Demographic Consequences of World War II on the Non-Russian Nationalities of the USSR," in S. J. Linz, ed., *The Impact of World War II,* pp. 211–249.

54. Millar, "Conclusion: Impact and Aftermath of World War II," p. 291.

55. *Ibid.,* p. 292.

56. Millar, "Financing the Soviet War Effort."

57. Zaleski, *Stalinist Planning for Economic Growth,* p. 326.

58. *Ibid.,* p. 311.

59. *Ibid.,* chap. 14; Millar, "Conclusion: Impact and Aftermath of World War II," 292 ff.; S. R. Lieberman, "Crisis Management in the USSR: The Wartime System of Administration and Control," in S. J. Linz, ed., *The Impact of World War II,* pp. 61–78.

60. Zaleski, *Stalinist Planning for Economic Growth,* p. 287.

61. For a discussion of the relaxation of controls and the currency reform in particular, see Zaleski, *Stalinist Planning for Economic Growth,* chap. 18; also S. Fitzpatrick, "Postwar Soviet Society: The 'Return to Normalcy' " in S. J. Linz, ed., *The Impact of World War II,* pp. 131–158.

SELECTED BIBLIOGRAPHY

Y. Avdakov and V. Borodin, *USSR State Industry During the Transition Period* (Moscow: Progress Publishers, 1977).

E. H. Carr and R. W. Davies, *Foundations of a Planned Economy, 1926–1929* (London: Macmillan, 1969), vol. 1, parts 1 and 2.

R. W. Davies, *The Industrialization of Russia,* vols. 1 and 2 (Cambridge, Mass.: Harvard University Press, 1980).

M. Dobb, *Soviet Economic Development Since 1917,* 5th ed. (London: Routledge & Kegan Paul, 1960).

T. Dunmore, *The Stalinist Command Economy* (New York: St. Martins Press, 1980).

A. Erlich, *The Soviet Industrialization Debate, 1924–1928* (Cambridge, Mass.: Harvard University Press, 1960).

N. Jasny, *Soviet Industrialization, 1928–1952* (Chicago, Ill.: University of Chicago Press, 1961).

————, *The Socialized Agriculture of the USSR* (Stanford, Calif.: Food Research Institute, 1949).

J. F. Karcz, "From Stalin to Brezhnev: Soviet Agricultural Policy in Historical Perspective," in J. R. Millar, ed., *The Soviet Rural Community* (Urbana: University of Illinois Press, 1971), pp. 36–70.

————, "Thoughts on the Grain Problem," *Soviet Studies,* vol. 18, no. 4 (April 1967), 399–434.

M. Lewin, *Russian Peasants and Soviet Power* (London: Allen & Unwin, 1968).

————, "The Immediate Background of Soviet Collectivization," *Soviet Studies,* vol. 17, no. 2 (October 1965), 162–197.

S. J. Linz, ed., *The Impact of World War II on the Soviet Union* (Totowa, N.J.: Rowman & Allanheld, 1985).

J. R. Millar, "Financing the Soviet Effort in World War II," *Soviet Studies,* vol. 32, no. 1 (January 1980).

A. Nove, *An Economic History of the USSR* (London: Penguin, 1969), chaps. 7–10.

————, *Economic Rationality and Soviet Politics* (New York: Praeger, 1964), pp. 17–40.

L. Smolinski, "Planning Without Theory, 1917–1967," *Survey,* no. 64 (July 1968), 108–128.

————, "Soviet Planning: How It Really Began," *Survey,* no. 64 (April 1968), 100–115.

N. Spulber, ed., *Foundations of Soviet Strategy for Economic Growth* (Bloomington: Indiana University Press, 1964).

————, *Soviet Strategy for Economic Growth* (Bloomington: Indiana University Press, 1964).

V. A. Vinogradov et al., eds., *Istoriia sotsialisticheskoi ekonomiki SSSR* [History of the socialist economy of the USSR], vols. 1–5 (Moscow: Nauka, 1976).

L. Volin, *A Century of Russian Agriculture* (Cambridge, Mass.: Harvard University Press, 1970), chaps. 9 and 10.

N. A. Voznesensky, *Soviet Economy During the Second World War,* translated from the Russian edition (New York: International Publishers, 1949).

E. Zaleski, *Planning for Economic Growth in the Soviet Union, 1918–1932* (Chapel Hill: University of North Carolina Press, 1971).

————, *Stalinist Planning for Economic Growth, 1933–1952* (Chapel Hill: University of North Carolina Press, 1980).

chapter *6*

The Soviet Economy in the Postwar Era (1950–1985)

Thus far, we have examined the historical underpinnings of the Soviet economic system. This story has been developed through the momentous organizational changes of the 1930s and the crushing impact of World War II. Before we turn to an in-depth analysis of how the Soviet economy works, it is appropriate that we bring the general story of Soviet economic development up to date.

The period between the 1950s and the 1980s is obviously of great importance to our ultimate assessment of the Soviet economy. This is, after all, the era in which the Soviet Union came to enjoy world status as a superpower. Moreover, it is as close as we can come to a period of "normal" operation for the Soviet system, a period in which we can begin to isolate and identify the various forces contributing to the Soviet economic performance.

Possibly most important, this period represents a gradual end to the forced-draft industrialization of the 1930s and an attempt to achieve maturity. Both in terms of our understanding of the planned socialist system and in terms of any projections of future Soviet economic prospects, it is imperative that we understand the Soviet economy in its contemporary setting, in its drive for maturity through efficiency.

It has been customary in Western analysis of the Soviet economy to periodize economic history, that is, to identify policies and performance with prevailing political leaders. This approach may be somewhat artificial, since, in fact, there is a good deal of continuity of basic economic policies from one Soviet leader to the next. However, to simplify our presentation in this chapter, we will follow this practice, beginning with the post-Stalin transition (Malenkov and Khrushchev), the long tenure of Brezhnev, the short tenures of Andropov and Chernenko, and finally the present era of Gorbachev in the 1980s.

THE EARLY YEARS—POSTWAR TRANSITION

After the end of World War II, a transition period saw much of the war-related administrative structure dismantled. The State Committee of Defense was abolished in late 1945. The fourth Five Year Plan (FYP) for the period 1946 through 1950 was a plan of reconstruction. As we have already noted, plan achievement is difficult to monitor due to frequent changes in basic targets; nevertheless, the postwar recovery seems to have been rapid. As the evidence in Table 17 suggests, by 1950, most prewar indices had been exceeded, in some cases by substantial amounts. There were two major exceptions to this record of rapid postwar recovery. Grain production in 1950 was well below the level of production achieved in 1940. In part, this must have resulted from the depressed conditions in rural areas and possibly from the low priority accorded to agriculture during the war years.[1] It is worth noting that the share of total investment devoted to agriculture declined steadily from 15.5 percent during the first Five Year Plan (1928–1932) to 9.3 percent during the war years.[2] While this trend would be reversed after the war, it would take time to rebuild the agricultural capital stock. According to the official Soviet capital stock series *(osnovnye fondy)*, the share of agricultural capital stock declined from roughly 31 percent in 1929 to 16 percent of the total in 1941 and remained at 14 percent throughout the 1950s.[3] In any event, agricultural production in general and grain production in particular would become the subjects of major controversy and concern in the 1950s and thereafter.

A second important exception to this overall postwar growth was the sharp difference in performance between heavy industry and light industry. For industrial output in the aggregate, the fourth Five Year Plan (1946–1950) was fulfilled by 117 percent. However, heavy industry (Group A) was fulfilled by 128 percent, while light industry (Group B) was fulfilled by 95 percent.[4] On the surface, this evidence would certainly seem to confirm the widely held view that in the immediate postwar years, the primacy of heavy industry so firmly established in the 1930s was reestablished. However, as Timothy Dunmore has noted in his study of

Table 17   THE SOVIET ECONOMY: SELECTED INDICATORS, 1940–1950

	1940	1945	1946	1950
National income (1940 = 100)	100	83	—	161
Industrial production	100	91	76	172
Heavy industry (Group A)	100	112	82	204
Light industry (Group B)	100	59	67	122
Gross agricultural product	100	60	—	99
Steel (million tons)	18,317	12,252	13,346	27,329
Oil (million tons)	31,121	19,436	21,746	37,878
Electricity (million kWh)	48,562	43,257	48,571	91,226
Transport (billion tons km)	494.4	374.8	395.5	713.3
Fertilizer (standard units)	3,290	1,121	1,711	5,497
Grain (million tons)	95.6	47.3	39.6	81.2
Meat (tons slaughter wt.)	4,695	2,559	—	4,867
Money wage (avg. monthly)	33.1	—	48.1	64.2

Source: Official Soviet series from *Narodone khoziaistvo SSSR za 60 let* [The national economy of the USSR over 60 years] (Moscow: Statistika, 1977). Data on meat production from *Sel'skoe khoziaistvo SSSR* [Agriculture of the USSR] (Moscow: Statistika, 1971).

policy-making and execution in this postwar period, the issue is more complex, involving such issues as a weakening of Stalin's personal authority, changing distribution of power among Soviet administrative agencies, and economic problems such as materials allocation.[5] Moreover, the issue of industrial priorities did not disappear with Stalin's death. Prior to Nikita Khrushchev's final ascendancy to power in the mid-1950s, he would vie for power with Georgi Malenkov, a major issue being the appropriate roles for the light and heavy industrial sectors in the Soviet economy.

The postwar transition of the Soviet economy was, in a number of respects, different from that experienced in other countries. The impact of the war continued to be felt long after the cessation of hostilities: shortages of labor, destruction of capital, and the general disruption of economic activity. Nevertheless, the economic system that had been successful in winning the war was gradually dismantled. The role of the Communist Party was once again established as an overseer of economic activity, budget allocations on both the income and expenditure side changed, and the labor force was gradually shifted back to earlier functions.[6]

The transition was not easy, nor would it take place in an unchanged economy. It was a time of rising consumer expectations, a sense of uncertainty as to whether Stalin would return to the policies practiced in the 1930s. Joseph Stalin, who would be remembered for his draconian measures of the 1930s, died in March 1953. His last major program was the 1948 Stalin program for the transformation of nature.[7] These programs reflected the Stalinist thinking of the 1930s; they were grandiose projects calling for major alterations to the Soviet countryside in the form of irrigation projects, shelter belts, and the like. While they were criticized in the subsequent Khrushchev era, substantial portions of these programs were, nevertheless, carried out in a less grandiose framework. For example, the expansion of irrigated farmlands remains as an important ingredient of Soviet agricultural policy to the present day. Moreover, the major expansion of sown area, ultimately to come to an end in the 1960s, would nevertheless be of major importance in the Khrushchev era.

THE KHRUSHCHEV YEARS

Nikita Khrushchev rose to power in the early and mid-1950s and was ousted in October 1964, being labeled a "hair-brained schemer" in an era of "subjectivism." However history may judge the Khrushchev years, many features make it seem distinctive.

From the standpoint of economic performance, the 1950s were years of rapid growth judged by international standards. In fact, Soviet rates of economic growth would never be as good again. Thus, in some respects, the 1950s were a "golden era" for Soviet economic performance. However, a close look at the record (see Table 18) indicates that the early years were very good years, the latter years markedly less so. Many have argued, based upon this record, that Khrushchev's downfall in 1964 was at least in part based upon economic failures.

Quite apart from how one might rate the Khrushchev years in terms of economic performance, Khrushchev certainly left his mark in terms of organizational and related changes in agriculture, industry, and the political sphere.

In the agricultural sphere, Khrushchev rose to power as an outspoken critic of Soviet agricultural performance at the Twentieth Congress of the Communist Party in 1953.[8] As a self-proclaimed agricultural specialist, Khrushchev would stake his career, in part, on his ability to solve the Soviet Union's agricultural problems. For purposes of exposition, we classify Khrushchev's agricultural policies as (1) campaigns, (2) organizational changes, and (3) economic adjustments.

Agricultural Campaigns

Khrushchev's most famous agricultural campaign was the virgin lands campaign.[9] Begun in 1954, the goal was initially quite modest, namely, to reclaim 13 million hectares (1 hectare is 2.47 acres) of land by 1955 in Siberia and Kahakhstan, using state farms as the mode of organization. As we shall see later, state farms are those farms owned and operated directly by the state, using state employees payed a guaranteed wage. However, by 1960, 42 million hectares, representing some 20 percent of all sown area in that year, had been seeded.[10] The vision was grandiose, although the results were less so. Although these new lands received substantial capital investment, the marginal soil and the variable climate resulted in modest yields and a fluctuating (and gradually declining) output. However, the program did contribute roughly 25 million tons of grain annually between 1958 and 1963, though performance in the early years of the program was generally better than in the later years.[11] It is interesting to note that this program, generally attributed to Khrushchev, was, in fact, an acceleration of a long-term trend. In part, it continued the eastward shift of agricultural activity begun much earlier and, in addition, replacement of sown area lost during the war years.[12] It was also representative of the extensive strategy of agricultural development that would persist through the 1950s into the 1960s.

A second major program initiated by Khrushchev was the corn program. Begun in 1955, it was intended to imitate practice in the United States where corn has been a major source of animal fodder. This program also expanded rapidly. In 1954, 4.3 million hectares were sown to corn, while corn sowings would reach 37 million hectares by 1962.[13] Thus as a portion of total sown area, the importance of corn increased from just under 10 percent in 1955 to over 17 percent in 1962. Corn has become an important element in Soviet fodder supplies, although Khrushchev's initial vision was overly grandiose and, moreover, neglected important differences between the U.S. and the Soviet cases, namely, U.S. development of hybrids and the fact that climatic conditions in the USSR were ill-suited to the production of corn.

Finally, Khrushchev's "plough up" campaign, begun in 1961, was designed to eliminate or sharply reduce the grassland system of crop rotation by drastically cutting the land area devoted to fallow. Undoubtedly, such a policy would have had beneficial short-run effects on production but with serious long-term consequences as soil nutrients were gradually used without adequate replacement.

These programs did alter the nature of Soviet agriculture and became the focus of controversy. Undoubtedly, they were overly grandiose in conception and, in some cases, lacked a sound scientific basis, not to mention readily available complementary inputs. On the other hand, they did represent a strategy of long-term standing, namely, an extensive strategy of development or the expansion of output by the expansion of inputs, a quite reasonable approach given the prevailing Soviet stage of economic development. If intensification would come later, these programs did, in a sense, help to buy time until agricultural modernization could become a major focus of Soviet policy in the 1960s and thereafter.

Organizational Changes in Agriculture

While the flamboyance of the campaigns caught the spotlight, Khrushchev's far-reaching organizational changes were no less important.[14] One change that would continue (though at a much reduced pace) in the post-Khrushchev era was the amalgamation of collective farms and the conversion of a number of collective farms to state farms. For example, between 1940 and 1969, the number of collective farms declined from 236,900 to 34,700, while the sown area per farm increased from approximately 500 hectares to 2,800 hectares.[15] The pace of amalgamation varied, as did the regional impact. Nevertheless, the pattern was similar: several collectives would be combined to form a new larger collective farm, with the original collective farms becoming brigades in the new larger units. The pursuit of scale economies was a major force motivating these amalgamations.

In addition to the changing organizational structure of the typical kolkhoz, also other important changes were introduced. Khrushchev placed great emphasis upon improvement of the quality of farm management personnel. Along with this emphasis on greater quality, there was also a tendency to enhance the decision-making power within the farm, especially at the brigade level, and to use new tools, especially accounting. The brigade grew in size over these years. Moreover, the abolition of the machine tractor stations in 1958 and the placement of agricultural specialists directly on the farms improved the technical input available to collective farms to some degree.[16] Although it is difficult to characterize the extent to which these changes actually decentralized decision-making, they must have moved in this general direction. An effort was made to begin targeting output (letting local managers decide details) rather than have central planners involved in every detail of land use, sowing, harvesting, and the like. There was also an effort to pay more attention to serious long-term planning— all themes that would surface again in the post-Khrushchev years.

Economic Adjustments in Agriculture

Khrushchev undertook major economic adjustments within Soviet agriculture. Improved collective farm management became a major focus. For example, cost accounting methods were introduced on a major scale in an effort to improve farm decision-making. The discovery that, in many cases, procurement prices did not cover production costs led to substantial increases in farm prices. At the same time, peasant rewards were changed. Historically, rewards to collective farmers had generally been paid on an in-kind basis, and on a very uncertain schedule. Increasingly, these rewards came to be paid at least partially in money form, and on a more regular and frequent basis. During the decade after 1953, peasant incomes increased significantly. Although industrial incomes were also increasing, they did so at a much slower pace, which substantially reduced the rural/urban difference.[17] This policy with regard to incomes was part of a more general strategy of making rural life more attractive and to stem the rapid flow of the labor force (especially the young labor force) out of rural areas and strengthen rural production incentives.

Although Khrushchev was criticized for his style of agricultural leadership, many of his reforms endured and became the basis of further modernization in the subsequent Brezhnev era.

The Industrial Sector: Programs and Reforms

Although Khrushchev became closely associated with the problems of Soviet agriculture, he also left a mark on the Soviet industrial establishment. Western observers tend to date the beginning of reform discussion to the early 1960s, but it is important to emphasize that Khrushchev was quite willing to experiment with organizational change in the Soviet economy. Much of this change was motivated by a desire to improve Soviet industrial performance.

In an atmosphere of continuing emphasis on heavy industry and on increases in investment ratios, the first major industrial reform of this period was the Sovnarkhoz Reform of 1957. The Sovnarkhoz Reform, though subsequently abolished by Brezhnev in 1965, was an attempt to change the Soviet planning scenario from a ministerial to a regional basis.[18]

Khrushchev argued that the industrial ministries had certain deficiencies— empire building within ministries, lack of attention to regional coordination, and bureaucratic delays, especially in the material technical supply system. Khrushchev thought that these deficiencies could be corrected by revamping the planning system along regional lines. Accordingly, in 1957, the ministries were abolished (except the ministries supervising the nuclear sector and electricity) and a system of 105 *sovnarkhozy* (regional economic councils) was introduced. Enterprises would be subordinated to a regional council rather than a ministry.

After Khrushchev's ouster, the *sovnarkhozy* were replaced by the former ministries. While the ministries had been blamed for empire building and bureaucratic inefficiencies, the regional economic councils, the *sovnarkhozy,* were criticized for favoring regional interests, for "localism." In a sense, the same problems which led to the initial reform program also led to its subsequent abandonment.

Khrushchev's campaign approach was not limited to agriculture. The chemical industry received major attention in the 1950s. Prior to the 1950s, the Soviet chemical industry was neglected, especially its ability to bring much needed chemical fertilizers to agriculture. The growth of output of chemicals and petrochemicals increased from an average annual rate of 9.8 percent in 1951 to a high of 14.9 percent in 1955.[19] Investment in chemicals and petrochemicals increased at an average annual rate of 18.3 percent in the decade between 1951 and 1960, compared to an overall annual average investment increase of 11.7 percent for the same period.[20] This priority would be relaxed in the 1960s.

The output of mineral fertilizers increased from 5.5 million tons in 1950 to 13.8 million tons in 1960 and 31 million tons in 1965.[21]

Living Standards

In the area of consumer well-being, Georgi Malenkov, Khrushchev's rival for power immediately after Stalin's death, had, in the earlier 1950s, emphasized the need to expand consumer goods production, a move generally seen as an attempt to enhance his political fortunes. In spite of Khrushchev's reassertion of the primacy of heavy industry after his ascendancy to power, he nevertheless did take a number of steps to improve the position of the consumer in Soviet society. In addition to reducing compulsory bond purchases and reducing some consumer goods prices, attention was given to increasing the production of consumer durables and introducing limited credit provisions to make these products more readily available. To the extent that these moves represented a concession to the consumer, they were generally thought to have arisen out of a debate about consumer goods in the early 1950s. In addition, Khrushchev's famous "secret speech" in 1956 in which he denounced Stalin's crimes was seen as further evidence of relaxation.[22]

In the period between 1951 and 1955, per capita consumption grew at an average annual rate of 4.5 percent, while for the period 1956 to 1960, it grew at 4.0 percent. For these same periods, consumer durable output grew at rates of 17.7 and 10.4 percent, respectively.[23]

Khrushchev emphasized the expansion of services, for example, educational facilities and medical services, though not without controversy. For example, in an attempt to emphasize technical education, compulsory schooling was reduced from ten years to eight years, a move that would later be reversed.[24]

Khrushchev devoted considerable attention to housing, a much neglected sector of the Soviet economy. The average annual growth rate of housing increased steadily from a low of 2.6 percent in 1951 to a high of 5.9 percent in 1959.[25] Indeed, in retrospect, the 1950s would turn out to be a golden age for housing construction, the only period in the entire postwar era in which the growth of housing construction in Soviet urban areas would exceed the growth of urban population demanding this housing. For the period 1951–1960, there was an average annual increase of fixed investment in the construction materials sector of the Soviet economy of 22.8 percent. The comparable figure for the period 1961–1965 was −2.8 percent.[26]

Foreign Trade

Finally, we would be remiss in not mentioning the reemergence of Soviet foreign trade in the 1950s.[27] While foreign trade will be discussed in depth in Chapter 10, we note here that after the formation of the Council for Mutual Economic Assistance (CMEA, or COMECON) in 1949, the Soviet Union promoted increasing integration with Eastern Europe and increasing participation in world markets in the 1950s. Although such efforts were limited in these years, the expansion of Soviet foreign trade and the various problems that this effort would encounter were important issues throughout the postwar period.[28]

The volume of Soviet foreign trade (imports plus exports) increased significantly during the Khrushchev years. Although the bulk of Soviet foreign trade during these years was with other socialist countries, the growth of Soviet trade with capitalist countries was more rapid than that with socialist countries. Thus, Soviet trade with capitalist countries accounted for a growing portion of total Soviet trade. Moreover, a basic pattern persisted: Soviet exports of raw materials in return for imports of machinery and equipment. Although the events of the early 1960s (the U-2 incident and the Cuban missile crisis) chilled trade relations between the Soviet Union and the United States, the Soviet need for grain would soon be a new factor in expanding East–West trade.

THE KHRUSHCHEV YEARS: AN ASSESSMENT

Considering the changes outlined above, how might we assess the Khrushchev years? Most Western observers consider the Khrushchev record to have two rather distinct phases.[29] In the first phase, that is, from the mid- through the late 1950s, Khrushchev could ride a crest of generally expanding economic performance. However, in the second phase, that is, the late 1950s and early 1960s, this trend was generally reversed.

The aggregate evidence presented in Table 18 supports this general interpretation. Of course, closer examination of individual data series would obviously yield exceptions, yet one cannot escape the conclusion of slackening performance in the later years. To what extent these reverses were associated specifically with policies implemented by Khrushchev or with other influences outside his immediate control (for example, climatic reverses affecting agriculture) is difficult to say. In practice, Khrushchev would bear the burden of failure.

For example, the newly cultivated virgin lands came to be a major contributor to Soviet total grain output, but with sharp year-to-year fluctuations. In 1956, for example, fully 68 percent of state grain purchases would come from these lands, while by 1963 this figure would drop to 36.4 percent.[30] While the product

Table 18   AGGREGATE ECONOMIC PERFORMANCE: THE KHRUSHCHEV YEARS

	Average annual growth		
	1951–1955	1956–1960	1961–1965
Gross national product	5.5	5.9	5.0
Industry	10.2	8.3	6.6
Agriculture	3.5	4.2	2.8
Services	1.9	3.5	4.4
Consumption	4.9	5.7	3.7
Investment	12.4	10.5	7.6

Source: U.S. Congress, Joint Economic Committee, *USSR: Measures of Economic Growth and Development, 1950–80* (Washington, D.C.: U.S. Government Printing Office, 1982).

contribution of this program of new cultivation continued to expand, yields and output were variable, and a good year in 1964 was too late to save Khrushchev.

To take another example, Khrushchev's reorganization of industry was the subject of attention and controversy in the 1960s. The problems of the newly created sovnarkhozy were in large part similar to those of the ministries they had replaced. Rather than pursue fundamental changes suggested initially in 1962 by Evsei Liberman, Khrushchev intended to pursue further organizational changes.[31] Indeed, in 1961, some sovnarkhozy were combined with coordination councils being set up to administer the economy in 17 large economic regions.[32] This was yet another attempt to discover the optimum set of organizational arrangements. In addition, Khrushchev split the Communist Party into an agricultural and an industrial branch and in 1963 established yet another superagency for economic coordination, the Supreme Council of the National Economy. Khrushchev continued to voice criticism of arrangements in agriculture and arrangements in industry. Doubtlessly, he would have continued to shuffle the arrangements had he not been removed in 1964.

AFTER KHRUSHCHEV: FROM BREZHNEV TO GORBACHEV

There is evidence that prior to his removal from power, Nikita Khrushchev was considering even more organizational change. Such was not the tone of the Brezhnev ascendancy. Indeed, as we look at the 1960s, 1970s, and 1980s, they seem dull when compared to the flamboyance of the Khrushchev style. But there were serious problems to which the new Soviet leadership would turn its attention.

As the evidence in Table 19 suggests, the average annual rate of growth of GNP would decline steadily in the post-Khrushchev years, as would its principal components.The average annual rate of growth of consumption and investment has declined, as has the rate of growth of factor productivity. The beginning of large-scale imports of Western grain would be an unwelcome signal to Soviet leaders that problems of agriculture demand more attention.

In assessing this period from the 1960s through the 1980s, it would be a

Table 19   AGGREGATE ECONOMIC PERFORMANCE AFTER KHRUSHCHEV

	Average annual growth				
	1966–1970	1970–1975	1976–1980	1981–82	1984[a]
Gross national product	5.2	3.7	2.7	2.1	2.6 [b]
Industry	6.3	5.9	3.4	2.4	4.2
Agriculture	3.5	−2.3	0.3	1.8	0.0
Services	4.2	3.4	2.8	n.a.	n.a.
Consumption	5.3	3.6	2.6	1.8	4.3 [c]
Investment	6.0	5.4	4.3	3.2	2.0

Source: U.S. Congress, Joint Economic Committee, *USSR: Measures of Economic Growth and Development, 1950–80* (Washington, D.C.: U.S. Government Printing Office, 1982); *Handbook of Economic Statistics* (Washington, D.C.: Directorate of Intelligence, 1983), 63; "The Report on 1984 Plan Fulfillment," *Current Digest of the Soviet Press* XXXVII, 4 (1985), 10.

[a]Official Soviet series for 1984 as a percent of 1983.
[b]National income.
[c]Production of consumer goods.

mistake to suggest that repudiation of the Khrushchev policies was paramount. While we have seen that some changes were reversed (the sovnarkhoz reform, the educational reform, and the Communist Party reform), other changes, for example, the new lands program and the corn program in agriculture, would be the basis of continuing policy. The heavy industry bias would continue and organizational change in agriculture (specifically the amalgamation and conversion of collective farms) would continue, as would emphasis (albeit at a lower level) on key sectors such as chemicals. The virgin lands program would remain intact but without further expansion and, one might note, without the attention given it in earlier times. Organizational change would continue, but in much more modest ways. Moreover, economic reform, or improvements without really changing the basic economic system, would become a central theme.

SOVIET AGRICULTURE AFTER KHRUSHCHEV

During the decade 1951–1960, Soviet net agricultural output grew at an average annual rate of 4.8 percent, a pace that would be reduced to an average annual rate of 1.8 percent in the 1970s.[33] At the same time, the rate of growth of agricultural inputs would slow down, but the slackening of output growth would exceed the slackening of input growth, which resulted in a continuing deterioration of the growth of productivity. Performance trends in the early 1980s were mixed. According to official Soviet sources, the gross output of agriculture increased between 1980 and 1984 at an average annual rate of just over 2.6 percent.[34] However, there were substantial fluctuations. Thus, gross output actually declined between 1980 and 1981, increased again in both 1982 and 1983, and once again stagnated in 1984.

Although the overall rates of growth of agricultural output would be viewed as good by international standards, a number of disquieting trends developed leading Soviet officials to continue their search for a solution to agricultural problems.

In the aggregate, the growth in demand for farm products seemed to outstrip the growth in supply, the result being sharp increases in agricultural imports. For example, grain output would grow from an average annual output of 167 million metric tons in the period 1966–1970 to 205 million metric tons in the period 1976–1980.[35] But while the production of all grains would exceed 237 million metric tons in 1978, it would be just over 179 million metric tons in 1979.[36] By the early 1980s, the Soviet Union imported over 40 million metric tons of grain annually.[37] Indeed, the Soviet Union was a net importer of grain throughout the 1970s.

A similar scenario prevails for meat. For example, average annual meat production increased from over 11 million tons in the period 1966–1970 to over 14 million tons in the period 1976–1980.[38] At the same time, meat imports increased significantly, roughly doubling between the mid-1970s and the early 1980s.

More generally, rising production costs and a large agricultural subsidy (to avoid increasing retail food prices) have led to further emphasis on intensification or to the improvement of agricultural efficiency.[39] In this respect, some traditional policies have been continued. For example, mineral fertilizers of all types were delivered to agriculture at an average annual rate of just over 8 million metric tons during the period 1966–1970. Deliveries for the period 1976–1980, also on an average annual basis, were at a rate of over 18 million metric tons.[40] Agricultural yields have risen steadily, if slowly. In the period 1966–1970, the average annual yield of all grains was 1.37 million metric tons per hectare. This yield would increase to 1.60 million metric tons per hectare in the period 1976–1980, although with significant year-to-year fluctuations.[41]

Official concern for improving agriculture has been evident in investment patterns. While the overall growth rate of gross fixed investment increased in the 1960s and declined thereafter, the share of investment devoted to agriculture increased from its usual 15 percent to a high of 27 percent. This represents a major emphasis on agriculture and a significant change in Soviet economic policies. Thus, if one views the 1930s as an era in which agriculture was supposed to subsidize the nonagricultural economy, today the pattern has clearly been reversed.

Turning to organizational matters, we observe that trends of earlier years would continue, though at a slower pace. For example, in 1965, there were almost 37,000 agricultural collectives, with an average sown area per collective of 3,000 hectares. By 1983, the number of collectives decreased to 26,000, and the average sown area had increased to 3,500 hectares. For the same period, the number of state farms increased from just under 12,000 with an average sown area of just over 7,600 hectares to over 22,000 with an average sown area of 4,900 hectares.[42]

Possibly more important in the long run, the 1970s was a decade of emphasis on agro-industrial integration, about which more will be said in Chapter 9. Basically, the emphasis was combining the production, processing, and distribution facilities in large integrated complexes, hoping to take advantage of economies of scale, and to lessen supply problems endemic to the Soviet system.[43] The number of such combines doubled in the 1970s from 4,580 in 1970 to 9,897 in 1983.[44] For the same period, the capital stock of these complexes increased by a factor of almost 23.[45]

In spite of these changes, the 1970s were not generally good times for Soviet agriculture. Recognition of this fact came in 1982 when Brezhnev announced the new Food Program, a major effort to solve the food supply problem through improvements in planning, organization, incentives and with greater emphasis upon the private sector.[46]

SOVIET INDUSTRY: CONTINUITY AND CHANGE

The post-Khrushchev era through the present (under the leadership of Mikhail Gorbachev) has been one of stability in the overall pattern of Soviet economic arrangements. However, it has also been a period of experimentation with economic reforms. Following the public discussion of economic reform in 1962 launched by the contributions of Evsei Liberman, Premier Alexei Kosygin announced a major economic reform in 1965, dubbed the Kosygin Reform.[47] Although we will leave for Chapter 13 a full discussion of the reform process in the Soviet economy, it is important to note here that this program, aimed at improving Soviet industrial performance, had two important threads: First, it was intended to simplify the enterprise planning system by lessening the number of plan indicators that would be given to enterprises by their superiors. Second, it emphasized a major change in the primary success indicator(s) guiding managerial decision-making. Specifically, there would be an attempt to move away from gross output toward sales and profitability as criteria for assessing managerial performance. These trends are discussed in detail in the following chapters.

As we shall see later, it is difficult to assess with precision the degree of implementation of these reform programs. Doubtlessly, and in spite of continuing criticism of gross output indicators in the 1970s, it has gradually come to the fore. At the same time, this program has been combined with a myriad of other reform changes, including incentive arrangements, price changes, and rules for the introduction of new technology, just to name a few.[48] As we shall see, intensification has become and remains a key basis for continuing reform efforts.

The most notable organizational reform in the 1970s was the introduction of industrial associations that essentially serve to decentralize decisions formerly made in the ministries while they, at the same time, centralize some decisions made within firms.[49] Thus, the industrial associations would be groupings of formerly independent firms below the ministry level.

The Consumer

For most observers, improvements in the standard of living must be an important criterion by which to judge the success of any economic system. According to Gertrude Schroeder, a Western authority on Soviet levels of living, "since 1950, real per capita consumption has risen at an average annual rate of 3.4 percent, resulting in a near tripling of the level of living of the average Soviet citizen."[50] However, Schroeder notes that "despite these gains, the Soviet Union has made little progress toward its often-avowed goal to overtake and surpass capitalist countries in levels of living of the people."[51]

Gains have been made with respect to the availability of most consumer goods, although progress has varied. Diets have improved and clothing is more readily available, as are most consumer durables. However, if progress was rapid in the 1960s, it was much less so in the 1970s and 1980s. The average annual rate of growth of real per capita consumption in the 1970s and 1980s has been roughly one-half the rate prevailing in the 1960s.

To some degree, recent declines in the rate of growth of Soviet consumption can be attributed to poor agricultural performance. However, reverses can also be noted in food processing, light industry in general, and the production of consumer durables. Trends for the remainder of the 1980s will clearly depend upon the overall performance of the Soviet economy. In turn, the reality of improved levels of living will be an important factor influencing attitudes of the Soviet labor force.

Foreign Trade

The Brezhnev era also witnessed a significant expansion of foreign trade.[52] While trade patterns changed, especially in the 1970s with the impact of the world energy crisis, the Soviet Union continued to seek expanded integration with Eastern Europe and more trade with the West while at the same time attempting to reform domestic foreign trade arrangements.

Trade between the Soviet Union and the United States, although small in absolute terms, increased significantly during the 1970s. However, year-to-year increases were very uneven due largely to the impact of a changing political climate. Although there have been important differences in Soviet trade relations with different Western countries, in general, the Soviet Union has pursued expanded trade with the West as a mechanism to improve Soviet domestic performance. At the same time, firms in the West have been attracted by potential Soviet markets, supported in part by the greater availability of hard currency credits in the 1970s. However, in spite of the era of detente in the early 1970s, the fate of the Trade Act of 1974 and subsequent Soviet behavior, especially Soviet actions in Afghanistan in the late 1970s and the resulting U.S. grain embargo imposed during the Carter administration, have chilled Soviet–U.S. trade relations. Indeed, under the Reagan administration, there had been a tendency to link trade to Soviet behavior in other spheres and to question the potential benefits to the U.S. of expanded technology exports to the Soviet Union.

Many forces have and will continue to influence patterns of trade between the Soviet Union and Western countries. Clearly, for many Western countries, most notably the U.S., the political climate will be of great importance.

THE SOVIET ECONOMY SINCE KHRUSHCHEV: AN ASSESSMENT

The Soviet economy of the 1980s has changed significantly from the system inherited by Khrushchev in the 1950s but subsequently modified by Khrushchev and the post-Khrushchev leadership. The Soviet Union has become a predominately urban society, with both the promises and the problems that generally accompany urbanization. Not unlike the Western experience, these problems require increases in support funds in a time of growing demands elsewhere, for example, by agriculture and the military. At the same time, Soviet economic performance has slackened, in both industry and agriculture. It is important to appreciate that while Soviet rates of economic growth are generally positive, the focus of attention is a decline in these rates of growth and a general slackening of the contribution of productivity growth, an element crucial to improved performance in an advanced economy.

Thus far, we have surveyed the economic development of the Soviet Union from the draconian policies of the Stalin era through the flamboyance of the Khrushchev era. The post-Khrushchev era has been one of both stability and change; but in contrast to earlier years, stability has prevailed over change. This does not mean that organizational arrangements and economic policies in the

Soviet Union remain constant through time. Rather, it means that the practical implementation of economic reform has been modest and has taken place in modest directions. Rather than experiment with the sorts of significant changes made in some other planned socialist economic systems, Soviet leaders have, thus far, been content with efforts to make existing arrangements work better. Only time will tell whether this trend will continue and whether it will work to improve the performance of the contemporary Soviet economy.

In the 1980s, the Soviet Union is, in a sense, at a crossroad. Since the late 1920s, the Soviet Union has used a particular economic system and economic policies to pursue economic growth and economic development. These arrangements, generally different from those familiar to us in the West, have produced a substantial measure of both growth and development. However, the question facing Soviet leaders in the 1980s is whether methods useful in the past can also be useful in the future. If the answer is negative, as many would argue, then the prospects for future Soviet economic performance rest very heavily on the ability of the present Soviet leadership to modify the existing system.

To assess future Soviet prospects, it is important that we understand both the nature of the contemporary Soviet economic system and the economic structure inherited from over 50 years of Soviet socialist planning. Both will influence future directions of the Soviet economy. Thus, before we turn to an in-depth examination of how the contemporary Soviet economy works, it seems useful to outline the essential features of what we term the Soviet Development Model (SDM).

THE SOVIET DEVELOPMENT MODEL

Description

The small amount of attention devoted to the Soviet Development Model (SDM) by Western economists is surprising in view of its importance as a major alternative development pattern—although the gaps in our knowledge on this subject have been narrowed in recent years.[53] Using available research on the SDM, we delineate the following as its most essential components.[54]

1. Planners' preferences, dictated by the Communist Party through the planning hierarchy, replaced consumer preferences. This changeover was made possible by the establishment of a political dictatorship that placed the means of production in the hands of the state. As a response to the imposition of planners' preferences, the structure of demand was changed dramatically within a brief period of time in favor of selected (priority) heavy industry branches—in particular, metallurgy, machine building, and electricity. The allocation of resources to light industry and agriculture was severely restricted. These two trends reflected themselves in prominent structural shifts: the aggregate investment rate rose markedly and rapidly while the share of GNP devoted to personal consumption fell. The share of communal consumption (public health, education, etc.) rose at the expense of private consumption. The rise in public consumption, however, was not sufficient to counter the relative decline in total consumption (as a percentage of GNP).

The growth of the service sector was retarded despite the rise in health and education services, thereby limiting the flow of resources into "nonproductive" sectors.* Development of commerce was especially restricted because the limitations placed on consumer goods retarded the growth of retail trade; the absence of property ownership limited the need for banking, legal, and other commercial services; and the material balance system in large measure replaced the wholesale trade network.

2. Sectorial relationships changed. Agriculture was collectivized and private trade was virtually eliminated. In this way, the state could ensure deliveries of agricultural products to the cities by making the deliveries mandatory. The prices at which farms had to sell produce to the state were set at low levels for two purposes. The first was to force a transfer of savings from the countryside to industry to finance the industrial investment (via the turnover tax on food products). The second purpose was to reduce rural real incomes to facilitate the transfer of labor out of agriculture into higher priority industrial occupations, offering relatively higher real wages. The depression of rural living standards encouraged the more productive age groups to leave the collective farms for the city, and organized state recruitment campaigns in the countryside were used to promote this movement.

3. In industry, especially in high-priority branches, highly capital-intensive factor proportions were adopted. In this manner, the movement of population from the rural to urban areas, though quite rapid, was held down. The result was a below-average ratio of urbanization, relative to the level of development, which enabled planners to restrict the flow of resources into nonproductive municipal services.[55] Urbanization was also held down by encouraging high labor participation rates among the existing urban population, especially of women. The low absolute real income levels and (in later years) laws against parasitism and absenteeism were used to encourage such high labor participation rates.

The rapid expansion of priority industrial branches was made possible by generous allocations of scarce capital by planning authorities. In addition, in the priority areas, relatively high wages were set to attract skilled industrial workers. On the other hand, the most neglected light industrial sectors were those with high capital-output ratios, notably printing, paper, and food products.[56]

Not having developed sophisticated planning techniques, the Soviets used "campaigns" to eliminate bottlenecks that arose as a result of taut planning. In addition, industrial planning was simplified by limiting product differentiation. This product strategy was expected to encourage standardization, limit the spare parts problem, and facilitate maintenance and repair. Scarce industrial capital was stretched by multiple shift arrangements (often three per day) and by utilizing capital until it was totally worn out. Further capital saving techniques involved the combining of advanced capital-intensive Western technology in primary processes with old-fashioned labor-intensive methods in auxiliary processes and the limiting of social overhead investment in transportation, roads, apartment

---

*We use "nonproductive" sectors in the Marxian meaning of an economic sector that produces services not directly connected with the production of a physical commodity.

buildings, schools, and hospitals.[57] Instead, social overhead capital carried over from earlier periods was simply utilized more intensively.

Large-scale integrated plants were chosen. This gigantomania was sanctioned for reasons of international prestige (having the world's largest dam, for example) and because it was hoped that unit costs would eventually be lower owing to economies of scale.[58] Furthermore, a long planning time horizon was adopted and interest rate calculations were not used, both of which condoned the long gestation periods involved in such projects. Highly integrated plants were chosen because of the primitive state of the material supply system, a factor that made less integrated plants quite vulnerable to supply interruptions. Machinery plants, for example, produced their own steel and shipped their finished products.[59] The integrated nature of industrial plants enabled planners to limit the size of wholesale trade.

4. Inflation, monetary controls, and the "money illusion" played important roles. The shift of resources away from consumer goods meant that the growth of real income would be held below the overall growth rate or, in its extreme manifestation, would even decline.* However, it was necessary to preserve worker incentives. Wages were allowed to rise out of pace with consumer goods, thereby creating inflation. Prices of consumer goods were raised at a more rapid rate than wages, on the grounds that workers would be more concerned with what was happening to their *money* wages than to their *real* wages. To preserve equity during this period of rapid inflation, some rationing of necessities was implemented. Sales at above-rationing prices were permitted—in fact, a complex multiple price system was used—to preserve the incentive effect of differential wages.

Personal income taxes were not used as a major source of state revenue because it was assumed that indirect taxes better preserve worker incentives. The form of indirect taxation adopted—the turnover tax—was a hidden tax, and consumers were unaware of the extent to which they were bearing the burden of industrialization.[60] In addition, the multiple price system was a rich source of tax revenue.

Tax revenues gathered in this fashion were then used to finance investment, the funds for which were allocated by an investment plan. Very little, if any, investment was determined at the plant level. The state bank monitored the cash in the hands of the public through its control of enterprise cash accounts and—via its control over credit and transactions—monitored plan fulfillment, thus providing a secondary source of information on enterprise operations for the planning apparatus.

5. A significant portion of government expenditure was used to finance industrial investment. The remainder served to finance defense, administration,

*One can question whether the decline in real income is a fundamental aspect of the SDM rather than an unforeseen result of the world depression, collectivization problems, poor harvest of 1931, and so on. In fact (as indicated in Chapter 3), the first Five Year Plan projected a substantial increase in consumer goods as well as falling consumer prices. Also, industrial wages were not supposed to rise as fast as they did. Our view is that the SDM does call for a *relative* shift in resources away from consumption and for holding the rate of growth of real incomes below attainable levels. Whether this policy will result in absolute declines, as was true in the Soviet case, will depend on the situation. It will, however, result in a relative decline.

and public consumption expenditures. Considerable public resources were channeled into public health and education, on the grounds that a healthy and well-trained labor force was required to man the economy. The focus of education was upon technical specialization. The state embarked on a mass campaign of vocational education that took place to a great extent on the job. In this manner, the state saved scarce capital by not having to build additional schools, universities, and technical institutes. A further device to stretch educational resources was the emphasis on night school training, correspondence courses, and self-instruction. Throughout, the worker was encouraged to acquire additional training by highly differentiated wages, which favored the skilled worker.

6. The expansion of transport capacity was limited to restrict investment in social overhead capital. Planners counted on substantial improvements in levels of *utilization*, coupled with a pattern of industrialization designed to minimize the need for transport services. To achieve this latter objective, strong emphasis was placed upon locating industrial establishments at the site of raw materials.[61] A further aspect was the emphasis on railways as opposed to other forms of surface transportation, thereby enabling authorities to avoid highway construction.[62]

7. The economy's relationships with the outside world changed as well. The state established a foreign trade monopoly to ensure that dealings with the outside world were in accordance with the needs of industrialization. Initially, agricultural products were exchanged for the machinery—in particular, machine tools that could be used to make other machinery—vital to the early stages of industrialization, and heavy reliance was placed on imports of foreign technology. However, the long-term emphasis was placed upon lessening dependence on the rest of the world, for such reliance was viewed as incompatible with the planned nature of the economy. This autarky approach dictated that a complete range of industrial and agricultural products should be produced domestically. Domestic production was, therefore, substituted for imports, and specialization according to comparative advantage was neglected.*

Comparison with Western Trends

The above summary outlines the major features of Soviet industrialization during the USSR economy's formative years. Upon closer examination, it could be argued that there is nothing patently new about Soviet development, for there are striking similarities with economic development in the West. For example, the share of heavy industry increases during the process of development.[63] The investment rate rises during the course of development. In most Western countries, import substitution has caused a lowering of foreign trade proportions, just as in

---

*One could perhaps argue that the Soviet autarky model was not a true component of the SDM, rather a historical accident of the world depression and the hostility of capitalist trading partners. While these factors were, of course, important in forcing the USSR into a position of low reliance on trade, it is also true that there are noteworthy factors in the system itself (the inability of a planned economy to tie itself to outside economies) that have caused both the USSR and Eastern Europe to maintain low foreign trade proportions in spite of changing political climates.

the Soviet case.[64] A further common feature is the rapid expansion of universal education and specialized training during the development process.

Thus, many aspects of the SDM are not new. Others—for example, material balance planning, the substitution of planners' preferences, the collective farm, the deemphasis of services, and many others—are new features of the SDM. One important fact, however, should not be neglected; that is, that the SDM involved considerable differences in magnitude and timing in the implementation of these common elements.

1. The relative increase in heavy industry that generally occurs during development was greater both in *magnitude* and in *speed* in the Soviet Union. The increase in the combined metallurgy and engineering product share of manufacturing in the USSR of 26 percentage points (from 19 percent to 45 percent) between 1928 and 1937 required from 50 to 75 years in other countries, and many industrialized Western countries have yet to attain a heavy industry share as large as the USSR's in 1937.[65]

2. The rapidity of the increase in the investment rate in the Soviet Union is another distinctive feature of the SDM. In 1928, gross investment as a percent of GNP (measured in 1937 factor costs) was 12.5 percent; by 1937, this figure was 25.9 percent, after peaking at 32 percent in 1935.[66] Such high investment rates have been matched and even surpassed by several Western countries. However, in Western countries, the rise in the investment rate was gradual and began several decades after industrialization was under way, not during its initial stages.[67]

3. Another distinctive feature of the SDM was its combination of a high investment rate with a relatively low marginal capital-output ratio during the initial stages of industrialization.* In Western countries, either investment rates and marginal capital-output ratios were both low, or high investment rates were combined with high marginal capital-output ratios. The Soviet marginal capital-output ratio did begin to rise substantially after 1958, but prior to that, it had remained stable. The Soviets were able to maintain the stability of the marginal capital-output ratio largely by limiting investment in residential construction and transportation (with high capital-output ratios) and by intensive multishift utilization of existing industrial capital stock.[68]

4. Extremely rapid shifts of resources out of agriculture into industry were also characteristic of the SDM. In the course of Western development, the labor force and product shares of agriculture generally declined, but the decline in the Soviet Union between 1928 and 1940 (Table 10, Chapter 4) required from 30 to 50 years in other countries.[69]

5. As far as sectoral productivity relationships are concerned, the Soviet experience was distinctive for the relatively low output per worker in agriculture compared to industry. In fact, ratios of sectoral product per worker were quite similar to the LDCs, where traditional and backward agricultural sectors prevail. There is evidence that labor productivity (in full-time equivalents) in Soviet

---

*The marginal (or incremental) capital-output ratio is the ratio of the change in capital stock to the change in output ($\Delta K/\Delta Q$).

agriculture actually declined between 1928 and 1940, quite in contrast to the industrialization experiences of other countries, where agricultural labor productivity generally kept pace with the overall productivity growth of the economy.[70]

6. The SDM also differed from the Western experience with respect to private consumption. In the West, the GNP share of private consumption normally declined. The distinctive feature of the trend in private consumption in the Soviet Union was the magnitude and rapidity of its relative decline—not to mention the *absolute* decline. In 1928, private consumption accounted for 80 percent of Soviet GNP. By 1940, this figure had dropped to 50 percent (Table 10, Chapter 4). In other countries, the drop was from 80 percent to between 60 and 70 percent—a decline that required from 30 to 80 years to be completed, versus 12 years in the Soviet case.[71]

7. A further distinctive feature of the SDM was the rapid rise in the labor participation rate. Between 1928 and 1940, the Soviet population grew at 1.2 percent annually, while the labor force grew at 3.7 percent. Thus, there was a 2.5 percent annual rate of growth of the labor participation rate. As Simon Kuznets notes: "No such accelerated use of labor relative to population appears to have occurred in other countries."[72]

8. The relatively low Soviet foreign trade proportions during industrialization were also a distinctive feature of the SDM. Commonly, a country's dependence on foreign trade is gradually reduced in the course of development.[73] In the Soviet case, the ratio of exports to national income dropped dramatically, from 3.5 percent in 1930 to 0.5 percent in 1937. Part of this drop can be explained by the collapse of world prices of primary products during the world depression, but Soviet trade ratios to and after the depression remained quite low by international standards. As Kuznets notes: "[The low Soviet foreign trade proportions] reflect a forced isolation of a large population from contact with the rest of the world, not paralleled in any non-Communist country within modern times."[74]

9. A final distinctive feature of the SDM was the extent to which the service sector, especially commercial services such as trade, banking, and insurance, was depressed below "normal" levels in the Soviet Union. When compared with the development experience of Western countries, a Soviet service gap is evident in the sense that the labor force share of services was much below that expected of a market economy at a similar level of development. Thus, the Soviet economy developed without devoting as much resources to services as have "normally" been required in the West.[75]

SOVIET ECONOMIC DEVELOPMENT: AN ASSESSMENT

The speed of the structural transformation of the Soviet economy in accordance with the proclaimed goals of heavy industry priority, massive capital accumulation, and the decline in private ownership indicates the success of the Soviet Development Model. The transformation that took place in the Soviet Union in the short span of 12 years (1928–1940) required a half-century or more in the industrialized West. It would be difficult to argue in the face of such evidence that the Soviet leadership's goal of accelerating economic development was not met.

These are the benefits of the Soviet Development Model. Its costs are more difficult to evaluate, primarily because a disentanglement of the basic features of the Soviet model from the unique features of the Stalin dictatorship is required. Were the substantial losses of forced collectivization a characteristic of the model or a historical accident linked to Stalin's personality? This issue has long been debated in Western literature in the context of Alec Nove's question: "Was Stalin necessary?"[76] We cannot hope to resolve such weighty issues here; what we can do is to list some of the costs of rapid development. The forced transformation of Soviet agriculture from a private to a collective basis entailed significant costs that probably could not have been avoided, with or without Stalin. The relative decline of light industry undoubtedly affected industrial incentives and labor productivity. The general neglect of agriculture has required extraordinary injections of resources into agriculture in the postwar era in the form of sharply increased investment, subsidies, and the like. The one-sided priority of heavy industry has probably resulted in the maldistribution of capital resources by Western standards. We could add to this list but choose instead to return to the basic point of trade-offs among economic objectives. Economic development was, indeed, accelerated in the Soviet case, but at the considerable expense of other areas.

Finally, as we have already emphasized, the issue facing the Gorbachev regime is modernization of the Soviet economic system to improve productivity performance and, hence, overall performance of the Soviet economy.

REFERENCES

1. For a discussion of the impact of the war in rural areas, see A. Nove, "Soviet Peasantry in World War II," in S. J. Linz, ed., *The Impact of World War II on The Soviet Union* (Totowa, N.J.: Rowman and Allanheld, 1985), pp. 79–92.

2. F. A. Durgin, Jr., "The Relationship of the Death of Stalin to the Economic Changes of the Post-Stalin Era," in R. C. Stuart, ed., *The Soviet Rural Economy* (Totowa: Rowman and Allanheld, 1984), pp. 119–123.

3. R. Moorsteen and R. P. Powell, *The Soviet Capital Stock, 1928–1962* (Homewood, Ill.: Richard D. Irwin, 1966), p. 615.

4. It is important to note two major issues relating to plan fulfillment in this era. First, the plans were changed so frequently that assessment of fulfillment is a difficult task, not to mention the problem of unrealistic plans developed to serve as an incentive for greater achievement. Second, Soviet official series on plan fulfillment and economic achievement during this period are based upon 1926/27 prices. For a host of reasons, these prices are suspect as conveyors of relative scarcities of the 1940s. It is not surprising, therefore, that Western estimates of achievement during this period are lower, in some cases significantly lower, than official Soviet series. For a detailed discussion of these issues and citation of the various estimates, see E. Zaleski, *Stalinist Planning for Economic Growth, 1933–1952* (Chapel Hill: University of North Carolina Press, 1980), pp. 396–402.

5. For a detailed discussion of policy-making in the immediate postwar era, see T. Dunmore, *The Stalinist Command Economy* (London and Basingstoke: Macmillan, 1980).

6. For a discussion of the role of the Communist Party during the war and the postwar transition, see C. S. Kaplan, "The Impact of World War II on the Party," in S. J. Linz, ed., *The Impact of World War II,* pp. 159–190.

7. For a discussion of agriculture during these transition years, see F. A. Durgin, Jr., "The Relationship of the Death of Stalin."

8. There is a considerable amount of literature pertaining to Khrushchev and Soviet agriculture. For Khrushchev's own views, see N. S. Khrushchev, *Stroitel'stvo kommunizma v SSSR i razvitie sel'skogo khoziaistva* [The construction of communism in the USSR and the development of agriculture] (Moscow: Gospolitizdat, 1962), 8 vols. For a useful survey of this period, see J. F. Karcz, "Khrushchev's Agricultural Policies," in M. Bornstein and D. Fusfeld, eds., *The Soviet Economy: A Book of Readings* 3d ed. (Homewood, Ill.: Richard D. Irwin, 1970), pp. 223–259. For a discussion of agricultural policy-making, see S. I. Ploss, *Conflict and Decision-Making in Soviet Russia: A Case Study of Agricultural Policy, 1953–1963* (Princeton, N.J.: Princeton University Press, 1965); and W. G. Hahn, *The Politics of Soviet Agriculture, 1960–1970* (Baltimore, Md.: The Johns Hopkins Press, 1973). For a survey of agricultural campaigns, see J. W. Willett, "The Recent Record in Agricultural Production," in U.S. Congress, Joint Economic Committee, *Dimensions of Soviet Economic Power* (Washington, D.C.: U.S. Government Printing Office, 1962), pp. 91–113. For a discussion of organizational changes, see R. C. Stuart, *The Collective Farm in Soviet Agriculture* (Lexington, Mass.: D. C. Heath, 1972). For a discussion of monetary incentives, see F. A. Durgin Jr., "Monetization and Policy in Soviet Agriculture Since 1952," *Soviet Studies,* vol. 15, no. 4 (April, 1964), 381–407; and D. W. Bronson and C. B. Krueger, "The Revolution in Soviet Farm Household Income, 1952–1967," in J. R. Millar, ed., *The Soviet Rural Community* (Urbana: University of Illinois Press, 1971), pp. 214–258. The virgin lands campaign is discussed in detail in M. McCauley, *Khrushchev and the Development of Soviet Agriculture* (New York: Holmes & Meier, 1976).

9. McCauley, *Khrushchev and the Development of Soviet Agriculture.*

10. *Ibid.,* pp. 79–83.

11. *Ibid.,* Tables 4.5 and 4.6.

12. For a discussion of this strategy, see McCauley, *Khrushchev and the Development of Soviet Agriculture.*

13. J. Anderson, "A Historical-Geographical Perspective on Khrushchev's Corn Program," in J. F. Karcz, ed., *Soviet and East European Agriculture* (Berkeley and Los Angeles: University of California Press, 1967), Table 2. The data include corn for all uses.

14. For a discussion of organizational changes, see Stuart, *The Collective Farm;* and R. D. Laird, "Khrushchev's Administrative Reforms in Agriculture: An Appraisal," in J. F. Karcz, ed., *Soviet and East European Agriculture,* pp. 29–56.

15. *Strana Sovetov za 50 let* [Country of the Soviets during 50 years] (Moscow: Statistika, 1967), p. 121; *Narodnoe Khoziaistvo SSSR v 1969 g* [The national economy of the USSR in 1969] (Moscow: Statistika, 1970), pp. 404 and 405.

16. For a detailed discussion of the evolution of the machine tractor stations, see R. F. Miller, *One Hundred Thousand Tractors* (Cambridge, Mass.: Harvard University Press, 1970).

17. For a discussion of rural/urban income differences during this period, see Bronson and Krueger, "The Revolution in Soviet Farm Household Income, 1952–1967."

18. For a discussion of the Sovnarkhoz Reform, see O. Hoeffding, "The Soviet Industrial Reorganization of 1957," *American Economic Review: Papers and Proceedings,* vol. 49, no. 2 (May 1959), 65–77.

19. U.S. Congress, Joint Economic Committee, *USSR: Measures of Economic Growth and Development, 1950–80* (Washington, D.C.: U.S. Government Printing Office), p. 193.
20. S. Butler, "The Soviet Capital Investment Program," in U.S. Congress, Joint Economic Committee, *Economic Performance and the Military Burden in the Soviet Union* (Washington, D.C.: U.S. Government Printing Office, 1970), p. 53.
21. *Narodnoe khoziaistvo SSSR za 60 let* [The national economy of the USSR during 60 years] (Moscow: Statistika, 1977), p. 213.
22. For a useful survey of this period, see H. Schwartz, *The Soviet Economy Since Stalin* (Philadelphia: J. B. Lippincott, 1965).
23. U.S. Congress, Joint Economic Committee, *USSR: Measures of Economic Growth and Development, 1950–80,* pp. 193, 326.
24. This educational reform was complex, but generally the basic ten-year school was to be replaced by a basic eight-year school. After the completion of eight years of schooling, the student might take an additional three years of schooling as prerequisite to higher education or, as an alternative, might go directly to work or additional training of a technical nature. For a discussion of the reform and a comparison to prevailing U.S. patterns, see N. DeWitt, "Education and the Development of Human Resources: Soviet and American Effort," in U.S. Congress, Joint Economic Committee, *Dimensions of Soviet Economic Power* (Washington, D.C.: U.S. Government Printing Office, 1962), pp. 235–268.
25. U.S. Congress, Joint Economic Committee, *USSR: Measures of Economic Growth and Development, 1950–80,* p. 56.
26. Butler, "The Soviet Capital Investment Program," p. 53.
27. For a general discussion, see F. D. Holzman, *International Trade Under Communism* (New York: Basic Books, 1976).
28. For a discussion of trade in the 1950s, see P. H. Thunberg, "The Soviet Union in the World Economy," in U.S. Congress, Joint Economic Committee, *Dimensions of Soviet Economic Power,* pp. 409–438.
29. For a survey of the economic aspects of Khrushchev's downfall, see H. Schwartz, *The Soviet Economy.*
30. McCauley, *Khrushchev and the Development of Soviet Agriculture,* Table 4–9.
31. The original paper by Evsei Liberman can be found in M. E. Sharpe, ed., *Planning, Profit and Incentives in the USSR,* vols. 1 and 2 (White Plains, N.Y.: International Arts and Sciences Press, 1966).
32. Schwartz, *The Soviet Economy,* pp. 148ff.
33. D. B. Diamond, L. W. Bettis, and R. E. Ramsson, "Agricultural Production," in A. Bergson and H. S. Levine, eds., *The Soviet Economy Toward the Year 2000* (Winchester, Mass.: George Allen & Unwin, 1983), p. 145.
34. "The Report on 1984 Plan Fulfillment." *Current Digest of the Soviet Press,* vol. XXXVII, no. 4 (1985), 10–16.
35. U.S. Department of Agriculture, *USSR: Outlook and Situation Report* (Washington, D.C.: U.S. Department of Agriculture, 1984), p. 22.
36. *Ibid.*
37. *Ibid.,* p. 29.
38. *Ibid.,* p. 24.
39. For a discussion of the Soviet agricultural subsidy, see V. G. Treml, "Subsidies in Soviet Agriculture: Record and Prospects," in U.S. Congress, Joint Economic Committee, *Soviet Economy in the 1980's: Problems and Prospects,* part 2 (Washington, D.C.: U.S. Government Printing Office, 1982), pp. 171–185.
40. Data on fertilizers are from U.S. Department of Agriculture, *USSR: Outlook and Situation Report,* p. 32.

41. *Ibid.,* p. 22.

42. Data are from *Narodnoe khoziaistvo SSSR v 1982* [The national economy of the USSR in 1982] (Moscow: Finansy i Statistika, 1983), pp. 255–256; and *Narodnoe khoziaistvo SSSR v 1983* [The national economy of the USSR in 1983] (Moscow: Finansy i Statistika, 1984), pp. 273–274.

43. For a discussion of the development of agricultural integration, see E. M. Jacobs, "Soviet Agricultural Management and Planning and the 1982 Administrative Reforms," in Stuart, ed., *The Soviet Rural Economy,* pp. 273–295.

44. *Narodnoe khoziaistvo SSSR v 1983* [The national economy of the USSR in 1983] (Moscow: Finansy i Statistika, 1984), p. 292.

45. *Ibid.*

46. For a survey, see A. F. Malish, "The Food Program: A New Policy or More Rhetoric?" in U.S. Congress, Joint Economic Committee, *The Soviet Economy in the 1980's: Problems and Prospects,* part 2, pp. 41–59.

47. This reform will be discussed in greater depth in Chapter 13. For a useful survey, see G. E. Schroeder, "Recent Developments in Soviet Planning and Managerial Incentives," in U.S. Congress, Joint Economic Committee, *Soviet Economic Prospects for the Seventies* (Washington, D.C.: U.S. Government Printing Office, 1973), pp. 11–44.

48. For a discussion of Soviet attitudes toward technology, see B. Parrott, *Politics and Technology in the Soviet Union* (Cambridge, Mass.: the MIT Press, 1983), chaps. 5 and 6. Even attempts in the late 1970s to relax traditional taut planning methods were apparently unsuccessful. For a discussion, see G. E. Schroeder, "The Slowdown In Soviet Industry, 1976–1982," *Soviet Economy,* vol. 1, no. 1 (January–March, 1985), 42–75.

49. For a discussion, see A. Gorlin, "Industrial Reorganization: The Associations," in U.S. Congress, Joint Economic Committee, *Soviet Economy in a New Perspective* (Washington, D.C.: U.S. Government Printing Office, 1976), pp. 162–188.

50. G. E. Schroeder, "Soviet Living Standards: Achievements and Prospects," in U.S. Congress, Joint Economic Committee, *Soviet Economy in The 1980's: Problems and Prospects,* part 2 (Washington, D.C.: U.S. Government Printing Office, 1982), p. 368.

51. *Ibid.*

52. See F. D. Holzman, *International Trade under Communism;* and U.S. Congress, Joint Economic Committee, *Soviet Economy In The 1980's: Problems And Prospects,* part 2, section VIII.

53. A comprehensive and controversial work is C. K. Wilber, *The Soviet Model and Underdeveloped Countries* (Chapel Hill: University of North Carolina Press, 1969). Other authors making significant contributions are O. Hoeffding, "State Planning and Forced Industrialization," *Problems of Communism,* vol. 8, no. 6 (November–December 1959); N. Spulber, *Soviet Strategy for Economic Growth* (Bloomington: Indiana University Press, 1964); A. Nove, "The Soviet Model and Underdeveloped Countries," *International Affairs,* vol. 36, no. 1 (January 1961); N. Dodge and C. K. Wilber, "The Relevance of Soviet Industrial Experience for Less Developed Economies," *Soviet Studies,* vol. 21, no. 3 (January 1970), 330–349.

54. Our elaboration of the components of the SDM is drawn from the following studies: Wilber, *The Soviet Model,* part I; G. Ofer, *The Service Sector in Soviet Economic Growth* (Cambridge, Mass.: Harvard University Press, 1973); G. Ofer, "Economizing on Urbanization in Socialist Countries," in A. A. Brown and E. Neuberger, eds., *Internal Migration: A Comparative Perspective* (New York: Academic Press, 1977), pp. 277–304; G. Ofer, "Industrial Structure, Urbanization, and the Growth Strategy of Socialist Countries," *Quarterly Journal of Economics,* vol. 90, no. 2 (May 1976),

219–243; P. R. Gregory, *Socialist and Nonsocialist Industrialization Patterns* (New York: Praeger, 1970); F. L. Pryor, *Public Expenditures in Communist and Capitalist Nations* (Homewood, Ill.: Irwin, 1968); F. D. Holzman, *Soviet Taxation* (Cambridge, Mass.: Harvard University Press, 1955); F. D. Holzman, "Foreign Trade," in A. Bergson and S. Kuznets, eds., *Economic Trends in the Soviet Union* (Cambridge, Mass.: Harvard University Press, 1963), pp. 283–332; H. Hunter, *Soviet Transportation Policy* (Cambridge, Mass.: Harvard University Press, 1957); E. W. Williams, Jr, *Freight Transportation in the Soviet Union* (Princeton, N.J.: Princeton University Press, 1962); S. Kuznets, "A Comparative Appraisal," in A. Bergson and S. Kuznets, eds., *Economic Trends in the Soviet Union* (Cambridge, Mass.: Harvard University Press, 1963). In this section, we do not cite references to summary material drawn from earlier chapters.

55. Ofer, *The Service Sector,* chap. 1.
56. Gregory, *Socialist and Nonsocialist Industrialization Patterns,* p. 144.
57. Dodge and Wilber, "The Relevance of Soviet Industrial Experience," part 2.
58. An empirical study of the costs of gigantism is provided by B. Katz, " 'Gigantism' as an Unbalanced Growth Strategy: An Econometric Investigation of the Soviet Experience, 1928–1940," *Soviet Union,* vol. 4, part 2 (1977), pp. 205–222. For a statistical comparison of the scale of Soviet industrial establishments with American establishments, see A. Woroniak, "Industrial Concentration in Eastern Europe: The Search for Optimum Size and Efficiency," *Notwendigkeit und Gefahr der Wirtschaftlichen Konzentration* (Basel: Kyklos Verlag), pp. 265–284.
59. D. Granick, *Soviet Metal Fabricating and Economic Development* (Madison: University of Wisconsin Press, 1967).
60. F. D. Holzman, "Financing Soviet Development," in M. Abramovitz, ed., *Capital Formation and Economic Growth* (Princeton, N.J.: Princeton University Press, 1955), pp. 229–287.
61. Soviet planners have long stressed the need for economic development in all regions of the country. The Ural-Kuznetsk Combine was designed to tap the mineral resources of the Ural mountains and the coal resources of the Kuznetsk area and to be appropriately combined to form a large industrial center. For a detailed discussion of the program, see, for example, F. D. Holzman, "The Soviet Ural-Kuznetsk Combine: A Study of Investment Criteria and Industrialization Policies," *Quarterly Journal of Economics,* vol. 71, no. 3 (August 1957), 367–405.
62. Hunter, *Soviet Transportation Policy,* chap. 3, especially chart 4, p. 49; Williams, *Freight Transportation,* pp. 136–137.
63. W. Hoffman, *The Growth of Industrial Economies* (Manchester, England: Manchester University Press, 1958); Gregory, *Socialist and Nonsocialist Industrialization Patterns,* p. 168.
64. S. Kuznets, *Modern Economic Growth* (New Haven, Conn.: Yale University Press, 1967), pp. 300–303.
65. Gregory, *Socialist and Nonsocialist Industrialization Patterns,* pp. 28–29, appendix B.
66. R. Moorsteen and R. Powell, *The Soviet Capital Stock, 1928–1962* (Homewood, Ill.: Irwin, 1966), pp. 358, 361. The 1935 figure is estimated by applying the Moorsteen and Powell investment rate index to the Bergson 1937 figure.
67. Kuznets, "A Comparative Appraisal," pp. 353–354.
68. Kuznets, "A Comparative Appraisal," pp. 354–357.
69. *Ibid.,* pp. 345–347.
70. *Ibid.,* pp. 350–352.
71. *Ibid.,* pp. 358–361.

72. *Ibid.,* p. 341.
73. Kuznets, *Modern Economic Growth,* pp. 300–302.
74. Kuznets, "A Comparative Appraisal," p. 367.
75. Ofer, *The Service Sector,* chap. 3.
76. A. Nove, *Economic Rationality and Soviet Politics* (New York: Praeger, 1964), essay 1.

SELECTED BIBLIOGRAPHY

A. Bergson and H. S. Levine, *The Soviet Economy Toward the Year 2000* (London: George Allen & Unwin, 1983).

M. Bornstein, ed., *The Soviet Economy: Continuity and Change* (Boulder, Colo.: Westview Press, 1981).

F. D. Holzman, *International Trade Under Communism* (New York: Basic Books, 1976).

———, *The Soviet Economy: Past, Present and Future* (New York: The Foreign Policy Association, 1982).

R. Hutchings, *The Soviet Budget* (Albany, N.Y.: State University of New York Press, 1983).

———, *Soviet Economic Development,* 2nd ed. (New York and London: New York University Press, 1982).

J. R. Millar, *The Soviet Rural Community* (Urbana: University of Illinois Press, 1971).

———, *The ABC's of Soviet Socialism* (Urbana: University of Illinois Press, 1981).

H. W. Morton and R. C. Stuart, eds., *The Contemporary Soviet City* (Armonk: M. E. Sharpe, 1984).

W. Moskoff, *Labour and Leisure in the Soviet Union* (New York: St. Martins Press, 1984).

A. Nove, *The Soviet Economic System* (London: George Allen & Unwin, 1977).

H. Schwartz, *The Soviet Economy Since Stalin* (Philadelphia: J. B. Lippincott, 1965.

R. C. Stuart, ed., *The Soviet Rural Economy* (Totowa, N.J.: Rowman & Allenheld, 1984).

two

HOW THE SOVIET
ECONOMY OPERATES

How the Soviet Economy Operates: Planning, Pricing, and Markets

INTRODUCTION TO SOVIET RESOURCE ALLOCATION

In this chapter, we turn from the history of the Soviet planned economy to its actual operation. Although arrangements for allocating resources in the Soviet Union have changed over time, we shall concentrate on how the Soviet economy operates in the early 1980s. The various Soviet economic reforms (discussed in Part IV) have at best brought about relatively minor changes in basic Soviet working arrangements. The Soviet economic system of the early 1980s is not fundamentally different from the system put in place in the 1930s. The description of resource allocation arrangements that follows, therefore, does not depend heavily on the exact time period chosen.

Our foremost concern in the next two chapters is to elaborate how resources are allocated in the Soviet Union, in particular by what arrangements goods and services are produced and distributed and how the major factors of production (labor and capital) are allocated. Particular attention will be given to both the formal and informal means through which resource allocation is achieved. To analyze the matter of goods production, we consider in this chapter the planning apparatus, the relationship between the planners and enterprises, and the process of price formation. We approach the latter question of factor allocation in Chapter 8 by examining the Soviet manager, the labor market, and the allocation of scarce capital among competing uses.

First, however, it is necessary to outline the institutional framework in which the Soviet economy operates, since these institutions—the state economic hierarchy and the Communist Party—provide much of the direction and control generally exerted by the market in capitalist economies.

THE SOVIET ECONOMIC BUREAUCRACY[1]

The political system of the Soviet Union was described briefly in the introductory chapter. This chapter focuses on the Soviet economic bureaucracy, defined to include the economic activities of the ruling Communist Party, the state bureaucracy including the state planning apparatus, the industrial ministries, the trusts intermediate between the industrial ministries and the enterprises, and the enterprises at the lowest level.

The Party and State Economic Apparatus

The Communist Party of the Soviet Union (CPSU) is the dominant ruling force in the Soviet Union. The CPSU deals with a multitude of matters—propaganda, media control, foreign policy—in addition to economics. Its economic functions range from devising overall economic policy, to controlling key appointments in the economy, to monitoring economic activity at the highest to the lowest level. The CPSU plays a vital and ongoing role in the area of economics. At the highest level, the Department of Planning and Finance Organs *(Otdel planovykh i finansovykh organov)* of the Central Committee of the CPSU is responsible for issuing instructions to the highest state planning organs and for coordinating overall plan activity. This party department is staffed by professional party bureaucrats and plays a crucial role in staffing key positions in the state planning apparatus and in determining appointments and promotions in the upper echelons of the state economic bureaucracy. The Central Committee also has industrial departments that supervise and monitor specific branches of the economy. For example, the Central Committee currently has separate departments of heavy industry, machine building, defense industries, chemicals, light industry and food, construction, transportation and services, and trade. These party industrial departments parallel the industrial departments of state planning organs and the industrial ministries themselves.

The CPSU exercises control over the economy not only from its apex in Moscow. Regional and local party organs—the oblast' party committees *(obkoms),* the city party committees *(gorkoms),* and the regional party committees *(raikoms)* are also involved in economic affairs. The first party secretary of a particular *obkom* oversees the economic affairs of his oblast' and is typically held responsible for the aggregate economic successes or failures of the oblast' economy. The first party secretary of a particular city (say, Moscow) tends to be judged according to the combined economic performance of enterprises in Moscow. This pattern is thought by political observers of the Soviet scene to lead to different goals pursued at the national and regional and local levels of the party organization. Whereas the Central Committee tends to be concerned with overall economic performance, regional and local party authorities tend to be concerned about the economic performance in the area of their jurisdiction. They are, therefore, prepared to intervene on behalf of local enterprises.

The primary party organizations (PPOs) of the productive enterprises represent party authority at the microeconomic level of the economy. Each enterprise has a PPO. In large enterprises, the PPO is headed by a full-time professional who is "freed" from other work responsibilities. In small enterprises, the PPO is more often headed by a party member who carries this responsibility on a part-time basis. Most political scientists agree that the power of the PPO is limited and does not strongly influence the operation of Soviet enterprises.

Whereas the CPSU involves itself in the making of economic policy, controlling key appointments, and in general monitoring and assistance, the state economic bureaucracy is charged with the formal implementation of party economic policy. Although there is an elected government, the Supreme Soviet, whose affairs are carried out by its presidium, the Council of Ministers *(Soviet ministrov)* conducts the routine business of government in the Soviet Union. The Council of Ministers is the government bureaucracy of the Soviet Union. Each of the 15 union republics has its own state apparatus, the organization of which parallels the USSR state apparatus. The USSR Council of Ministers is staffed by the industrial ministers, the chairmen of various state committees, and the chairmen of other agencies with ministerial status. The chairman of the Council of Ministers occupies the most powerful position in the state apparatus.

Of the more than 20 state committees, the most important to planning and managing the national economy are *Gosplan* (the State Planning Commission), *Gosbank* (the State Bank), *Gossnab* (the State Committee for Material Technical Supply), *Gosstroi* (the State Committee for Construction), and the Central Statistical Administration. Although nominally responsible to the USSR Council of Ministers, *Gosplan* is by far the most important agency of the state economic bureaucracy. It maintains close ties with the Central Committee and is viewed by members of the Soviet economic bureaucracy as representing the will of the Central Committee. *Gosplan* itself is organized along functional lines in branch departments that parallel the various branches of the economy. For example, *Gosplan* has branch departments of coal, ferrous metals, machine building, and the like. In addition to branch departments, *Gosplan* has various summary departments (such as the departments of finance and costs, the department for the annual national economic plan, and the department of capital investment) which deal with issues that cross functional boundaries such as the development of an integrated national plan. *Gosplan* is headed by a chairman, and its most important operational affairs are handled by *Gosplan*'s collegium (staffed by the various department heads, the chairman, and the deputy chairmen). *Gosplan* USSR has branches in the 15 republics.

Gosplan, the State Planning Commission, was established in 1921 and engaged primarily in nonoperational long-term planning during the 1920s. During the 1920s, the role of *Gosplan* as the central coordinator of national planning was challenged by the People's Commissariat of Finance *(Narkomfin),* by VSNKh, and the ministerial planning bodies; but by the late 1920s, *Gosplan* was fairly well recognized as the principal planning body in the Soviet Union.[2] After its reorganization in 1928, it came to play an important coordinating function, especially after the ministerial system was introduced in 1932. Although the ministries themselves performed most of the current planning within the ministry, *Gosplan* was given the task of coordinating these ministerial plans by drawing up *material balances,* the basic planning system to be discussed shortly. The structure and functions of *Gosplan* have changed over the years, though to relate these changes in detail would be confusing to the reader and would not add significantly to our understanding of Soviet planning.* The important point to note is that in spite of continuing changes in the organizational structure of planning agencies, *Gosplan* has played a central coordinating role throughout the plan period, especially with the application of material balance planning. *Gosplan*'s main charge is devising national economic plans. Currently, *Gosplan* draws up both long-term plans (five years and longer) and annual economic plans. The annual economic plans are the plans according to which the economic bureaucracy operates, and *Gosplan*'s planning work guides the activities of the other state committees that manage the nation's economy.

    Gossnab, the State Committee for Material Technical Supply, is charged with managing the distribution of material inputs required to fulfill the national economic plan. *Gosbank* monitors fulfillment of financial plans and manages the credit and cash accounts of enterprises. *Gosstroi,* the State Committee for Construction, coordinates construction activity carried out throughout the national economy. The Central Statistical Administration monitors plan fulfillment and gathers statistics for the use by the state economic bureaucracy.

Ministries, Industrial Associations, and Enterprises

The ministries fulfill several functions. They supervise the productive enterprises that fall within their functional domain. The Ministry of Ferrous Metals, for example, supervises the enterprises in the economy that produce ferrous metals. The ministries break down the aggregated plan activities handed down by *Gosplan* into detailed targets for individual enterprises. The ministries are charged with carrying out the allocation of various supplies and materials among their enterprises. In the Soviet planning jargon, ministries are "fund holders" *(fondoderzhateli)*. They, in effect, carry the responsibility for the orderly allocation of scarce inputs to their enterprises.

    The ministries are headed by a minister who has various deputy ministers. Each ministry is divided into chief administrations (or *glavks*) that are responsible for the different activities of the ministry. The ministry of construction materials, for example, is broken down into chief administrations that handle the different types of construction materials (cement, asphalt, bricks, etc.) produced by the ministry's enterprises. The routine business of the ministry is handled by its

---

    *In 1948–1949, *Gosplan* was weakened by the establishment of what had formerly been its material allocation department, technical department, and Central Statistical Agency as separate agencies. After Stalin's death, these departments (with the exception of the Central Statistical Agency) were returned to *Gosplan.* In 1955, *Gosplan* was split into two agencies: *Gosplan,* which was to concentrate on long-term planning, and the State Economic Commission, which was to be concerned with short-term plans. As a result of the regionalization reforms (the *Sovnarkhozy*) of 1957, *Gosplan* took on new responsibilities. It absorbed the planning functions of the defunct ministries and was the crucial coordinating agency at the all-union level. In 1960, *Gosplan* was again split into the State Economic-Science Council, in charge of long-range planning, and *Gosplan,* in charge of current planning.

collegium, which is staffed by the minister, the deputy ministers, the heads of the chief administrations, and the directors of major enterprises. The collegium deals with supply and output problems, makes personnel changes, and advises the minister.

Ministries are of three types. The all-union ministries manage directly from Moscow all the enterprises in that branch. Branches that are organized as all-union ministries tend to be key industrial branches (such as machine building, electronics, defense, and communications equipment) that maintain enterprises throughout the Soviet Union. The second type of ministry is the union-republican ministry, whose enterprises are subject to the dual subordination of the Moscow ministry and the republican ministry. Branches that tend to be organized on the union-republican basis are those in which production is concentrated in one or several republics (such as coal production, which is concentrated in particular republics, or agriculture, where the same is true) or where activities are carried out broadly among the republics but on a more decentralized basis (such as construction). The third type of ministry is the republican ministry, which is charged primarily with managing enterprises producing for the local economy. Republican ministries also deal with construction projects of more local significance. In this latter activity, they share responsibility with the republican council of ministers.

The Soviet economic bureaucracy also contains a large number of semi-independent consulting institutes, called scientific research institutes, project-making institutes, or scientific-technical institutes. These institutes can be technically subordinated to ministries, to *Gosplan,* to the Academy of Sciences, or to republican organs. They contract with the various planning organs and ministries to perform detailed planning studies, feasibility studies for major construction projects, scientific input norm calculations, and the like. Much of the detailed planning work in the Soviet economy is actually carried out by these institutes.

Since 1973, increased emphasis has been placed on developing an intermediate management level between the ministries and the enterprises, called industrial associations. The industrial associations *(obedineniia)* are generally organized corresponding to the chief administrations, the *glavks,* of the ministry. In construction materials, for example, the industrial associations would be organized according to the main product lines handled by the main administrations. The industrial associations are, relatively speaking, a new phenomenon in the Soviet economic bureaucracy, and a number of operating rules remain to be firmly established. How much autonomy do individual enterprises that are members of the industrial association have? What supervisory and management tasks are left to the ministry? What tasks are carried out by the management of the industrial association? Apparently, the two motivating forces behind the idea of the industrial association were the desire to involve technical ministerial experts in the direct administration of enterprises and to simplify the planning and management process by allowing planners to deal with combinations of industrial enterprises rather than individual enterprises.

The productive enterprises *(predpriiatiia)* form the microeconomic core of the Soviet economy. Much more will be said about them in the next chapter. For now, we can say that Soviet enterprises are headed by a professional manager (director), who is aided by a management staff of accountants, engineers, designers, technologists, and economists. The enterprise runs on an independent accounting system, which means that it is supposed to cover its costs with its revenues and to (hopefully) earn a profit. The enterprise operates according to detailed instructions from the ministry main administration and from the industrial association but retains considerable independent decision-making authority.

The Principal/Agent Problem and the Economic Bureaucracy

As the above illustrates, the Soviet economic bureaucracy is a complex, multilayered organization. The discussion also brings home the point that the Soviet economic bureaucracy is organized according to hierarchical principles, with organization A being superior to organization B which is itself superior to organization C. The superiority of A over B and of B over C is evidenced by the fact that A can issue binding orders to B, and B can issue binding orders to C. In the Soviet case, these orders are instructions on what to produce and permission to use certain resources. In the language of modern economics, organization A is the principal and organization B is the agent of A. Organization B is the principal of C, or, stated otherwise, C is the agent of B. Organizations in the Soviet economic bureaucracy are tied together in principal/agent relationships.[3]

When two organizations are involved in a principal/agent relationship, the agent is charged with carrying out the instructions of the principal according to an agreed-upon contractual arrangement. In market economies, principal/agent relationships of all kinds exist: a professional management team (the agent) represents the interests of the stockholders of a corporation (the principal). A home builder (the agent) carries out the orders of a family contracting with him to build a home (the principal). A professional baseball player is the agent of the team's owner. An agency problem arises when the agent fails to pursue the interests of the principal without formally violating the contractual agreement between the principal and agent. For example, the stockholders of a corporation wish to maximize the long-run market price of their shares, while the professional management team wishes to maximize their job security. Accordingly, the management team resists corporate takeovers that benefit the stockholders. The contract between the stockholders and the management team does not prevent the agents from behaving contrary to the interests of the principal. The home builder may build a home that is of lower quality than the buyer perceives as contracted for, but the contract has been written in such a way that the agent has formally met his or her contractual obligations to the principal. When the interests of the principal and agent diverge, the principal must either devote resources to monitoring the contractual performance of the agent or attempt to devise an incentive scheme that causes the agent to pursue automatically the interests of the principal. Whether the principal chooses monitoring or automatic incentive schemes depends upon the cost and feasibility of monitoring. If monitoring is costless, the agent simply watches every move of the agent to prevent the agent from acting contrary to the interests of the principal. When monitoring costs are present, perfect monitoring is typically not rational. The principal, therefore, must find incentive schemes that will encourage agents, who cannot be perfectly monitored, to pursue their interests as closely as possible. In the real world, where monitoring costs are present, principals select a combination of monitoring and incentive mechanisms, the combination depending upon the costs of monitoring.

This chapter shows that agency problems are present in the Soviet context. Within the Soviet economic bureaucracy, principals issue orders and instructions to their agents, monitor the performance of agents, and reward or punish agents on the basis of established performance criteria. The Soviet economic bureaucracy is a complex organization. It is difficult to monitor the detailed activities of agent organizations, and information reported by agents tends to be distorted; so, principals in the Soviet system must combine performance monitoring with incentive mechanisms to encourage agents to act in the principal's interests. It is the task of the principal to find an incentive system that encourages their agents to follow the spirit of the principal's instructions as closely as possible. The importance of the incentive system depends upon the principal's ability to monitor the performance of the agent. The better the principal's monitoring, the less important the incentive mechanism.

Figure 7 gives an impressionistic picture of the various principal/agent relationships that exist in the Soviet economic bureaucracy. In this discussion, we focus on the agency relationship between the Central Committee and *Gosplan* and the ministries and between the ministries and the enterprises. As the figure shows, there are a multitude of agency relationships that we cannot touch on in this discussion. The chief principals in the Soviet economy are the Central Committee and *Gosplan* (we know too little of their relationship to determine if an agency problem exists here). It is the principal to the various industrial ministries, *Gosplan* issues directives to its agent ministries, telling them how much to produce (and in what assortments) and the resources (both real and financial) that will be made available to them. The principal would like the agent to meet these output targets with a minimal expenditure of society's resources (or to produce a maximum output with the allotted quantity of resources). Besides setting up monitoring procedures, it seeks to devise incentive schemes to encourage the agent ministries to pursue the interests of the principal. Within the general constraint of performance monitoring by the principal, the agent ministries wish to achieve maximal rewards from the established incentive scheme (either in the form of income, adulation, promotion, or job security). If the incentive scheme is imperfectly devised (and monitoring is imperfect), the agent ministries will engage in behavior (such as achieving output targets at the sacrifice of quality or the wastage of resources) that is contrary to the interests of the principal as long as this perverse behavior is neither detected nor punished by the established incentive scheme.

The ministries, on the other hand, are the principals to the industrial associations and industrial enterprises that serve as their agents. They issue instructions to their agent enterprises concerning what they are to produce (and in what qualities and assortments) and concerning the real and financial resources at their disposal. The ministries cannot monitor their agents perfectly, and there-

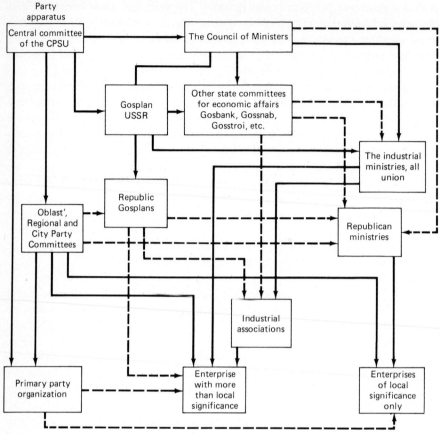

Figure 7

fore, to supplement direct monitoring, they must devise incentive systems that encourage their agents to carry out instructions in the spirit of the principal. It is too costly to the principal to monitor all the activities of its many agents. The ministry would like its agents to produce the outputs ordered in the appropriate assortments and qualities with minimal expenditure of the ministry's scarce resources. Unless the incentive scheme is perfect, the agent enterprises will be tempted to earn the rewards offered by their principals (in the form of bonuses, promotion, etc.) by engaging in perverse behavior. If the principal's incentive system rewards output without rewarding quality or cost savings, the agent is tempted to sacrifice quality or cost savings in meeting its output directives.

The basic theme of this chapter and the next is how the Soviet economic system deals with the principal/agent problem. The agency problem provides a convenient framework for studying Soviet resource allocation practices. We first identify the major principal/agent problems in the Soviet economy. Second, we treat the various monitoring techniques used by principals. Third, we consider why the Soviet system tends to generate false information that raises monitoring costs. Finally, we discuss the different incentive systems that have been designed to treat the agency problem and show why it is difficult in the Soviet context to find incentive systems that eliminate agency problems. The chapter on economic reform (Chapter 13) describes the Soviet search for better incentive systems to ameliorate principal/agent problems.

SOVIET PLANNING: THE BASIC BALANCES

The official guide for Soviet economic planners emphasizes that planning in the Soviet Union proceeds from a series of basic balances.[4] This chapter concentrates specifically on only two of these balances—the material balance and the income balance—but it is useful to begin with an overview of the basic balances of the Soviet planned economy.[5] In market economies, market forces bring about a number of balances: the supplies and demands for particular goods, services, and resources are equalized by the price system. The supply and demand for loanable funds are equalized through market interest rates. The aggregate supply and demand for goods and services are balanced by income adjustments and price level changes, and so on.

The Soviet planned economy must likewise achieve similar balances. There are negative consequences to underutilizing goods and resources. Resources are wasted if trained labor is standing idle due to lack of demand. If capital goods, produced at high opportunity cost, are not used, society has wasted its resources. Excess demands for goods, resources, and capital have similarly negative consequences. If the quantity of a good or resource demanded exceeds the quantity supplied, some means must be found to ration out the available supply in a reasonable manner to prevent chaos. The next two chapters discuss in some detail how the Soviet planned economies achieve balances, largely without the aid of automatic market forces.

The Consumer Goods Balance

In the consumer goods market, planners aim to achieve a balance between the supplies and demands for individual goods and services at the micro level and between the aggregate supply and the aggregate demand for consumer goods at the macro level. The use of the price system to achieve micro balances is discussed later in this chapter. Let us briefly consider the problem of the macrobalance. There are reasons why Soviet planners would want a balance between the aggregate demand and aggregate supply of consumer goods. If there were excess demand that is not compensated by inflation, disappointed consumers might lose their interest in the monetary rewards offerred by the economic system. For this reason, excess demand might have to be countered by inflation, which might unleash a political backlash against the system's leaders. Soviet planners, therefore, seek a balance between the desired money outlays for goods and services of the population and the money value of goods and services offered to consumer markets. If planners wish to have stable prices and a general clearing of markets, then the two major means of bringing about this equality are to control the flow of income to the population or to control the output of goods and services desired by the population.

In notational form, a macrobalance is achieved in the consumer goods market (at established prices) when

$$PQ = wL + O - T - R$$

where P = the prevailing price level
$\quad\quad\quad Q$ = the real output of consumer goods
$\quad\quad\quad w$ = the average annual wage rate
$\quad\quad\quad L$ = average annual employment
$\quad\quad\quad O$ = earnings other than wage earnings
$\quad\quad\quad T$ = tax payment
$\quad\quad\quad R$ = personal savings.

The $wL + O - T$ term equals personal disposable income. When personal savings are subtracted from this term, we get the demand for consumer goods.

The Labor Balance

In labor markets, planners desire to have microbalances between the supplies of the different labor services offered by the able-bodied population and the demands for these different labor services. The next chapter discusses how the Soviet labor market seeks to achieve microbalances. At the macro level, Soviet planners wish to have an aggregate labor force balance, whereby the aggregate demand for labor services equals the aggregate supply of labor services. In market economies, both the micro and macro labor balances are brought about by relative wage adjustments (especially in the long run). In the Soviet Union, both micro- and macrobalances are brought about by labor force planning (planning the supply of and the demand for professional and manual labor force) which uses relative wages as an instrument of labor force policy. Obviously, both micro- and macrobalances are desired because underutilized labor resources mean that the economy is producing below potential.

At the macro level, Soviet planners concentrate on balancing the demand for new positions in the economy with the flows of people into and out of the labor force. In notational form, a macrobalance is achieved when

$$\Delta D^L = E - R$$

where ΔD^L = new jobs projected by planning authorities
$\quad\quad\quad E$ = new entrants into the labor market (primarily from the educational establishment)
$\quad\quad\quad R$ = departures from the labor force (largely due to retirements)

The Credit Balance

Soviet planners must also aim for a balance of the demand for credit by Soviet enterprises and organizations and the supply of credit. In capitalist economies, this balancing is achieved primarily through interest rate changes, while in the Soviet Union, planners determine the credit needs of the economy and the state bank supplies credit in accordance with planned credit requirements. The credit balance, like most other Soviet macrobalances, is achieved administratively, largely without adjustments in the opportunity costs of credit to the participants. One set of planners determines the credit needs of the microeconomic units, while another set of planners (theoretically working in tandem with the first group) supplies the credit needs of the microunits.

In notational form, macrobalance is achieved in credit markets when:

$$D^C = S^C$$

where D^C = the aggregate demand for credit
S^C = the aggregate supply of credit

The Capital Goods Balance

Soviet planners are also charged with ensuring a micro- and a macrobalance of the demand for and supply of capital goods. The supply of capital goods is determined by the output of various capital goods (machinery, structures, and housing), while the demand for capital goods is determined by investment planners through investment plans for the various enterprises and organizations throughout the economy. In capitalist economies, the demand and supply of capital goods is balanced by adjustments in real interest rates. In the Soviet planned economy, the balance is brought about by administrative decree by those who plan the output of capital goods and their distribution. As the next chapter will show, the microunit has surprisingly little to say about the process.

Although capital goods tend to be treated separately by Soviet planners, the investment goods balance illustrates the general problem of material balances. Basically, Soviet planners must ensure that the economy produces sufficient supplies of individual materials and capital goods to enable the enterprises to meet their production targets and to meet the demand for exports and for final consumption. The next section concentrates on material balance planning.

Material Balances[6]

Soviet planning authorities must balance the supplies and demands for the basic raw materials and commodities that are used in the production process or flow to final consumers such as households or foreign exports. In any economy, there are literally millions of such goods (thousands of types of steel products, hundreds of different building materials, thousands of chemical products, a few types of coal, and so on). In market economies, the supplies and demands for such goods are brought into balance by relative price changes. If the quantity of coal demanded exceeds the quantity of coal supplied at prevailing prices, the relative price of coal will rise until the quantity demanded equals the quantity supplied. Under normal circumstances, users of materials in market economies do not have to stand in line to obtain materials; the price system allows buyers who are prepared to pay the going market price to buy the product.

In the Soviet planned economy, the supply and demand for materials are brought into balance by administrative procedures. One of the principal tasks of the Soviet planning apparatus is the achievement of balances of materials. *Gosplan* plays a key role in this activity—called material balance planning—and is assisted by the ministries and by *Gossnab* (the state supply committee). We shall begin our discussion of material balance planning with the idealized version reported by official Soviet texts on the subject.[7] We then turn to a discussion of how material balance planning is conducted in Soviet practice.

Our discussion begins with the construction of the annual plan.[8] The key to Soviet success in dealing with the enormous complexities of planning is that only a limited number of commodities are centrally planned and distributed by *Gosplan SSSR*. Even then, industrial supply and distribution plans compiled by *Gosplan* have been known to total 70 volumes of almost 12,000 pages and to deal with well over 30,000 commodities.

The most important industrial products—such as steel, cement, machinery, building materials—are called *funded commodities*. *Gosplan SSSR* is in charge of drawing up output and distribution plans for these funded commodities, which are specifically approved by the USSR Council of Ministers. Between 1928 and the present, *Gosplan* has developed annual balances for between 277 and 2390 separate funded product groups. Currently, *Gosplan* prepares some 2000 balances. Output and distribution plans are also drawn up for two other categories of industrial products. *Planned commodities* are those industrial products jointly planned and distributed by *Gosplan, Gossnab* (State Committee for Material-Technical Supply) and the All-Union Main Supply and Sales Administrations—under the approval of the heads of these organizations. In recent years, 25,000 or more commodities have been planned according to this system. Finally, *decentrally planned* commodities are planned and distributed by the territorial administrations of *Gossnab* and by the ministries without the explicit approval of higher organs. In recent years, over 50,000 industrial products have been planned according to this system.

In addition to these three categories, the ministries plan and allocate "nonplanned" industrial commodities, largely for internal use. In the 1970s, for example, the ministries allocated 26,000 products in this category.

An idealized version of *Gosplan's* planning of funded commodities through the industrial supply and output planning system is as follows (the breakdown into distinct steps is somewhat arbitrary, for there is considerable overlapping):

1. The first step in the planning process is for the party (the Politburo or the Central Committee) to establish its priorities for the forthcoming planning period. This is usually done in the spring preceding the planning period. The party expresses its priorities by setting output targets (generally in the form of desired rates of growth) for a number of crucial funded commodities.

2. The second step is the control figure phase. Output targets are sent down through the state apparatus to *Gosplan,* which has been active gathering data on past plan fulfillment and bottlenecks. *Gosplan* then formulates a preliminary set of *control figures* (tentative output targets) for 200 to 300 product groups that fulfills the priorities set by the party. *Gosplan* also tentatively estimates, on the basis of past performance, the inputs required to achieve the control figures. The ministries are informed of their projected material "limits." At this stage, the planning departments of the ministries aid *Gosplan* in the formulation of the full

set of control figures and project input requirements—a process that involves considerable negotiation and friction as the ministries bargain for reasonable targets and sufficient resources.

The objective of the next three phases is the preparation of a draft plan. Ministries react to their control figures and resource limits and bargain with *Gosplan.* Enterprises bargain with their ministries over their own control figures and proposed material limits.

3. The ministries send down control figures through the planning hierarchy via the ministerial organizations until they reach the individual enterprises. As the control figures progress through the planning hierarchy, they are disaggregated into specific tasks. For example, the all-union ministry will receive its control targets, which are then disaggregated by branches within the ministry, and so on, until each enterprise under the purview of the ministry receives its own control figures. At this stage, the planning branch of the ministry will prepare a list of tentative input requirements, based on the ministry's control figures, for internal use by each enterprise.

4. Information now begins to flow up the planning hierarchy from the enterprise to *Gosplan.* The enterprise will relate its input requirements to its immediate superior, which in turn will aggregate the requirements of all enterprises under its control. These will be related to its superior, and so on, up to the ministry and then to *Gosplan.* At each stage in this process, the requested inputs are compared with estimated input needs and the so-called *correction principle* is used to adjust for differences between the two (after considerable bargaining among the various levels). If ministries propose higher material limits than those calculated by *Gosplan,* the ministries must "defend" their requests before *Gosplan.* Similarly, enterprises must "defend" requests for deviations from output and input targets before their ministries. An authoritative observer of this process reports a "siege" of *Gosplan* during the draft plan process as ministerial officials flood into *Gosplan* with their arguments and requests.[9]

5. After this phase of bargaining has been completed, *Gosplan* must check the consistency of the control figures, that is, determine whether an equilibrium exists. An equilibrium is achieved when the planned supplies of each commodity equal its targeted material input requirements and final uses. Assuming a total of 2000 funded commodities to be balanced, a material balance is achieved when:

Exhibit 1

$$S_1 = D_1$$
$$S_2 = D_2$$
$$\cdot$$
$$\cdot$$
$$\cdot$$
$$S_{2000} = D_{2000}$$

where S = the planned supplies
           D = the estimated demands for the (2000) materials

The planned supply of the first commodity (S_1), for example, is the sum of its planned output (the control figure), denoted as X_1; available stocks (V_1); and planned imports (M_1). The total demand for the first commodity (D_1) is the sum of its intermediate (interindustry) demands $(X_{11}, X_{12}, X_{13}, \ldots X_{1,2000})$* and its final demand (investment, household demand, and exports), which is denoted as Y_1. From Exhibit 1, it is noted that a consistent set of control figures requires that

Exhibit 2

    Sources   *Distribution*

$$X_1 + V_1 + M_1 = X_{11} + X_{12} + \cdots + X_{1,2000} + Y_1$$

$$X_2 + V_2 + M_2 = X_{21} + X_{22} + \cdots + X_{2,2000} + Y_2$$

$$X_{2000} + V_{2000} + M_{2000} = X_{2000,1} + X_{2000,2} + \cdots + X_{2000,2000} + Y_{2000}$$

In most cases, planned production (the X_1) is the most important supply source, accounting for as much as 95 percent of the total supply of funded materials. On the other hand, imports are usually an insignificant source of supply. It is *Gosplan's* task to ensure that a material balance exists.

A simplified hypothetical material balance consisting of four product categories—coal, steel, machinery, and consumer goods—is provided in Table 20 to illustrate the concepts of intermediate demand, final demand, balance, and so on.

Usually, when *Gosplan* first compares supplies and demands, it finds a tendency for demands to exceed supplies because of large interindustry requirements and taut planning in general. In those cases where excess demand prevails, the commodities are called "deficit" *(defitsitny)* commodities. *Gosplan* must then equate supplies and demands for deficit commodities by adjusting their different components (Exhibit 2). To illustrate this process in the simplest possible manner, assume that an overall balance has been achieved with the exception of the first commodity, which is, say, steel—that is, the supplies of all other commodities equal their demands, but the demand for steel exceeds its supply. This material imbalance can be equilibrated in five different ways:

    a. *Gosplan could order an increase in the planned output of the deficit commodity (raise X_1).* This approach, however, could throw the remaining sectors out of balance because additional coal, electricity, and other inputs used to make steel would be required, and their targets would have to be increased accordingly, which would in turn require increased outputs of commodities used in producing them, and so on. If an output target is changed to achieve a balance, a chain of *secondary effects* is set

---

*The X_{ij} refer to interindustry demands. For example, X_{13} would refer to the quantity of commodity 1 required to produce the planned output of commodity 3. In more general terms, X_{ij} would refer to the quantity of commodity i required to produce the planned output of commodity j. Such input requirements are also called *intermediate* inputs.

Table 20 A SAMPLE BALANCE OF MATERIALS

	Sources			Intermediate inputs required by:				Final use	
	Output	Stocks	Imports	Coal industry	Steel industry	Machinery industry	Consumer goods industry	Exports	Domestic uses
Coal (tons)	1000	10	0	100	500	50	50	100	210
Steel (tons)	2000	0	20	200	400	1000	300	100	20
Machinery (units)	100	5	5	20	40	10	20	10	10
Consumer goods (units)	400	10	20	0	0	0	100	100	230

Demonstration that a balance exists: Sources of coal: 1010 tons = uses of coal: 1010 tons. Sources of steel: 2020 tons = uses of steel: 2020 tons. Sources of machinery: 110 units = uses of machinery: 110 units. Sources of consumer goods: 430 units = uses of consumer goods: 430 units off that affects balances in other sectors. For this reason, Soviet planners have generally been reluctant to use this approach to achieve a balance, finding it difficult to adjust for the secondary impacts of such changes. When Soviet planners have used this approach, they have tended to adjust only for secondary effects in obvious cases.[10] A more common approach has been to call for increased production without raising planned inputs, thus pressuring enterprises to economize on inputs and increasing the tautness of planning.

b. *Gosplan could increase imports* (M_1) *of the deficit commodity.* The major drawback of this approach is that it would make the consistency of the overall balance dependent on foreign suppliers and would require use of essential foreign exchange reserves (if imported from the West). Even utilizing trade connections within the communist bloc would be an uncertain alternative because of the risk that delivery deadlines will not be met. This second approach has generally been of limited importance in Soviet material balance planning, although during the first Five Year Plan (1928–1932), it was used to make up deficits of certain types of machinery; during the postwar period, it has been used to import grain and, in recent years, advanced technology products from the West.

c. *Gosplan could reduce interindustry demands for the deficit commodity* (X_{ij}). This could be done by directing enterprises to use substitutes not in short supply or by reducing their overall inputs. The danger inherent in this approach is that by reducing planned intermediate inputs or by forcing enterprises to use inferior substitutes, the affected enterprises may not be able to meet their own output targets, thus creating further bottlenecks.

d. *Gosplan could reduce final demands for the deficit commodity* (Y_1). This could be done by reducing either exports, household demand, or investment demand. The positive feature of this approach is that household demand (such as coal for home heating) in particular can be treated as a residual in the planning process, with little impact upon interindustry balances. Its negative feature is that such final demands are required to meet the material needs of the populace and could tend to be too readily sacrificed simply to achieve a balance of interindustry demands.

e. *Gosplan could draw upon stocks of the deficit commodity* (V_1). This approach is generally impractical because of either the lack of adequate stockpiles or the unwillingness of planners to draw down strategic supplies, and it has been used only rarely.

Gosplan has historically favored the third and fourth balancing techniques and has generally applied them within the context of a priority system, which has limited the flow of inputs to low-priority industrial branches (generally consumer goods) and has restricted the availability of final consumer goods. In the former case, planners have assumed that the neglect of low-priority consumer goods branches will not jeopardize plan fulfillment in the high-priority heavy industry branches, which tend to be fairly independent of the consumer good branches. For example, if a garment-producing enterprise were to fall short of its output goal owing to inadequate materials, this failure would not jeopardize plan fulfillment in the steel industry. In the latter case, if coal were in deficit, a simple balancing method would be to reduce coal available for household heating, which would have little immediate impact on the crucial interindustry balance. Over time (especially during the 1930s), the consumer sector has tended to be neglected for the sake of achieving balances, so much so that it has at times been called the "buffer" sector of the Soviet economy.

This neglect can be seen from the evidence presented in Table 21. For example, if one examines official Soviet estimates for plan achievement in producer and consumer goods for the period 1928 through 1980, the achievement in producer goods has been substantially greater than that in consumer goods. Although in recent years there has been continuing emphasis on the need to improve both the quantity and the quality of consumer goods, plan adjustments and shortfalls still seem to predominate in the consumer goods sector.

After *Gosplan* achieves (or approximates) the balances, the final version of the plan is submitted to the Council of Ministers for approval (and sometimes modification), after which the finalized targets are sent down the hierarchy to the individual firm. In its final form, the enterprise plan is called the *techpromfinplan* (the technical-industrial-financial plan) and establishes enterprise output targets as well as input allocations, supply plans, delivery plans, financial flows, wage bills, and many other targets.

The final stage of material balance planning occurs during the actual operation of the finalized plan. During this stage, *Gosplan* checks plan fulfillment at the various levels and gathers information upon which next year's plan will be based. An important element of the plan fulfillment stage is the response of *Gosplan* and the ministries to bottlenecks, that is, their manipulation of available resources to ensure fulfillment of priority targets.

It would be a mistake to think that the process of resource allocation is completed with the approval of the final version of the plan. Rather, important shifts of resources occur during the course of plan fulfillment as the planning agencies respond in a pragmatic manner to the various crises and bottlenecks that arise. The national economic plan is only the first stage of Soviet resource allocation. The real process of resource allocation commences with plan fulfillment. As bottlenecks develop, it becomes evident that certain targets must be sacrificed, and it is at this stage that centralized management supercedes centralized planning. As Table 21 indicates, plan fulfillment can vary dramatically by sector, even when one deals with broad aggregates. Those who control the flow of resources during plan implementation, therefore, play a crucial role in determining economic outcomes. The numerous adjustments that take place during the course of plan fulfillment have caused some experts to question whether the Soviet economy is indeed a "planned" economy. This issue is discussed later in this chapter.

THE PLANNING PROBLEM—AN INPUT-OUTPUT FRAMEWORK*

We have presented a sanitized version of Soviet material balance planning. Our description neglects what goes on behind the scenes as all the interested parties

---

*This technical section can be skipped without loss of continuity.

Table 21 FULFILLMENT OF PRINCIPAL GOALS OF SOVIET FIVE YEAR PLANS (5YPs), 1928–1980 (PERCENT FULFILLMENT)

	1st 5YP (1928–1932)	2nd 5YP (1933–1937)	4th 5YP (1946–1950)	5th 5YP (1950–1955)	7th 5YP (1959–1965)	8th 5YP (1966–1970)	9th 5YP (1971–1975)	10th 5YP (1976–1980)[a]
National income								
Official estimate	92	96	119		98	101	95	95[E]
Western estimates	70	67	84–90	94				
Industrial output								
Official estimates	101	103	117		102	101	97	93[E]
Western estimates	60–70	76–93	84–95	97				
Producer goods								
Official estimates	128	121	128		106	100	100	
Western estimates	72	97	97	94				
Consumer goods								
Official estimates	81	85	96		99	103	92	98[E]
Western estimates	46	68	81	94				
Agricultural production								
Official estimates	58	63–77	90		77	97		
Western estimates	50–52	66–78	76–79	80				
Labor productivity								
Official estimates	65		101					
Western estimates	36–42	86	81	85			96	
Retail trade								
Official estimates	39	54	86			106	96	91[E]
Western estimates				109				

Sources: N. Jasny, *Essays on the Soviet Economy* (New York: Praeger, 1962), p. 266; E. Zaleski, *Stalinist Planning for Economic Growth: 1933 to 1952* (Chapel Hill: University of North Carolina Press, 1980), p. 503; A. Nove, *An Economic History of the USSR* (London: Penguin, 1969), p. 353; Department of Commerce, *State Five Year Plan for the Development of the USSR National Economy for the Period 1971–1975*, JPRS 56970-1, Washington, D.C., September 1972, part 1, p. 65, part 2, pp. 356–358; D. Green et al., "An Evaluation of the 10th Five-Year Plan Using the SRI-WEFA Econometric Model of the Soviet Union," in Joint Economic Committee, *Soviet Economy in a New Perspective* (Washington, D.C.: U.S. Government Printing Office, 1976), p. 305; *Narodnoe khoziaistvo SSSR v 1979 g.* [The national economy of the USSR in 1979]. (Moscow: Statistika, 1980).

[a] E denotes estimated plan fulfillment.

(*Gosplan,* the ministries, regional and local authorities, the enterprises, and party officials) struggle, bargain, and cajole for resources. As this process remains behind the scenes and out of Soviet textbooks, the Western observer can only imagine its intensity.

Soviet material balancing is carried out largely independently of the theoretically powerful input-output approach to planning, which could provide an alternative for Soviet plan formulation. An examination of input-output planning facilitates understanding of present Soviet planning practices and will help us to assess future improvements in Soviet planning procedures.[11]

Conceptually, the basic problem of plan formulation is quite simple. In the Soviet case, the planner *(Gosplan)* receives plan directives from the Communist Party. At this level, plan objectives must be highly aggregated and require that the planner disaggregate them to an operational level. The planner might begin the task of plan formulation from a list of final demands for various products to be produced in various sectors of the economy. The planner must then prepare a plan relating inputs to outputs and bearing in mind two important considerations.

First, the plan must be *feasible,* that is, it must be capable of being achieved, given existing resource availabilities and the state of technology. Second, it would be desirable that the plan be *optimal.* Among all plan variants that are feasible, the *best* should be chosen. A plan that is best would be one that achieves the maximum level of output for a given input—or what amounts to the same thing, a minimum input for a given level of output. The maximum level of output is that which yields the greatest level of "satisfaction" to the political authorities of the USSR. The implication here is that a number of variants of the plan should be prepared and the best variant (as defined above) be chosen. Given the fact that the preparation of a plan for an economy the size of the USSR is a massive task, the application of mathematical techniques capable of computer manipulation has obvious appeal. Indeed, the basic planning problem as we have outlined it is the classic case of maximization under constraints, for which a large body of techniques is available. Let us turn to the input-output model, examining first the basic model, second its application to the Soviet case, and finally, the implications for future applications in Soviet planning procedures.

A basic input-output table such as Exhibit 3 is in essence a graphic presentation of the national accounts of an economic system, showing the interrelationships among the producing and the using sectors. The rows consist of producing sectors (in our simple example, industry, agriculture, and other sectors are shown) while the columns are consuming sectors. Each producing sector will generate output, some of which will be used as an *intermediate input* for the production of more output by that sector and by the other sectors. The remaining output will be used to satisfy the various components of final demand, such as consumption, exports, government, and so on. The table in Exhibit 3 is divided into four quadrants. The interindustry transactions quadrant (upper left), for example, shows the amount of industrial output that is needed to produce agricultural output (X_{12}), a relationship that can be expressed as a technical coefficient (a_{ij}).

Exhibit 3

Hypothetical input-output table

Columns:		1	2	3	4	5	6	7	8	9
	Input: Consuming sectors Outputs: Producing sectors	Industry	Agriculture	Other sectors	Total intermediate production	Consumption (C)	Exports	Government and defense (G)	Total final demand (D)	Total gross output (GO)
1	Industry	X_{11}	X_{12}	X_{13}	Σ_{X1j}	C_1	E_1	G_1	D_1	$D_1 + \Sigma_{X1j}$
2	Agriculture	X_{21}	X_{22}	X_{23}	Σ_{X2j}	C_2	E_2	G_2	D_2	$D_2 + \Sigma_{X2j}$
3	Other sectors	X_{31}	X_{32}	X_{33}	Σ_{X3j}	C_3	E_3	G_3	D_3	$D_3 + \Sigma_{X3j}$
4	Total intermediate use	Σ_{Xi1}	Σ_{Xi2}	Σ_{Xi3}	$\Sigma\Sigma_{Xij}$	ΣC	ΣE	ΣG	$D_1 + D_2 + D_3$	
5	Labor	L_1	L_2	L_3	ΣL_j	L_C	L_E	L_G	ΣL	
6	Capital	K_1	K_2	K_3	ΣK_j	K_C	K_E	K_G	ΣK	
7	Land	LA_1	LA_2	LA_3	ΣLA_j	LA_C	LA_E	LA_G	ΣLA	
8	Total inputs	I_1	I_2	I_3	ΣI_j	I'_C	I'_E	I'_G	$\Sigma I'$	

Notes: $D_i = C_i + E_i + G_i$; $I_j = L_j + K_j + LA_j$; $I'_C = L_C + K_C + LA_C$ etc.

The technical coefficients are computed as follows:

$$a_{ij} = \frac{X_{ij}}{X_j}$$

where a_{ij} = the amount of commodity i required to produce one unit of commodity j

X_{ij} = the amount of good i actually used by industry j

X_j = the gross output of industry j

Such a coefficient can be computed for each cell of this quadrant and indicates the amount of item i that is needed to produce one unit of j. This technical relationship is crucial in the development of a plan, a point to which we return shortly.

The final use quadrant (upper right of Exhibit 3) shows the distribution of production to final use, while the value-added quadrant (lower left) shows the contribution of the primary inputs (land, labor, and capital) to output. Finally, the direct factor purchase quadrant (lower right) shows the distribution of primary inputs to final users.

The matrix of technical coefficients is derived from the interindustry transactions quadrant and provides the planner with crucial information, namely, how much intermediate input is necessary to produce a unit of a particular output. The use of the input-output model is limited (unless the I-0 table is recomputed regularly) insofar as it assumes constancy of these coefficients. Thus, it is assumed that the production function underlying the relationship exhibits constant returns to scale and is without factor substitution. Although such assumptions may seem unduly restrictive, there has been considerable support for the use of this method of planning, at least in the short run. Let us return to the Soviet case, illustrating how a feasible plan could be formulated using the input-output approach.

Assuming that Soviet planners have a matrix of technical coefficients (A) derived from past performance, the plan process would begin with the specification by the planner of the final demands (Y) to be produced in the forthcoming plan year. The next step, matrix inversion, provides the planner with a list of gross outputs of each sector (X) that will, if produced, satisfy the planners demand for final output* The power of this model lies in the fact that within reason, even for

---

*If the matrix of technical coefficients is known, and the input-output table is entirely in physical units, then the consistency of a set of control figures can be checked almost immediately by using the formula $(I - A)X = Y$, where X is the proposed vector of control figures (in gross output terms), A is the familiar Leontief matrix of technical coefficients, I is the identity matrix, and Y is the vector of final outputs. An inconsistency in the proposed control figures would be indicated by a negative Y element, or by a Y element that is unacceptably small in light of planned investment, consumption, and exports. Thus, the internal consistency of alternative vectors of control figures could be readily determined simply by matrix multiplication.

If, on the other hand, Soviet planners desired to compute the vector of gross outputs (X) required to produce a proposed vector of final output targets (Y), then the following formula can be used: $(I - A)^{-1}Y = X$, where $(I - A)^{-1}$ is the inverse of $(I - A)$ and X is the set of required gross outputs. The feasibility of producing Y would be determined by considering the primary factor requirements (such as labor, capital, etc.) of the various programs relative to their availabilities.

an economy disaggregated into a considerable number of producing and using sectors, the computation of sectoral outputs can be computerized. Furthermore, the matrix inversion process takes into account both initial *and* second round effects (something material balancing cannot do), a feature crucial to the development of a balanced plan.

If the planner decides to increase the output of steel, obviously it will be necessary to increase the output of electricity, since electricity is used in the production of steel. However, when the output of electricity is increased, more inputs used in the generation of electricity will be needed, and so on. The process of matrix inversion is powerful in the sense that it can take into account all these "second round" effects and, with the aid of a computer, permit the rapid calculation of a number of feasible plan variants. It is in this capability that the real power of the input-output method lies. The process of adjustment to changing outputs can be captured and the feasibility of numerous variants checked. If adjustments are necessary, the alternatives can be calculated quickly. The process of plan formulation is iterative or sequential. The input-output approach facilitates the rapid execution of a complicated iterative process.

If the input-output approach were the theoretical basis of material balance planning, it would provide a powerful basis for plan formulation. Why is it not, then, the basis of Soviet planning practice? There are a number of basic problems with the input-output approach, all of which have tended to limit its practical application in the Soviet case.[12]

First, there has always been an element of ideological bias against such methods, a bias that was particularly strong during the Stalin era but that has slackened in recent years. In the early years, when economic laws and the notion of balance and equilibrium were rejected, one can understand official distrust of input-output procedures. Furthermore, the input-output framework as we have outlined it suggests that land and capital are scarce factors, for which scarcity prices exist.* This thinking is (or was) contrary to the labor theory of value.

---

*If the matrix B represents a matrix of primary resource coefficients, where b_{kj} represents the amount of the kth primary factor (land, labor, capital, etc.) required to produce one unit of output of commodity j, then

$$B(I-A)^{-1}=T$$

is the matrix of full primary resource coefficients. Each element of T (t_{kj}) indicates the amount of primary factor k required *both directly and indirectly* to produce one unit of commodity j. The price of j would, therefore, be computed by multiplying the p_k by the t_{kj}, where p_k is the price of the kth primary factor; and summing over the k's (assuming n primary factors) yields

$$p_j = \sum_{k=1}^{n} p_k t_{kj}$$

The "optimality" problem could be solved by determining all the Y vectors that meet the following condition:

$$TY=Z$$

where Z is the vector of primary resource availabilities. These Y vectors would represent a "production possibilities schedule" from which the *optimal* vector could be chosen as defined by the planners' objective function.

Second, the present Soviet system of data gathering does not adapt itself well to input-output technology. Data are gathered on an administrative basis rather than on the product basis required to compute input-output tables. Material balances are prepared on an industrial branch basis and result in concrete plans for the various industrial ministries. Yet these ministries tend to produce internally a broad range of products (steel, machinery, and consumer goods in one ministry, for example) that should show up in different commodity categories in an input-output table. A far more serious data problem is the generally poor and unreliable data base underlying both the construction of input-output balances and industrial planning. This tends to result in what one Soviet economist has termed "natural calamities"[13] when the technological coefficients are actually estimated.

Third, it has proved difficult to compute complete input-output tables in physical terms. As one might expect, certain products are heterogeneous and must be aggregated in value terms. This leads to further problems. Because of the distortive impact of the turnover tax (different users pay different prices), it is difficult to convert from the value figures (for example, rubles of steel) to the physical figures (for example, tons of steel) of primary concern to supply planners. Also, the computed input-output tables reflect in value terms the existing non-scarcity industrial prices and are therefore of dubious value.

Fourth, material balance planners have traditionally derived balances for between 300 and 2000 materials. At the distribution stage, they have planned about 10 times the higher figure. Yet the Central Statistical Agency's 1959 national input-output table was a 73 by 73 matrix, and the 1966 and 1972 tables were 110 by 110.[14] Work has been done on a 600-branch national table by the Academy of Sciences (Siberian branch).[15] Input-output tables of much larger dimensions would have to be developed to preserve the current level of disaggregation of the material balance system. Given the current data-gathering capacity and computational sophistication of the Soviet Union, this would probably prove to be too complicated a task. Thus, the input-output tables used for planning would have to be at a higher level of aggregation than the material balance and industrial supply system. This aggregation would be done in value terms, and the technical coefficients would be weighted averages of disaggregated coefficients. To be useful for Soviet planning purposes, some method of meaningful disaggregation would have to be devised, which is an extremely thorny problem.

AN EVALUATION OF MATERIAL BALANCE PLANNING

The input-output approach is a powerful theoretical base for material balance planning. However, for a number of important reasons that we have discussed, planning practice is really material balance planning. What are the strengths and weaknesses of the material balance approach? On the positive side, by placing severe pressure on enterprises in the form of taut targets designed to strain enterprise capacity, Soviet supply planning has brought about rapid growth of industrial output in selected priority sectors and has presided over the vast and rapid transformation of the Soviet economy. Thus, the major strength of Soviet planning seems to be its ability to direct resources into areas selected by planners with more speed and force than can a market-directed economy. An example is the ability of Soviet planners to direct resources to the military effort.

The material balance system works in an indirect sense to equate supply and demand within the priority system. That is, although taut output targets often exceed enterprise capacities and create supply shortages, ultimately the administration can equate supplies and demands by directing available resources into higher-priority enterprises. The Soviets themselves stress this very point: their planning system is seen to replace the "anarchy of the market" by rational direction of resources into socially necessary ends.[16] In fact, Soviet planners recognized from the very outset of the industrialization drive that taut planning would result in severe strains and pressures on the economy, but they considered the risks well worth taking. Taut (*naprazhennye*) plans continue to be demanded by the Soviet leadership and remain a basic fact of industrial planning up to the present. For example, *Gosplan* was directed by the Central Committee of the CPSU to undertake three separate revisions of the ninth Five Year Plan (1971–1975) so as to uncover further "hidden reserves" of the economy—a euphemism for increasing the tautness of the plan. As growth has continued to decline in the 1980s, *Gosplan* continues to be pressured into finding further "hidden reserves."

One reason for taut planning was its role in helping to maintain plan discipline. As has been pointed out by Western students of Soviet planning,[17] the greater the degree of slack in the economy, the greater the flexibility exercised by managers at the local level and the greater the likelihood that production may stray from strict adherence to the priority system. In other words, taut planning is required to enable central authorities to maintain strict control over the economy.

Second, arguments can be made for Soviet-style taut industrial planning on other grounds, using the theories of Western development economics. The argument here is that by setting taut (often unattainable) targets rather than setting moderate targets that avoid bottlenecks, enterprises will be forced to expand to the limits of their production possibilities and the economy will be pulled up to higher production levels in the process. This pressure, combined with an appropriate degree of administrative flexibility, could lead to more rapid economic development than would have occurred under more "rational" balanced planning. In the language of Soviet planning, the plan should serve not to balance resources but to "mobilize" the economy.[18]

On the negative side, it is also recognized that excesses result from the Soviet material balance system.[19] First, the pressured Soviet system often forces Soviet managers to engage in dysfunctional forms of behavior. Faced with over-ambitious targets and lacking flexible access to supplies, managers have frequently engaged in excessive stockpiling. They strive to build up emergency stocks as "safety factors," which they can use for future plan fulfillment or for trading, by overstating input requirements to their immediate superiors. As a result of such actions, which are often required to make the system work, the economy loses on two counts: scarce materials tend to stand idle (resources are wasted) and planners receive inaccurate information. On another score, the over-taut planning system has created a definite sellers' market, which has meant that managers can generally unload their output irrespective of its quality and design. This feature has been an important source of the quality problems so widely noted in the Soviet press.

A second weakness of Soviet planning is that as long as the consumer sector is used as a buffer, personal incentives and productivity suffer, and productivity increases are most important as the major source of growth as the economy becomes more mature. The Soviets have relied heavily on using material incentives to promote labor productivity, but if consumer goods are not available in the desired quantities and qualities (because they have been sacrificed for heavy industry), the incentive system will be less effective.

As we argued earlier, it is apparent that the consumer sector was a buffer for plan imbalances during the Stalin years. To what extent this is still the case is a difficult question to answer. Although consumption grew at very respectable rates during the 1950s and 1960s, this growth slipped steadily in the 1970s and 1980s, and the share of consumption in gross national product declined steadily in the past 20 years. Thus, while there was substantial rhetoric in the 1970s about the need to expand consumer goods output, the attention paid to quality, imports, better food products, and so on, may not have kept pace with the growing expectations of the average Soviet citizen.

Third, material balance planning is quite cumbersome and slow. Enterprises invariably get their finalized targets well into the operating year (often as late as March) and must work without clear knowledge of what their targets actually are. When the targets are received, enterprises often desperately attempt to meet production targets at the end of each period by engaging in what the Soviets called *Shturmovshchina*—"storming"—a fairly inefficient method of scheduling production. Informal methods have been developed to get around this problem. One, the "correction principle," involves the use of advance estimates at each stage of the planning process prior to receipt of the information on the current production targets. Another device is the "advance fund allotment," which gives enterprises about one-quarter of the previous period's input allotments to tide them over until the final plan is received. A further device used by the ministries is "reserving," whereby ministries reserve a portion of enterprise material allotments to aid in combatting bottlenecks.[20] With the tendency toward planning delays and the use of informal methods, Soviet administrators have found that planning is less of a problem when targets change only marginally from year to year. Thus, there is a built-in tendency in the Soviet planning system to avoid dramatic change. Soviet planning, as the emigré economist Igor Birman has emphasized, is based on the "achieved level."[21] Because of planning complexity, *Gosplan* must begin its projections with the output levels achieved in the past. It then adds on a growth factor (often arbitrarily) to determine current planned output levels. There is no opportunity to consider whether the "achieved level" from which planning begins is the appropriate level. At the enterprise level, the manager is reluctant to introduce new technologies that require a restructuring of established supply channels. In general, the introduction of new technology and of new ways of doing things are retarded by the material balance system.[22]

Fourth, the Soviet planning system, with its stress on output goals, generates dysfunctional behavior at various planning levels. The enterprise will pursue output targets even if they lead to clearly irrational results.[23] The ministry tends to be primarily concerned with the success of enterprises under its own control and places the input needs of its own enterprises over those of enterprises outside its control. The planning system does not foster concern for the environment, because enterprise managers are judged on the basis of output target fulfillment, not on the basis of environmental protection or conservation of natural resources. Also, the uncertainties of the material supply system have caused enterprises to adopt peculiar production patterns. Soviet enterprises have been known to integrate vertically as many operations as possible to provide their own material inputs—it is not rare in the Soviet Union for machinery-producing enterprises to fabricate their own steel.[24] Thus, vital specialization of production is limited by the planning system.

A fifth criticism of central economic planning is the notion that it requires a very large bureaucracy to generate and implement the plan. The theme of a rapidly growing cadre of administrative personnel is a subject of continuing complaint in the Soviet press.[25] At the same time, Western evidence, and indeed Soviet official statistics, do not support the view that the administrative apparatus is especially large. A study by Gur Ofer, attempting to assess the size of the Soviet service sector, comes to the conclusion that the size of the administrative aparatus is smaller than one would expect, based upon the evidence of development patterns in other countries.[26] Ofer's results have been challenged, but they suggest at a minimum that fears of a cancerous growth of the Soviet bureaucracy have not been upheld.

Finally, one can evaluate Soviet material balance planning in terms of its *consistency* and *optimality*. A consistent plan is one in which supplies and demands of funded commodities are equal. Consistency is one of the main objectives of the Soviet material balance system. From the point of view of Soviet planners, consistency is a desirable goal: if the plan were highly inconsistent, plan fulfillment would become a competitive struggle for deficit inputs that the planner would have difficulty in controlling, even with the priority system. Instead, connections, prestige, and ability to maneuver (already important factors in plan fulfillment) would primarily determine who would be able to fulfill the target— a definitely undesirable situation in a controlled economy.

On the other hand, *optimality* should also be a desirable goal in a planned economy. To illustrate the concept of optimality, consider a situation where five different sets of control figures are consistent. From the point of view of the state, it would be desirable to be able to choose the "best," or optimal, figures; to do otherwise would be to misallocate scarce resources.* This kind of choice is currently beyond the reach of Soviet planners, however, because the Soviet material balance system works so slowly that planners are fortunate if they approxi-

---

*The optimal set of control figures could be defined in technical terms as the one that yields the maximum value of all consistent sets when entered into the planners' objective function, that is, the consistent set of control figures that the planners regard as the "best" in terms of their preferences and biases.

mate just one consistent plan variant in the allotted planning period. Current Soviet balancing techniques, time, and manpower are inadequate to find several consistent plan variants from which to choose the optimal one, and the Soviet's disregard of the importance of optimality is a major weakness of material balance planning.[27]

IS THE SOVIET ECONOMY A "PLANNED" ECONOMY?

Both formal and informal aspects of the Soviet planning system result in a good deal of both unplanned and uncontrolled activity. Indeed, one long-time observer of the Soviet economy, Eugene Zaleski, argues that the Soviet economy might better be described as a centrally *managed* rather than a centrally planned economy.[28] By this, Zaleski means that the construction of the plan is only the first step in the resource allocation process. The decisions made during the implementation stage are just as important. Moreover, much economic activity remains out of the purview of planners and is controlled by local officials, enterprises, and even private markets. The extent of economic activity not controlled by planners has caused observers to question whether the Soviet economy is "planned" after all.[29]

The discussion about whether the Soviet economy is "planned" or not has led to the search for fixed reference points in Soviet planning. If enterprises are able to bargain easily for adjustments in plan targets or manipulate their own plans, and if long-run plans are continuously violated by the annual plans, are there indeed operational plans in the Soviet economy that are binding on their recipients? Moreover, if enterprises are punished for good plan performance by being given even more difficult plan targets in the next period, will not enterprises react counterproductively by holding plan fulfillment below potential? A "ratchet effect" exists when planners make current plan targets dependent upon last year's plan overfulfillment (and thus discourage plan overfulfillment). The evidence (to be discussed in the next chapter) is overwhelming that enterprise plans are not firm and that Soviet enterprises are subject to a ratchet effect.

David Granick has advanced the proposition that ministerial output plans are firm binding plans, and, in this sense, Granick argues that the Soviet economy does operate ultimately on the basis of economic plans.[30] Moreover, Granick maintains that Soviet planners do not subject the ministries to the ratchet effect because of its known counterproductive long-run effects on economic performance. Granick notes that if plans are not firm, in the sense that plans depend upon the actual performance of the planned agent, agents will manipulate their performance to change the plan to better suit the agent's interests. With changing plans that depend on ongoing performance, the agent will engage in a gaming exercise to elicit more favorable plans from his principal. This gaming can take place with reference to the current period, and it can also take place with reference to future periods if next period's plan is dependent upon this year's performance (the ratchet effect).

As Granick notes, it is an empirical issue whether Soviet planners assign firm plans to ministries. This empirical issue is not easy to clarify because of the difficulty of relating actual plan fulfillment by the appropriate economic organizations to their original plan targets. Soviet economic data do not make this an easy comparison. Granick's own empirical analysis covering Soviet data for 1966–1977 suggests that Soviet ministries do tend to fulfill the plans assigned to them by superior planning organizations and that the next period's plan is not affected by ministry plan fulfillment in the current period. Granick's conclusion is supported by the empirical research for the same time period of Alice Gorlin and David Doane, who find that Soviet ministerial plans are firm and that the ministries do indeed succeed in fulfilling these firm plans.[31] Moreover, differences among ministries in plan fulfillment appear to be random and not systematically related to any explanatory factors. As in the case of many empirical issues, contrary evidence has been brought forth. Michael Keren maintains, using alternate econometric methods, that Soviet data reveal that ministerial plan targets are indeed affected by ministerial plan fulfillment during the previous plan period. Keren also presents theoretical arguments as to why Soviet planners might be willing to base current plan targets on previous plan fulfillment, especially if they have a short time horizon.[32] Presumably, further study of this issue will eventually resolve the controversy over the firmness of ministry plans, but it does appear that, relatively speaking, ministry plans are much firmer than enterprise plans. Enterprise plans and the ratchet effect will be discussed again in the next chapter.

MONEY IN THE SOVIET ECONOMY

In market economic systems, money plays a crucial role in coordinating the activities of enterprises, households, and the government.[33] Our discussion of Soviet planning has, thus far, focused on input and output determination in physical terms. We turn now to an examination of the financial side of Soviet planning. In a basic sense, money in the Soviet economy plays a role similar to that in other systems, namely, as a store of value, a medium of exchange, and a unit of account. There is, however, a very basic difference between the role of money in the Soviet economy and its role in market economic systems. Money is assumed to influence real economic activity in the market system; monetary policy influences real economic events through interest rates, unanticipated inflation, and changes in relative prices. In the case of the Soviet economy, no connection between monetary and real phenomena is argued, and money plays a *passive* role in the execution of economic activity. Thus, money should not be a factor that either encourages or inhibits the economic activity of enterprises.

The present-day Soviet monetary system derives in large part from the credit reforms of 1930–1932 and subsequent modifications, especially in 1947. In the Soviet economy, there are three basic economic units—the enterprise, the state, and the household. Although enterprises are owned by the state, they are nevertheless separate entities, the accounts of which are kept in value terms, under the *khozraschet* (economic accounting) system.

There are two monetary channels in the Soviet economy—the enterprise and the household. Money in both channels arises from the provision of credit and cash to enterprises through the state bank. Credit and cash accounts are closely controlled through a credit plan that provides for the financing of capital investment in the case of the enterprise and for the payment of other expenses—notably, the wages of labor. Both flows are closely monitored, although the rules for each flow differ. In general, however, state-granted and state-controlled credit provides the means for financing enterprise activity. That activity, in turn, provides revenue for the state budget through profits taxes, where, under strict state control, redistribution can take place. Thus, in the Marxian schema, surplus value is redistributed by the state.

THE ENTERPRISE PLAN AND FINANCIAL CONTROLS

Let us now turn to the financial side of enterprise planning. The enterprise *techpromfinplan* (technical-industrial-financial plan) includes, as its name suggests, a pervasive financial plan as well as physical input and output indicators. This financial plan parallels the physical section of the industrial supply and output plans and acts as a check on enterprise performance. The financial plan consists of a wage bill, planned cost reductions, and credit plans for purchasing inputs, along with many other targets. The amount of detail contained in the financial plan has varied over the years, but financial targets continue to serve as the monetary counterparts of enterprise output and input targets.

Soviet managers have tended to regard the fulfillment of financial plans (cost reduction targets, wage bills, credit plans, etc.) as less important than output plans and have tended to sacrifice the former as a result. Despite this, financial targets have remained important to the planners because they serve to enhance the planners' control over enterprise operations. In the Soviet terminology, this is called *ruble control (kontrol' rublem),* a system that works as follows: Because the financial plan is the monetary counterpart of a firm's input and output plans, deviations from the financial plan signal deviations from the physical plan. If a firm's labor input plan calls for the employment of 500 workers, the enterprise can draw only enough cash from its bank account to pay that number. If the input plan calls for 10 tons of steel, the enterprise can draw upon its funded input account only enough for that particular transaction, nothing in excess. If the firm is in need of working capital, short-term credit will be granted only if the transaction is called for in the plan. Reinforcing the system of ruble control is the fact that all (legal) interfirm transactions are handled by *Gosbank* (the State Bank), which supervises all such transactions and is the sole center for the settling of accounts.[34]

The Soviet manager, in response to this system of financial supervision, has developed informal sources of supply that do not require bank clearing operations and other informal devices to circumvent many financial controls.[35] Also, successful firms are often not strictly held to their financial plans. Financial controls are used primarily to detect significant deviations from planned activities, and desired corrections are normally made administratively. However, in recent years, state control over funds for wages has become very strict. The wage fund is, in many instances, a binding constraint. Despite the flexibility and circumventions of financial controls, ruble control remains an important monitoring device in the Soviet planning system.

PUBLIC FINANCE AND FINANCIAL PLANNING
IN THE SOVIET UNION

The major allocation decisions in the Soviet Union are reflected in the annual budget of the USSR, which determines the allocation of total output by end use among private consumption, investment, public consumption, defense, and administration. The annual budget of the USSR is a consolidated budget, which encompasses the all-union budget, the state budgets of the republics, and the local budgets of provinces, regions, and districts.[36] It is a much more comprehensive system of accounts than the budget of the United States, which encompasses only federal receipts and expenditures.

As one might expect, a much larger portion of the Soviet GNP flows through its state budget than is the case with the American GNP. Between 1929 and the present, 10 to 30 percent of American GNP has been channeled through government budgets (including state and local government). In the Soviet Union, the cumulative average for the postwar period has been about 45 percent.[37] The relatively greater importance of the state budget in the Soviet economy derives from the financing of most investment directly from the state budget and because communal consumption (public health, education, and welfare) represents a larger share of total consumption in the Soviet Union. Thus, the scope of public goods is broader in the USSR than in the United States. In a sense, one could argue that all products produced by the Soviet economy are public because they are produced by state or collective enterprises. However, in dealing with the Soviet economy, the convention is that if the enterprise operates on its own accounting system, independently of the state budget, it is not considered a public enterprise.

The budget of the USSR directs resources into consumption, investment, defense, and administration in the following manner: The state collects revenues from sales taxes (the so-called turnover tax), deductions from enterprise profits, direct taxes on the population, and social insurance contributions (see Table 22). The first two alone have consistently accounted for over 60 percent of total revenues throughout most of the plan period. These revenues are then directed through the national budget, the republican budgets, and through provincial and local budgets to various uses: to finance investment in the form of grants, which at various times has accounted for between 33 and 64 percent of total expenditures (the "national economy" category in Table 22); to finance communal consumption ("social and cultural undertakings"), which has accounted for from 14 to 36 percent of the total; and to finance defense and administration.

Once the overall allocation of budget resources into nonprivate consumption uses (investment, communal consumption, defense, and administration) is made and the physical outputs of consumer goods are specified by *Gosplan,* financial authorities (the State Bank and the Ministry of Finance) must ensure that a macroequilibrium of supply and demand exists.

The objective of Soviet financial planning at the macro level is to balance the aggregate money demand for consumer goods with the aggregate supply at established prices. This is done centrally, because planning authorities must ensure the compatibility of the output of consumer goods at established prices with employment levels and wage rates. The smaller the planned output of

Table 22   THE BUDGET OF THE USSR, 1931–1984 (SELECTED YEARS)

	1931	1934	1937	1940	1950	1960	1970	1978	1984
Receipts (percent of total)									
Turnover tax	46	64	69	59	56	41	32	32	30
Deductions from profits	8	5	9	12	10	24	35	30	30
Social insurance	9	10	6	5	5	5	5	5	7
Taxes on population	4	7	4	5	9	7	8	8	8
Other revenue	33	14	12	19	20	23	20	25	25
Expenditures (percent of total)									
National economy	64	56	41	33	38	47	48	54	56
Social and cultural undertakings	14	15	24	24	28	34	36	34	33
Defense	5	9	17	33	20	13	12	7	5
Administration and justice	4	4	4	4	3	2	1	1	1
Other expenditures	13	16	14	6	11	4	3	4	5

Sources: Narodnoe khoziaistvo SSSR v 1970 g. [The national economy of the USSR in 1970] (Moscow: Statistika, 1971), p. 731; M. V. Condoide, *The Soviet Financial System* (Columbus: Bureau of Business Research of Ohio State University, 1951), pp. 84–87; *Narodnoe khoziaistvo SSSR v 1978 g.* [The national economy of the USSR in 1978] (Moscow: Statistika, 1979), p. 534; *SSSR v tsifrakh v 1984 godu* [USSR in figures in 1984] (Moscow: Finansyi Statistika, 1985), pp. 50–51. As will be explained in a later chapter, the defense share is grossly understated by Soviet budget figures.

consumer goods and the larger the number employed and the higher the wages, the more likely that aggregate money demand will exceed available supply at established prices.

An algebraic example illustrates this relationship. This example is the same as the consumer goods balance given above, but now broken down into consumer and producer goods.[38] Assume that the output plan calls for enterprises to produce Q_1 "units" of consumer goods and Q_2 "units" of producer goods. The planners determine, through the use of labor input coefficients, that L_1 man-years of labor are required to produce Q_1 and that L_2 man-years are required to produce Q_2, and these employment levels are accordingly targeted by *Gosplan*. The workers are paid the prevailing wage rates in the consumer and producer goods sectors, respectively, and average annual wages are denoted in the two sectors as W_1 and W_2, respectively. In this manner, an annual wage income of $W_1L_1 + W_2L_2$ from public sector employment is created.

The total demand for consumer goods, therefore, is that portion of total income that is not taxed away or saved. If personal taxes are denoted by T and personal savings by R, the total money demand (D) for consumer goods is

$$D = W_1L_1 + W_2L_2 + O - T - R$$

where O denotes other earnings (from interest or private economy earnings). The total supply of consumer goods at established prices (S) is the total value of all consumer goods (denoted as P_1Q_1):

$$S = P_1Q_1$$

where P_1 denotes the existing consumer price level.

The task of the financial authorities is to strike an appropriate balance

between consumer demand and supply at prevailing prices, that is, between
$W_1L_1 + W_2L_2 + O - T - R$ and P_1Q_1.

BALANCING CONSUMER DEMAND: A HISTORICAL EXAMPLE*

We illustrate the various balancing techniques used by Soviet planners by review-
ing their handling of the inflationary pressures of the 1930s. The setting was as
follows: The industrialization drive of the early 1930s had created severe inflationary pressures on both the supply and demand sides of the consumer market. On
the supply side, the structure of the economy had shifted drastically during this
period in favor of producer goods and away from consumer goods, and the output
of consumer goods had declined in real terms.[39] At the same time, Soviet planners
were practicing "overfull" employment planning by confronting enterprises with
output goals that were obviously unattainable with the targeted enterprise labor
force. This forced enterprise managers to compete vigorously among themselves
for labor, and average wages were bid up in the process. Although wage rates were
centrally determined, managers could still offer higher wages by upward reclas-
sification of workers and by setting low piece rate norms.[40]

The rising industrial wages were only one inflationary force driving up the
demand for consumer goods. Labor was also being drawn at rapid rates out of
agriculture into higher-paying industrial jobs, thereby raising average wages for
the entire economy as well—a further inflationary factor on the demand side.[41]
Another complication was the rapid expansion of the full-time labor force, due
mainly to the rising participation rates of women and to the decline in part-time
agricultural employment. Thus, while the supply of consumer goods was declining, both average wages and employment were rising, generating substantial
increases in money incomes. An indication of the scope of the rise in money wages
was the increase in currency in circulation (used almost exclusively for wage
payments) from 3 billion rubles in 1930 to about 16 billion rubles in 1940.[42] The
inflationary implications of these trends are obvious.

As the algebraic example shows, several methods could have been used to
deal with the growing inflationary problem.[43] One obvious approach would have
been a wage freeze (the W's in the equation) enforced by strict limitations on
enterprise wage funds. On the other hand, flexible wages were required to attract
labor into high-priority sectors and to maintain incentives. The figures[41] on industrial wage increases during the 1930s show clearly that this approach was not
chosen. A second approach would have been to increase personal taxes (T),
thereby reducing personal disposable income; but high tax rates also would have
reduced labor incentives and retarded industrialization. Inflationary pressures
were so great during the early 1930s that tax rates perhaps as high as 60 percent
of personal income would have been required.

A third alternative would have been to encourage personal savings (R)—
a difficult feat during a period of rapid inflation. The Soviets did make government
bond purchases compulsory (as automatic payroll deductions) between 1930 and

*This section can be skipped without loss of continuity.

1957, a policy that did create some resentment and tended to reduce work incentives. The Soviets also established a network of savings banks in an attempt to encourage voluntary savings.[44]

A fourth method for balancing supply and demand would be to raise consumer retail prices (P_1) to soak up the excess consumer demand, and this is exactly what the Soviets did in large measure. The *turnover tax* was the formal device used. The turnover tax was a differentiated sales tax levied primarily on consumer products and will be discussed in detail in the section on prices. As the state determined retail prices, excess demand for a commodity could be eliminated quite simply by raising the turnover tax and hence the retail price. The extent to which this method was used can be seen from the much more rapid increase of retail prices between 1928 and 1937 than average costs of production, as measured by material costs (wholesale prices of industrial commodities) and wage costs. For example, wholesale prices of basic industrial commodities increased 75 percent. Average industrial wages increased 430 percent, but retail prices of consumer goods rose 700 percent between 1928 and 1937. These differential rates illustrate the increasing role of the turnover tax, which averaged 22 percent of the retail price in 1928–1929 and 64 percent in 1935.[45] For example, in 1934, the state sold rye for 84 rubles per centner, of which 66 rubles were turnover tax, and wheat for 104 rubles per centner, of which 89 rubles were turnover tax.[46]

Thus, inflation via increased indirect taxation was used to soak up excess consumer demand during the 1930s. A prominent authority on Soviet taxation, Franklyn Holzman, postulates that Soviet tax authorities preferred indirect commodity taxes (the turnover tax) over direct income taxes because the former would have less of a disincentive effect on workers. It was hoped that industrial workers would pay more attention to increases in their money wages than to the reduction in their real wages, which resulted as retail prices rose faster than money wages (the so-called money illusion), and that incentives would be maintained. In addition, the turnover tax was administratively easier to collect and administer than direct taxation in a populous, semiliterate agricultural country.[47] To this day, the turnover tax remains an important source of government revenue in the Soviet Union.

The final balancing method employed heavily by the Soviets in the 1930s was *repressed inflation.* What this means is that Soviet authorities simply allowed some of the excess consumer demand to persist. Despite rapidly rising retail prices during the 1930s, consumer demand still exceeded supply. Soviet authorities were therefore called upon to ration consumer goods either formally or indirectly during most of the 1930s. Such rationing proved necessary because Soviet financial authorities found it difficult to keep prices high enough to eliminate inflationary pressures in the face of the numerous unplanned wage increases and shortfalls in plan fulfillment in the consumer sector.

Rationing of essential consumer goods was introduced in the winter of 1928–1929, first on foodstuffs and then on manufactured consumer goods.[48] To maintain labor incentives, to preserve the effectiveness of wage differentials, and to reward special groups, Soviet pricing authorities sanctioned a complex system of multiple prices during the early 1930s.[49] They consisted of (1) retail prices of rationed goods sold in state and cooperative stores ("normal fund" prices); (2) the so-called prices of the "commercial fund," which were higher than the "normal fund" prices (yet even these were often available only in "closed shops," open only to special groups); (3) *Torgsin* shop prices of items which could only be bought with precious metals and foreign currency; (4) free-market prices (primarily on the collective-farm markets); and (5) several other prices, including inflated black-market prices.[50] The collective-farm markets where peasants could sell their private produce were especially useful in siphoning off the excess purchasing power of industrial workers and in preserving industrial incentives, for extra earned income could be used to buy scarce food products in these markets.

While prices in state and cooperative stores doubled between 1928 and 1932, collective-farm market prices, the only free-market prices in the Soviet Union, rose 30 times, a clear indication of the extent of repressed inflation during this period.* After 1932, this differential was reduced and nearly closed in 1937, but it was opened again by the outbreak of World War II. Because of the complex multiple price system, it is difficult to gauge trends in the general price level during the 1930s. What is known for sure, however, is that retail prices rose substantially, but not by enough to eliminate the excess consumer demand entirely—as is witnessed by the long queues and the multiple prices of the 1930s.

SOVIET PLANNING FOR INFLATION

Although inflationary pressures were high during the industrialization drive of the 1930s and the war years of the 1940s, inflationary pressures have subsided in the postwar era. The Soviet history of inflation is a chronological reverse of that of the capitalist West. In the 1930s, prices were generally falling in the West at a time when inflation was high in the Soviet Union. In the West, the postwar era saw accelerating inflation from the mid-1960s on at the time when inflationary pressures were easing in the Soviet Union. From the official price statistics published by Soviet statistical authorities, it appears that overt inflation has been virtually eliminated in the postwar era. According to official indexes, Soviet retail prices declined substantially in the immediate postwar years. From 1965 to 1982 (the period of greatest price acceleration in the West), the official Soviet price index rose by only 8 percent.[51] We shall examine Soviet price statistics in this section, but first let us consider the means by which Soviet pricing and monetary authorities have reduced (or even eliminated) inflationary pressures.

First, wholesale price increases have either been very limited (such as in industry) or have not resulted in increases in retail prices (such as in agriculture). Over the 1965–1982 period, industrial wholesale prices rose only 15 percent, according to official statistics. In the case of agricultural products, where wholesale purchase prices have been raised to make farm production profitable, retail prices of these products have not been raised, the difference being absorbed by

*We define inflation as an upward trend in the price level; repressed inflation, as persistent excess demand at prevailing prices.

the state as a subsidy. In other instances, the turnover tax rate has been reduced, thus allowing wholesale prices to increase without commensurate increases at the retail level. The important exception is where the prices of what planners consider to be luxuries (for example, automobiles, coffee, tea, jewelry) have been raised sharply. In this pattern lies a basic element of Soviet price policy, namely, to attempt to keep the prices of "necessities" stable, while increasing the prices of "luxuries" sufficiently to absorb excess purchasing power.

As the money balance equation shows, fundamental inflationary pressures are determined by the relationship between money income and the output of consumer goods. Although the average monthly money wage has grown steadily since the 1950s, so, too, has the output of consumer goods and services. Average annual wages increased by 90 percent between 1965 and 1982, while the real output of consumer goods increased by about 83 percent. In the postwar years, planners have been better able to control inflationary forces than was the case in the 1930s. Methods of control used by *Gosbank* have improved, and the use of overfull employment planning may have lessened. No longer can enterprises draw excess funds for wage payments from their *Gosbank* accounts, and state control over wage payments has increased. The upshot of these changes is that average annual wage increases have been held to modest rates (by Western standards) throughout the postwar era. Wage inflation, a major source of inflationary pressure in the 1930s, has been kept under control in the postwar years.

The picture presented thus far seems to support the view that inflation has not been a serious problem in the postwar Soviet experience. However, this interpretation is subject to challenge. What is the evidence that there may, in fact, be a problem with inflation in the Soviet economy?

First, it has been pointed out that lack of detailed knowledge about Soviet price indices, along with the traditional problems with such measures, could lead one to question the validity of the official retail price index as an accurate measure of retail prices.[52] However, an alternative retail price index computed by Gertrude Schroeder and Barbara Severin, while showing generally declining retail prices in the 1950s and 1960s, suggests only modest growth of retail prices in the 1970s —at an average annual rate of approximately 1.5 percent.[53] Western recalculations of Soviet industrial price indices reveal that, although they are understated, the actual inflation rate was in the range of 1.5 to 2.25 percent per annum for the period 1960–1975. These recalculations seem to point to the conclusion that although the official Soviet retail price indexes are biased on the downward side, the extent of inflation has been quite limited. The above recalculations refer to indexes of inflation in official markets. Western research (to be discussed later in this chapter) has revealed that a significant volume of consumer transactions takes place in the unofficial second economy. Insofar as there are no published indexes of second-economy prices, we have no way of knowing the rate at which second-economy retail prices are rising. Theoretically speaking, if official prices do not rise sufficiently to choke off repressed inflation, purchasing power can spill over into the second economy and cause second-economy prices to rise much more rapidly than official prices. Recent emigrés from the Soviet Union, for example, when asked to estimate their personal rate of inflation for the goods they generally bought between 1973 and 1979, reported a perceived annual inflation rate of around 5 percent.* It should be emphasized that these are perceived inflation rates and not necessarily actual inflation rates, but they are consistent with the proposition that second-economy prices have been rising more rapidly than official prices.

The actual rates of inflation experienced in retail and wholesale markets in the Soviet Union in recent years will likely never be known with any precision. The evidence, however, does suggest that prices have risen less rapidly in the Soviet Union than in the capitalist West. The main reason for the relatively slow inflation in the Soviet Union appears to be the control by Soviet authorities over wage inflation. By keeping wage increases close to productivity increases, Soviet authorities have been able to keep Soviet inflation well below inflation in the West. The relatively slow rate of growth of prices in the Soviet Union does not mean that inflation is not a problem. In fact, some authorities argue that the slow growth of prices has meant serious repressed inflation and that repressed inflation has had a serious negative impact on incentives and output.

There is no question about the magnitude of repressed inflation in the Soviet Union from the 1930s to the early 1950s. The question is the extent of repressed inflation in the Soviet Union from the mid-1960s to the present and the impact of repressed output on Soviet economic performance. The classic indicators of repressed inflation are queues for consumer goods, consumer complaints of short-ages of goods, prices rising more rapidly in uncontrolled markets (such as the collective-farm markets and the second economy) than in official markets, and rising savings that are the result of not having anything to buy. What has been the extent of repressed inflation in the Soviet Union since the mid-1960s?

The approach to answering this question has been the development and application to the Soviet case of a disequilibrium model of household behavior. This model, developed by R. J. Barro and H. I. Grossman, suggests that both labor supply responses and savings responses will be influenced by the availability of consumer goods. Thus, in a case of repressed inflation (excess demand), it is argued that an increase in the availability of consumer goods will lead to a decrease in savings and an increase in labor supplied.[54] This model, with modifica-tions, has been applied to the Soviet case by D. H. Howard.[55] Howard finds that the Barro–Grossman model fits the Soviet case quite well, thus supporting the view of a disequilibrium situation in which there is repressed inflation.[56] However, these results have been challenged by Barbara Katz and by Machiko Nissanke, who criticize the nature and the measurement of the variables examined and the econometric difficulties of applying the Barro–Grossman model to the Soviet case.[57] Also, it should be noted that the application of the disequilibrium approach to the East European case by Richard Portes and others does not lend support to the hypothesis of repressed inflation.[58] In view of the differences between the Soviet Union and Eastern Europe, one does not know whether these results can

*The data on Soviet emigré inflationary perceptions were gathered by the Soviet Interview Project, James Millar, director, funded by the National Council for Soviet and Eastern European Research. These results, based on interviews with 2793 emigrés, were reported by Paul Gregory in a State Department briefing, October 1984.

be applied to the USSR. Joyce Pickersgill finds that the savings behavior of Soviet households can be accounted for by rational consumer behavior and that the increase in household savings of the postwar era does not necessarily suggest repressed inflation.[59]

Econometric studies of the extent of repressed inflation (using disequilibrium models and analyzing saving behavior) yield uncertain results. They do not yield conclusive evidence that repressed inflation has been a serious problem in the Soviet Union in recent years. More direct emigré evidence, however, suggests that an overriding concern of individuals who lived in the Soviet Union in the 1970s was about the availability of goods. Goods shortages, queues, and the like definitely had a negative impact at least on people's perception of the quality of life in the Soviet Union, as judged by emigré experiences.[60]

Gregory Grossman and Igor Birman have investigated the growth of the USSR money supply (data on currency in circulation are not published) and suspect that monetary growth has been much more rapid than the growth of real output of consumer goods. Savings account data are published by the Soviets, and they do show substantial rises in household savings. From their investigations, Grossman and Birman believe that Soviet macroinflationary pressures may be greater that the average wage data cited above would cause us to expect.[61]

We would draw the following conclusion from the above evidence. We believe it is true that the growth of disposable income has been kept more in line with the growth of the real output of consumer goods in the Soviet Union in recent years. Thus, severe inflationary pressures in the sense of balance between aggregate demand and aggregate supply have been avoided. Official Soviet price indexes (and their recalculated versions) bear witness to this point. Such a macrobalance is not inconsistent with testimony on goods shortages. A macrobalance does not rule out severe microimbalances in which excess inventories of one type of good build up while there are long lines for other goods. Even with a macrobalance, Soviet consumers could form negative impressions about living standards when confronted with severe microimbalances in the consumer sector. We shall return to this point in our discussion of Soviet prices.

THE SOVIET BANKING SYSTEM

The Soviet banking system plays an integral role in the planning process. Soviet banking is quite unlike its Western counterpart, for it is dominated by a single bank, *Gosbank,* which is a monopoly bank in its purest form. As a monopoly bank, *Gosbank* combines the functions of central and commercial banking, but owing to the absence of money and capital markets, some traditional banking functions (open-market operations, commercial-paper transactions, etc.) are not performed by *Gosbank.*

The tremendous scope of *Gosbank's* organization is difficult to conceptualize: it has more than 150,000 employees and more than 300 main offices, about 3500 local branches, and 2000 collection offices. *Gosbank's* customers include approximately 250,000 enterprises, 40,000 collective-farm accounts, and nearly one-half million government organizations. Since 1954, *Gosbank* has been independent of the Ministry of Finance, and its director has ministerial status in the government. Since 1963, the savings bank system (with over 70,000 branches) has been incorporated into *Gosbank's* operations. The only other banks in the Soviet Union are the specialized banks—the Investment Bank (*Stroibank*) and the Foreign Trade Bank (*Vneshtorgbank*). The former is concerned with the disbursing of funds budgeted for capital investment, and the latter handles international transactions; neither competes with *Gosbank.* [62]

Throughout its history, *Gosbank* has had two primary functions: first, to make short-term loans for the working capital needs of enterprises. In the process, it creates money (it is the only money-creating institution in the Soviet Union) by creating cash for consumers and workers as firms draw on cash accounts for wage payments and noncash accounts for interenterprise transactions. Its second purpose is to oversee enterprise plan fulfillment and to monitor payments to the population by acting as the center of all accounts in the Soviet Union. Let us now consider how these two objectives are pursued.

Each Soviet enterprise deals directly with a local *Gosbank* branch. It is dependent upon *Gosbank* for short-term credit to finance inventories and working capital. Its receipts are automatically deposited at *Gosbank,* and it draws cash for wage payments at the discretion of the branch bank. In addition, the portion of its own profits that the enterprise is allowed to retain remains on deposit at, and under the supervision of, *Gosbank. Gosbank* is the sole legal grantor of short-term credit. Interfirm credit is forbidden, and a strict discipline on payments is enforced in interfirm transactions to prevent spontaneous interfirm lending. In addition, all transactions between firms involving funds in enterprise accounts are handled by, and are subject to, the supervision of *Gosbank* (with the exception of small payments).

As far as the control function of *Gosbank* is concerned, its supervision of enterprise accounts and its short-term lending operations are important. As the single clearing agent for the economy and the sole source of short-term credit, *Gosbank* is in a unique position to monitor the activities of enterprises. In drawing up short-term credit plans and in controlling enterprise accounts, *Gosbank* plays a largely passive role in the planning process by providing the monetary resources required to implement the physical plan. In making short-term loans for working capital, *Gosbank* has tended to grant production credit for specific purposes: if a particular transaction is called for in the input plan, the firm is automatically granted credit for this specific purpose. Not only is credit granted for specific purposes, but all interfirm transactions are cleared by *Gosbank,* and *Gosbank* must receive evidence of the transaction—such as a lading bill—before the clearing operation is completed. In this way, as the enterprise financial plan is the monetary counterpart of the physical plan, deviations from the physical plan will reveal themselves as deviations from the financial plan. This is a further extension of *ruble control.* Even if an enterprise builds up excess balances at *Gosbank,* this liquidity still does not represent a command over producer goods unless thay are specifically called for in the plan.*

As the social accounting center monitoring cash payments to the popula-

---

*Reforms since 1965 have resulted in the granting of credit for more general purposes rather than restricting the use of credit for very specific purposes.

tion, *Gosbank* plays a role in the macroeconomic planning described previously. It provides financial authorities with data on disposable income—information that is vital in macroplanning. In case of a projected imbalance, *Gosbank* will act to limit the flow of wage payments to the population as much as possible, within the limits of the plan. This is accomplished primarily by restricting the convertibility of enterprise accounts into cash for wage payments and by permitting wage payments in excess of the planned wage bill only if the output target is overfulfilled.

The monopoly powers of *Gosbank* are seldom used to influence the flow of production. Instead, *Gosbank's* audit operations serve primarily to reveal to planning authorities deviations from planned tasks, which are then corrected by the planners. Throughout its history, *Gosbank* has tended to automatically meet the credit needs of the economy (as specified in the plan) instead of regulating the flow of money and credit on a discretionary basis in order to direct the level of economic activity.

THE SOVIET PRICE SYSTEM

In our discussion of Soviet central planning, it was noted that the planning hierarchy is responsible for the allocation and distribution of resources in the Soviet Union. One may rightly be puzzled over the role that prices play, insofar as they, not central planners, carry the primary allocative responsibilities in market economies.

In this section, we consider the Soviet price system. First, the actual system of industrial wholesale, retail, and agricultural price setting is discussed. Second, the role that prices are supposed to play in the Soviet economic system—allocation, control, measurement, and income distribution—is considered. Last, we provide an evaluation of the Soviet price system.

Price Setting in the Soviet Union

Most prices in the Soviet Union are fixed by central authorities rather than by the interaction of supply and demand. Price-setting responsibilities have at various times been shared by the Price Bureau of *Gosplan SSR,* the Ministry of Trade, the Ministry of Finance, the Union-Republican Councils of Ministers, and various republican and *oblast'* authorities.[63] The most important prices established by the forces of supply and demand have been the collective-farm market prices. It is useful to discuss price setting in the Soviet Union in terms of four different types of prices, for the principles observed in each case are quite different: (1) industrial wholesale prices, (2) retail prices, (3) agricultural procurement prices, and (4) collective-farm market prices.[64]

Industrial Wholesale Prices   Industrial wholesale prices perform less of an allocative function than other Soviet prices. Contrary to retail price setting, where an attempt is generally made to set market-clearing prices, industrial wholesale prices tend to serve primarily as accounting prices, used to add together heterogeneous inputs and outputs. That industrial wholesale prices play no real allocative role should come as no surprise, in view of our earlier discussion of industrial supply planning.

At the wholesale level, there are two important types of prices. First, the *factory wholesale price* is the price at which the industrial enterprise sells its product to the wholesale trade network. Second, the *industry wholesale price* is the price at which goods are sold to buyers outside the industry. In the latter case, a turnover tax will likely be included (on the average, about 8 percent of the industry wholesale price in heavy industry).[65] In the former case, there is seldom a turnover tax. Although the rules of price setting have changed somewhat over time, generally speaking, this function has tended to remain centralized. Thus, agencies in the planning hierarchy establish wholesale prices on the basis of *average branch cost* of production plus a small profit markup (generally 5 to 10 percent). Included in enterprise costs are wage payments, costs of intermediate materials, depreciation, insurance, and payments to overhead. Interest and rental charges are not normally included in costs, and depreciation charges do not include charges for obsolescence. While market prices in a competitive market system tend toward marginal costs, they are, in the Soviet case, average cost prices. Using average branch costs means that many enterprises will, in fact, take losses at the established prices because the cost figures are averages of low- and high-cost producers, and historically such has been the case. The consequences of such losses in the Soviet system have generally been small.

During the early years of planning, the prices of important industrial inputs were purposely kept low, and many industrial enterprises were operated under state subsidies. Since enterprise survival is not based on profits or losses, as in a market system, such losses are of little particular importance, since subsidies are granted almost automatically to enterprises to cover operating losses. In these cases, minimization of losses (which might be a short-run objective for a capitalist firm) becomes a long-run criterion of operation and price setting in the Soviet Union.

Profit calculations have always existed in the Soviet schema; they simply have not been a dominant criterion of enterprise performance, and the presence or absence of profits has therefore not been the basis for action by Soviet planning authorities. A fundamental reason for this is the inability of pricing authorities to establish "fair" prices, under which the level of profits serves as a true indication of enterprise performance.

In some cases, especially the extractive industries, in which marked cost variations among producers occur, so-called accounting prices have been used. Producers, in effect, receive different prices (depending upon cost differences) while all buyers pay the same price, with the state providing the intermediate cushion. Thus, the low-cost producers are, in effect, paying a differential rent to the state.

In rare cases, attempts have been made by pricing authorities to adjust the prices of close substitutes for differences in "use value," the most notable cases being the pricing of fuel oil and coal, and nonferrous and ferrous metals. In both instances, it was determined that the "use values" of fuel oil and nonferrous metals were higher than those of coal and ferrous metals, respectively; therefore, prices in excess of average branch costs were set for fuel oil and nonferrous metals (the difference between average branch costs and the whole-

sale prices being the turnover tax). Nevertheless, such instances are rare because generally it is difficult to distinguish among industrial commodities according to their "use values."

Further problems are created by the treatment of "new" products and of
products bought and sold in Western markets.[66] If the labor theory of value is to
be observed, "new" products produced by a new technology that results in labor
savings should be priced relatively low. The enterprise director who therefore
takes the risk of introducing new labor-saving technology faces the prospect of
having what would have been increased profits passed on to the users of his
product in the form of price reductions. The reader can understand that such a
pricing formula would not be conducive to technological innovation, and Soviet
pricing authorities have (without great success) sought ways to exempt such
"new" products from the labor theory of value formula. Cases of large differentials between domestic wholesale prices and world market prices have also been
troublesome to pricing authorities. In the case of imports, planners may have to
pass on to the Soviet enterprise at a low domestic price equipment that has been
purchased at a high price in the world market. In the case of exports (oil, for
example), the product may sell for a much higher price in the world market than
the producing enterprise receives at home. Because of these discrepancies, there
has been an increased tendency in recent years to adjust Soviet domestic prices
on the basis of movements in world prices.

A major problem of industrial price setting is that owing to the administrative complexities of price reform, industrial prices have seldom conformed to
average branch costs. It has proved too difficult to change prices regularly along
with costs. Instead, industrial prices have tended to remain rigid over long
periods. As a result, general subsidies have often been required as the wholesale
prices of many commodities gradually fell below rising costs. Industrial wholesale
prices remained roughly constant between 1929 and 1936, despite rapidly rising
wage costs, and by 1936, subsidies were the rule rather than the exception. A price
reform in spring of 1936 sharply increased prices to cover costs, while in 1949,
another large general price increase was required to eliminate subsidies. Despite
the general rule that prices should cover costs, industrial prices remained virtually
unchanged from the 1955 price reform to the 1966–1967 price reform despite
changing wage costs and changing technology.[66] Since 1966–1967, there have
been only modest official adjustments in industrial wholesale prices, and familiar
complaints that the 1966–1967 prices did not reflect current costs were already
being heard shortly after the reform was completed. A general price reform is
being carried out in the mid-1980s.

Official Soviet industrial wholesale price indexes indicate a very modest
degree of inflation throughout the postwar era, but there is reason to suspect that
the official indexes suffer from the same deficiencies as the retail-price indexes.
Yet Western recalculations also fail to reveal significant inflation in the industrial
wholesale-price sphere.[67]

Retail Prices   At the retail level, most prices are also formed by state planning
authorities. They are basically designed to *clear the market* (to equate supply and

demand), although this standard is often not met. This basic policy is in line with the Soviet policy of market distribution of consumer goods to preserve the incentive to work: for wage differentials to be meaningful, it is essential that they represent a differential command over consumer goods. In reality, retail prices have often tended to be somewhat below market clearing levels, and thus queues have often served, in part, as a rationing device.

The retail price is simply the industry wholesale price, plus the retail margin (and costs, where additions to the product are generated at the retail level), plus the turnover tax. Unlike Western sales taxes, where consumers are generally aware of the tax rate they are paying, the Soviet turnover tax is included in the retail price without the purchaser knowing how large it is. The level of the tax is a function of supply-and-demand conditions in the given market and of the prevailing industry wholesale price. Where the price without turnover tax is below the market clearing level, a tax sufficient to raise the retail price to the clearing level is added. In Figure 8, if the industry wholesale price is OP and the resulting equilibrium price is OP', the turnover tax will be PP' (or slightly below if the price is set below clearing levels).* Thus, the level of taxation is price-determined rather than price-determining.

At this point, the reader might well ask, what happens if the industry wholesale price is greater than OP'? Obviously, in such a case there will be no turnover tax, and unless there is a subsidy that permits the setting of the retail price *below* the industry wholesale price, surplus unsold stocks will result. Two comments are in order. First, throughout much of the plan period, a sellers' market has prevailed—obviating the subsidy problem at the retail level. Second, the matter of unsold stocks is more fundamental than simply a question of price setting. In particular, as economic development proceeds and greater attention is given to consumer goods in the Soviet Union, one would expect the sellers' market to subside. Such indeed has been the case—for example, in the clothing industry and more recently in the consumer durables area.[68] In these cases, there have been unsold stocks in recent years, unlike the old sellers' market where producers could be unresponsive to consumers without losing sales. Thus, the current problem is a combination of matching output to consumer tastes and setting appropriate prices. In recent years, the simultaneous existence of surpluses of some commodities and shortages of others have demonstrated the magnitude of this structural problem. There are also financial implications involved: if stocks are unsold, the state is not able to collect the turnover tax—an important source of revenue. A fundamental problem of economic reform revolves around this question: when the sellers' market subsides, how can producers be made responsive to the consumer if the price system fails to provide effective information concerning consumer demand? What was not so much a problem in the past may well be an increasing problem in the future.

---

*The supply schedule in Figure 8 is drawn to be perfectly inelastic. This is done under the assumption that the quantity of output is determined by the state plan, irrespective of price. This would apply largely to enterprises producing a single homogeneous product. For a multiproduct firm attempting to fulfill a gross output target, the supply schedule would likely be less than perfectly inelastic, that is, would have a positive slope.

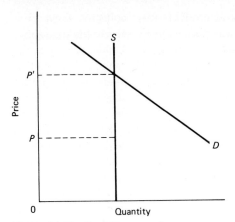

Figure 8   The Soviet turnover tax.

If retail prices are to serve as mechanisms to transmit consumer preferences to producers, fundamental changes will be necessary. In this regard, the two-tiered price system shown in Figure 8 is an obstacle. Because retail prices are essentially demand-determined and factory wholesale prices are cost-determined, it may happen that *relative* retail prices diverge significantly from *relative* factory wholesale prices. Yet producers will be more responsive to the relative wholesale prices that they receive rather than to the retail prices paid by consumers, which reflect consumer preferences. Thus, the signal sent by the consumer in the form of a market-clearing retail price is not received by the producer, who is paid a different factory wholesale price. For some products, the two-tiered system is being gradually and automatically eliminated, namely, in food processing and in clothing and textiles. Their retail prices have been held roughly constant in recent years, whereas their factory wholesale prices have risen along with rising wage and material costs, thus squeezing out the turnover tax.

Although there has been a continuing effort to vary prices on a zonal basis and to change them over time, this sort of variability has been highly restricted, given the magnitude of the administrative task involved. One can expect this problem to become more difficult in the future, as the economy grows more complex and the product range widens. Finally, it might be noted that the level of turnover tax (as one would expect) has varied widely among products and is as high as 80 percent of the price on some products. The average light-industry turnover tax in 1983 was 23 percent of the wholesale price, while it was 7 percent in heavy industry.[69] As we have seen, the revenue from this tax accounts for a substantial portion of state budgetary revenues and therefore remains an important consideration in both financial planning and price setting.

Agricultural Procurement Prices   Turning to agricultural pricing, we note that until 1958 (and again for grain after 1965), there existed a two-level pricing system for state purchases of agricultural products from collective farms. For compulsory deliveries, a low fixed price was paid, while for sales to the state above the compulsory level, a higher fixed price was established. Unlike pricing in the industrial sector, these prices, until recently, bore little relation to the production costs of the collective farm. There was no cost accounting whatsoever on collective farms until the mid-1950s, at which time initial cost studies revealed that for most collective farms, production costs were substantially above even the above-quota prices. In this manner, state pricing policy was placing the collective farms in a most difficult financial position by purchasing output at less than cost. At the same time, the state farms, operating essentially as industrial enterprises, were receiving subsidies from the state to compensate them for the low procurement prices and were not financing their own capital investment, as were the collective farms.

The two-level system was abandoned in 1958 and, although revived in 1965 for grain and then some other products, the differential between the below- and above-quota grain prices has been small relative to earlier differentials. Most notably, however, throughout the 1950s and 1960s, purchase prices were raised substantially, so that average purchase prices would cover production costs.* This pricing policy is in line with the agricultural policy that collective-farm production should be "profitable" in the general sense of revenues covering costs. This policy remains in a state of active debate, since the problem of agricultural land rental charges remains unresolved. Finally, there has been a preliminary effort to revise agricultural purchase prices not only in terms of their levels but also in terms of their flexibility over time and in regions.

Collective-Farm Market Prices   The most significant example of a true market price in the Soviet economy is the collective-farm market price. In these markets, the collective farmers sell their produce (from private plots and after meeting state targets) at prices determined by demand and supply. While these prices fluctuate, they have generally been substantially above the level of state food prices, a phenomenon explained in part by quality differentials and by the maintenance of state prices at artificially low (below equilibrium) levels. For example, collective-farm market prices were on the average more than double state retail prices in 1940. After considerable variation throughout the postwar period, collective-farm market prices were 63 percent greater than state retail prices in 1972.[70] The collective-farm markets have been especially important in large cities, where standard sources of supply have been inadequate. How important are these markets? Although measurement is rather complex, collective-farm markets accounted for 13.9 percent of aggregate food sales in 1960 and for 8.8 percent in 1978. However, for certain products, these markets are of much greater significance. In 1957, for example, when the aggregate collective-farm market share of food sales was 18.2 percent, they accounted for 63 percent of potato sales, 48

---

*Thus, a squeeze is put on food processing establishments, which are forced to make planned losses as the line is held on retail food prices.

percent of egg sales, and 35 percent of meat sales. In 1970, they accounted for 67, 54, and 35 percent, respectively, of sales of these products.[71]

The Functions of Soviet Prices

Our discussion of the Soviet price system suggests that Soviet prices are formed quite differently from their market economy counterparts. However, to evaluate Soviet prices, we must consider them in the context of the various roles that prices are supposed to play in the Soviet command economy. To judge the Soviet price system exclusively as an instrument for allocating resources (as is sometimes done) would be a mistake, for Soviet authorities have generally not intended it to be used as such. Instead, industrial supply and output planning are supposed to allocate resources, with prices playing other roles. Soviet prices can be considered in terms of four possible functions: (1) allocation, (2) control, (3) measurement, and (4) income distribution. A biased picture of Soviet prices would inevitably be drawn if one were to concentrate only on the first function.

Allocation   In any economic system, prices can reflect relative scarcities on the basis of which economic decisions are made. As any standard economics textbook will explain, the profit-maximizing producer will employ inputs so as to equate marginal factor outlays and marginal revenue products. The utility-maximizing consumer will purchase goods and services so as to equate marginal utilities per dollar, and so on. In this manner, supply-and-demand schedules arise, and prices that reflect *relative scarcities* are determined. Under ideal conditions, such an arrangement will result in a maximum output produced at a minimum cost irrespective of the economic system and is, in this sense, optimal.[72] It is only necessary for the consumer and producer to be aware of relative prices to respond correctly in such a system; no planner is required to tell either one how to behave.

Such perfect price allocation is scarcely to be found in either planned or market economies in the real world, since imperfect competition, price controls, public goods, government regulations, and so on, prevail almost everywhere.

What we have in the real world is a mixture of price allocation and administrative allocation. In the United States, for example, resource allocation is accomplished primarily through the price mechanism, though not necessarily in the optimal manner described above. In the Soviet Union, administrative planning bears the primary responsibility for allocation, although prices do play a limited role. Thus, while both systems have scarce resources to be marshaled toward the achievement of given (although different) goals—for which the price system might be utilized—the fundamental differences are, first, the extent to which prices are utilized for these purposes and, second, the manner in which price formation is executed.

Soviet industrial wholesale prices, being centrally determined and based on the ideological definition of average branch costs, do not represent relative scarcities—as Soviet planners are well aware. This is one of the reasons why the administrative planning structure remains so much in charge of resource allocation and why there is so little price allocation in the Soviet Union. Like any generalization, there are exceptions. In the labor sector, differential wages are used largely to allocate labor. Also, retail prices are used largely to distribute *available* consumer goods among the population, although such prices generally play an unimportant role in the decision to produce such goods. The most striking feature of the Soviet economic system remains the minor role that prices play in the allocative process.

That Soviet prices generally fail to reflect relative scarcities is important despite their lack of use as allocative instruments, since Soviet prices do play other roles. This may sound rather abstract, but it is important. The Soviets have chosen administrative allocation over price allocation. Yet it is difficult to administratively allocate resources on a day-to-day basis without knowing relative scarcities, and it is even more difficult to relegate decision-making to lower echelons without scarcity prices. How to introduce a degree of price allocation into such a system and how to make the prices themselves more "rational" are recurrent themes in the reform discussions in the Soviet Union and Eastern Europe.

Control   The control function of prices is perhaps the most important in the Soviet context. Even in a centralized economy, some delegation of authority and responsibility is required, ranging from the central planning agencies to the enterprises. This necessitates a mechanism for control of subordinates. In market economies, the profit mechanism and variants thereof can act as a control device as well as an allocative device. In the Soviet case, however, profits have played virtually no allocative role in the industrial enterprise (at least prior to 1965). Nevertheless, many of the directives of higher planning authorities must be stated and verified in value terms—for example, rubles of steel output rather than tons. Thus, the extensive use of value categories—the most famous being *valovaia produktsia,* or *val* (gross production)—in Soviet planning means that prices have been used in a control function to evaluate and assess performance at all levels. However, value indicators have been largely used to indicate *deviations* from planned activities. Actual control has been carried out mainly through physical controls and directives.

Measurement   The measurement role of Soviet prices is also important and is similar to the control function in various aspects. Prices are required to measure the results of economic activity, especially if one's scope extends beyond individual products: the measurement of economic activity requires the aggregation of dissimilar products, and aggregation requires valuation. Without prices, one cannot determine at what rate the economy is growing, whether the capital/output ratio is rising or falling, and so on, and these are important variables in the planning process. For example, the total output of the economy ("gross material product" as the Soviets call it) must be valued to be measured, and in an important sense, the results of this measurement will depend upon the nature of the prices used. For example, the Soviets used 1926–1927 "constant" prices until the 1950s to measure Soviet total output. Over such a long period of time, these prices came to reflect prevailing prices and costs less and less, and eventually, because of their questionable economic significance, they were abandoned for a more up-to-date price base.

This illustration points out an important potential conflict among the various roles that a price system can play in the Soviet command economy, and this applies to both the control and the measurement functions. Control and measurement are more easily carried out when prices are not changed frequently. However, if prices remain unchanged, after awhile they will not reflect current cost relationships and therefore will be even less useful as a guide to allocation. Soviet authorities have been reluctant to change prices for two basic reasons. First, it is administratively difficult to gather the mass of wage and cost data required for a reform of prices. Second, it has proved a complex task to plan and evaluate when prices are in the process of change. In such a case, value targets must be stated in two variants—one for the old, the other for the new prices—and general confusion tends to reign until the new prices are firmly established.

Income Distribution   Finally, Soviet prices play an important role in the distribution of income. In addition to the centrally determined wage scales that, of course, affect the distribution of income, pricing authorities can influence the distribution of real income through retail prices. In fact, some Soviet pricing policies can be partially explained in terms of their impact on income distribution. For example, low housing rents have been charged (despite a severe housing shortage) throughout the plan period, and below-equilibrium prices have generally been charged in state and cooperative shops for basic food products.[73] In line with these price-setting policies has been the practice of charging nothing or only nominal prices for health care and education.[74]

One can view the Soviet policy of setting low prices for necessities such as basic food products and health and education as an attempt to improve the distribution of real income. It is noteworthy that the most direct method of equalizing the distribution of income—the leveling of wage income—has not been used on the grounds that this would weaken the incentive system.

An Evaluation of Soviet Prices

Thus far, we have described the operation and functions of the Soviet price system. We now turn to a partial evaluation of Soviet pricing. Is the Soviet price system really unsatisfactory and "irrational," as many Western observers claim?[75] It is, of course, difficult to answer this question because the response depends to a great extent upon the criteria used to judge Soviet prices. If one accepts the criterion that "good" prices should smoothly allocate scarce resources among competing goals by equating supply and demand, then the Soviet price system will show up poorly. If, on the other hand, one judges the price system on the basis of how well it leads to the accomplishment of goals desired by leaders (say, Soviet planners), then the judgment may be quite different. While we cannot hope to provide conclusive answers to the relative "goodness" of Soviet prices, some plausible generalizations are in order.

We must recognize that when one judges the Soviet price system in absolute terms, it has become apparent to both Soviet and Western observers that the Soviet price system does not perform its postulated functions especially well. This dissatisfaction among observers on both sides is reflected in the long-standing Western criticisms of the lack of scarcity pricing and price inflexibility, and in the Soviet's own criticisms along these same lines. In particular, the conflict between the price flexibility required for scarcity pricing and smooth distribution of goods and the price inflexibility required for effective control and measurement has led to numerous problems. The absence of an interest charge on capital (prior to 1965) caused managers to treat capital as a free good, with ensuing capital wastage. For many years, natural gas was allowed to disappear into the air as a by-product of oil production. There are many more examples. Perhaps most disturbing have been the strict limitations imposed by the inflexible Soviet price system on the devolution of decision-making through decentralization.

To evaluate Soviet prices on their own terms, one must determine to what extent the Soviet price system has promoted or retarded the attainment of the long-run economic, military, and political goals of the Soviet leadership. For example, has the Soviet price system furthered the Soviet economic goals of rapid economic growth, world military power, and the preservation of internal stability? From the leadership's point of view, flexible equilibrium prices may be generated only by allowing more decisions to be made at the micro level. The price of Western-style prices may be the loss of decision-making authority. Are key decisions to be made administratively or by marketlike forces? There is a clear trade-off. The Soviets must recognize that dissatisfaction with goods scarcities is one of the most common concerns of the man on the street. The inability to price consumer goods properly drives consumers into the second economy both as consumers and producers.

The major problem of the Soviet price system appears to be its inability to communicate relative scarcities to participants in the economy. Enterprise managers and ministry officials, for example, are not informed by Soviet prices of the true opportunity costs of their various inputs and outputs. Without such information, resources cannot be combined in an efficient manner. There is general agreement that Soviet prices do not provide accurate information on opportunity costs, but is there some substitute mechanism? Raymond Powell has argued that economic planners (in ministries, *Gosplan, Gossnab,* and the party industrial departments) may be in a position to gather and analyze information on relative scarcities.[76] Planners will be confronted with various kinds of information concerning relative scarcities: enterprises will clamor more for one resource than another; long-time associates will informally tell their planning superiors that a particular goods shortage is more acute than others. Through a variety of signals, an experienced economic planner will learn how to detect true signals of high-opportunity costs from false signals. Planners can, therefore, to a degree, substitute their own information for the opportunity cost information not provided by the price system. Accordingly, planners will be able, albeit imperfectly, to correct for gross misallocations of resources. It is Powell's claim that this ability to detect relative scarcities has prevented the Soviet economy from performing as poorly as might be expected in an economy in which relative scarcities are not known.

THE SECOND ECONOMY OF THE SOVIET UNION

The major "unplanned" component discussed to this point has been the private plot of the farm population. State regulations govern (or seek to govern) the size of such plots and the proportion of work time devoted to private farming, but such activity is legal according to Soviet law—as is the practice of selling private-plot produce at market prices. Yet hidden from view is a broad range of private, unplanned, and generally illegal economic activities, called the "second economy," or "counter economy," by students of this phenomenon.

The second economy has been analyzed extensively by Gregory Grossman, Vladimir Treml, Dimitri Simes, and Aron Katsenelinboigen.[77] It consists of a number of market-type activities of varying degrees of legality, all involving "unplanned" exchange. According to Grossman, second-economy activities must fulfill at least one of the two following tests: (1) the activity is for private gain; (2) the activity knowingly contravenes existing law.

Examples of second economy activities are easily found in the Soviet press, court reports, and emigré interviews. A physician or dentist may treat private patients for higher fees. A salesperson may set aside high-quality merchandise for customers who offer large tips (bribes). A manager of a manufacturing firm sets aside the highest-quality production for sale to the black market. A collective farmer may divert collective-farm land and supplies to his private plot ("theft of socialist property"). Black marketeers in port cities deal in contraband merchandise. Owners of private cars transport second-economy merchandise. In many cases, official and second-economy transactions are intertwined. A manager may divert some production into second-economy transactions to raise cash to purchase unofficially supplies needed to meet the plan. The official activities of an entire enterprise may serve as a front for a prospering second-economy undertaking. Workers may engage in private production on the job (repairing private automobiles in state garages). Private construction teams may build structures for private individuals. Information sellers (apartment brokers) may provide information on the availability of apartments or imported goods. The list could be expanded indefinitely. An important area of second-economy activity is bribery and corruption—influence buying, purchasing favors that only state and party officials can provide.

According to available accounts, second-economy activities are concentrated in collective farms and in the transportation network. Apparently, the supervision of collective farms is more lax, and they therefore serve as better fronts for the second economy. Transportation enterprises are also critical to the second economy, for second-economy merchandise must be transported somehow. The increase in private ownership of automobiles has apparently enhanced the operation of the second economy and has led to a growing market in stolen gasoline.

We cannot establish how important the second economy is, say, as a percent of retail sales or GNP, but those who have studied the second economy argue that it is quite significant. Exact estimation of the importance of the second economy will never be possible, for measurement of an illegal activity is a virtually impossible task. To take one isolated example where estimates are available: in 1970, one-fourth of all alcohol consumed in the Soviet Union was produced and supplied through the second economy. In 1972, 500 million liters of stolen gasoline are estimated to have been sold by the second economy. Some 80 percent of the USSR fur market and 25 percent of fish sales are handled by the second economy. House repairs and decoration are dominated by the second economy. The most reliable information on the scope of the second economy comes from the emigré surveys conducted by Gur Ofer and Aaron Vinokur in Israel, which show that earnings derived from an activity other than that in the main place of employment account for some 10 percent of earnings.[78] The magnitude of the second economy would come as no surprise, for the official planning system has assigned low priority to "nonessential" services (beauty shops, appliance repairs, and so on), and expenditures on these items typically rise with rising income. Moreover, the official supply system has failed to offer the Soviet consumer sufficient supplies of quality merchandise, and the second economy would serve as a means of channeling available quality merchandise to the highest bidder. Moreover, the Soviet taxation system imposes almost confiscatory marginal tax rates on professionals who are legally licensed to carry out private professional activity. As in many Western countries, the tax system of the Soviet Union drives professionals into the second economy. The immense power over resources placed in the hands of officials is another reason for the existence of the second economy. Rather than the market, officials allocate many of the scarce commodities treasured by the Soviet consumer—automobiles and auto licenses, apartments, building permits, and so on. This situation opens up the possibility of bribery and corruption, much as it does in the West.

The second economy has its advantages and disadvantages as far as the planners are concerned. It helps to preserve incentives because higher wages and bonus payments can be spent in the second economy. Moreover, the second economy serves to reduce inflationary pressures in the official economy. On the negative side, the second economy diverts participants in the economy from planned tasks and loosens planners' control over the economy. The Soviets do not publish data on currency in circulation, and it is likely that second-economy transactions are conducted largely in cash. For this reason, studies of savings based on savings account deposits (see previous section) may be biased. The brisk market in jewelry and precious metals also provides the participants in the second economy with a means of storing value.

REFERENCES

1. This section is based on the following sources: F. Kushnirsky, *Soviet Economic Planning, 1965–1980* (Boulder, Colo.: Westview Press, 1982); A. Nove, *The Soviet Economic System* (London: Allen & Unwin, 1977), chaps. 1–4; W. J. Conyngham, *Industrial Management in the Soviet Union* (Stanford: Hoover Institution Press, 1973); W. J. Conyngham, *The Modernization of Soviet Industrial Management* (Cambridge: Cambridge University Press, 1982); A. C. Gorlin, "The Soviet Economic Associations," *Soviet Studies,* vol. 26, no. 1 (January 1974), pp. 3–27; G. Grossman, "The

Party as Manager and Entrepreneur," in G. Guroff and F. Carstensen, eds., *Entrepreneurship in Russia and the Soviet Union* (Princeton, N.J.: Princeton University Press, 1983), pp. 284–305.

2. E. H. Carr and R. W. Davies, *Foundations of a Planned Economy, 1926–1929,* vol. 1, part 2 (London: Macmillan, 1969), pp. 802–836.

3. The principal/agent literature has been applied to the Soviet context by D. Granick, "Institutional Innovation and Economic Management: The Soviet Incentive System, 1921 to the Present," in G. Guroff and F. Carstensen, eds., *Entrepreneurship in Imperial Russia and the Soviet Union* (Princeton, N.J.: Princeton University Press), 1983, pp. 223–257; and by J. B. Miller, "The Big Nail and Other Stories: Product Quality in the Soviet Union," *ACES Bulletin,* vol. 26, no. 1 (Spring 1984), pp. 43–58.

4. Gosplan SSSR, *Metodicheskie ukazaniia k razrabotke gosudarstvennykh planov i sotsial'nogo razvitiia SSSR* [Methodological directives to working out state plans and the social development of the USSR] (Moscow: Ekonomika, 1980). The authors are grateful to G. Schroeder for bringing this book to our attention.

5. The notion of various macrobalances of the Soviet economy has been investigated by J. Millar, *The ABCs of Soviet Socialism* (Urbana: University of Illinois Press, 1981) and by J. Millar and J. Pickersgill, "Aggregate Economic Problems in Soviet-Type Economies," *ACES Bulletin,* vol. 19, no. 1 (Spring 1977), pp. 5–20.

6. We avoid detailed listing of sources in this section. The material presented here is largely based on the following sources: Bergson, *The Economics of Soviet Planning,* chap. 7; Nove, *The Soviet Economy,* pp. 87–96; R. W. Davies, "Soviet Planning for Rapid Industrialization," *Economics of Planning,* vol. 6, no. 1 (1966); R. W. Davis, "Planning a Mature Economy in the USSR," *Economics of Planning,* vol. 6, no. 2 (1966); M. Ellman, "The Consistency of Soviet Plans," *Scottish Journal of Political Economy,* vol. 16, no. 1 (February 1969). The last three are reprinted in M. Bornstein and D. Fusfeld, eds., *The Soviet Economy: A Book of Readings,* 3rd ed. (Homewood, Ill.: Irwin, 1970). See also H. Levine, "The Centralized Planning of Supply in Soviet Industry," in Joint Economic Committee, *Comparisons of the United States and Soviet Economies* (Washington, D.C.: U.S. Government Printing Office, 1959), pp. 151–176, reprinted in M. Bornstein and D. Fusfeld, eds., *The Soviet Economy: A Book of Readings,* rev. ed. (Homewood, Ill.: Irwin, 1965), pp. 49–65; M. Ellman, *Soviet Planning Today: Proposals for an Optimally Functioning Economic System* (Cambridge: Cambridge University Press, 1971); G. E. Schroeder, "The 'Reform' of the Supply System in Soviet Industry," *Soviet Studies,* vol. 24, no. 1 (July 1972), 97–119; G. E. Schroeder "Recent Developments in Soviet Planning and Managerial Incentives," in Joint Economic Committee, *Soviet Economic Prospects for the Seventies* (Washington, D.C.: U.S. Government Printing Office, 1973), pp. 11–38; M. Ellman, *Socialist Planning* (Cambridge: Cambridge University Press, 1979); Nove, *The Soviet Economic System;* G. E. Schroeder, "The Soviet Economy on a Treadmill of 'Reforms,' " in Joint Economic Committee, *Soviet Economy in a Time of Change* (Washington, D.C.: U.S. Government Printing Office, 1979), pp. 312–340, vol. 1; E. Zaleski, *Stalinist Planning for Economic Growth, 1933–1952* (Chapel Hill: University of North Carolina Press, 1980); Kushnirsky, *Soviet Economic Planning, 1965–1980.*

7. As examples, see A. N. Efimov et al., *Ekonomicheskoe planirovanie v SSSR* [Economic planning in the USSR] (Moscow: 1967) and A.N. Efimor et al., *Metodicheskie ukazaniia.*

8. This chapter deals only with annual plans, which are the operational plans in the Soviet economy, and omits long-term "perspective planning," since historically there seems to have been little relationship between the perspective and annual plans. See

N. Jasny, *Essays on the Soviet Economy* (New York: Praeger, 1962), essay 6. In theory at least, annual plans should be compiled on the basis of the five- or seven-year perspective plans, in such a manner that at the end of five (or seven) annual plans, the perspective plan targets are met. This was not generally the case for the first eight Five [Seven] Year Plans. The ninth and tenth Five Year Plans (1971–1980) apparently sought to remedy this situation by upgrading the role of the long-range plan by requiring more conformity between it and the annual operational plans. Although there was pressure during the 1970s to improve long-term planning, it is not clear that substantial gains were made. For evidence on this, see Schroeder, "Recent Developments in Soviet Planning," pp. 13–15, and Schroeder, "The Soviet Economy on a Treadmill of 'Reforms,' " pp. 318–319.

9. Kushnirsky, *Soviet Economic Planning, 1965–1980,* p. 66.

10. In practice, Soviet planners have generally adjusted only for *first-order relationships* when output targets are changed because of the tremendous amount of time required to make the necessary computations. By first-order changes, we mean the additional coal, electricity, ore, and other commodities required to produce the additional steel in our example above. No account is taken of the additional resources required to produce the extra coal, electricity, and ore. For a detailed discussion of this point, see Levine, "The Centralized Planning of Supply," in Bornstein and Fusfeld, pp. 55–57.

11. For an introductory discussion on planning, see P. R. Gregory and R. C. Stuart, *Comparative Economic Systems,* 2nd ed. (Boston: Houghton Mifflin, 1985), pp. 173–178. For a discussion of the basic input-output model and its application to Soviet planning, see M. P. Todaro, *Development Planning* (Nairobi: Oxford University Press, 1971).

12. To what extent is input-output analysis actually used in the USSR? For a recent discussion and analysis of this point, see A. Tretyakova and I. Birman, "Input-Output Analysis in the USSR," *Soviet Studies,* vol. 28, no. 2 (April 1976), 157–186; V. G. Treml, "A Comment on Birman-Tretyakova," *Soviet Studies,* vol. 28, no. 2 (April 1976), 187–188. For more background material, see V. G. Treml, "Input-Output Analysis and Soviet Planning," in J. P. Hardt et al., *Mathematics and Computers in Soviet Planning* (New Haven, Conn.: Yale University Press, 1967), pp. 68–120; H. Levine, "Input-Output Analysis and Soviet Planning," *American Economic Review,* vol. 52, no. 2 (May 1962); J. M. Montias, "On the Consistency and Efficiency of Central Planning," *Review of Economic Studies,* vol. 29, no. 81 (October 1962); B. N. Ward, *The Socialist Economy* (New York: Random House, 1967), chap. 3; V. G. Treml et al., "Interindustry Structure of the Soviet Economy," in Joint Economic Committee, *Soviet Economic Prospects for the Seventies* (Washington, D.C.: U.S. Government Printing Office, 1973), pp. 246–269; V. G. Treml et al., "The Soviet 1966 and 1972 Input-Output Tables," in Joint Economic Committee, *Soviet Economy in a New Perspective* (Washington, D.C.: U.S. Government Printing Office, 1976), pp. 332–376; D. M. Gallik et al., "The 1972 Input-Output Table and the Changing Structure of the Soviet Economy," in Joint Economic Committee, *Soviet Economy in a Time of Change* (Washington, D.C.: U.S. Government Printing Office, 1979), vol. 1, pp. 423–471.

13. Statement of S. Shatalin quoted in Treml et al., "Interindustry Structure of the Soviet Economy," p. 249.

14. *Narodnoe khoziaistvo SSSR v 1969 g* [The national economy of the USSR in 1969] (Moscow: Statistika, 1970), pp. 50–75; Treml et al., "The Soviet 1966 and 1972 Input-Output Tables."

15. F. Baturin and P. Shemetiv, "Activities of Siberian Economists," *Problems of Econom-*

ics: A Journal of Translations, vol. 7, no. 7 (November 1969), 69. Translated from *Voprosy ekonomiki* [Problems of economics], no. 5 (1969).

16. M. Bor, *Aims and Methods of Soviet Planning* (New York: International Publishers, 1967), chap. 6.

17. R. D. Portes, "The Enterprise Under Central Planning," *Review of Economic Studies,* vol. 36, no. 106 (April 1969), 197–212. Also see M. Keren, "On the Tautness of Plans," *Review of Economic Studies,* vol. 39, no. 4 (October 1972), 469–486.

18. H. Hunter, "Optimum Tautness in Developmental Planning," *Economic Development and Cultural Change,* vol. 9, no. 4, part 1, (July 1961), 561–572. A similar argument has been made by A. Hirschman, *The Strategy of Economic Development* (New Haven, Conn.: Yale University Press, 1958), pp. 29–33. Hunter is careful to recognize that there is a level of "optimal tautness" and that Soviet planning may have exceeded this optimal limit. Western experts concluded that the ninth Five Year Plan, for example, went well beyond this optimal limit and that serious shortfalls in metals, timber, and electricity hindered its implementation. On this, see J. Noren and F. Whitehouse, "Soviet Industry in the 1971–75 Plan," in Joint Economic Committee, *Soviet Economic Prospects for the Seventies* (Washington, D.C.: U.S. Government Printing Office, 1973), pp. 207, 239–242. For a discussion of the pressure on planners to "mobilize" resources rather than formulate balanced plans, see Kushnirsky, *Soviet Economic Planning, 1960–1980.*

19. Hunter, "Optimum Tautness," 567–571; and H. Levine, "Pressure and Planning in the Soviet Economy," in H. Rosovsky, ed., *Industrialization in Two Systems: Essays in Honor of Alexander Gerschenkron* (New York: Wiley, 1966), pp. 266–285. Reprinted in M. Bornstein and D. Fusfeld, eds., *The Soviet Economy: A Book of Readings* (Homewood, Ill.: Irwin, 1970), pp. 64–82.

20. Levine, "Pressure and Planning in the Soviet Economy," in Bornstein and Fusfeld, p. 73.

21. I. Birman, "From the Achieved Level," *Soviet Studies,* vol. 31, no. 2 (April 1978), pp. 153–172.

22. J. Berliner has extensively investigated the problems of introducing new technology in the context of the Soviet planned economy; see J. Berliner, *The Innovation Decision in Soviet Industry* (Cambridge, Mass.: MIT Press, 1983).

23. In the oil industry, drilling enterprises are given targets in thousands of meters to be drilled. Theoretically, a dry hole is treated the same as a gusher. Enterprises therefore refuse to move their drilling equipment and continue to drill in the established fields. On this, see "Soviet Oil Expert Warns of Reliance on Old Fields," *The New York Times,* February 13, 1980.

24. D. Granick, *Soviet Metal Fabricating and Economic Development* (Madison: University of Wisconsin Press, 1967), pp. 159–160; Schroeder, "The Soviet Economy on a Treadmill of 'Reforms,' " p. 336.

25. L. Smolinski, "What Next in Soviet Planning?" *Foreign Affairs,* vol. 42, no. 4 (July 1964), 604.

26. This evidence can be found in G. Ofer, *The Service Sector in Soviet Economic Growth* (Cambridge, Mass.: Harvard University Press, 1973). For more recent evidence, see F. L. Pryor, "Some Costs and Benefits of Markets: An Empirical Study," *Quarterly Journal of Economics,* vol. 91 (February 1977), 81–102. For additional discussion of this theme, see F. A. Durgin, "What Is Left for the Market in Our Market Economy?" *ACES Bulletin,* vol. 16, no. 3 (Winter 1974), 41–51; G. E. Schroeder, "A Critique of Official Statistics on Public Administration in the USSR," *ACES Bulletin,* vol. 18, no. 1 (Spring 1976), 23–44; F. A. Durgin, "A Commentary on Gertrude Schroeder's

'Critique of Official Statistics on Public Administration in the USSR,' " *ACES Bulletin*, vol. 19, no. 1 (Spring 1977), 109–116; and G. E. Schroeder, "Reply," *ACES Bulletin*, vol. 19, no. 1 (Spring 1977), 117–118.

27. Schroeder, "Soviet Economy on a Treadmill of 'Reforms,' " pp. 319–322, discusses the computerization of Soviet planning. About one-half of the calculations involved in the 1978 plan were aided by computers.

28. Zaleski, *Stalinist Planning*.

29. J. Wilhelm, "Does the Soviet Union Have a Planned Economy?" *Soviet Studies*, vol. 31, no. 2 (April 1979), 268–274; J. Wilhelm, "The Soviet Union Has an Administered, Not a Planned Economy, *Soviet Studies*, vol. 37, no. 1 (January 1985), pp. 118–130.

30. D. Granick, "The Ministry as the Maximizing Unit in Soviet Industry," *Journal of Comparative Economics*, vol. 4, no. 3 (September 1980), pp. 255–273.

31. A. C. Gorlin and D. P. Doane, "Plan Fulfillment and Growth in Soviet Ministries," *Journal of Comparative Economics*, vol. 7, no. 4 (December 1983), pp. 415–431.

32. M. Keren, "The Ministry, Plan Changes, and the Ratchet Effect in Planning," *Journal of Comparative Economics*, vol. 6, no. 4 (December 1982), pp. 327–342.

33. Our discussion of the role of money in the Soviet economy is based on G. Garvy, *Money, Financial Flows, and Credit in the Soviet Union* (Cambridge, Mass.: Ballinger, 1977), and A. Zwass, *Money, Banking, and Credit in the Soviet Union and Eastern Europe* (White Plains, N.Y.: M. E. Sharpc, 1979). For a history of money in the Soviet Union, see, for example, Z. V. Atlas, *Sotsialisticheskaia denezhnaia sistema* [Socialist monetary system] (Moscow: Finansy, 1969).

34. See Garvy, *Money, Financial Flows, and Credit*, pp. 101–105.

35. For an analysis of informal sources of supply, see A. Katsenelinboigen, "Coloured Markets in the Soviet Union," *Soviet Studies*, vol. 29, no. 1 (January 1977), 62–85.

36. M. V. Condoide, *The Soviet Financial System* (Columbus: Bureau of Business Research of Ohio State University, 1951), pp. 78–79; Nove, *The Soviet Economic System*, chap. 9. For a Soviet textbook on the subject, see M. K. Shermenov, ed., *Finansy SSSR* [Finances of the USSR] (Moscow: Finansy, 1977); R. Hutchings, *The Soviet Budget* (Albany: State University of New York Press, 1983); I. Birman, *Secret Incomes of The Soviet State Budget* (Boston: Martimus Nighoff, 1981).

37. A. Becker, *Soviet National Income, 1958–1964* (Berkeley: University of California Press, 1969), pp. 92–93; Joint Economic Committee, Congress of the United States, *USSR: Measures of Economic Growth and Development, 1950–1980* (Washington, D.C.: U.S. Government Printing Office, 1982), pp. 66–67.

38. This algebraic approach is a modification of the model used by H. Sherman, *The Soviet Economy* (Boston: Little, Brown, 1969), chap. 10, appendix A.

39. Per capita real consumption (not including communal services) declined at an annual rate of −0.3 percent between 1928 and 1937. See J. G. Chapman, "Consumption," in A. Bergson and S. Kuznets, eds., *Economic Trends in the Soviet Union* (Cambridge, Mass.: Harvard University Press, 1963), pp. 238–239.

40. F. D. Holzman, "Soviet Inflationary Pressures, 1928–1957: Causes and Cures," *Quarterly Journal of Economics*, vol. 74, no. 2 (May 1960), 176–180.

41. *Ibid.*, 176.

42. *Ibid.*, 180.

43. For a detailed discussion of the alternative methods of financing Soviet economic development, see F. D. Holzman, "Financing Soviet Economic Development," in M. Abramovitz, ed , *Capital Formation and Economic Growth* (Princeton, N.J.: Princeton University Press, 1955), pp. 229–287.

44. *Ibid.*, pp. 230–238.

45. Holzman, "Soviet Inflationary Pressures," 168, 173.
46. A. Nove, *An Economic History of the USSR* (London: Penguin, 1969), p. 210.
47. Holzman, "Financing Soviet Economic Development," pp. 231–237.
48. On rationing in the 1930s, see V. A. Vinogradov et al., eds., *Istoriia sotsialisticheskoi ekonomiki SSSR* [History of the Socialist economy of the USSR] (Moscow: Nauka, 1978), vol. 4, chap. 13.
49. On pricing, see A. L. Vainshtein, *Tseny i tsenoobrazovanie v SSSR v vostanovitel'ny period* [Prices and price formation in the USSR in the transition period] (Moscow: Nauka, 1972).
50. Nove, *An Economic History of the USSR,* pp. 203–207.
51. The following figures are from *Narodnoe khoziaistvo SSSR v 1978 g.* [The national economy of the USSR in 1978] (Moscow: Statistika, 1979), p. 447; *Statisticheski ezhegodnik stran-chelenov SEV 1983* [Statistical yearbook of member countries of CME 1983] (Moscow: Finansy i Statistika, 1983), p. 301; *Vestnik Statistiki* [Herald of Statistics], no. 9 (1983), p. 67; *SSR v tsifrakl 1983* [USSR in figures 1983], pp. 170–171; *USSR: Measures of Economic Growth,* pp. 66–67.
52. For a discussion of Soviet price indices, see M. Bornstein, "Soviet Price Statistics," in V. G. Treml and J. P. Hardt, eds., *Soviet Economic Statistics* (Durham, N.C.: Duke University Press, 1972), pp. 355–396. The argument has been made that, over time, there has been a systematic and continuing disappearance of the lower price variants of a particular product, thus effectively raising the average retail price.
53. G. E. Schroeder and B. S. Severin, "Soviet Consumption and Income Policies in Perspective," in Joint Economic Committee, *Soviet Economy in a New Perspective* (Washington, D.C.: U.S. Government Printing Office, 1976), pp. 620–660. Also see *USSR: Measures & Economic Growth,* p. 334. For a discussion of this and other evidence on inflation, see J. Pickersgill, "Soviet Inflation: Causes and Consequences," *Soviet Union,* vol. 4, part 2 (1977), 297–313; see also J. Pickersgill, "Soviet Household Saving Behavior," *The Review of Economics and Statistics,* vol. 58, no. 2 (May 1976), 139–147. More generally, see M. Yves Laulan, ed., *Banking, Money and Credit in the USSR* (Brussels: NATO Directorate of Economic Affairs, 1973); M. Yves Laulan, ed., *Economic Aspects of Life in the USSR* (Brussels: NATO Directorate of Economic Affairs, 1975). For evidence on recalculations of industrial price indexes, see J. E. Steiner, "Disguised Inflation in Soviet Industry," *Journal of Comparative Economics,* vol. 6, no. 3 (September 1982), 278–287.
54. R. J. Barro and H. I. Grossman, "A General Disequilibrium Model of Income and Employment," *American Economic Review,* vol. 61, no. 1 (March 1971), 83–93.
55. For a complete statement, see D. H. Howard, *The Disequilibrium Model in a Controlled Economy* (Lexington, Mass.: Heath, 1979).
56. D. H. Howard, "The Disequilibrium Model in a Controlled Economy: An Empirical Test of the Barro-Grossman Model," *American Economic Review,* vol. 66, no. 5 (December 1976), 871–879.
57. B. Katz, "The Disequilibrium Model in a Controlled Economy: Comment," *American Economic Review,* vol. 69, no. 4 (September 1979), 721–725; M. K. Nissanke, "The Disequilibrium Model in a Controlled Economy: Comment," *American Economic Review,* vol. 69, no. 4 (September 1979), 726–732; D. H. Howard, "The Disequilibrium Model in a Controlled Economy: Reply and Further Results," *American Economic Review,* vol. 69, no. 4 (September 1979), 733–738.
58. See, for example, R. Portes, "The Control of Inflation: Lessons from East European Experience," *Economica,* vol. 44, no. 174 (May 1977), 109–130; R. Portes and D. Winter, "The Demand for Money and for Consumption Goods in Centrally Planned

Economies," *The Review of Economics and Statistics,* vol. 60, no. 1 (February 1978), 8–18; R. Portes and D. Winter, "The Supply of Consumption Goods in Centrally Planned Economies," *Journal of Comparative Economics,* vol. 1, no. 4, (December 1977), 351–363.

59. Pickersgill, "Soviet Household Saving Behavior," pp. 139–147.

60. This finding is from the Soviet Interview Project and is reported by J. Millar and E. Clayton, "Quality of Life in the USSR," SIP Working Paper series.

61. I. Birman, *Secret Incomes of the Soviet State Budget* (Hague: Nijhoff, 1981); G. Grossman, "A Note on Soviet Inflation," Joint Economic Committee, *Soviet Economy in the 1980s,* part I (Washington, D.C.: U.S. Government Printing Office, 1982), pp. 267–286.

62. G. Garvy, *Money, Banking and Credit in Eastern Europe* (New York: Federal Reserve Bank of New York, 1966); P. Gekker, "The Banking System of the USSR," *Journal of the Institute of Bankers,* vol. 84, part 3 (June 1963), 189–197; Garvy, *Money, Financial Flows, and Credit;* Zwass, *Money, Banking, and Credit.*

63. P. Hanson, *The Consumer Sector in the Soviet Economy* (Evanston, Ill.: Northwestern University Press, 1968), pp. 175–176.

64. For general treatments of Soviet pricing policies, the reader is referred to the following sources: M. Bornstein, "Soviet Price Theory and Policy," in M. Bornstein and D. Fusfeld, eds., *The Soviet Economy: A Book of Readings* (Homewood, Ill.: Irwin, 1970), pp. 106–137; Hanson, *The Consumer Sector,* chap. 8; M. Bornstein, "The Soviet Price Reform Discussion," *Quarterly Journal of Economics,* vol. 78, no. 1 (February 1964), pp. 15–48; Bergson, *The Economics of Soviet Planning,* chap. 8; M. Bornstein, "The Soviet Debate on Agricultural Prices and Procurement Reforms," *Soviet Studies,* vol. 21, no. 1 (July 1969), pp. 1–20; M. Bornstein, "The Administration of the Soviet Price System," *Soviet Studies,* vol. 30, no. 4 (October 1978), pp. 466–490; M. Bornstein, "Soviet Price Policy in the 1970s," in Joint Economic Committee, *Soviet Economy in a New Perspective* (Washington, D.C.: U.S. Government Printing Office, 1976), pp. 17–66.

65. Bornstein, "Soviet Price Theory and Policy," p. 110; *Narodnoe khoziastvo SSR v 1978 g.* [The National economy of the USSR in 1978], p. 141.

66. The problems of pricing "new" products and the impact of world prices on Soviet prices are discussed in J. S. Berliner, *The Innovation Decision in Soviet Industry* (Cambridge, Mass.: MIT Press, 1976), part 2; V. G. Treml, "Foreign Trade and the Soviet Economy: Changing Parameters and Interrelationships," in E. Neuberger and L. Tyson, eds., *Transmission and Response: The Impact of International Disturbances on the Soviet Union and Eastern Europe* (New York: Pergamon Press, 1980).

66. A. Bergson, and L. Turgeon, "Basic Industrial Prices in the USSR, 1928–1950," The Rand Corporation, Research Memorandum RM-1522, August 1, 1955; *Narodnoe khoziastvo SSSR v 1969 g.* [The national economy of the USSR in 1969] (Moscow: Statistika, 1970), p. 190.

67. For Western recalculations of industrial prices, see A. Becker, "The Price Level of Soviet Machinery in the 1960s," *Soviet Studies,* vol. 26, no. 3 (July 1974), 363–380; J. E. Steiner, *Inflation in Soviet Industry and Machine Building and Metalworking,* SRM78–10142, Office of Strategic Research, Washington, D.C., 1978.

68. For example, sales of clothing and leather footwear grew at an annual rate of around 8 percent between 1968 and 1971. During the same period, clothing and footwear stocks grew at an annual rate of around 19 percent, largely because the types of goods produced failed to correspond to the wishes of the consumer. See *Planovoe khoziaistvo* [The planned economy], no. 10 (1972), pp. 5–7. This growing selectivity also applies

to consumer durables. For example, the "Baku" refrigerator proved to be of such low quality that Azerbaijan SSR consumers refused to buy it. The quick-witted manager in charge of its production then changed the name and appearance and released it as a new model. For an account of this, see *Sotsialisticheskaia industria* [Socialist industry], no. 14 (1969), p. 2.

69. *Vestnik Statistiki* [Journal of Statistics], no. 9 (1984), 80.
70. D. W. Bronson and B. S. Severin, "Consumer Welfare," Joint Economic Committee, *Economic Performance and the Military Burden in the Soviet Union* (Washington, D.C.: U.S. Government Printing Office, 1970), p. 381.
71. Data from *Narodnoe khoziaistvo SSSR v 1978 g.* [The national economy of the USSR in 1978], p. 433; J. F. Karcz, "Quantitative Analysis of the Collective Farm Market," *American Economic Review,* vol. 54, no. 4, part 1 (June 1964), 315–333; see especially the discussion on page 315.
72. See, for example, F. Bator, "The Simple Analytics of Welfare Maximization," *American Economic Review,* vol. 47, no. 1 (February 1957), 22–59. Of course, this definition of optimality (called Pareto Optimality) does not take the optimality of the distribution of income into consideration.
73. Political factors have also been important in maintaining low prices on basic foods such as meat and dairy products. In the post-Stalin era, the Soviet leadership risked popular discontent and sometimes civil unrest when such prices were raised. An example of this was the 30 percent increase in meat and butter prices in 1962. On this, see Hanson, *The Consumer Sector,* pp. 171–177.
74. While charges for such services are generally very low, they do appear more substantial when considered as a portion of family income. Also, it is possible to contract some services—for example, those of a doctor—privately. In such cases, charges will be higher. For a discussion of this point, see R. J. Osborn, *Soviet Social Policies: Welfare, Equality, and Community* (Homewood, Ill.: Dorsey Press, 1970), pp. 89–94.
75. For this view, see Bergson, *The Economics of Soviet Planning,* pp. 166–170.
76. R. P. Powell, "Plan Execution and the Workability of Soviet Planning," *Journal of Comparative Economics,* vol. 1, no. 1 (March 1977), 69–73.
77. See Katsenelinboigen, "Coloured Markets in the Soviet Union"; D. K. Simes, "The Soviet Parallel Market," *Economic Aspects of Life in the USSR* (Brussels: NATO Directorate of Economic Affairs, 1975), pp. 91–100; G. Grossman, "The 'Second Economy' of the USSR," *Problems of Communism,* vol. 26 (September–October 1977), 25–40; G. Grossman, "Notes on the Illegal Private Economy and Corruption," in Joint Economic Committee, *Soviet Economy in a Time of Change* (Washington, D.C.: U.S. Government Printing Office, 1979), vol. 1, pp. 834–855; V. G. Treml, "Production and Consumption of Alcoholic Beverages in the USSR: A Statistical Study," *Journal of Studies on Alcohol,* vol. 36 (March 1975), 285–320; G. E. Schroeder and R. Greenslade, "On the Measurement of the Second Economy in the USSR," *ACES Bulletin,* vol. 21, no. 1 (Spring 1979), 3–22. D. O'Hearn, "The Consumer Second Economy: Size and Effects," *Soviet Studies,* vol. 32, no. 2 (April 1980), 218–234; F. J. M. Feldbrugge, "Government and the Shadow Economy in the Soviet Union," *Soviet Studies,* vol. 36, no. 4 (October 1984), 528–543; B. Rumer, "The 'Second' Agriculture in the USSR," *Soviet Studies,* vol. 33, no. 4 (October 1981), 560–572; R. E. Erickson, "The 'Second Economy' and Resource Allocation Under Central Planning," *Journal of Comparative Economics,* vol. 8, no. 1 (March, 1984), 1–24; R. E. Erickson, "An Allocative Role of the Soviet Second Economy," in P. Desai, ed., *Marxism, Central Planning and the Soviet Economy* (Cambridge, Mass.: The MIT Press, 1983).

78. G. Ofer and A. Vinokur, *Family Budget Survey of Soviet Immigrants in the Soviet Union* (Jerusalem: Soviet and East European Research Center, Hebrew University, June 1977), table 14. G. Ofer and A. Vinokur, *Private Sources of Income of the Soviet Urban Household,* Rand Corporation, R-2359-NA, August 1980.

SELECTED BIBLIOGRAPHY

Political Institutions and Control of the Economy

W. Conyngham, *The Modernization of Soviet Industrial Management* (Cambridge: Cambridge University Press, 1982).
J. F. Hough and M. Fainsod, *How the Soviet Union Is Governed* (Cambridge, Mass.: Harvard University Press, 1979).
A. Nove, *The Soviet Economic System* (London: Allen & Unwin, 1977).
L. Shapiro, *The Government and Politics of the Soviet Union* (Essex: Hutchison Publishing Group, 1978).

Supply and Output Planning

A. Bergson, *The Economics of Soviet Planning* (New Haven, Conn.: Yale University Press, 1964), chap. 7.
P. Bernard, *Planning in the Soviet Union* (Oxford: Pergamon Press, 1966).
M. Bor, *Aims and Methods of Soviet Planning* (New York: International Publishers, 1967).
R. W. Davies, "Planning a Mature Economy," *Economics of Planning,* vol. 6, no. 2 (1966), 138–153.
———, "Soviet Planning for Rapid Industrialization," *Economics of Planning,* vol. 6, no. 1 (1966), 53–67.
M. Ellman, "The Consistency of Soviet Plans," *Scottish Journal of Political Economy,* vol. 16, no. 1 (February 1969), 50–74.
———, *Socialist Planning* (Cambridge: Cambridge University Press, 1979).
F. Kushnirsky, *Soviet Economic Planning, 1965–1980* (Boulder, Colo.: Westview Press, 1982).
H. Levine, "The Centralized Planning of Supply in Soviet Industry," *Comparisons of the United States and Soviet Economies* (Washington, D.C.: U.S. Government Printing Office, 1959).
M. Manove, "A Model of Soviet-Type Economic Planning," *American Economic Review,* vol. 61, no. 3, part 1 (June 1971), 390–406.
J. Marczewski, *Crisis in Socialist Planning, Eastern Europe and the USSR* (New York: Praeger, 1974).
J. M. Montias, "Planning with Material Balances in Soviet-Type Economies," *American Economic Review,* vol. 49, no. 5 (December 1959), 963–985.
G. E. Schroeder, "Recent Developments in Soviet Planning and Managerial Incentives," in U.S. Congress, Joint Economic Committee, *Soviet Economic Prospects for the Seventies* (Washington, D.C.: U.S. Government Printing Office, 1973), pp. 11–38.
———, "The 'Reform' of the Supply System in Soviet Industry," *Soviet Studies,* vol. 24, no. 1 (July 1972), 97–119.
———, "Soviet Economic 'Reform' Decrees: More Steps on the Treadmill" in U.S. Congress, Joint Economic Committee, *Soviet Economy in the 1980s* (Washington, D.C.: U.S. Government Printing Office, 1982), vol. 1, pp. 312–340.

J. Wilhelm, "The Soviet Union has an Administered, not a Planned Economy," *Soviet Studies,* vol. 37, no. 1 (January 1985), 118–130.

E. Zaleski, *Stalinist Planning for Economic Growth* (Chapel Hill: University of North Carolina Press, 1980).

The Soviet Price System

A. Abouchar, ed., *The Socialist Price Mechanism* (Durham, N.C.: Duke University Press, 1977).

A. Becker, "The Price Level of Soviet Machinery in the 1960s," *Soviet Studies,* vol. 26, no. 3 (July 1974), 363–380.

A. Bergson, *The Economics of Soviet Planning* (New Haven, Conn.: Yale University Press, 1964), chap. 8.

M. Bornstein, "The Administration of the Soviet Price System," *Soviet Studies,* vol. 30, no. 4 (October 1978), 466–490.

———, "The 1963 Soviet Industrial Price Revision," *Soviet Studies,* vol. 15, no. 1 (July 1963), pp. 43–52.

———, "The Soviet Debate on Agricultural Prices and Procurement Reforms," *Soviet Studies,* vol. 21, no. 1 (July 1969), 1–20.

———, "Soviet Price Policy in the 1970s," in U.S. Congress, Joint Economic Committee, *Soviet Economy in a New Perspective* (Washington, D.C.: U.S. Government Printing Office, 1976), 17–66.

———, "The Soviet Price Reform Discussion," *Quarterly Journal of Economics,* vol. 78, no. 1 (February 1964), 15–48.

———, "Soviet Price Theory and Policy," in M. Bornstein and D. Fusfeld, eds., *The Soviet Economy,* 3rd ed. (Homewood, Ill.: Irwin, 1970), pp. 106–137.

R. W. Campbell, "Marx, Kantrovich and Novozhilov: Stoimost' Versus Reality," *Slavic Review,* vol. 20, no. 3 (October 1961), 402–418.

P. Hanson, *The Consumer Sector in the Soviet Economy* (Evanston, Ill.: Northwestern University Press, 1968), chaps 7 and 8.

D. H. Howard, "The Disequilibrium Model in a Controlled Economy: An Empirical Test of the Barro-Grossman Model," *American Economic Review,* vol. 66, no. 5 (December 1966), 871–879.

R. Hutchings, "The Origins of the Soviet Industrial Price System," *Soviet Studies,* vol. 13, no. 1 (July 1961), 1–22.

A. Nove, *The Soviet Economic System* (London: Allen & Unwin, 1977), chaps. 2 and 3.

J. Pickersgill, "Soviet Household Savings Behavior," *The Review of Economics and Statistics,* vol. 58, no. 2 (May 1976), 139–147.

R. Powell, "Plan Execution and the Workability of Soviet Planning," *Journal of Comparative Economics,* vol. 1, no. 1 (March 1977), 69–73.

G. E. Schroeder, "The 1966–67 Soviet Industrial Price Reform: A Study in Complications," *Soviet Studies,* vol. 20, no. 4 (April 1969), 462–477.

J. Steiner, "Disguised Inflation in Soviet Industry," *Journal of Comparative Economics,* vol. 6, no. 3 (September 1982), 278–287.

Public Finance and Financial Planning in the Soviet Union

V. P. Diachenko, *Istoriia finansov SSSR* [History of USSR finance] (Moscow: Nauka, 1978).

G. Garvy, *Money, Financial Flows, and Credit in the Soviet Union* (Cambridge, Mass.: Ballinger, 1977).

G. Grossman, "A Note on Soviet Inflation," in U.S. Congress, Joint Economic Committee, *Soviet Economy in the 1980s* (Washington, D.C. U.S. Government Printing Office, 1982), pp. 267–286.

F. D. Holzman, "Financing Soviet Economic Development," in M. Abramovitz, ed., *Capital Formation and Economic Growth* (Princeton, N.J.: Princeton University Press, 1955), pp. 229–287.

F. D. Holzman, "Soviet Inflationary Pressures, 1928–1957: Causes and Cures," *Quarterly Journal of Economics,* vol. 74, no. 2 (May 1960), 167–188.

————, *Soviet Taxation: The Fiscal and Monetary Problems of a Planned Economy* (Cambridge, Mass.: Harvard University Press, 1955).

R. Hutchings, *The Soviet Budget* (Albany: State University of New York Press, 1983).

M. Yves Laulan, ed., *Banking, Money and Credit in the Soviet Union and Eastern Europe* (Brussels: NATO Directorate of Economic Affairs, 1975).

F. L. Pryor, *Public Expenditures in Communist and Capitalist Nations* (Homewood, Ill.: Irwin, 1968).

A. Zwass, *Money, Banking, and Credit in the Soviet Union and Eastern Europe* (White Plains, N.Y.: M. E. Sharpe, 1979).

Second Economy in the Soviet Union

F. J. M. Feldbrugge, "Government and the Shadow Economy in the Soviet Union," *Soviet Studies,* vol. 36, no. 4 (October 1984), 528–543.

G. Grossman, "Notes on the Illegal Private Economy and Corruption," in Joint Economic Committee, *Soviet Economy in a Time of Change* (Washington, D.C.: U.S. Government Printing Office, 1976), pp. 834–855.

————, "The 'Second Economy' of the USSR," *Problems of Communism,* vol. 26 (September–October 1977), 25–40.

A. Katsenelinboigen, "Coloured Markets in the Soviet Union," *Soviet Studies,* vol. 29, no. 1 (January 1977), 62–85.

D. O'Hearn, "The Consumer Second Economy: Size and Effects," *Soviet Studies,* vol. 32, no. 2 (April 1980), 218–234.

D. K. Simes, "The Soviet Parallel Market," *Economic Aspects of Life in the USSR* (Brussels: NATO Directorate of Economic Affairs, 1975), pp. 91–100.

G. Ofer and A. Vinokur, *Private Sources of Income of the Soviet Urban Household,* Rand Corporation, R-2359-NA, August 1980.

chapter 8

How Resources Are Allocated in the Soviet Union

The Soviet Manager, Labor, and Capital

THE SOVIET ENTERPRISE MANAGER

The Soviet manager plays a key role in the Soviet resource allocation process. We begin this chapter with a discussion of Soviet enterprise management—the framework in which managers operate, Soviet managerial personnel, and their responses to enterprise and plan goals under prevailing incentives and constraints. Once the Soviet managerial setting is established, we examine managerial allocation of labor and capital.

The Soviet Firm

The enterprise is the basic unit of production in the Soviet economy. The enterprise is headed by a director (manager), who has a professional management staff. The management staff consists of a deputy director and a chief engineer, chief accountant, chief economist, and chief technologist. Structurally, the Soviet enterprise is specialized in the sense that the subunits, or shops *(tsekh),* are organized to perform specific production tasks. The staff of the enterprise is broken down into white-collar and blue-collar components, and foremen are responsible for the routine activities of blue-collar workers at the shop level. The organizational structure above the enterprise is hierarchical. Managers receive directives from the planning apparatus. Directives come from the responsible chief administration *(glavk)* of the ministry, from the production association, and from *Gosplan.* It is the responsibility of the manager, within constraints both formal and informal, to achieve plan directives. Rewards, both monetary and nonmonetary,

215

are designed to induce the appropriate managerial response to plan directives. Planning authorities recognize that managerial staff, like the staff of workers, require incentives to encourage work effort.

An authority on Soviet management, William G. Conyngham, notes that "Historically, Soviet management has been characterized by centralism, verticalism, and one-man management."[1] In effect, these are the basic principles underlying the Soviet managerial system.

Centralism refers to the concept of democratic centralism, long a basic feature of the Soviet political system. Under this concept, discussion is encouraged on any particular issue until a decision is formalized. At this point, centralism prevails, and the decision is binding upon subordinates. Thus, enterprise managers can contribute to plan formulation through discussion of control figures and supply targets; the plan, however, once formulated, is law. The Soviet system is a vertically organized hierarchy. Although Soviet enterprises can be subordinated to more than one external organization, for example, both to a ministry and to a local political (or state) unit, directives come from above, and the task of the manager is to achieve the wishes of those in power.

Although emphasis on the collective prevails in Soviet society, the principle of one-man management *(edinonachalie)* means that the enterprise manager is, in fact, responsible for the operations of the enterprise. "Edinonachalie" means that the manager has the authority to direct the labor and capital resources of the enterprise (within the constraints imposed by the plan). The manager's staff is obliged to obey the manager's directives, according to Soviet law. The principle of one-man management has been a key feature of the Soviet management system since the early 1930s. It clearly establishes the responsibility and authority of the Soviet manager over the collective of workers.[2]

This is a managerial structure familiar to students of the Western corporation. It is a structure in which there is managerial input but where rules imposed from above are important. The manager is held responsible for the success or failure of enterprise operations and derives considerable personal benefit from successful operation. Success is not automatic. There are a number of risks and obstacles that make the managerial outcome uncertain. In this sense, the Soviet manager, like his Western counterpart, operates under considerable pressure.

Enterprise Planning and the Soviet Manager

The operation of the Soviet industrial enterprise is governed in most every respect by the *techpromfinplan* (technical-industrial-financial plan). This plan is the annual (semiannual, quarterly, monthly) subplan of long-term (five- to seven-year) "perspective" plans (although we have noted that the link between the two is often difficult to find) and is itself composed of subplans, each comprising a number of appropriate indicators or targets pertaining to the operation of the enterprise. In its broadest sense, the *techpromfinplan* sets forth the social goals—in the Soviet case, planners' preferences—that the enterprise is to implement. In a narrow sense, the *techpromfinplan* specifies output levels (in quantity and value terms), output assortment, labor and other inputs, productivity indexes, profit norms, and so on, which the enterprise is expected to observe.

The most important component of the *techpromfinplan* has been the production plan. Based upon the capacity of the enterprise (normally defined as past performance plus some increment to incorporate planned capacity expansion), expected resource utilization, and estimated productivity increases, the production plan has typically specified the ruble value of output *(valovaia produktsia)*, the commodity assortment, and the delivery schedule of this output.*

In addition to the production plan, the *techpromfinplan* includes a number of other component plans, the most important of which are the financial plan (the monetary expression of the physical plan), the plan of material and technical supply, the delivery plan, the plan of plant and equipment utilization, the plan of labor and wages, and, finally, indexes of labor productivity.

In the above plans, state goals and the means for their achievement are elaborated, and within the plan framework, the enterprise is exhorted by the state and party to perform all these tasks at the best possible levels.

One might conclude from this formal version of Soviet planning that the Soviet managers' freedom to make decisions is severely restricted. The *techpromfinplan* governs their choice of enterprise inputs and outputs, and they are morally and legally obligated to implement the plan, with bonuses geared to motivate them in this direction. Looking beneath the surface, however, one unearths a significant area of managerial flexibility. Due in large part to the inability of central organs to specify and control all details of local enterprise operation, Soviet managers do have a sphere of decision-making freedom.

Plan Execution by the Soviet Manager

Both formally and informally, one of the most important functions of the factory manager is the translation of state goals into daily tasks. If one considers the enterprise plan, it is readily apparent that the Soviet manager is confronted with both multiple targets (outputs, cost reduction, innovation, deliveries, etc.) and multiple constraints. Yet the enterprise plan fails to specify formally either the nature of the maximand (enterprise goal) or, for that matter, the nature of the trade-offs among possibly competing goals. The plan does not tell the manager which goals are more important than others, except informally—through party campaigns, bonuses, word of mouth, and other means. The manager is thus faced with a dilemma. If all plan indicators cannot be simultaneously and harmoniously achieved,† which ones should be met and which sacrificed and to what degree

---

*Enterprises producing homogeneous products often have their output targets stated in physical units rather than value terms—such as tons of cement, square meters of textiles, or tons of plastic —with a specified assortment. It is here that the reform of 1965 sought to make a substantial impact by moving away from gross output toward sales as an important success indicator. These changes are examined in detail in Chapter 13.

†A common conflict under conditions of ambitious output targets occurs between profit maximization and output target fulfillment. The graph below illustrates how this conflict may arise. The enterprise's output target is Q', which it produces at an average cost above the price that it

in each case?[3] This question is resolved in the capitalist enterprise by the use of profit as an enterprise goal and a set of scarcity prices such that the trade-offs among various objectives are readily apparent.

While profits have always formally been a part of the economic calculus of the Soviet enterprise, their maximization has generally not been an important enterprise goal either in theory or practice.[*] In fact, quite apart from the meaning of profit in the light of Soviet prices, profits have tended to be of minimal importance in the operation of an enterprise. What then replaces profits in the Soviet managerial calculus? In essence, the plan, the formal and informal constraints, and the managerial incentive structure have made *gross output*—and more recently, refinements such as "realized" gross output (sales) or net output —the most important indicator of enterprise performance. In short, managers have been rewarded primarily for the achievement of output targets, and, accordingly, those targets not directly related to output have tended to be of secondary importance.

A frequent misconception should be cleared up at this point. Soviet enterprises do operate on an independent "economic accounting" *(khozraschet)* system, which is often taken to mean that Soviet enterprises operate to maximize profits. The *khozraschet,* or official managerial accounting system of the Soviet industrial enterprise, cannot, however, be understood to imply that profit and other monetary variables are of prime importance. Enterprise profits are calculated, but the *khozraschet* system simply guarantees that enterprises have financial relations with external organs such as *Gosbank* and, further, that their operations are elaborated and evaluated in terms of value indicators using official prices. The minimal practical significance of *khozraschet* to the Soviet economy must be understood, for, in the first instance, the structure of Soviet prices makes such calculations suspect, and, in the second, the result of such value calculations have had little impact upon the present and future direction of enterprise activities. Future production targets are generally not a function of current profits. This aspect of the Soviet managerial system should be emphasized in view of the crucial role of profits in market economies.

---

receives (and thus makes losses denoted by the area of the loss rectangle). To maximize enterprise profits, the enterprise would restrict its output to Q (and fail to fulfill its output target) but would maximize profits denoted by the profit rectangle.

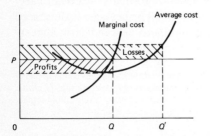

[*]The enhanced role of profits in the Soviet enterprise after 1965 as a consequence of the September 1965 economic reform will be discussed in Chapter 13. The reform theoretically increased the importance of two performance indicators: "realized" output (sales) and enterprise profits.

The Success Indicator Problem

The choice of gross output instead of profits as the crucial "success indicator" of managerial performance generates a series of problems. In most cases, maximands relating to output (whether in value or quantity terms) cannot be defined in perfect detail by central authorities, and in the Soviet case in particular, gross production "success indicators" have led to considerable managerial freedom and often distortion. Where the weight of the output has been the success indicator in the production of castings, for example, castings tend to be made heavier than necessary, thus wasting scarce inputs. Where size has been the indicator, in the production of cloth, for example, managers favor large sizes and largely ignore assortment goals. These distortions are only a part, however, of what has been described as the problem of success indicators in Soviet industry.[4]

We noted that the planners estimate plant capacity—a crucial aspect of plan formulation—as a direct function of past performance plus allowances for productivity improvements. At the enterprise level, however, managers face a dilemma: if they significantly overfulfill output targets in the current year, they may receive a sizable bonus, but in subsequent years, targets will be substantially increased (the "ratchet effect"), thereby diminishing the likelihood of bonus earnings in the immediate future. As a result, managers will tend to be cautious about overfulfilling plan targets even if overfulfillment is well within their grasp. Another problem arises from the stress upon the expansion of output in combination with a bonus system that reinforces this narrow production-oriented conception of performance. A rapid expansion of physical output this year is unambiguously "good" according to the success indicator, irrespective of poor performance in other areas. Thus, technological change, cost reduction, quality improvements, and on-time deliveries, all very important indicators for the Soviet economy as a whole, tend to be secondary considerations as far as the manager is concerned.

The uncertain supply system imposes risk and uncertainty on Soviet managers. Soviet managers are faced by continual pressure from above in the form of taut production targets. Therefore, management must rely heavily on the efficient functioning of the material and technical supply system, a system over which management has little formal control. Yet enterprise output depends to a great extent upon the availability of appropriate inputs in the proper quantity and quality and at the appropriate time. In the absence of a genuine wholesale market, the enterprise must rely upon all other supplier enterprises to meet its plan obligations, and a failure by a single enterprise can cause continuing reverberations throughout the system.[5] The supply system is crucial to enterprise plan fulfillment; yet its manifold weaknesses outlined above continue to impede enterprise target fulfillment.[6]

Informal Behavior Patterns

The emphasis on taut production targets has led to certain informal behavior patterns by enterprise management. First, the manager must make decisions based upon his perception of what is important to his superiors in the hierarchy.

The astute manager uses plan directives, the bonus system, informal and formal communications from the party, and simple intuition as indicators of the prevailing priority structure.

Historically, the priority system has consistently signalled the priority of output performance over other plan targets. Thus, the priority system directs them to emphasize output performance over other plan targets, with the resulting neglect of costs, innovations, quality, and so on. Second, the priority system signals to managers the relative importance of the various enterprises with whom they conduct business. If managers find themselves unable to meet delivery obligations to both enterprises X and Y, they must rely on their priority awareness to make their choice.

The major reason for the important role of priorities in the world of the Soviet manager is the existence of supply uncertainty, which itself is due to the tautness of planning and to planning errors. The priority system does have its positive aspect, because, in an imperfect system, it ensures that planners get their high-priority targets irrespective of planning errors and supply deficiencies; yet it does force managers to seek informal sources of supply and to engage in dysfunctional practices.

A second informal behavior pattern is the *safety factor* phenomenon. The combination of ambitious targets, uncertain supply, and substantial rewards for fulfillment of priority targets, causes the manager to search for organizational slack, or a *safety factor,* as it is called in the Soviet parlance. This search leads the manager into patterns of dysfunctional behavior, for example, the hoarding of material supplies (especially those most likely to be in short supply), thus immobilizing scarce resources.[7] This stockpiling is not totally dysfunctional, for the Soviet manager will use his *tolkach* (expediter) to barter and exchange stockpiled materials with other enterprises. Nevertheless, this informal supply system operated by the tolkach (and tolerated by planning and legal authorities) results in a weakening of centralized control over material allocation—a definitely undesirable feature from the planning authorities' point of view. Yet the toleration of the informal supply system indicates that the authorities have reluctantly accepted it as a necessary evil, required by the frequent breakdowns in the official supply system.

Third, under the existing priority system, there is a tendency for managers to avoid change, for the manager is not suitably rewarded for process and product innovation. Such innovations are considered risky because they might endanger plan fulfillment during the current period, and they carry little potential reward because output targets will simply be ratcheted upward if the innovations are successful. At the same time, quality, which is typically very difficult to incorporate effectively into quantitative indicators, has tended to be of secondary importance to the manager, who tends to be judged on the basis of *production,* not quality of product. Also, in a sellers' market, those searching for supplies will be less likely to complain about inferior quality. In this case, the economic facts of life dictate against the use of legal and other channels to seek redress of supply grievances pertaining to quality or quantity.

Fourth, the bonus structure has tended to penalize 99 percent fulfillment, but offers substantial rewards for 101 percent fulfillment. This discontinuous aspect of the bonus system, plus the other characteristics outlined earlier (especially supply inadequacy), lead to *storming,* or the production of a substantial portion of the monthly output in the final few days of the month. The result of *storming* is a reinforcement of other dysfunctional features—irregular delivery on supply contracts, improper utilization of capacity, poor quality, and so forth.[8]

Soviet Management and Incentives[9]

The basic problems of management are not peculiar to the Soviet industrial enterprise; their counterparts can be found for the most part in capitalist industrial enterprises. Given a set of goals (whether from a board of directors or a central planner), and given that appropriate information for both plan formulation and execution is held largely at local levels (in the branch plant of a capitalist enterprise, for example), how is a managerial environment and incentive structure to be constructed such that (1) managers know precisely what is expected from them, and (2) they are motivated to carry out the directives of their superiors in the true spirit of the directive?

The relationship between the Soviet manager and his planning superiors is a classic principal/agent problem (see previous chapter). The planning authorities (in this case, typically the ministry) want the manager (the agent) to implement a number of goals imposed by the principal. These goals, explicitly stated in the enterprise's *techpromfinplan*, translate into concrete targets given to him in proper assortment and qualities, with a minimal expenditure of the resources allocated by the principal. If the principal had perfect information about the operations of the enterprise and could perfectly monitor the actions of the agent, there would be no principal/agent problem. In fact, under these circumstances, there would be no need for a manager because the principal could directly manage the enterprise from above. Because the principal's information is not perfect and because the principal cannot perfectly monitor the agent, the agent must be given the flexibility to make certain key decisions concerning the output and inputs of the enterprise. With the agent able to exercise decision-making authority, the principal must devise a monitoring and incentive scheme to cause the agent to act in the best interests of the principal.

If the principal and agent have identical goals, there is no principal/agent problem because the agent will automatically act in the interests of the principal. However, if the agent has different goals from the principal, then it is up to the principal's monitoring and incentive schemes to ensure that the agent does not act contrary to the interests of the principal. If the main goal of managers is to achieve a quiet, secure life, the manager may wish to bargain for easy output targets and liberal input allocations, and may supply misleading information to the principal to convince the principal that the manager's requests are legitimate. The principal, however, wants the agent to produce the maximum output with minimum expenditure of resources. When the fundamental goals of principal and agent conflict, the principal must devise an incentive and a monitoring system to encourage the agent to pursue the goals of the principal, not the agent's own goals.

The Soviet answer to the principal/agent problem is a managerial framework that combines a relatively high degree of centralization of decision-making within a rather formal bureaucratic structure with a significant degree of managerial freedom through informal decentralization. Thus, the hierarchical centralized planning structure implies that managers respond to "rules" while, at the same time, the *khozraschet* enterprise system implies that managers have a degree of local freedom and initiative in the operation of the enterprise.

It must be recognized that in almost any organization, there will exist both a formal and an informal sphere of managerial decision authority. In a sense, the latter oils the operation of the former. In the Soviet case, to the degree that the latter does not smooth the operation of the former, there exists a myriad of internal and external enterprise controls to reorient enterprise behavior along desirable paths. These controls will be examined as we consider the Soviet managerial reward structure.

Managerial Personnel and Rewards

Before considering the Soviet managerial reward system, let us consider the profile of Soviet industrial management. From the evidence gathered by Western authorities on Soviet management,[10] we know that the typical Soviet manager is probably well-educated (usually at the college level)—most likely in the field of engineering, with minimal emphasis on finance and what we would describe as "business" courses. This is an interesting deviation from the American pattern where, for example, the manager has to be primarily conversant with financial and sales matters. Instead, the Soviet managers' engineering training prepares them more for technological production problems. While Soviet managers are typically not from a working-class background, they will, during the course of their educational experience and also throughout the period of managerial advancement, receive more practical training than their American counterparts.

The rewards for successful managerial performance can be significant. Although data in this area are limited, it is probably safe to generalize that the typical Soviet manager earns a base pay substantially higher than the average Soviet worker, and further, that monetary bonuses are a significant portion of total earnings. Bonus payments have varied substantially both over time and by regions. In 1934, the share of bonus earnings in managerial incomes averaged 4 percent, rising to 11 percent by 1940. It was allowed to rise to 33 percent under wartime pressures but declined after the war to 12 to 15 percent in the mid-1950s. In 1961, the share dropped to 8 percent. The renewed emphasis on material incentives after 1961 caused the relative importance of managerial bonuses to rise again, to 16 percent in 1965 and to 35 percent in 1970.[11] Thus, bonus earnings are important for the Soviet factory manager, although, as a portion of aggregate managerial earnings, they were of no greater importance in the Soviet Union than in the United States in the 1960s.[12] It should be noted, however, that while participation in bonus schemes is generally universal for Soviet managerial personnel, such is not the case in the United States.

The bonus system has changed since 1965 in one important dimension.

While gross output (or some variant thereof) remains an important determinant of bonuses, they are now awarded for the achievement of a variety of plan indicators, specified in advance of the operational period. The managerial bonus formula has changed over the years. During periods when labor productivity is of great concern, labor productivity performance is an important determinant of bonuses. When planners are concerned with raising product quality, quality indicators become an important ingredient in managerial bonuses. In this sense, managers are aware of the importance placed by the planners on the achievement of various plan indicators. The inclusion of a number of indicators in the managerial bonus formula means that planning authorities wish managers to turn in a good performance for each indicator. It also means that managers can trade off one performance indicator for another. The weights attached to each indicator help determine the nature of this trade-off. David Granick, an expert on Soviet management practices, views the change in bonus-setting arrangements as being an important departure from past practices.[13]

Executive bonuses in the United States tend to be paid for achievement of both short-run and long-run objectives. For example, the American manager is expected to strike a proper balance between short-run and long-run profitability. Insofar as stock prices tend to reflect investor perceptions of long-run profitability, American corporate managers must pay attention to the effect of current actions on long-run profitability. In addition, bonus arrangements in the United States are more likely to be based on subjective evaluations of performance.[14] In the Soviet Union, however, bonus payments tend to be for short-run rather clearly defined tasks, such as the quantitative fulfillment of a specific output target or specific cost reductions. The short-run nature of Soviet bonuses tends to create an environment of pressure, and this in itself becomes a mechanism through which short-run priorities can readily be identified by managers. It is in this sense that some longer-run targets, such as quality, innovation, and new technology may well be set aside in favor of more rewarding short-run achievements.

In the Soviet case, the monetary bonus awards are normally awarded on a short-run basis (i.e., monthly), while the nonmonetary rewards are in greater measure long-run rewards, although they, too, can be thought of as defining priority goals and delineating the sphere of informal managerial behavior. Enterprises may, for example, provide the manager with living quarters and an automobile, the latter most likely with a driver. Both are significant amenities in present-day Soviet society when one considers the shortage of housing space (and the lack of a formal market for the purchase of same) and the prestige and convenience of an automobile. Finally, the enterprise manager can anticipate participation in local, state, and party organs, adulation in the press for particularly good performance, and also upward mobility to positions of greater prestige and reward.

While the Soviet manager's position is one of potentially significant monetary rewards, it is also one of significant risk. First, in an environment of uncertainty where the manager lacks decisive control over all inputs (for example, the delivery of material supplies to the enterprise on time), the manager is clearly in danger of not being able to meet priority targets. There are two possible consequences of such failure: loss of bonus, which represents a substantial portion of total income, or loss of job. A third consequence, execution or imprisonment, was widespread during the 1930s, when failures to fulfill targets were seen to be the work of saboteurs. Fortunately, Soviet managers no longer work under this threat.* Executive turnover was very high in the 1930s, although it is clear that this pattern has changed significantly in recent years. Thus, for the postwar years, turnover of Soviet managerial personnel at both the middle and upper levels has been substantially less than that of comparable managerial personnel in American corporations. This represents significantly increased job security for Soviet managers of the 1960s, 1970s, and 1980s as opposed to those of the 1930s.[15] At the same time, it may suggest a degree of stagnation in the management system and the aging of managers, deemed an important factor in recent years.[16]

EXTERNAL CONSTRAINTS UPON SOVIET MANAGERS

Numerous internal and external constraints upon managerial flexibility make the job of the Soviet manager even more difficult. The planning and administrative bodies external to the firm also have targets to meet, which depend upon the performance of subordinate enterprises. Regional and ministerial authorities are therefore interested in forcing enterprises under their control to exert themselves to the maximum. This relationship is significant, whether industry is arranged on a territorial or ministerial basis, for higher bodies will place pressure upon the subordinate enterprises to ensure fulfillment of their own targets. The ministry practice of holding back enterprise supply allotments ("reserving") and of planning enterprise targets to exceed the aggregate ministry target are part of this pressure. In this manner, managers are subjected to increased pressure from their immediate supervisors. In addition, while the *khozraschet* system of management implies a degree of autonomy for the enterprise, it also suggests the establishment of financial rewards and connections with the State Bank—a further form of external control. The system of "ruble control" implies that the funds of the enterprise must be deposited in the bank and that the bank will exercise control over enterprise funds.

The role played by external forces is not necessarily negative. The regional or local party or state organization tends to be judged on the basis of the success or failure of enterprises under its jurisdiction. Thus, the local party organization is often prepared to represent the interests of local enterprise managers in disputes over input allocations or the lowering of plan targets. There is evidence that enterprises that experience plan fulfillment difficulties are able to get plan reductions *(korrektirovki)* and that the influence of the party can be helpful in this regard. The role of the supervising ministry remains unclear. The ministry is ultimately judged by the success or failure of the enterprises it supervises, so it would want to avoid the appearance of widescale failure. Thus, there are reasons to suspect that ministries would want to help out struggling enterprises. On the other hand, the ministry itself has targets that it must meet (such as producing

---

*One can better understand the dysfunctional behavior of Soviet managers and their search for the "safety factor" by remembering that these practices originated during the 1930s, when managers faced severe consequences if they failed to meet plan obligations.

a certain number of tons of steel, or trucks, or cement). If it is too easy on its own enterprises, then the ministry target will be jeopardized. An important research task of Western researchers is to determine the working relationships between the ministry and its enterprises.

INTERNAL CONSTRAINTS: THE TRADE UNION

Assessing the role of labor unions in Soviet society is a difficult task. In Western economics, labor unions are perceived as performing extra-market allocation functions. Since Soviet ideology views the objectives of the individual worker and the state as identical, one might question the role of an organization generally thought to defend the rights of the worker vis-à-vis the employer. Moreover, since Soviet trade unions do not have a formal role in wage setting and are not permitted legally to organize strikes, important functions of Western trade unions seem to be absent. What, then, is the nature and role of trade unions in the Soviet economic system?

As Blair A. Ruble, a Western authority on Soviet labor, notes, socialist unions in general and Soviet unions in particular ". . . have two divergent functions: on the one hand, they exhort workers to produce more; on the other, they defend the rights and interests of union members as those interests are defined by law."[17] The balance between these functions and the methods used for their achievement have varied over time. Indeed, as we have already emphasized, the Khrushchev and post-Khrushchev periods have witnessed varying degrees of emphasis on incentives versus controls as a way to achieve desired objectives. Although recent changes in labor regulations seem to imply a growing support for controls over incentives, it is not this clear within the trade union movement, where the general issue of working conditions is paramount for the union.

Soviet trade unions are organized on the production principle, meaning that workers in a given sector of the economy will belong to a particular union. There are approximately 31 such unions, with a membership of roughly 130 million workers.[18] The structure of Soviet trade union is exceedingly complex, but it begins with general meetings of union members at the enterprise level culminating in the Congress of Soviet Trade Unions—the All Union Central Council of Trade Unions (AUCCTU) as the highest governing body.

Within the enterprise, a union chairman is elected.[19] This election is subject to a number of important constraints such as the nomenklatura procedure described earlier (Chapter 1). Nevertheless, it is the function of this union representative, now responsible to higher levels of union authority, to work within the additional confines of party and managerial authority. In the enterprise, then, the key relationship is among the enterprise director, the head of the party, and the union representative.

In a Soviet enterprise, the union and the manager negotiate a collective agreement operating under the general principle of democratic centralism, a concept discussed earlier. This agreement governs the conditions of labor in the enterprise. There is a formal and complex grievance procedure for those arguing that provisions of the agreement are not being implemented.

Understanding the formal structure of Soviet trade unions is a complicated task. Assessing their practical operation and impact is considerably more difficult, for a variety of reasons. There is little or no uniformity in collective agreements, so it is not surprising that reported outcomes of the union process differ significantly from one case to another. The nature of the union function is much more complicated than is implied by the traditional Western interpretation. On the one hand, it is true that with regard to important issues such as wages, Soviet trade union power is limited. It is also true that much of Soviet trade union activity at all levels is devoted to broad cultural issues, recreation facilities, and the like.[20] But in terms of the take-home pay of the Soviet worker, the trade union can have an impact not only at upper levels as pay scales are established, but also at local levels in terms of interpreting those pay scales and the many supplements (for example, bonus arrangements) that can and do vary locally.[21] Finally, the area of enforcement is also a matter of complexity. For example, safety is of major concern to Soviet trade unions. However, recent evidence seems to support the view that in spite of sometimes very successful trade union action in support of improved safety rules and conditions, Soviet safety standards and enforcement should be a matter of major concern.[22]

Soviet trade unions are complex organizations functioning in a peculiar environment. In recent years, there have been reports of labor unrest, though frequently these seem to be related to unenforced rights rather than efforts to make fundamental changes.[23] However, as the Soviet economy enters the 1990s, the Soviet trade union movement bears watching as it attempts to come to grips with increased worker unrest in countries such as Poland and with attempts by Soviet leaders to pursue an egalitarian distribution of income while at the same time motivating Soviet workers to work harder and be more efficient.

LABOR ALLOCATION IN THE SOVIET UNION

The allocation of labor in the Soviet economy is accomplished through a combination of administrative controls and market forces. The latter, in the form of voluntary responses to wage differentials, primarily affect the supply of labor in various occupations and regions, whereas administrative controls have been used to affect both the supply and demand sides of the Soviet labor market, with the mix of market forces and administrative controls changing over time. In describing labor allocation, we first concentrate on general long-run trends, after which consideration will be given to periods when labor allocation has diverged distinctly from the central tendency. Given the important role played by the market in labor allocation, we shall consider both the demand and supply of labor in the Soviet economy. Let us consider first the determination of enterprise demand for labor through the planning system.

Labor Planning in the Soviet Union

In the Soviet Union, the amount of labor required by an industrial enterprise is decided largely outside of the firm by superior authorities. In fact, the determination of enterprise labor staffing is an integral part of the general planning process.

The enterprise *techpromfinplan* contains not only enterprise output and material input targets but also instructions on labor inputs. The amount of detail on labor staffing has varied over the years. However, throughout most of the plan era, *techpromfinplan* labor staffing instructions have tended to be quite detailed, specifying the enterprise wage bills, the distribution of enterprise labor force by wage classes, average wages, planned increases in labor productivity, and so on. As one might recognize from our discussion of the Soviet manager, the manager has tended to exercise some discretion in the area of labor staffing within the constraints of the *techpromfinplan*; nevertheless, enterprise labor staffing is basically a decision made by planning authorities in accordance with the production plans that they also determine.

Gosplan derives a balance for the Soviet labor force just as it derives balances for material inputs. The most important part of such Soviet manpower balancing is the estimation of available manpower resources, which is carried out by *Gosplan* with the help of regional and local governments and planning authorities. This is not an easy task, for the reserve labor force in agriculture must be estimated along with the potential reserves among the female population, in addition to existing urban labor resources. Also, demographic factors such as birth and death rates and migration rates between regions and between the countryside and towns must be considered.

Once the available supply (both actual and potential) of labor resources has been estimated, *Gosplan* must estimate the demands for labor resources. The labor requirements of the various economic branches are determined in much the same manner as material input requirements. The planning authorities estimate in detail (after considerable bargaining and consultation with lower echelons)— on the basis of coefficients (norms) relating labor inputs to outputs—the labor staffing required to produce the given output targets. As in the case of material inputs, enterprises and lower planning echelons have commonly exaggerated their labor staffing needs for the purpose of adding to their safety factor, and planning authorities have had to allocate labor resources below enterprise requests to balance supplies and demands. Another complication is the fact that labor productivity tends to increase over time, meaning that the relationship between enterprise outputs and labor inputs varies over time, adding another variable to the problem of estimating required labor inputs.[24]

Once the planning authorities draw up the balance of labor resources, a second problem arises: How are they to bring the appropriate amount of labor into the various enterprises, or to use the Soviet terminology, how are they to "guarantee the labor requirements of the national economy"?[25]

Population Growth: Long-Run Supply

The supply of labor to the Soviet economy is a function of the population base from which it is derived and the manner in which members of households decide to participate in the labor force. Both sets of forces are interrelated, but first we examine some salient features of Soviet population dynamics, turning thereafter to incentive arrangements.[26]

The Soviets inherited from the tsars a population that had been growing rapidly since the 1860s due to high fertility and declining mortality. Despite enormous losses during World Wars I and II, high rates of natural increase and territorial annexations caused the population of the USSR to grow at an annual rate of slightly under 1.5 percent between 1926 and 1985. During the early postwar period, Soviet population growth was especially rapid (1.7 percent per annum between 1951 and 1966). Since the early 1960s, there has been a sharp and continuing decline in the rate of growth of the Soviet population due to declining Soviet fertility. Although expansion of the labor force has continued due to the continuing growth of population in the able-bodied ranges (16 through 54 years for women and 16 through 59 years for men), this growth will largely end in the mid- and late 1980s. At the same time, overall labor force participation rates are very high, suggesting limited, if any, addition to the labor supply from this source. Although there has been a serious female/male imbalance in the Soviet population resulting from the impact of World War II, this imbalance has been declining along with the general aging of the population.

Beyond the basic demographic patterns outlined above, there are other factors that affect labor supply. In the Soviet case, regional redistribution has been important, most notably the outmigration from rural to urban areas. While serving as a major source of industrial labor in the past, the importance of the rural sector as a supplier of labor to urban areas has declined due to the aging of the rural population, the need to maintain the growth of agricultural output, and the difficulty of accommodating rural migrants in already crowded Soviet cities.[27] Regional migration must be used to alleviate regional labor shortages, although Soviet past experience in this area suggests limited potential. In the case of Siberia, for example, higher wages have attracted new workers, but high turnover rates inhibit the development of a stable productive labor force. In Central Asia, the one region of the Soviet Union where the rate of growth of population remains high (and well above that prevailing in European Russia), migration of the able-bodied population has not been significant.[28]

Soviet policies have been modified to encourage the greater overall participation of younger and older people. For example, students are used to offset seasonal imbalances and for short-term needs in agriculture. Rules have been modified to enable older person (specifically pensioners) to return to work yet still retain pension benefits.

All of these measures can make a contribution to increasing the Soviet labor supply and improving the regional distribution of labor. However, at the present level of labor productivity, the Soviet economy is perceived to have a significant labor shortage. According to existing demographic projections, this problem will persist through the 1990s. But it is one thing to have people available and another to have them participate in the labor force at the appropriate level and with the maximum effort. Let us examine this aspect of the labor supply decision.

There are a number of alternative means by which eligible participants could be induced to contribute effectively to the labor effort. First, administrative means could be used. In an extreme form, the state could conscript (or incarcerate) labor and assign it to particular regions and particular sectors of the economy. A second alternative would be the use of material and moral rewards, differentiated to attract labor to those regions and sectors where it is needed most. Finally, as a long-term variant, the supply of labor could be influenced through manpower training, education, and organized recruitment.

In the Soviet case, all of these mechanisms have been used. In times other than collectivization of war, emphasis has been placed upon the use of market-type mechanisms—wages, education, and training—to influence household decision-making. Although the importance of controls has increased somewhat in recent years, we view relative wages as the most important force influencing Soviet labor force allocation. At the same time, market forces have been constrained in a number of ways—such as closed cities, the passport system, and labor mobilization.[29] Let us examine each of the allocational mechanisms in greater detail.

Differential Wages in the Soviet Union

Soviet wage-setting authorities have long recognized the allocative function of differential wages, and the principle has been accepted that wage determination should be governed by the needs of labor allocation rather than by considerations of equality.[30] Problems of poverty and income inequality should therefore be corrected by the social security system, not by the manipulation of wage differentials. Wage authorities point out that the "wrong" set of wage differentials will adversely affect labor productivity and promote excessive labor turnover. Ideologically, wage differentials are justified by the socialist distribution principle of "equal pay for equal work" and by Lenin's admonition against "equality mongering." Differentials are justified by Marx's labor theory of value, which recognizes that different types of labor must be converted into a common denominator. The Soviets call this the "principle of the reduction of labor." Insofar as labor consists of six dimensions—the length of time worked, the skill required, the region, the industry, the enterprise in which the work is performed, and working conditions—a socialist wage scale must differentiate among workers according to these dimensions.

Industrial wages are set by central authorities in the Soviet Union. Various agencies have over time participated in wage scale determination—the ministries, the Council of Ministers, the Central Council of Trade Unions, the State Committee on Labor and Wages, and many others—but the trend since 1956 has been toward uniformity in regulating wages by increasing centralization and standardization. A nationwide reform of industrial wages ongoing from 1956 to 1965, but largely completed between 1958 and 1960, established a more simplified uniform system of industrial wages for the Soviet labor force.[31] A new round of reforms between 1972 and 1976 extended the earlier reforms to other economic branches and continued the process of standardization of wage scales.

Industrial wage rates are set in the following manner: in each industrial branch, base rates *(stavka)* specifying the absolute wage of the lowest paid occupation are established. Then for each branch, a schedule *(tarifnaia setka)* is designated, which gives the wages of higher-grade occupations as percentages of the lowest-grade rate.[32] By altering the base rate, the state can direct labor into and out of branches according to the plan. In this manner, high average wages in high-priority sectors such as machinery, metallurgy, electricity, and coal were used to effect the dramatic shifts of labor out of agriculture and light industry into heavy industry during the early plan era. During NEP, average wages in the consumer goods sector exceeded those in heavy industry. Beginning with the first Five Year Plan, average wages in heavy industry grew more rapidly than in light industry, with a resulting shift of labor.[33] In the postwar period, a close correlation still persists between average branch wages and the national importance of the branch,[34] although recent statements suggest that wage authorities are now attempting to reduce differentials between light and heavy industries.[35]

By manipulating the *tarifnaia setka,* the state can encourage workers to acquire the skills that it requires. Thus, Stalin established schedules in 1931 that heavily favored skilled workers, to encourage the then untrained labor force to acquire industrial skills. As a result of the Stalin wage policy, large differentials arose between the earnings of skilled and nonskilled industrial workers. In fact, some evidence suggests that industrial wage differentials during the 1930s were larger than in the United States.[36] With the growing level of education of the labor force, the extreme differentials of the 1930s have been gradually reduced since World War II, especially after 1956; and between 1956 and 1976, new ratios were established that set the rates of the most-skilled categories at a maximum of 2.1 times those of unskilled categories—as opposed to the 4:1 to 8:1 ratios of the 1930s and 1950s. Two other factors have contributed to the leveling of industrial wages in the postwar period: minimum wage rates have been increased dramatically (they doubled between 1957 and 1968 and then were raised another 17 percent in 1971) and the numbers (and percentage) of workers making low wages have declined markedly. In August 1982, industrial workers were divided into six *tarifnaia setkas,* with over 50 percent in the third and fourth categories. Some workers in ferrous metallurgy, iron ores, and machine building worked according to eight *tarifnaia setkas,* with 75 percent congregating in the third through the fifth categories.[37]

Industrial wages are also differentiated by region to encourage labor mobility into such rapidly growing areas as Siberia, Kazakhstan, Central Asia, and the Far North, which have harsh climates and lack the cultural amenities of European Russia. Such regional differentials are computed by means of a uniform system of coefficients, which are multiplied by the standard wage rates to yield regionally differentiated wages. For example, the coefficients used to compute wages in the Far North range from 1.5 to 1.7;[38] that is, wages between 50 and 70 percent higher than the standard rates are paid to workers in the Far North for performing the same basic tasks as workers in European Russia. Supplements are also used, which bring the basic wage rate in the Far North to as high as 2.8 times that in European Russia.[39] By 1968, there were 10 regional coefficients used to establish regional wage differentials—a much simplified system from the 90 regional coefficients that existed prior to 1956.[40] In addition to regional differentiation, some higher rates are provided in cases of dangerous work and work performed under arduous conditions. For example, underground mining occupations receive basic monthly wages 14 to 33 percent higher than those for above-ground occupations. In the chemicals industry, work performed under especially hot, heavy, and unhealthy conditions receives payment 33 percent above that for work performed under normal conditions.[41]

The *total* wage of Soviet industrial workers is actually the sum of two components. On the one hand, the worker receives the basic wage computed according to the *setka* and *stavka* system described above. This component does not vary relative to the performance of the individual or the enterprise, and is guaranteed by the state. In addition, the worker receives a variety of supplementary bonus and incentive payments that vary with performance. These supplementary payments are in the form of bonuses for overfulfillment of plan norms, of premiums paid from the wage fund or material incentive fund of the enterprise, and of supplements for special working conditions. For example, in 1957, 56 percent of the average industrial worker's full wage was the basic wage, the remaining 44 percent being incentive payments of one kind or another. Of the latter, about 29 percent was for overfulfillment of norms, 6 percent was from premium payments, and 15 percent was supplements for region and special working conditions. In 1972, the figures were as follows: the basic wage accounted for 59 percent; bonuses, for 20 percent; premiums for norm overfulfillment, for 11 percent; and regional and special working conditions differentials, for 10 percent of average monthly earnings in industry.[42]

Prior to the general reform of wages that began in 1956, bonuses and incentive payments made up a larger share of industrial wages owing to the greater importance of piece rates and incentive schemes. During the early 1950s, such payments accounted for slightly more than 40 percent of average industrial incomes. As a result of the 1956–1965 wage reform, bonuses and supplements now account for around 30 percent of industrial wage income. This decrease is a consequence of the substantial decline in the percentage of workers paid according to piece rates, which dropped from two-thirds to one-third of all industrial workers between 1957 and 1961. According to more recent statistics, the proportion of industrial workers working according to some form of piece rates was slightly above 50 percent in both 1972 and 1982. Apparently, there has been a resurgence in piece-rate work since the early 1960s. In construction, the percentage of workers on piece rates was a much higher 80 percent in 1982.[43]

The common current in Soviet wage policy has been that wage rates should be set to equate supply and demand for labor. If the state wants an increase of employment in metallurgy, for example, wage rates should be raised to attract additional labor into metallurgy. If the state wants to develop the Far North, it must take labor supply factors into account and set a highly differentiated wage to overcome the workers' aversion to the region. As Leonard Kirsch has pointed out, in actual practice, the equation of supply and demand has been accomplished by combining centralized wage setting with enterprise flexibility in the area of incentive payments.[44] Thus, if the basic wage rates established by central authorities create labor shortages or surpluses at the enterprise level, managers have made needed adjustments at the local level by raising or lowering incentive payments. According to Kirsch, the trend toward more simplicity and national uniformity in wage rates may therefore result in a loss of flexibility and a weakening of central control over labor allocation.

EXTRAMARKET CONTROLS OVER LABOR ALLOCATION

While Western economists have tended to view market-type forces as being important for the allocation of labor in the Soviet economy, it would be a mistake not to consider the importance of extramarket mechanisms. If it is true, as generally argued, that the importance of controls generally declined in the 1950s and 1960s, the same cannot be said for the 1970s. As we will see, legislation of the 1970s has strengthened the state's hand in a number of important areas such as distribution of graduates, controls over work discipline, and the allocation of labor through special programs.

We turn now to an examination of the important mechanisms used to control labor allocation, namely, education, organized recruitment, direct controls over labor mobility, the nomenklatura system, and Soviet labor unions.

The Education System

In the Soviet Union, the educational system provides an important centralized mechanism for control over the labor force.[45] This control derives from a number of basic characteristics of the Soviet educational system. Like other aspects of Soviet economic life, the educational training of qualified labor is planned by central authorities. The key actors are Gosplan, the ministries (most of which maintain educational establishment), and the Ministry of Higher and Secondary Specialized Education. Education policy emanates from the highest levels of the CPSU. The main features of Soviet education policy are described below.

First, the completion of secondary education (through eighth grade since 1973) in general education schools is compulsory.[46] Beyond and in addition to this basic preparation, the Soviet Union has developed a large and complex net of specialized educational institutions under differing jurisdictions devoted to particular educational tasks such as technical training, training in specialized subjects such as foreign languages, graduate training, and the like. At the highest level, universities and research institutes train higher-degree candidates. The rapid expansion of the Soviet educational establishment is an indicator of its priority (Table 23).

Second, the content of Soviet education reflects the official view that the educational system must serve both the economy and Soviet society within a Marxist–Leninist framework.[47] Accordingly, there is no equivalent of what in the West would be described as a "liberal arts" education. Soviet education is devoted to the development of the new Soviet man, Communist morality, and, above all, skills useful to the economy. Soviet education is skewed in the direction of science, engineering, and technical specialities and restricts entry into the study of arts and humanities. Although career paths through the various different types of schools create familiar problems of choice for Soviet students, service to Soviet society

Table 23   THE SOVIET EDUCATIONAL ESTABLISHMENT

	1960/61	1970/71	1983/84
General education schools	224,000	190,000	141,000
Enrollment	36,187,000	49,193,000	44,479,000
Graduates (full completion: day and evening students)	1,055,000	2,581,000	3,628,000
Specialized secondary schools	3,328	4,223	4,438
Enrollment	2,060,000	4,388,000	4,503,000
Graduates	483,500	1,033,300	1,265,600
Vocational-technical schools	3,684	5,351	7,624
Enrollment	1,064,000	2,380,000	3,770,000
Graduates	741,000	1,638,000	2,518,000
Higher educational institutions	739	805	890
Enrollment	2,396,000	4,581,000	5,301,000
Graduates	343,300	630,800	849,500

Source: TsSU, *Narodnoe khoziaistvo SSSR v 1983 g.* [The national economy of the USSR in 1983] (Moscow: Finansy i statistika, 1984), 402, 484–504. *Note:* The data in this table are to be viewed as approximate. In most cases, the numbers are rounded. Some refer to the academic year (for example, 1970/71), while others refer to a calendar year (for example, graduates in 1970).

is a theme that remains strong in the 1970s and 1980s. In keeping with their emphasis on scientific and technical training, the Soviet educational establishment relies heavily on specialized secondary schools that provide professional vocational training to medical assistants, draftsmen, and skilled mechanics at a level between university and high school training.

Third, while service to the economy is reinforced by the nature of the school curriculum, it is also achieved in other ways. For example, an attempt is made at all levels of the hierarchy from Gosplan down through the local districts to plan in advance for labor requirements and, on this basis, to provide the educational capacity necessary to meet these planned needs. This feature is seen in the fact that the different education ministries take their orders from Gosplan. Moreover, there is a strong emphasis on vocational work experience in the Soviet school setting. Practical work experience was emphasized in the Khrushchev years and has resurfaced in recent educational reforms. Richard B. Dobson, a specialist on Soviet education, writes of recent Soviet efforts to expand "production training combines" whereby local enterprises build special workshops staffed by local students for the purpose of improving their technical skills and general work experience.[48]

Finally, Soviet authorities use a variety of control mechanisms to allocate labor, especially highly trained manpower. The most important of these is the work placement of graduates of higher and secondary specialized educational institutions. Decrees of the late 1970s and early 1980s have strengthened the role of the state in this regard. For example, graduates of vocational technical schools (since 1980) can be required to complete two years of work assignment at a specified location.[49] Similar types of required assignments have been used for more highly skilled graduates and have been employed to offset labor shortages in areas such as Siberia.

In theory, state control of the educational system should be a powerful mechanism of guaranteeing the labor needs of the Soviet economy. The task of actually meeting these needs is, however, exceedingly difficult. For this and a host of related reasons, the system does not always work smoothly. The Soviet press contains accounts of university graduates whose specialities are no longer required by the ministry that ordered those specialties four years earlier. It also contains accounts of trained specialists who are working in areas outside their speciality. There are also reports of too many trained engineers. What is of interest here is that the objective of meeting the needs of the economy through the educational system remains intact and has been reinforced in recent years. Moreover, administrative methods to achieve desired ends have been upgraded.

Organized Recruitment

A second important mechanism for the administrative allocation of labor in the Soviet Union is organized recruitment.[50] Since 1976, the All-Union Resettlement Committee and the Administration for Organized Recruitment *(Orgnabor)* have gained substantial strength, having been placed under the State Committee for Labor and Social Problems *(Goskomtrud)*. Organized recruitment has been important in the past. During the 1930s, Orgnabor facilitated the vast transfer of labor from countryside to the cities by recruiting labor for industrial enterprises from collective and private farms. In this manner, some 3 million peasants were transferred from the village to the city through Orgnabor contracts. After World War II, Orgnabor became more involved in the transfer of workers among industrial enterprises rather than from agriculture to industry; and by the late 1950s, Orgnabor's role in supplying industrial labor had become a limited one. Its major role, instead, became the recruiting of labor for vast construction projects and new industries located in the east and the north. Although there is evidence to suggest that the importance of Orgnabor has been increasing, a recent source suggests that in 1976, only about 3 percent of job placements were handled by this agency.[51]

　　In the general task of worker placement, especially in the less desirable areas of the Soviet Union, the use of these formal mechanisms has always been supplemented by general appeals of the Communist Party and the Komsomol, the latter designed to attract youth to fulfill special tasks.

Labor Mobility: Legal Controls

The competitive bidding for industrial workers plus the vast influx into the cities of untrained peasants from the countryside created excessive job turnover during the 1930s. To take one example, the average worker in the food industry changed jobs on the average of three times a year in 1930 and 1931; and for the economy as a whole, the average industrial worker changed jobs more than once per year.[52] This forced the state and the enterprises to adopt additional extramarket controls over labor mobility.

　　During the 1930s, a series of measures was adopted to reduce the excessive turnover. Absenteeism was deterred by severe penalties (eviction from factory housing and loss of social insurance benefits), "closed shops" were used to reward select groups of reliable workers, and enterprise control over limited housing was used as leverage to promote labor stability. After 1938, such controls became even more severe. Labor books (in which a person's work record would be recorded) were issued to all employed persons, an internal passport system was used to monitor the movements of population, and permission was required to change jobs (failure to comply being a criminal offense). Administrative controls over labor increased during the war with the mobilization of specialists, the lengthening of the workday, the making of absenteeism a criminal offense, and the establishment of labor reserve schools. Most of the laws pertaining to labor control during the war were passed in 1940. They were quite severe and resulted in numerous instances of criminal prosecution and imprisonment.[53] They remained on the books until their full repeal in 1956, although they had actually fallen into disuse during the early 1950s. In 1956, the workday was shortened, criminal liability for leaving work without permission and for absenteeism was abandoned, and social benefits were raised. As an immediate response to this liberalization, turnover in industry rose to 38 percent in 1956, after which it declined to a fairly steady 20 to 22 percent, which is below comparable turnover rates in manufacturing in the United States.[54] Nevertheless, the problem of "rolling stones" (workers who change jobs too frequently) remains a source of official concern, especially in the outlying republics where labor is quite scarce. This concern has been sufficiently serious for the state to introduce a series of measures—special bonuses for uninterrupted employment (1965), a labor code of 1971 giving reliable workers special privileges and priority in job advancement, and experimental programs in various urban areas to reduce job turnover—designed to combat what the state perceives as excessive job turnover. This theme, emphasized in the 1970s, has remained a point of focus in the 1980s under both Andropov and Gorbachev. Beyond the repetition of the general theme on the need to tighten labor discipline, specific steps have been taken to lessen turnover. In addition to the development of positive incentives (for example, expanded pension benefits for continuous service), negative sanctions have been increased. Thus, the notice period for voluntary separations was increased from two weeks to one month in a 1980 decree.[55]

Soviet authorities have also taken another step to lessen the impact of labor turnover. The role of labor placement bureaus, first introduced in the late 1960s, has been expanded. Between 1977 and 1980, the number of such bureaus increased from 370 to 650, and they are now responsible for the placement of roughly 15 percent of the workforce. Moreover, Soviet authorities have initiated scientific surveys of labor turnover in an effort to identify the sources of turnover. A 1978 study of the food processing industry, for example, identified unattractive work conditions, overtime requirements, poor housing, inability to use specialization, and low wages as significant causes of turnover. The study found further that turnover was greatest among women, young people, persons on the job for less than one year, and manual workers.[56]

As we shall see later when we examine Soviet economic performance, the rate of growth of labor productivity in the Soviet Union has declined significantly in recent years. While many factors can account for this outcome, there is no question that Soviet authorities place increasing emphasis upon the need for better work discipline. Lack of work discipline is perceived to come from many sources, among them excess turnover, lack of adequate incentives, alcohol, and the like. The evidence from recent years supports the view that in the face of a continuing slow growth of the labor force, considerable attention will be paid to various means for improving work discipline. Administrative means, especially controls of various sorts, are likely to play an important role.

Penal Labor[57]

The most glaring deviation from the principle of a free labor market was the creation of a large penal labor force in the Soviet Union beginning in 1929. The number of prisoners in Soviet concentration camps (the *gulag* population) cannot be estimated with precision, but disparate sources—an occasional official reference, comparisons of official labor force figures with the able-bodied population, accounts of ex-prisoners, the materials published by Alexander Solzhenitsyn—all point to astonishing numbers of forced laborers. The literature has witnessed heated debate over the size of the *gulag* population. We shall never know the exact numbers, but we believe there would be agreement on the following points: The *gulag* population received its first large influx with the collectivization drive, reaching 1 to 2 million in the early 1930s. The second large influx came with the Stalin purges of the mid- and late 1930s. Estimates for 1939 vary from 2 to 11 million. The camp population reached its peak size during World War II and its immediate aftermath. The figures for the 1945–1950 period range from 4 to 15 million. Ex-prisoners of war, resettled minorities, citizens of occupied territories, and many other groups were incarcerated during the war years. The official abolition of the *gulag* by Khrushchev in 1956 did not immediately spell the end of the large *gulag* population, the size of which was between 2 and 4 million in 1959. The proportion of the labor force in concentration camps was probably 5 percent in the mid-1930s and rose to over 10 percent during the war years.[58]

The legal foundation for mass political internments was provided by Article 58 of the 1926 Soviet criminal code, which declared actions directed toward weakening state power a crime against the state. Falling under this classification were a wide variety of offenses—including sabotage, propaganda, agitation, conscious failure to carry out one's duties, subversion of industry, and suspicion of espionage.

It would be difficult to justify the internment of large percentages of the population in forced labor camps on moral and economic grounds. One may classify the *gulags* as the product of an irrational Stalin and his associates and not regard them as being consciously designed for economic purposes. The *gulag* population was put to work principally in mining and on construction projects in harsh climates to which free labor could not be attracted. Apparently, the state did seek to derive economic benefit from forced labor. However, the costs of this penal labor were immense. The high death rates in the concentration camps caused a substantial loss of population.

It is difficult to estimate the loss of life in the camps because of conceptual and data problems. One measure, however, is excess mortality between 1926 and 1939. "Excess mortality" measures the number of people alive in 1926 who died between 1926 and 1939 in excess of the number that would have died under normal circumstances. Excess mortality between 1926 and 1939 was likely in the range of 3 to 6 million.[59] Excess mortality is only one cost of the camps. The sense of alienation of former prisoners and their families (along with deteriorated health) would not render them enthusiastic "builders of socialism" after their release. Furthermore, it is likely that forced labor is less productive than free labor. The diversion of labor from the labor market into concentration camps more than likely caused a loss of output due to a general lowering of labor productivity.

Nomenklatura Controls

Another source of extramarket control over labor is the nomenklatura system (Chapter 1). Under the nomenklatura procedure, the most important appointments in the economic system are filled from a party nominations list of candidates. This list, maintained by the various cadres departments of the Communist Party, allows the party to maintain direct control over most important administrative appointments. This control is important insofar as it can cover all aspects of the appointment process, whether it be technical skills required for the job or more general issues of party loyalty. The nomenklatura system means that those individuals who desire high-level appointments must demonstrate their acceptability to the party. This means following party directives, cultivating the favors of influential party officials, and avoiding behavior that would be frowned upon by the party.

AN EVALUATION OF SOVIET LABOR POLICY

One way to evaluate Soviet labor policy would be to consider its role in the process of resource allocation. How well have Soviet authorities utilized available labor resources? Are there notable labor shortages or surpluses either by occupation or by region? Has aggregate unemployment been avoided? How well does the system correct structural unemployment? This is the criterion of *allocative efficiency*.[60] Although the allocative efficiency of the Soviet labor market is an important criterion, a broader criterion may also be in order. The effectiveness of Soviet labor policy may also be evaluated in light of its contribution to the economic and social goals of the state, which we denote as *goal achievement efficiency*.[61] Although these two efficiency measures are not necessarily incompatible, they may be in some cases. The restrictive labor policies of the late 1930s and World War II definitely reduced allocative efficiency in order to achieve the political, economic, and military objectives of the state.

Quantitative and Structural Changes

Despite the slower population growth after the revolution, the Soviets were able to expand their total labor force at an annual rate of 2.5 percent between 1928 and 1937,[62] a quite high rate by international standards.[63] Even more important than the overall rate of growth in employment was its sectoral distribution. In keeping with the state policy of rapid industrial transformation, the nonagricultural labor force expanded at an annual rate of nearly 9 percent, while the agricultural labor force contracted at an annual rate of -2.5 percent. Light industry suffered a decline in its labor force between 1928 and 1937 that was as dramatic as the shift of labor out of agriculture.

How did Soviet labor policy effect these shifts? The rapid growth of the total labor force can in part be explained by the large rise in the participation rate (the percentage of total population employed on a full-time basis).[64]

Various labor policies contributed to the high participation rate. First, low wages in agriculture, coupled with the organized recruitment of workers in agriculture by *Orgnabor,* resulted in the wholesale transfer of labor out of agriculture, where days worked per year were few relative to industry (owing to seasonal and other factors). Second, in the city, the authorities introduced moral and legal, as well as economic, inducements for all able-bodied individuals to work. "Parasitism" was subject to severe penalties. Such pressures increased throughout the 1930s and peaked in the late 1930s (during the Stalin purges), when cases are recorded of nonworking mothers with newborn infants being criminally prosecuted for "parasitism."[65] The low real wages of the 1930s made it necessary for both husband and wife to work to make ends meet.[66] By 1939, 71 percent of able-bodied women were members of the labor force.[67]

In 1926, 54 percent of the Soviet population over 60 years of age participated in the labor force; by 1939, this number had been reduced to 49 percent.[68]

Soviet wage policy was also used to effect the distribution of labor within industry. In particular, the setting of higher relative wages in heavy industry than in light industry, the use of "closed shop" privileges to reward workers in high-priority branches, and the setting of low piece rate norms to allow large supplemental earnings in heavy industry encouraged the rapid transfer of labor into priority branches. Of 17 industrial branches, average wages in coal and in iron and steel ranked tenth and thirteenth, respectively, in 1924. By 1940, they ranked first and second, respectively.[69] The rankings of the consumer goods branches declined generally. These dramatic shifts in relative wages go a long way toward explaining the radical shift of labor within industry.

In recent years, the matter of labor supply for the Soviet economy has become a major problem. Put simply, the Soviet economy may use its available labor ineffectively, but within this constraint, there is a significant shortage of labor, a shortage that will ease to some degree in the 1990s but will effectively continue until the end of the present century. Although demand is a factor that we have considered (overstaffing, excessive turnover, etc.), supply considerations are most important.

Supply-side problems stem fundamentally from adverse demographic patterns in the Soviet Union. Although there are important regional differences, to be considered later, the following general trends should be noted.

The rate of growth of the Soviet population has declined significantly in recent years. For example, during the period 1959–1970, the average annual rate of growth of the Soviet population was 1.34 percent. The comparable figure for the period 1970–1979 was 0.92 percent, a sharp decline in a relatively short span of years.[70] Although the specific changes have varied from one republic to another, all republics experienced a decline during this period. This trend is expected to continue. Murray Feshbach has noted that "by the last decade of the century the rate of growth of the population will drop to 0.6% per year, about one-third the 1951–1955 rate."[71]

This dramatic change in the growth rate of the Soviet population can be accounted for by changes in both birthrates and death rates. Again, we focus on national trends, leaving regional issues for subsequent discussion.

Broadly speaking, Soviet crude birthrates (number of births divided by population) have declined significantly. For example, in the USSR as a whole, the crude birthrate has declined from 26.7 births per 1000 population in 1950 to 19.2 per 1000 in 1980 and is projected to reach 16.1 per 1000 by the year 2000.[72] Projections for all union republics indicate similar trends, though naturally with different absolute rates and with some intermediate differences between 1950 and 2000. This decline in crude birthrates is, in part, a result of declining fertility and declining age-specific fertility. Put another way, there are fewer women in the child-bearing age, but, in addition, the women in this age group are choosing to have fewer children. This pattern is typical of the development process, especially with rapid urbanization, increasing levels of educational attainment, and the already very high female labor force participation rates in the Soviet Union.

On the other side of the coin, the Soviet crude death rate has risen from 9.7 per 1000 population in 1950 to 9.8 per 1000 population in 1980, and it is projected to reach 10.6 by the year 2000.[73] Again, Murray Feshbach has noted in his analysis of mortality rates that "the three major components underlying the increases are the aging of the population, infant mortality, and death rates for males aged 20–44."[74]

In part, then, increases in the Soviet crude death rate can be explained by an aging of the population. Also, it is important to note that this results in a growth in the size of the pension-aged population. While this increases the dependence ratio, it also provides a small but nevertheless additional source of labor.

More troubling, though, are the other factors accounting for the increase in the crude death rate. For the period 1963–1964 to 1973–1974, the age-specific death rate for prime-aged males (males aged 20 to 44) has increased for every age bracket.[75] For females over the same period, the age-specific mortality rate has declined for every age bracket except the 40–44 bracket, for which there was a very small increase. This pattern for males has generally been attributed to health problems (specifically coronary disease and cancer) and the excess consumption of alcohol. It may, however, also be related to other important though less quantifiable factors such as work stress.

Finally, for the period from the mid-1960 to the mid-1970s, there was a significant increase in the rate of infant mortality. Indeed, the reasons for this pattern have been the subject of discussion and controversy. What do these trends tell us about quantitative changes in the Soviet labor force? For the period 1950 to 2000, the Soviet able-bodied population and the Soviet labor force have and will continue to grow. But the rates of growth of both have declined sharply. For example, in the 1970s, net annual increments to the Soviet labor force averaged 2.38 million persons. The comparable increment for the 1980s is 0.65 million, or roughly one-third of the 1970 figure.

In sum, increments to the Soviet labor force have and will continue to slow sharply for a variety of basic demographic reasons. Although the slowdown will abate, it will do so only slowly in the mid- and late 1990s.

The Regional Distribution of Labor

Issues relating to the regional distribution of labor in the Soviet Union have assumed much greater importance in recent years. This importance arises in several dimensions.

First, the rural-urban balance has always been a crucial aspect of labor allocation. The Soviet Union became a predominantly urban society in a relatively short period of time. The single most important source of this urban growth has been rural-to-urban migration.[76] Both administrative and market-type mechanisms have been used to manipulate this process, and the empirical evidence shows that wage differentials have been important in explaining the rural-to-urban shifts of the labor force.[77] In fact, rural-to-urban migration has been a crucial source of urban labor supply in the sense that it is rural youth who are most likely to migrate, motivated by the perception of better opportunities in the urban/industrial sector.

However, while the urban sector may have benefited, increasingly the rural sector has been facing a labor shortage, especially for peak season needs. Although there are important regional differences, the rural sector can no longer be viewed as a major source of incremental urban labor. In fact, policies have been implemented (for example, sharp improvements in rural levels of living) to make rural life more attractive and thus stem the migratory flows.

Second, a critical dimension of the contemporary Soviet labor force is its regional distribution. Whether we define a region in broad and general terms, related to specific economic characteristics, or simply in terms of political units such as the union republics, an examination of basic demographic patterns reveals major problems.

Fertility rates are sharply higher in the southern regions of the Soviet Union, broadly speaking, Central Asia and Kazakhstan (territory of predominantly Muslim population), than in other areas of the Soviet Union.[78] The result is a significantly higher rate of growth of population, able-bodied population, and hence labor force in these regions. The implications of differential growth are important. For example, a Western study published in 1982 commenting on Central Asia and Kazakhstan notes that "of the roughly 9.5 million workers who will be added to the labor force in the next decade, about ninety percent will come from these five republics."[79]

This picture presents both demand and supply problems. On the demand side, Soviet industrial capacity is not, of course, located in Central Asia, but rather primarily to the north.[80] This means that the demand for labor located where the labor supply is and will be available. Supply problems are also evident. Central Asia is a less developed region of the Soviet Union, with population and labor force characteristics reflecting this lower level of development. The labor force participation rate is generally lower than elsewhere, and there is a greater tendency to remain in rural activity. In addition, educational levels are lower, all of which suggests lesser market orientation, especially for women. Finally, the kinds of differences suggested here would lead one to doubt the possibility of significant migration, that is, of shifting the available labor supply from the south to the labor-short areas of the north.[81] Likewise, it is doubtful that Soviet planners will want to implement any major shift of industrial activity toward the south.

It is important to note that these regional imbalances result from basic underlying demographic and other relatively long-term factors. In this sense, the problem of regional labor imbalances is not likely to be solved in the near future.

Qualitative Changes

Soviet labor policy was successful in bringing about significant qualitiative changes in the Soviet labor force. The Soviet labor force was poorly equipped to meet the needs of all-out industrialization. The 1897 census showed 78 percent of the over-15-year-old population as illiterate, with only 1.4 million having education beyond the seventh grade out of a population of 126 million and only 93,000 with completed higher education. The immediate preindustrialization figures of the 1926 census show considerable improvement preparatory to the industrialization drive: the illiteracy rate had dropped to 56 percent, 6 million had received education beyond the seventh grade, and roughly half a million had completed higher education.[82]

The major spurt in educational achievement occurred during the industrialization drive of the 1930s. By 1939, the illiteracy rate had dropped to 20 percent, 14 million had completed education beyond the seventh grade, and more than 1 million had completed higher education.[83] Thus, the Soviet educational system did a very significant job in meeting the manpower needs of a modernizing economy.

Soviet labor policy contributed to this modernization of Soviet manpower in several ways. First, labor codes were put into effect forbidding the employment of younger people, a factor that enhanced the effectiveness of the universal education decrees. Large wage differentials were established between skilled and unskilled laborers, providing positive incentives for laborers to acquire highly rewarded skills. Stalin in 1931 cast aside "left equalitarianism" and introduced large incentives for skilled occupations. Wage differentials widened substantially between 1928 and 1934 and continued to increase throughout the 1930s.[84] The wage revision beginning in 1956 narrowed wage differentials, a policy made possible by the vast increases in skilled labor during the prewar period. For example, 4.5 percent of the Soviet labor force were specialists with a higher or secondary specialized education in 1928. By 1967, this ratio had risen to 14 percent. In 1983, 28 percent of the Soviet labor force were specialists with a higher or secondary specialized education.[85]

In contemporary times, the Soviet educational establishment remains a major priority in the system. As we have already noted, educational levels of the Soviet population continue to increase, although major controversies surround the educational process in important areas, for example, in managerial training.

Soviet Full-Employment Policies

Long-term unemployment should not be a serious aggregate problem in the Soviet planned economy. The output of goods and services is planned as a function of available capital and labor. Planners automatically plan to produce an aggregate level of output that provides employment for the able-bodied adult population. In fact, official Soviet concern is more about labor shortages (not having enough labor to meet the needs of the national economy). According to official statistics, unemployment was "liquidated" during the first Five Year Plan.* On the eve of the first Five Year Plan (1927–1928), unemployment averaged 8 percent of the Soviet labor force.[86]

Modern economic theory recognizes that frictional unemployment is required for a smoothly functioning dynamic economy. Of course, societies would like to keep the amount of frictional unemployment to a minimum, but the economy would be ill-served if a zero percent unemployment rate were indeed achieved. In the course of economic growth, some branches rise while others decline. Some regions of the country grow, others lose population. A natural consequence of the ebb and flow of economic fortunes is that people change jobs; whenever there are job changes in a dynamic economy, frictional unemployment will result.

One cannot get an accurate picture of the extent of unemployment in the Soviet Union with the available data. A study by Peter Wiles, based on official turnover data from the late 1960s, suggests that Soviet short-term unemployment is in the neighborhood of 1 to 1.5 percent, a rate well below current short-term unemployment rates in the West but not far below rates achieved in the West in the 1960s. Another study based on Soviet emigré work experiences of the late 1970s finds that the long-term Soviet unemployment rate (unemployment of one

---

*The Soviet figures on the liquidation of unemployment are as follows:

	Year	Unemployed (in thousands)
	1922	407
	1924	1344
	1929	1741
April	1930	1081
October	1930	240
December	1930	No unemployment

Source: Danilov and Matrozova, "Trudovye resursy," 245–248.

month or more) is between 1 and 1.5 percent of the Soviet labor force.[87] The Soviet long-term unemployment rate is well below recent Western experience but only slightly below the Western rates of the 1960s.

It should come as no surprise that there is unemployment in the Soviet Union. In any dynamic economy, there must be unemployment. The economy could not function without unemployment unless it is totally static.

A number of indications show that Soviet full-employment policies may have certain efficiency costs. First, the official Soviet concern with reducing labor turnover means that the Soviet leadership has set a goal of limiting the amount of frictional unemployment. Labor turnover has both its positive and negative sides. On the positive side, labor turnover allows the economy to adjust to differential growth patterns among employers. It allows workers to shift to employment where their productivity (and hence pay) will be higher. On the negative side, excessive turnover can raise training costs and employee search costs.

It is unclear where the line should be drawn between healthy and unhealthy turnover rates. Soviet policies may be aiming for too little turnover. The Soviet leadership has paid little attention to the legitimate role of employment exchanges; in a society that claims to have liquidated unemployment, state unemployment services are not necessary by definition. Local unemployment exchanges were abolished in the 1930s. Although local state and party organizations involve themselves in job placement (especially for graduates of local schools), there is little in the way of organized job information. In the postwar era, there have been efforts to reinstitute labor exchanges,[88] but most Soviet workers still find their jobs by informal means, such as inquiring at the factory gate, billboards, and information from friends.

Limited geographic mobility is another contributing factor to low turnover rates. About half the Soviet population reports never having moved since the date of birth. This very limited geographic mobility is likely tied to the difficulty of obtaining housing in faraway cities and to the internal passport system. Or it may be due to the limited financial incentives to move. In an economy that requires shifts in population to supply labor for new industries and to populate new regions, the limited geographic mobility of the Soviet population would be a problem; it also helps explain the low Soviet frictional unemployment rates. When people stick with prevailing housing and jobs, frictional unemployment is down.

The ultimate cost of Soviet full-employment policies is the widespread phenomenon of underemployment. Managers are reluctant to let workers go (although this is not a totally rare phenomenon).[89] Hoarding labor now often protects managers against overambitious plan targets in the future. Yet if workers know that it is unlikely they will be fired for mediocre performance, they will have little incentive to turn in their best performance. Guaranteed job tenure can definitely have negative effects on allocative efficiency.

Discrimination by Sex in the Soviet Union

An evaluation of Soviet labor and manpower policy would not be complete without reference to the role of women in the Soviet economy.[90] The traditional

Western view prompted by Soviet writings has been that Soviet women have enjoyed relatively free access to the various occupations and professions, thus avoiding the allocative inefficiency that might derive from discrimination. This view has been supported by a rather general view of the role of women in the Soviet labor force—in particular, the high participation rates and child care and other support services to facilitate this role. In addition, it has been noted that women play an important role in key professions, for example, medicine.

In recent years, increasingly sophisticated analysis of Western labor markets and notably the role of women in these markets has led to a renewed interest in, and examination of, the role of women in the Soviet economy. Thus far, this reappraisal lends only partial support to the traditional scenario outlined above.

The overall participation rate of both men and women in the Soviet economy is very high, an aggregate rate of approximately 88 percent.[91] It is unlikely that the participation rate for women will increase. Although steps have been taken to increase female employment, increases are most likely to come from women in Central Asia, where female participation rates are lower than elsewhere in the Soviet Union.[92] At the same time, efforts are being made to stimulate larger families in non-Muslim areas, policies likely to reduce female participation rates, at least in the short run.

Although female labor force participation rates are very high in the Soviet Union, it has been pointed out that there tends to be an inverse relationship between the rate of pay and the proportion of women in a particular occupation or sector.[93] Women tend to predominate in sectors with relatively low pay. For example, in 1975, women accounted for only 21 percent of the labor force in construction and 21 percent in forestry, whereas they accounted for 76 percent in trade and services and 84 percent in health services.[94]

Furthermore, within these sectors, women occupy a lower proportion of the technical and higher-paying positions than would be true for the lesser-paying positions. Thus, the evidence suggests that women earn less than men due to their higher representation in lower-paying sectors and occupations.

A recent study of the Soviet urban sector (based upon an emigré sample) provides strong, though rather preliminary, evidence to support the above view. This study, by Gur Ofer and Aaron Vinokur, concludes that the hourly pay for Soviet urban women is roughly 0.68 to 0.70 of that for men, a figure closely approximating the gap that is found for the United States.[95] Furthermore, these authors find that rather traditional factors such as the return to schooling and the role of experience are important in explaining these Soviet differences, just as they are in the United States.

Clearly, additional research will be necessary to elucidate the nature and causes of male-female earnings differentials in the Soviet Union and in other socialist countries.[96] However, the evidence presented above suggests that equality in the workplace may have to be a goal for the future.

It will take considerable effort to unravel the forces underlying this pattern. Soviet women have enjoyed substantial achievement in terms of education and participation in the labor force. These achievements have, in part, been the result of changing values and policies, possibly also as a function of the industrialization experience. At the same time, the typical Soviet woman bears a rather high share of the household work burden.[97] High participation rates may also be, in part, functions of a severe labor shortage and of the impact of World War II on the Soviet population. However, it remains true that Soviet women do not participate equally with Soviet men in the better-paying jobs and in jobs of administrative responsibility, for example, enterprise director or farm head, where women are almost nonexistent.[98]

The role of women in the Soviet economy is rather different from traditional Western perceptions. It is true that women have participated actively in the economy through expansion of educational levels and participation in the labor force. At the same time, Soviet women seem to bear a "double burden" insofar as they are largely responsible for work in the home. Econometric evidence thus far seems to suggest that the overall role of women in the Soviet population, labor force, and home is not particularly unique, inasmuch as it exhibits patterns of behavior found elsewhere.[99] Moreover, as we have noted, it would appear that Soviet women tend to earn less than Soviet men, and for about the same reasons found to explain male-female earnings differences in the United States.

THE ALLOCATION OF CAPITAL IN THE SOVIET ECONOMY: THE INVESTMENT DECISION

Investment Planning

By designating the physical outputs of the economy in the process of material balance planning, authorities must plan at the same time the expansion of enterprise capacity, that is, capital investment in plant and equipment.[100] To meet the expansion of output called for by either current or prospective plans, the capacity of the enterprise must be expanded accordingly to ensure the consistency of the output plan. Earlier, it was noted that enterprise output plans are based on past performance plus projected increases from additional plant and equipment. Although there has, at times, been an imperfect meshing of output and investment plans, the latter have been primarily determined by the former.

Most of the research and development (R&D) work in the Soviet Union is conducted outside of the enterprise, although large enterprises do have R&D facilities. They are more centralized than in capitalist economies. There are three types of R&D organizations. First, there is the research and development institute, which conducts applied research in a specialized technological area; there were 1700 such institutes in 1969. The second type of R&D establishment is the engineering design organization, which specializes in the design of new products and of production processes. It is called a project-making organization; in 1964, there were approximately 1000 engineering design organizations. The third type of R&D establishment is the construction engineering organization. It determines matters such as the location of the plant, the kind of equipment, and the scale of production; in 1970, there were 1400 such organizations.

Most of these R&D organizations are attached to ministries, and they are charged with the design and implementation of innovation and the expansion of existing facilities. Unlike capitalist enterprises, in which routine investment decisions and technological innovation are taken within the enterprise, in their Soviet counterparts such matters are handled by external R&D establishments, whose responsibility ends when the project design is completed. This explains, in part, the reluctance of Soviet managers to risk introducing new technology.

The task of the project-making organization is first to elaborate and then to choose among alternative projects that yield the expansion of enterprise capacity specified by higher planning authorities. In this section, we deal with how project-making organizations choose among alternative projects. In a broad sense, they actually have little to do with the basic allocation of capital among competing ends, for they are concerned primarily with allocating fixed amounts of investment in accordance with centralized directives within their own administrative unit. The allocation of capital *among* administrative units, which, after all, is the decision most basic to the allocation of capital, remains in the hands of higher planning authorities.

In the Soviet Union, an annual investment plan for the entire economy that has been formulated by *Gosplan,* the ministries, and various state committees is submitted to the Council of Ministers. Once approved, the various R&D organizations, *Gosplan,* and the ministries supervise its implementation by the project-making organizations. Just as the material balance plan has its financial counterpart, so does the investment plan. The Ministry of Finance provides a portion of the funds required to finance the various projects directly from the state budget—the financial institution directly in charge of disbursing such investment funds is the Investment Bank *(Stroibank),* with *Gosbank* providing the funds for general repairs.[101] In this manner, the financial counterpart of the investment plan is used to locate deviations from the investment plan in much the same manner as it is used to monitor other enterprise operations. An overcommitment of investment resources (a situation where the materials and equipment required for approved projects exceed available supplies) will usually result in financial authorities providing insufficient financial resources to complete the project as scheduled. This practice tends to bring investment supplies and demands into balance but builds costly delays into underfinanced investment projects. One important source of this tendency to overcommit investment resources has been the ministries' desire to get as many projects started as early as possible so as to establish a priority claim on future investment supplies. This problem had become so serious that by 1971, 85 percent of investment projects begun the previous year were still unfinished.[102] The problem of unfinished construction remains serious. One Western author writing in the early 1980s observed that "the amount of unfinished construction has more than doubled since 1970 and in 1980 was equivalent to about 6 percent of the value of the total capital stock in the economy, and to almost 80 percent of the total fixed capital investment."[103]

Problems of Investment Choice in the Soviet Economy

The choice among alternative investment projects, all of which yield the same increase in capacity, is not easy to resolve in the Soviet context. How is the project-making enterprise to choose among them? Ideally, a choice should be made that would minimize the consumption of scarce capital resources while achieving the required capacity expansion. On the surface, this seems like a simple criterion; yet for Soviet investment planners, it can be very complex.

First, there is an ideological constraint. The Marxian labor theory of value attributes all value to the current and past labor that has gone into the production of a commodity. From this, Soviet ideologists concluded during the early plan period that capital does not create value; therefore, enterprises should not pay interest charges for its use—a view that prevailed until the 1965 economic reform. Thus, using interestlike calculations to rank investment alternatives seemed out of line with Marxian ideology. As Alfred Zauberman has expressed it, "Where yield on capital is rejected as the motive force of the economy, its maximization could not serve as a guide for investment decisions."[104] In line with this reasoning, fixed capital from 1930 through 1965 was allocated to enterprises as an interest-free grant. Enterprises therefore came to regard capital as a free factor of production, to be sought after as long as its marginal productivity remained positive. The only legitimate capital cost definitely allowable by Marxian value theory is depreciation, which supposedly compensates the state for the past labor being used up in production. There is no room in this strict Marxian framework, however, for technological obsolescence that does not represent a using up of past labor. As a result, the sole capital cost to enterprises, depreciation, has generally been small because of the omission of charges for obsolescence.[105]

The conflict between the strict interpretation of the labor theory of value and Soviet growth strategy is obvious. Whereas Marxian value theory dictates that capital does not create value, the basis of Soviet growth strategy has been to direct as much additional capital as possible into growth-producing sectors such as electricity, machinery, and metallurgy. Rapid industrial growth is the objective of the system; yet the instrument crucial to generating this growth was said to create no value of itself and carried a zero price. In practice, this conflict between ideology and growth strategy was resolved by having Soviet planners allocate capital administratively according to a strict set of priorities and without reference to relative rates of return.[106]

The Soviet industrial price system represents a second problem. If more than one project yields the planned capacity increase, the project-making organization must generally evaluate the costs and benefits of alternative projects in value terms. If one of two equally expensive investment projects economizes on coal inputs while the other saves natural gas, the final choice will depend to a great extent on the relative prices of coal and gas. If these prices fail to reflect relative scarcities, then the "wrong" choice can be made. Because of the inconsistencies of the Soviet price system, one can understand the reluctance of planners to rely exclusively on value criteria in making investment decisions. Instead, most official guidelines suggest that value criteria be combined with physical indicators such as labor productivity and savings of specific material inputs, rather than relying exclusively on single value indicators.[107]

A third problem, closely related to the first, has been the lack of recognition of the importance of the time factor in capital investment decisions—a consequence of the absence of a recognized *time discount factor,* or interest rate. In market economies, investment projects that promise to yield large returns in the distant future will be ranked against projects yielding smaller but quicker returns by computing the present discounted value of each project using the interest rate as a common discount factor. A high interest rate (that supposedly reflects both society's time preferences and the scarcity of capital) will discourage long-term projects with delayed returns.

In the Soviet Union, there has historically been little recognition (at least until recently) of the time factor in choosing among alternative investment projects, and the perceived opportunity cost—either to the Soviet enterprise or to the ministry—of tying scarce resources down in long-term projects has been small. The lack of a time discount factor explains to a great extent the undue delays in the completion of investment projects (a problem frequently referred to in the Soviet press) and the tendency to select projects with long gestation periods (the gigantomania of the early thirties) despite the considerable scarcity of capital resources. Such behavior can be attributed, in part, to the expansion of planners' time horizons beyond sight during the "heroic phase of growth" during the 1930s.[108]

The Development of Investment Choice Criteria

Beginning in 1930, interest was outlawed as a capitalistic vestige no longer required when capital is the property of the state. In keeping with the general sentiment of the early 1930s, it was argued that the economic laws of capitalism were no longer operative and that capital should be allocated administratively, without resort to the economic criteria of the old capitalist order. Thus, Stalin argued that the allocation of investment according to rates of return or other profitability measures would be contrary to the interests of the state, for resources would then be directed away from heavy industry into light industry, where profit rates would be higher. In addition, it was argued in some quarters that the liberation from economic rules would permit planners to choose more advanced technology than would be justified if standard economic rules were strictly observed, and thus the rapid industrial transformation of the Soviet Union would be promoted.[109]

The intersectoral allocation of investment became an administrative decision of higher planning authorities after 1930, and open discussion of investment choice criteria at the economywide level disappeared. The practical problem of allocating investment funds within specific sectors led, however, even during the barren Stalin years, to the development of informal investment allocation rules that were eventually officially formalized between 1958 and 1960. During this early period, ministerial project-making organizations were forced to develop more specific rules for making decisions rather than simply choosing the investment variant yielding the lowest operating costs (the only rule officially sanctioned), since the ministry had a limited capital allotment that had to be stretched as far as possible. This problem was especially troublesome in the railroad and electrical power industries, where continuous substitutions between ever-increas ing capital outlays and ever lower operating costs were possible. Thus, project-making engineers and industry officials began to develop investment rules for internal use that implicitly introduced rates of return and other capital profitability criteria into the investment decision. Disguised under such acceptable terminology as "effectiveness of investment" and "periods of recoupment," these investment criteria came into fairly wide use within selected ministries by the late 1930s.[110]

The use of such interestlike calculations was officially sanctioned in 1958 by an all-union conference on capital effectiveness, after roughly three decades of pioneering work by engineers and economists.[111] The appearance of the USSR Academy of Science publication *Typical Method of Determining the Economic Effectiveness of Capital Investment and New Technology* in 1960 further substantiated the official acceptance of interestlike criteria for allocating investment within administrative units. Let us turn to the rules suggested by this 1960 publication.

Investment Decision Rules, 1960–1969

The most important decision rule suggested by *Typical Method* was the *coefficient of relative effectiveness (CRE)*, which was designed to evaluate the trade-offs between capital outlays and operating expenses. Such a measure was easily rationalized in terms of Marxian value theory, since operating expenses ultimately reflect labor costs, and capital should be evaluated according to how well it economizes the use of labor. To illustrate how the CRE measure operates, we assume that a project-making organization must choose between two alternative projects, both yielding the planned capacity increase. The two differ in terms of initial capital outlays *(K)* and resulting annual operating expenses *(C)*, which, let us say, do not vary over time. Under normal circumstances, the higher the capital outlay, the lower the operating costs, and the CRE must evaluate this trade-off. It should be noted that a capital charge is *not* included in operating expenses— only a depreciation charge—an omission that may bias the CRE measure in favor of capital-intensive projects. In our example, the CRE is given by the following formula, where the *a* and *b* subscripts refer to two projects *a* and *b*:

$$\text{CRE} = \frac{C_b - C_a}{K_a - K_b}$$

Thus, if project *b* costs 1 million rubles and project *a* costs 2 million rubles of capital outlay,[112] and the operating expenses of project *b* are 0.2 million and those of project *a* are 0.1 million, then the CRE of project *a* (relative, of course, to project *b*) would be 10 percent. This should be interpreted to mean that for every additional ruble of capital outlay on project *a*, 0.1 ruble of operating costs would be saved over project *b*.[113]

Typical Method further suggested that a norm be established—the standard coefficient of efficiency—for *each* branch. If a project's CRE fell below the norm, it should be rejected unless there were special reasons for not doing so. In this manner, a minimum profitability, or capital effectiveness, rate would be established for each branch. Because these norms varied by branch (with the higher the priority, the lower the profitability norm for a given branch), capital profitability rates would not equalize among branches, as had been advocated by several prominent Soviet economists and many Western economists.[114] This result, however, was to be expected, in view of the state's desire to promote priority industrial and military sectors independently of restrictive economic criteria. Although there is no definite evidence, the CRE norms actually established were most likely not high enough to equate the supply and demand for capital, and administrative capital rationing remained the primary mechanism for investment allocation, despite the CRE.[115]

Although the CRE was just one of many rules suggested between 1960 and 1969, it became the most important and most widely used. It is important to note how crude a measure it actually was, for it failed to come to grips with varying patterns of capital expenditures, different service lives of projects, risk differences, and different time spacing of operating cost economies, as well as a host of other problems.

An important question raised by the CRE criterion was whether a single, uniform standard coefficient should be established for the entire economy, promoting eventual equalization of marginal rates of returns on investment projects in all branches.[116] *Typical Method* was clearly in favor of differentiated standard branch norms. For the state to surrender its control over investment allocation and to replace it by a uniform mechanical rule was judged as contrary to the long-range vision of the Soviet leadership. The 1958 all-union conference on capital effectiveness leading up to the publication of *Typical Method* was quite clear on this point: "Some projects with smaller effectiveness may be approved . . . because they accelerate the solution of the basic economic problem, and are necessary for defense, political and other reasons . . ." and further, "capital investments are made on the basis of the economic laws of socialism which require the preferential development by the means of production. . . ."[117] An important point often overlooked in these discussions of the CRE is that the suggested rules generally pertain to the internal allocation of fixed sums of investment within a branch, and that only those investment alternatives would be evaluated that yield the planned increases in capacity. Also, the norms were generally not set to equate supply and demand, thus requiring a continuation of administrative rationing independently of the suggested rules. Thus, the leadership's acceptance of interestlike calculations in 1960 really represented no significant deviation from the centrally planned nature of the Soviet economy. Instead, the objective throughout was to make the allotted investment more effective and efficient within the context of planned choice.

Another common current running through official pronouncements during this period was the reluctance of planning authorities to rely too heavily upon a single criterion. For example, the 1958 conference report made it quite clear that while the conference favored the CRE measure, it was to be used in combination with a number of other indicators when the situation required. If industrial prices failed to reflect relative scarcities, physical indicators were to be used along with the CRE criterion. The possibilities of substantial delays in project completion were also to be considered, as well as the interrelation of the project with other branches. Social factors such as the workers' safety were to enter into the calculation as well.[118]

Revised Investment Rules, 1969

In September of 1969, a new methodology for evaluating the relative effectiveness of investment projects was approved. The new *Standard Methodology for Determining the Economic Effectiveness of Capital Investments*[119] (referred to here as *Standard Methodology*) is identical to the CRE method, except for the acceptance of a *uniform* standard norm to apply to all branches of the economy. The measurement suggested for comparing alternative investment projects is the *comparative economic effectiveness of capital investments,* referred to here as the CEE. The CEE measure requires that investment projects be selected so that

$$C_i + E_n K_i = \text{minimum}$$

where C_i = the current expenditures of the ith investment variant
K_i = the cost of the investment project
E_n = the uniform *normative coefficient of effectiveness* of capital investments, which is the same for all branches

Standard Methodology suggests that this normative coefficient be set at 12 percent. Thus, *Standard Methodology* (like *Typical Method*) calls for evaluating investment projects on the basis of their *full* costs (operating costs plus imputed capital costs), with imputed capital costs calculated using a uniform coefficient for all branches.

An example of how the CEE method works would perhaps be helpful at this point. Assume three alternative investment projects (Table 24). As one might expect, there is a trade-off between operating costs and investment outlays in our example (the higher the K, the lower the C).

In our example, the projects should refer to investment projects within a branch or in different branches. Because the normative coefficient is uniform for the entire economy, this should make no difference in the evaluation process. The CEE investment criterion calls for the selection of the project having the lowest costs, that is, the lowest *full* cost (the sum of operating expenses plus a capital charge). In the table, the project with the lowest full cost, project 2, should be

**Table 24   COMPUTATION OF THE "COMPARATIVE ECONOMIC EFFECTIVENESS"
(CEE) OF THREE INVESTMENT PROJECTS**

Project	Operating costs *(C)*	Investment outlay *(K)*	Uniform normative coefficient	Full costs $(1 + 3 \times 2)$
1	300	510	12%	361.2
2	290	525	12%	353.0
3	285	590	12%	355.8

selected, for it yields the optimal trade-off between greater investment outlays and lower operating costs.*

In addition to establishing the CEE concept, *Standard Methodology* provides detailed discounting procedures for evaluating in present value terms projects whose operating expenditures and capital outlays change over time. *Standard Methodology* suggests using a discount rate of 8 percent, which it claims is in line with current depreciation procedures.

On the surface, the use of a uniform normative coefficient for the entire economy would seem to violate the branch priority principle and call for the allocation of investment strictly on the basis of rates of return. This conclusion seems to be further supported by the fact that *Standard Methodology* calls upon the investment plan to allocate investment among branches according to a uniform coefficient of effectiveness. In fact, this may not prove to be so. First, the suggested normative coefficient (12 percent) will probably not be high enough to equate the supply and demand for capital—a point already noted by Soviet critics.[120] As long as this remains true, much capital allocation will be handled by administrative procedures. Second, *Standard Methodology* states that deviations from the normative coefficient may be approved by *Gosplan* in order to stimulate technological progress, to allow for differences in wage and price levels, and to promote regional development. For example, a lower (8 percent) normative coefficient was established for the Far North, and there is talk of establishing an 8 percent norm for electrical power generation. The generally liberal allowance for exceptions to the uniform coefficient rule quickly became a matter of concern to reform-minded Soviet economists, one of whom wrote that they "open the door to the broadest degree of arbitrariness" in investment decisions.[121] Third, *Standard Methodology* suggests that the CEE index be supplemented by further indexes—productivity of labor, capital/output ratios, capital investment per unit of output, and selected physical indexes—to "take account of the influences of the most important factors on the economic effectiveness of capital investments and to take account of the interaction of this effectiveness with other divisions of the plan.[122] Fourth, *Standard Methodology* states that the investment plan should follow the output plan of the national economy; for example, the allocation of investment among branches is still to be predetermined by the industrial supply and output plan. This statement seems to contradict one of the key provisions of the new investment rules, namely, that capital should be allocated among branches according to a uniform normative coefficient of effectiveness.[123]

Thus, the *Standard Methodology* was a step in the direction of investment allocation on the basis of rates of return irrespective of branch of production, but it clearly did not call for a clear break with investment allocation according to the priority principle. We emphasize that efficiency indexes are brought into play only *after* the basic investment allocation decisions are made in the investment plan. Investment funds are allocated in the investment plan. The efficiency in-

---

*The importance of differential normative coefficients in preserving the branch priority system can be illustrated using Table 24. Suppose that project 2 is in light industry, whereas projects 1 and 3 are in heavy industry. Instead of using 12 percent as a norm for light industry, a higher 30 percent rate is set. The CEE of project 2 now becomes 447.5, which eliminates it from selection.

dexes play a relatively minor role: they assist in selecting that investment project which yields the capacity expansion called for in the investment plan.

Investment Rules: The 1970s and 1980s

Decrees of 1974 reinforced the 1969 rule that capital projects should be selected to minimize the sum of operating costs and imputed annual capital costs ($C_i + E_n K_i$ = minimum). It was emphasized that this approach would be used to compare *project variants,* and it was not intended to change centrally determined investment priorities. However, discussion in the Soviet press has indicated that, in some instances, this criterion was interpreted more generally as a measure of overall effectiveness of investment.[124]

Throughout the 1970s, there was considerable discussion concerning the normative coefficients (E_i) to be used in project evaluation. A key question in these discussions was whether the normative coefficient would be the same for all branches. In 1981, a new *Methodology* (with no reference to being standard or typical) was published.[125] The 1981 *Methodology* elaborates the same basic method for evaluating project variants and suggests that for the period 1981– 1985, normative coefficients should be set at 0.12. This apparently is the average rate, which will be allowed to vary from a minimum of 0.08 to a maximum of 0.25.[126]

David Dyker, in his analysis of Soviet investment rules, points out a difference in the 1981 *Methodology*: "The 1981 *Methodology* has laid down norms for levels of absolute effectiveness which are to operate as 'gateways' through which blocks of investment projects should have to pass."[127] In other words, investment projects should yield certain minimum rates of return to qualify for funding. Rate-of-return norms are not to fall below the actual average rate for the preceding five-year period. Dyker notes that the actual average rate for the period 1976–1980 was 0.14.[128] As the continuing flow of investment allocation rules indicates, Soviet authorities remain interested in injecting more rate-of-return decision-making into the Soviet capital investment process. Yet, the same authorities recognize that capital allocation determines the basic future direction of the economy. They remain reluctant, therefore, to turn such decisions over to "rules." Whether the 1981 rule of meeting minimum rate-of-return requirements will actually be implemented remains to be seen.

SUMMARY: RESOURCE ALLOCATION IN THE SOVIET UNION

In the last two chapters, we have surveyed how resources are allocated in the Soviet economy. With several significant exceptions, resources are allocated administratively by the central plan. Material balance planning is used to allocate industrial supplies almost without reference to their prices, which are designed to equal average branch costs of production. Throughout the planning process, financial authorities and party officials monitor plan fulfillment, the former through the use of "ruble control." Soviet managers are supposed to direct their enterprise in accordance with the *techpromfinplan,* which has been formulated by superior planning agencies. In fact, managers do exercise some discretion in the operation of the enterprise, and, in this area, they are motivated by the managerial reward system, which has tended to be output-oriented. The enterprise's investments are determined external to the enterprise, with the basic allocation of investment funds being determined administratively in the investment plan.

The major exceptions to administrative allocation are the labor and the consumer goods market. In the Soviet Union, labor has been allocated primarily by differential wages, supplemented by other controls such as organized recruitment, placement of selectively educated graduates, and other administrative arrangements. Consumer goods, once produced in planned quantities, have primarily been allocated to consumers through the market. Thus, retail prices have tended to approach market clearing prices, just as wage rates have tended toward market clearing rates.

REFERENCES

1. W. J. Conyngham, *The Modernization of Soviet Industrial Management* (New York: Cambridge University Press, 1982), p. 2.
2. H. Kuromiya, "Edinonachalie and the Soviet Industrial Manager, 1928–1937," *Soviet Studies,* vol. 36, no. 2 (April 1984), 185–204.
3. For a discussion of the "success indicator" problem in Soviet industry, see A. Nove, "The Problem of Success Indicators in Soviet Industry," in *Economic Rationality and Soviet Politics* (New York: Praeger, 1964), pp. 83–98.
4. Nove, "The Problem of Success Indicators," p. 88. A striking example of the possible distortion as pictured by the Soviet humor magazine *Krokodil* and cited by Nove is the nail factory whose gross output target is specified in *weight.* The month's output is one gigantic nail being hauled away with a crane. See A. Nove, *The Soviet Economy,* rev. ed. (New York: Praeger, 1969), p. 174.
5. Enterprise failures to meet delivery targets are generally not severely punished. Fines tend to be nominal and difficult to collect, and generally enterprises do not bother to pursue those who break contracts. Because of the lack of coordination of supply plans between the State Committee for Material-Technical Supply *(Gossnab), Gosplan,* and the ministries, no particular agency has been willing to take the responsibility for contract violations. For Soviet discussions of these problems, see *Planovoe khoziaistvo* [The planned economy], no. 6, 1978, 101–109; *Pravda,* February 18, 1978.
6. For a discussion of the problems imposed by the supply system, see G. E. Schroeder, "The 'Reform' of the Supply System in Soviet Industry," *Soviet Studies,* vol. 24, no. 1 (July 1972), 105–107; G. E. Schroeder, "The Soviet Economy on a Treadmill of 'Reforms,' " in U.S. Congress, Joint Economic Committee, *Soviet Economy in a Time of Change* (Washington, D.C.: U.S. Government Printing Office, 1979), vol. 1, pp. 323–224.
7. For a mathematical demonstration that supply uncertainty leads to over demanding of inputs, see S. Linz and R. Martin, "Soviet Enterprise Behavior under Uncertainty," *Journal of Comparative Economics,* vol. 6, no. 1 (March 1982), 24–36.
8. R. Hutchings, *Seasonal Influences in Soviet Industry* (London: Oxford University Press, 1971), pp. 187–195.

9. The discussion of Soviet management is based primarily upon the following works: J. S. Berliner, *Factory and Manager in the USSR* (Cambridge, Mass.: Harvard University Press, 1957)—a study of the early years of Soviet management experience based primarily upon emigré interviews; D. Granick, *Management of the Industrial Firm in the USSR* (New York: Columbia University Press, 1954)—an in-depth study of industrial management of the 1930s, based primarily upon a detailed reading of the Soviet local and specialized press; B. M. Richman, *Soviet Industrial Management* (Englewood Cliffs, N.J.: Prentice-Hall, 1965)—a general survey of material similar to that discussed by Berliner and Granick. More recent material on the Soviet as compared with other industrial managers can be found in D. Granick, *Managerial Comparisons of Four Developed Countries: France, Britain, United States, and Russia* (Cambridge, Mass.: MIT Press, 1972). For treatment of the Soviet managerial system in the language of organization theory, see David Granick, *Soviet Metal Fabricating and Economic Development* (Madison: University of Wisconsin Press, 1967), chap. 7. The Soviet manager and innovation are treated in J. S. Berliner, *The Innovation Decision in Soviet Industry* (Cambridge, Mass.: MIT Press, 1976), part 3; G. Guroff and F. V. Carstensen, eds., *Entrepreneurship in Imperial Russia and The Soviet Union* (Princeton, N.J.: Princeton University Press, 1983); W. J. Conyngham, *The Modernization of Soviet Industrial Management* (New York: Cambridge University Press, 1982); J. C. Thompson and R. F. Vidmer, *Administrative Science and Politics in The USSR and The United States* (New York: Praeger, 1983); H. Bhérer, *Management Soviétique* (Paris: Presses de la Fondation Nationale des Sciences Politiques, 1982).

10. Notably, Berliner, *Factory and Manager;* Granick, *Management of the Industrial Firm;* Granick, *Managerial Comparisons of Four Developed Countries;* Richman, *Soviet Industrial Management.*

11. Richman, *Soviet Industrial Management,* pp. 134–135; Berliner, *The Innovation Decision,* pp. 478–484.

12. Granick, *Managerial Comparisons of Four Developed Countries,* chap. 9.

13. D. Granick, "Institutional Innovation and Economic Management: The Soviet Incentive System, 1921 to the Present," in G. Guroff and F. V. Carstensen, eds., *Entrepreneurship in Imperial Russia and the Soviet Union*, pp. 245ff.

14. Granick, *Managerial Comparisons of Four Developed Countries,* chap. 9.

15. Granick, *Managerial Comparisons of Four Developed Countries,* chap. 8.

16. For a discussion, see Conyngham, *The Modernization of Soviet Industrial Management,* p. 13.

17. B. A. Ruble, "Soviet Trade Unions and Labor Relations After 'Solidarity' " in U.S. Congress, Joint Economic Committee, *Soviet Economy in the 1980s: Problems and Prospects,* part 2 (Washington, D.C.: U.S. Government Printing Office, 1982), p. 349. There is a large body of literature pertaining to Soviet labor unions. See, for example, B. A. Ruble, *Soviet Trade Unions* (New York: Cambridge University Press, 1981); A. Broadersen, *The Soviet Worker* (New York: Random House, 1966); E. Clark Brown, *Soviet Trade Unions and Labor Relations* (Cambridge, Mass.: Harvard University Press, 1966); D. C. Heldman, *Trade Unions and Labor Relations in The USSR* (Washington, D.C.: Council on American Affairs, 1977); P. Barton, "Trade Unions in The USSR," *AFL-CIO Free Trade Union News* 26 (September 1979), 1–16; A. Kahan and B. R. Ruble, eds., *Industrial Labor in The USSR.*

18. Ruble, "Soviet Trade Unions and Labor Relations After 'Solidarity'," 355.

19. For a discussion of Soviet unions at the enterprise level, see Ruble, *Soviet Trade Unions,* chap. 4.

20. The major source of trade union income is membership dues. In 1981, just under 65 percent of union expenditure was for "mass cultural" and sports activities. See Ruble, "Soviet Trade Unions and Labor Relations After 'Solidarity'," 356.

21. The legal rights of Soviet workers are elaborated in Ruble, *Soviet Trade Unions,* chap. 4.

22. Ruble, *Soviet Trade Unions,* chap. 6.

23. For a recent discussion on worker influence over enterprise decisions, see D. Slider, "Reforming the Workplace. The 1983 Soviet Law on Labour Collectives," *Soviet Studies,* vol. 37, no. 2 (April 1985), 173–83.

24. Detailed discussions of Gosplan's labor balances can be found in *Metodicheskie ukazaniia k razrabotke gosudarstuennykh planov ekonomichiskogo i sotsialnogo razvitiia SSSR* (Moscow: Ekonomika, 1980), chap. 19; A. N. Efimov et al., *Ekonomicheskoe planirovanie v. SSSR* [Economic planning in the USSR], (Moscow: 1967), chap. 6; and in Y. Dubrovsky, ed., *Planning of Manpower in the Soviet Union,* translated from the Russian (Moscow: Progress Publishers, 1975). For discussions of the construction of the labor balance for the 1971–1975 plan, see M. Feshbach and S. Rapawy, "Labor Constraints in the Five-Year Plan," in U.S. Congress, Joint Economic Committee, *Soviet Economic Prospects for the Seventies* (Washington, D.C.: U.S. Government Printing Office, 1973), pp. 485–507; and M. Feshbach and S. Rapawy, "Soviet Population and Manpower Trends and Policies," in U.S. Congress, Joint Economic Committee, *Soviet Economy in a New Perspective* (Washington, D.C.: U.S. Government Printing Office, 1976), pp. 113–154.

25. Efimov et al., *Ekonomicheskoe planirovanie,* p. 171.

26. For a discussion of population and labor force issues, see M. Feshbach, "Population and Labor Force," in A. Bergson and H. S. Levine, eds., *The Soviet Economy: Toward the Year 2000* (Boston: George Allen & Unwin, 1983), chap. 3; A. Kahan and B. A. Ruble, eds., *Industrial Labor in the U.S.S.R.* (New York: Pergamon, 1979); J. Chinn, *Manipulating Soviet Population Resources* (New York: 1977); A. Coale, et al., *Human Fertility in Russia Since the Nineteenth Century* (Princeton, N.J.: Princeton University Press, 1979); S. Rapawy and G. Baldwin, "Demographic Trends in the Soviet Union: 1950–2000," in U.S. Congress, Joint Economic Committee, *Soviet Economy in the 1980s: Problems and Prospects,* part 2 (Washington, D.C.: U.S. Government Printing Office, 1982), pp. 265–296; A. Goodman and G. Schleifer, "The Soviet Labor Market in the 1980s," in U.S. Congress, Joint Economic Committee, *Soviet Economy in the 1980s: Problems and Prospects,* part 2, pp. 323–348. The latest Soviet population census (1979) can be found in TsSU, *Chislennost' i sostav naseleniia SSSR* (Moscow: Finansy i statistika, 1984).

27. The urban labor force is discussed in W. Moskoff, "The Soviet Urban Labor Supply," in H. W. Morton and R. C. Stuart, *The Contemporary Soviet City* (Armonk, N.Y.: M. E. Sharpe, 1984), chap. 4. The specifics of rural to urban migration are developed in R. C. Stuart and P. R. Gregory, "A Model of Soviet Rural-Urban Migration," *Economic Development and Cultural Change,* vol. 26, no. 1 (October 1977), 81–92. General discussion of regional labor force problems can be found in S. Rapawy, "Regional Employment Trends in The U.S.S.R.: 1950–1975," in U.S. Congress, Joint Economic Committee, *Soviet Economy in a Time of Change,* vol. 1 (Washington, D.C.: U.S. Government Printing Office, 1979), pp. 600–617.

28. For an examination of this case, see M. Feshbach, "Prospects for Outmigration from Central Asia and Kazakhstan in the Next Decade," in Joint Economic Committee, *Soviet Economy in a Time of Change* (Washington, D.C.: U.S. Government Printing Office, 1979), vol. 1, pp. 656–709; M. Feshbach, "Trends in The Soviet Muslim

Population—Demographic Aspects," in U.S. Congress, Joint Economic Committee, *Soviet Economy in The 1980's: Problems and Prospects,* part 2, pp. 297–322.

29. V. Zaslavsky and Y. Luryi, "The Passport System in the USSR and Changes in Soviet Society," *Soviet Union,* vol. 6, no. 2 (1979), 137–153.

30. This discussion is based upon A. McCauley, *Economic Welfare in the Soviet Union* (Madison: University of Wisconsin Press, 1979), pp. 174–186.

31. L. J. Kirsch, *Soviet Wages: Changes in Structure and Administration Since 1956* (Cambridge, Mass.: MIT Press, 1972), pp. 1–8; J. G. Chapman, "Labor Mobility and Labor Allocation in the USSR," paper presented at the joint meeting of the Association for the Study of Soviet-Type Economics and the Association for Comparative Economics, Detroit, Mich., December 1970, p. 3; J. G. Chapman, "Soviet Wages Under Socialism," in A. Abouchar, ed., *The Socialist Price Mechanism* (Durham, N.C.: Duke University Press, 1977), pp. 246–281; McCauley, *Economic Welfare in the Soviet Union,* chap. 8.

32. Prior to 1956, this system was extremely complex. In all, there existed around 1900 different *setka* schedules and about 1000 different *stavka* assignments. In the 1957–1961 system there were 10 *setka* schedules and 50 different *stavka* assignments. The 1972–1976 reforms reduced the number of *setka* to 3 and the number of *stavka* to 17. On this, see B. M. Sukharevsky, "Zarabotnaia plata i material'naia zainteresovannost" [The wage and material incentives], in A. P. Volkova et al., eds., *Trud i zarabotnaia plata v SSSR* [Labor and wages in the USSR] (Moscow: 1968), p. 302; see also Kirsch, *Soviet Wages,* Table 4-2, p. 75; and McCauley, *Economic Welfare in the Soviet Union,* p. 202.

33. E. C. Brown, "The Soviet Labor Market," *Soviet Trade Unions and Labor Relations* (Cambridge, Mass.: Harvard University Press, 1966), pp. 11–37, reprinted in M. Bornstein and D. Fusfeld, eds., *The Soviet Economy: A Book of Readings,* 3rd ed. (Homewood, Ill.: Irwin, 1970), pp. 217–220.

34. A. Bergson, *The Economics of Soviet Planning* (New Haven, Conn.: Yale University Press, 1964), p. 115. Soviet labor experts have noted in recent years that this system tends to create excessive turnover problems in branches having low base rates. In the eastern regions during the 1960s, turnover was highest in the food industry, where wages were lowest, and lowest in ferrous metals, where wages were highest. Attempts are being made to reduce the turnover problem in consumer branches by raising the minimum wage (in 1968 and 1971). On this, see Chapman, "Labor Mobility," p. 13; McCauley, *Economic Welfare in the Soviet Union,* pp. 200–207.

35. Sukharevsky, "Zarabotnaia plata," p. 292; McCauley, *Economic Welfare in the Soviet Union,* pp. 206–207.

36. A. Bergson, *The Structure of Soviet Wages* (Cambridge, Mass.: Harvard University Press, 1944), chap. 8; Sukharevsky, "Zarabotnaia plata," p. 291.

37. McCauley, *Economic Welfare in the Soviet Union,* p. 201; Kirsch, *Soviet Wages,* chap. 4; M. Yanowitch, "The Soviet Income Revolution," *Slavic Review,* vol. 22, no. 4 (December 1963), reprinted in M. Bornstein and D. Fusfeld, *The Soviet Economy,* 2nd ed. (Homewood, Ill.: Irwin, 1966), pp. 228–241. See also Sukharevsky, "Zarabotnaia plata," p. 196; and *Vestnik Statistiki* [Herald of Statistics], no. 6 (1983), 61–62.

38. Brown, "The Soviet Labor Market," p. 219; Sukharevsky, "Zarabotnaia plata," p. 302.

39. Chapman, "Labor Mobility," p. 23. Even these differentials have not proven sufficient to maintain an adequate labor force in the Far North and Siberia. Recent Soviet studies have suggested that the established regional differentials are not sufficient to

compensate for cost-of-living differentials, not to mention the low level of services (child care, health, education) available in these regions. On this, see *ibid.,* pp. 13–16.

40. Sukharevsky, "Zarabotnaia plata," p. 302; McCauley, *Economic Welfare in the Soviet Union,* p. 202.
41. Sukharevsky, "Zarabotnaia plata," p. 292; Kirsch, *Soviet Wages,* Table 6-1, p. 125.
42. McCauley, *Economic Welfare in the Soviet Union,* p. 248.
43. Sukharevsky, "Zarabotnaia plata," pp. 297–302; Kirsch, *Soviet Wages,* chap. 2; *Vistnik Statistiki* [Herald of Statistics], no. 6 (1983), 63–68.
44. Kirsch, *Soviet Wages,* chap. 8.
45. There is a large body of literature devoted to Soviet education. See, for example, M. Matthews, *Education in The Soviet Union: Policies and Institutions Since Stalin* (Boston, Mass.: Allen & Unwin, 1982); R. B. Dobson, "Education and Opportunity," in J. Pankhurst and M. P. Sacks, eds., *Contemporary Soviet Soviety: Sociological Perspectives* (New York: Praeger, 1980); R. B. Dobson, "Soviet Education: Problems and Policies in The Urban Context," in H. W. Morton and R. C. Stuart, eds., *The Contemporary Soviet City* (Armonk, N.Y.: M. E. Sharpe, 1984), pp. 156–179; National Foreign Assessment Center, *USSR: Trends and Prospects in Educational Attainment 1959–85* ER79-10344 (Washington, D.C.: June 1979).
46. Dobson, "Soviet Education," p. 156.
47. Dobson, "Soviet Education," pp. 172ff.
48. Dobson, "Soviet Education," p. 174. According to a recent Soviet source, 99 percent of day students in general education schools receive work-related experience as part of schooling. See TsSU, *Narodnoe Khoziaistvo SSSR v 1983 g.* [The national economy of the USSR in 1983] (Moscow: Finansy i statistika, 1984), p. 490.
49. For a discussion of recent changes, see Goodman and Schleiter, "The Soviet Labor Market in the 1980s," pp. 336–339.
50. For a discussion of controls, see E. Nash, "Recent Changes in Labor Controls in the Soviet Union," in U.S. Congress, Joint Economic Committee, *New Directions in the Soviet Economy,* part 3 (Washington, D.C.: U.S. Government Printing Office, 1966), pp. 849–871; for recent evidence, see Goodman and Schleifer, "The Soviet Labor Market in the 1980s."
51. Goodman and Schleifer, "The Soviet Labor Market in the 1980s," p. 338.
52. J. G. Chapman, "Labor Mobility and Labor Allocation in The USSR," paper presented at the ACES Meeting, Detroit, Michigan, December 1970, p. 8.
53. For a detailed discussion of labor controls from the mid-1930s to 1956, see A. Nove, *An Economic History of the USSR* (London: Penguin, 1969), pp. 195–198, 260–263.
54. Chapman, "Labor Mobility," 7–8.
55. Goodman and Schleiter, "The Soviet Labor Market in the 1980s," p. 336, Note 14, 338.
56. *Zaniatost' naseleniia: izuchenie i regulirovanie* [Employment of the population: study and regulation] (Moscow: Finansy i statistika, 1983), pp. 49–65.
57. This discussion is based on the following references: S. Rosefielde, "How Reliable Are Available Estimates of Forced Concentration Camp Labor in the Soviet Union?" *Soviet Studies,* vol. 32, no. 4 (October 1981); D. Dallin and B. Nicolevsky, *Forced Labor in Soviet Russia* (New Haven, Conn.: Yale University Press, 1947); N. Jasny, "Labor and Output in Soviet Concentration Camps," *Journal of Political Economy,* vol. 59, no. 5 (October 1951), 405–419; A. Solzhenitsyn, *The Gulag Archipelago* (New York: Harper & Row, 1973 and 1974), vols. 1 and 2; S. Swianiewicz, *Forced Labor and Economic Development* (London: Oxford University Press, 1965); S. Rosefielde, "An Assessment of the Sources and Uses of Gulag Forced Labor," *Soviet Studies,* vol. 32, no. 1 (January 1981), 51–87; S. G. Wheatcroft, "On Assessing the

Size of Forced Concentration Camp Labour in the Soviet Union, 1929–56," *Soviet Studies,* vol. 32, no. 2 (April 1981), 265–295; R. Conquest, "Forced Labour Statistics: Some Comments," *Soviet Studies,* vol. 34, no. 3 (July 1982), 434–439; S. G. Wheatcroft, "Towards a Thorough Analysis of Soviet Forced Labour Statistics," *Soviet Studies,* vol. 35 (April 1983), 223–237.

58. For a summary of estimates, see Rosefielde, "How Reliable are Available Estimates?" Tables 1 and 4; and Wheatcroft, "On Assessing the Size of Forced Concentration Camp Labor," pp. 267–268.

59. S. Rosefielde, "Excess Mortality in the Soviet Union: A Reconsideration of the Consequences of Forced Industrialization 1929–1949," *Soviet Studies,* vol. 35, no. 3 (July 1983), 385–409; B. Anderson and B. Silver, "Demographic Analysis and Population Catastrophes in the USSR," *Slavic Review,* vol. 44 (Fall 1985).

60. Our approach to allocative efficiency is quite intuitive and should not be confused with a formal development of Pareto optimality. The optimality of Soviet labor policy in terms of the Pareto conditions is discussed by Bergson, *The Economics of Soviet Planning,* pp. 118–126.

61. A similar standard is suggested by Kirsch, *Soviet Wages,* chap. 8.

62. R. Moorsteen and R. Powell, *The Soviet Capital Stock, 1928–1962* (Homewood, Ill.: Irwin, 1966), pp. 643, 648.

63. S. Kuznets, *Economic Growth of Nations* (Cambridge, Mass.: Harvard University Press, 1971), p. 74.

64. One finds varying estimates of trends in the Soviet labor participation rate. The reason is that prior to 1928, the major portion of the Soviet labor force was engaged in agriculture, and, by definition, just about all in agriculture are considered employed, even if they only work part time. Thus, the measure cited here is for full-time labor equivalents. See Eason, "Labor Force," pp. 53–56; L. M. Danilov and I. I. Matrozova, "Trudovye resursy i ikh ispol'zovanie" [Labor resources and their utilization], in A. R. Volkova et al., eds., *Trud i zarabotnaia plata v SSSR* [Labor and wages in the USSR] (Moscow: 1968), p. 247.

65. Nove, *An Economic History of the USSR,* p. 262.

66. Chapman, "Labor Mobility," p. 31.

67. W. W. Eason, "Labor Force" in A. Bergson and S. Kuznets, eds., *Economic Trends in The Soviet Union* (Cambridge, Mass.: Harvard University Press, 1963), p. 57.

68. Eason, "Labor Force," 57.

69. Bergson, *The Economics of Soviet Planning,* 115.

70. Feshbach, "Population and Labor Force," Table 3.2; see also the sources cited in reference 26.

71. Feshbach, "Population and Labor Force," p. 79.

72. Feshbach, "Population And Labor Force," Table 3.4.

73. Feshbach, "Population and Labor Force."

74. Feshbach, "Population and Labor Force," p. 83.

75. Feshbach, "Population and Labor Force," Table 3.7. For a discussion of health issues, see M. Feshbach "Issues in Soviet Health Problems," in U.S. Congress, Joint Economic Committee, *Soviet Economy in the 1980s: Problems and Prospects,* part 2 (Washington D.C.: U.S. Government Printing Office, 1982) pp. 203–227; Davis, "The Economics of the Soviet Health System," in *Soviet Economy in the 1980s: Problems and Prospects,* pp. 228–264.

76. For a discussion, see R. C. Stuart, "The Sources of Soviet Urban Growth," in H. W. Morton and R. C. Stuart, *The Contemporary Soviet City* (Armonk, N.Y.: M. E. Sharpe, 1984), chap. 2.

77. For evidence, see Stuart and Gregory, "A Model of Soviet Rural-Urban Migration."

78. In addition to sources cited in reference 17, see especially M. Feshbach, "Trends in the Soviet Muslim Population-Demographic Aspects," in U.S. Congress, Joint Economic Committee, *Soviet Economy in the 1980s: Problems and Prospects,* part 2 (Washington, D.C.: U.S. Government Printing Office, 1982), pp. 297–322.

79. Goodman and Schleifer, "The Soviet Labor Market in the 1980s," p. 333.

80. The question of labor from central Asia has received considerable attention. See, for example, Feshbach, "Trends in the Soviet Muslim Population—Demographic Aspects"; M. Feshbach, "Prospects for Outmigration from Central Asia and Kazakhstan in the Next Decade," in U.S. Congress, Joint Economic Committee, *Soviet Economy in a Time of Change,* vol. 1 (Washington, D.C.: U.S. Government Printing Office, 1979), pp. 656–709; S. E. Wimbush and D. Ponomarett, *Alternatives for Mobilizing Central Asian Labor: Outmigration and Regional Development* (Santa Monica, Calif.: The Rand Corporation, 1979).

81. The question of outmigration from Central Asia has been one of controversy. For an analysis, see Feshbach, "Prospects for Outmigration from Central Asia and Kazakhstan in the Next Decade."

82. N. DeWitt, "Education and the Development of Human Resources: Soviet and American Effort," in U.S. Congress, Joint Economic Committee, *Dimensions of Soviet Economic Power* (Washington, D.C.: U.S. Government Printing Office, 1962), p. 244.

83. DeWitt, "Education and the Development of Human Resources," p. 243.

84. Bergson, *The Structure of Soviet Wages,* chaps. 8 and 14; Sukharevsky, "Zarabotnaia Plata," pp. 291–292; Kirsch, *Soviet Wages,* pp. 174–179.

85. Data are from *Narodnoe Khoziaistvo 1983.*

86. Bergson, *The Economics of Soviet Planning,* p. 105.

87. P. J. D. Wiles, "A Note on Soviet Unemployment in U.S. Definitions," *Soviet Studies,* vol. 23, no. 2 (April 1972), 619–628. The emigré unemployment rate data come from the Soviet Interview Project in a report by P. Gregory, "Unemployment and Job Security in the Soviet Union: Results from the Soviet Interview Project," SIP Working Paper, Summer 1985.

88. A Soviet source from the early 1970s suggests that roughly one-half of industrial jobs are mediated by employment agencies in operation since the late 1960s. See F. D. Romma and K. P. Urzhinsky, *Pravovye voprosy podbora rasstanovki kadrov* [Legal questions concerning the selection and arrangement of cadres] (Moscow, 1971), chaps. 1 and 2; and Chapman, "Labor Mobility," Chap. 4. Recent sources suggest that such agencies place about 15 percent of those employed in the *entire* national economy. See Goodman and Schleifer, "The Soviet Labor Market in The 1980s," 336 (footnote 14).

89. A 1978 study conducted by Soviet statistical authorities of the food-processing industry finds that 8.5 percent of the recorded separations were separations initiated by the enterprise administration for poor work. On this, see *Zaniatost' naselenie: izuchenie i regulirovanie* [Employment of the population: study and regulating] (Moscow: Finansy i statistiki, 1983), p. 57.

90. For the role of women in the Soviet economy, in addition to sources dealing with population and labor force, in general, the interested reader should consult N. T. Dodge, *Women in the Soviet Economy* (Baltimore, Md.: The Johns Hopkins University Press, 1966); D. Atkinson et al., eds., *Women in Russia* (Stanford: Stanford University Press, 1977); M. P. Sacks, *Work and Equality in Soviet Society* (New York: Praeger, 1982); M. P. Sacks, *Women's Work in Soviet Russia: Continuity in the Midst of Change* (New York: Praeger, 1976); W. Moskoff, *Labor and Leisure in*

the Soviet Union (New York: St. Martin's Press, 1984); G. W. Lapidus, *Women in Soviet Society* (Berkeley and Los Angeles: University of California Press, 1979); G. Ofer and A. Vinokur, "Earnings Differentials by Sex in the Soviet Union: A First Look," in S. Rosefielde, ed., *Economic Welfare and the Economics of Soviet Socialism* (New York: Cambridge University Press, 1981), pp. 127–162; P. R. Gregory, "Fertility and Labor Force Participation in The Soviet Union and Eastern Europe," *Review of Economics and Statistics,* vol. 64, no. 1 (February 1982), 18–131.

91. Feshbach, "Population and Labor Force," Table 3.9.
92. Goodman and Schleiter, "The Soviet Labor Market in the 1980s," 329–330.
93. W. Moskoff, "An Estimate of the Soviet Male-Female Income Gap," *ACES Bulletin,* vol. 16, no. 2 (Fall 1974), 21–31.
94. *Vestnik Statistiki* [Herald of Statistics], no. 1 (1976), 85. Since 1976, the proportion of women in the labor force of various sectors is no longer published in *Vestnik Statistiki,* although the section in which the information appeared, *Zhenshchiny v SSSR* [Women in the USSR], appears annually in the January issue.
95. G. Ofer and A. Vinokur, "Earnings Differentials by Sex in the Soviet Union: A First Look," in S. Rosefielde, ed., *Economic Welfare and The Economics of Soviet Socialism* (New York: Cambridge University Press, 1981), pp. 127–162.
96. J. R. Moroney, "Do Women Earn Less Under Capitalism?" *Economic Journal,* vol. 89, no. 355 (September 1979), 601–613.
97. Moskoff, *Labor and Leisure in the Soviet Union,* chap. 7.
98. Discussions of the role of women in the Soviet rural economy are given in N. T. Dodge, "Recruitment and the Quality of the Soviet Agricultural Labor Force," in J. R. Millar, ed., *The Soviet Rural Community* (Urbana: University of Illinois Press, 1971), pp. 180–213; and R. C. Stuart, "Women in Soviet Rural Management," *Slavic Review,* vol. 38, no. 4 (December 1979). For an examination of the role of women in industrial management, see K. M. Bartol and R. A. Bartol, "Women in Managerial and Professional Positions: The United States and the Soviet Union," *Industrial and Labor Relations Review,* vol. 28, no. 4 (July 1975), 524–534.
99. Gregory, "Fertility and Labor Force Participation in the Soviet Union and Eastern Europe."
100. Investment choice in the Soviet Union has been discussed in a number of articles and books: Bergson, *The Economics of Soviet Planning,* chap. 11; G. Grossman, "Scarce Capital and Soviet Doctrine," *Quarterly Journal of Economics,* vol. 67, no. 3 (August 1953); A. Zauberman, *Aspects of Planometrics* (New Haven, Conn.: Yale University Press, 1967), chaps. 13 and 14; A. Abouchar, "The New Soviet Standard Methodology for Investment Allocation," *Soviet Studies,* vol. 24, no. 3 (January 1973), 402–410; Berliner, *The Innovation Decision,* chap. 21; S. H. Cohn, "Deficiencies in Soviet Investment Policies and the Technological Imperative," in U.S. Congress, Joint Economic Committee, *Soviet Economy in a New Perspective* (Washington, D.C.: U.S. Government Printing Office, 1976), pp. 447–459; S. H. Cohn, "Soviet Replacement Investment: A Rising Policy Imperative," in U.S. Congress, Joint Economic Committee, *Soviet Economy in a Time of Change* (Washington, D.C.: U.S. Government Printing Office, 1979), pp. 230–245; Michael Ellman, *Socialist Planning* (Cambridge, Mass.: Cambridge University Press, 1979), chap. 5; D. A. Dyker, *The Process of Investment in the Soviet Union* (New York: Cambridge University Press, 1983); J. Giffen, "The Allocation of Investment in the Soviet Union: Criteria for the Efficiency of Investment, *Soviet Studies,* vol. 33, no. 4 (October 1981), 593–609; R. Leggett, "Soviet Investment Policy in the 11th Five-Year Plan," in U.S. Congress, Joint Economic Committee, *Soviet Economy in the 1980s: Problems and Prospects,* part 1

(Washington, D.C.: U.S. Government Printing Office, 1982), pp. 129–152; S. H. Cohn "Sources of Low Productivity in Soviet Capital Investment," in *Soviet Economy in the 1980s,* p. 1969–1994.

101. After the Kosygin reform of 1965, the importance of decentralized investment increased. However, in the 1970s, even where decentralized funds (for example, from enterprises) were financing investment, the distinction between centralized and decentralized investment lost its former significance, with central control being maintained over all investment. For a discussion, see Dyker, *The Process of Investment In The Soviet Union,* p. 31.

102. *Voprosy ekonomiki* [Problems of economics], nos. 9 and 11 (1972). Also see Nove, *The Soviet Economy,* pp. 97–98, 231–240.

103. Leggett, "Soviet Investment Policy in the 11th Five-Year Plan," 142–143.

104. Zauberman, *Aspects of Planometrics,* p. 139.

105. G. Leptin, *Methode und Effizienz der Investitionsfinanzierung durch Abschreibungen in der Sowjetwirtschaft* [Methods and efficiency of investment financing through depreciation in the Soviet economy] (Berlin: Osteuropa-Institut, 1961), part 2.

106. For a detailed discussion of these points, see Grossman, "Scarce Capital," 311–314, reprinted in F. D. Holzman, *Readings on the Soviet Economy* (Skokie, Ill.: Rand McNally, 1962).

107. "Recommendations of the All-Union Scientific-Technical Conference on Problems of Determining the Economic Effectiveness of Capital Investment and New Techniques in the USSR National Economy," *Problems of Economics: A Journal of Translations,* vol. 1, no. 9 (January 1959), 86–90, reprinted in Holzman, *Readings on the Soviet Economy,* pp. 383–392. Also see "Standard Methodology for Determining the Economic Effectiveness of Capital Investments," *Ekonomicheskaia gazeta* [The economic gazette], no. 39 (1969), 11–12, translated in *The ASTE Bulletin,* vol. 13, no. 3 (Fall 1971), 25–36.

108. Zauberman, *Aspects of Planometrics,* p. 139.

109. Nove, *The Soviet Economy,* p. 233.

110. For a detailed discussion of the various techniques used during this period, see Grossman, "Scarce Capital," 315–343.

111. "Recommendations of the All-Union Scientific-Technical Conference," 86–90.

112. Capital outlay includes the cost of buildings, equipment, and installation but excludes the cost of the site: Zauberman, *Aspects of Planometrics,* p. 142.

113. An equivalent test would be: Let E be the "standard coefficient of efficiency." Then, the projects should be compared by comparing their full costs—including an imputed interest cost: $C_i + EK_i$ = minimum. The project with the lowest *full* cost would be chosen. See Bergson, *The Economics of Soviet Planning,* p. 254.

114. Bergson, *The Economics of Soviet Planning,* pp. 225–265; J. Thornton, "Differential Capital Charges and Resource Allocation in Soviet Industry," *Journal of Political Economy,* vol. 79, no. 3 (May-June 1971), 545–561.

115. Bergson, *The Economics of Soviet Planning,* pp. 262–263.

116. See Bergson, *The Economics of Soviet Planning,* p. 258, for a demonstration that a uniform norm will result in the equalization of the marginal productivities.

117. "Recommendations of the All-Union Scientific-Technical Conference," 88.

118. *Ibid.,* 88–89.

119. "Standard Methodology for Determining the Economic Effectiveness of Capital Investments," translated in *The ASTE Bulletin,* vol. 13, no. 3 (Fall 1971), 25–36. It originally appeared in *Ekonomicheskaia gazeta* [The economic gazette], no. 39 (1969), 11–12.

120. V. Cherniavski, "The Measure of Effectiveness," *Problems of Economics: A Journal of Translations,* vol. 15, no. 8 (December 1972); and L. V. Kantorovich, *Essays in Optimal Planning* (White Plains, N.Y.: International Arts and Sciences Press, 1976), essays 8–10.
121. Quoted in V. Vainshtein, "On Methods of Determining the Economic Effectiveness of Capital Investment," *Problems of Economics: A Journal of Translations,* vol. 15, no. 3 (July 1972), 12.
122. "Standard Methodology," p. 31.
123. Abouchar, "The New Soviet Standard Methodology," 407.
124. This discussion is based on Giffen, "The Allocation of Investment in the Soviet Union: Criteria for the Efficiency of Investment," 600–601.
125. "Methodika opredeleniia ekonomicheskoi effektivnosti kapital'nyich vlozhenii" [The method of determining the economic effectiveness of capital investment], *Ekonomicheskaia gazeta* [The economic gazette], 2–3 (1981).
126. Dyker, *The Process of Investment in the Soviet Union,* p. 107.
127. *Ibid.,* p. 108.
128. *Ibid.*

SELECTED BIBLIOGRAPHY

Soviet Enterprise Management

J. S. Berliner, *Factory and Manager in the USSR* (Cambridge, Mass.: Harvard University Press, 1957).
———, *The Innovation Decision in Soviet Industry* (Cambridge, Mass.: MIT Press, 1976).
———, "Managerial Incentives and Decision-making: A Comparison of the United States and the Soviet Union," in M. Bornstein and D. Fusfeld, eds., *The Soviet Economy,* 3rd ed. (Homewood, Ill.: Irwin, 1970), pp. 165–195.
W. J. Conyngham, *The Modernization of Soviet Industrial Management* (New York: Cambridge University Press, 1982).
D. Granick, *Management of the Industrial Firm in the USSR* (New York: Columbia University Press, 1954).
———, *Managerial Comparisons of Four Developed Countries: France, Britain, United States, and Russia* (Cambridge, Mass.: MIT Press, 1972).
———, *The Red Executive* (Garden City, N.Y.: Doubleday, 1960).
———, *Soviet Metal Fabricating and Economic Development* (Madison: University of Wisconsin Press, 1967), chap. 7.
G. Guroff and F. V. Carstensen, eds., *Entrepreneurship in Imperial Russia and the Soviet Union* (Princeton, N.J.: Princeton University Press, 1983).
A. Nove, *Economic Rationality and Soviet Politics* (New York: Praeger, 1964), chap. 5.
B. M. Richman, *Management Development and Education in the Soviet Union* (East Lansing: Michigan State University Press, 1967).
———, *Soviet Industrial Management* (Englewood Cliffs, N.J.: Prentice-Hall, 1965).

Labor Allocation in the Soviet Union

A. Bergson, *The Economics of Soviet Planning* (New Haven, Conn.: Yale University Press, 1964), chap. 6.
———, *The Structure of Soviet Wages* (Cambridge, Mass.: Harvard University Press, 1944).

E. C. Brown, *Soviet Trade Unions and Labor Relations* (Cambridge, Mass.: Harvard University Press, 1966).

A. Coale et al., *Human Fertility in Russia Since the Nineteenth Century* (Princeton, N.J.: Princeton University Press, 1979).

J. G. Chapman, "Labor Mobility and Labor Allocation in the USSR," paper presented at the joint meeting of the Association for the Study of Soviet-Type Economics and the Association for Comparative Economics, Detroit, Mich., December 1970.

———, *Real Wages in Soviet Russia Since 1928* (Cambridge, Mass.: Harvard University Press, 1963).

———, "Soviet Wages Under Socialism," in A. Abouchar, ed., *The Socialist Price Mechanism* (Durham, N.C.: Duke University Press, 1977), pp. 246–281.

W. W. Eason, "Labor Force," in A. Bergson and S. Kuznets, eds., *Economic Trends in the Soviet Union* (Cambridge, Mass.: Harvard University Press, 1963).

M. Feshbach, "Trends in the Soviet Muslim Population—Demographic Aspects," in U.S. Congress, Joint Economic Committee, *Soviet Economy in the 1980s: Problems and Prospects* (Washington, D.C.: U.S.Government Printing Office, 1982).

———, "Labor Force," in A. Bergson and H. S. Levine, eds., *The Soviet Economy Towards the Year 2000* (Boston: Allen & Unwin, 1983).

M. Feshbach and S. Rapawy, "Labor Constraints in the Five-Year Plan," in U.S. Congress, Joint Economic Committee, *Soviet Economic Prospects for the Seventies* (Washington, D.C.: U.S. Government Printing Office, 1973).

———, "Soviet Population and Manpower Trends and Policies," in U.S. Congress, Joint Economic Committee, *Soviet Economy in a New Perspective* (Washington, D.C.: U.S. Government Printing Office, 1976), pp. 113–154.

A. Goodman and G. Schleifer, "The Soviet Labor Market in the 1980s," in U.S. Congress, Joint Economic Committee, *Soviet Economy in the 1980s: Problems and Prospects,* part 2 (Washington, D.C.: U.S. Government Printing Office, 1982).

A. Kahan and B. Ruble, eds., *Industrial Labor in the USSR* (New York: Pergamon, 1979).

L. J. Kirsch, *Soviet Wages: Changes in Structure and Administration Since 1956* (Cambridge, Mass.: MIT Press, 1972).

A. McAuley, *Economic Welfare in the Soviet Union* (Madison: University of Wisconsin Press, 1979).

M. McAuley, *Labor Disputes in Soviet Russia 1957–1965* (Oxford: Oxford University Press, 1969).

S. Rapawy, "Regional Employment Trends in the U.S.S.R.: 1950 to 1975," in U.S. Congress, Joint Economic Committee, *Soviet Economy in a Time of Change* (Washington, D.C.: U.S. Government Printing Office, 1979), vol. 1, pp. 600–617.

S. Rapawy and G. Baldwin, "Demographic Trends in The Soviet Union: 1950–2000," in U.S. Congress, Joint Economic Committee, *Soviet Economy in The 1980s: Problems and Prospects,* part 2 (Washington, D.C.: U.S. Government Printing Office, 1982).

B. A. Ruble, *Soviet Trade Unions* (New York: Cambridge University Press, 1981).

The Investment Decision

A. Abouchar, "The New Soviet Standard Methodology for Investment Allocation," *Soviet Studies,* vol. 24, no. 3 (January 1973).

A. Bergson, *The Economics of Soviet Planning* (New Haven, Conn.: Yale University Press, 1964), chap. 11.

F. A. Durgin, "The Soviet 1969 Standard Methodology for Investment Allocation Versus

'Universally Correct' Methods," *The ACES Bulletin,* vol. 19, no. 2 (Summer 1977), 29–54.

D. A. Dyker, *The Process of Investment in the Soviet Union* (New York: Cambridge University Press, 1981).

J. Giffen, "The Allocation of Investment in the Soviet Union: Criteria for the Efficiency of Investment," *Soviet Studies,* vol. 32, no. 4 (October 1981), 593–609.

P. Gregory, B. Fielitz, and T. Curtis, "The New Soviet Investment Rules: A Guide to Rational Investment Planning?" *Southern Economic Journal,* vol. 41, no. 3 (January 1974).

G. Grossman, "Scarce Capital and Soviet Doctrine," *Quarterly Journal of Economics,* vol. 67, no. 3 (August 1953).

G. Leptin, *Methode und Effizienz der Investitionsfinanzierung durch Abschreibungen in der Sowjetwirtschaft* [Methods and efficiency of investment financing through depreciation in the Soviet economy] (Berlin: Osteuropa-Institut, 1961).

A. Zauberman, *Aspects of Planometrics* (New Haven, Conn.: Yale University Press, 1967), chaps. 13 and 14.

———, *Mathematical Theory in Soviet Planning* (New York: Oxford University Press, 1976), chap. 4.

chapter 9

Soviet Agriculture

The development of Soviet agriculture forms a very important part of the overall story of Soviet economic development. This importance stems, in part, from the role that agriculture has played in early Soviet development and the particular organizational arrangements utilized to fulfill this role. We have already considered this story.

Soviet agriculture is also of great importance to the contemporary Soviet economy for its ability to produce adequate food and fiber at reasonable costs in what is now primarily an industrial and urban society. In short, Soviet agricultural performance assumes major importance as Soviet leaders move toward the modernization of this traditionally controversial sector.

Westerners are accustomed to the notion that Soviet agriculture does not perform very well. This conception generally assumes sharp fluctuations in annual grain output, significant increases in the volume of Soviet grain imports, inadequate distribution of food products, periodic food shortages, rationing, and the like. How serious is the Soviet food problem and what contributes to it? If low productivity is a problem, why have recent resource shifts into agriculture not increased efficiency?

In this chapter, we consider three major themes. First, we examine the organizational arrangements of Soviet agriculture and the manner in which agriculture fits into overall Soviet planning. Second, we examine Soviet agricultural performance in terms of output, inputs, and associated factor productivity. Finally, we will examine more general performance considerations such as the contribution of agriculture to the Soviet diet and the role of agriculture in foreign trade. Our objective is an assessment of contemporary Soviet agriculture, the nature and origin of its problems, and its prospects for the future.

SOVIET AGRICULTURE: ORGANIZATION AND PLANNING

As we have already noted, Soviet agricultural production takes place in a variety of institutions.[1] The most basic production units are the collective farm *(kolkhoz)* and the state farm *(sovkhoz)*. In addition, agricultural production also takes place in the private or subsidiary sector that arises in both the state and cooperative sectors.

Beyond the *kolkhozy* and *sovkhozy,* in recent years there has been a tendency to integrate various facets of agricultural production, processing, and distribution in single administrative units broadly classified as agro-industrial enterprises. While difficult to measure in terms of simple numbers, integration, cooperation, and the development of more complex organizational arrangements have been a major and important theme in Soviet agriculture in the 1970s and 1980s.

The importance of these various organizational arrangements can be measured in a number of ways. The basic indicators assembled in Table 25 prompt a number of observations.

First, as we noted in Chapter 5, in terms of simple numbers, state farms have been replacing collective farms since the 1940s. Both *kolkhozy* and *sovkhozy* are large by Western standards, though with some reversal of the shift to larger scale in the 1980s. Moreover, in terms of sown area, the growing importance of the *sovkhoz* and the minimal role of the private sector are both evident.

Second, the number of interfarm organizations and enterprises has grown significantly in recent years. Although these numbers are difficult to interpret, as we shall see shortly, they nevertheless represent an important contemporary trend. Indeed, according to official Soviet statistics, the capital funds of interfarm enterprises increased from just under 400 million rubles in 1970 to almost 9000 million rubles in 1983. For the same period, the average annual labor force of interfarm organizations and enterprises increased from just over 78,000 to 765,000 at a time when the overall agricultural labor force had been declining.[2]

If one considers the importance of various organizational arrangements in terms of their contribution to output, a different picture emerges (Table 26). In terms of the basic distribution of production activity, the roles of the *kolkhoz* and *sovkhoz* differ. For example, in the production of meat and vegetables, the roles of *kolkhozy* and *sovkhozy* are pretty similar, but with the private sector being a major though declining contributor. Finally, despite recent relaxation in attitudes toward the private sector (about which more later), the importance of the private sector has been great but has been slowly declining in recent years.[3] We now turn to a brief examination of each of the major organizational types.

The *Kolkhoz*

The *kolkhoz* is, in theory, a cooperative form of organization in which the peasants voluntarily join to till the soil, using the means of production contributed by those who join but that now are owned jointly by all in the *kolkhoz.* Under the original *kolkhoz* charter developed in 1935 (a new charter was created in

Table 25 THE ORGANIZATION OF SOVIET AGRICULTURE (SELECTED INDICATORS)

	1928	1932	1940	1953	1957	1960	1965	1970	1978	1983
Number of collective farms (in thousands)	33.3	211.7	236.9	97.0	78.2	44.9	36.9	33.6	26.7	25.0
Sown area of collective farms as a portion of total sown area (%)	1.2	70.5[a]	78.3	83.9	68.4	60.6	50.2	47.9	44.2	43.75
Size of collective farms (acres per farm)	237	2,218	3,530	10,374		16,302	15,067	15,067	16,549	16,055
Number of state farms	1,407	4,337	4,159	4,857	5,905	7,375	11,681	14,994	20,500	22,313
Sown area of state farms as a portion of total sown area (%)	1.5[b]	n.a.	7.7	9.6	25.7	33.1	42.6	44.4	51.2	53.35
Size of state farms (acres per farm)			30,134	32,357	60,021	64,714	60,762	51,376	43,472	41,002
Number of interfarm enterprises and organizations							3,354	4,580	8,907	9,897
Sown area of the private sector as a portion of total sown area (%)[c]	97.3	n.a.	13.0	4.4	3.8	3.3	3.2	3.2	3.0[d]	2.89

Sources: Selected volumes of *Narodnoe khoziaistvo SSSR* [The national economy of the USSR]; *Sel'skoe khoziaistvo SSSR* [Agriculture of the USSR]; and *SSSR v tsifrakh* [The USSR in figures].

[a] Based upon aggregate sown area for 1933.

[b] Includes state farms and other state agricultural enterprises.

[c] The private sector consists of three parts: (1) private plots of collective farm members; (2) private plots of workers in industry and other state organizations; (3) the private peasant economy. The last was of minimal importance after the 1930s.

[d] 1975.

Table 26   **SOVIET AGRICULTURAL PRODUCTION BY TYPE OF PRODUCING UNIT (% OF TOTAL PRODUCTION)**

Product	Year	*Kolkhoz* and inter-*kolkhoz* organizations	*Sovkhoz* and other state enterprises	Private sector
Meat	1965	30	30	40
	1975	33	35	31
	1983	30	41	29
Milk	1965	35	26	40
	1975	39	30	31
	1983	41	34	25
Eggs	1965	13	20	67
	1975	11	49	39
	1983	7	63	30

Source: TsSU, *Narodnoe khoziaistvo SSSR* [The national economy of the USSR] (Moscow: Statistika), selected volumes. *Note:* Total production may not sum to 100 percent due to rounding.

1969), the means of production are said to be *"kolkhoz-*cooperative" property belonging to the *kolkhoz* in perpetuity. In addition to the socialized sector (land, equipment, buildings, etc.) belonging to the farm as a whole, the use of which is governed by a chairman and a management board, each peasant household is entitled to cultivate a private plot.

In reality, much of the voluntary and cooperative nature of the *kolkhoz* has been lost. Those who depart from the *kolkhoz* to the city do not, in fact, receive their equity from the farm. Moreover, mobility has been limited because, until recently, members of collective farms did not possess internal Soviet passports.

Historically, the *kolkhoz* has been administered by a general meeting of its membership or, more recently, in large farms through a meeting of elected representatives. In theory, this general meeting elects the chairman of the *kolkhoz,* although, in fact, the position of chairman is on the nomenklatura list and is therefore a local party appointee. In addition, the general meeting is supposed to select the operative management team, the management board, although here, again, the party-appointed chairman and the party secretary are powerful.[4]

It is important to recall that prior to their abolition in 1958, the Machine Tractor Stations (MTS) played an important role in the day-to-day operations of the *kolkhoz.*[5] The MTS were responsible for the provision of machinery and equipment and agricultural specialists to the *kolkhozy.* Indeed, the fulfillment of *kolkhoz* tasks was the joint responsibility of the *kolkhoz* chairman and the director of the MTS, a scenario described by Khrushchev as "two bosses" at the time of the abolition of these stations.

An important and distinguishing feature of any cooperative that is beyond its distinctive managerial system is its method of labor payment, normally a dividend, as opposed to payment of a wage. In this sense, the *kolkhoz* was distinctive until 1966, when a regular wage payment system was introduced.

Prior to 1966, all work tasks were rated in terms of a unit called the labor day, or *trudoden'.* The labor day was an artificial measure of labor input and bore little relation to the nature of the task. Thus, the labor days awarded for a particular task might differ from one farm to another and from one region to another, with little difference in effort required to complete the particular task. However, for each task assigned, the *kolkhoznik* would receive a specified number of labor days, the total to be recorded in an individual workbook. At the time of earning the labor day, its ultimate value in terms of money and product would be unknown. However, at the end of the year, when required state deliveries had been made, the value of each labor day would be determined simply by summing all of the earned labor days and dividing this sum into the available product remaining after fulfillment of state delivery obligations. After the value of the labor day had been determined, individual distributions in product and in money could take place. In light of the extreme uncertainty surrounding the eventual worth of a labor day at any time and place, it is not suprising that Khrushchev's moves to regularize payments were very popular. Moreover, distributions to labor were increasingly paid in money rather than in-kind. In effect, the peasant was expected to expend effort now for an unknown future reward.

Western observers have tended to view the *kolkhoz* as an organization bearing little formal resemblance to a cooperative.[6] Moreover, the incentive system has been viewed as inadequate, with little immediate connection between effort expended and reward gained. However one views the *kolkhoz,* it is evident, as we have seen earlier, that it has been changed significantly such that the contemporary *kolkhoz* closely resembles a *sovkhoz* in many important dimensions.

The *Sovkhoz*

The second major form of production enterprise in Soviet agriculture is the state farm, or *sovkhoz.* The *sovkhoz* has always been structurally similar to a Soviet industrial enterprise. Specifically, this means that the *sovkhoz* is budget-financed (unlike the *kolkhoz,* which has been primarily self-financed), operates (or is intended to operate) under the *khozraschet* system of management, and pays a state-specified wage.[7] Ideologically, the *sovkhoz* with full state property is an organizational form favored over the *kolkhoz.* Moreover, the *sovkhoz,* directly under state control, has been favored where policy changes have necessitated implementing major changes in the countryside. Important examples are the virgin lands program discussed earlier and, more recently, the campaign to develop potato and vegetable specialization around large Soviet cities.[8] Finally, as we shall see, both forms of organization have played a role in agro-industrial integration, though the *sovkhoz* is the cornerstone of this program. It has been argued that, in the long run, the *kolkhoz* will eventually disappear to be replaced by the *sovkhoz* and other integrated forms of organization. Much of the available evidence supports this contention in the sense that changes within *kolkhozy* have made them increasingly similar to *sovkhozy*; many *kolkhozy* have been directly converted to *sovkhozy*; and, finally, many *kolkhozy* have lost their unique character in recently developed integration arrangements.

The Private Sector

As we have already noted, the private sector is important in terms of product contribution, but much less so in terms of the land area it occupies. By most indicators, the importance of the private sector has declined slowly over a relatively long period of time. This decline reflects, in part, a changing and generally hostile environment created by official attitudes and policies regarding the private sector. Recent modest changes in these policies may arrest past trends.

The private sector can be perceived in several different contexts. First, families on *kolkhozy* are entitled to the use of plots of land by virtue of their membership on the collective farm and their participation in the socialized sector of the farm. This allottment has varied over time and continues to vary on a regional basis. Its magnitude was reinforced in the 1969 charter as approximately 1.23 acres.[9] In addition, a small but generally limited number of animals may be held privately.

The products of the private sector may be consumed on the farm, they may be sold in farm markets, or they may be purchased by the state. State purchases of meat, milk, and eggs have generally represented a very small share of private output, although for some products, for example, wool, state purchases are important.

Second, workers and employees are also entitled to plots of land, although this entitlement varies depending upon where they live and where they work. For example, after 1964, state farm workers are entitled to plots which ". . . should not normally exceed 0.30 hectare . . . ," or roughly three-quarters of an acre.[10] Workers and employees who live in rural areas but who don't work directly in agriculture have a smaller entitlement of roughly 0.37 acre.

Finally, workers and employees residing in urban areas are also entitled to garden plots varying from 0.15 to 0.30 acre, depending upon whether the plot is located inside or outside city boundaries.

As we have noted, there has been considerable variability in these land allotments. However, in 1981, 13 million collective-farm families held plots averaging just over three-quarters of an acre in size; 10 million state farm workers held plots averaging just over one-half acre; and, finally, 10 million families of workers and employees held plots averaging 0.17 acre in size in urban areas and 0.42 acre in size in rural areas.[11]

In the late 1970s and 1980s, there has been a relaxation of official restrictions on private agricultural activity. Specifically, the limits on the numbers of livestock held in the private sector have been removed where such livestock is being raised on a contract basis for subsequent transfer to the socialized sector. Moreover, credits have been made available to finance this activity.

In spite of a more supportive attitude toward the private sector in the Brezhnev and post-Brezhnev years, it is not yet clear that the decline of private agricultural activity will, in fact, be reversed. Future trends will depend on the nature of future policies; the relative size of the constituent members of the private sector (the *kolkhoz,* from which much private activity derives, is gradually disappearing); and, finally, the nture and magnitude of the benefits that can actually be derived under recent changes to be discussed later.

Agro-Industrial Integration and Cooperation

Thus far, we have discussed the traditional organizational forms operative in Soviet agriculture—the *kolkhoz,* the *sovkhoz,* and private activity. However, various integration arrangements are the essence of Soviet policy since the early 1970s.[12] Postponement of our discussion of these trends allows us to bring the story of organizational change up to date, to see what has happened to the traditional organizational units, and what new arrangements have been introduced in recent years.

Soviet leaders have long tended to downplay basic differences between industrial and agricultural production, arguing that it is possible to "industrialize" agriculture. While there are varying perspectives on this theme, fundamentally it involves improving agricultural performance by industrial-type organizational and managerial arrangements. Moreover, as in industry, this argument represents an important theme in Soviet economic thought, namely, that benefits are to be derived from organizational change.

These ideas are not new in the Soviet Union. What is new is the intensity of application. For example, in the 1960s, there was continuing pressure to industrialize agriculture, but it found relatively limited application and only in a few regions, and only for selected types of activities. For example, construction was, and is, frequently organized on an interfarm basis. Selected types of production and/or processing activity, for example, wine making, might be organized on an industrial-type basis.

In the 1970s, however, there was a renewed emphasis upon organizational change to reap the benefits of integration, both horizontal and vertical. These changes, of the 1970s and 1980s, have been developed and implemented with many important variations. There is no single, uniform mode of classification. Thus, we must be content with a broad picture to illustrate the major directions of change.

From a Western perspective, Soviet agro-industrial integration can best be understood by comparison with Western experience. For example, in American agriculture, integration would generally be termed the development of "agribusiness." In this context, there may be both vertical and/or horizontal integration in which a single administrative unit produces an agricultural product encompassing basic production, processing, and distribution. Horizontal integration may be achieved, for example, where a number of farms contribute a basic product to the integrated processing and distribution facility.

The process of "specialization and concentration of agricultural production on the basis of interfarm cooperation and agro-industrial integration" has become the operative phrase of Soviet agriculture in the 1970s and 1980s.[13]

Interfarm cooperation in the 1960s was largely associated with the development of inter-*kolkhoz* associations. These associations, initially in traditional areas such as construction, were expanded in the 1970s to include other activities and, in some cases, multiple activities. Although there were variations, the basic approach was the formation of an association with capital contributed by individual *kolkhoz* participants, with profit-sharing based on a formula related to this capital contribution. Although affiliation with such an association was to be on a voluntary basis, important elements of managerial power from individual *kolkhozy* were shifted to the association level and vested in a representative assembly and a chairman.

Integration, specifically vertical integration, received new impetus in the mid-1970s and involved the combination of industrial-type activity (for example, food processing) with constituent agricultural producing units. The latter were to be *kolkhozy, sovkhozy,* or a mixture of the two, although, in practice, *sovkhozy* tended to predominate. It is from this movement of the mid-1970s that the phrase agro-industrial integration and the notion of creating agro-industrial enterprises take on new importance.

Like the inter-*kolkhoz* associations, agro-industrial enterprises were formed with shareholder contributions managed by elected representatives, usually within the boundaries of a single raion.[14] *Sovkhozy* have predominated in this type of activity, in part because, in some regions, *sovkhoz* trusts had already been formed to bring *sovkhozy* together with other state enterprises and organizations in a single integrated unit. These units combined partially centralized management along with a degree of autonomy for participating individual *sovkhozy.*

In the late 1970s, statutes for agricultural production associations were formulated. These associations were to be broad-based, encompassing *kolkhozy, sovkhozy,* and other state agricultural and nonagricultural enterprises and organizations. Again, the association would operate as a legal entity with contributions to capital funds from constituents and mixed managerial powers at the association and the constituent levels.

Through the 1970s and into the 1980s, various forms of integration and cooperation continued to expand, though not without problems and reverses. Changes would be forthcoming.

Not infrequently, the distribution of decision-making authority, for example, in the areas of plan formulation and execution, remained unclear. Specialization, said to be important at the farm level, was not always promoted by upper-level associations. There were important regional variations.

The problems that arose in the 1970s were, in part, addressed by several major experiments conducted in various regions of the country. Ultimately, changes would be introduced as part of the Brezhnev "food program" of 1982.

While we leave for later discussion the economic aspects of the food program, in the administrative sphere, it called for the establishment of *raion* agro-industrial associations and a complete organizational hierarchy above the *raion* level. At the raion level, agro-industrial associations would incorporate *kolkhozy, sovkhozy,* state enterprises, and other state organizations. Management would be conducted by a *raion* agricultural council chaired by the first deputy chairman of the *raion* Soviet executive committee. This council would serve as the management authority between the members of the association and upper-level administrative agencies. At the *oblast'* level (and in other similar regional units), a similar structure will be duplicated with an administrative council made up of members from the councils of constituent associations and agricultural officials from the *oblast'* level. In addition, in each republic, a commission was created to oversee the agro-industrial complexes subordinate to the presidium of the union republic council of ministers. Finally, a commission on agro-industrial complexes was created under the presidium of the USSR Council of Ministers.

Considerable power rests at the *oblast'* level, for example, in the areas of plan formulation and execution, redistribution of resources, suggestions for change, and the like.

Only time will tell to what extent these important changes will fundamentally alter the Soviet agricultural system. They are aimed at basic problems such as the lack of specialization. While *raion oblast'* and republic levels may better see the possibilities of specialization, the large and potentially unwieldly structure that has been created may make it difficult to oversee the best utilization of local resources. However, it is an attempt once again to handle the problems of territorial versus branch organization through integration and within a framework familiar to Soviet reform methods.

SOVIET AGRICULTURAL PERFORMANCE

Earlier in this book, we considered the performance of Soviet agriculture by focusing on its sectorial contribution to economic development. Contemporary interest focuses on a different issue. To what extent does Soviet agriculture contribute adequate supplies of food and fiber to the Soviet population with reasonable outlays of land, labor, and capital?

Our assessment of Soviet agriculture will be based on a variety of indicators. We begin with an examination of broad measures of output and input growth and thereafter turn to more sophisticated productivity measures.

In Table 27, we present evidence on basic output trends for the period 1960 through 1984. A number of observations seem relevant. First, a simple interpretation of these figures would suggest that there has been considerable output growth over these years. Although there are exceptions, for example, virtual stagnation of output of sunflower seeds, the output of major agricultural products such as grain and meat has risen considerably over the long haul.

Second, in spite of what seems to be, at first glance, a reasonable growth of output, closer examination of these figures indicates a slowdown in growth of output into the 1980s. Also, year-to-year fluctuations, though not shown by our use of averages, are, nevertheless, important. For example, while the average annual output of grain for the period 1976–1980 was 205 million metric tons, annual output during this period varied from a low of 179 million metric tons in 1979 to a high of 237 million metric tons in 1978. This represents an output reduction of 24 percent, clearly a major change for a single production year. But if one compares the average annual output data for the period 1976–1980 with the same data for the period 1981–1984 (see Table 28), a striking picture emerges. With the exception of cotton, meat, milk, and eggs, the average annual output

Table 27   SOVIET AGRICULTURAL PRODUCTION, 1961–1984 (AVERAGE ANNUAL
           BASIS)[a]

Product	1961–1965	1966–1970	1971–1975	1976–1980	1981–1984
Grain (total)	130,335	167,562	181,554	205,028	175,000
Raw cotton	4,996	6,099	7,667	8,932	9,185
Sunflower seeds	5,068	6,389	5,975	5,309	4,890
Sugarbeets	59,170	81,118	75,984	88,732	74,832
Potatoes	81,628	94,813	89,782	82,571	79,671
Vegetables	16,877	19,472	22,974	26,310	29,216
Meat	9,320	11,583	14,004	14,844	15,930
Milk	64,714	80,553	87,446	92,704	93,492
Eggs	28.7	35.8	51.4	63.1	73.6

Source: Compiled from U.S. Department of Agriculture, Economic Research Service, *USSR: Outlook and Situation Report* (Washington, D.C.: U.S. Department of Agriculture, May 1984), tables 1, 5, and 7; TsSU, *Narodnoe khoziaistvo SSSR v 1983 g.* [The national economy of the USSR in 1983] (Moscow: Finansy i statistika, 1984); "The Report on 1984 Plan Fulfillment," *Current Digest of The Soviet Press,* vol. 37, no. 4 (1985); U.S. Department of Agriculture, Economic Research Service, *USSR: Outlook and Situation Report* (Washington, D.C.: U.S. Department of Agriculture, April 1985).
[a]Units of measure: thousands of metric tons, except eggs, which are in billions.

in the early 1980s was lower than in the late 1970s. Fortunately, this trend seems to have been reversed in 1984, with increases in all products considered except sunflower seeds.

Later, we examine in some detail the various forces that have influenced contemporary Soviet agricultural performance. But what about the growth of available inputs? Evidence on the growth of inputs is assembled in Table 29. While examining this evidence on agricultural inputs, it is important to bear in mind that factor substitution would suggest substitution of capital for labor and, in particular, a growing role for purchased inputs. In addition, these figures tell us about the growth of inputs through time, though they do not provide a comparison of absolute levels with those found elsewhere.

Bearing in mind these reservations, two important conclusions can be derived from Table 29. First, there has been a significant increase in the amount

Table 28   AGRICULTURAL PRODUCTION: PLAN AND PERFORMANCE (ANNUAL
           AVERAGE, 1981–1990)

Product	Plan 1981–1985	Plan 1986–1990	Actual 1981–1983	Actual 1984
Grain	238–243	250–255	178.3	170.0
Sugarbeets	100–103	102–103	71.4	85.3
Potatoes	82–89	90–92	77.7	85.3
Sunflower seeds	6.7	7.2–7.5	5.10	4.5
Meat	17.0–17.5	20.0–20.5	15.5	16.7
Milk	97–99	104–106	92.1	97.6

Source: U.S. Department of Agriculture, *USSR: Outlook and Situation Report* (Washington, D.C.: U.S. Department of Agriculture, May 1984), Tables 1 and 5; Current Digest of The Soviet Press, "The Report on 1984 Plan Fulfillment,") vol. 37, no. 4 (1985), 10–16; A. F. Malish, "The Soviet Food Program: A New Policy or More Rhetoric?" in U.S. Congress, Joint Economic Committee, *Soviet Economy in the 1980s: Problems and Prospects,* part 2 (Washington, D.C.: U.S. Government Printing Office, 1982), p. 51; U.S. Department of Agriculture, Economic Research Service, *USSR: Outlook and Situation Report* (Washington, D.C.: U.S. Department of Agriculture, April 1985).

Table 29   INPUTS TO SOVIET AGRICULTURE: SELECTED INDICATORS

Input	1960	1970	1978
Mineral fertilizer (tons of effective nutrient/100 ha.)	0.9	3.6	6.2
Tractor power (Total motor h.p./100 ha.)	17	38	61
Electricity (million kWh used per 100 ha.)	3.5	13.2	32.4
Sown area (million ha.)	203.0	206.7	218.2
Average annual labor force (millions)	29.4	26.8	26.4
Capital investment (billion rubles in "comparable" prices)	6.5	17.5	31.2
As a share of total investment (percent)	20	24	27

Sources: Lines 1 through 3 from K.-E. Wädekin, *Agrarian Policies in Communist Europe: A Critical Introduction* (Totowa, N.J.: Allanheld, Osmun & Co., 1982), table 8–13. Remaining data from TsSU, *Sel'skoe khoziaistvo SSSR* [Agriculture in the USSR] (Moscow: Statistika, 1971); and TsSU, *Narodnoe Khoziaistvo SSSR* [The national economy of the USSR], various issues. *Note:* Per 100 ha. refers to compound land units; 1 hectare (1 ha.) of land under arable and perennial crops is given unit weight; other agricultural land is weighted at 0.20 of its actual amount.

of capital investment going to Soviet agriculture both in terms of the absolute amount and the importance of agricultural capital investment as a portion of total capital investment. Thus, in the early 1960s, capital investment in agriculture amounted to roughly 9.6 billion rubles, or roughly 20 percent of total capital investment on an average annual basis. For the period 1981 through 1983, the average annual investment in agriculture had increased to 38.7 billion rubles, which represents 27 percent of total capital investment.[15]

In addition, there have been sharp improvements in the application of purchased inputs such as mineral fertilizers and electricity. Direct evidence on these inputs is instructive. For example, the average annual fertilizer delivery to Soviet agriculture during the period 1966–1970 (calculated on a nutrient weight basis and including feed additives) was just over 8 million metric tons. The equivalent delivery for the period 1981–1984, again on an average annual basis, was almost 21 million tons.[16] Inventories of agricultural equipment have increased significantly. For example, in the late 1960s, there were approximately 1.8 million tractors in Soviet agriculture. By 1984, this number had increased to 2.7 million.[17]

It is interesting to note that while sown area has been increasing and agricultural labor force has been declining, the rates of change in both cases have been modest in recent times. Particularly striking is the slowdown in the outflow of labor from rural areas. For example, between 1970 and 1983, the average annual agricultural labor force (in millions) declined from 26.8 to 26.1, a change so small it could be accounted for by statistical error.

The trends observed here suggest that output increases, slowing in the late 1970s and early 1980s, have, in part, been achieved with increases in factor inputs. This evidence deserves closer attention. In Table 30, we have assembled several indexes to facilitate our examination of output and input patterns in Soviet agriculture.It is evident from an examination of both the Soviet and Western indexes that the average annual rate of growth of Soviet agricultural production for the period 1950 to 1980 has been quite good, approximating 3 percent.

It is also interesting to note that, for the most part, output performance in the livestock sector has been much better than performance in the crop sector.

Table 30   SOVIET AGRICULTURAL PRODUCTION: SELECTED OUTPUT INDEXES,
1950–1979

Index	Average annual percentage rate of growth			
	1951–1979	1951–1960	1961–1970	1971–1979
USDA index				
Crops	2.7	3.2	3.7	0.9
Net livestock	4.0	5.9	3.5	2.5
Total	3.1	4.1	3.6	1.5
CIA index				
(net in 1970 prices)				
Crops	2.4	2.6	3.7	0.7
Livestock	3.7	6.1	3.7	1.0
Total	3.0	4.3	3.7	0.9
Soviet official				
(1965 prices)				
Crops	2.8	4.1	3.3	0.8
Livestock	3.9	6.4	3.3	2.0
Total	3.2	4.8	3.3	1.4

Sources: B. Severin and M. Hughes, "An Index of Agricultural Production in the USSR," in U.S. Congress, Joint Economic Committee, *USSR: Measures of Economic Growth and Development, 1950–80* (Washington, D.C.: U.S. Government Printing Office, 1982), pp. 245–284; appendixes A–C.

Every index shows a slowdown in the average annual rate of growth of output, a slowdown that becomes greater in the 1970s than in the 1960s.* Why has this slowdown occurred in a decade when the Soviet leadership has clearly been expanding the resources available to the agricultural sector?

Factor Productivity in Soviet Agriculture

To understand costs in Soviet agriculture, it is necessary to examine outputs, inputs, and associated changes in factor productivity. A recent study by Diamond, Bettis, and Ramsson examines these trends for the period 1951 through 1979.[18] The results are reported in Table 31. The figures in this table tell a familiar story. Output growth since the 1950s has been generally very good but has been declining markedly. The same can be said for the growth of inputs, though the slackening in the growth rate of inputs has been less than that for output. If we accept the traditional assumption that the growth of output results from the growth of inputs and the growth of factor productivity (better use of available inputs), it is apparent that the latter has accounted for a declining share of output growth. Indeed, according to the figures presented here, improvement of factor productivity accounted for approximately 44 percent of the increase in agricultural output during the period 1951–1960, while it accounted for approximately 11 percent during the period 1971–1979. The implication is that costs have increased. We turn to direct evidence.

*A more recent index provided to the authors by the U.S. Department of Agriculture shows very modest growth in total agricultural output. From a base of 1976–1978 = 100, this index grows to 102 in 1984.

Table 31 FACTOR PRODUCTIVITY IN SOVIET AGRICULTURE, 1951–1979

	Average annual rate of growth			
	1951–1960	1961–1970	1971–1979	1951–1979
Output	4.8	3.0	1.8	3.4
Inputs	2.7	2.1	1.6	2.1
Factor productivity	2.1	1.0	0.2	1.2

Source: D. B. Diamond, L. W. Bettis, and R. E. Ramsson, "Agricultural Production," in A. Bergson and H. S. Levine, eds., *The Soviet Economy: Toward the Year 2000* (Winchester, Mass.: Allen & Unwin, 1983), p. 146.

Agricultural Costs and Prices

Since the 1950s when Khrushchev introduced cost accounting into Soviet collective farms, it has been widely recognized that cost/price ratios have been very unfavorable to agriculture. Specifically, for many products in many regions, state purchase prices simply did not cover basic production costs, leaving farms to make up the difference. Viewing the price/cost ratios as an important incentive for farm production and specialization, Soviet leaders have, over the years, increased prices with the objective of making agricultural production profitable. These increases have been designed to stimulate greater agricultural productivity.

For purposes of our appraisal, cost/price data are assembled in Table 32. Interpretation of Soviet agricultural cost and price data should proceed with caution, because the computation of both costs and prices is subject to complications.

Examination of cost price data reveals a number of important trends in Soviet agriculture. Obviously, production costs have risen, in some cases sharply. For example, the cost of meat, milk, and potatoes have roughly doubled. In addition, while the degree of profitability differs significantly from one product to another, generally speaking, crop production has been much more profitable than the production of meat-related products. Moreover, the general stability of

Table 32 AGRICULTURAL COSTS AND PRICES: 1967–1968 AND 1983 (RUBLES PER TON)

	Cost 1967–1968		Price 1965	Cost 1983		Price 1977
	Sovkhoz	*Kolkhoz*		*Sovkhoz*	*Kolkhoz*	
Grain	54	48	89.6	84	76	107.1
Cotton	321	354	442.2	629	561	608.0
Sugarbeets	25	21	28.5	46	34	36.7
Potatoes	65	50	n.a.	147	124	n.a.
Vegetables	77	86	n.a.	117	134	n.a.
Meat	1139	1153	993.5	2550	2271	1569.3
Milk	171	165	148.5	391	312	234.7
Eggs	66	71	78.8	63	86	92.4

Source: TsSU, *Narodnoe Khoziaistvo v USSR* [The national economy of the USSR] (Moscow: Statistika) various volumes. Price data are from U.S. Department of Agriculture, *Agricultural Situation: Review of 1978 and Outlook for 1979* (Washington, D.C.: U.S. Department of Agriculture, April 1979), Table 15. *Note:* Cost is prime cost *(sebestoimost')*; prices are average state procurement prices for the given years.

food prices at the retail level has resulted in a large and growing agricultural subsidy.[19]

Soviet agricultural subsidies arise in several ways, though generally through efforts to hold down the price of purchased inputs and to raise procurement prices making farms profitable. According to estimates compiled by Vladimir G. Treml, "since the system was introduced in 1965, subsidies have risen from about 2 billion rubles to 37 billion rubles in 1980."[20] The latter figure, according to Treml, amounts to roughly 54 percent of the value of national income generated in agriculture.[21]

The impact of the subsidy system on Soviet agriculture is a matter of substantial complexity. In general, however, it is clear that Soviet authorities have been unwilling to pass increases in the cost of production on to the retail level. At the same time, there has been continuing pressure to expand inputs to agriculture in the anticipation of output improvement. Clearly, the 1970s were years in which Soviet leaders paid a great deal of attention to agriculture. Agriculture seems to claim a growing share of the nation's resources; and yet, despite a reasonable long-term rate of growth of output, imports have risen significantly and the Soviet domestic agricultural product has become much more costly. Why have costs increased so rapidly in Soviet agriculture?

Recent studies of Soviet agriculture by a number of Western scholars shed light on this issue.[22] While cost increases can be traced to a number of factors, the bottom line is that Soviet agriculture does not use its inputs effectively, although the reasons for such a pattern are not always clear. Moreover, to the extent that Soviet agriculture has not been able to increase its efficiency, increases in output have been obtained with inordinate input increases, the prices of which have risen sharply. On both counts, the result has been an increasingly costly agricultural product.

Western studies have generally concluded that the effectiveness of resource utilization in Soviet agriculture is highly variable and not generally good. Although direct comparisons between the Soviet Union and other countries such as the United States involve a number of measurement difficulties, they are nevertheless instructive. In the postwar era, the capital stock of Soviet agriculture has increased much more rapidly than that of American agriculture. But, for the 1970s, the capital/output ratio of Soviet agriculture was three times that of American agriculture.[23] Labor productivity in Soviet agriculture is roughly 6 percent of labor productivity in American agriculture.[24]

Comparison of yields not only sheds light on the effectiveness of land utilization but also on the question of climatic impact both in the long term and on a year-to-year basis. It has been widely argued that Soviet climatic peculiarities (inadequate amounts and distribution of warmth and moisture) account for Soviet crop production difficulties, especially year-to-year variability.[25]

The evidence on this question is mixed. Analysts have studied crop yields using climatic analogs, that is, comparing Soviet yields with yields in other countries having similar climatic conditions. For example, when Soviet grain yields are compared with those in North America, Soviet yields are lower but generally quite good.[26] On the other hand, Soviet hay yields are at best one-half those obtained in climatically similar areas elsewhere.[27] Finally, if one examines technical crops, especially those of high priority such as cotton, yields are generally good.

What, then, of the role of climate? In his recent study of Soviet agriculture, D. Gale Johnson concludes that "there can be no doubt that climatic factors affect both the level of agricultural output and its variability in the USSR. But I believe that it has been shown that policy choices have influenced a significant proportion of these two effects."[28]

Although it is difficult to clearly demarcate systemic and policy factors that may have influenced Soviet agricultural performance, plainly both are important. The organizational arrangements in Soviet agriculture have clearly been a factor that influences outcomes. Decision-making has been historically relatively centralized, while agricultural activity must be guided in large part by the use of local information. This centralization stems, in part, from lack of effective decision-making procedures at the local level. From a technical perspective, Soviet agriculture at the local level has been poorly served by agricultural specialists in spite of efforts to make it otherwise. Historically, most specialists have found it both possible and attractive to work outside the rural economy. Moreover, from an economic perspective, local (and indeed upper-level) decision-making must have been impaired by inadequate information. The development of useful cost information is a recent phenomenon, not to mention the perennial problem of pricing.[29] Thus, the concept of profitability has had little meaning; some activities have been highly profitable, while others have been persistently unprofitable, with neither having any relation to the achievement of desired objectives. While the capital stock of Soviet agriculture has been increased at a very rapid pace in recent years, we have seen that capital productivity is very low when compared to agriculture elsewhere. To take a case in point, the level of utilization of machinery and equipment is very low for a variety of reasons, not the least important of which is inadequate support facilities to keep equipment functional.

While it is difficult to offer firm figures, most observers of Soviet agriculture would argue that the agricultural infrastructure is a major problem. Whether one considers nonagriculture serving agriculture or the reverse, there are major problems. For example, Soviet economists have long argued that losses between the field and the table are great. Historically, processing and storage have been inadequate, and the transportation system (especially roads) is ill-suited for the tasks at hand. On the input side, similar considerations prevail. To take another example, the production of chemical fertilizer has increased dramatically, and yet significant portions of this increase never find their way to the fields due to transportation and storage losses and the like. These problems, in spite of reform efforts, tend to persist to one degree or another. They must have had a negative impact upon the cost and the availability of the Soviet agricultural product.

Our earlier discussion of Soviet agricultural yields concluded with the argument that policy factors may have an important influence on Soviet agricultural performance. For example, it is argued that Soviet use of fallow land is inappropriate, namely, too low. D. Gale Johnson notes that "despite evidence from both foreign and Soviet sources of the merits of clean fallow for many agricultural areas, Soviet fallow area remains very low."[30]

Another example of policy failure is the evidence that Soviet seeding rates are inordinately high, especially for certain crops such as grain. As Johnson notes in his analysis of this issue, high seeding rates are inefficient, whether they result from ignorance or improper seeding procedures, or both.[31]

Finally, it is instructive to note that similar problems exist in the livestock sector production activity, where climatic and other unfavorable natural conditions should be of lesser importance than in crop production. As we have already noted, performance of the Soviet livestock sector, specifically, meat production, has been a matter of continuing concern. Efforts to expand meat production at a faster pace have resulted in sharp cost increases. Once again, problems in this sector can be found throughout the production process. Soviet hay yields are poor. More generally, animal fodder is deficient in protein content which, in combination with inappropriate feeding procedures and lack of specialization in the Soviet cattle sector, results in poor output per unit of input. This outcome is partly a result of Soviet organizational and other systemic arrangements, but it also results from questionable policies such as the lack of specialization.[32] It remains to be seen to what extent organizational and policy changes of the 1970s and 1980s will alleviate the problems outlined here.

ASSESSING THE RESULT: FURTHER EVIDENCE

We have now assembled sufficient information to return briefly to the theme developed at the beginning of this chapter. Has Soviet agriculture been able to supply adequate food and fiber for its population at reasonable cost?[33] But what are adequate amounts, and what is a reasonable cost?

One useful way to assess supply is to consider the ability of the system to meet self-imposed dietary norms. Evidence of dietary achievement is assembled in Table 33. The evidence in this table suggests that there has been a steady improvement in the Soviet diet, based upon the extent to which official Soviet dietary norms have been achieved. Clearly, the achievement is variable, but it nevertheless reflects traditional trends away from starchy foods toward proteins. In addition, the share of a worker's income devoted to food has declined from 38 percent in 1960 to just over 30 percent in 1983.[34]

The reader may well be puzzled at this point. We have observed that during the period 1950–1980, Soviet agricultural output grew at an average annual rate of roughly 3 percent, while Soviet population grew at an average annual rate of roughly 1.6 percent. Thus, on an average annual basis, there has been an increase of 1.4 percent in per capita food production. But how can the rate of improvement be maintained if the rate of growth of output has been declining in recent years? The answer lies in the increasing utilization of foreign trade.[35]

In Table 34, we present some basic numbers on Soviet agricultural trade. Western attention is frequently captured by the grain question. Obviously, grain is a crucial product of agriculture used for consumption, for industrial processing, and as animal food. During the 1960s, the Soviet Union was a net grain exporter,

Table 33   SOVIET FOOD CONSUMPTION AND NORMS: SELECTED YEARS, 1966–1990

	Meat and fat	Fish	Milk	Eggs	Potatoes	Grain	Veg.	Fruits
Norm	78	18.2	405	292	110	115	130	91
Actual 1966–1970	47	14.3	287	144	132	150	78	n.a.
Actual 1976–1980	57	17.3	318	227	116	139	92	39
Plan 1990	70	19.0	330–340	260–266	110	135	126–135	66–70

Source: U.S. Department of Agriculture, *USSR: Outlook and Situation Report* (Washington, D.C.: U.S. Department of Agriculture, May 1984), Table 6.

that is, it generally sold more than it purchased. In the 1970s, however, this position was reversed. Throughout the 1970s and 1980s, Soviet grain requirements have exceeded domestic grain production; the difference was made up by a growing volume of imports. Soviet requirements have also exceeded Soviet domestic production in other critical areas, as the evidence in Table 34 indicates. At the same time, there have been products, such as cotton, where the Soviets have continued to be major net exporters. How should we interpret this trade posture?

Soviet agricultural trade in the 1970s and 1980s has been the focus of much attention, largely because of its impact on a number of different interest groups.[36] For the farmers of the major grain-exporting countries, for example, Canada, the United States, and Australia, sales to the Soviet Union provide a large if sometimes unpredictable market. Moreover, in this context, grain becomes a major issue in the more general framework of East–West relations.[37]

Agricultural trade, and especially the large volume of grain sales to the Soviet Union, are of interest to trade economists as a major component of overall Soviet foreign trade with important implications for Soviet decision-making arrangements, payments mechanisms, and the like.

What does this trade posture tell us with respect to Soviet domestic agricultural production capability? There is nothing wrong with trade. Indeed, economists have long argued that specialization and exchange are rational. Moreover, the trends that we have observed may not persist in the late 1980s and early 1990s. But the growing importance of Soviet agricultural imports suggests that domestic production has, in recent times, been increasingly incapable of meeting Soviet needs in spite of a growing effort by Soviet leaders to solve the agricultural problem. In this sense, it worries Soviet leaders, and it necessarily limits their available options.

Leaving aside the specifics of policies, organizational arrangements, and the like, how might we assess the present state of Soviet agriculture and its prospects for the future? As we examine the recent record of Soviet agriculture, it is evident that many of the changes taking place are quite familiar. Overall, the relative importance of the agricultural sector has been declining. Within agriculture, labor has been departing to be replaced by capital. These are familiar trends, and they appear in conjunction with reasonable, if not good, long-term rates of output growth. Structurally, Soviet agriculture seems to have been moving in familiar directions when judged against agricultural development in other countries.

Table 34   TRENDS IN SOVIET AGRICULTURAL TRADE (NET BALANCE IN THOUSANDS OF METRIC TONS)

Product	1975	1978	1980	1982	1983
Grain	−12,117	−21,014	−28,794	−37,429	−31,551
Meat and meat products	−471	−145	−786	−907	−960
Vegetable oil (edible)	+355	−18	−233	−752	−598
Cotton (lint)	+633	+743	+794	+923	+597

Source: Compiled from U.S. Department of Agriculture, *USSR: Outlook and Situation Report* (Washington, D.C.: U.S. Department of Agriculture, May 1984), Tables 11 and 14; and U.S. Department of Agriculture, *USSR: Outlook and Situation Report* (Washington, D.C.: U.S. Department of Agriculture, April 1985).

On the negative side, Soviet agriculture has continued to be the subject of domestic controversy, in large part due to the perception of inadequate performance, especially the instability of agricultural production over time, and its sharply varying performance from one product to another. These are the traditional worries that occupied much space in the Soviet press 30 years ago.

In addition, trends in the 1970s and 1980s are troubling. The rate of output growth, while generally positive, has declined sharply. The rate of growth of inputs, also positive, has declined at the same time, but to a much lesser degree. The net result has been sharply rising costs of production and a large and growing state subsidy in an era when Soviet leaders seem to be paying more rather than less attention to agriculture. Put another way, if one could successfully argue that Soviet agriculture was, in fact, neglected in the past, surely such an argument would not hold in contemporary times. As we have seen, there has been a vast infusion of resources into Soviet agriculture precisely at a time when output performance has lagged. Soviet leaders, through the remainder of the 1980s and into the 1990s, must address this basic issue.

SOVIET AGRICULTURE: THE 1980s AND THEREAFTER

The thrust of Soviet agricultural policies in the 1980s became evident in the 1970s and need not be repeated. Organizational change, along with an infusion of inputs was important. In our earlier discussion of organizational arrangements, we noted that the food program of 1982 was a major program to redirect Soviet agriculture in the 1980s.[38] It is worth examining the basic thrust of this program.

In the late 1970s and early 1980s, Leonid Brezhnev was suprisingly outspoken about the problems of Soviet agriculture. The changes and the output projections announced in May of 1982 (see Table 28) were Brezhnev's response to his perception that the Soviet Union did indeed have a food problem. There are several major components to the new program.

First, new attention is to be devoted to the private sector. As noted earlier, there has been a relaxation of rules pertaining to the holding of animals and renewed emphasis on the contract system in which cattle raised in the private sector would be sold to the socialized sector. Bank credits and other supports are to be provided to encourage this effort.

Second, there is renewed emphasis on increased flexibility of decision-making at the farm level. This attitude reflects a continuing interest in improved incentives, namely, changing the rules to relate reward to performance more closely. Specifically, bonus arrangements are to reflect the importance of the final result rather than changes in inputs, for example, sown area.

Third, discussion of the late 1970s and early 1980s has reinforced the strength of decision-making arrangements at upper levels, regionally and within the state and party apparatus. This pattern reflects a more general picture of Soviet economic reform and change, namely, adjustments to improve the existing system.

Finally, procurement prices have been increased in 1983. These increases will doubtless impact on farm profitability and also on individual earnings of farm workers.

With the exception of grain and sunflower seeds, Soviet agricultural production in 1984 (see Table 28) was generally good compared to the early 1980s. Moreover, climatic conditions and seeding patterns suggest that 1985 may well be a good year. But what are the basic trends to watch?

Clearly, Soviet leaders have made a commitment to organizational change and input expansion designed to improve Soviet agriculture. Change cannot be expected overnight, but within the traditional fluctuations, output growth must be sufficient to support the growing urban food demands. Moreover, as the cost of the agricultural product rises, Soviet leaders will face the inevitable dilemma of whether to hide the real cost or to pass it on to the retail level in the form of higher prices. In both these crucial areas, the performance of Soviet agriculture in the latter half of the 1980s will be an important element of overall Soviet economic performance.

REFERENCES

1. For historical development, see D. J. Male, *Russian Peasant Organization Before Collectivization* (Cambridge: Cambridge University Press, 1971); R. G. Wesson, *Soviet Communes* (New Brunswick, N.J.: Rutgers University Press, 1963); R. W. Davies, *The Industrialization of Soviet Russia,* vol. 2 (Cambridge, Mass.: Harvard University Press, 1980). For a discussion of contemporary arrangements, see R. C. Stuart, *The Collective Farm in Soviet Agriculture* (Lexington, Mass.: D. C. Heath, 1972); K.-E. Wädekin, *The Private Sector in Soviet Agriculture* (Berkeley: University of California Press, 1973).

2. TsSU, *Narodnoe Khoziaistvo SSSR v 1983g.* [The national economy of the USSR in 1983] (Moscow: Finansy i statistika, 1984), p. 292.

3. For recent evidence on the private sector, see A. Lane "U.S.S.R.: Private Agriculture on Center Stage," in U.S. Congress, Joint Economic Committee, *Soviet Economy in the 1980s: Problems and Prospects,* part 2 (Washington, D.C.: U.S. Government Printing Office, 1982), pp. 23–40.

4. For details, see Stuart, *The Collective Farm in Soviet Agriculture.*

5. The MTS are discussed in depth in R. F. Miller, *One Hundred Thousand Tractors* (Cambridge, Mass.: Harvard University Press, 1970).

6. There is a considerable body of literature on this issue. See, for example, E. D. Domar, "The Soviet Collective Farm as a Producer Cooperative," *American Economic Review,* vol. 56, no. 4, part I (September 1966), 734–757; W. Y. Oi and E. M. Clayton, "A Peasant's View of a Soviet Collective Farm," *American Economic Review,* vol. 58, no. 1 (March 1968), 37–59. For recent analysis, see M. L. Wyzan, "The Kolkhoz and the Sovkhoz: Relative Performance as measured by Productive Technology," in R. C. Stuart, ed. *The Soviet Rural Economy* (Totowa, N.J.: Rowman & Allanheld, 1983), pp. 173–198; Clark Chandler, "The Effects of the Private Sector on the Labor Behavior of Soviet Collective Farmers," in Stuart, ed. *The Soviet Rural Economy,* pp. 223–237.

7. For a discussion of financing, see J. R. Millar, "Financing the Modernization of Kolkhozy," in J. R. Millar, ed., *The Soviet Rural Community* (Urbana: University of Illinois Press, 1971), pp. 276–313.

8. The virgin lands program is discussed in M. McCauley, *Khrushchev and the Development of Soviet Agriculture* (New York: Holmes & Meier, 1976). Urban specialization

is discussed in F. M. Leversedge and R. C. Stuart, "Soviet Agricultural Restructure and Urban Markets." *Canadian Geographer,* vol. 19, no. 1 (1975), pp. 73–93.

9. For a detailed discussion of rules, see Wädekin, *The Private Sector in Soviet Agriculture,* chap. 3.

10. *Ibid.,* p. 35.

11. A. Lane, "U.S.S.R.: Private Agriculture on Center Stage," 24 (note 2), 29 (note 16).

12. For a discussion of integration, see E. M. Jacobs, "Soviet Agricultural Planning and Management and the 1982 Administrative Reform," in Stuart, ed., *The Soviet Rural Economy,* pp. 273–295; V. Litvin, "Agro-Industrial Complexes: Recent Structural Reform in the Rural Economy of the USSR," in Stuart, ed., *The Soviet Rural Economy,* pp. 258–272; R. C. Stuart, "Aspects of Soviet Rural Development," *Agricultural Administration,* vol. 2 (1975), pp. 165–178; A. Kahan "The Problems of the Agrarian-Industrial Complexes in the Soviet Union," in Z. Fallenbuchl, ed., *Economic Development in The Soviet Union and Eastern Europe* (New York: Praeger, 1976) pp. 205–222, K.-E. Wädekin, *Agrarian Policies in Communist Europe: A Critical Introduction* (Totowa, N.J.: Allanheld & Osmun, 1982), chap. 12.

13. E. Jacobs, "Soviet Agricultural Planning and Management and the 1982 Administrative Reform," p. 274.

14. This discussion is based on Jacobs, "Soviet Agricultural Planning and Management and the 1982 Administrative Reform," pp. 273–295.

15. Official Soviet data from TsSU, *Narodnoe Khoziaistvo SSSR v 1983g.* [The national economy of the USSR in 1983] (Moscow: Finansyi statistika, 1984), p. 362.

16. U.S. Department of Agriculture, Economic Research Service, *USSR: Outlook and Situation Report* (Washington, D.C.: U.S. Department of Agriculture, 1985), p. 28.

17. *Ibid.*

18. D. B. Diamond, L. W. Bettis, and R. E. Ramsson, "Agricultural Production," in A. Bergson and H. S. Levine, eds., *The Soviet Economy: Toward The Year 2000* (London: Allen & Unwin, 1983), chap. 3.

19. For a discussion of recent trends, see V. G. Treml, "Subsidies in Soviet Agriculture: Record and Prospects," in U.S. Congress, Joint Economic Committee, *Soviet Economy in the 1980s: Problems and Prospects* (Washington, D.C.: U.S. Government Printing Office, 1982), pp. 171–186.

20. Treml, "Subsidies in Soviet Agriculture," pp. 171–172.

21. *Ibid.,* p. 172.

22. For a general discussion of factors underlying cost increases, see D. G. Johnson and K. McC. Brooks, *Prospects for Soviet Agriculture in the 1980s* (Bloomington: Indiana University Press, 1983). For a discussion of the livestock sector, see K. R. Gray, "Soviet Livestock: Stymiel Growth Increased Cost and Search for Balance," in U.S. Congress, Joint Economic Committee, *Soviet Economy in the 1980s: Problems and Prospects,* pp. 86–108; and Diamond, Bettis, and Ramsson, "Agricultural Production."

23. Johnson and Brooks, *Prospects For Soviet Agriculture in the 1980s,* p. 56.

24. *Ibid.*

25. *Ibid.,* chap. 6 and pp. 123–128. See also R. A. Ambroziak and D. W. Carey, "Climate and Grain Production in the Soviet Union," in U.S. Congress, Joint Economic Committee, *Soviet Economy in the 1980s: Problems and Prospects,* pp. 109–123.

26. Johnson and Brooks, *Prospects for Soviet Agriculture in the 1980s,* pp. 73–79. See also R. C. Stuart, "Wheat Yields in Socialist and Capitalist Economic Systems: A Statistical Comparison," *The Aces Bulletin,* vol. 26, no. I (Spring 1984), pp. 77–85.

27. Johnson and Brooks, *Prospects for Soviet Agriculture in the 1980s,* pp. 80–82.

28. *Ibid.*, p. 91.
29. For empirical evidence on the rationality of Soviet factor proportions, see M. L. Wyzan, "Empirical Analysis of Soviet Agricultural Production and Policy," *American Journal of Agricultural Economics* vol. 63, no. 3 (August 1981), 475–483; E. M. Clayton, "Productivity in Soviet Agriculture," *Slavic Review,* vol. 39 (1980), 446–458; Johnson and Brooks, *Prospects for Soviet Agriculture,* chap. 9.
30. Johnson and Brooks, *Prospects for Soviet Agriculture,* p. 41.
31. *Ibid.*, pp. 41–44.
32. See, for example, K. R. Gray, "Improved Agricultural Location: Econometric Evidence from the Ukraine," in Stuart, ed., *The Soviet Rural Economy,* chap. 10; K. R. Gray, "Soviet Agricultural Specialization and Efficiency," *Soviet Studies,* vol. 31, no. 4 (October 1979), 542–558.
33. K. R. Gray, "Soviet Consumption of Food: Is the Bottle 'Half-Full,' 'Half-Empty,' 'Half-Water,' or 'Too Expensive'?" *The Aces Bulletin* vol. 23, no. 2 (Summer 1981), 31–50.
34. TsSU, *Narodnoe Khoziaistvo SSSR v 1983g.* [The national economy of the USSR in 1983] (Moscow: Finansyi statistika, 1984), p. 415.
35. According to a recent study, net imports of farm products in the 1970s replaced sown acreage as the second most important source of increased supply, with increased yields being the most important source when the 1970s are compared with the 1960s. See Diamond, Bettis, and Ramsson, "Agricultural Production," p. 151.
36. See, for example, P. L. Kelley, "Implications for World Food System Strategies with Special Regard to the Role of the United States," in K.-E. Wädekin, ed., *Current Trends in the Soviet and East European Food Economy* (Berlin: Duniker & Humbolt, 1982), pp. 339–361; K.-E. Wädekin, "Soviet Agriculture's Dependence on the West," *Foreign Affairs*; A. O. Byrne, J. E. Cole, T. Bickerton, and A. F. Malish, "U.S.–U.S.S.R. Grain Trade," in U.S. Congress, Joint Economic Committee, *Soviet Economy in the 1980s: Problems and Prospects,* pp. 60–85.
37. See, for example, discussion of the U.S. grain embargo of 1980–1981 in J. C. Roney, "Grain Embargo as Diplomatic Lever: A Case Study of the U.S.–Soviet Embargo of 1980–81," in U.S. Congress, Joint Economic Committee, *Soviet Economy in the 1980s: Problems and Prospects,* pp. 124–140.
38. A. F. Malish, "The Food Program: A New Policy or More Rhetoric?" U.S. Congress, Joint Economic Committee, *Soviet Economy in the 1980s: Problems and Prospects,* pp. 41–59; E. M. Jacobs, "Soviet Agricultural Management and Planning and the 1982 Administrative Reform," in Stuart, ed., *The Soviet Rural Economy,* chap. 14.

SELECTED BIBLIOGRAPHY

D. B. Diamond, L. W. Bettis, and R. E. Ramsson, "Agricultural Production," in A. Bergson and H. S. Levine, eds., *The Soviet Economy: Toward The Year 2000* (London: Allen & Unwin, 1983), ch. 5.

F. A. Durgin, Jr., "Monetization and Policy in Soviet Agriculture Since 1952," *Soviet Studies,* vol. 15, no. 4 (April 1964).

K. R. Gray, "Soviet Agricultural Specialization and Efficiency," *Soviet Studies,* vol. 31, no. 4 (October 1979), pp. 542–548.

S. Hedlund, *Crisis in Soviet Agriculture* (New York: St. Martins Press, 1984).

W. A. D. Jackson, ed., *Agrarian Policies and Problems in Communist and Non-Communist Countries* (Seattle: University of Washington Press, 1971).

N. Jasny, *The Socialized Agriculture of the USSR* (Stanford, Calif.: Stanford University Press, 1949).

D. G. Johnson and K. McC. Brooks, *Prospects For Soviet Agriculture* (Bloomington: Indiana University Press, 1983).

J. F. Karcz, ed., *Soviet and East European Agriculture* (Berkeley and Los Angeles: University of California Press, 1967).

R. D. Laird, ed., *Soviet Agricultural and Peasant Affairs* (Lawrence: University of Kansas Press, 1963).

R. D. Laird and E. L. Crowley, eds., *Soviet Agriculture: The Permanent Crisis* (New York: Praeger, 1965).

R. D. Laird, J. Hajda, and B. A. Laird, eds., *The Future of Soviet Agriculture in the Soviet Union and Eastern Europe* (Boulder, Colo.: Westview Press, 1977).

J. R. Millar, ed., *The Soviet Rural Community* (Urbana: University of Illinois Press, 1971).

R. F. Miller, *One Hundred Thousand Tractors* (Cambridge, Mass.: Harvard University Press, 1970).

R. C. Stuart, *The Collective Farm in Soviet Agriculture* (Lexington, Mass.: Heath, 1972).

————, ed., *The Soviet Rural Economy* (Totowa, N.J.: Rowman and Allenheld, 1984).

U.S. Congress, Joint Economic Committee, *Soviet Economy in the 1980s: Problems and Prospects,* part 2 (Washington D.C.: U.S. Government Printing Office, 1983), section VI.

U.S. Congress, Joint Economic Committee, *Soviet Economy in a Time of Change* (Washington, D.C.: U.S. Government Printing Office, 1979), vol. 2, part 3.

U.S. Department of Agriculture, Economic Research Service, *USSR: Outlook and Situation Report* (Washington, D.C.: U.S. Department of Agriculture, April 1985).

L. Volin, *A Century of Russian Agriculture* (Cambridge Mass.: Harvard Universuty Press, 1970).

K.-E. Wädekin, *Agrarian Policies in Communist Europe: A Critical Introduction* (Totowa, N.J.: Rowman & Allanheld, 1982).

————, ed., *Current Trends in the Soviet and East European Food Economy* (Berlin: Duncker & Humbolt, 1982).

chapter *10*

Soviet Foreign Trade

In this chapter, we examine the role of the foreign sector in the Soviet economy. We begin with a discussion of trade in the Soviet planned economy—in particular, the state trade monopoly and the trade planning instruments utilized throughout the plan era. In addition to developing an understanding of how trade is conducted, it is necessary to examine both the volume and the structure of Soviet trade, especially its distribution among various trading partners in the world—notably among capitalist countries (developed and underdeveloped) and socialist bloc member countries of the COMECON organization. These trends can give us a picture of how Soviet trade policies have functioned in practice.

Finally, we examine the role of foreign trade in economic development and especially its role in the Soviet development experience.

TRADE IN THE SOVIET PLANNED ECONOMY

The Organization of Foreign Trade[1]

The organizational mechanisms used to conduct Soviet foreign trade are numerous, and over the years they have grown in number and complexity. Altogether, these organizations comprise the foreign trade monopoly of the Soviet Union. The basic organization responsible for the conduct of foreign trade is the Ministry of Foreign Trade, which itself is subordinate to *Gosplan,* and the USSR Council of Ministers (see Figure 9). The operative trade units, that is, the organizations that actually do the buying and selling in foreign markets, are Foreign Trade Organizations (FTOs)—or the All-Union Import-Export Associations, as they are described in Soviet parlance. These foreign trade organizations are usually subordinate to the Ministry of Foreign Trade and are financially independent, operating on a *khozraschet* basis. Most of the FTOs are organized by product. Thus, the FTO *Avtoeksport* ("auto export") deals in automobiles, and *Mezhdunarodnaia kniga* ("international book") deals in books. These organizations may handle imports, exports, or both. Reforms of the late 1970s were directed toward combining both the import and the export tasks within a single FTO. In addition to those FTOs dealing with specific products, others exist for the servicing of foreign trade and conducting trade on a regional basis. An example of the former would be *Vneshtorgreklama* ("foreign trade advertising"), which handles advertising in foreign trade. An example of the latter would be *Vostokintorg,* which is the Eastern Trade Association.

The FTOs have within them the means of conducting foreign trade, and they provide necessary technical and financial services. Their revenue is calculated as a percentage of their foreign trade turnover (exports plus imports). In addition to the individual FTOs, the Ministry of Foreign Trade is divided into main administrations or branches that are concerned with a wide range of issues relating to foreign trade. These administrations provide technical and financial services, including research on foreign trade.

The financial arrangements for Soviet foreign trade are handled by a special bank, *Vneshtorgbank.*[2] Though traditionally under the jurisdiction of *Gosbank,* the *Vneshtorgbank* has had significantly expanded powers and functions since the

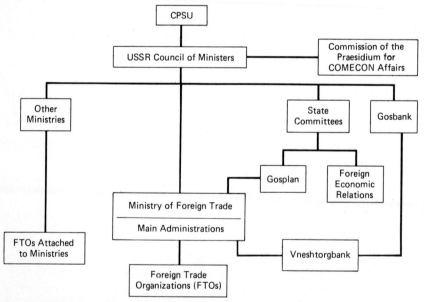

Figure 9   The organization of Soviet foreign trade. (*Source:* Compiled from V. P. Gruzinov, *The USSR's Management of Foreign Trade* [White Plains, N.Y.: M. E. Sharpe, 1979], pp. 26, 75, 79; E. A. Hewett, "Most-Favored Nation Treatment in Trade Under Central Planning," *Slavic Review,* vol. 37, no. 1 [March 1978], 28; Paul K. Cook, "The Political Setting," in Joint Economic Committee, *Soviet Economy in a Time of Change* [Washington, D.C.: U.S. Government Printing Office, 1979], vol. 1, no. 2, face p. 50.)

early 1960s. It now operates under policy guidance from *Gosbank,* but in close cooperation with the main foreign exchange administration of the Ministry of Foreign Trade. In addition to a large number of correspondent banks in foreign countries, *Vneshtorgbank* also operates through Soviet-owned banks abroad—for example, the Moscow Narodny Bank of London.

There are other more specialized organizations for the conduct of trade, the importance of which has been growing in recent years. A number of special FTOs do not fall under the jurisdiction of the Ministry of Foreign Trade. *Intourist,* the FTO responsible for Soviet tourism, falls within the jurisdiction of the administration for foreign tourism under the Council of Ministers. Another example was SOOC (Soviet Olympic Organizing Committee), operating independently of the Ministry of Foreign Trade and the FTOs but fully empowered to sign agreements with foreign firms for the conduct of the 1980 Olympic Games held in Moscow. Finally, the Soviet Union has Joint Stock Companies, for example, Belarus Machinery Inc., which sells and services Belarus tractors in the United States.

The Planning of Foreign Trade

Soviet foreign trade, like other sectors of the Soviet economy, is managed as an integral part of the system of material balance planning.[3] Soviet foreign trade planners have tended to use imports and exports as balancing items in the national economic plan (imports where there were shortages and exports where there were surpluses). Planners have sought to avoid heavy reliance on trade to balance the plan for reasons discussed later in this chapter. In trade with COMECON countries,* Soviet authorities planned for trade to play a more important role, namely, to promote the integration of these countries with the Soviet economy. Specifically, the Soviet Union was to serve as the basic source of raw materials for Eastern European development, with manufactured products supplied in return.

In recent years, a combination of reforms in the Soviet foreign trade sector plus a new Soviet posture in foreign trade (the greater use of Western imports to stimulate economic performance and a more aggressive export posture to pay for imports) have led to the evolution of an increasingly sophisticated foreign trade planning structure, but the main features of foreign trade planning have remained basically intact since the 1930s.

Trade objectives are expressed in three plans: (1) an import-export plan, (2) a plan for support materials and services for Soviet projects outside the Soviet Union, and (3) a balance-of-payments plan. These plans are segregated according to region, and in the case of trade with COMECON, they are supposed to be coordinated with the general (and trade) plans of each member country. This coordination function is supported by long-range programs to promote joint planning among COMECON members—efforts to plan integration on a five-year time horizon in terms of industrial branches, projects, and joint ventures.

*The Council for Mutual Economic Assistance, called COMECON or, alternatively, CMEA, is the Soviet bloc's equivalent to the European Common Market and will be discussed in this chapter. The member countries, in addition to the USSR, are Bulgaria, Hungary, East Germany, Cuba, Mongolia, Poland, Rumania, and Czechoslovakia.

The foreign trade plans contain detailed plan targets. The import-export plan indicates the regional distribution of exports and imports, the tasks of each organization involved (the foreign trade and other ministries, the FTOs), and the schedule of deliveries. The balance-of-payments plan is developed by the Ministry of Foreign Trade in conjunction with the Ministry of Finance and shows both payments and receipts (on both a current and a credit basis) for various categories of goods and services distinguished by currency type—for example, by specific convertible currencies and transferable rubles. The transferable ruble (or *valuta* ruble) is used as an accounting tool and often has little relationship with internal ruble prices. In addition to the balance-of-payments plan, a capital plan is also prepared by the Ministry of Finance, *Gosplan,* and the *Vneshtorgbank.* It summarizes claims and credits on an annual basis.

The integration of the foreign trade plans and the national economic plan is incomplete in that there is no comprehensive plan that translates foreign trade flows into domestic prices. The trade plans are expressed in terms of foreign trade rubles, whose relationship to domestic prices is unclear. This separation of financial plans into those in *valuta* rubles and in domestic rubles has complicated Soviet economic planning; yet no solution has been offered to this point.

The apparatus for the conduct of Soviet foreign trade is fundamentally different from that of a market economy. The most basic difference is that the foreign trade monopoly serves to isolate Soviet internal producers and consumers of export and import items, respectively, from direct contact with the outside world. From this basic difference stems a set of arrangements in international trade that are very different from those typically observed in the West.

The operative unit for carrying out the foreign trade plan is the FTO. While the FTOs have been the focus of substantial attention and reform effort in recent years, their basic function remains to connect the internal producer or consumer with the external world. The FTO purchases authorized export items from the Soviet producer at internal ruble prices and sells them in foreign markets at agreed upon (typically, world market) prices. Within COMECON, the sale will be transacted in transferable rubles.* Likewise, an FTO will purchase authorized items in foreign markets at negotiated or world market prices, and the internal Soviet consuming firm will be charged the internal ruble price for the imported item. The financial side of these transactions is the responsibility of the various financial organs involved with foreign trade, along with the Ministry of Foreign Trade. If the imported item is sold to the using enterprise at a higher price than that paid by the FTO, a surplus is created for the state budget. In the late 1970s, surplus earnings accounted for some 10 percent of state revenues.[4]

Soviet Foreign Trade Policy

Thus far, we have examined only the mechanisms for organizing Soviet foreign trade and how foreign trade is included in the national economic plan. But what

---

*As we shall see below, the pricing of goods and services in Soviet foreign trade is a matter of great complexity. The influence of world market prices is only a beginning point in the discussion.

are the rules that determine the level and distribution of Soviet foreign trade? We turn now to a discussion of Soviet foreign trade policy.

Western observers have noted that the volume of Soviet foreign trade has been significantly less than one would find in market economies at similar levels of economic development.[5] This pattern is said to demonstrate a Soviet bias against trade or a "policy of trade aversion." Data on the volume of Soviet trade and trade proportions are given in Table 35. What factors explain the Soviet bias against trade?

From the earliest days of the Soviet regime, the prevailing Marxist–Leninist ideology called for rejection of traditional Western arguments concerning the benefits to be gained from international trade—the thesis of *comparative advantage* —just as it has called for the rejection of other Western "economic laws." Western markets were viewed as subject to chaotic fluctuations that could jeopardize the planned nature of the Soviet economy. Moreover, it was argued that "socialism in one country" was possible due to the vast resources of the Soviet Union.

A second major factor explaining the Soviet policy of trade aversion was the early perception (and, in large part, reality) of a "hostile capitalist encirclement," which encouraged the Soviet regime to avoid reliance on foreign markets for its economic development. Events over the years have tended to bolster Soviet distrust of Western markets. In the immediate postwar era, the United States spearheaded a movement to restrict credits and the flow of "strategic" goods to the USSR. The United States has also used cutoffs of high-technology trade and, in 1980, of grain to punish the Soviets for political misdeeds.

Third, as a sector to be incorporated into an already complex planning system, foreign trade as a priority sector might significantly complicate the overall planning process—in particular, by introducing outside forces not directly controlled by Soviet planners and thus increasing the degree of plan uncertainty. One can find the tendency to avoid reliance on outsiders at all levels of the Soviet economy,[6] and this reluctance is intensified when foreign suppliers (even ideologically compatible suppliers from COMECON) are involved. It is noteworthy that Soviet trade potential within COMECON remains "underutilized," although there can be no ideological objections to such trade.

Fourth, the Soviets stress that the capitalist countries have erected barriers against trade with the Soviet Union, beginning with the embargoes following the 1917 revolution to the present-day restrictions on lending, failure to grant tariff reductions, and controls on strategic commodities.

Fifth, and possibly most important, the very mechanisms for the conduct of Soviet foreign trade have themselves served to complicate the conduct of foreign trade, to limit Soviet participation in the international financial community, and to necessitate peculiar arrangements that inhibit foreign trade. We turn to these arrangements in the following section.

Internal Barriers to Foreign Trade

We have already noted that the arrangements for conducting foreign trade and for the pricing of traded commodities have isolated Soviet enterprises from for-

Table 35   REAL VOLUME OF IMPORTS AND EXPORTS OF THE USSR (1913 = 100)
AND TRADE RATIOS, 1913–1982

Year	Exports composite index	Imports composite index	Exports as percent of national income	Year	Exports composite index	Imports composite index	Exports as percent of national income
1913	100.0	100.0	10.4	1948	51.1	64.3	
1917	6.9	176.3		1949	58.2	72.4	
1918	0.5	7.7		1950	80.7	82.0	
1919	0.0	0.2		1951	94.6	101.4	
1920	0.1	2.1		1952	114.2	123.4	
1921	1.3	15.3		1953	120.0	133.1	
1922	5.4	19.6		1954	132.6	154.4	
1923	14.3	10.4		1955	142.3	149.2	3.0
1924	22.2	18.9		1956	150.7	173.8	3.0
1925	25.1	37.8		1957	179.2	186.7	3.6
1926	32.2	33.8		1958	184.2	223.8	3.1
1927	34.7	38.9		1959	242.9	264.7	3.9
1928	37.7	49.4		1960	242.6	290.1	3.7
1929	44.4	48.3	3.1	1961	265.7	299.4	3.9
1930	57.0	72.1	3.5	1962	311.8	334.6	4.3
1931	61.4	82.4	3.0	1963	321.7	364.3	4.4
1932	53.7	59.1	2.6	1964	333.9	378.9	4.4
1933	49.8	31.9	2.3	1965	371.5	401.5	4.5
1934	43.2	24.0	1.8	1966	422.9	396.3	4.6
1935	38.0	26.3	1.3	1967	458.0	423.0	5.0
1936	28.6	30.3	0.8	1968	503.4	479.5	5.9
1937	30.0	27.8	0.5	1969	558.8	514.1	6.0
1938	26.2	32.3		1970	590.8	552.9	6.3
1939	10.6	20.4		1971	608.5	586.1	6.4
1940	21.8	27.7		1972	626.3	685.6	5.7
1941	14.4	29.1		1973	714.9	785.1	6.0
1942	4.8	17.6		1974	809.3	812.8	6.5
1943	4.3	15.5		1975	833.0	962.1	6.3
1944	6.6	16.5		1976	898.0	1022.9	6.5
1945	15.5	20.0		1977	980.7	1039.5	
1946	27.2	49.4		1978	1028.0	1194.3	
1947	30.0	43.9		1980	1572.8	1528.3	
				1982	2004.6	1934.3	

Sources: M. Kaser, "A Volume Index of Soviet Foreign Trade," *Soviet Studies,* vol. 20, no. 4 (April 1969), 523–526; *Vneshnaia torgovlia SSSR v 1978 g.* [USSR foreign trade 1978] (Moscow: Statistika, 1979), p. 16; F. D. Holzman, "Foreign Trade," in A. Bergson and S. Kuznets, eds., *Economic Trends in the Soviet Union* (Cambridge, Mass.: Harvard University Press, 1963), p. 290, V. G. Treml, "Foreign Trade and the Soviet Economy: Changing Parameters and Interrelationships," in E. Neuberger and L. Tyson, eds., *Transmission and Response: The Impact of International Disturbances on the Soviet Union and Eastern Europe* (New York: Pergamon Press, 1980). The indexes are updated to 1982 using official Soviet data on the real exports and real imports.

eign market influences. If there is a difference between the internal ruble price and the foreign price of a particular product, this difference appears as a subsidy or as a revenue source in the state budget, with no immediate implications for the internal Soviet enterprise. This isolation of the Soviet enterprise both as a producer and as a consumer sets it apart from capitalist enterprises, which enter directly into foreign trade arrangements and can respond more readily to foreign markets. The isolation of Soviet producing enterprises makes it difficult for them to be competitive in world markets by not knowing what the changing world market requires. The Soviets' inability to compete in capitalist markets in the areas of manufactured goods and in the service fields is, in part, accounted for by this isolation.[7] The weak Western market for Soviet manufacturers has limited Soviet foreign exchange earnings over the years, which has, in turn, restricted Soviet imports from the West.[8] The Soviet Union has been unable (or unwilling) to expand its exports of petroleum products and other raw materials to offset its expanding import requirements from the West. Trade deficits vis-à-vis Western countries therefore have had to be financed with credits granted by capitalist countries.[9]

Existing arrangements for conducting trade inhibit trade in other ways. First, the Soviet ruble is an inconvertible currency, not listed on world currency markets and not accepted by (or available to) trading partners. Ruble inconvertibility, along with the Soviet system of centralized planning and price setting, means that the Soviet prices used in foreign transactions (*valuta* rubles) bear little relation either to relative scarcities in the domestic economy or to world market prices. There is, therefore, no common scale of value through which the potential advantages or disadvantages of trade can be measured. In the absence of an effective way to assess the costs and benefits of trade, bilateral agreements have to be negotiated between the Soviet Union and its trading partners, balanced usually in terms of some approximation of world market prices. The use of bilateral arrangements is almost inevitable, given Soviet internal controls over trade flows, the nature of Soviet prices, and the lack of meaning of the ruble (or any other socialist currency) in world markets.

Since the ruble is not a convertible currency, its real value in terms of other currencies (its exchange rate) is not known.[10] The exchange rate set administratively by the Soviet government tends to be arbitrary and not necessarily reflective of the relative purchasing power of the ruble. Thus, the exchange rate as a means to assess the benefits from trade is of little use in this case.

Unlike capitalist economies, where the gains from trade are obvious from comparisons of domestic and foreign prices, what goods should be traded and with what countries is not clear in the Soviet case. Internal Soviet prices themselves may not reflect domestic relative scarcities, and internal prices are difficult to compare with foreign prices due to the lack of appropriate rates of exchange. The absence of firm information on relative foreign and domestic costs and prices explains in part the depressed levels of Soviet trade. Even if there were substantial gains to specialization of production and exchange (say, trading Soviet machines for Bulgarian consumer goods) due to large differences in costs of production, this would likely not be evident to foreign trade planners. Thus, in the Soviet Union, an important pressure in favor of trade expansion is absent, namely, a clear appreciation of the fact that certain products can be obtained abroad with less sacrifice of resources than if produced domestically.

Soviet trade authorities (along with their COMECON counterparts) have sought to remedy this situation by developing criteria—Foreign Trade Efficiency Indexes (FTEI)—for evaluating on a rational basis exports and imports.[11] The FTEI have been in use within COMECON since the mid-1960s and seek to provide rules for calculating the ratios of domestic to foreign costs of potential export and import items.* The general principle underlying these formulas is that foreign trade prices should be translated into domestic prices by calculating the amount of domestic production required to earn the foreign exchange (*valuta* rubles) needed to purchase the foreign item (in the case of the FTEI, for imports). Although these formulas bear a certain resemblance to the relative cost comparisons made by capitalist economies, the approximation is very rough. To be an accurate index of the opportunity costs of domestic production versus foreign production, internal prices must reflect domestic relative scarcities, and the implicit exchange rates used in the indexes must indicate the relative purchasing power of the foreign exchange accounting units. These conditions are not met in most instances. Moreover, the FTEI are used only as an aid for foreign trade planners. Most trading decisions are made administratively—without consulting foreign trade efficiency indexes as a part of long-term agreements—and are often based on political decisions.

The second important consequence of Soviet trade arrangements is the difficulty of devising appropriate financial arrangements to handle the financing of trade imbalances. Specifically, since a nonconvertible currency cannot be used in payment for goods and services, Soviet trade with each partner must balance. If not, the Soviet Union must pay in gold or convertible Western currencies or arrange credit. In contrast, if the United States were to purchase more goods and services from Canada than Canada buys from the United States, there would be no immediate problem, since Canada would be willing to accept U.S. dollars either for purchases in the United States or for use in other countries where dollars are readily acceptable at the established rate of exchange. Thus, the U.S. trade deficit with Canada is automatically financed, and a trade imbalance is possible. This cannot be done in the case of Soviet transactions with other countries, for currency inconvertibility leads to "commodity inconvertibility." If the

---

*Typically, FTEI are calculated separately for potential exports and imports. In simplified form, the *import index* is

$$X_{ie} = \frac{Z_i X_{i \cdot eq}}{V_i}$$

where X_{ie} = the index of import effectiveness of the product
   V_i = the foreign exchange cost of one unit of the product
   Z_i = the domestic cost of producing one unit of the product
   $X_{i \cdot eq}$ = the ratio of foreign exchange receipts from the country in question from exported goods to the domestic cost of producing these goods

The import effectiveness index is easy to understand except for $X_{i \cdot eq}$, which plays the role of a crude exchange rate. The Z values represent the internal ruble prices of imported items, and the V values represent foreign prices expressed in transfer (valuta) rubles. These transfer rubles are determined administratively and will vary for each of the USSR's trading partners. The problem is translating these foreign prices into domestic prices—a role played by exchange rates in capitalist countries. For this purpose, a form of opportunity cost measure is calculated for each trading partner. For this import index, this is the average domestic cost of producing goods domestically to earn the foreign exchange necessary to import the item from the particular country. It is calculated by taking the foreign exchange earnings from Soviet exports to that country and dividing by the domestic cost of producing these goods for export.

Soviet Union were to have a trade deficit with Poland, for example, the Soviet Union could not automatically finance the deficit by paying in rubles. Insofar as Poland cannot use rubles to freely purchase what it wants from the Soviet Union or another country, they are of no value to the Polish trade authorities. The tendency, therefore, is to balance transactions with all countries, even though a "rational" trading plan would call for surpluses or deficits vis-à-vis individual trading partners. In this manner, trade is restricted to the amount that one trading partner is willing to accept from the other a form of barter transaction. Within COMECON, trade imbalances must be cleared by hard currency payments, and, in rare instances, credits are granted to finance deficits.

THE EXTERNAL ENVIRONMENT: THE SOCIALIST COUNTRIES

In terms of geographic distribution, the Soviet Union distinguishes between its trade with socialist countries (COMECON and other) and capitalist countries (developed and underdeveloped). The Council for Mutual Economic Assistance, COMECON, was established in 1949 on the initiative of the Soviet Union for the expressed purpose of integrating the socialist planned economies of Eastern Europe with the Soviet Union through the specialization of trade and production among member countries.[12] Trade with COMECON members has accounted for more than 50 percent of Soviet foreign trade throughout the postwar era (see Table 36), and the Soviet Union is in many respects the dominant partner in this organization. Although there have been some changes in the trading arrangements and cooperative agreements among COMECON countries since the 1960s, only a relatively limited degree of integration among these countries has been achieved, for a number of basic reasons.[13]

First, in spite of Soviet economic and political pressure for integration, the countries of Eastern Europe have focused upon developing their own diversified industrial economies, including an adequate base of heavy industry.[14] During the postwar era, the COMECON countries have not been content to specialize in specific product lines as desired by the USSR, for they have viewed this as a loss of national economic independence. This stance is buttressed by the fact that COMECON possesses no supranational authority over its members. Each member has veto power, and various Soviet efforts to give COMECON supranational powers have been successfully opposed by other members.

Second, although some coordination has been developed, there has been less effective development of integrated planning arrangements, and only preliminary steps have been taken to develop common yardsticks (such as common costs and prices, and a convertible COMECON trading currency) to direct specialization and to achieve a more optimal pattern of bloc trade.[15] The most important efforts to date to promote COMECON integration are the Comprehensive Program of 1971, the Agreed Plan for Multilateral Integration Measures of 1975, and the Long-Term Special-Purpose Program for Cooperation signed in 1979. These cooperation programs are a series of bilateral agreements for bilateral economic and scientific cooperation and for joint economic planning among individual COMECON members. The agreement signed in 1979 calls for cooperative pro-

Table 36   SOVIET FOREIGN TRADE TURNOVER—GEOGRAPHIC DISTRIBUTION IN SELECTED POSTWAR YEARS (PERCENTAGES)

	1946	1950	1953	1956	1959	1962	1965	1970	1975	1982
1. Socialist countries[a]	54.5	81.1	83.2	75.7	75.3	70.2	68.8	65.2	56.3	54.3
COMECON member countries	40.6	57.4	59.3	49.6	52.0	57.5	58.0	55.6	51.7	49.1
2. Capitalist countries	45.5	18.9	16.8	24.3	24.7	29.8	31.2	34.7	43.6	45.7
Industrial	38.4	15.1	14.5	16.8	15.9	18.1	19.3	21.2	31.2	31.6
Less developed countries (LDCs)	7.1	3.8	2.3	7.5	8.8	11.7	11.9	13.5	12.4	14.1

Source: Compiled from official Soviet foreign trade handbooks, in particular, from annual editions of *Vreshnaia torgovlia SSSR* [Foreign trade of the USSR] and *Statisticheski ezhegodnik Stran-chlenov S.E.V.* [Statistical yearbook of the member countries of S.E.V.].
[a]Includes China, Cuba, Vietnam, North Korea, and Yugoslavia.

grams to be implemented through 1990. The latest cooperative agreements focus on the development of Soviet energy and raw materials using Eastern European labor and capital.

Since the economic mechanisms and pricing arrangements are similar among the bloc countries (with the exception of Hungary, where major reforms have been undertaken), the USSR's COMECON trading partners conduct trade much like the Soviet Union does. Intrabloc trade is conducted largely on a bilateral basis, with five-year and one-year planning horizons. To facilitate multilateral clearing, the Bank for International Cooperation (IBEC) was created in 1964. However, most intra-COMECON trade is conducted in transferable rubles, a nonconvertible currency used basically in bilateral arrangements. Trade in hard currencies is small, and multilateral clearing is minuscule, perhaps 5 percent of the total.[16] Where there is a bilateral deficit, it is normally settled by adjusting future plan targets or by the shipment of "soft goods" (goods that are relatively unattractive because they are overpriced in COMECON relative to world market prices). Preference would be for "hard goods" that would have a market in the West, but hard goods are typically not offered to correct imbalances.

As with Soviet trade, the trade of bloc members is determined by their national planning agencies and with little or no cost-benefit frame of reference. The pricing of traded commodities in intrabloc trade has been complicated by the absence of a set of internal prices (say, USSR ruble prices) suitable for valuing transactions among member countries. As a general rule, the pricing principle for intrabloc trade is to begin by determining what the commodity would have cost in the world market. Such calculations are not easy to make in the case of machinery and equipment not sold in the West, since authorities can only guess at the price the commodity would command in world markets. This ambiguity has led to controversy between the Soviet Union and its COMECON partners over whether the terms of trade are "fair" and to claims that the USSR pays too little for manufactured imports from other COMECON countries. For example, Michael Marrese and Jan Vañous claim that the USSR has deliberately subsidized Eastern Europe by selling Soviet raw materials at low prices to gain political leverage. On the other hand, Josef Brada finds that Soviet export pricing to Eastern Europe is the natural result of relative resource endowments.[17]

Prior to 1975, COMECON prices were fixed over the life of long-term national plans. According to the pricing formula agreed upon in Bucharest in 1958, the world market prices of 1957 were applied to intrabloc transactions until 1965. For the planning period 1966–1970, average 1961–1965 world market prices were used, and then average world prices of 1966–1970 were used for the period 1971–1975.[18] The explosion of energy and other raw material prices in the 1970s caused the USSR to change this pricing formula, as the Soviet Union is the dominant supplier of energy to Eastern Europe. COMECON adopted in 1975 a new "sliding pricing formula," whereby average world market prices of the preceding five years are used. Thus, rising energy prices are passed on to COMECON partners gradually over time. Also, provision was made to pay for Soviet energy deliveries above targeted levels in hard currencies at prevailing world market prices. These changes led to a substantial improvement in the USSR's terms of trade with Eastern Europe after 1975.

In spite of attempts at reform of institutional arrangements, the basic problems of integrating the COMECON countries remain. It has proved especially difficult to integrate the industrialized members (the USSR, East Germany, and Czechoslovakia) with the less industrialized countries (Bulgaria and Rumania), due to the unwillingness of the latter to specialize in low-technology products and agriculture. Disputes among these countries have arisen, and with East European products finding a growing market in the West and with increasing hard-currency credits, imports of more advanced technology from the West (rather than from the Soviet Union) have become increasingly attractive. It is from this basic pattern that the problem of an expanding COMECON hard-currency debt has arisen, an issue we examine below.

SOVIET TRADE WITH CAPITALIST COUNTRIES

Soviet trade with capitalist countries has increased significantly during the postwar years. If one excludes the atypical immediate postwar period, Soviet trade with capitalist countries as a portion of total Soviet foreign trade has increased from roughly 19 percent in 1950 to 46 percent in 1982 (see Table 36). This expansion in trade with capitalist countries has been accompanied by a reduction of trade with socialist countries (especially with the People's Republic of China).

The expansion of Soviet trade with capitalist countries can be divided into two different components: Soviet trade with the industrialized West (North America, Western Europe, and Japan) and with the less developed countries (LDCs). Let us examine each in turn.

Soviet trade with the LDCs has expanded from minuscule levels in the early 1950s but has not expanded as a share of Soviet trade since the early 1960s, stabilizing between 12 and 14 percent of trade turnover. The composition of Soviet trade with the LDCs is markedly different from that with the industrialized West. The Soviet Union exports primarily machinery and equipment to LDCs, along with some raw materials and petroleum (for "client" states). Whereas the USSR has difficulty marketing its heavy industry manufactures in the West, an LDC market does exist for such exports. It is, therefore, a puzzle why Soviet trade with the LDCs has not expanded more rapidly.

A dominant theme of Soviet relations with LDCs is its economic and military aid. The thrust of Soviet assistance to LDCs is broadly political and concentrates upon a limited number of strategic nations. From its inception in the mid-1950s, Soviet aid has grown in magnitude but remains well below levels of U.S. aid. Between 1956 and 1978, Soviet aid agreements totaled just under 47 billion dollars, though actual deliveries amounted to just under 33 billion dollars. This figure is about one-fifth the volume of U.S. economic and military aid for the same period.[19]

The features of Soviet aid to LDCs are distinctive when compared to those of other aid-granting nations. First, Soviet aid is dominated by military as opposed to general economic aid. For the period 1956 through 1978, 63 percent of aid agreements were military, while 77 percent of actual aid deliveries were military.[20] Second, Soviet aid is typically for specific projects and combined with technical and service support provided on the site by Soviet advisers. In 1978, there were 75,000 technicians from the Soviet Union and Eastern Europe in the LDCs.[21] Third, Soviet aid is frequently repayable in the form of long-term low-interest loans. Finally, Soviet aid is usually directed at a few recipients and seldom offers hard-currency credits for purchases outside of the Soviet Union. From 1954 to 1978, six countries received over 60 percent of all Soviet economic aid to the LDCs.[22]

The share of Soviet trade with the industrialized West remained fairly constant at nearly 15 percent during the 1950s, then almost doubled from 1960 to 1982. Thus, Soviet trade with the industrialized West has been expanding more rapidly than that with its other trading partners; yet currently, trade with the USSR accounts for only 2.5 percent of the exports of the major industrialized countries. It should be emphasized that exports to the Soviet Union still represent a relatively minor market for the industrialized West, although it looms large for selected products. Soviet trade with Western industrialized countries has been dominated by a very different set of issues. These have revolved around the nature of Soviet foreign trade arrangements in an era of growing Soviet import needs from the West (especially industrial technology and grain) and the Soviet drive to expand exports to pay for these imports. During the early 1970s, in trade with the West, the rate of growth of imports outstripped the rate of growth of exports by a significant margin, the result being a growing hard-currency deficit with the West.[23] Let us examine the pattern of Soviet trade in greater detail.

The growth of imports from the industrialized West has been concentrated in two broad areas—industrial goods and services designed to support the technological needs of the Soviet economy, and agricultural goods (largely grain and fertilizer) to offset serious climatic (and thus harvest) reverses and to stimulate agricultural productivity in general and meat production in particular.[24]

The rapid growth of Soviet imports from the West slowed substantially in the mid-1970s, but Soviet exports to the industrialized West have not kept up with the pace of imports, so the hard-currency debt continues to grow. Since Soviet manufactures typically do not compete well in Western markets (they are sold primarily to socialist bloc nations and the LDCs), the result has been a growing Soviet hard-currency debt estimated to be $20.9 billion in 1981.[25] The burden of this debt can be measured in two ways. The first is to determine the ratio of annual payments on hard-currency debt to hard-currency export earnings. In 1981, this "debt service ratio" stood at 17 percent. A second measure is to determine the ratio of gross hard-currency debt to hard-currency export earnings. This ratio equaled 64 percent in 1981. Although the Soviet debt position remains within reason, it has had its costs in terms of gold sales abroad, increased reliance on Western credits, and the need to expand arms sales. Moreover, the debt position of Eastern Europe is more alarming, and Eastern Europe may some day require assistance to service its hard-currency debt. The effect of this growing debt has been twofold since the mid-1970s. First, Soviet authorities have trimmed the growth of imports from the industrialized West for the purpose of regaining control over the hard-currency balance, a policy that has cut the annual trade deficit substantially. The second element of Soviet trade policy of the 1970s and 1980s has been the continuing campaign to increase participation in Western markets. This effort has several goals.

First, there has been a long-standing effort to improve both the political and the economic bases of trade with Western countries such as the United States.[26] The most significant breakthroughs have come in commercial relations with Western Europe and Japan, in which the USSR has gained tariff reductions and has had relatively easy access to private and government credit. United States legislation on trade with the Soviet Union remains restrictive, focusing especially upon limiting sales of "strategic" goods, restricting governmental credits, and failing to grant general trade concessions. The 1960s and 1970s were a period of considerable discussion on trade matters between the Soviet Union and the United States, culminating in the negotiation of the U.S.-USSR Trade Agreement in 1972. This agreement, which was to grant most favored nation (MFN) status, was annulled in 1975 by the Soviets when it was linked with the question of Jewish emigration. The question of granting MFN status remains up in the air, a matter of substantial emotional and political (though possibly dubious economic) importance to the Soviet side, especially when China was granted MFN in January of 1980. The Soviets have argued that not being granted MFN has made their manufactured products less competitive in U.S. markets, but there is some controversy about the future effect of granting MFN on USSR exports to the United States.[27]

Second, the Soviet Union has been more aggressive in devising arrangements for increasing imports from the West without an immediate increase in exports.[28] For example, the importance of compensation agreements between the Soviet Union and the United States has increased in recent years.[29] Compensation agreements were almost nonexistent in the early 1960s but grew substantially thereafter, involving Western Europe, Japan, and the United States.[30]

The compensation agreement underscores an important problem in Soviet-Western trade, especially in the area of capital imports. Because of prohibitions against private ownership, the Soviets are denied the advantages (and avoid the disadvantages) of direct foreign investment. Foreign companies cannot own and manage subsidiaries in the USSR. However, near substitutes have been sought, and the compensation agreement is one, for it promises the Western investor a share in the resulting output. Joint ventures, coproduction, and licensing have been used as well to promote industrial cooperation without Western ownership.

Another device for trade expansion has been direct investment by the Soviet Union in the West.[31] This phenomenon, which grew significantly in the 1970s, is diversified geographically and by type of economic activity, varying from production (on a limited basis) through trade and service organizations to banking. However, with these organizations typically wholly owned, controlled, and managed by the Soviet Union, Western nations express the usual concern that one might connect with a multinational enterprise, adding the participation of a foreign and sometimes antagonistic government.

The future of Soviet trade with the Western industrialized nations and especially with the United States will hinge upon the fruitful development of these new strategies along with the improvement of the mechanisms with which the Soviet planned economy conducts its foreign trade. However, basic problems such as restrictions on strategic goods, limitations on direct investment, product quality, and marketing difficulties—issues to which we return at the end of this chapter—will remain dominant throughout the 1980s.

THE STRUCTURE AND VOLUME OF SOVIET COMMODITY TRADE

Over the years, the composition of Soviet trade has changed with the evolving requirements of the domestic economy. In 1913, imports were concentrated in three areas: raw materials (for the textiles industry), 22 percent; consumer goods, 21 percent; and machinery and equipment, 16 percent. On the export side, raw materials, grain, and animal products accounted for virtually all of Russian exports. In 1928, on the eve of the Five Year Plan era, the structure of exports and imports was much like that of the late tsarist era.[32]

The forced industrialization program of the 1930s brought about significant shifts in the structure of Soviet trade. On the import side, there was a distinct movement away from importing consumer goods and toward importing producer goods. Producer goods and consumption goods accounted respectively for 27 and 7 percent of aggregate Soviet imports in 1918; by 1931, the figures were 95 and 5 percent for production and consumption goods, respectively.[33] Also notable during the early years of Soviet industrialization was the increasing importance of imports of machinery and equipment. From a level of 15.9 percent of imports in 1913, machinery and equipment imports grew to account for 55.2 percent of imports in 1932.[34] This pattern changed significantly after the first Five Year Plan, basically through the development of domestic capacity in key industrial sectors. Nevertheless, if we look at the portion of Soviet utilization of key industrial commodities (those of crucial importance to the industrialization effort) accounted for by imports, the result is striking and suggests that foreign technology may have been a very important element in the industrialization process.[35] In 1930, for example, 89 percent of the aggregate Soviet consumption of turbines, boilers, and generators came from imports. In 1932, 66 percent of the machine tools used in the Soviet Union were imported.

Export patterns did not change radically during the early years of Soviet industrialization. Fuels, raw materials, and consumer goods remained important as a portion of aggregate export volume. Exports of grain, which had virtually disappeared by 1928, increased significantly during the First Five Year Plan but fluctuated significantly thereafter, depending on the harvest. It is significant that grain exports were never again to regain the import role they played throughout the tsarist era.

Since the 1950s, there have been important shifts in Soviet commodity trade patterns on both the import and the export sides (Tables 37 and 38). These shifts have been a focus of concern by Soviet policy makers in the 1970s and 1980s and from one of the more important arguments in support of upgrading the trade mechanism, a matter that we examined earlier in this chapter.

On the import side, there have been increases in the relative importance of machinery and equipment and of food-related items since the 1950s. In 1982, 34 percent of Soviet imports were for machinery. Since 1977, the Soviets have reduced the detail of published trade data, so it is now difficult to calculate the percentage share of agricultural imports. We would guess that they represent nearly 20 percent of the total. Imported grains in 1981–1982 accounted for about one-quarter of Soviet grain utilization.[36] On the export side, fuels have grown to a dominant position, along with the traditionally important exports of raw materials. In 1982, the two accounted for almost 60 percent of Soviet exports. The aggregate data, however, hide the important underlying issue of geographic distribution. In the hard-currency markets, fuels and raw materials are dominant, with machinery and equipment (exported mainly to Eastern Europe and the LDCs) playing only a very small role. Unless the Soviet Union can continue to expand fuel and raw materials sales in hard-currency markets, trade diversification in the direction of manufactures will be essential in the late 1980s and beyond.[37]

Finally, the development of Soviet foreign trade since World War II has been distinctive on several fronts, all of which deserve closer attention. The volume of trade has grown significantly—more rapidly than the economy. Thus, in 1950, exports and imports accounted for 2.1 and 2.9 percent, respectively, of GNP. By 1977, these shares had grown to 6.7 and 9.2 percent.[38] The rapid growth of trade volume has caused Vladmir Treml[39] to argue that the USSR has abandoned at long last its policy of trade aversion. Does the Soviet Union still "underutilize" its trade potential, as it obviously did from the 1930s to the early

Table 37   THE STRUCTURE OF SOVIET EXPORTS (PERCENTAGES)

	1950	1955	1960	1965	1970	1975	1977	1982
Machinery	11.8	17.5	20.5	20.0	21.3	18.5	18.7	12.9
Fuels and energy	3.9	9.6	16.2	17.2	15.6	31.4	35.0	52.1
Metals, ores, minerals	12.3	18.6	21.6	23.2	21.5	17.0	13.1	5.5
Chemicals, fertilizer, rubber	4.0	2.7	2.9	2.8	3.5	3.5	2.8	2.5
Construction products	0.2	0.5	0.3	0.5	0.6	0.6	0.5	.1
Forest products, paper	3.0	5.0	5.5	7.2	6.5	5.7	5.0	2.4
Fibers	11.2	10.1	6.4	5.1	3.4	3.0	3.2	2.8
Agricultural raw materials	3.8	1.9	2.0	1.3	1.0	.5	0.5	1.7
Grain and oilseed	12.9	8.6	8.6	3.4	3.3	1.6	1.1	
Sugar	0.9	0.7	0.5	0.6	0.8	0.07	0.05	
Other foodstuffs	3.3	2.5	3.8	4.3	4.1	2.0	1.4	
Cloth, clothing, shoes	2.2	1.5	1.2	0.8	0.7	0.5	0.4	22.0
Small consumer durables	0.2	0.2	0.8	0.7	0.9	1.1	0.9	
Other consumer manufacturing	2.4	1.4	0.8	0.8	1.1	1.5	1.4	
Unclassified	27.7	19.0	8.8	11.8	15.5	12.9	15.7	

Source: Computed from M. R. Dohan, "Export Specialization and Import Dependence in the Soviet Economy, 1970–77," in U.S. Congress, Joint Economic Committee, *Soviet Economy in a Time of Change* (Washington, D.C.: U.S. Government Printing Office, 1979), vol. 2, pp. 370–371, and *Vneshniaia torgovlia SSSR v 1982 g.* [Foreign trade of the USSR in 1982], p. 19.

Table 38 THE STRUCTURE OF SOVIET IMPORTS (PERCENTAGES)

	1950	1955	1960	1965	1970	1975	1977	1982
Machinery	21.5	30.2	29.7	33.4	35.1	33.2	37.5	34.4
Fuels and energy	11.5	8.1	4.2	2.5	2.0	3.9	3.6	4.6
Metals, ores, minerals	15.1	16.6	17.0	10.0	10.7	12.5	10.2	9.9
Chemicals, fertilizer, rubber	6.9	3.4	6.0	6.2	5.7	4.7	4.4	4.4
Construction products	1.4	0.6	0.8	0.7	0.4	0.3	0.4	n.a.
Forest products, paper	3.9	3.0	1.8	1.9	2.2	2.1	1.8	1.5
Fibers	7.8	5.4	6.4	4.4	4.8	2.4	2.7	1.5
Agricultural raw materials	0.4	2.2	2.2	1.0	2.0	1.4	1.7	1.6
Grain and oilseed	1.0	0.8	1.0	5.0	1.1	7.4	3.4	
Sugar	3.1	2.8	2.3	3.8	3.4	5.9	6.1	
Other foodstuffs	11.9	16.3	9.7	12.0	11.1	9.1	10.2	
Cloth, clothing, shoes	5.6	3.8	13.8	9.3	12.3	8.9	8.6	43.6
Small consumer durables	0.07	0.2	0.5	0.2	0.3	0.1	1.4	
Other consumer manufacturing	1.7	0.8	3.0	4.7	5.7	3.9	4.2	
Unclassified	6.5	5.5	1.5	5.0	3.0	4.0	5.0	

Source: Computed from M. R. Dohan, "Export Specialization and Import Dependence in the Soviet Economy, 1970–77," in U.S. Congress, Joint Economic Committee, *Soviet Economy in a Time of Change* (Washington, D.C.: U.S. Government Printing Office, 1979), vol. 2, pp. 370–371; and *Vneshniaia torgovlia SSSR v 1982 g.* [Foreign trade of the USSR in 1982], p. 18.

1970s? This question remains unresolved at this time because of the difficulty of translating foreign trade prices into domestic prices. What is clear is that the 1970s witnessed a dramatic increase in foreign trade volume, starting from extremely depressed rates in the immediate postwar period.

The structure of Soviet imports and exports has been planned largely by administrative decree throughout the era of central planning. There is no strong reason, therefor, to expect the observed Soviet pattern of trade to correspond to its relative resource endowments. It is thus interesting to find that the Soviet Union does appear to have the pattern of trade one would expect of a capitalist country having the relative resource endowments of the USSR.[40]

TRADE IN SOVIET ECONOMIC DEVELOPMENT

Western trade theory suggests that with varying resource availabilities in different countries, specialization of production and exchange with other countries can serve to promote economic development. According to such theorizing, during the early stages of modernization, an LDC should export those goods and services in which it has a comparative advantage, and it should utilize export earnings to finance imports of those goods and services needed for industrialization that would be produced at high relative cost domestically. As the economy grows more sophisticated over a long period of time, it will be able to substitute domestic production for imports and lessen its dependence upon trade.

The role of trade in Soviet economic development was discussed seriously in the Industrialization Debate of the 1920s, with the right wing of the party emphasizing the comparative cost advantages of international trade. The trade strategy eventually adopted by Stalin during the forced industrialization of the 1930s rejected traditional comparative advantage principles and called for a policy of isolation from the outside world. It was argued that socialism could be "built in one country," without reliance on the capitalist world, and the Soviet Union's use of trade during the 1930s represents a case study of an industrialization that had only minimal reliance on other economies. We now examine the role played by foreign trade during the early years of Soviet economic development.

A hallmark of Soviet economic development over the years has been the emphasis on self-sufficiency as a desirable economic goal. Self-sufficiency was most prominent during the 1930s, when trade proportions were negligible, but the policy of trade aversion has been continued into the postwar era. Soviet reasoning in support of self-sufficiency has already been described (capitalist encirclement, planning uncertainty, etc.), and the Soviet leadership's vision of capitalist world markets as chaotic underscored the theoretical legitimacy of trade aversion.

Possibly more important than such theoretical considerations was the Soviet development strategy of treating agriculture as a low-priority sector throughout the 1930s. Thus, the very nature of Soviet development strategy prohibited extensive reliance upon foreign trade. As Bukharin had argued, a prosperous peasantry was the key to expanding trade; once the collectivization decision was made, the Soviet Union's role as a major supplier of grain and animal products to the world market was effectively terminated. Moreover, the Soviet economy of the 1930s had certain basic features that could support a minimal role for the foreign sector. With a favorable and varied resource base, a political mechanism to enforce high internal saving rates, and a reasonable scale for heavy industrial development from which to begin in 1928, substantial reliance upon foreign products and capital could be avoided. In particular, the existence of a state monopoly in foreign trade enabled the Soviet authorities to avoid noncritical imports (a pressing problem for many present-day LDCs) and to focus upon those imports most crucial for economic growth—in particular, machinery and equipment and associated technology. Strict controls over the flow of exports and imports allowed the promotion of specific industrialization goals with relatively low foreign trade volumes.

Soviet trade patterns prior to 1917 were, as Franklyn Holzman has pointed out, "what one would have expected from such a nation."[41] Exports were primarily agricultural products or semifabricates, while imports were mostly producers goods and raw materials. In 1913, for example, 60 percent of Russian exports were agricultural, 34.4 percent were raw materials and semifabricates, while 27 percent of imports were consumer goods, the remainder being raw materials and producer goods.[42]

Although trade was important in the period prior to 1900—for example, between 1886 and 1890, 46 percent of Russian wheat production was exported—this importance declined immediately prior to the revolution, due in large part to the onset of World War I. In addition, what had previously been a favorable balance-of-payments position—commodity exports typically exceeding commodity imports offset by capital inflows—was sharply reversed by 1917. The portion of grain output exported during World War I declined sharply, as did the foreign exchange earnings on this grain, largely due to growing competition in the world grain market.[43] In addition, while imports initially declined, by 1917 they were once again increasing, thus leading to an unfavorable Russian trade position and the expansion of Russian debts abroad.

From the relatively low levels of the immediate prerevolutionary period, the volume of Soviet foreign trade increased quite significantly between 1917 and 1928. However, the prerevolutionary trade level was not regained by 1928; trade volume that year was well below 50 percent of the 1913 level (Table 35). The instigation of the industrialization drive in that year significantly altered Soviet thinking on appropriate trade patterns and levels.

During the first three years of the first Five Year Plan (1928–1933), the volume of both Soviet exports and imports increased significantly. Thus, the volume of exports (1913 = 100) increased from 37.7 in 1928 to a high of 61.4 in 1931 while the volume of imports increased at a more rapid rate from 49.4 in 1928 to a high of 82.4 in 1931, declining thereafter (Table 35). The expansion of imports was directed almost exclusively to meeting the needs of heavy industry. In 1932, 66 percent of machine tools, 55 percent of metal cutting tools, and 77 percent of turbines and generators were imported.[44] Equipment was imported for two purposes: to generate electricity and to build other machines. In light of this significant expansion of foreign trade during the first Five Year Plan, it may well be that Soviet planners did not, in fact, initially plan to pursue a deliberate policy of autarky, rather that later economic events forced them into that course. The volume of Soviet foreign trade declined very sharply after the conclusion of the first Five Year Plan, but this trend was in some part the result of a collapse in world markets (especially grain prices) brought on by the world depression of the 1930s.[45]

After the onset of the depression, the prices of Soviet exports and imports declined significantly, though the rate of decline of the former greatly outstripped that of the latter. The index of the prices of Soviet exports fell from 100 in 1929 to 48.7 in 1931, while the prices of Soviet imports declined from 100 in 1929 to 68 in 1931. The result of these price changes was a substantial decline in the Soviet commodity terms of trade.[46]

Although the significant increase in the volume of trade during the first Five Year Plan must be considered important to the initial industrialization effort, the decline in the terms of trade must have been an important factor—in addition to ideological and strategy considerations—in leading the Soviet economy toward a different role for the foreign sector. After the first Five Year Plan, the volume of Soviet foreign trade declined sharply and steadily, increasing again only after World War II. For example, the share of exports in national income declined from 10.4 percent in 1913 to 0.5 percent in 1937.[47] Thus, at the peak of the forced industrialization drive of the late 1930s, the Soviets were operating a virtually autarkic economy. It was not until the early 1950s that the volume of trade turnover exceeded that of 1913, despite the fact that national income had been expanding at a rapid rate since 1928. Thus, the Soviet Union represents a case study of a country that was able to generate rapid growth of output and substantial shifts in the structure of output in the direction of heavy industry with only modest levels of industrial imports. Since the early 1950s, there has been a moderation of the Soviet policy of autarky as practiced during the 1930s, so that now it is more appropriate to speak of trade aversion rather than autarky.

SOVIET FOREIGN TRADE: PROSPECTS FOR THE FUTURE

In this chapter, we have examined the role of foreign trade in the Soviet economy. In addition to looking at the long-term role of foreign trade in the Soviet development experience, we have also investigated postwar trends in the organization and execution of foreign trade. In light of the Soviet long-term experiences with foreign trade, what are the events and forces that will shape the Soviet foreign economy in the late 1980s and the 1990s?[48]

In the past, foreign trade has not been a particularly important element in the overall Soviet economy. However, Soviet institutional arrangements—in particular, the state monopoly over foreign trade—have greatly facilitated the ability of Soviet planners to direct trade toward the fulfillment of state objectives—in particular, the importation of advanced technology.

In recent years, as with other sectors of the economy, Soviet authorities have sought to improve the mechanisms for the conduct of trade, many of which have outlived their usefulness in an era of increasing domestic economic complexity and diversity. Soviet authorities have sought to bring more rationality into foreign trade decisions via foreign trade efficiency indexes, and there are signs of erosion of the complete control of the Ministry of Foreign Trade over foreign transactions.[49] Export manufacturers and ministries are gaining more direct access to foreign exchange and to foreign markets. If foreign trade is to be used more effectively in the future, the price may be a loosening of central control over trade and a resubjection of the Soviet domestic economy to the "chaotic" forces of capitalist markets.[50] It remains to be seen whether Soviet political authorities will be willing to pay this price.

There is little doubt that the events of recent years, and especially of the decade of the 1970s, represent a Soviet reappraisal of the appropriate role for foreign trade in the Soviet economy. The 1970s were a period of reform and change. In addition to the changing internal factors affecting Soviet trade, turbulent forces in the world economy—notably the sharp rise in petroleum prices—and in international affairs contributed to the Soviet reappraisal. Evidence presented by Vladimir Treml suggests that the Soviets may be in the process of abandoning their traditional policy of trade aversion. In our view, it would be premature to make this argument. From the viewpoint of Soviet authorities, there would be substantial costs to such a move. The planned Soviet economy would become increasingly subject to the ups and downs of capitalist markets and to political decisions by its adversaries to withhold products (grain, high technology) required by the plan. Yet these costs may ultimately be viewed smaller than the alternatives—namely, significant reform of domestic industry and agriculture.

Soviet trade with some countries, notably the United States, remains small and one-sided, with little U.S. interest in Soviet goods. This experience is, to some degree, a function of the peculiar relations between the two superpowers. It is, however, also a function of much more basic forces, the nature of which will change only very slowly in the late 1980s. These forces—for example, the problems of the quality, design, serviceability, and financing of Soviet exports—are familiar to Western observers of the Soviet scene. Such problems—in addition to the traditional difficulty of Western business participation in the Soviet environment, problems of security, and so on—will limit the growth of trade in the late 1980s.

Finally, the Soviet Union is itself a large and potentially rather self-sufficient nation. While the desire to stimulate better agricultural and industrial performance through trade is strong, it is at the same time balanced by the reluctance to let outside economic events influence the planned Soviet economy as Soviet political objectives are pursued in the external world. Whether or in what ways this balance may change in the late 1980s will depend largely upon the ability of the Soviet leaders and their planned economy to withstand two sorts of pressures: those from outside, as world economic arrangements and realities change, and those from inside, as Soviet consumers increasingly demand that their ruble incomes be able to purchase more and better consumer goods and services. These issues, and, in particular, the general role of foreign trade and the impact of technology transfer from the West, will be considered in more detail in a later chapter.

REFERENCES

1. For a general discussion of foreign trade in centrally planned economies, see F. D. Holzman, *International Trade Under Communism* (New York: Basic Books, 1976); and A. A. Brown, "Towards a Theory of Centrally Planned Foreign Trade," in A. A. Brown and E. Neuberger, eds., *International Trade and Central Planning* (Berkeley and Los Angeles: University of California Press, 1968), pp. 57–93. For a survey of the literature and basic issues, see F. D. Holzman, *Foreign Trade Under Central Planning* (Cambridge, Mass.: Harvard University Press, 1974), chap. 1. For details of organizational arrangements, see V. P. Gruzinov, *The USSR's Management of Foreign Trade* (White Plains, N.Y.: M.E. Sharpe, 1979). For details of recent organizational changes, see S. Bozek, "The U.S.S.R.: Intensifying the Development of Its Foreign Trade Structure," in Joint Economic Committee, *Soviet Economy in a Time of Change* (Washington, D.C.: U.S. Government Printing Office, 1979), vol. 2, pp. 506–525; and H. S. Gardner, *Soviet Foreign Trade: The Decision Process* (Boston: Kluuer-Nijhoff, 1983).
2. For more detail on financial arrangements, see G. Garvy, *Money, Financial Flows, and Credit in the Soviet Union* (Cambridge, Mass.: Ballinger, 1977), pp. 152–155.
3. This discussion is based on L. J. Brainard, "Soviet Foreign Trade Planning," in U.S. Congress, Joint Economic Committee, *Soviet Economy in a New Perspective* (Washington, D.C.: U.S. Government Printing Office, 1976), pp. 695–708; V. G. Treml, "Foreign Trade and the Soviet Economy: Changing Parameters and Interrelationships," in E. Neuberger and L. Tyson, eds., *Transmission and Response: The Impact of*

International Disturbances on the Soviet Union and Eastern Europe (New York: Pergamon Press, 1980); H. Levine, "The Effects of Foreign Trade on Soviet Planning Practices," in A. A. Brown and E. Neuberger, eds., *International Trade and Central Planning* (Berkeley and Los Angeles: University of California Press, 1968), pp. 255–276; and *Metodicheskie ukazaniia k razrabotke gosudarstvennykh planov ekonomicheskogo i sotsial'nogo razvitia SSSR* [Methodological directives to working out the state plan of economic and social development of the USSR] (Moscow: Ekonomika, 1980), chap. 25.

4. Treml, "Foreign Trade." This surplus is the consequence of overvalued exchange rates used to translate *valuta* ruble prices into domestic prices and the rise in the world prices of Soviet raw material exports.

5. For empirical evidence on this point, see, for example, P. R. Gregory, *Socialist and Nonsocialist Industrialization Patterns* (New York: Praeger, 1970), pp. 119–120; and F. L. Pryor, *The Communist Foreign Trade System* (Cambridge, Mass.: MIT Press, 1963), chap. 1. According to Treml, "Foreign Trade," the Soviets in the 1970s abandoned their "policy of trade aversion" and now have a trade share of national income of 21 percent. The confusion lies in the manner of translating Soviet trade data in *valuta* rubles into domestic prices, and there is much controversy over this issue. On this controversy, consult Treml, *ibid.,* footnote 1.

6. The tendency toward self-reliance (autarky) on the part of Soviet enterprises and ministries has been chronicled by G. E. Schroeder, "The Soviet Economy on a Treadmill of 'Reforms,' " in U.S. Congress, Joint Economic Committee, *Soviet Economy in a Time of Change* (Washington, D.C.: U.S. Government Printing Office, 1979), vol. 1, pp. 335–336; and by D. Granick, *Soviet Metal Fabricating and Economic Development* (Madison: University of Wisconsin Press, 1967).

7. P. G. Ericson, "Soviet Efforts to Increase Exports of Manufactured Products to the West," in U.S. Congress, Joint Economic Committee, *Soviet Economy in a New Perspective* (Washington, D.C.: U.S. Government Printing Office, 1976), pp. 709–727; H. H. Kravalis et al., "Soviet Exports to the Industrialized West: Performance and Prospects," in U.S. Congress, Joint Economic Committee, *Soviet Economy in a Time of Change* (Washington, D.C.: U.S. Government Printing Office, 1979), vol. 2, pp. 414–462.

8. F. D. Holzman, "Some Theories of the Hard Currency Shortages of Centrally Planned Economies," in U.S. Congress, Joint Economic Committee, *Soviet Economy in a Time of Change* (Washington, D.C.: U.S. Government Printing Office, 1979), vol. 2, pp. 297–316.

9. P. G. Ericson and R. S. Miller, "Soviet Foreign Economic Behavior: A Balance of Payments Perspective," in U.S. Congress, Joint Economic Committee, *Soviet Economy in a Time of Change* (Washington, D.C.: U.S. Government Printing Office, 1979), pp. 208–243.

10. For a discussion of the long-term impact of exchange rate prices, see F. D. Holzman, "The Ruble Exchange Rate and Soviet Foreign Trade Pricing Policies, 1929–1961," *American Economic Review,* vol. 57, no. 4 (September 1968), 807–812. For a discussion of how ruble-dollar exchange rates are determined, see Garvy, *Money, Financial Flows, and Credit,* chap. 7.

11. For discussions of FTEIs, consult L. Brainard, "Soviet Foreign Trade Planning," pp. 701–707; C. H. McMillan, "Some Recent Developments in Soviet Foreign Trade Theory," *Canadian Slavonic Papers,* vol. 12, no. 3 (Fall 1970), 243–272; A. Boltho, *Foreign Trade Criteria in Socialist Economies* (Cambridge: Cambridge University Press, 1971).

12. The members of COMECON are Bulgaria, Cuba (since 1972), Czechoslovakia, the German Democratic Republic, Hungary, Poland, Rumania, Mongolia, and the Soviet Union. For a more extensive discussion of bloc trade, see M. Kaser, *COMECON, Integration Problems of the Planned Economies,* 2nd ed. (London: Oxford University Press, 1967); F. L. Pryor, *The Communist Foreign Trade System* (Cambridge, Mass.: MIT Press, 1963), J. M. van Brabant, *East European Cooperation: The Role of Money and Finance* (New York: Praeger, 1977); and E. A. Hewett, *Foreign Trade Prices in the Council for Mutual Economic Assistance* (Cambridge: Cambridge University Press, 1974).

13. For discussions of the degree of integration of the COMECON countries, see J. Pelzman, "Trade Integration in the Council for Mutual Economic Assistance: Creation and Diversion, 1954–1970," *ACES Bulletin,* vol. 18, no. 2 (Fall 1976), 39–60; and J. van Brabant, "Trade Creation and Trade Diversion in Eastern Europe: A Comment," *ACES Bulletin,* vol. 19, no. 1 (Spring 1977), 79–98.

14. For a discussion of one particular but important case, see J. Michael Montias, *Economic Development in Communist Rumania* (Cambridge, Mass.: MIT Press, 1967), chap. 4. Also see J. M. Montias, "Socialist Industrialization and Trade in Machinery Products," in A. A. Brown and E. Neuberger, eds., *International Trade and Central Planning* (Berkeley and Los Angeles: University of California Press, 1968), pp. 130–158.

15. For a discussion of recent developments in the process of integration, see M. Bornstein, "East-West Economic Relations and Soviet-East European Economic Relations," in U.S. Congress, Joint Economic Committee, *Soviet Economy in a Time of Change* (Washington, D.C.: U.S. Government Printing Office, 1979), vol. 1, pp. 291–311; A. Smith, "The Council for Mutual Economic Assistance in 1977: New Economic Power, New Political Perspectives, and Some Old and New Problems," in U.S. Congress, Joint Economic Committee, *East European Economies Post-Helsinki* (Washington, D.C.: U.S. Government Printing Office, 1977), pp. 152–173; and M. Lavigne, "The Soviet Union Inside Comecon," *Soviet Studies,* vol. 35, no. 2 (April 1983), 135–153.

16. For in-depth discussions, see van Brabant, *East European Cooperation,* chaps. 3 and 4; and M. Kohn and N. Lang, "The Intra-CMEA Foreign Trade System: Major Price Changes, Little Reform," in U.S. Congress, Joint Economic Committee, *East European Economies Post-Helsinki* (Washington, D.C.: U.S. Government Printing Office, 1977), p. 137.

17. M. Marrese and J. Vañous, *Soviet Subsidization of Trade with Eastern Europe: A Soviet Perspective* (Berkeley: University of California Institute of International Studies, 1983); J. Brada, "Soviet Subsidization of Eastern Europe: The Primacy of Economics over Politics," *Journal of Comparative Economics,* vol. 9 no. 1 (March 1985), 80–85.

18. For a detailed discussion of these issues, see R. Dietz, "Price Changes in Soviet Trade with CMEA and the Rest of the World Since 1975," in U.S. Congress, Joint Economic Committee, *Soviet Economy in a Time of Change* (Washington, D.C.: U.S. Government Printing Office, 1979), vol. 1, pp. 263–299; Bornstein, "East-West Economic Relations," pp. 299–308.

19. For a survey of Soviet economic and military aid, see O. Cooper and C. Fogarty, "Soviet Economic Military Aid to the Less Developed Countries, 1954–78," in U.S. Congress, Joint Economic Committee, *Soviet Economy in a Time of Change* (Washington, D.C.: U.S. Government Printing Office, 1979), vol. 2, pp. 648–662, and especially Appendix Table 1. For worldwide data, see National Foreign Assessment Center, *Handbook of Economic Statistics 1979,* ER79–10274, Washington, D.C., August 1979, pp. 110–126.

20. Cooper and Fogarty, "Soviet Economic Military Aid," Appendix Table 4.
21. National Foreign Assessment Center, *Handbook of Economic Statistics 1979*, p. 125.
22. *Ibid.*, pp. 118–119.
23. For a discussion of theoretical issues underlying the hard-currency debt, see Holzman, "Some Theories of the Hard Currency Shortages," pp. 297–316. For measurement, see Ericson and Miller, "Soviet Foreign Economic Behavior," pp. 208–243; Bornstein, "East-West Economic Relations," p. 297; and J. Zoeter, "USSR: Hard Currency Trade and Payments," U.S. Congress, Joint Economic Committee, *Soviet Economy in the 1980s,* part II (Washington, D.C.: U.S. Government Printing Office, 1982), p. 494.
24. For a discussion of the role of agriculture in Soviet foreign trade, see D. M. Schoonover, "Soviet Agricultural Trade and the Feed-Livestock Economy," in U.S. Congress, Joint Economic Committee, *Soviet Economy in a New Perspective* (Washington, D.C.: U.S. Government Printing Office, 1976), vol. 2, pp. 813–821. For recent developments, see D. M. Schoonover, "Soviet Agricultural Policies," in U.S. Congress, Joint Economic Committee, *Soviet Economy in a Time of Change* (Washington, D.C.: U.S. Government Printing Office, 1979), vol. 2, pp. 103ff, and J. G. Goldich, "U.S.S.R. Grain and Oilseed Trade in the Seventies," in U.S. Congress, Joint Economic Committee, *Soviet Economy in a Time of Change* (Washington, D.C.: U.S. Government Printing Office, 1979), pp. 133–164.
25. Zoeter, "USSR: Hard Currency Trade," p. 494.
26. For a background of U.S.-Soviet trade and commercial relations, see Holzman, *International Trade Under Communism,* pp. 159–173. For a survey of recent developments, see H. W. Heiss, A. J. Lenz, and J. Brougher, "United States-Soviet Commercial Relations Since 1972," in U.S. Congress, Joint Economic Committee, *Soviet Economy in a Time of Change* (Washington, D.C.: U.S. Government Printing Office, 1979), vol. 2, pp. 189–207; and M. Goldman, "Interaction of Politics and Trade: Soviet-Western Interaction," U.S. Congress, Joint Economic Committee, *Soviet Economy in the 1980s,* part I, pp. 117–128; Cooper, "Soviet Western Trade," in same volume, pp. 454–478.
27. For a discussion of this issue, see E. A. Hewett, "Most-Favored Nation Treatment in Trade Under Central Planning," *Slavic Review,* vol. 37, no. 1 (March 1978), 25–39; H. Raffel, M. Rubin, and R. Teal, "The MFN Impact on U.S. Imports from Eastern Europe," in U.S. Congress, Joint Economic Committee, *East European Economies Post-Helsinki* (Washington, D.C.: U.S. Government Printing Office, 1977), p. 1427.
28. For useful background, see J. Brougher, "USSR Foreign Trade: A Greater Role for Trade with the West," in U.S. Congress, Joint Economic Committee, *Soviet Economy in a New Perspective* (Washington, D.C.: U.S. Government Printing Office, 1976), pp. 677–694; Ericson, "Soviet Efforts to Increase Exports," pp. 709–726.
29. For a recent discussion of compensation agreements, see D. J. Barclay, "U.S.S.R.: The Role of Compensation Agreements in Trade With the West," in U.S. Congress, Joint Economic Committee, *Soviet Economy in a Time of Change* (Washington, D.C.: U.S. Government Printing Office, 1979), vol. 2, pp. 462–481.
30. M. Smith, "Industrial Cooperative Agreements: Soviet Experience and Practices," in U.S. Congress, Joint Economic Committee, *Soviet Economy in a New Persepctive* (Washington, D.C.: U.S. Government Printing Office, 1976), pp. 767–785; C. H. McMillan, "East-West Industrial Cooperation," in U.S. Congress, Joint Economic Committee, *East European Economies Post-Helsinki* (Washington, D.C.: U.S. Government Printing Office, 1977), pp. 1175–1224.

31. This discussion is based upon C. H. McMillan, "Soviet Investment in the Industrialized Western Economies and in the Developing Economies of the Third World," in U.S. Congress, Joint Economic Committee, *East European Economies Post-Helsinki* (Washington, D.C.: U.S. Government Printing Office, 1977), pp. 625–647; C. H. McMillan, "Growth of External Investments by the COMECON Countries," *World Economy,* vol. 2, no. 3 (September 1979), 363–386.

32. F. D. Holzman, "Foreign Trade," in A. Bergson and S. Kuznets, eds., *Economic Trends in the Soviet Union* (Cambridge, Mass.: Harvard University Press, 1963), pp. 291–300.

33. *Ibid.,* p. 297.

34. *Ibid.,* p. 296.

35. It is important to recognize that the shift in trade patterns during the first Five Year Plan not only provided producer goods so necessary for the immediate expansion of output but also—and this may be the more crucial factor—provided prototypes of the best Western technology that could then be duplicated. For a discussion of the role of Western technology during the early years, see A. C. Sutton, *Western Technology and Soviet Economic Development 1930 to 1945* (Stanford, Calif.: The Hoover Institution, 1971).

36. A. Bryne, J. Cole, T. Brickerton, and A. Malish, "US-USSR Grain Trade," in *Soviet Economy in the 1980s,* part 2, p. 75.

37. For an elaboration, see Bozek, "The U.S.S.R.: Intensifying the Development of Its Foreign Trade Structure."

38. M. R. Dohan, "Export Specialization and Import Dependence in the Soviet Economy, 1970–77," in U.S. Congress, Joint Economic Committee, *Soviet Economy in a Time of Change* (Washington, D.C.: U.S. Government Printing Office, 1979), vol. 2, p. 369. There is controversy over the share of imports of national income, with Treml, "Foreign Trade," Table 1, estimating the import share much above Dohan and other researchers. The share figures cited in Table 35 are those of Treml for the years 1955 to 1976.

39. Treml, *ibid.*

40. S. Rosefielde, "Factor Proportions and Economic Rationality in Soviet International Trade," *American Economic Review,* vol. 64, no. 4 (September 1974), 670–680.

41. See Holzman, "Foreign Trade," p. 284.

42. *Ibid.*

43. *Ibid.,* p. 286.

44. *Ibid.,* p. 290.

45. For a discussion of the role of foreign trade in the preplan and early planning years, see M. R. Dohan, *Soviet Foreign Trade in the NEP Economy and Soviet Industrialization Strategy,* unpublished doctoral dissertation, Massachusetts Institute of Technology, 1969.

46. Holzman, "Foreign Trade," pp. 287–288.

47. *Ibid.,* pp. 289–290.

48. For an examination of trends and prospects, see L. J. Brainard, "Foreign Economic Constraints on Soviet Economic Policy in the 1980s," in U.S. Congress, Joint Economic Committee, *Soviet Economy in a Time of Change* (Washington, D.C.: U.S. Government Printing Office, 1979), vol. 1, pp. 98–109.

49. Treml, "Foreign Trade."

50. For a series of papers on this subject, see Neuberger and Tyson, *Transmission and Response.*

SELECTED BIBLIOGRAPHY

G. Adler-Karlsson, *Western Economic Warfare: 1947–1967* (New York: Humanities Press, 1968).

A. Boltho, *Foreign Trade Criteria in Socialist Economies* (Cambridge: Cambridge University Press, 1971).

J. C. Brada, ed., *Quantitative and Analytical Studies in East-West Economic Relations* (Bloomington: Indiana University Press, 1976).

A. A. Brown and E. Neuberger, eds., *International Trade and Central Planning* (Berkeley and Los Angeles: University of California Press, 1968).

R. Campbell and P. Marer, eds., *East-West Trade and Technology Transfer* (Bloomington, Ind.: International Development Research Center, 1974).

M. R. Dohan, *Soviet Foreign Trade in the NEP Economy and Soviet Industrialization Strategy,* unpublished doctoral dissertation, Massachusetts Institute of Technology, 1969.

Z. Fallenbuchl and C. H. McMillan, eds., *Partners in East-West Economic Relations: The Determinants of Choice* (London: Pergamon Press, forthcoming).

H. S. Gardner, *Soviet Foreign Trade: The Decision Process* (Boston: Kluwer-Nijhoff, 1983).

M. I. Goldman, *Soviet Foreign Aid* (New York: Praeger, 1967).

G. Grossman, "U.S.-Soviet Trade and Economic Relations: Problems and Prospects," *ACES Bulletin,* vol. 15, no. 1 (Spring 1973), 3–22.

V. P. Gruzinov, *The USSR's Management of Foreign Trade* (White Plains, N.Y.: M.E. Sharpe, 1979).

E. A. Hewett, *Foreign Trade Prices in the Council for Mutual Economic Assistance* (Cambridge: Cambridge University Press, 1974).

————, "Most-Favored Nation Treatment in Trade Under Central Planning," *Slavic Review,* vol. 37, no. 1 (March 1978), 25–39.

F. D. Holzman, "East-West Trade and Investment Policy Issues," *United States International Economic Policy in an Interdependent World* (Washington, D.C.: U.S. Government Printing Office, 1971), pp. 363–395.

————, "Foreign Trade," in A. Bergson and S. Kuznets, eds., *Economic Trends in the Soviet Union* (Cambridge, Mass.: Harvard University Press, 1963), pp. 283–332.

————, "Foreign Trade Behavior of Centrally Planned Economies," in H. Rosovsky, ed., *Industrialization in Two Systems: Essays in Honor of Alexander Gerschenkron* (New York: Wiley, 1966).

————, *Foreign Trade Under Central Planning* (Cambridge, Mass.: Harvard University Press, 1974).

————, *International Trade Under Communism* (New York: Basic Books, 1976).

M. Kaser, *COMECON: Integration Problems of the Planned Economies,* 2nd ed. (London: Oxford University Press, 1967).

C. H. McMillan, ed., *Changing Perceptives in East-West Commerce* (Lexington, Mass.: Heath, 1974).

A. Malish, Jr., *United States-East European Trade: Considerations Involved in Granting Most-Favored-Nation Treatment to the Countries of Eastern Europe* (Washington, D.C.: United States Tariff Commission, Staff Research Studies, no. 4, 1972).

P. Marer, *Soviet and East-European Trade (1946–1969): Statistical Compendium and Guide* (Bloomington: Indiana University Press, 1972).

M. Marrese and J. Vañous, *Soviet Subsidization of Trade With Eastern Europe: A Soviet Perspective* (Berkeley: University of California Institute of International Studies, 1983).

J. M. Montias, *Economic Development in Communist Rumania* (Cambridge, Mass.: MIT Press, 1967), chap. 4.

F. L. Pryor, *The Communist Foreign Trade System* (Cambridge, Mass.: MIT Press, 1963).

J. Quigley, *The Soviet Foreign Trade Monopoly: Institutions and Laws* (Columbus: Ohio State University Press, 1974).

G. A. Smith, *Soviet Foreign Trade: Organization, Operations, and Policy, 1918–1971* (New York: Praeger, 1973).

A. C. Sutton, *Western Technology and Soviet Economic Development 1917 to 1930* (Stanford, Calif.: The Hoover Institution, 1968).

——, *Western Technology and Soviet Economic Development 1930 to 1945* (Stanford, Calif.: The Hoover Institution, 1971).

——, *Western Technology and Soviet Economic Development 1945 to 1965* (Stanford, Calif.: The Hoover Institution, 1973).

V. G. Treml, "Foreign Trade and the Soviet Economy: Changing Parameters and Interrelationships," in E. Neuberger and L. Tyson, eds., *Transmission and Response: The Impact of International Disturbances on the Soviet Union and Eastern Europe* (New York: Pergamon, 1980).

U.S. Congress, Joint Economic Committee, "Foreign Economic Activities," in *Soviet Economy in a New Perspective* (Washington, D.C.: U.S. Government Printing Office, 1976), part 3.

——, "Foreign Economic Activities," in *Soviet Economy in a Time of Change* (Washington, D.C.: U.S. Government Printing Office, 1979), vol. 2, Part 4.

——, "Foreign Economic Relations," in *East European Economies Post-Helsinki* (Washington, D.C.: Government Printing Office, 1977), part 3.

——, "Foreign Economy," in *Soviet Economic Prospects for the Seventies* (Washington, D.C.: U.S. Government Printing Office, 1973), part 7.

——, *Soviet Economy in the 1980s: Problems and Prospects* (Washington, D.C.: U.S. Government Printing Office, 1982), papers by Goldman, Bryne et al., and part VIII.

J. M. van Brabant, *East European Cooperation: The Role of Money and Finance* (New York: Praeger, 1977).

J. Wilczynski, *The Economics and Politics of East-West Trade* (New York: Praeger, 1969).

P. J. D. Wiles, *Communist International Economics* (Oxford: Blackwell, 1968).

T. Wolf, *U.S. East-West Trade Policy* (Lexington, Mass.: Heath, 1973).

three

SOVIET ECONOMIC GROWTH AND PERFORMANCE

chapter *11*

Soviet Economic Growth and Performance

How well the Soviet economy has performed relative to other economies is an important question. In fact, this is ultimately what the study of differing economic systems is all about: which economic organization seems to function the "best"? Although we recognize that it is risky to generalize from the performance of one economy to the performance of the system,[1] that is, to treat Soviet economic performance as representative of the command socialist system as a whole, we compare the performance of the Soviet command economy with that of industrialized market economies in this chapter. Of special interest are the comparisons between the USSR and the United States, despite the different levels of development of the two countries. This is not to deny that other comparisons, such as the USSR with West Germany or Japan, are just as relevant.[2] The United States and the Soviet Union are nonetheless the world's two largest economic powers, with fairly equal population sizes. Considerable research has already gone into Soviet-American comparisons, and the Soviets themselves tend to judge their economic performance relative to that of the United States. In this chapter, we emphasize long-run performance and concentrate on secular trends. The often considerable variation around the secular trend is not considered in detail.[3]

In comparing the economic performance of countries, there are two major problems. First, it is often difficult to measure the various economic performance criteria in an unambiguous manner. For example, measures of economic growth —frequently used performance criteria—are often dramatically affected by the choice of price weights—the index number problem. Thus, direct comparisons of growth rates tend to be difficult to interpret. It is difficult to evaluate the relative growth performance of countries, although one can narrowly define economic growth in rather specific terms. It is even more difficult to measure less easily quantifiable performance criteria, such as environmental quality or dynamic efficiency.

The second major problem is even more difficult to come to grips with. In view of the multitude of possible performance criteria—economic growth, environmental quality, efficiency of resource utilization, relative standards of living, equity of income distribution, military power, and so on—how can one rank the performance of one economy relative to another unless one economy outperforms the other in all categories? As an example, let us assume that the Soviet economy has outperformed the American economy in terms of growth and equity of income distribution, but that the United States economy has outperformed the USSR in all other categories. Which country deserves the higher overall rating? This depends, of course, on the relative importance of the various performance criteria, which is a matter of individual judgment, not of objective economics.[4]

In sum, there seems to be no unambiguous way to objectively evaluate the performance of one economy relative to another except in obvious (and rare) cases where one outperforms the other in all categories. Given, however, the widespread interest in performance evaluation, what can be done? Our answer is to examine the performance of the Soviet economy and market economies in terms of what we consider the most important performance criteria; the reader can then supply his or her own subjective weights to aggregate the individual performance indicators. In this chapter, we deal with the "conventional" economic success indicators commonly used to assess economic performance: economic growth; static and dynamic efficiency; the equity of the distribution of income; consumer welfare, including both private and public goods; and economic stability (or security). Less conventional indicators of economic performance—military strength, environmental quality, and technological change—will be considered in the following chapter. The stroke of our pen is quite broad: how well has the Soviet economy performed in each of these areas during the era of central planning (a time span encompassing almost 60 years) vis-à-vis the long-term performance of the industrialized capitalist countries? The time horizon of each comparison is dictated by the availability of data, and some series do not go back past World War II, but our objective is to assess the entire plan era with broad data aggregates. Shorter-term performance is considered in the final chapter.

SOVIET ECONOMIC GROWTH

Although it is not widely recognized, measures of the long-term growth of real GNP are sensitive to the choice of constant price weights. If one measures the growth rate of an economy that has successfully transformed itself into an advanced industrial country, the computed real growth rate will often be much higher if constant preindustrialization prices are used as weights. This phenomenon is called *index number relativity,* or the "Gerschenkron Effect," after Alexander Gerschenkron, who analyzed it in his study of Soviet industrial production.[5]

Although the explanation of index number relativity might seem a digression to the reader, we attempt to provide an explanation of this phenomenon because of its importance in evaluating USSR growth, especially during the 1930s. Moreover, index number effects play important roles in the assessment of Soviet military power (Chapter 12) and of the size of Soviet GNP relative to other countries.

An intuitive account of index number relativity would be as follows. In the course of industrialization, a negative correlation exists between the rates of growth of sector outputs and the rates of growth of sector prices. The fastest growing sectors—machinery, electricity, transportation equipment—all tend to experience *relative* declines in prices (relative to the prices of the slowly growing sectors, such as food products and textiles) as advanced technology is introduced and economies of scale are achieved. Thus, if constant preindustrialization prices are used, the most rapidly expanding sectors will receive large relative weights, whereas the other sectors will receive small relative weights. Conversely, if post-industrialization prices are used, the rapidly expanding sectors will receive small relative price weights (which reflect the reductions in their relative prices), and the other sectors will receive large relative price weights. The same logic would apply to comparisons of the relative size of the total output of two countries, one "industrialized," the other "backward." The industrialized country produces larger relative volumes of "advanced" goods, whose relative prices are low, and produces relatively small volumes of "traditional" goods, whose relative prices are high. The backward country produces relatively large volumes of traditional goods at relatively low prices and relatively small volumes of advanced goods at relatively high prices. If the relative output of the two countries is calculated using the prices of the advanced country, the differential will be smaller than if the prices of the backward country were used. A hypothetical example is supplied in the accompanying note to assist the reader.[6]

This may seem quite academic to the reader, but Soviet 1976 GNP was three-quarters that of the United States in *dollar* prices but one-half that of the United States in *ruble* prices. Moreover, the annual growth rate of Soviet real GNP between 1928 and 1937, as calculated by Abram Bergson, was 11.9 percent using the preindustrialization prices of 1928 and 5.5 percent when calculated in postindustrialization prices of 1937.[7] The complexity of the question is increased when one realizes that comparable estimates of American growth in preindustrialization prices, say, of the 1800s, are not available.[8] What, then, is the "true" growth rate (or relative GNP) of the Soviet Union or of the United States? There is, in fact, no single "true" growth rate. Instead, there is a whole series of growth rates, one for each set of price weights, which yield a *range* of growth rates. Fortunately, for purposes of intercountry comparisons, truly significant differences arise only when comparing growth rates computed using pre- versus postindustrialization prices, owing to the large structural changes that occur during industrialization. Differences between growth rates in constant postindustrialization or constant preindustrialization prices tend to be smaller. Nevertheless, index number relativity continues to operate in industrialized countries, but only to a smaller degree.

With these reservations in mind, we shall contrast "comparable" Soviet and Western growth rates; in other words, we shall concentrate on growth rates that employ "late" year (postindustrialization) price weights. This method, however, does not eliminate all biases resulting from index number problems but acts instead only as a crude adjustment. The cited Soviet growth rates have been estimated by American economists who have recalculated Soviet GNP using Western GNP definitions[9] to ensure the comparability of Soviet and American rates.[10] For reference purposes, we include the official estimates of growth rates of Soviet *net material product,* which differs from the standard Western concept by its exclusion of services not directly connected with physical production.

In Table 39, we supply annual growth rates of tsarist GNP (1885–1913), of Soviet real GNP during the plan era (1928–1983), and of the United States between 1834 and 1984. The Soviet figures to 1950 are based on the estimates by Abram Bergson, which are the most widely accepted Western estimates of Soviet growth. Bergson's figures are available through 1958. Estimates of the Central Intelligence Agency (CIA) are available for the entire postwar era and are used to extend the Bergson series.[11]

What conclusions can be drawn from Table 39 concerning Soviet growth performance relative to that of the United States? First, it is obvious that Soviet growth since 1928 has been more rapid than American growth during the same period. The average annual growth rate of the Soviet economy between 1928 and 1984 was 4.3 percent, whereas the rate for the United States between 1929 and 1984 was 3.1 percent. If one measures Soviet growth only during "effective years,"[12] that is, if one eliminates the war years, Soviet growth rises to 4.8 percent, 1.7 percentage points above the American annual growth rate.

Second, the Soviet growth rate during the postwar period (1950–1984) of 4.4 percent exceeded the comparable American rate of 3.4 percent (1950–1984) —a difference of 1.0 percentage points annually.

Third, Soviet growth in the postwar period has been declining, from a high of 6.0 percent between 1950 and 1960 to 3.7 percent between 1970 and 1980 and dropping further to a rate of 2 percent between 1980 and 1984. During this latter period, the worst growth years were 1963 (2.2 percent), 1969 (2.3 percent), 1972 (2.0 percent), and 1975 (1.7 percent).[13] As the table shows, growth was quite slow from 1980 to 1984. In each year, growth failed to exceed 2 percent. This declining growth rate has had a depressing effect upon the long-term Soviet growth rate, which is a combination of relatively rapid growth from 1928 to 1940 and from 1950 to 1960 and relatively slower growth after 1960. As the Soviet growth slowdown continues, the growth rate differential between the United States and the Soviet Union has declined.

Fourth, the official Soviet estimates of the growth of net material product in constant prices are much larger than the American estimates of Soviet growth using Western GNP concepts and different price weights. Such differences are greatest when comparing the 1928–1940 period, part of which is explained by the Soviets' use of preindustrialization 1926–1927 prices until 1950.[14] From the Soviet viewpoint, this is more than a matter of academic interest; it is difficult to determine how much Soviet growth has actually declined in recent years because

Table 39   LONG-TERM GROWTH OF GNP IN THE USSR AND THE UNITED STATES (ANNUAL RATES OF GROWTH)

USSR	American estimates	Official Soviet estimates (net material product)
1885–1913	3.3[c]	—
1928–1940	5.4[a]	14.6[d]
1950–1960	6.0[c]	10.1
1960–1970	5.1[c]	7.0
1970–1980	3.7[c]	5.3
1980–1984	2.0[c]	3.2
1928–1984	4.3[b]	8.8
1928–1984, effective years	4.8[b]	9.7
1950–1984	4.4[c]	7.6

United States	1860 prices	1929 prices	1958 and 1972 prices
1834–1843 to 1879–1888	4.4	—	—
1879–1888 to 1899–1908	3.7	3.8	—
1899–1908 to 1929	—	3.4	—
1929–1950	—	—	2.5
1950–1960	—	—	3.3
1960–1970	—	—	3.9
1970–1984	—	—	3.0
1929–1984	—	—	3.1
1950–1984	—	—	3.4

Sources: A. Bergson, *The Real National Income of Soviet Russia Since 1928* (Cambridge, Mass.: Harvard University Press, 1961), p. 210; H. Block, "Soviet Economic Performance in a Global Context," in U.S. Congress, Joint Economic Committee, *Soviet Economy in a Time of Change* (Washington, D.C.: U.S. Government Printing Office, 1979), vol. 1, p. 135; P. Gregory, *Russian National Income, 1885–1913,* (Cambridge: Cambridge University Press, 1982). Table 1; A. L. Vainshtein, *Narodny dokhod Rossii i SSSR* [The national income of Russia and the USSR] (Moscow: Statiska, 1969), p. 119; *Narodnoe khoziaistvo SSSR v 1983 g.* [The national economy of the USSR in 1983], (Moscow: Statistika, 1979), pp. 31–33; National Foreign Assessment Center, *Handbook of Economic Statistics 1984,* ER79–10274, Washington, D.C., August 1984, p. 22; *The Economic Report of the President* (selected years); *Dostizheniia sovetskoi vlasti za 40 let v tsifrakh* [The accomplishments of the Soviet regime over 40 years in numbers] (Moscow: 1957), p. 327; R. Gallman, "Gross National Product in the United States, 1834–1909," *Output, Employment and Productivity in the United States after 1800* (New York and London: National Bureau of Economic Research, 1966), p. 26. The 1984 USSR figures are based on preliminary Soviet figures.

[a] 1950 prices.
[b] Combined index, 1950 prices 1928–1950, 1970 prices thereafter.
[c] 1970 weights.
[d] 1926–1927 prices.
[e] 1913 prices.

the earlier rate (1928–1940) is difficult to interpret. Another cause of the differences between American and Soviet estimates is the Soviets' omission from net material product of selected service categories (such as passenger transportation, government employees, lawyers, housing), which have been among the slowest growing sectors in the Soviet Union.

Fifth, United States growth rates during early periods of industrial transformation are closer to the Soviet plan period rates than are the twentieth-century American rates. Thus, the American economy grew 4.4 percent annually between 1834–1843 and 1879–1888, which is 1 percentage point less than the Soviet rate

during the 1928–1940 period and is roughly equal to the Soviet 1950–1984 rate.*
In fact, the United States growth rate of 6.6 percent during the 1869–1878 to
1879–1888 period exceeded the Soviet 1928–1940 rate.

Sixth, whereas the Soviet growth rate of 6.0 percent between 1950 and 1960
was rapid by international standards, it was by no means unprecedented among
the major industrial powers during this period. The annual West German growth
rate between 1950 and 1960 was 7.8 percent, and the Japanese rate for the same
period was almost 9 percent.[15] It may not be a coincidence that those major
industrial powers that suffered the most extensive wartime destruction also experienced the most rapid growth rates in the immediate postwar period. More
important, both Japan and West Germany (especially Japan) have been able to
sustain high rates of growth after 1960, in contrast to the USSR's declining rate
of growth. Since 1970, the USSR growth rate has been only slightly above that
of Western Europe.

Seventh, Soviet growth rates during the plan era well exceeded the growth
rate during the "industrialization era" of the tsarist period (1885–1913). In fact,
the long-run Soviet growth rate during 1928–1984 was roughly 50 percent above
the 1885–1913 rate. Thus, the Soviet period has seen an acceleration of economic
growth. If the decline in the Soviet growth rate continues, however, the difference
between the tsarist and Soviet growth rates could become negligible. In fact, the
Soviet growth rate after 1970 (3.3 percent) is identical to growth during the late
tsarist period.

Eighth, Soviet growth between 1928 and 1984 exceeded the long-term
growth rates of the other industrialized economies, including the United States
(Table 40). Only the long-term Japanese growth rate (4.5 percent) roughly equals
the Soviet 1928–1984 rate. The above comparison does, however, assume that the
1928–1984 Soviet rate was indeed the long-term growth rate of the Soviet economy, although it is computed using a much shorter time period than the other
rates. This assumption may eventually not prove to be the case, in view of the
declining Soviet growth pattern. For the other countries, however, there seems
to be no consistent difference between early-period and late-period rates,[16] so
perhaps the shorter Soviet period does not distort our overall conclusion that the
long-term Soviet growth rate is the highest recorded (along with Japan's). We
emphasize that we are dealing with long-term rates, which conceal the fact that
growth rates as high or higher than the long-term Soviet rate have been attained
by many of these countries (Japan, the United States, Germany, and others)
during various subperiods in the past.

Thus, we conclude that Soviet economic growth during the plan era was
more rapid than American growth throughout the twentieth century and was
more rapid than the long-run growth of other industrialized countries—except

---

*In these comparisons, we use early-year price weights for the United States (1860 prices) and
late-year price weights for the USSR—a seeming violation of the principle stated above. Index number
relativity does not show up in these calculations for the United States, probably because of different
calculating methods used by Gallman (the 1860 price estimates) and Kuznets (the 1929 price estimates). Note that for the same period (1879–1888 to 1899–1908), the 1929 price weights yield a higher
growth rate (Table 35).

Table 40 LONG-TERM GROWTH OF GNP OF SELECTED COUNTRIES (AVERAGE ANNUAL GROWTH RATE)

United Kingdom	1855–1864 to 1984	2.1
France	1831–1840 to 1984	2.4
Belgium	1900–1904 to 1984	2.2
Netherlands	1860–1870 to 1984	2.5
Germany (West Germany after 1945)	1850–1859 to 1984	2.8
Denmark	1865–1869 to 1984	3.0
Sweden	1861–1869 to 1984	3.0
Italy	1895–1899 to 1984	2.8
Japan	1874–1879 to 1984	4.5
United States	1834–1843 to 1984	3.4
Canada	1870–1874 to 1984	3.5
USSR	1928 to 1984	4.3–4.8

Sources: S. Kuznets, *Economic Growth of Nations* (Cambridge, Mass.: Harvard University Press, 1971), pp. 11–14; and Table 39. The Kuznets figures are updated from *Handbook of Economic Statistics 1984,* p. 22, and *Economic Report of the President,* February 1985, p. 356.

Japan. Soviet growth during the 1950s was rapid but was surpassed by the two other major industrial powers—West Germany and Japan—which had also suffered extensive war damage. Only during its period of industrial transformation did American growth approach the Soviet rate during the plan era. Soviet growth was also above the growth rate of the tsarist economy after 1885. These conclusions are probably sufficiently general not to be notably affected by the index number problem and the other measurement problems mentioned above.

Let us now turn to a deeper question: to what extent was the rapid Soviet growth a consequence of the Soviet economic system per se or of other special factors unrelated to the system? This is a fundamental issue in appraising alternative systems, for we are interested in the merits of the system independent of special circumstances.[17] In this regard, certain special factors probably affected long-run Soviet growth performance. First, the Soviets industrialized late and could, therefore, borrow more advanced technology from the West. Second, the large Soviet population, concentrated as it was in agriculture at the beginning of the plan era, provided, as we have seen, a plentiful supply of labor for industry. Economies of scale could, therefore, be achieved in the course of Soviet industrialization without diminishing the marginal productivity of capital. On the negative side, Soviet agricultural resources were limited relative to population, with only a small proportion of land suitable for cultivation.[18] Although it is impossible to weigh the impact of each of these factors on Soviet growth, one can speculate that the Soviets' borrowing of more advanced technology was an important factor in explaining rapid growth, especially during the 1930s and the immediate postwar period.

Special factors aside, to what extent was the more rapid Soviet growth a product of the Soviet system of central planning and political dictatorship? It would seem that much of the superior Soviet growth performance can be explained by the substitution of growth-oriented planners' preferences for consumer sovereignty. In this manner, the state was able to opt for a pattern of development conducive to rapid economic growth by planning high investment and labor participation rates and by expanding the education of the labor force. In the case of educational levels, for example, in 1926 only 6 percent of the over-15-year-old population (of 89 million) had received education beyond the seventh grade. By 1959, this percentage had risen to 39 percent (of 148 million).[19] The high investment ratios (Chapter 4) and labor participation rates (Chapter 8) have already been discussed.

The growth bias of Soviet planning can be illustrated by comparing the pattern of Soviet growth (the growth of household consumption vis-à-vis gross investment) with that of the United States (Table 41). The major difference between the two is the much more rapid growth of investment than consumption in the USSR as opposed to the more rapid growth of consumption—with the exception of the very early 1834–1888 period and the period 1970–1984—in the United States. The most extreme case of this is the negligible growth of household consumption in the USSR between 1928 and 1937, a period when investment was expanding at over 14 percent annually. Although investment expanded more rapidly than consumption in the United States between 1834 and 1888 and between 1970 and 1984, the extreme differences noted in the Soviet case were avoided. This growth orientation is also reflected in the differential growth pattern of the various originating sectors of Soviet GNP (Table 42). The consumption-oriented sectors (trade, services, and agriculture) expanded more slowly than total output in the USSR, whereas in the United States they have expanded (during the period in question) at roughly the same rate as GNP, with the exception of agriculture.

DYNAMIC EFFICIENCY AND THE GROWTH OF PRODUCTIVITY

A second criterion for evaluating the performance of economies is *dynamic efficiency,* which "relates to the community's capacity to add to its technological knowledge and to exploit such knowledge with increasing effect."[20] We use this criterion in addition to economic growth because, as we just noted, the Soviet Union deliberately adopted a rapid growth strategy of high investment rates, high labor participation rates, borrowing of more advanced technology, and rapid expansion of education and training. Thus, one would be surprised if the Soviets had *not* attained relatively high rates of economic growth. This is not to detract from their growth achievement, but just to place it in its proper perspective.

Theory

In such a case, dynamic efficiency might prove a useful second performance criterion, for it measures the rate at which a country is able to increase the efficiency of resource utilization over time, that is, the rate of increase of the amount of output derived from a given amount of factor inputs. Dynamic efficiency can be measured only imperfectly and indirectly. Its most common measure is the rate of growth of output per unit of *combined* factor inputs.[21] A less general measure would be the rate of growth of output per unit of labor (or

Table 41   DIFFERENTIAL GROWTH PATTERNS: GNP BY FINAL USE, USSR AND UNITED STATES (ANNUAL GROWTH RATES)

	Household consumption	Gross investment	GNP	(1 ÷ 2)
USSR				
1928–1937[a]	0.7	14.5	5.5	0.05
1950–1955[a]	8.7	8.7	7.6	1.00
1958–1964[b]	4.8	7.4	5.9	0.65
1965–1969[f]	6.2	6.8	4.9	0.91
1970–1980[g]	3.1	4.8	3.2	0.64
1928–1955[a]	2.8	7.9	4.8	0.35
United States				
1834–1843 to 1879–1888[c]	4.0	6.5	4.4	0.62
1879–1888 to 1899–1908[d]	3.8	3.8	3.8	1.00
1899–1908 to 1914–1923[d]	3.1	3.0	3.1	1.03
1929–1950[e]	2.7	2.6	2.6	1.04
1950–1970[e]	3.6	2.0	3.6	1.80
1970–1984[h]	3.3	4.3	3.0	.77
1929–1984[e]	3.2	2.9	3.1	1.10

Sources: Bergson, *The Real National Income of Soviet Russia,* p. 210; A. Becker, *Soviet National Income 1958–1964* (Berkeley: University of California Press, 1969), p. 256; *USSR: Measures of Economic Growth and Development, 1950–80,* pp. 66–67. S. Kuznets, *National Product Since 1869* (New York: National Bureau of Economic Research, 1946), table II-16; R. Gallman, "Gross National Product in the United States, *Output, Employment and Productivity in the United States After 1800,* (New York and London: National Bureau of Economic Research, 1966), pp. 26–34; *The Economic Report of the President* (Washington, D.C.: U.S. Government Printing Office, 1985); S. H. Cohn, "The Economic Burden of Defense Expenditures," in *Soviet Economic Prospects for the Seventies,* p. 151; Block, "Soviet Economic Performance," p. 136.

[a] 1937 ruble factor cost.
[b] 1958 adjusted factor cost.
[c] 1860 prices.
[d] 1929 prices.
[e] 1958 prices.
[f] 1955 prices.
[g] 1970 prices.
[h] 1972 prices.

capital) input. One measures the rate of growth of output per unit of input by subtracting the growth rate of the input from the growth rate of output. For example, if GNP grows at 5 percent annually and combined factor inputs grow at 3 percent annually, the annual rate of growth of output per unit of combined factor input would be 2 percent.

From this description of total factor productivity, one can see that it provides only an indirect link to dynamic efficiency because one can only imperfectly measure the rates of growth of factor inputs in both qualitative and quantitative terms. For example, it is extremely difficult to measure changes in the quality of Soviet capital and labor force relative to such changes in the United States or other countries. Further, how does one measure nonconventional inputs such as management? As a result, only conventional inputs such as land, labor, and capital can be measured and generally only in quantitative terms.[22] The danger, therefore, is that important changes in nonconventional inputs and qualitative changes of conventional inputs will be ignored, thus distorting the estimation of the growth of output per unit of input.

Table 42 ANNUAL RATES OF GROWTH: MAJOR ECONOMIC SECTORS

	USSR, 1928–1982		United States, 1947–1984	
	Sector growth	Sector growth ÷ GNP growth	Sector growth	Sector growth ÷ GNP growth
Agriculture	1.5	0.32	1.2	0.36
Industry	6.8	1.45	3.2	0.97
Construction	6.5	1.38	1.9	0.58
Transportation and communications	7.9	1.68	3.5	1.06
Trade	4.1	0.87	3.5	1.06
Services	3.8	0.81	2.5	0.76
GNP	4.7		3.3	

Sources: R. Moorsteen and R. Powell, *The Soviet Capital Stock, 1928–1962* (Homewood, Ill.: Irwin, 1966), pp. 622–624; S. H. Cohn, "General Growth Performance of the Soviet Economy," in U.S. Congress, Joint Economic Committee, *Economic Performance and the Military Burden in the Soviet Union* (Washington, D.C.: U.S. Government Printing Office, 1970), p. 17; *The Economic Report of the President,* 1985 (Washington, D.C.: U.S. Government Printing Office, 1985), p. 245; Block, "Soviet Economic Performance," p. 135; *USSR: Measures of Economic Growth and Development, 1950–80,* p. 63; *Handbook of Economic Statistics 1983,* p. 63.

The Record

In Table 43, we relate several measures of the rates of growth of factor productivity in the Soviet Union, United States, and selected other countries, both over the long run and for the postwar period. The table includes both the rate of growth of output per unit of combined (capital and labor) input (column 5) and also the growth of output per unit of specific factor input, namely, labor productivity (column 6) and capital productivity (column 7).

Looking at the long-term trends in panel A, we see that the Soviet Union distinguishes itself from the United States and other countries by a more rapid growth of both labor and capital—2.2 percent and 7.4 percent, respectively, between 1928 and 1966. This reinforces our earlier point that one would expect more rapid Soviet output growth because of the more rapid growth of inputs— thus our hesitancy to use growth as our sole performance criterion. In the USSR, about 65 percent of long-term growth (column 1 ÷ column 4, panel A) is accounted for by growth of inputs, whereas in the United States and other countries (the United Kingdom is somewhat of an exception), a much smaller portion of growth can be attributed to the growth of inputs. The significance of this pattern is that Soviet growth has tended to be quite dependent upon an expanding labor force and capital stock, rather than upon expanding output per unit of input. Thus Soviet growth has tended to be *extensive* (based upon expanding inputs) rather than *intensive* (based upon better utilization of inputs)—a rather expensive growth pattern in terms of economic costs, for capital is expanded at the expense of current consumption and labor is expanded at the cost of leisure.

The postwar trends in panel B show that Soviet input growth was indeed

Table 43 ANNUAL RATES OF GROWTH OF INPUTS AND PRODUCTIVITY: USSR, UNITED STATES, AND SELECTED COUNTRIES

Panel A: Long-term trends	(1) Output	(2) Labor, man hours	(3) Fixed capital	(4) Combined inputs	(5) Output per unit of combined input (1–4)	(6) Labor productivity (1–2)	(7) Capital productivity (1–3)
USSR (GNP) 1928–1966	5.5[a]	2.2	7.4[b]	3.5[a]	2.0	3.3	−1.9
United States (GNP) 1929–1969	3.3	0.8	2.0[b]	1.1	2.2	2.5	1.3
United Kingdom (GDP) 1925–1929 to 1963	1.9	0.8	1.8[b]	1.1	0.8	1.1	0.1
France (GDP) 1913–1966	2.3	−0.5	2.0[b]	0.2	2.2	2.8	0.3
Canada (GNP) 1926–1956	3.9	0.8	2.9[b]	1.2	2.7	3.1	1.0
Norway (GDP) 1899–1956	2.8	0.3	2.5[b]	0.7	2.1	2.5	0.3

Panel B: Postwar trends	(1) Output	(2) Employment	(3) Fixed capital	(4) Combined inputs	(5) Output per unit of combined input (1–4)	(6) Labor productivity (1–2)	(7) Capital Productivity (1–3)
USSR							
1950–1960	5.8	1.2	9.4	4.1	1.7	4.6	1.7
1960–81	4.1	1.4	7.6	3.3	0.8	2.7	−3.5
United States							
1948–1960	3.2	1.4	3.2	2.0	1.2	1.7	0.0
1960–1981	3.5	2.0	3.6	2.6	0.9	1.4	−0.1
Canada							
1960–1980	4.6	2.9	4.9	3.6	1.0	1.7	−0.3
Belgium							
1950–1962	3.2	.6	2.3	1.2	2.0	2.6	0.9
Denmark							
1950–1962	3.5	.9	5.1	2.4	1.1	2.6	−1.6

(continued on overleaf)

Table 43 (*Continued*)

Panel B: Postwar trends	(1) Output	(2) Employment	(3) Fixed capital	(4) Combined inputs	(5) Output per unit of combined input (1–4)	(6) Labor productivity (1–2)	(7) Capital Productivity (1–3)
France							
1950–1962	4.9	.1	4.2	1.5	3.4	4.8	0.7
1960–1980	4.6	.8	5.0	2.3	2.3	3.6	−0.4
West Germany							
1950–1962	7.3	2.0	6.9	3.5	3.8	5.3	0.9
1960–1980	3.8	.0	4.8	1.7	2.1	3.8	−1.0
Italy							
1950–1962	6.0	.6	3.5	1.6	4.4	5.4	2.5
Netherlands							
1950–1962	4.7	1.1	4.7	3.1	1.6	3.6	0.0
Norway							
1950–1962	3.5	.2	4.2	1.6	1.9	3.3	−0.7
1950–1980	4.7	.5	4.1	1.7	3.1	4.2	0.6
United Kingdom							
1950–1962	2.3	.7	3.4	1.7	0.6	1.6	−1.1
1960–1980	2.3	.4	3.4	1.5	0.8	1.9	−1.1
Japan							
1953–1970	10.0	1.7	9.8	4.5	5.5	8.3	0.2
1970–1980	5.0	.9	8.4	3.5	1.5	4.1	−3.4
Greece							
1960–1980	6.1	.0	6.2	2.2	3.9	6.1	−0.1

Sources: Panel A: Moorsteen and Powell, *The Soviet Capital Stock,* pp.38, 166, 315, 361–362, 365; A. Becker, R. Moorsteen, and R. Powell, *Soviet Capital Stock: Revisions and Extension, 1961–1967* (New Haven, Conn.: The Economic Growth Center, 1968), p. 11, 25, 26; Kuznets, *Economic Growth of Nations,* p. 74; E. Denison, *Accounting for United States Economic Growth 1929–1969* (Washington, D.C.: The Brookings Institution, 1974), p. 54, p. 186; B. J. Wattenberg, ed., *The Statistical History of the United States from Colonial Times to the Present* (New York: Basic Books, 1976), pp. 257–258. Panel B: *Handbook of Economic Statistics* (various years), employment; U.S. Department of Labor, *Trends in Multifactor Productivity, 1948–81,* Bul'etin 2178, September 1983, p. 22; *Growth Rates of Employment, Reproducible Capital, and Output:* E. Denison, *Why Growth Rates Differ* (Washington, D.C.: Brookings, 1967), pp. 42, 190, and chap. 21; E. Denison, *Accounting for United States Economic Growth, 1929–1969* (Washington, D.C.: The Brookings Institution, 1974), pp. 32, 58; E. Denison and W. Chung, *How Japan's Economy Grew So Fast* (Washington, D.C.: The Brookings Institution, 1976), pp. 19, 31; OECD, Department of Economics and Statistics, *Flows and Stocks of Fixed Capital, 1955–1980* (OECD: Paris, 1983), pp. 1–39; *Handbook of Economic Statistics 1980,* p. 47; *World Tables, 1982,* country tables and Table 5 (social indicators).

rapid by international standards, but it was not unique. Canada (which experienced rapid labor force growth), West Germany (rapid growth of both labor and capital), and Japan (rapid growth of labor and capital) matched the Soviet postwar growth rate of combined inputs. It is notable that in the case of West Germany (1950–1962) and Japan (1953–1970), the payoff to rapid input growth was higher (in terms of growth) than in the Soviet Union.

Can one argue that rapid input growth forced the USSR into an extensive growth pattern? The example of Japan is instructive, for Japan was able to combine rapid input growth with a relatively intensive growth pattern. Some 60 percent of Japanese postwar growth is explained by increasing output per unit of input.

Turning to the rate of growth of output per unit of combined input (panel A, column 5), we see that the long-term Soviet rate (1928 to 1966) is perhaps somewhat below, or roughly equivalent to, the long-term productivity growth rates in the United States, France, Canada, and Norway. It is difficult to generalize on the basis of such narrow differences because the impact of wartime destruction on Soviet productivity is difficult to gauge; such estimates are quite sensitive to measurement errors. As far as the postwar period is concerned, while the annual rate of growth of output per unit of combined input in the Soviet Union 1950 to 1960—1.7 percent—exceeded the American rate of 1.2 percent, it was only average as far as Western Europe was concerned; it was well exceeded by France, West Germany, and Italy and dwarfed by the Japanese rate. After 1960, the Soviet factor productivity growth rate—0.8 percent—was below all the other factor productivity growth rates, just equaling the anemic English productivity rate. It was dwarfed by the Greek and Norwegian rates.

The long-term growth of Soviet labor productivity (3.3 percent annually) is slightly above the average rates in the other countries examined (but well above that of the United Kingdom). Soviet labor productivity growth in the early postwar period was extremely rapid (4.6 percent annually) and far exceeded the American rate. It was matched by the productivity growth in France, West Germany, and Italy but was dwarfed by the Japanese rate of 8.3 percent.

After 1960, Soviet labor productivity growth dropped to 60 percent of its earlier rate. At 2.7 percent per annum, it exceeded the American and English rates, but was well below France, West Germany, Japan, and Greece. Trends in Soviet capital productivity relative to the other countries (the rate of growth of output per unit of capital input) are interesting to note. The long-term growth rate of Soviet capital productivity is −1.9 percent annually, which indicates a rising capital/output ratio over the long run. Of the surveyed countries, none has a long-term negative rate of growth of capital productivity. In the early postwar era, the Soviet Union registered healthy growth of capital productivity at 1.7 percent per annum, exceeded only by the Italian rate. After 1960, Soviet capital productivity dropped at an annual rate of −3.5 percent. Most other countries also experienced slightly negative growth of capital productivity, but only Japan matched the Soviet Union's precipitous decline.

In sum, both the long-term and postwar comparisons show Soviet dynamic efficiency, as measured indirectly by the rate of growth of output per unit of combined input, to be neither exceptionally large nor small when compared to trends in the United States and other industrialized Western countries. Instead, Soviet productivity performance could be described as average. What these figures do indicate quite clearly is the extent to which the fast Soviet growth rate may be attributable to the policy of rapidly expanding inputs. The impersonal statistics of input and output growth rates veil a very significant point concerning long-term Soviet economic growth. The relatively low proportion of output growth explained by productivity growth means that Soviet growth was of the "high cost" variety. Rapid growth rates of labor and capital occasion significant sacrifice from the population in the form of lessened consumption, leisure, and "home production." If the USSR had been able to grow as "intensively" as the industrialized market economies (let us say, two-thirds of output growth accounted for by productivity growth), then the same long-term rate of economic growth could have been achieved with considerably less sacrifice demanded of the population. The USSR-Japanese postwar productivity comparison is notable, for it illustrates this point well. Both countries experienced roughly comparable input growth rates (equal sacrifice); yet the Japanese output growth rate for the 1953-to-1980 period was almost 2 percentage points above that of the Soviet Union. One cannot argue *a priori* that the Japanese experience is representative of capitalism under conditions of rapid input growth (just as one cannot argue that the USSR is representative of command socialism), but the Japanese counterexample must be recognized.

Factors Behind the Soviet Productivity Decline

Table 43 showed the decline in Soviet combined factor productivity, labor productivity, and capital productivity after 1960. Table 44 provides more detail, breaking Soviet productivity performance down into subperiods and into individual years. It shows productivity growth for the aggregate economy (as in Table 43) and for the crucial industrial sector. The magnitude of the Soviet productivity problem is shown by the fact that combined factor productivity was negative at the economywide level between 1971 and 1975, and was negative in each year after 1975 (except for 1976). Labor productivity remained positive (except for 1979) but fell to near 1 percent or below after 1978. The factor productivity picture in industry is not any better. Combined factor productivity growth was negative between 1961 and 1965, was 1 percent or below between 1966 and 1975, and was negative in each year after 1975. Labor productivity dropped from between 3 and 4.4 percent in the period 1961 to 1975 to between 0.7 and 1.8 percent after 1975 (with the exception of 1977).

What has been the relative productivity performance of Soviet industry (the branch of highest official priority) relative to the industrialized capitalist economies? This appears to be the crucial test of the productivity performance of the Soviet planned economy. In this regard, Abram Bergson has demonstrated that even if one uses a wide range of estimates of Soviet industrial technology (encompassing all positions in the debate), the annual growth rate of productivity has been roughly equal to the disappointing records of the United States and the

Table 44 SOVIET FACTOR PRODUCTIVITY, AGGREGATE ECONOMY, AND INDUSTRY (AVERAGE ANNUAL RATES OF GROWTH)

	1961–1965	1966–1970	1971–1975	1976	1977	1978	1979	1980	1981	1982
Factor productivity, aggregate economy	0.5	1.1	−0.05	1.0	−0.1	−0.3	−2.6	−1.1	−1.6	−1.3
Labor productivity, aggregate economy	3.4	3.2	2.0	3.5	2.1	1.7	−0.8	0.6	1.2	0.9
Factor productivity, industry	−0.1	0.6	1.0	−0.9	−0.3	−0.9	−2.2	−1.1	−1.6	−1.3
Labor productivity, industry	3.5	3.1	4.4	1.8	2.6	1.6	0.7	1.7	1.6	1.5

Sources: Handbook of Economic Statistics, 1980, p. 59; 1983, p. 66.

United Kingdom (1955–1970) and well below the other industrialized countries.[23] Insofar as the growth rate of industrial output in the USSR was higher than that of the industrialized countries, this again points to a highly extensive pattern of industrial growth.

The pattern of declining factor productivity growth has been a major factor of concern to the Soviet leadership. Western scholars, along with the Soviet leadership, are interested in explaining the collapse of Soviet productivity growth. The various explanations offered have concentrated on the declining rate of growth of industrial labor productivity.

There has been a substantial debate in Western literature concerning the productivity performance of postwar Soviet industry, principally directed toward an explanation of its declining rate of growth. This discussion is highly technical and involves debates over the appropriate measurement of industrial output and the specification of Soviet industrial technology (via econometric and other methods). One explanation for the Soviet industrial productivity decline has been advanced by Martin Weitzman. Weitzman argues that the explanation lies in the difficulty of substituting capital for labor.[24] Throughout the postwar era, industrial capital has grown at a much more rapid rate than industrial labor (from 1960 to 1970, labor grew at 3 percent and capital at 10 percent per annum).[25] With such divergent rates of input growth, how successfully capital can be substituted for labor depends upon the technology ("production function") of Soviet industry. If capital can be easily substituted for labor, then these divergent rates should not impair the growth of output. If, however, it becomes increasingly difficult to substitute capital for labor (the technical measure is called the "elasticity of substitution"),* then one would expect a declining pattern of output growth. The measurement of the elasticity of substitution of Soviet industry is a complicated theoretical and econometric matter, as the debate over this issue suggests, and competing estimates have been offered, most of which suggest that Soviet indus-

---

*A simple technical explanation of the substitution problem is as follows. The increase in output (dQ) can be decomposed (assuming a linear homogeneous production function and other "usual" assumptions concerning the shape of the production function) into that increase due to increase in labor (L) and capital (K) inputs and a residual due to technical progress (T). Thus,

$$dQ = \frac{\delta Q}{\delta L}\, dL + \frac{\delta Q}{\delta K}\, dK + dT$$

Dividing through by Q yields

$$\frac{dQ}{Q} = \eta_L \frac{dL}{L} + \eta_K \frac{dK}{K} + \frac{dT}{T}$$

where

$$\eta_L = \frac{\delta D}{\delta L} \cdot \frac{L}{Q} \quad \text{and} \quad \eta_K = \frac{\delta D}{\delta K} \cdot \frac{K}{Q}$$

are the partial elasticities of output with respect to each factor input. If the elasticity of substitution is less than unity, then it follows (Weitzman, "Soviet Postwar Growth," p. 679) that η_L will increase if K grows more rapidly than L (definitely true in the Soviet case). Thus, the weight of the slower-growing factor input (L) increases over time, while that of the faster-growing input (K) declines. The growth rate of combined factor inputs declines over time, therefore partially (or fully) offsetting the decline in the rate of growth of output.

trial technology does not allow "easy" substitution of capital for labor. The whole point of this exercise is to demonstrate that the declining rate of growth of industrial output may (partially or fully) be the consequence of growing substitution difficulties rather than the result of declining productivity performance per se.

Padma Desai offers a different interpretation of declining industrial factor productivity performance. Through a careful analysis of industry and the individual industrial branches, Desai concludes that the decline in factor productivity growth is not due to the difficulty of substituting capital for labor. In fact, Desai's estimated production functions indicate that capital can be readily substituted for labor in most industrial branches. The output decline is not due to substitution difficulties but rather to a declining growth rate of the unexplained productivity differential.[26]

If Desai's interpretation is correct, the decline in the growth of the productivity residual remains to be explained. Gertrude Schroeder has analyzed the industrial productivity slowdown between 1961 and 1982 at both an industrywide and branch level and attempts to account for its precipitous decline, especially after 1975. Schroeder offers a number of explanations, not being able to single out any one as the dominant factor. First, she points to the decision of the central planners to reduce growth targets after 1976 in the hopes that reduced pressure would cause managers to use resources more efficiently. According to her analysis, this policy backfired in that output growth did indeed contract as planned but the efficiency of resource use did not improve. Second, the Soviet economy began to encounter severe shortfalls of key raw materials such as steel and coal after 1976 and was beset by transportation and energy bottlenecks as well. A third factor—the most difficult to quantify—may have been a decline in worker morale and discipline in the late years of the Brezhnev reign. Schroeder is able to rule out one factor—agricultural shortfalls—which she finds to be an insignificant factor behind the productivity slowdown.[27]

Growth and productivity slowdowns are difficult to understand in any setting. We imagine that Soviet and Western economists will never fully understand why Soviet output growth and productivity growth have declined so dramatically in recent years. The productivity slowdown is apparently so pronounced that it is readily recognized by emigrés from the Soviet Union who witnessed the productivity slowdown first-hand. They tend to blame a decline in material incentives for Soviet productivity problems.[28]

SOVIET STATIC EFFICIENCY

Not only is the changing efficiency of an economy over time—*dynamic efficiency* —a valuable performance criterion, but one might also consider its efficiency at one point in time—*static efficiency*. The two concepts are interrelated in that an economy's dynamic efficiency in the long run will determine its static efficiency at a distant point in time, and static efficiency, in turn, may have an important impact upon dynamic efficiency in the long run. In any case, the efficiency of the economy today is a matter of concern and interest. In this section, the focus is upon the static efficiency of the Soviet economy relative to that of the United States and selected other market economies.

Static efficiency is defined intuitively by Bergson as "the degree to which, *equity apart* [our italics], the community is, in fact, able to exploit the economic opportunities that are open."[27] The degree of static efficiency, therefore, will depend on the available stock of technological knowledge and on the effectiveness of its utilization, both of which serve to define the economic opportunities open to the community at a given point in time.*

How, then, is the relative static efficiency of the Soviet economy to be measured? Again, as in the case of dynamic efficiency, static efficiency can only be measured indirectly by comparing the magnitude of the output that is derived from a unit of "combined" factor inputs at one point in time. It is immediately obvious from our discussion of dynamic efficiency that such "factor productivity" comparisons measure static efficiency indirectly because inputs differ in quality, and some of them cannot be measured at all. In measuring output per unit of input at one point in time, differences in climate and soil fertility (an important factor in determining agricultural productivity), scale differences, cultural factors, and many other variables that may or may not affect productivity tend to be ignored, for they cannot readily be included.[28] There is yet another problem: to compute the relative magnitudes—as opposed to rates of growth—of output per unit of combined factor inputs suitable for intercountry comparisons, both output and factor inputs must be measured in a common unit. Soviet output must either be valued in foreign prices (American prices, for example), or the output of the other country must be valued in ruble prices. The same is true of combined factor inputs (land, labor, and capital). As we have shown, index number relativity will affect such measurements because output mixes and relative prices vary among economies, and what one country produces in abundance at relatively low prices will likely be produced in smaller quantities at relatively higher prices by another country. In this manner, the relative GNP of one country valued in its own prices will be smaller than when valued in the prices of another country.[29]

A further problem in the Soviet case is that combined factor inputs (capital, land, and labor), which are measured by the total cost of such inputs, cannot be measured directly because capital and land fail to generate rent and interest—

---

*This static efficiency concept can be illustrated in the figure below using the Production Possibilities Schedule (PPS). If the economy is operating on its PPS (point *A*), then it has attained maximum static efficiency. If it operates below the PPS (point *B*, for example), it has failed to attain maximum static efficiency. The available stock of technological knowledge will determine the location of the schedule, and an increase in this stock will move the schedule out. Thus, with an increase in the stock of technological knowledge, point *A* will now be below the new PPS, and if the economy is to remain statically efficient, it must advance to a higher point on the new PPS.

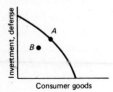

under the labor theory of value—as they do under capitalism. Therefore, "synthetic" capital charges must be computed by applying an "arbitrary" rate of return to the value of net capital stock, and the choice of this rate of return can significantly affect the outcome of factor productivity comparisons.[30]

Despite all the shortcomings noted above, we relate Abram Bergson's estimates of national income per unit of combined factor (labor and reproducible capital) input in American prices to the Soviet Union, the United States, and several European countries in 1960 (Table 45). The United States price-weighted index was chosen because Soviet factor productivity makes its best showing using this variant.

The calculations of national income per unit of factor input show that the Soviet economy in 1960 derived slightly less than 50 percent as much output per unit of combined input as did the American economy, about 65 percent as much as France, West Germany, and the United Kingdom, and slightly below the output per unit of input in Italy. When the comparison is for industry alone, the Soviet productivity ratios improve (this is reflective of the relatively poor performance of agriculture and services). USSR factor productivity in 1960 was roughly equal to that of Italy and the United Kingdom and was 80 percent that of France and West Germany. Although it is possible that a substantial portion of the computed productivity differentials could be accounted for by input quality differences[31] and by omitted factor inputs, such as land or entrepreneurship, this seems unlikely.[32]

Thus, one would have to conclude that the level of output per unit of combined capital and labor input in the Soviet Union was low relative to the other countries surveyed (except Italy) in 1960. These productivity rankings have changed significantly since 1960 (the West German ratio is likely equal to that of the United States in 1980), but the Soviet Union's ranking, as we have shown above, has not changed appreciably relative to the industrialized capitalist countries. The potential sources of low Soviet productivity have been described in Chapters 7 and 8—the managerial bonus system, irrational prices, deficient investment allocation criteria, lack of incentives to innovate and to introduce new technology—and may be more severe than the sources of economic inefficiency

Table 45   **NATIONAL INCOME PER UNIT OF COMBINED**
FACTOR (LABOR AND REPRODUCIBLE
CAPITAL) INPUTS, 1960 U.S. PRICE WEIGHTS
(UNITED STATES = 100)

	National income	Industry
United States	100	100
France	63	71
West Germany	65	69
United Kingdom	64	61
Italy	47	60
USSR	41	58

Source: Bergson, *Productivity and the Social System: The USSR and the West* (Cambridge, Mass.: Harvard University Press, 1978), pp. 101, 111.

in the industrialized West. It is interesting to note that Soviet estimates show Soviet industrial efficiency (output per production worker) to be slightly above one-half that of American industry.[33]

Just what does the low Soviet output per unit of input tell us about static efficiency in the Soviet Union? Can one attribute low productivity to weaknesses in the Soviet economic system or are factors independent of the economic system involved? On the one hand, it might be argued that low output per unit of input and low levels of economic development tend to go together, and the Soviet Union, like Italy—whose factor productivity is also low—is less developed (in terms of development indicators such as per capita income and percentage of rural population) than the other countries in Table 44. Thus, the Soviet productivity deficit should perhaps be regarded as a function of the low level of development of the Soviet Union and not as an indicator of its static inefficiency.* To determine the extent to which low Soviet static efficiency is a product of the stage of economic development requires firm information on the relationship between efficiency levels and economic development. Moreover, if one attempts to make hypothetical adjustments for the level of development, the outcome in the Soviet case depends upon which development indicator one employs. After examining this matter, Bergson concludes that "the low Soviet factor productivity does not seem fully explicable in such terms."[34] It is also not clear whether Soviet static efficiency should improve (in relative terms) as the stage of development advances, for the ability of the command economy to deal with the growing complexities of a modern economy remains to be demonstrated. The growth of Soviet factor productivity over time (Table 43) has been only average when compared with other industrialized countries; therefore, the Soviet Union does not seem to have reduced its productivity gap as it gradually closed its development gap— a result that one would expect if low productivity were solely the result of low economic development.

The low level of static efficiency in the Soviet Union has evoked considerable discussion among Western students of the Soviet economy. We summarize briefly two representative points of view. On the one side, Alec Nove and Peter Wiles,[35] both English economists, argue that the Soviets deliberately sacrificed static efficiency to achieve their long-run political objectives—the restructuring of the economy, the transformation of property relations, the expansion of military

---

*The problem of comparing the productivity performance of two countries at different levels of development is illustrated in the figure below using the Production Possibilities Schedule (PPS). The country at a higher level of development would have a higher PPS (*aa*) than the country at a lower level of development (*bb*). Thus both countries may be operating at maximum static efficiency (at points *A* and *B*), yet the computed productivity at *A* will be greater than at *B*.

Consumer goods

power, and rapid economic growth. Static efficiency, they argue, could have been achieved only at the expense of these goals, by adopting a more gradual marginalist approach and by eliminating political control over economic decisions. Thus, the static inefficiency of the Soviet economy today can be viewed as a deliberate policy decision, just as the rapid Soviet growth rate can be considered a deliberate policy choice of the Soviet leadership—with static inefficiency as the price that the Soviet leadership willingly paid for rapid economic development.

In opposition to this line of reasoning, Abram Bergson[36] argues that rapid economic development and static efficiency are not necessarily incompatible, as Nove and Wiles maintain, for an economy with greater static efficiency will produce a larger output and consequently a larger volume of savings (with the same savings rate), which will promote economic growth. Bergson does grant, however, that in a centrally planned economy, the state may opt to promote growth by autonomously increasing the savings rate through the introduction of forced savings, administrative economic controls, collectivization, and autarky—measures that may reduce static efficiency yet generate growth. If the state does so, however, it is at the expense of reduced living standards, which is in itself a significant cost to be considered in evaluating the performance of economies. According to Bergson, the basic question, therefore, should be: to what extent could similar rates of growth or slightly lower rates have been attained in the Soviet case through maximum utilization of resources (static efficiency) without sacrificing living standards?

One further aspect of the relative efficiency of the Soviet economy that fails to show up in output or input measures is that such figures often indicate output per unit of *employed* labor and capital inputs.[37] Although the Soviets do not publish aggregate unemployment figures, one can probably safely assume that aggregate unemployment in the Soviet Union is less than in the United States, where unemployment occasionally rises to 8 or 10 percent of the entire labor force, with 6 percent considered as normal. Thus, unemployment is a major source of inefficient resource utilization in the United States that the Soviets have largely avoided, although the Soviets do seem to suffer from "underemployment," as discussed in Chapter 8. In addition, capital capacity in the United States also tends to stand idle during downturns in the business cycle. On the other hand, it is difficult to predict the magnitude of the waste of capital resources in the Soviet Union that results from the stockpiling of fixed and working capital by the Soviet manager for the sake of building a safety factor and from poor choices of investment projects. In the American economy, such stockpiling adds to inventory costs and interest expenses, thereby reducing profits, and is therefore avoided as much as possible.

An even thornier issue in estimating factor productivity concerns the relative quality of output. Factor productivity measures relate the volume of output per unit of input, whereas the output measures (especially in the case of Soviet consumer goods) inadequately reflect the relative quality of output, which, according to numerous reports, is poor in the Soviet Union.[38] The production of a large quantity of defective goods using minimal inputs would show up well in factor productivity estimates, introducing a bias into such measures.

...IE DISTRIBUTION IN THE SOVIET UNION

... performance criterion for evaluating economies is how "equitably" ...me is distributed among members of the population. Of all the suggested criteria, this is the most difficult to evaluate objectively because different individuals and different societies have different views on what constitutes an "equitable" or "inequitable" distribution of income. Some may argue that income is equitably distributed when divided equally; others may argue that equity requires large income differentials to reward risk, effort, and past frugality. Income derived from ownership of property is a very thorny question; in the United States, for example, large income differences among spending units result from differences in property income as opposed to wage and salary incomes. Whether it is equitable to allow such disparities in property income is a subjective judgment, yet it is crucial when contrasting equity in the Soviet Union and the United States. In view of these issues, we suggest that the definition of "good" or "poor" income distribution must remain subjective over a fairly wide range.

The Soviets have not published much data on the distribution of income among families. This is more likely the result of the relatively low priority attached to the gathering of such information than to any official policy of secrecy. The available data on income distribution have been analyzed extensively by Alastair McCauley, Peter Wiles, Stefan Markowski, Abram Bergson, Gur Ofer, Aron Vinokur, and Murray Yanowitch.[39] Although such data are far from complete and omit important income groups (the upper strata of the state and party bureaucracy, the state farmers), they do allow the researcher to draw certain conclusions. From the evidence that is available on industrial wage income, we note that Soviet wage differentials within industrial branches between high- and low-paid workers during the 1930s and early 1950s were probably greater than in the United States, but since the mid-1950s, Soviet differentials have been narrowed substantially until they are now probably smaller than American differentials. In general, the trend in recent years has been toward the concept of "equal pay for equal work," with wages to be determined by job content—working conditions, skill requirements, on-the-job incentives—rather than by some measure of productivity, which may be viewed as an attempt to introduce more equality into Soviet wage determination.[40] Such intercountry wage differential comparisons are quite crude and inexact, but the important point is that Soviet industrial wage differentials have at times been as large as in the United States. This result is in keeping with the Marxian theory of income distribution in the transitional stage of socialism, during which the workers' contribution to society should determine their share of society's output; inequality of income distribution would only be eliminated when society attained a higher stage of socialism—a stage of absolute abundance—when distribution would proceed according to need.[41]

Beginning in the early 1930s, the Soviet leadership waged a consistent battle against "equality mongering" *(uravnilovka)*, a policy linked with utopian socialism and even Trotskyism. Indeed, during the 1930s, there was strong evidence of increasing inequality in the distribution of wage income, which persisted into

the mid-1950s. Since the mid-1950s, there has been a remarka
inequality. In 1956, the average wage earned by the top 10 perc
and salaried workers exceeded that of the bottom 10 percent
By 1981, this ratio had been reduced to 3.0. For wage earne
ratio dropped from 3.36 in 1956 to 2.63 in 1972.[42] Although
greater equality in the distribution of wage income has been jus ....gically
by the "law of reimbursement,"[43] we suspect that economic considerations—
namely, the greater supply of educated workers—served as the impetus for the
leveling of wage incomes.

Comparisons of the *overall* distribution of income in the Soviet Union with
that of other countries, both capitalist and socialist, is a risky business because
of the omission of significant groups from the Soviet data and the questionable
reliability of the data on included families.[44] With these reservations in mind, we
cite some preliminary conclusions. The first is that the distribution of income
probably became more equal between the late 1950s (1958) and the late 1960s
(1967). This conclusion follows from evidence on state employees, a group accounting for 70 percent of all employment in 1967. It would be surprising if such
a leveling had not occurred in light of the marked reduction in industrial wage
differentials during this period. The second conclusion (derived from a measure
of income distribution that does cover most, but not all, population groups) is that
the overall distribution of money income after taxes (including income earned or
retained by the farm population) in the USSR in 1967 was more unequal than
in the other planned socialist economies of Eastern Europe.[45]

Third, the USSR distribution of income is not very different from the
distributions of income in a number of industrialized capitalist countries, especially on an after-tax basis. The available evidence (gathered by Abram Bergson)
is given in Table 46 for the USSR and for a number of industrialized capitalist
countries. It should be noted that farm households are not included in the Soviet
data, an omission that probably understates income inequality. Also the incomes
of the Soviet elite are not included, but their numbers are so small that this
omission is likely not significant. As the income distributions show, the USSR
1972–1974 distribution looks very much like the Swedish, Norwegian, and U.K.
after-tax distributions. The Soviet distribution is more equal than the U.S., Aus-
tralian, French, and Canadian distributions. To quote Abram Bergson:

> Inequality in the USSR may not be much less than that in Norway and the United
> Kingdom, but is no doubt less than that in the United States and France.
> According to especially incomplete data, inequality in the USSR could some-
> times fall short of that in countries at a comparable development stage, though
> that need not be markedly so in the case of Japan.[46]

Fourth, contrary to the popular impression of the countryside, there is as
much differentiation in the distribution of income among the farm population as
among the city population.[47]

The final conclusion is a striking one: namely, the high incidence of "poverty" among the Soviet population, not only among the rural population and the

Table 46 DISTRIBUTION OF INCOME, SOVIET UNION AND WESTERN COUNTRIES, HOUSEHOLDS BY PER CAPITA HOUSEHOLD INCOME

	Income share of			
	Lowest 10%	Lowest 20%	Highest 20%	Highest 10%
USSR, nonfarm households, before tax 1967 (McAuley)	4.4	10.4	33.8	19.9
USSR, urban households, after tax 1972–1974 (Ofer–Vinokur)	3.4	8.7	38.5	24.1
All households				
Australia, 1966–1967				
'Before tax	3.5	8.3	41.0	25.6
After tax	3.5	8.3	40.9	25.5
Norway, 1970				
Before tax	3.5	8.2	39.0	23.5
After tax	4.7	10.5	35.6	22.4
United Kingdom, 1973				
Before tax	3.5	8.3	39.9	23.9
After tax	4.2	9.7	38.3	22.7
France, 1970				
Before tax	2.0	5.8	47.2	31.8
After tax	1.9	5.8	47.1	31.2
Canada, 1969				
Before tax	2.2	6.2	43.6	27.8
After tax	2.8	7.2	41.3	25.7
United States, 1972				
Before tax	1.8	5.5	44.4	28.6
After tax	2.3	6.5	42.5	26.8
Sweden, 1972				
After tax	3.5	9.3	35.2	20.5

Source: A. Bergson, "Income Inequality Under Soviet Socialism," *Journal of Economic Literature,* vol. 22, no. 3 (September 1984), pp. 1070, 1072. Bergson uses the work of McAuley, Ofer and Vinokur, and Sawyer in his comparisons. *Note:* The post-tax figures (except for Sweden) are calculated from the post-tax/pre-tax ratios for total household income (Bergson, p. 1072).

pensioners but also among nonagricultural state employees. If one takes the Soviet's own "minimum material satisfaction budget" (the MMS budget), described as containing the "volume and structure of necessaries of life required for the reproduction of labor power among unskilled workers,"[48] then, McCauley estimates, in 1967, 42 million nonagricultural employees and their dependents, 5 to 10 million state farm families, and 32 million *kolkhoznik* families had incomes at or below the MMS level. These figures add up to an astonishing 79 million persons (or one-third of the Soviet population) living at or below the minimum material satisfaction budget. Given this large proportion, it is likely that the Soviet MMS budget is a liberal estimate of contemporary subsistence norms. However, if one adopts as the poverty norm one-half of the MMS budget, in 1967 approximately 25 million Soviet citizens were living at or below the poverty level (10 percent of the population).[49] From these figures, McCauley concludes that "there are significant lacunae in the network of support provided by Soviet social welfare programs."[50]

The cited income distribution data are based upon money incomes and fail to incorporate social services provided free of charge and perquisites (the use of official cars, dachas, foreign vacations, and other fringe benefits). Moreover, they do not include the income of top government and party officials, but the number of Soviet elite is so small (maybe 0.15 to 0.3 percent of the population[51]) that their inclusion would be unlikely to change any of the above results. Moreover, most of their income comes to them in the form of payments in kind and perquisites (Katsenelinboigen's law[52]) so that it would be difficult to incorporate them in the distribution. The distribution of noncash social consumption services (primarily education, child care, and medical services) received by Soviet workers cannot be specified with any degree of precision; such information must be culled from socioeconomic studies of workers at individual factories or municipalities. From this scattered information, it appears that noncash social services form a larger percentage of total family income among low-paid workers (as would be expected) but that higher-paid workers receive larger absolute benefits.

CONSUMER WELFARE IN THE SOVIET UNION

How well an economy meets the material wants and needs of its population with its *given productive capacity* is yet another way to evaluate economic performance. By "material wants and needs" we refer to those who can be satisfied through the consumption of material goods and services; items relating to mental and spiritual well-being are omitted, even though they are potentially important in determining overall welfare.

The level of consumer satisfaction in any given country must be evaluated in terms of existing productive capacity, for countries rich in terms of productive potential would naturally be expected to provide higher living standards than poor countries. This fact should be kept in mind throughout this section.

If one attempts to measure the level of consumer satisfaction in the Soviet Union relative to that of the United States or Western Europe, one encounters difficulties. First, the most frequently used measure of the relative level of consumer satisfaction is the per capita quantities of consumer goods and services made available to the consumer. According to this standard, either per capita quantities of selected consumer goods and services or aggregate per capita consumption may be compared. Both measures have their own deficiencies, aside from the almost impossible task of measuring quality differences. If one compares per capita consumption of selected commodities, one must realize that consumption patterns vary according to the level of development and cultural differences. For example, the per capita consumption of wheat products in the Soviet Union exceeds that of the United States, but the per capita consumption of most personal services and consumer durables in the United States exceeds that of the USSR. In this example, these differences are explained to a great extent by differences in per capita income, which means that single consumption indicators can provide misleading impressions of consumer welfare. The aggregative measure—total per capita consumption—must be computed in value terms; therefore, in comparisons between two countries, the prices of one country must be used to weigh the quantities of consumer goods and services available in both countries. Yet relative consumer prices vary among countries: commodities that are important consumption items in one country (where the price is relatively cheap) tend to be unimportant in another country (where the price is relatively expensive). Thus, the relative per capita consumption level of one country will be *higher* when valued in the prices of a second country and vice versa—another example of index number relativity.

A further problem in the measurement of consumer satisfaction is that *average* consumption figures veil the underlying distribution of goods and services among the population, and the nature of this distribution has a great deal to do with the level of consumer satisfaction. Prominent Western economists have argued that relative, not absolute, consumption levels are most important in determining consumer satisfaction, for individuals tend to judge their own economic well-being relative to the standard of living of their neighbors.[53] If income is distributed fairly evenly, the chances of feeling deprived relative to someone else are smaller than if income is unevenly distributed. For example, in 1957, the average personal income of the poorest fifth of American families was about the same as the *average* income in the Soviet Union.[54] Is, then, the conclusion proper that the American poor are as "well off" as the average Soviet citizen? In terms of how well both are provisioned with physical quantities of goods and services (index number problems aside), the answer may be yes. Yet in terms of perceived welfare levels, the answer is probably no, because the American poor feel relatively deprived because of the much higher living standards around them.

The point of this discussion is that, once a relatively comfortable standard of physical subsistence is reached, absolute measures of living standards may reflect the state of mental satisfaction less than relative measures do. In the foregoing section, we noted that a surprisingly large proportion of the Soviet population does not earn an income high enough to have a minimum material satisfaction budget. Does this mean that poverty is rampant in the Soviet Union? The answer is probably no, as perceived by the Soviet populace—a population that has experienced significant increases in its level of material well-being in recent years and that would be inclined to judge its contemporary well-being relative to its past experience. Insofar as the minimum material satisfaction budget has been recognized (tolerated?) by Soviet officialdom, this reflects the dissatisfaction of committees of specialists (health officials and sociologists) with existing consumption levels, which is itself a telling point.

Another problem in evaluating Soviet consumer welfare involves the relatively large share of communal consumption in the Soviet Union. Communal consumption—for example, communal services such as health care and education, provided free of charge—accounts for a substantial share of total consumption in the Soviet Union.[55] Such services are provided free of charge and are not subject to a market test as to the value of the satisfaction they provide. In fact, their value is determined by the costs of supplying them. Thus, it is difficult to compare the consumption levels of countries having different shares of communal consumption.

The foregoing discussion points to the loose relationship between the consumption of commodities and the level of satisfaction derived therefrom; yet it is perceived satisfaction that is of most interest. Thus, it is possible to argue (as the Soviets have done) that the underprovisioning of the Soviet consumer relative to American or Western European standards does not imply lower levels of satisfaction because of the new social consciousness of the Soviet people, who will accept this as a necessary cost of building socialism and whose recognition of their patriotism enhances their perceived level of welfare. The validity of such arguments is well outside the scope of this work.

With the above reservations in mind, we present estimates of total per capita consumption in the Soviet Union (including communal services) as a percent of total per capita consumption in the United States and several other countries (Table 47). All figures are calculated in United States prices to present the Soviet figures in the most favorable light (in view of index number relativity).

The striking feature of Soviet per capita consumption is that it is quite low relative to the United States, the United Kingdom, France, and West Germany, both in 1955 and in 1970. In 1955, it was roughly one-third of the American level and one-half of the British, French, and West German levels, and was more than three-quarters of the Italian level. Between 1955 and 1970, there was a catching up in relative terms. By 1970, Soviet per capita consumption was one-half that of the United States, 60 to 70 percent that of the United Kingdom, France, and West Germany, and 86 percent that of Italy. Data are available for Japan for 1970, with the Soviet level 84 percent of the Japanese level.

We suggested above that consumer welfare must be evaluated not in terms

Table 47   **TOTAL PER CAPITA CONSUMPTION AND PER CAPITA GNP OF THE SOVIET UNION AS A PERCENT OF THE UNITED STATES AND OTHER COUNTRIES, 1955 AND 1970 (VALUED IN UNITED STATES PRICES)**

USSR as a percent of:	1955		1970	
	Total per capita consumption	GNP per capita	Total per capita consumption	GNP per capita
United States	27	36	47	60
United Kingdom	41	53	67	88
France	47	59	61	73
West Germany	48	57	69	75
Italy	79	94	86	109
Japan	—	—	84	88

Sources: U.S. Congress, Joint Economic Committee, *Economic Performance and the Military Burden in the Soviet Union* (Washington, D.C.: U.S. Government Printing Office, 1970), pp. 14, 97; United Nations, *Yearbook of National Accounts Statistics* (1978); M. Gilbert and Associates, *Comparative National Products and Price levels* (Paris: Organization for European Economic Cooperation), p. 36; Irving Kravis et al., *A System of International Comparisons of Gross Product and Purchasing Power* (Baltimore and London: Johns Hopkins University Press, 1975), pp. 11, 189; Imogene Edwards, Margaret Hughes, and James Noren, "U.S. and USSR: Comparisons of GNP," in U.S. Congress, Joint Economic Committee, *Soviet Economy in a Time of Change* (Washington, D.C.: U.S. Government Printing Office, 1979), vol. 1, pp. 378–379. The USSR-U.S. 1976 relatives are backcast to 1970, using GNP and consumption indexes.

of absolute magnitudes but relative to productive capacity. Thus, one should ask to what extent the relatively low Soviet per capita consumption is a consequence of relatively low per capita GNP. Table 47 indicates that the major portion of the low Soviet per capita consumption can be accounted for by low per capita GNP, which shows that even if the Soviets had devoted the same proportion of their resources to consumption as the other countries shown, there would still be a substantial "gap" in Soviet per capita consumption.[56] In all cases, Soviet per capita consumption compares much less favorably than per capita GNP, which shows that the Soviets directed a relatively larger share of total resources to nonconsumption items such as investment and defense, and this was, of course, an administrative decision. In the Japanese case, the difference is small because of the similar allocation of resources in Japan and the USSR. As Table 48 indicates, the Soviets devote a much larger share of GNP to investment than the major Western countries. The sole exception is Japan, which devotes only a negligible proportion of its resources to defense.

The reader should now well understand the importance of using multiple criteria to evaluate economies. The Soviet economy grew at such a rapid pace largely because it was decided to devote labor and capital resources to this pursuit. Per capita consumption remained below levels attainable from Soviet productive capacity as a consequence of these policies—thus a trade-off between growth and consumption. In a long-run sense, the two are not incompatible, for economic growth will raise productive capacity, which can eventually be used to raise consumption levels.

The structure of Soviet consumption reflects both the relatively low per capita income of the Soviet Union and the efforts of the state to educate and keep the population healthy. Relative to the United States, Soviet per capita consumption compares more favorably in necessities such as basic food products and health care than in nonnecessities such as durable goods. For example, in 1977, Soviet per capita consumption of food products was 54 percent that of the United

Table 48   GROSS INVESTMENT EXPENDITURES AS A PERCENT OF GNP, USSR AND SELECTED COUNTRIES, 1964 AND 1978 (SOVIET DATA IN FACTOR COST, OTHER DATA IN MARKET PRICES)

	1964	1978	1982
USSR	35	31	33
United States	17	16	14
France	23	21	21
West Germany	28	22	23
United Kingdom	19	18	17
Italy	22	19	21
Japan	39	33	31

Sources: A. Becker, *Soviet National Income, 1958–1964* (Berkeley: University of California Press, 1969), pp. 220, 271; National Foreign Assessment Center, *Handbook of Economic Statistics 1979,* p. 29, 1983, p. 62; World Bank, *World Tables,* 3rd ed. (Baltimore: Johns Hopkins, 1983).

States (up from 39 percent in 1955); education was 75 percent and health expenditures were 37 percent those of the United States (both down from 1955). On the other hand, expenditures for consumer durables were only 13 percent of the United States 1977 level.[57] A few individual comparisons bring this point home. In 1968, the average caloric intake of grain products and potatoes in the USSR exceeded that of the United States; yet the caloric intake of meat and fish was less than 50 percent of the United States figure, and this figure does not take quality differences into consideration—which may be substantial. In 1968, there were 412 automobiles per 1000 persons in the United States; the Soviet figure was 5 per 1000. On the other hand, in the Soviet Union, the number of doctors per person, hospital beds per person, and teachers per person exceeded that of the United States. The Soviet consumer remains relatively deprived as far as housing is concerned. The 1969 per capita availability of 77 square feet of housing space, although it represented a 20 percent improvement over 1960, was still well below the 97 square-foot minimum standard required for health and decency established by Soviet authorities.[58]

Let us now consider to what extent the Soviets have been able to reduce their per capita consumption gap between 1928 and the present. This is an important question because the current low Soviet consumption level would seem less significant if it was being steadily eliminated. We therefore compare the long-term growth rate of per capita consumption (including communal services) in the Soviet Union during the plan era with comparable United States rates (Table 49).

Table 49 indicates the very respectable performance of Soviet per capita consumption during the plan era as measured against long-term United States rates. The long-term Soviet rate of 2.7 percent (1928–1982) far exceeds the comparable rate for the United States (1.7 percent) during the same period. It

Table 49 ANNUAL RATES OF GROWTH OF PER CAPITA
CONSUMPTION: USSR, 1928–1978—UNITED STATES,
1869–1978 (INCLUDING COMMUNAL SERVICES)

USSR		United States	
1928–1982	2.7	1869–1873 to 1927–1929	2.4
1928–1937	1.1	1929–1984	1.7
1950–1969	4.5	1950–1969	2.3
1970–1982	2.2	1970–1984	2.3

Sources: J. G. Chapman, "Consumption" in A. Bergson and S. Kuznets, eds., *Economic Trends in the Soviet Union* (Cambridge, Mass.: Harvard University Press, 1963), pp. 238, 245–246; D. W. Bronson and B. S. Severin, "Consumer Welfare" in U.S. Congress, Joint Economic Committee, *Economic Performance and the Military Burden in the Soviet Union* (Washington, D.C.: U.S. Government Printing Office, 1970), p. 97; M. E. Denton, "Soviet Consumer Policy: Trends and Prospects," in U.S. Congress, Joint Economic Committee, *Soviet Economy in a Time of Change* (Washington, D.C.: U.S. Government Printing Office, 1979), vol. 1, p. 768. The Soviet figures are in 1937 factor cost for the 1928-to-1958 period and in 1955 weights for 1958 to 1969. For the period 1970–1978, 1978 prices are used. The Soviet figures are updated from 1978 to 1982 using *Handbook of Economic Statistics 1983,* p. 62. The United States figures are from *Historical Statistics of the United States, Colonial Times to 1957,* pp. 7, 144; *Statistical Abstract of the U.S., 1970,* p. xiii; *The Economic Report of the President, 1985,* p. 261. The 1869–1873 to 1927–1929 figures are in 1929 dollars. The 1929–1978 figures are in 1958 dollars.

should be noted, however, that the United States rate from the Civil War to the Great Depression (1869–1873 to 1927–1929) compares more favorably with the Soviet plan era rate. The rate of growth of Soviet consumption during the first two Five Year Plans (1928–1937) was very slow compared with the postwar rate. Thus, the fairly high long-term Soviet growth rate of per capita consumption is an average of the slow growth of per capita consumption during the 1930s and of the rapid growth of the early postwar period. Since 1970, Soviet and U.S. per capita consumption have grown at identical rates.

To sum up trends in Soviet per capita consumption, we note that per capita consumption in the Soviet Union is low compared to consumption levels in the United States and Western Europe. The major portion of the Soviet consumption gap can be accounted for by low per capita income, but some of it is attributable to the administrative decision to devote a relatively larger proportion of total resources to investment. The pattern of Soviet consumption also reflects the decision of Soviet authorities to deemphasize nonnecessities and to concentrate on essential goods and health and education, all of which are required to maintain and increase the productivity of the Soviet labor force. Looking at trends in Soviet consumption over time, one must conclude that the rate of growth of per capita consumption in the Soviet Union during the plan era has been quite respectable, exceeding comparable United States rates. Since 1970, however, Soviet per capita consumption has not grown more rapidly then the U.S. rate. Thus, since 1970, the Soviet Union has not narrowed the prevailing consumption gap.

ECONOMIC STABILITY (SECURITY) IN THE SOVIET UNION

The ability of an economic system to provide economic stability to its population is yet another indicator of economic performance. Economic stability is an amorphous concept, but it conveys the notion of "reasonable" stability of employment and real incomes. The economic stability (or security) of a nation's citizens can be threatened by declines in real output (or a declining rate of growth of real output), resulting in significant losses of jobs, and by unanticipated inflation, which leads to substantial declines in the real incomes of population subgroups. The sources of economic instability can be either internal or external. In the latter category, one would have inflation transmitted into a country from abroad or by the interruption of petroleum deliveries. Economic stability, like consumer welfare, is a relative concept. In democratic countries, the electorate will determine "acceptable" and "unacceptable" levels of economic instability. In command systems, this function will be performed by political authorities, who may allow themselves to be influenced by public opinion. Different societies will have different attitudes, determined in part by past experience. American society is said to be more tolerant of inflation than German society because of Germany's experience with hyperinflation in the 1920s.

Three empirical measures are typically employed to quantify the degree of economic instability: the unemployment rate, the rate of inflation, and fluctuations in the growth of real output. These three measures are not independent, as the well-known short-run trade-off between employment and inflation attests.

Which stability goals to pursue is, therefore, an important decision for a society to make. How well has the Soviet economy succeeded in providing economic stability, as measured by these three indicators? We begin with unemployment.

One has little notion of how much involuntary unemployment there is in the Soviet Union, as Soviet authorities claim to have "liquidated" unemployment in the early 1930s.[59] Such Soviet claims are exaggerated, for no society can completely eliminate unemployment. Frictional unemployment (the time spent unemployed while in the process of changing jobs) will be present at all times. In the Soviet Union in 1967–1968, the average period spent between jobs was 33 days for all workers and 47 days for female workers.[60] Because unemployment is said to no longer exist, there is no unemployment pay in the USSR. However, by any conceivable measure, the amount of involuntary unemployment in the Soviet Union is small relative to that of capitalist market economies.[61] Soviet law requires citizens of working age to be employed unless there are strong reasons against it; and in 1970, 92.4 percent of the working age population was either employed or engaged in full-time studies. The remaining 7.6 percent were either engaged in child care activities, incapacitated, or working on private agricultural plots.[62]

One would thus have to conclude that Soviet citizens do have a greater degree of economic security with regard to job protection. This conclusion should come as no surprise to the reader, for we have already pointed out (Chapter 8) that Soviet planners have engaged throughout the plan era in deliberate full-employment planning. Enterprises and local authorities are given quotas for hiring new entrants into the job market; national and regional planners must ensure the full utilization of labor resources. Unsuccessful enterprises are not allowed to fail, thereby eliminating a major source of job loss under capitalism. The guaranteeing of job security has not been without costs, however. Unproductive workers cannot be laid off except under extreme circumstances, even if the enterprise (which typically hoards labor anyway) desires to do so. That Soviet authorities have been willing to engage in experiments since 1967 to encourage the laying off of redundant workers, which indicates an understanding of the efficiency and incentive costs of total job security. However, the major incentive lever remains the differential wage, not the threat of dismissal.

The Soviet Union has, to this point, avoided episodes of negative real growth, unlike its capitalist competitors, who have experienced a depression in the 1930s and a series of recessions in the postwar era. The Soviet economy has, however, had "growth recessions," that is, episodes of reductions in the rate of growth; and, as we demonstrated earlier in this chapter, the rate of Soviet growth has been declining steadily in recent years. In general, the command economies of the Soviet Union and Eastern Europe, although they do experience cycles in output and trade (see reference 3), have been able to avoid the larger fluctuations suffered periodically by the capitalist world. This result is also not unexpected, given the manner in which the Soviet economy is planned and managed. Planners ensure that there is no deficiency in aggregate demand; output is credited to the enterprise (which is not permitted to fail), even if the output remains unsold. Workers continue to hold their jobs and receive their paychecks even if they are redundant. Under these circumstances, real output will continue to grow unless factor productivity declines to such an extent to offset increases in factor inputs. Thus negative real growth would require severe declines in productivity—a phenomenon that has not occurred to this point but may in the future.

The measurement of the rate of inflation in the Soviet Union is a matter of great complexity. The official retail price index claims that consumer prices were basically unchanged between 1955 and 1975. From 1970 to 1983 (a period of rapid inflation in the West), the official price indexes show only an 8.6 percent increase (0.6 percent per annum). The official wholesale price index for industrial output shows an increase of 15 percent between 1965 and 1982.[63] If accurate, these indexes reveal a remarkable degree of price stability in a period when retail prices were rising elsewhere at annual rates of from 5 to 20 percent in the West.[64] Western analysts distrust official Soviet price statistics for a variety of reasons, the most important being the lack of representativeness of included products, the omission of commodities sold in relatively free markets, the common practice of claiming nonexistent quality improvements to raise prices, and so on.[65] Moreover, Western authorities (and Soviet emigrés) point to signs of repressed inflation— queues, waiting lists, and growing savings accounts "forced" by the inadequate supplies of consumer goods—as further indicators that Soviet inflation has been grossly understated by official statistics.[66]

The relative question here is the Soviet Union's relative performance vis-à-vis the industrialized West, and there is fairly firm evidence that the Soviet inflation rate has been well below that of the West. Recalculations of official Soviet price indexes (which probably understate Soviet inflation) show retail and wholesale prices rising at some 1.5 percent annually after 1960,[67] and this rate (even if understated somewhat) is only a small fraction of the inflation rate in the industrialized capitalist nations. Such independent studies demonstrate that Soviet claims of total price stability are grossly exaggerated, but they fail to yield more than modest rates of price increase. Nor would one expect rapid inflation if the official wage series are to be believed. Between 1960 and 1983, wages rose at an annual rate of 3.6 percent.[68] It only takes an annual growth rate of labor productivity of 2.1 percent to yield an annual growth rate of unit labor costs of 1.5 percent, the inflation rate revealed by independent studies. Official Soviet wage policy over the years has been to permit wage increases equivalent to or below the rate of growth of labor productivity; thus, wage inflation as a source of inflation has been held to moderate levels. The negative growth of labor productivity in recent years should increase Soviet inflationary pressures from the cost side.

There is little doubt that repressed inflation was substantial during the period from 1929 to the mid-1950s, and individual products (automobiles, cooperative housing, imported consumer goods) remain in excess demand to the present day. Recent empirical studies of the savings behavior of Soviet households have revealed, however, that the accumulation of personal savings since the mid-1950s has followed normal patterns of rational consumer behavior and is not necessarily a sign of repressed inflation.[69] Soviet financial authorities are apparently less convinced than Western analysts on this point; these savings are regarded as postponed demand that could descend unexpectedly at any point on the consumer market or into the second economy.[70]

The fact that the Soviet economy was not caught up in the worldwide inflation of the 1970s may be regarded as justification of the long-standing pattern of trade aversion and economic independence. There are growing signs, however, that the domestic economy is coming to be influenced by capitalist inflation. The transmission mechanism is still not clearly defined, but Soviet pricing authorities now tend to pass on world market price increases of luxuries to the domestic consumer. Moreover, internal pricing decisions are influenced by world prices of machinery and oil. In general, there is an increased willingness to accept world market prices as the standard for domestic pricing decisions.[71] The point should be emphasized, however, that Soviet authorities are still in a position to insulate the domestic economy from external price disturbances if they choose to do so (for example, in the case of subsidized food prices).

SOVIET ECONOMIC PERFORMANCE: AN ASSESSMENT

There is a unifying theme in this evaluation of Soviet economic performance: the crucial role of trade-offs. Over the years, the Soviet Union has consistently "traded off" consumption (and leisure) for rapid (by international standards) economic growth. Had the Soviets adopted the input growth patterns of the West, their output growth would have been lower, *ceteris paribus*. The existence of this trade-off alone underscores the deficiencies of relying upon a single performance indicator to assess economic performance. The trade-offs are not limited to consumption and output growth, although these other trade-offs are more difficult to capture. The full employment and price stability policies of the Soviet government have likely reduced worker and management incentives and have made rational economic decision-making more difficult. Moreover, the impact of Soviet consumption policies upon incentives in general is an important unresolved issue.

The "high cost" nature of Soviet economic growth is evident from the productivity comparisons. Only one-third of Soviet output growth is accounted for by efficiency growth, whereas in the West this figure is generally in the range of two-thirds. Moreover, the declining rate of productivity growth in the Soviet Union suggests that this situation is not improving. Although one cannot argue *a priori* that the Japanese experience is representative of capitalism under conditions of rapid input growth, the Japanese case does suggest that capitalism is capable of combining rapid growth of inputs with an "intensive" pattern of growth. Had the Soviets emulated this experience, they could have achieved the same rate of growth with considerably less sacrifice.

REFERENCES

1. P. Hanson, "East-West Comparisons and Comparative Economic Systems," *Soviet Studies,* vol. 22, no. 3 (January 1971), 327–343. We have shown that the performance of the USSR economy is in many respects different from that of other planned socialist

economies. See P. R. Gregory and R. C. Stuart, *Comparative Economic Systems*, 2d. ed. (Boston: Houghton Mifflin, 1985), chap. 10.

2. A. Maddison, *Economic Growth in Japan and the USSR* (New York: Norton, 1969); A. Bergson, *Productivity and the Social System: The USSR and the West* (Cambridge, Mass.: Harvard University Press, 1978), chap. 11.

3. The reader interested in pursuing the question of cyclical instability in socialist economic systems should consult G. J. Staller, "Fluctuations in Planned and Free Market Economies," *American Economic Review,* vol. 54, no. 4, part 1 (June 1964), 385–395; O. Kyn, W. Schrettel, and J. Slama, "Growth Cycles in Centrally Planned Economies: An Empirical Test," Osteuropa Institute, Munich, working paper no. 7, August 1975; J. Goldman, "Fluctuations and Trends in the Rate of Economic Growth in Some Socialist Countries," *Economics of Planning,* vol. 4, no. 2 (1964), 89–98; C. W. Lawson, "An Empirical Analysis of the Structure and Stability of Communist Foreign Trade," *Soviet Studies,* vol. 26, no. 2 (April 1974), 224–238.

4. For a discussion of the success criteria problem, see B. Belassa, *The Hungarian Experience in Economic Planning* (New Haven, Conn.: Yale University Press, 1959), pp. 5–24. Also see A. Eckstein, ed., *Comparison of Economic Systems* (Berkeley and Los Angeles: University of California Press, 1971), parts 1 and 2; and J. M. Montias, *The Structure of Economic Systems* (New Haven, Conn.: Yale University Press, 1976), chap. 4.

5. A. Gerschenkron, "The Soviet Indices of Industrial Production," *Review of Economics and Statistics,* vol. 29, no. 4 (November 1947), 217–226.

6. For example, consider a hypothetical case in which the USSR in 1928 produced 100 "units" of textiles and 50 "units" of machinery, and that is all. The 1928 per unit prices of textiles and machinery were *1 R* and *2 R,* respectively. Assume further that in 1980, the USSR produced 200 "units" of textiles and 1000 "units" of machinery, and the prices of textiles and machinery had risen to *10 R* and *10 R,* respectively. If one values both 1928 and 1980 outputs in 1928 prices, 1980 output is *11 times* the 1928 output. If one values both 1928 and 1980 output, in 1980 prices, 1980 output is *8 times* the 1928 output. Formal analyses of the index number problem are found in R. Moorsteen, "On Measuring Productive Potential and Relative Efficiency," *Quarterly Journal of Economics,* vol. 75, no. 3 (August 1961), 451–467; and G. W. Nutter, "On Economic Size and Growth," *Journal of Law and Economics,* vol. 9, no. 2 (October 1966), 163–188.

7. A. Bergson, *The Real National Income of Soviet Russia Since 1928* (Cambridge, Mass.: Harvard University Press, 1961), p. 261. The 1976 relative GNP figures are from I. Edwards, M. Hughes, and J. Noren, "U.S. and U.S.S.R.: Comparisons of GNP," in U.S. Congress, Joint Economic Committee, *Soviet Economy in a Time of Change* (Washington, D.C.: U.S. Government Printing Office, 1979), vol. 1, p. 378.

8. Growth in the United States between 1834 and 1908 has been estimated in 1860 prices. See R. Gallman, "Gross National Product in the United States, 1834–1909," *Output, Employment and Productivity in the United States After 1800* (New York and London: National Bureau of Economic Research, 1966), pp. 3–75. These estimates are not comparable with the figures in 1929 prices cited in Table 35 because the two differ on current price estimates. Thus, these figures are not tests of the impact of index number relativity on the measurement of U.S. GNP.

9. Of course, there is the problem of valuation of Soviet GNP, because established prices often fail to reflect costs of production owing to substantial subsidies and indirect taxes. The figures cited employ the factor cost concept, which eliminates subsidies and indirect taxes. There is still a problem in that such factor costs fail to adequately reflect

capital costs, but various adjustments show that overall growth rates are not substantially altered by the inclusion of capital costs. See Bergson, *Real National Income,* p. 219. For a discussion of conceptual differences in measures of aggregate output, see J. Pitzer, "Reconciliation of Gross National Product and Soviet National Income," *NATO Colloquium* (Brussels, July 1977).

10. For studies of the availability and reliability of Soviet statistics, see V. G. Treml and J. P. Hardt, eds., *Soviet Economic Statistics* (Durham, N.C.: Duke University Press, 1972). Also see A. Bergson, "Reliability and Usability of Soviet Statistics," *The American Statistician,* vol. 7, no. 3 (June-July, 1953), 19–23.

11. The cited Bergson figures are in 1950 prices, and the CIA figures employ 1959 or 1970 weights; thus, this is a mixed index. Differences that arise as a result of the mixed weighting scheme are most likely minimal. Differences between this index and one based on the Bergson 1937 price-weighted figures (to 1958) are negligible. Individuals associated with the Rand Corporation and various governmental agencies have made contributions to the estimation of Soviet GNP using Western accounting practices. See, for example, S. H. Cohn, "General Growth Performance of the Soviet Economy," in U.S. Congress, Joint Economic Committee, *Economic Performance and the Military Burden in the Soviet Union* (Washington, D.C.: U.S. Government Printing Office, 1970); A. Becker, *Soviet National Income, 1958–1964* (Berkeley: University of California Press, 1969). The most complete source is: U.S. Congress, Joint Economic Committee, *USSR: Measures of Economic Growth and Development, 1950–80* (Washington, D.C.: U.S. Government Printing Office, 1982).

12. The practice of computing Soviet growth for "effective years" was originated by Gregory Grossman, as a suggested measure of what long-term Soviet growth might have been in the absence of the war: G. Grossman, "Thirty Years of Soviet Industrialization," *Soviet Survey* (October 1958). One could perhaps argue that the Great Depression should be omitted from computing the long-term United States growth rate, except that it could be argued that the business cycle is inherent to the capitalist system and should be included.

13. Cohn, "General Growth Performance," p. 9; H. Block, "Soviet Economic Performance in a Global Context," in U.S. Congress, Joint Economic Committee, *Soviet Economy in a Time of Change* (Washington, D.C.: U.S. Government Printing Office, 1979), vol. 1.

14. Bergson calculates Soviet growth between 1928 and 1937 as 11.9 percent annually in 1928 prices, compared with the official claim of 16.9 percent: Bergson, *The Real National Income of Soviet Russia,* p. 216. In recent Soviet publications, the official estimates of Soviet growth during the 1930s have been severely criticized as being unrealistic and inconsistent; on this, see Vainshtein, *Narodnii dokhod Rossii i SSSR,* pp. 99–108. For a further discussion of the official Soviet figures, see A. Nove, "1926/7 and All That," *Soviet Studies,* vol. 9, no. 2 (October 1957), 117–130.

15. National Foreign Assessment Center, *Handbook of Economic Statistics 1979,* p. 22; World Bank, *World Tables 1976* (Baltimore, Md.: Johns Hopkins University Press, 1976), pp. 262–263.

16. S. Kuznets, *Economic Growth of Nations* (Cambridge, Mass.: Harvard University Press, 1971), pp. 37–43.

17. On this point see Abram Bergson, "Comparative Productivity and Efficiency in the USA and USSR," in Alexander Eckstein, ed., *Comparison of Economic Systems* (Berkeley and Los Angeles: University of California Press, 1971), pp. 161–240.

18. Bergson, *The Real National Income of Soviet Russia,* p. 260.

19. N. DeWitt, "Education and Development of Human Resources: Soviet and American

Effort," in U.S. Congress, Joint Economic Committee, *Dimensions of Soviet Economic Power* (Washington, D.C.: U.S. Government Printing Office, 1962), p. 244.

20. A. Bergson, *Planning and Productivity Under Soviet Socialism* (New York: Columbia University Press, 1968), p. 52.

21. To determine the rate of growth of combined inputs—labor and capital—the individual growth rates of labor and capital, respectively, must be combined in some manner. In similar studies for Western countries, the two growth rates are generally combined by computing a weighted average, the weights being the labor and capital shares of total income. In the Soviet case, capital does not generate income; therefore, there is no real "capital share" of total income. For this reason, "synthetic" factor shares have been used for the Soviet case, based largely upon factor shares found in Western countries. For examples of the use of "synthetic" factor shares, see A. Bergson, *The Economics of Soviet Planning* (New Haven, Conn.: Yale University Press, 1964), pp. 341–343; and R. Moorsteen and R. Powell, *The Soviet Capital Stock, 1928–1962* (Homewood, Ill.: Irwin, 1966), pp. 264–266.

22. Attempts have been made to adjust for quality differences and to measure nonconventional inputs, but they rest very heavily upon rather tenuous assumptions made by the researchers themselves. See, for example, E. Denison, *Why Growth Rates Differ* (Washington, D.C.: The Brookings Institution, 1967); and E. Denison, *Accounting for United States Economic Growth 1929–1969* (Washington, D.C.: The Brookings Institution, 1974). For an attempt to adjust Soviet inputs for quality differences, see E. R. Brubaker, "The Age of Capital and Growth in the Soviet Nonagricultural Nonresidential Sector," *Soviet Studies,* vol. 21, no. 3 (January 1970), 350–359; and E. R. Brubaker, "Embodied Technology, the Asymptotic Behavior of Capital's Age, and Soviet Growth," *Review of Economics and Statistics,* vol. 50, no. 3 (August 1968), 304–311.

23. Bergson, "Notes on the Production Function," p. 124. For example, Bergson finds the range of possible rates of growth of factor productivity in Soviet industry (1955–1970) to run from 1.6 to 2.3 percent per annum, depending upon the elasticity of substitution and the method of calculating the rate of return to capital. Using the same procedures, Bergson calculates the following ranges for other countries (1955–1970): United States, 1.5 (no variation); France, 3.6–3.9; West Germany, 3.2–3.6; United Kingdom, 1.8–2.2; Italy, 4.2–4.7; Japan, 5.9–7.0.

24. This discussion was spurred by Martin Weitzman's seminal paper of 1970. See M. Weitzman, "Soviet Postwar Growth and Capital-Labor Substitution," *American Economic Review,* vol. 60, no. 4 (September 1970), pp. 676–692. Contributors to this debate are P. Desai, "The Production Function and Technical Change in Postwar Soviet Industry," *American Economic Review,* vol. 66, no. 3 (June 1976), 372–381; S. Gomulka, "Soviet Postwar Industrial Growth, Capital-Labor Substitution, and Technical Changes: A Reexamination," in Z. M. Fallenbuchl, ed., *Economic Development in the Soviet Union and Eastern Europe* (New York: Praeger, 1976); S. Rosefielde and C. A. Lovell, "The Impact of Adjusted Factor Cost Valuation on the CES Interpretation of Postwar Soviet Economic Growth," *Economica,* vol. 44 (November 1977), 381–392; S. Rosefielde, "Index Numbers and the Computation of Factor Productivity: A Further Appraisal," *Review of Income and Wealth,* forthcoming; A. Bergson, "Notes on the Production Function in Soviet Postwar Industrial Growth," *Journal of Comparative Economics,* vol. 3, no. 2 (June 1979), 116–126.

25. National Foreign Assessment Center, *Handbook of Economic Statistics 1979,* p. 65; F. D. Whitehouse and R. Converse, "Soviet Industry: Recent Performance and Future Prospects," in U.S. Congress, Joint Economic Committee, *Soviet Economy in a Time*

of Change (Washington, D.C.: U.S. Government Printing Office, 1979), vol. 1, pp. 402–422.

26. P. Desai, "Total Factor Productivity in Soviet Postwar Industry and its Branches," *Journal of Comparative Economics,* vol. 9, no. 1 (March 1985), pp. 1–23.

27. G. Schroeder, "The Slowdown in Soviet Industry, 1976–1982," *Soviet Economy,* vol. 1, no. 1 (January–March 1985), pp. 42–74.

27. Bergson, *Planning and Productivity,* p. 15. See also Joseph S. Berliner, "The Static Efficiency of the Soviet Economy," *American Economic Review,* vol. 54, no. 2 (May 1964), 480–490.

28. Hanson, "East-West Comparisons," 332–343; Bergson, *Productivity and the Social System,* pp. 95–107.

29. An illustration and explanation of this phenomenon in American-Soviet GNP comparisons is found in R. Campbell, "Problems of United States-Soviet Economic Comparisons," in U.S. Congress, Joint Economic Committee, *Comparisons of the United States and Soviet Economies* (Washington, D.C.: U.S. Government Printing Office, 1959), part 1, pp. 13–30.

30. Hanson, "East-West Comparisons," 340, argues that perhaps Soviet labor was (for the period in question, the early 1960s) in "excess supply" because of labor hoarding in industry and seasonal unemployment in agriculture. A low weight should, therefore, be attached to labor and a high weight to capital. This would raise Soviet factor productivity considerably relative to the United States because the Soviet labor force is larger than the American labor force.

31. Bergson has made adjustments for quality differences in the Soviet and American labor forces—as indicated by the larger Soviet female labor force and lower educational levels of Soviet workers. These adjustments, which are admittedly very crude, raise Soviet factor productivity relative to the United States by about 10 percentage points but fail to alter the overall conclusion of the relatively low productivity of the Soviet economy. Bergson, *The Economics of Soviet Planning,* p. 342.

32. The major source of the low factor productivity of the Soviet economy seems to be the low productivity of the commerce and service sectors. On this, see E. R. Brubaker, "A Sectoral Analysis of Efficiency Under Market and Plan," *Soviet Studies,* vol. 23, no. 3 (January 1972), 443.

33. G. E. Schroeder, "The Economic Reform as a Spur to Technological Progress in the USSR," *Jahrbuch der Wirtschaft Osteuropas* [Yearbook of Eastern European Economics], Band 2 (Munich: Gunter Olzog Verlag, 1971), p. 346.

34. Bergson, *Productivity and the Social System,* p. 104.

35. See A. Nove, "The Politics of Economic Rationality," in A. Nove, *Economic Rationality and Soviet Politics* (New York: Praeger, 1964), p. 53; and P. J. D. Wiles, *The Political Economy of Communism* (London: Blackwell, 1963), chap. 11.

36. See Bergson, *Planning and Productivity,* pp. 16–19, and *The Economics of Soviet Planning,* chap. 14.

37. Hanson, "East-West Comparisons," 338.

38. Bergson, *The Economics of Soviet Planning,* pp. 293–297, and Philip Hanson, *The Consumer in the Soviet Economy* (Evanston, Ill.: Northwestern University Press, 1968), p. 63.

39. P. J. D. Wiles and S. Markowski, "Income Distribution Under Communism and Capitalism: Some Facts About Poland, the U.K., the USA and the USSR," *Soviet Studies,* vol. 22, nos. 3 and 4 (January and April 1971), 344–369 and 487–511; P. J. D. Wiles, *Economic Institutions Compared* (New York: Halsted Press, 1977), p. 443; A. McCauley, *Economic Welfare in the Soviet Union* (Madison: University of Wiscon-

sin Press, 1979); M. Yanowitch, *Social and Economic Inequality in the USSR* (White Plains, N.Y.: M. E. Sharpe, 1977); A. Bergson, "Income Inequality Under Soviet Socialism," *Journal of Economic Literature,* vol. 22, no. 3 (September 1984), 1052–1099.

40. L. J. Kirsch, *Soviet Wages: Changes in Structure and Administration Since 1956* (Cambridge, Mass.: MIT Press, 1972), chaps. 1 and 8; M. Yanowitch, "The Soviet Income Revolution," *Slavic Review,* vol. 22, no. 4 (December 1963), reprinted in M. Bornstein and D. Fusfeld, eds., *The Soviet Economy,* 2nd ed. (Homewood, Ill.: Irwin, 1966), pp. 228–241; Bergson, *The Economics of Soviet Planning,* pp. 106–120; Wiles and Markowski, "Income Distribution," 501–507.

41. A. Bergson, "Principles of Socialist Wages," in *Essays in Normative Economics* (Cambridge, Mass.: Harvard University, Belknap Press, 1966).

42. Yanowitch, *Social and Economic Inequality,* p. 25; Bergson, "Income Inequality Under Soviet Socialism."

43. The "law of reimbursement" means that workers should receive wages sufficient to cover the normal costs of production of labor power; e.g., workers should receive sufficient income to cover their basic living requirements. Yanowitch, *Social and Economic Inequality,* pp. 27–28.

44. McCauley, *Economic Welfare,* provides surveys of the available data on Soviet income distributions. The major omitted categories are the Soviet elite and state farm families.

45. This conclusion follows from McCauley, *Economic Welfare,* p. 66; and Wiles, *Economic Institution Compared,* p. 443. Also see P. J. D. Wiles, *Distribution of Income: East and West* (Amsterdam: North-Holland, 1974), p. 48.

46. Bergson, "Income Inequality under Soviet Socialism," p. 1092.

47. McCauley, *Economic Welfare,* pp. 59–61.

48. *Ibid.,* p. 18.

49. *Ibid.,* pp. 78–88.

50. *Ibid.,* p. 74.

51. M. Mathews, "Top Incomes in the USSR," in NATO Economics Directorate, *Economic Aspects of Life in the USSR* (Brussels: NATO, 1975), pp. 131–158.

52. A. Katsenelinboigen, p. 150. Katsenelinboigen contends that the proportion of total income received in the form of perquisites increases with the responsibility of the position. He believes this is a device used by the Soviet leadership to ensure the loyalty of high officials.

53. J. Duesenberry, *Income, Saving and the Theory of Consumer Behavior* (Cambridge, Mass.: Harvard University Press, 1949).

54. J. G. Chapman, "Consumption," in A. Bergson and S. Kuznets, eds., *Economic Trends in the Soviet Union* (Cambridge, Mass.: Harvard University Press, 1963).

55. Between 1937 and 1964, communal consumption accounted for between 8 and 9 percent of Soviet GNP. In the United States, it accounts for about 3 percent (1956). See Bergson, *The Real National Income of Soviet Russia,* p. 237; Becker, *Soviet National Income,* p. 220; Chapman, "Consumption," p. 263.

56. For further evidence on the Soviet consumption "gap," see P. Gregory, *Socialist and Nonsocialist Industrialization Patterns* (New York: Praeger, 1971), p. 152.

57. Edwards, Hughes, and Noren, "U.S. and USSR," p. 385.

58. All of the above figures are from D. W. Bronson and B. S. Severin, "Consumer Welfare," in U.S. Congress, Joint Economic Committee, *Economic Performance and the Military Burden in the Soviet Union* (Washington, D.C.: U.S. Government Printing Office, 1970), pp. 97–98. For more recent figures, see National Foreign Assessment Center, *Handbook of Economic Statistics 1979,* pp. 16–17.

59. The Soviets delight in contrasting the absence of unemployment in the USSR since

October 1, 1930, with the high unemployment rates in the capitalist world. For an example, see *SSSR v tsifrakh v 1977 g.* [The USSR in figures 1977] (Moscow: Statistika, 1978), pp. 78–79.

60. McCauley, *Economic Welfare,* p. 209.
61. For an attempt to estimate the Soviet unemployment rate, see P. J. D. Wiles, "A Note on Soviet Unemployment in US Definitions," *Soviet Studies,* vol. 23, no. 2 (April 1972), 619–628.
62. D. I. Valentei and M. Liatukh, eds., *Vosproizvodstvo naseleniia sotsialisticheskikh stran* [Reproduction of population of socialist countries] (Moscow: Statistika, 1977), p. 37.
63. *Vestnik Statistiki* [Herald of Statistics], no. 9 (1983), p. 67; *Narodnoe khoziaistvo SSSR v. 1978 g.* [The National economy of the USSR in 1978] (Moscow: Statistika, 1979), pp. 138, 448. Also see the 1983 volume, p. 471.
64. National Foreign Assessment Center, *Handbook of Economic Statistics 1979,* pp. 46–47.
65. M. Bornstein, "Soviet Price Statistics," in V. G. Treml and J. P. Hardt, eds., *Soviet Economic Statistics* (Durham, N.C.: Duke University Press, 1972), pp. 355–376.
66. There is a substantial literature on this subject. See, for example, Bronson and Severin, "Consumer Welfare"; K. Bush, "Soviet Inflation," in M. Y. Laulan, ed., *Banking, Money and Credit in Eastern Europe* (Brussels: NATO, 1973); A. Katsenelinboigen, "Disguised Inflation in the Soviet Union," in NATO Economics Directorate, *Economic Aspects of Life in the USSR* (Brussels: NATO, 1975), pp. 101–109; G. E. Schroeder, "Consumer Goods Availability and Repressed Inflation in the Soviet Union," in NATO Economics Directorate, *Economic Aspects of Life in the USSR* (Brussels: NATO, 1975).
67. J. E. Steiner, *Inflation in Soviet Industry and Machine-Building and Metalworking,* Office of Strategic Research, Washington, D.C., SRM78–10142, 1978, p. 44; G. E. Schroeder and B. S. Severin, "Soviet Consumption and Income Policies in Perspective," in U.S. Congress, Joint Economic Committee, *Soviet Economy in a New Perspective* (Washington, D.C.: U.S. Government Printing Office, 1976), p. 631; M. E. Denton, "Soviet Consumer Policy: Trends and Prospects," in U.S. Congress, Joint Economic Committee, *Soviet Economy in a Time of Change* (Washington, D.C.: U.S. Government Printing Office, 1979), vol. 1, p. 766; *USSR: Measures of Economic Growth and Development, 1950–80,* p. 334.
68. *Narodnoe khoziaistvo SSSR v 1983 g.,* p. 393.
69. J. Pickersgill, "Soviet Household Saving Behavior," *Review of Economics and Statistics,* vol. 58, no. 2 (May 1976), 139–147.
70. For a discussion of current Soviet attitudes toward accumulated savings, see Schroeder and Severin, "Soviet Consumption," pp. 637–639.
71. V. G. Treml, "Foreign Trade and the Soviet Economy: Changing Parameters and Interrelationships," in E. Neuberger and L. Tyson, eds., *Transmission and Response: The Impact of International Disturbances on the Soviet Union and Eastern Europe* (New York: Pergamon, 1980).

SELECTED BIBLIOGRAPHY

Overall Evaluation Problems

B. Belassa, *The Hungarian Experience in Economic Planning* (New Haven, Conn.: Yale University Press, 1959), pp. 5–24.
A. Bergson, "East-West Comparisons and Comparative Economic Systems: A Reply," *Soviet Studies,* vol. 23, no. 2 (October 1971), 282–295.

————, *The Economics of Soviet Planning* (New Haven, Conn.: Yale University Press, 1964), chap. 14.

————, "National Income," in A. Bergson and S. Kuznets, eds., *Economic Trends in the Soviet Union* (Cambridge, Mass.: Harvard University Press, 1963), pp. 1–37.

R. Campbell et al., "Methodological Problems Comparing the US and USSR Economies," in U.S. Congress, Joint Economic Committee, *Soviet Economic Prospects for the Seventies* (Washington, D.C.: U.S. Government Printing Office, 1973), pp. 122–146.

A. Eckstein, ed., *Comparison of Economic Systems* (Berkeley and Los Angeles: University of California Press, 1971).

I. Edwards, M. Hughes, and J. Noren, "U.S. and USSR: Comparisons of GNP," in U.S. Congress, Joint Economic Committee, *Soviet Economy in a Time of Change* (Washington, D.C.: U.S. Government Printing Office, 1979), vol. 1, pp. 369–401.

P. Hanson, "East-West Comparisons and Comparative Economic Systems," *Soviet Studies,* vol. 22, no. 3 (January 1971).

V. G. Treml and D. Gallik, *Soviet Studies on Ruble/Dollar Parity Ratios,* Foreign Economic Reports, no. 4, U.S. Department of Commerce, November 1973.

V. G. Treml and J. P. Hardt, eds., *Soviet Economic Statistics* (Durham, N.C.: Duke University Press, 1972).

C. K. Wilber, "Economic Development, Central Planning, and Allocative Efficiency," *Yearbook of East-European Economics* (Munich: Günter Olzog Verlag, 1971), pp. 221–246.

Soviet Economic Growth

A. Becker, *Soviet National Income, 1958–1964* (Berkeley: University of California Press, 1969).

A. Bergson, *Productivity and the Social System: The USSR and the West* (Cambridge, Mass.: Harvard University Press, 1978), part 3.

————, *The Real National Income of Soviet Russia Since 1928* (Cambridge, Mass.: Harvard University Press, 1961).

H. Block, "Soviet Economic Performance in a Global Context," in U.S. Congress, Joint Economic Committee, *Soviet Economy in a Time of Change* (Washington, D.C.: U.S. Government Printing Office, 1979), vol. 1, pp. 110–140.

M. Bornstein, "A Comparison of Soviet and United States National Product," in M. Bornstein and D. Fusfeld, eds., *The Soviet Economy* (Homewood, Ill.: Irwin, 1962).

S. Cohn, *Economic Development in the Soviet Union* (Lexington, Mass.: Heath, 1969), chap. 7.

S. H. Cohn, "General Growth Performance of the Soviet Economy," in U.S. Congress, Joint Economic Committee, *Economic Performance and the Military Burden in the Soviet Union* (Washington, D.C.: U.S. Government Printing Office, 1970).

R. Greenslade, "The Real Gross National Product of the USSR, 1950–1975," in Joint Economic Committee, *Soviet Economy in a New Perspective* (Washington, D.C.: U.S. Government Printing Office, 1976), pp. 269–300.

Joint Economic Committee, *USSR: Measures of Economic Growth and Development, 1950–80* (Washington, D.C.: U.S. Government Printing Office, 1982).

Narodnoe khoziaistvo SSSR za 60 let [National economy of the USSR for 60 years] (Moscow: Statistika, 1977).

A. L. Vainshtein, *Narodnii dokhod Rossii i SSSR* [The national income of Russia and the USSR] (Moscow: Statistika, 1969).

Dynamic Efficiency and the Growth of Productivity

A. Bergson, "Development Under Two Systems: Comparative Productivity Growth Since 1950," *World Politics,* vol. 23, no. 4 (July 1971), 579–617.

———, *Planning and Productivity Under Soviet Socialism* (New York: Columbia University Press, 1968).

———, *Productivity and the Social System: The USSR and the West* (Cambridge, Mass.: Harvard University Press, 1978), part 3.

E. Brubaker, "Embodied Technology, the Asymptotic Behavior of Capital's Age, and Soviet Growth," *Review of Economics and Statistics,* vol. 50, no. 3 (August 1968), 304–311.

R. Moorsteen and R. Powell, *The Soviet Capital Stock, 1928–1962* (Homewood, Ill.: Irwin, 1966).

G. Schroeder, "The Slowdown in Soviet Industry, 1976–1982," *Soviet Economy,* vol. 1, no. 1 (January-March 1985), 42–74.

F. Douglas Whitehouse and Ray Converse, "Soviet Industry: Recent Performance and Future Prospects," in U.S. Congress, Joint Economic Committee, *Soviet Economy in a Time of Change* (Washington, D.C.: U.S. Government Printing Office, 1979), vol. 1, pp. 402–422.

Consumer Welfare in the Soviet Union

D. W. Bronson and B. S. Severin, "Consumer Welfare," in U.S. Congress, Joint Economic Committee, *Economic Performance and the Military Burden in the Soviet Union* (Washington, D.C.: U.S. Government Printing Office, 1970), pp. 93–99.

———, "Soviet Consumer Welfare: The Brezhnev Era," in U.S. Congress, Joint Economic Committee, *Soviet Economic Prospects for the Seventies* (Washington, D.C.: U.S. Government Printing Office, 1973), pp.-376–403.

J. G. Chapman, "Consumption," in A. Bergson and S. Kuznets, eds., *Economic Trends in the Soviet Union* (Cambridge, Mass.: Harvard University Press, 1963), pp. 235–282.

———, *Real Wages in the Soviet Union* (Cambridge, Mass.: Harvard University Press, 1963).

M. E. Denton, "Soviet Consumer Policy: Trends and Prospects," in U.S. Congress, Joint Economic Committee, *Soviet Economy in a Time of Change,* (Washington D.C.: U.S. Government Printing Office, 1979), vol. 1, pp. 759–798.

B. Q. Madison, "Social Services: Families and Children in the Soviet Union Since 1967," *Slavic Review,* vol. 31, no. 4 (December 1972), 831–852.

———, *Social Welfare in the Soviet Union* (Stanford, Calif.: Stanford University Press, 1968).

R. J. Osborn, *Soviet Social Policies: Welfare, Equality, and Community* (Homewood, Ill.: Dorsey Press, 1970).

G. E. Schroeder and B. S. Severin, "Soviet Consumption and Income Policies in Perspective," in U.S. Congress, Joint Economic Committee, *Soviet Economy in a New Perspective* (Washington, D.C.: U.S. Government Printing Office, 1976), pp. 620–660.

Economic Stability (Security) in the Soviet Union

M. Bornstein, "Unemployment in Capitalist Regulated Market Economies and Socialist Centrally Planned Economies," *American Economic Review, Papers and Proceedings,* vol. 68, no. 2 (May 1978), 38–43.

K. Bush, "Soviet Inflation," in M. Y. Laulan, ed., *Banking Money and Credit in Eastern Europe* (Brussels: NATO, 1973), 97–105.

NATO Economics, Directorate, *Economic Aspects of Life in the USSR* (Brussels: NATO, 1976), contributions by G. E. Schroeder and A. Katsenelinboigen.

J. Pickersgill, "Soviet Household Saving Behavior," *Review of Economics and Statistics,* vol. 58, no. 2 (May 1976), 139–147.

P. J. D. Wiles, "A Note on Soviet Unemployment in US Definitions," *Soviet Studies,* vol. 23, no. 2 (April 1972), 619–628.

Soviet Static Efficiency

A. Bergson, "Comparative Productivity and Efficiency in the USA and USSR," in A. Eckstein, ed., *Comparison of Economic Systems* (Berkeley and Los Angeles: University of California Press, 1971), pp. 161–218.

———, *The Economics of Soviet Planning* (New Haven, Conn.: Yale University Press, 1964), chap. 14.

———, *Planning and Productivity Under Soviet Socialism* (New York: Columbia University Press, 1968).

J. S. Berliner, "The Static Efficiency of the Soviet Economy," *American Economic Review,* vol. 54, no. 2 (May 1964), 480–490.

E. Domar, "On the Measurement of Comparative Efficiency," in A. Eckstein, ed., *Comparison of Economic Systems* (Berkeley and Los Angeles: University of California Press, 1971), pp. 219–232.

Equity of Income Distribution in the Soviet Union

A. Bergson, *The Structure of Soviet Wages* (Cambridge, Mass.: Harvard University Press, 1944).

———, "Income Inequality under Soviet Socialism," *Journal of Economic Literature,* vol. 22, no. 3 (September 1984), 1052–1099.

A. McCauley, "The Distribution of Earnings and Income in the Soviet Union," *Soviet Studies,* vol. 29, no. 2 (April 1977), pp. 214–237.

———, *Economic Welfare in the Soviet Union* (Madison: University of Wisconsin Press, 1979).

P. J. D. Wiles, *Distribution of Income: East and West* (Amsterdam: North-Holland, 1974).

P. J. D. Wiles and S. Markowski, "Income Distribution Under Communism and Capitalism: Some Facts About Poland, the U.K., the USA and the USSR," *Soviet Studies,* vol. 22, nos. 3 and 4 (January and April 1971), 344–369 and 487–511.

M. Yanowitch, *Social and Economic Inequality in the USSR* (White Plains, N.Y.: M. E. Sharpe, 1977).

———, "The Soviet Income Revolution," *Slavic Review,* vol. 22, no. 4 (December 1963).

chapter *12*

Soviet Performance: Military Power, Technology, and the Environment

FURTHER PERFORMANCE INDICATORS

In Chapter 11, we assessed the performance of the Soviet economy in terms of conventional economic performance criteria: economic growth, efficiency, living standards, income distribution, and economic stability. This list is a restrictive one in the Soviet context because other goals, pursued consistently by the Soviet leadership, are not included. The first of these is the objective, first sought by an "encircled" Bolshevik regime in 1917, of achieving a degree of military power sufficient to protect the Soviet experiment from its capitalist foes and, later, to expand the Soviet sphere of influence. One can debate current Soviet military objectives—are they designed to achieve parity or dominance? But one thing is clear: there is a consistent priority assigned to military power. Soviet economic performance, especially in the postwar era, cannot be understood without an assessment of the resources devoted to the military and the military might these resources have produced, for these resources had to be diverted from consumption and investment. Trade-offs between military and civilian objectives would therefore be expected.

The second objective—the establishment of a high level of technology in the Soviet Union—is another that has been emphasized since the early days of the Soviet regime, when high-technology heavy industry was proclaimed the instrument through which socialism would be built. To what extent has this objective been achieved? Has the Soviet economy succeeded in creating and utilizing advanced technology to its maximum potential, given the resource constraints in which it has had to operate? To a limited extent, this issue has been addressed in the previous chapter, for efficiency gains will depend upon the production and utilization of improved technology (including improved organizational arrangements). In this chapter, we examine this issue directly by considering the Soviet record in the technology area. Unlike other performance indicators, global measures of technological performance (other than measures of productivity) are not available; therefore we must make do with partial indicators of technological achievement. The manner in which new technologies are created and utilized by the Soviet economic system will be considered as well, for in the absence of accurate global measures of technological performance, analyses of Soviet "rules of the game" for technological innovation may provide insights overlooked by empirical measures.

The third performance criterion not encompassed in the conventional performance indicators is the degree to which the Soviet economy has been able to produce "environmental quality" or, expressed in the negative form, has been able to prevent "environmental disruption." Widespread concern and analysis of environmental disruption is a postwar phenomenon. Many LDCs still view environmental protection as a luxury that only affluent countries can afford; and as the Soviet Union was engaged in a program of rapid industrialization, and thereafter in a world war, one can understand that environmental concerns were of low priority during those early periods. Environmental disruption in the Soviet Union provides an interesting test case of the effect of the economic system on environmental quality, especially for those who have argued that environmental disruption is a product of capitalism.

SOVIET MILITARY POWER

We approach the topic of Soviet military power by posing two questions. The first is: how much military power have the Soviets been able to produce, given the limitations imposed by their economic base? This question is analogous to our earlier discussion of living standards, where we argued that per capita consumption levels must be judged relative to economic capacity. If one compares Soviet and American military power, it must be done with an appreciation of the different resource bases available to the two countries. To deal with this first question, we must above all have measures of military power, and as we shall point out, the measurement of military power raises severe conceptual and practical problems. The second question concerns the burden imposed on the Soviet domestic economy by the diversion of resources to military uses.

Problems of Measurement[1]

The military power of the Soviet Union can be quantified in two ways. The first is to list the physical quantities of the various inputs into the military power equation—armed service personnel, tanks, missiles, submarines, strategic supplies, and so on—and compare them with a similar list for the Soviet Union's major military competitors, the United States and its NATO allies and the People's Republic of China. In Table 50, such a compilation is supplied for the USSR and the United States.

Table 50   MILITARY STRENGTH: USSR AND USA, 1964, 1978, 1984

	1964	1978	1984
USSR			
Intercontinental ballistic missiles (ICBMs)	200	1400	1398
Submarine-launched ballistic missiles (SLBMs)	120	1015	981
Long-range bombers	190	135	143
Armed services personnel (millions)	3.4	4.2	4.3
USA			
Intercontinental ballistic missiles (ICBMs)	834	1054	1037
Submarine-launched ballistic missiles (SLBMs)	416	656	592
Long-range bombers	630	432	297
Armed services personnel (millions)	2.7	2.1	2.1

Sources: These data are based on studies of the International Institute for Strategic Studies, London. They are cited in *The 1979 Hammond Almanac* (Maplewood, N.J.: Hammond Almanac, Inc., 1978), pp. 733–735; *The Official Associated Press Almanac 1973* (New York: Almanac Publishing Company, 1972), pp. 616–617; and *The World Almanac 1985,* p. 339. The Soviet armed services figures are from M. Feshbach and S. Rapawy, "Soviet Population and Manpower Trends and Policies," in U.S. Congress, Joint Economic Committee, *Soviet Economy in a New Perspective* (Washington, D.C.: U.S. Government Printing Office, 1976), p. 132; Hearings Before the Subcommittee on Priorities and Economy in Government, *Allocation of Resources in the Soviet Union and China—1978; Part 4: Soviet Union* (Washington, D.C., June 26 and July 24, 1978), p. 68.

Comparisons of physical quantities of military inputs are useful, and they confirm the general increase in Soviet military power vis-à-vis the United States. Yet such comparisons suffer from a series of deficiencies. Military hardware tends to be quite complex and heterogeneous; therefore, the simple counting of physical units will not reveal their contribution to military power. To make such a judgment, one must have detailed information on the (perhaps thousands) characteristics of each type of military hardware. In the case of ICBMs, for example, one must know their payload, accuracy, speed of launch, degree of protection from nuclear attack, and so on. Even if this wealth of information were available, an *overall* measure of Soviet military power would still be lacking, for some means must be found of *aggregating* all the heterogeneous inputs (military personnel, tanks, bombs, ICBMs, strategic supplies, etc.).

The most straightforward means of converting physical indicators of military force into a common denominator is to multiply each by its price and then sum, that is, to compile a value aggregate of military power. Under ideal circumstances, relative prices will reflect both the opportunity cost of resources embodied in the commodity and the marginal rates at which defense planners are willing to substitute one item for another (holding the level of military power constant).* In our discussion of the Soviet price system (Chapter 7), we noted that Soviet ruble prices rarely mirror the opportunity costs of production (or the marginal rates of substitution of users); and, in the case of pricing the defense commodities of the United States, it is difficult to know how rational such prices are (for example, until 1973, the wage rates of draftees were set well below opportunity costs). Thus, in making value comparisons of USSR and U.S. military power, one is unsure of the "rationality" of the prices used in aggregation.

In the case of compiling value aggregates of Soviet defense outlays, practical

---

*Efficiency in the choice of military goods and services would require that the defense planners' marginal rates of substitution be equal to the marginal rates of transformation.

problems caused by data deficiencies are as serious as underlying theoretical issues. Official Soviet budgetary sources report defense spending as a single line item, and reported defense outlays are often manipulated to suit political needs. The announced state budget claims virtually no increase in defense spending (even prior to adjustment for inflation) between 1967 and 1978, a period when massive investments in military hardware systems were being made.[2] For these reasons, defense analysts in the United States have felt it necessary to make independent estimates of Soviet defense spending by employing U.S. defense budgetary practices. Two types of independent calculations have been made. The first, undertaken by the American intelligence community,[3] uses the "building block" approach, whereby the physical quantities of defense inputs (rockets, manpower, equipment, etc.) are multiplied by the presumed cost of producing the items in the United States (to obtain Soviet defense spending in U.S. prices for comparison with U.S. defense spending)* and by Soviet ruble prices.[4] The advantages of the building block approach are that the estimates are independent of official Soviet budgetary data and that they are in a form suitable for comparison with U.S. defense spending. The disadvantages are that one cannot assess the reliability of intelligence data on Soviet military hardware and that it is difficult to determine accurately costs in the United States and the Soviet Union. The second approach calls for the estimation of Soviet outlays on military hardware by subtracting civilian uses of industrial production from the ruble value of industrial production; the resulting residual is presumed to equal defense outlays.[5] The accuracy of both types of estimates is subject to serious question (although they have tended to agree with each other in recent years),[6] and skepticism concerning their reliability was increased in 1976, when the Central Intelligence Agency raised its estimate of Soviet defense spending by 100 percent.[7]

CIA Estimates

Using its building block approach, the CIA has derived estimates of the dollar cost of Soviet defense activities for the period 1967–1978. These dollar cost figures can then be contrasted with the actual dollar costs of U.S. defense outlays. The CIA findings are supplied in Figure 10. They show that from 1967 (and earlier), U.S. defense spending outdistanced Soviet defense outlays (by a factor of about one-third in 1967). Around 1971, Soviet defense spending came to equal American spending and, thereafter, exceeded American defense outlays. In 1978, Soviet spending was estimated to exceed American outlays by 45 percent.

Expenditures on defense in any one year will not yield the total of military power, for military power is the product of cumulated past expenditures.[8] Therefore, a more accurate measure of Soviet military power vis-à-vis the United States would be the sum of military expenditures (in constant prices) over a substantial period of time. According to CIA calculations, cumulative Soviet defense outlays for the decade 1968–1978 exceeded American totals by 12 percent.[9] The implica-

---

*Information on Soviet military hardware is supplied to American defense contractors, who are asked to indicate what the system would have cost if produced in the United States.

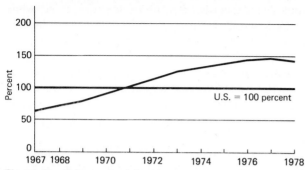

Figure 10 Dollar cost of Soviet activities as a percent of U.S. defense outlays. (*Source:* National Foreign Assessment Center, *A Dollar Cost Comparison of Soviet and U.S. Defense Activities, 1968–78*, SR79-10004, Washington, D.C., January 1979, p. 10. The 1967 figure is from the previous year's publication, which covers the years 1966–1977.)

tion of these findings is that the Soviet Union has overtaken the United States in its real defense spending and that, if current trends continue, it will outdistance the United States in military power in the future. This conclusion is not inconsistent with the evidence of the physical indicators presented in Table 50. Some reservations can be cited, however.

There is a range of considerable uncertainty surrounding these estimates, although the CIA believes its estimates are not more than 15 percent in error. For example, the CIA has made two substantial changes in its previous assessments of Soviet military spending. In 1976, the CIA increased its estimate of Soviet military spending in U.S. dollars as a consequence of raising its estimates of the dollar costs of Soviet procurement. In 1983, the CIA lowered its estimate of the growth of military spending after 1976 from 4–5 percent per annum to 2 percent per annum.[10] Given the problems of intelligence gathering and then of translating physical indicators into dollar or ruble values, one can understand why a substantial margin of error must be attached to these estimates. Second, the relationship between cumulated spending totals and military power is not clearly defined.[11] Military power depends not only upon sheer spending ability but also upon the wisdom of defense planners and the uses to which they put the expenditures. Third, there is the ambiguity introduced by the index number problem, which requires some comment.[12]

The dollar cost estimates of Soviet defense spending translate Soviet defense outlays into U.S. prices. Soviet ICBM systems are valued at U.S. prices, Soviet manpower is valued at U.S. military pay scales, fuels used by the military are computed in U.S. fuel prices. The United States is "rich" in advanced technology and "poor" in manpower relative to the Soviet Union; therefore, the prices of high-technology products will be low in the United States relative to Soviet ruble prices. The structure of Soviet defense outlays, however, is geared to domestic resource constraints, that is, Soviet defense planners will place relatively less emphasis on advanced technology (less use of advanced computer circuitry in ICBMs and greater use of large payloads) and more emphasis on labor-intensive military expenditures (larger armed forces). When Soviet defense outlays are translated into U.S. prices, products that play a relatively small role (advanced technology computer products) are accorded a relatively low U.S. price, while those products that play a heavy role (manpower, rifles, etc.) are valued in relatively high U.S. prices. Thus, dollar cost estimates of defense spending will yield a higher relative value for the USSR than comparisons conducted in ruble prices. To this point, the most reliable estimates are those in dollar values, but the available estimates in ruble prices do confirm the expected relationship, namely, that if ruble prices are employed, the USSR spending advantage is reduced (to a 25 percent from a 45 percent advantage in 1978 according to the CIA).*

Despite these reservations, the conclusion to be drawn from figures on defense spending and physical indicators of military potential is that the Soviet Union has achieved an impressive degree of military might. Most analysts would agree that Soviet military might is at least equivalent to that of the United States, a nation that possesses considerably more economic power (as measured by the size of GNP). Soviet authorities have, therefore, achieved their objectives as far as the military power equation is concerned.

The Burden of Soviet Defense Expenditures

Obviously, these military power achievements have not taken place without sacrifice. The diversion of resources from the civilian economy has cost the Soviet economy production for consumption and investment. These costs can be illustrated in a number of ways: Soviet males reaching the age of 18 become subject to conscription; and in 1975, 87 percent of males turning 18 were drafted. It is projected that if current military manpower levels are to be maintained, over 100 percent of 18-year-olds must be conscripted in the 1980s, meaning that conscripts will have to be sought in other age groups.[13] Not only does Soviet defense require a drain of manpower from the civilian economy, it is also estimated that one-third of the product of the machine building industry (the primary source of investment goods) is devoted annually to the defense sector.[14] In general, defense takes a large share of the highest quality scientific, technical, and managerial talent, as well as having preferential access to scarce resources of all kinds.

The most frequently used measure of the total defense burden is the ratio of defense spending to GNP, as this denotes the share of total resources devoted to defense activities. From 1967 to 1978, the Soviets devoted approximately one-eighth of their output to defense, versus 5 percent for the United States.[15] Recent revisions by the CIA may lower somewhat this burden estimate.

The exact costs of this military burden, as measured by the sacrifice of current consumption and the longer-run effects on growth of reduced investment, are not known, but econometric estimates suggest that they are substantial.[16] Projections into the future are necessarily uncertain, primarily because it is difficult to predict productivity gains, but the ultimate cost of Soviet defense

---

*Holzman argues[12] that the CIA grossly underestimates the effects of index number relativity. He maintains that it is quite possible that the United States outspends the Soviets if ruble prices would be correctly calculated. Holzman further argues that the higher quality of American manpower and military hardware is not captured by the CIA figures.

spending may prove to be a growth rate unacceptably low to Soviet authorities. In fact, if the Soviets have indeed slowed down the rate of growth of defense spending in recent years, this may have been dictated by lagging economic growth. The defense burden had simply become too large.

SOVIET TECHNOLOGY[17]

Measurement of Soviet technological performance is, like the assessment of Soviet military power, a complicated problem. Direct measures of Soviet technological achievement relative to that of capitalist countries can be made only on an industry case study basis, and the researcher will not know whether such results are representative for the economy as a whole. Moreover, case studies require the evaluation of the operating characteristics of the technology (reliability, power/weight ratios, energy efficiency, etc.) and of the quality of the end products produced, and the number of such technical-engineering characteristics is so large that the evaluation may depend upon the particular characteristics studied. Also, the characteristics of the technology will depend upon the resource endowments of the country; so it may be optimal for one nation to adopt technology that is less "advanced" because factor proportions dictate such a choice.

Indirect measurement of technology represents the alternate to direct case studies. The relative factor productivity of the USSR vis-à-vis other countries can be calculated (Chapter 11), but the relationship between factor productivity and Soviet technological achievement is not clearly defined. It is not directly apparent whether low Soviet factor productivity is a consequence of lagging technological performance or of "omitted factors" (qualitative differences in inputs, economies of scale, and so on). A low technological level is only one of several explanations of low Soviet factor productivity, as the factor productivity calculation represents "a measure of our ignorance."[18] Further measures of the technology level (lead time to the utilization of a new technology, number of patents, volume of scientific papers, scientific awards, citations in scientific papers) supplement our understanding of Soviet technology, but all suffer from serious deficiencies.

Granted that no single measure of technological performance will be adequate, we can nevertheless cite some of the basic results of research on Soviet technology. First, we should refer the reader back to the factor productivity results (Chapter 11), which show Soviet factor productivity to be low relative to the advanced industrialized countries. This finding is consistent with the conclusion that Soviet technological performance is below that of the industrialized West, but such evidence is not conclusive by itself. Case studies of the technological level of Soviet industry (even when chosen so as to select priority branches) suggest as well a relatively low level of Soviet technology, although this conclusion applies less strongly to the defense and iron and steel industries.[19] The most striking conclusion of case study research is that, in most sectors, "there is no evidence of a substantial diminution of the technological gap between the USSR and the West in the past 15 to 20 years, either at the prototype/commercial application stages or in the diffusion of advanced technology."[20] This conclusion is generally consistent with the factor productivity studies, which show the rate of growth of factor productivity in the USSR to be only average relative to the industrialized West.

Another source of evidence concerning the relatively low technological level of the Soviet economy is its continued reliance on imports from the West to meet its advanced technology requirements. Case studies of computer and machine tool imports can be cited to confirm this continuing dependence.[21]

The technological level of a country will depend not only on the availability of new technology but also upon its diffusion throughout the economy. The limited evidence that is available suggests that the lead time between the granting of a patent for a new invention and its practical implementation are longer in the Soviet Union than in the United States and West Germany. In fact, the United States and West Germany tend to implement over one-half of their inventions in little more than a year, while the Soviets require three years to attain this ratio.[22] The slowness of diffusion of new technology applies to imported technology as well as domestic inventions.[23]

What conclusions are to be drawn from this mass of data? Our overall conclusion is that the information supplied by factor productivity studies, direct investigations of the technology of Soviet industry, reliance on high-technology imports, lead times, and diffusion point to a relatively low level of technological achievement in the Soviet economy (with the exception of the military). Moreover, data over time suggest that the Soviet's technology gap has not been narrowed over the past two decades.

Microeconomic Causes of the Technology Gap

The probable causes of the Soviet technology gap have been identified by Joseph Berliner,[24] who argues that Soviet organizational structure, pricing system, and incentive rules discriminate against technological innovation. Although the Soviet economic system does have certain features favorable to innovation (patent restrictions do not limit the spread of an invention), other features inhibit technological innovation. The existing organizational structure gives maximal encouragement to decision-makers to discriminate against innovations and to managers to shy away from doing new things. As noted in Chapter 8, Soviet managers have learned to minimize the risk of failure by developing secure channels of supply. Once a Soviet manager has established reliable supply relationships, the chance of failure is reduced. The installation of a new technology would change routine patterns and disrupt existing supply channels built up carefully over the years. New ways of doing things would also change established distribution arrangements and add another source of uncertainty to plan fulfillment. Moreover, most research and development work is done by research institutes and ministerial project-making organizations whose responsibility for a project ends when a new design is approved by the ministry. The need for enterprises to rely on an outside supply of R&D services compounds the risk of failure.

As Berliner points out, innovation does increase managerial risks; but if the rewards to managers for innovation were large enough, managers could more readily be induced to innovate. One way to reward managers would be to grant them high prices relative to costs of production (and thus larger profits) for new products and then to pay them bonuses, either directly for innovative activity or through an increased share in enterprise profits. The existing pricing and incentive structures do neither. The principle of pricing according to the labor theory of value discriminates against product innovation, for savings in labor costs are passed on to the user in the form of lower prices rather than to the producer as higher profits. Efforts to exempt new products from branch-average cost pricing have been largely unsuccessful, although some of the cruder disparities of earlier years have been eliminated.

The managerial bonus system also discourages innovation. Over the years, managers have been paid bonuses primarily for fulfillment of current year production targets. It was not until the mid-1950s that special bonuses for innovation were developed. But even after introducing a variety of rewards for innovation, it remains true that the managerial bonus still depends primarily upon fulfilling basic enterprise plan targets. Moreover, the bonus system is geared to rewarding short-term results. Innovative activity, by disrupting existing channels of supply and distribution, typically causes a short-term reduction in enterprise output, which is compensated for by a long-term increase as an innovation comes onstream. Yet during this period, the manager will lose bonus funds and will thus be discouraged from innovation.

An economic reform begun in 1965 sought to reduce managerial resistance to change. Special bonuses for innovation were established, amended pricing rules for new products were introduced, and greater emphasis was placed upon longterm plan fulfillment. But as we shall note in Chapter 13, economic reform has not altered the fundamentals of the Soviet economic system, and this conclusion applies to innovative activity as well. Berliner, after analyzing Soviet efforts to improve the incentive system, concluded that "the current incentive structure does not lend very strong support to the new growth strategy [based upon technological progress]."[25] Berliner's work provides a vivid account of why Soviet enterprises are reluctant to engage in innovation and thus focuses on the micro context of innovation.

SCIENTIFIC LABOR FORCE IN THE SOVIET UNION

Berliner's work focuses on the microeconomic incentive problems of generating and implementing new technology in the Soviet economic system. This is one obvious cause of the Soviet technology gap. A second possible cause would be an inferior stock of trained science and technology (S&T) manpower, which would mean that the Soviet Union simply has not succeeded in creating the stock of S&T manpower required to bring about significant improvements in science and technology.

In the Soviet Union, the task of training S&T manpower is undertaken by the higher educational establishment, the so-called VUZ system. The VUZ system consists of traditional universities and a large number of scientific research institutes. The scientific research institutes may fall under the jurisdiction of the Soviet Academy of Sciences (and tend to concentrate on pure research), or they may fall under the jurisdiction of the various ministries (in which case they tend to concentrate on applied research). Both the universities and the scientific research institutes are charged with training advanced S&T manpower at the undergraduate and graduate levels. In fact, the specific positions opened to VUZ enrollees are determined through the interaction of *Gosplan,* the ministries, and the Ministry of Higher and Secondary Specialized Education. This interaction is to ensure that the VUZ system produce the S&T specialists required by the national economy.

The Soviet S&T training system can be judged according to its ability to select the most qualified candidates for advanced S&T training, by the quality of S&T training, by the rational placement of S&T personnel in the economy, and by the proper utilization of scientific and technical experts once they are at work in the nation's research network. As to the first point, it appears that admittance to advanced S&T training in the Soviet VUZ system is, with some exceptions, largely done on the basis of the scientific potential of the applicant. It is more difficult to judge the quality of Soviet S&T training at the VUZ level. Like in the United States, there is great variety among the best VUZs and the worst. The best higher educational establishments tend to be located in Moscow and Leningrad, and these institutions appear to offer advanced scientific training that is equal to the best training offered in the United States and Western Europe. On the other hand, the VUZs located in the provinces attract less-qualified candidates and function with less-qualified faculty; therefore, to draw an overall judgement is difficult. The Soviet S&T curricula tend to be highly standardized by central authorities, and examination of various S&T curricula suggests that they are on a par with S&T curricula in the West.

Long-run achievements of the Soviet S&T training establishment are impressive. High-level S&T manpower trends can be gleaned indirectly from the numbers of persons completing higher education because of the concentration of S&T in higher education training. In 1914–1915, 127,000 students were enrolled in higher educational establishments. By 1940–1941, this number had risen to 812,000; and by the 1980s, there were over 5 million students enrolled in higher education. In 1914, 136,000 people employed in the national economy had a higher education. In 1959, 3.8 million persons had a higher education. By 1982, this number had increased to 17.0 million. As for the over-10 population, the increase in the proportion of persons with higher education between 1959 and 1983 was from 2.3 percent to 7.6 percent.

The number of scientific workers with advanced degrees and titles tripled during the decade of the 1950s and tripled again during the decade of the 1960s. The 1970s saw a slowdown in the growth in the number of scientific workers with advanced degrees. The number increased from roughly 1 million to almost 1.5 million between 1970 and 1983. While the number had been tripling every decade from 1950 to 1970, from 1970 to 1980 the increase was limited to under 50 percent.

The growth of Soviet higher educational establishments has been impressive. In 1914–1915, there were 105 higher education establishments in tsarist Russia of which 13 had the stature of university. By 1970, there were 805 higher education establishments (42 universities), and by 1984, there were 891 higher education establishments in the USSR. The number of teachers in higher education rose from 61,000 in 1940, to 263,000 in 1967, to approximately 510,000 in 1984. The latter figure includes 19,000 doctors of science and 200,000 candidates of science.

Trends in enrollment in S&T higher education programs can be read from trends in overall enrollment in higher educational establishments. In 1976–1977, of the 4.95 million students in higher education, 1.6 million were enrolled in areas of study outside science and technology (teacher training, economics, law, arts, and humanities). Thus, about two-thirds of Soviet higher education enrollment tends to be in science and engineering (including medicine). Of the 840,000 graduates of higher educational establishments in 1982, roughly 50 percent were in science and technology.[26]

According to the best calculations available, the number of scientists and engineers employed in R&D in the United States around 1980 (some 600,000) was about three-quarters the number of R&D scientists and engineers employed in R&D in the USSR (about 830,000). The numerical superiority of the Soviet Union is a relatively new phenomenon dating to the late 1960s. In 1950, for example, the number of R&D scientists and engineers in the United States was around 50 percent higher than in the Soviet Union.

The number of R&D scientists with advanced degrees is more equal in the two countries, but the Soviet Union has clear numerical superiority. In the mid-1970s, the United States employed some 212,000 S&T specialists with advanced degrees, while the Soviet Union employed 271,000. The number of advanced-degree specialists in the physical and life sciences is about the same in the United States and the USSR, but the USSR has about twice the number of engineers as the United States.

Looking more generally at advanced-degree holders in both science and nonscience fields, we see that the United States devotes proportionally more resources to social sciences and humanities than the Soviet Union. A similar overall proportion of advanced degrees are in physical and life sciences. The major difference is that some 30 percent of Soviet advanced degrees are in engineering, while only 15 percent of American advanced degrees are in that field. The United States retains numerical superiority at the advanced-degree level only in the social sciences and humanities. The number of American advanced-degree specialists in social sciences and humanities is about 60 percent greater than the corresponding Soviet number. The sole exception is economics, an area (due to the enormous task of managing a centrally planned economy) in which there are more Soviet advanced-degree specialists than in the United States. The relative figures on specialists with advanced degrees bring home the fact that, although both the United States and the Soviet Union train roughly similar numbers of advanced-degree specialists, the Soviets have chosen to concentrate their higher educational resources on training science and engineering specialists at the expense of social sciences and humanities.[27]

Most Western observers agree that the Soviet Union now has the world's largest science and training establishment. It is much more difficult to assess the quality of Soviet S&T education in similarly broad strokes. There is nevertheless some evidence that sheds light on this issue. Let us first consider the side of the ledger that points to quality achievements and then turn to evidence of quality deficiencies.

Studies of Soviet S&T training in different science and engineering specialties yield mixed results on the relative quality of Soviet graduates relative to American graduates. In the area of physics, for example, expert Western opinion suggests that Soviet university training in physics is comparable (or even perhaps superior) to that found in American universities. Other studies have produced mixed results on the quality of engineering training in Soviet and American engineering colleges, but there appears to be enough difference of opinion to suggest that differences in the quality of engineering training are not overwhelming. To quote from U.S. specialists on this matter:

> Comparisons of the level of training received in specific specialty areas, however, indicate that the level of professional attainment of a science or engineering graduate of Soviet higher education establishments (in the full-time programs at least) is about the same as or occasionally higher than the level of attainment of a science or engineering graduate of a U.S. college or university.[28]

One caveat should be attached to the above conclusion: Just as in American science and technology education, there is variation in the quality of training among institutions. In the Soviet case, there is another source of quality variation —the quality difference between full-time training at higher education institutions and evening or correspondence training. There is universal agreement among Western and Soviet experts that the quality of evening and correspondence training is inferior. It will also be noted below that the majority of Soviet enrollment in higher educational establishments is in evening and correspondence programs, so this is a major adjustment that must be considered. On the matter of variation in quality among institutions, we have no way of knowing whether this variation is greater in the Soviet Union or in the United States. Soviet S&T training is more strictly controlled and standardized by government authorities, so it may be that there is less variation in the Soviet Union, but this is only speculation. The conclusion that Soviet advanced degree science training is roughly comparable to that of the United States is based on comparisons of the premier institutions in each country.

Other evidence on the quality of Soviet S&T training is fairly anecdotal, but may become a better established proposition as further studies of the third Soviet emigration are completed. There is some preliminary evidence that U.S. employers have found that the level of training of former Soviet citizens holding advanced degrees in science (based upon full-time study programs) is roughly comparable to that of U.S.-trained scientists with advanced degrees. Moreover, in-depth interviews with former Soviet scientists reveal that they personally rate the quality of their basic training as high.[29] This type of testimony is revealing because many Soviet emigré scientists have had an opportunity to compare themselves and their training with their American counterparts.

Additional evidence is derived from international scientific awards and citation indexes. In general, this evidence suggests that although Soviet scientists have received fewer prestigious science awards and are less widely cited by world scientists, they have achieved respectable world reputations in Soviet science priority areas. It must be emphasized that the relative numbers of international awards or citations are distorted measures of the qualitative achievements of Soviet science. There are obvious linguistic barriers; few world scientists read Russian. Soviet scientists tend to fall outside established scientific networks, and it is harder for Soviet scientists to obtain permission to travel to the West to establish contacts. Recognizing these problems, we note that in physics—a field in which Soviet scientists have historically excelled—Soviet scientists have captured seven Nobel prizes since 1950, as compared to the 31 captured by American-located physicists. In scientific fields not emphasized in Soviet resource allocation policies, Soviet scientists have performed less well.

Citation indexes reveal that Soviet scientists have established international reputations in mathematics, physics, and earth and space sciences. Despite language barriers, American mathematicians cite approximately as many Soviet mathematical articles as Soviet mathematicians cite American mathematical articles. The number of citations by U.S. scientists of Soviet publications in physics and earth and space sciences is also quite high, although the numbers of citations are far from parity.[30]

There is some evidence of weaknesses and flaws in the Soviet S&T training curriculum. In the standard Soviet University, 8 to 12 percent of classroom time is devoted to ideological training, and 4 to 6 hours per week are devoted to military training. Experts point out that Soviet scientists and engineers are trained in narrowly defined specialties (a comprehensive set of 499 numbered specialty fields) rather than receiving a broader scientific or technical background.[31] The extreme narrowness of Soviet S&T education may make it difficult for Soviet scientists to adapt to changes in scientific and technical fields. It may even lead to unemployed or underemployed S&T specialists when there are shifts in demand for the various specialties.

Another piece of evidence that points to systematic problems with Soviet S&T training is the bias in favor of passing students or graduating unqualified students. The Soviet press contains numerous complaints of grade inflation, lazy students, and the unwillingness of faculty to fail students. These complaints sound very much like those found in the American press, but the bias is possibly more systematic in the Soviet case. The reason is that Soviet educational establishments, like their factory counterparts, are judged on the basis of fulfillment of plans. The plans of higher educational establishments often consist of turning out target numbers of graduates in specific fields. If large numbers of students are failed, then the educational establishment fails to meet its plan. Moreover, activists in educational organizations (like activists in factory organizations) are judged on the basis of fulfillment of plan quotas. These pressures on the administration of higher educational establishments may lead to the release of poorly qualified S&T graduates on the R&D establishment.[32]

Although general conclusions of this sort are risky, we would conclude that the Soviet technology gap is not due to the low level of training and qualifications of Soviet S&T manpower. If anything, we would conclude that the Soviet economic system has done a relatively poor job utilizing the S&T manpower base with which it is working. It would thus appear that the microeconomic incentive problems emphasized by Berliner play the major role in explaining why the USSR, with its vast numbers of trained S&T experts, has not done a better job in closing the Soviet technology gap with the West.

SOVIET ENVIRONMENTAL QUALITY

Under capitalism, environmental disruption (ED) is thought to be caused by external effects. External effects arise whenever the private costs (or benefits) of a particular action diverge from its social costs (or benefits). If a profit-maximizing capitalist firm is able, for example, to pollute the air without being charged a price for this activity, the social cost of production will exceed the private cost and a greater than optimal level of environmental disruption will emerge. Only if private enterprises can be charged for the social costs (via a tax, for example) of their pollution or if such activities are internalized will the level of environmental disruption be optimal.* The optimality criterion is such that pollution should be allowed up to that level at which its marginal social cost equals the marginal cost of pollution abatement.[32] This is the standard adopted by most economists to the chagrin of many environmental groups, who deny the existence of "optimal" levels of pollution.

Advocates of socialism have long argued on theoretical grounds that ED will not arise in a socialist society. Although specifics have varied, the essential thread is the *level* of decision-making. Where decisions are centralized and the objective function—the outcome that planners are trying to achieve—includes environmental quality, there need never be externalities, since there is literally nothing external to the decision makers. A similar argument is made for local decision-making if the planners develop an incentive structure that ensures the harmony of local decisions with central goals (assuming the necessary concomitant of perfect information). It is necessary that appropriate resource valuations, which reflect central goals, be available to the central decision-makers.[33]

Oskar Lange, a classic advocate of the socialist cause, argued in his famous article, *On the Economic Theory of Socialism,*[34] that under socialism, the price system will be more comprehensive and, in effect, a high value will be placed by the Central Planning Board upon a clean environment. Maurice Dobb makes a similar argument when he suggests that, although information availability and digestion may be a problem in the real world, socialist planners will tend to make decisions with maximum global vision and an eye to their environmental impact.[35] Jan Tinbergen, the noted Dutch economist, has also endorsed the notion that, in general, decisions made at the highest possible levels will minimize the problem of externalities.[36]

---

*Internalization occurs when costs that were previously external to the polluting enterprise become internal costs. For example, if all enterprises located along a river are merged, then the water pollution abatement costs of these enterprises become private costs.

Such theoretical arguments to the contrary, there is a well-documented literature that environmental disruption is, in fact, a problem in the Soviet Union.[37] The Soviet press and literature abound with cases of soil erosion, poisoning of rivers and lakes with industrial effluents and chemical fertilizers, industrial air pollution, and so on—problems that have become common in the industrialized West. Growing concern in the Soviet Union is reflected in the formation of conservationist groups, increasing press attention, and the passage of a number of (generally ineffective) laws concerned with environmental quality.[38]

Measurement of Environmental Pollution

To assess the Soviet record of environmental protection, one must begin with some notion of the stock of pollution in the USSR relative to the stock in the industrialized capitalist countries. Of all the performance criteria, we are on the most treacherous footing with regard to the measurement of pollution levels.[39] Although it may be possible to establish the physical quantities of harmful air pollutants, water pollutants, noise pollution, and radiation, there is no established system of weights that allows the researcher to aggregate environmental disruption into a single global measure. In place of a global measure, one must rely on various partial measures, the firmest of which are for air pollution. According to calculations by Victor Mote (for 1968–1969), the gross weights of air pollutants produced in the USSR were as follows: dust, 61 percent of U.S.; sulfur dioxide, 49 percent of U.S.; carbon monoxide, 19 percent of U.S.; and hydrocarbons, 22 percent of U.S.[40] Although a number of studies of Soviet water, noise, and radiation pollution have been undertaken, the USSR production of these forms of environmental disruption relative to other countries cannot yet be estimated.

The air pollution data, however, suggest (by all conceivable weighting schemes) that the USSR produces less air pollution than does the United States. Does this demonstrate superior Soviet performance? A number of conditioning factors must be considered, some of which would contribute to higher levels of expected pollution (the greater frequency of air inversions, the lesser emphasis on "clean" industry and services) and others to lower expected levels. The USSR's lower level of economic output and lower per capita income are factors that would be expected to lower Soviet levels of environmental disruption. Soviet GNP in 1976 was roughly three-quarters that of the United States, while expenditures on consumption were 54 percent of those of the United States.[41] Given lower levels of output and consumption, one would expect lower levels of pollution, independent of environmental performance.

The lower level of consumption, especially the decision not to produce automobiles, is a significant explanatory factor behind the lower observed levels of Soviet pollution. The Soviets have yet to reach the age of mass motoring, with the stock of passenger automobiles roughly equivalent to American 1913 levels.[42] The flush toilet, with its tremendous demand on fresh water, is still not universal in Soviet urban housing. The density of population is still relatively low. Packaging in light industries and food industries is still a rarity, thus reducing the solid waste disposal problem that has plagued industrialized Western countries.

Because environmental disruption does seem to be a concomitant of the industrialization process, it is difficult to evaluate the performance of the Soviet system without some quantifiable notion of what constitutes a "normal" level of pollution for a given level of economic development. Only in this way can one judge whether the Soviet economy has performed "better" or "worse" in providing a suitable environment. In some areas, the Soviet system may have natural advantages over market economies—for example, the unwillingness of Soviet planners to meet the pent-up demand for private automobiles and their stress upon cheap mass urban transit, the ability of urban and regional planners to develop master plans for areas independently of private developers, the stress on multifamily dwellings that make use of centrally supplied warm water for washing and heating, and so on. However, it is not possible to draw an overall balance.

Even if we were able to determine whether Soviet environmental performance is better or worse than that of capitalist countries at the same stage of economic development, a measure of the *efficiency* of Soviet environmental policy is still lacking.[43] An efficient environmental program is one that equates the marginal costs and benefits of pollution abatement, and as different societies have varying preferences concerning the costs and benefits of environmental protection, it is theoretically possible to combine efficiency with relatively high (or low) environmental disruption.

Causes of Pollution in the Soviet Union

Why is there pollution in the Soviet economy? Three possible reasons might be considered. First, it may be that planners were not concerned with environmental quality until the level of development became such that, in combination with the international demonstration effect, its presence became pervasive. More important, however, is the possibility that environmental quality had been consciously discarded as one of the costs of rapid economic growth. In effect, the Soviets raised growth in the short run by simply not placing a high price on pollution costs—in effect, postponing some of the costs by letting them accumulate in the form of a stock of pollution. Thus disinvestment in the environment would be considered as a rather typical aspect of Soviet economic development, just as it has characterized economic growth generally in market economies.

A second factor leading to environmental disruption in the Soviet Union is the breakdown of *valuation,* a problem not unique to the Soviet Union. Planners are simply unaware of appropriate resource valuations, including the costs of environmental disruption, and hence may be unable to allocate them in a "rational" manner even if they so desired. This, in effect, is a breakdown of the information mechanism common to both market and planned economies. We suggest that this is a likely partial explanation in view of the Soviets' inability to compute scarcity prices in general either with or without social costs.[44] In the Soviet context, the valuation problem is further complicated by Marxian theory, which is prejudiced against charging for natural resources (the labor theory of value). Like the right to pollute the environment, natural resources have, in effect, been given to enterprises free of charge, thereby encouraging them to overuse depletable natural resources.[45]

Third, perfectly centralized decision-making as visualized in the idealized versions of the socialist economic model has not proved to be practical in the real world. In fact, most crucial economic decisions are made not by a small group of planners at the apex of the planning hierarchy who take the broad overview of the economy, but by ministerial and regional authorities and by plant managers, none of whom can see (or cares to see) the total impact of his actions. In effect, there has been no pressure group concerned with the environment. Instead, administrators and managers are concerned with performing well, in line with directives given them by their superiors; and as we noted above, success in the Soviet economy has been determined primarily on the basis of fulfilling short-term output goals. Less easily quantifiable goals (especially in view of the price system) such as cost reductions, innovations, and environmental quality have not played a role in influencing decision-making. Thus, where environmental groups exist in the Soviet Union, they find themselves in the awkward position of having to lobby against regional Gosplan organizations, national ministries, or even the party itself on projects that create environmental disruption; in other words, against the very organizations that, in theory, are to prevent environmental disruption from taking place.[46] In fact, there is no all-union agency for protecting the environment. Rather, environmental protection has tended to be placed in the hands of various agencies, all with limited powers.

The final source of environmental disruption in the Soviet Union is the lack of a clear assignment of "property rights" (the assignment of rights to use, benefit from, and bear the costs of scarce resources).[47] Under capitalism, property rights belong to private owners, who bear the costs and reap the benefits from the use of the resource. In the case of resources with a long life span (renewable and nonrenewable natural resources, capital equipment), the capitalist owner will weigh current and future benefits and will forgo current use if the prospect of future reward is sufficiently high. Thus, there is a natural incentive to conserve. Under socialism, property rights are assigned to society as a whole, not to individual workers or to plant managers. These persons are rewarded according to short-term performance criteria and will not personally benefit from refraining from current use for the sake of future use. The incentive to conserve is therefore lacking, unless imposed from above via a change in the existing incentive system.

REFERENCES

1. This discussion is based upon the following sources: A. Becker, "The Meaning and Measure of Soviet Military Expenditure," in U.S. Congress, Joint Economic Committee, *Soviet Economy in a Time of Change* (Washington, D.C.: U.S. Government Printing Office, 1979), vol. 1, pp. 352–368; H. W. Shaeffer, "Soviet Power and Intentions: Military-Economic Choices," in U.S. Congress, Joint Economic Committee, *Soviet Economy in a Time of Change* (Washington, D.C.: U.S. Government Printing Office, 1979), vol. 1, pp. 341–351; W. T. Lee, *The Estimation of Soviet Defense Expenditures, 1955–1975* (New York: Praeger, 1977); National Foreign Assessment

Center, *Estimated Soviet Defense Spending: Trends and Prospects,* SR78–10121 (Washington, D.C., June 1978); National Foreign Assessment Center, *A Dollar Cost Comparison of Soviet and U.S. Defense Activities, 1968–78,* SR79–10004 (Washington, D.C., January 1979); F. Holzman, "Are the Soviets Really Outspending the U.S. on Defense?" *International Security* (Spring 1980), 86–104.

2. Hearings Before the Subcommittee on Priorities and Economy in Government, *Allocation of Resources in the Soviet Union and China—1978; Part 4: Soviet Union* (Washington, D.C., June 26 and July 24, 1978), pp. 11, 49.

3. National Foreign Assessment Center, *Estimated Soviet Defense Spending;* and National Foreign Assessment Center, *A Dollar Cost Comparison.*

4. There is no direct information on the ruble costs of military hardware, so analysts convert dollar values into ruble values using conversion rates for similar products (relative U.S.–USSR machinery costs, for example). For a critique of these conversions, see Holzman, "Are the Soviets Really Outspending the U.S. on Defense?"

5. This is the procedure used by Lee, *Estimation of Soviet Defense Expenditures.*

6. The various estimates for 1975, cited in Becker, "Soviet Military Expenditure," p. 362, are: Official Soviet: 17.4 (billion rubles); CIA: 50–60; Lee: 72; French estimate: 42.3; Chinese estimate: 69.4.

7. P. Hanson, "Review of Estimating Soviet Defense Expenditures," *Soviet Studies,* vol. 30, no. 3 (July 1978), 403.

8. For a discussion of this point, see Becker, "Soviet Military Expenditure," pp. 352–366.

9. National Foreign Assessment Center, *A Dollar Cost Comparison,* p. 4.

10. *Allocation of Resources in the Soviet Union and China,* p. 37; R. F. Kaufman, "Causes of the Slowdown in Soviet Defense," *Soviet Economy,* vol. 1, no. 1 (January-March 1985), 9–36.

11. See Becker, "Soviet Military Expenditure," pp. 352–358, for a discussion of the tenuous relationship between outlays and military power; also see Holzman, "Are the Soviets Really Outspending the U.S. on Defense?" pp. 86–104.

12. Holzman, "Are the Soviets Really Outspending the U.S. on Defense?" pp. 87–93.

13. M. Feshbach and S. Rapawy, "Soviet Population and Manpower Trends and Policies," in U.S. Congress, Joint Economic Committee, *Soviet Economy in a New Perspective* (Washington, D.C.: U.S. Government Printing Office, 1976), p. 150.

14. National Foreign Assessment Center, *Estimated Soviet Defense Spending,* p. i.

15. See Holzman, "Are the Soviets Really Outspending the U.S. on Defense?" pp. 86–102, for a critique of estimates of defense expenditure shares.

16. For a simulation of the effects of defense spending during the 1960s, see D. Green and C. Higgins, *Sovmod I: A Macroeconometric Model of the Soviet Union* (New York: Academic Press, 1977), pp. 71–74. For a study of the 1970s and projections, see H. Bergendorff and P. Strangert, "Projections of Soviet Economic Growth and Defense Spending," in U.S. Congress, Joint Economic Committee, *Soviet Economy in a New Perspective* (Washington, D.C.: U.S. Government Printing Office, 1976), pp. 394–430. Another important econometric study of the defense-consumption-GNP relationship is L. Calmfors and J. Rylander, "Economic Restrictions on Soviet Defense Expenditure," in U.S. Congress, Joint Economic Committee, *Soviet Economy in a New Perspective* (Washington, D.C.: U.S. Government Printing Office, 1976), pp. 377–392.

17. This discussion is based largely on the following sources: J. S. Berliner, *The Innovation Decision in Soviet Industry* (Cambridge, Mass.: MIT Press, 1976); J. Berliner, "Prospects for Technological Progress," in U.S. Congress, Joint Economic Committee, *Soviet Economy in a New Perspective* (Washington, D.C.: U.S. Government Printing Office, 1976), pp. 431–446; R. Amman, J. Cooper, and R. W. Davies, *The Technologi-*

cal Level of Soviet Industry (New Haven, Conn.: Yale University Press, 1977); J. R. Thomas and U. Kruse-Vaucienne, eds., *Soviet Science and Technology* (Washington, D.C.: George Washington University, 1977), parts 3 and 4; E. Zaleski et al., *Science Policy in the USSR* (Paris: OECD, 1969); J. Martens and J. P. Young, "Soviet Implementation of Domestic Inventions: First Results," in U.S. Congress, Joint Economic Committee, *Soviet Economy in a Time of Change* (Washington, D.C.: U.S. Government Printing Office, 1979), vol. 1, pp. 472–509; J. Grant, "Soviet Machine Tools: Lagging Technology and Rising Imports," in U.S. Congress, Joint Economic Committee, *Soviet Economy in a Time of Change* (Washington, D.C.: U.S. Government Printing Office, 1979), vol. 1, pp. 524–553; P. Hanson, "International Technology Transfer from the West to the USSR," in U.S. Congress, Joint Economic Committee, *Soviet Economy in a New Perspective* (Washington, D.C.: U.S. Government Printing Office, 1976), pp. 786–812; R. Amann and J. Cooper, eds., *Industrial Innovation In the Soviet Union* (New Haven: Yale University Press, 1982); B. Parrott, *Politics and Technology in the Soviet Union* (Cambridge, Mass.: The MIT Press, 1983).

18. A statement of R. Nelson cited by R. Amman, "Soviet Technological Performance," in J. R. Thomas and U. Kruse-Vaucienne, eds., *Soviet Science and Technology* (Washington, D.C.: George Washington University Press, 1977), p. 329.

19. This is the basic conclusion of the Amman, Cooper, and Davies study, conducted at the University of Birmingham, England. See Amman, Cooper, and Davies, *The Technological Level of Soviet Industry.*

20. Amman, "Soviet Technological Performance," p. 328.

21. Grant, "Soviet Machine Tools," pp. 524–553; K. Tasky, "Soviet Technology Gap and Dependence on the West: The Case of Computers," in U.S. Congress, Joint Economic Committee, *Soviet Economy in a Time of Change* (Washington, D.C.: U.S. Government Printing Office, 1979), vol. 1, pp. 510–523.

22. Martens and Young, "Soviet Implementation," pp. 505–507.

23. P. Hanson, "The Diffusion of Imported Technology," in NATO Economics Directorate, *Economic Aspects of Life in the USSR* (Brussels: NATO, 1975).

24. This discussion is based upon Berliner, *The Innovation Decision,* and Berliner, "Prospects for Technological Progress."

25. Berliner, "Prospects for Technological Progress," p. 445.

26. The above figures are from *Naselenie SSSR* [Population of the USSR] (Moscow, 1983), pp. 102–121; *Obrazovatel'naia i sotsial'no-professional'naia struktura naseleniia SSSR* [Educational and social professional structure of the USSR population] (Moscow, 1975), *Vestnik Statistiki,* no. 11 (1984), 71; *Narodnoe khozaistvo SSSR za 60 let* [National Economy of USSR for 60 Years] p.477; V. Yelyutin, *Higher Education in the USSR* (Moscow: Novosti, 1970), pp. 22, 79; *Narodnoe khoziaistvo SSSR v 1982 g.,* p.462; I.M. Makarov, "Povysit effektivnost nauchnykh issledovanii," [To raise the effectiveness of scientific research] *Vestnik vysshei shkoly,* no. 7 (1984) 4; *Vestnik statistiki,* no. 8 (1983), 63.

27. These general conclusions are drawn from L. Nolting and M. Feshbach, "R&D Employment in the USSR," *Science,* vol. 207 (February 1980), 493–503; C. Ailes and F. Rushing, *A Summary Report on the Educational Systems of the United States and the Soviet Union,* SRI International, SSC-TN-7557-12, March 1980; S. Kassel and C. Campbell, *The Soviet Academy of Sciences and Technological Development,* Rand Corporation, R-2533-ARPA

28. Ailes and Rushing, *A Summary Report,* p. 11.

29. M. Kuchment and H. Balzer, An Interim Report on the Project: A Net Assessment of Soviet R&D Capabilities: Information and Insights From the 3rd Soviet Emigra-

tion, prepared for the National Council for Soviet and East European Studies, Washington, D.C., August 1981.

30. Based on data in the 1979 *Science Indicators,* published by the National Science Foundation and cited in U. M. Kruse-Vaucienne and J. Logsdon, *Science and Technology in the Soviet Union: A Profile* (National Science Foundation, George Washington University, Washington, D.C., 1979), p. 5.

31. M. Mathews, "Long Term Trends in Soviet Education," in J. J. Tomiak, ed., *Soviet Education in the 1980s* (New York: St. Martin's Press, 1983), pp. 1–24.

32. See, for example, *Current Digest of the Soviet Press,* July 4, 1984, for a typical series of complaints about Soviet university students.

32. R. McIntyre and J. Thornton, "On the Environmental Efficiency of Economic Systems," *Soviet Studies,* vol. 30, no. 2 (April 1978), 173–192.

33. A. Wright, "Environmental Disruption and Economic Systems: An Attempt at an Analytical Framework," *The ASTE Bulletin,* vol. 13, no. 1 (Spring 1971), 11–12.

34. Lange's paper appears in B. E. Lippincott, ed., *On the Economic Theory of Socialism* (Minneapolis: University of Minnesota Press, 1938), pp. 103 ff., reprinted by McGraw-Hill, 1964.

35. M. Dobb, *Welfare Economics and the Economics of Socialism* (Cambridge: Cambridge University Press, 1969), p. 133.

36. For a discussion of this point, see Dobb, *Welfare Economics,* pp. 133–134. For a survey of theorizing on environmental quality, see M. I. Goldman, *The Spoils of Progress: Environmental Pollution in the Soviet Union* (Cambridge, Mass.: MIT Press, 1972), pp. 12–22.

37. M. I. Goldman, "Externalities and the Race for Economic Growth in the Soviet Union: Will the Environment Ever Win?" *Journal of Political Economy,* vol. 80, no. 2 (March-April, 1972); K. Bush, "Environmental Disruption: The Soviet Response," *L'Est,* no. 2 (June 1972); D. Kelley, K. Stunkel, and R. Wescott, *The Economic Superpowers and the Environment: The United States, the Soviet Union, and Japan* (San Francisco, Calif.: Freeman, 1976); W. A. Jackson, ed., *Soviet Resource Management and the Environment* (Columbus, Ohio: Anchor Press, 1978); V. Mote, "Environmental Protection and the Soviet Tenth Five Year Plan," *Geographical Survey,* vol. 7, no. 2 (April 1978); P. R. Pryde, *Conservation in the Soviet Union* (Cambridge, Mass.: Harvard University Press, 1972); F. Singleton, *Environmental Misuse in the USSR* (New York: Praeger, 1976).

38. Although the power of the state and the Soviet view of the superiority of the public sector should be positive forces in the control of environmental disruption, the specific techniques used in the Soviet case, notably administrative penalties and criminal prosecution, seem to have been most ineffective. On this see Goldman, *The Spoils of Progress,* pp. 28–37.

39. For a discussion of measurement problems, see McIntyre and Thornton, "Environmental Efficiency," pp. 182–183.

40. *Ibid.,* p. 181.

41. I. Edwards, M. Hughes, and J. Noren, "US and USSR: Comparisons of GNP," in U.S. Congress, Joint Economic Committee, *Soviet Economy in a Time of Change* (Washington, D.C.: U.S. Government Printing Office, 1979), vol. 1, pp. 378 and 385.

42. K. Bush, "Environmental Disruption: The Soviet Response," *L'Est,* no. 2 (June 1972).

43. This point is stressed by McIntyre and Thornton, "Environmental Efficiency," p. 174.

44. Some Soviet economists have argued that each factory should be accountable for both direct *and* social costs. However, such has not been the case, primarily due to the absence of appropriate cost measurement and the potential conflict with Marxian ideology. On this see Goldman, *The Spoils of Progress,* pp. 46 ff.

45. J. Thornton, "Resources and Property Rights in the Soviet Union," in W. A. Jackson, ed., *Soviet Resource Management and the Environment* (Columbus, Ohio: Anchor Press, 1978), pp. 1–12.
46. The Ministry of Power's handling of Lake Baikal is a case in point. Despite protests from residents concerning the environmental damage that such a project would cause, dam construction was pushed through, although other sources of electricity were already available at cheaper cost. See Goldman, "Externalities." Another case in point is the Central Committee's irrigation program that calls for the diversion of Siberian rivers to irrigate dry regions in Kazakhstan and Central Asia, which will have an important impact on the climate of the Far North. On this, see Bush, "Environmental Disruption."
47. This discussion is based on Thornton, "Resources and Property Rights," pp. 1–12.

SELECTED BIBLIOGRAPHY

Soviet Military Power

A. Becker, "The Meaning and Measure of Soviet Military Expenditure," in U.S. Congress, Joint Economic Committee, *Soviet Economy in a Time of Change* (Washington, D.C.: U.S. Government Printing Office, 1979), vol. 1, pp. 352–368.

H. Bergendorff and P. Strangert, "Projections of Soviet Economic Growth and Defense Spending," in U.S. Congress, Joint Economic Committee, *Soviet Economy in a New Perspective* (Washington, D.C.: U.S. Government Printing Office, 1976), pp. 394–430.

L. Calmfors and J. Rylander, "Economic Restrictions on Soviet Defense Expenditure," in U.S. Congress, Joint Economic Committee, *Soviet Economy in a New Perspective* (Washington, D.C.: U.S. Government Printing Office, 1976), pp. 377–392.

J. Collins, *US/Soviet Military Balance, Statistical Trends, 1970–1982* (Washington, D.C.: Congressional Research Service, 1983).

R. E. Kaufman, "Causes of the Slowdown in Soviet Defense," *Soviet Economy,* vol. 1, no. 1 (January/March 1985), 9–31.

W. T. Lee, *The Estimation of Soviet Defense Expenditures, 1955–1975* (New York: Praeger, 1977).

National Foreign Assessment Center, *A Dollar Cost Comparison of Soviet and U.S. Defense Activities, 1968–78,* SR79–10004, Washington, D.C., January 1979.

———, *Estimated Soviet Defense Spending: Trends and Prospects,* SR78–10121, Washington, D.C., June 1978.

H. W. Shaeffer, "Soviet Power and Intentions: Military-Economic Choices," in U.S. Congress, Joint Economic Committee, *Soviet Economy in a Time of Change* (Washington, D.C.: U.S. Government Printing Office, 1979), vol. 1, pp. 341–351.

Soviet Technology

C. Ailes and F. Rushing, *A Summary Report on the Educational Systems of the United States and the Soviet Union,* SRI, SSC-TN-7557-12, March 1980.

R. Amann and J. Cooper, *Industrial Innovation in the Soviet Union* (New Haven: Yale University Press, 1982).

R. Amman, Julian Cooper, and R. W. Davies, *The Technological Level of Soviet Industry* (New Haven, Conn.: Yale University Press, 1977).

J. Berliner, *The Innovation Decision in Soviet Industry* (Cambridge, Mass.: MIT Press, 1976).

J. Grant, "Soviet Machine Tools: Lagging Technology and Rising Imports," in U.S. Congress, Joint Economic Committee, *Soviet Economy in a Time of Change* (Washington, D.C.: U.S. Government Printing Office, 1979), vol. 1, pp. 524–553.

P. Hanson, "The Diffusion of Imported Technology," in NATO Economics Directorate, *Economic Aspects of Life in the USSR* (Brussels: NATO, 1976).

———, "International Technology Transfer from the West to the USSR," in U.S. Congress, Joint Economic Committee, *Soviet Economy in a New Perspective* (Washington, D.C.: U.S. Government Printing Office, 1976), pp. 786–812.

S. Kassel and C. Campbell, The Soviet Academy of Science and Technological Development, Rand Corporation R-2533-ARPA, p. 1.

J. Martens and J. P. Young, "Soviet Implementation of Domestic Inventions: First Results," in U.S. Congress, Joint Economic Committee, *Soviet Economy in a Time of Change* (Washington, D.C.: U.S. Government Printing Office, 1979), vol. 1, pp. 472–509.

M. Mathews, "Long Term Trends in Soviet Education," in J. J. Tomiak, ed., *Soviet Education in the 1980s* (New York: St. Martin's Press, 1983), pp. 1–24.

B. Parrott, *Politics and Technology In the Soviet Union* (Cambridge, Mass.: The MIT Press, 1983).

J. R. Thomas and U. Kruse-Vaucenne, eds., *Soviet Science and Technology* (Washington, D.C.: George Washington University Press, 1977), parts 3 and 4.

E. Zaleski et al., *Science Policy in the USSR* (Paris: OECD, 1969).

Environmental Quality

K. Bush, "Environmental Disruption: The Soviet Response," *L'Est,* no. 2 (June 1972).

M. I. Goldman, "Externalities and the Race for Economic Growth in the Soviet Union: Will the Environment Ever Win?" *Journal of Political Economy,* vol. 80, no. 2 (March/April, 1972).

W. A. Jackson, ed., *Soviet Resource Management and the Environment* (Columbus, Ohio: Anchor Press, 1978).

D. Kelley, K. Stunkel, and R. Wescott, *The Economic Superpowers and the Environment: The United States, the Soviet Union, and Japan* (San Francisco, Calif.: Freeman, 1976).

R. McIntyre and J. Thornton, "On the Environmental Efficiency of Economic Systems," *Soviet Studies,* vol. 30, no. 2 (April 1978), 173–192.

V. Mote, "Environmental Protection and the Soviet Tenth Five Year Plan," *Geographical Survey,* vol. 7, no. 2 (April 1978), 25–34.

P. R. Pryde, *Conservation in the Soviet Union* (Cambridge, Mass.: Harvard University Press, 1972).

———, "The Decade of the Environment in the USSR," *Science,* vol. 220 (April 1983), 274–279.

F. Singleton, *Environmental Misuse in the USSR* (New York: Praeger, 1976).

J. Thornton, "Resources and Property Rights in the Soviet Union," in W. A. Jackson, ed., *Soviet Resource Management and the Environment* (Columbus, Ohio: Anchor Press, 1978), pp. 1–12.

four

REFORM AND CHANGE: PROSPECTS FOR THE FUTURE

chapter *13*

Soviet Economic Reform: Theory, Practice, Prospects

We have focused our attention on how the Soviet works and with what results. Our emphasis has been on what is actually done rather than on the theory of resource allocation in a centrally planned socialist economy. In part, this applied approach is dictated by the uncertain state of the literature on theoretical alternatives to the current Soviet economic system. Alec Nove, a veteran observer of the Soviet economic system, has noted that the Soviets had "virtually no theory to guide them; and no theory of planning emerged from their activities."[1]

This chapter is on economic reform. This is largely a theoretical topic because the Soviets have yet to reform their economic system in a significant way. To consider reform of an economic system, one must first identify the basic features of the existing system. Contemporary Soviet authors generally refer to the planning principle as the guiding force for resource allocation in the Soviet economy. The basic theory is Marxism–Leninism. To quote a recent Soviet book on national economic planning, "the theoretical basis for planning of the national economy is provided by Marxist–Leninist economic theory, especially the theory of social extended reproduction."[2] Thus, in contemporary Soviet thinking, planning derives from the basic economic laws of socialism. It is from these "objective preconditions" that the basic principles of an integrated, balanced, goal-oriented and effective plan mechanism for guiding the development of the national economy emerge.

The Soviet economic system is an example of centrally planned socialism because a national economic plan replaces the market as the dominant mechanism for the allocation of resources and public ownership of the means of production replaces private ownership. Planning and public ownership are the two main

387

features of the planned socialist economy.[3] If the Soviet system is a planned and socialist system, can one apply the contemporary theory of planning, as developed in East and West, as a theoretical basis for the Soviet economic system? Interestingly enough, Soviet authors would probably agree that planning theory applies to the Soviet case, though they would likely disagree that the theory of economic planning has common roots and common applications in socialist and capitalist economic systems. One Soviet source describes the difference between socialist and capitalist planning as follows:

> Socialist planning presumes a combination of the obligatory nature of the basic planned tasks with application of economic management methods, using prices, credit, and material incentives. Capitalist planning (programming) is, by nature, indicative (nonobligatory) and serves to supplement the machinery of the capitalist market economy, which can no longer satisfactorily function on the basis of free enterprise.[4]

As we have shown in Chapter 7, the characterization of the Soviet economy as a planned economy does not receive unanimous support from Western economists. Some have argued that it is an "administered" economy. In part, this characterization arises from Eugene Zaleski's painstaking analysis of Soviet planning from the 1930s to the early 1950s.[5] In his foreword to Zaleski's work, John H. Moore notes the following:

> Zaleski concludes that the planning system is best seen as a mechanism for managing the economy. The system is less important as a means for planning for the future, in the sense of setting out alternative courses of action to be pursued under different contingencies, or even for projecting outcomes to be achieved, than it is as a tool for maintaining the grip of the leadership and economy.[6]

Although characterization of the Soviet economy as an "administered" economy may arise from the particular conditions faced by early Soviet planners, the question of an appropriate characterization of the Soviet economy in contemporary times remains a matter of dispute.[7]

How we characterize the Soviet economic system is important. The topic of this chapter is economic reform, and by economic reform we mean changes in the economic system, as opposed to changes in economic policies or environmental factors. Specifically, we are concerned with changes in the economic system per se, that is, changes in the organizational arrangements of the economy or changes in what the Soviets term the economic levers, or mechanisms that guide economic activity within the prevailing organizational arrangements. The introduction of agro-industrial complexes is an example of the reform of organizational arrangements, and the changing of managerial success indicators is an example of reform of levers.[8]

If economic reform is change of the economic system and/or the system mechanisms (levers), the chapters on economic history have already dealt with considerable Soviet economic reform. The changes in the economic system during the 1920s, 1930s, and 1940s were discussed in some detail. These changes served to establish the Soviet economic system as we know it today. This chapter deals with reform of the Soviet economic system that was created using the reforms of the earlier period.

There is no general theory of economic reform. In some respects, the Soviet economy of 1985 resembles quite closely the Soviet economy of 1935, and in other respects it does not. To the extent that it does not, the outcome is the result of two types of changes: ongoing changes that continually affect the ways things are done, and major isolated reform programs. The latter are the primary focus of this chapter. Specifically, we are interested in examining the various Soviet reform programs, how these programs were intended to change Soviet working arrangements, and their actual outcomes. It is not always easy to distinguish between ongoing change and economic reform. However, during the past 25 years, there have been several major announced reform programs. These major reforms have been the thrust of intended change and will be the focus of this chapter.

Western economists have generally been skeptical about economic reform in the Soviet Union. Some argue the impact of economic reform has been inconsequential and not worth extended analysis. Although it is difficult to measure the impact of economic reform, this skepticism is based upon a number of considerations. First, although Soviet reform programs are announced with great fanfare, problems of implementation arise, public discussion of the program fades, and subsequently a new program is announced, again with great fanfare. Second, the skeptics cite evidence that reform programs are not successfully implemented because of bureaucratic resistance and problems of introducing changes in a piecemeal fashion. Third, skeptics note that, even if authorities were to follow through, the reforms call for such modest changes that their ultimate effect on efficiency would be trivial. However, even if this view is correct, it is important that we examine Soviet reforms. They indicate the direction in which Soviet leaders feel their economic system should go, and, in addition, they tell us a great deal about the actual operation of the system. There is no sign that the idea of reform will be abandoned. Indeed, the major reason for studying past reform is to gauge the prospects for future reform. Indeed, under Gorbachev, a leader committed to raising productivity, we might expect a greater emphasis on change in the Soviet economic system. Few would argue that there has been no change in the Soviet economic system; so, whether the change be small in degree or not, it is important that we understand the process of change.

TWO CURRENTS IN REFORM THINKING: HISTORICAL BACKGROUND

The problems associated with the Soviet type of planning and management system are familiar. For example, the Soviet press abounds with discussion of an appropriate management system: how can managers be induced to complete all the tasks assigned to them, meet plan targets, produce an appropriate mix of products, pay attention to quality, reduce costs, and so on?

Although it is simplistic to classify reform in just two dimensions, we can think of economic reform as either "centralizing" or "decentralizing." The centralizing approach to reform is based on the notion that administrative planning techniques can be perfected, that planners can obtain and act on all necessary information, and that subunits can be made to act "rationally" through better instructions and appropriate monitoring procedures.

The decentralizing school of reform argues that the effectiveness of planning is needlessly hampered by trying to make all decisions at the center. Important decisions can be made at the center; but to solve both information and incentive problems, more decisions must be made at local levels, that is, within individual producing units.[9]

This dichotomy between "decentralization" and "better centralization" can be traced all the way back to the discussions of the 1920s. The supporters of NEP were, in effect, advocates of the first approach: let the routine day-to-day decisions be made by managers and "experts," with the state controlling the commanding heights. In the NEP environment, the bulk of economic decisions would be made at micro levels, and the task of the planners would be limited to devising grand strategy. The mechanism that would make this all possible would be the market, which would coordinate the actions of producers and consumers. In words of Stephen Cohen, the "first great reform in Soviet history was the introduction of . . . NEP in 1921."[10] The appeal of NEP as a model of reform persists, largely due to Lenin's writings in its support.

The coming demise of NEP forced Soviet planners and theorists to grapple with a different scenario, one in which the market was eliminated and resource allocation decisions were to be made administratively. The guiding mechanism of the market was absent, and new methods of rational resource allocation had to be sought.

The 1920s was a productive period for theorizing about the administrative planning option. During this period, rough outlines began to emerge that probably would have eventually led to full-fledged theories of socialist resource allocation through central planning. Talented economists and statisticians were busy estimating national balances, an example being the well-known 1923–1924 balance of the national economy prepared by the Central Statistics Board under the direction of P. I. Popov.[11] Such efforts, the intellectual predecessors of input-output techniques later sophisticated by Professor Wassily Leontief in the United States, pointed the way toward the future development of mathematical planning techniques involving both balancing and optimization of resource allocation—an approach that was blocked by the harsh reaction against mathematical economics during the Stalin years. Nevertheless, such efforts (premature, given the state of knowledge at the time) were based on the premise that the socialist economy can be directed by mathematical planning models expressing input-output relationships among branches. It was not until the post-Stalin years that Soviet economists were allowed to return to their work and to develop the relatively sophisticated theories of mathematical planning in a centrally directed socialist economy.

With the establishment of the Stalinist dictatorship, discussion of the theory of Soviet planning ceased. The NEP system was anathematized, and the search for rational administrative planning procedures was halted by the brutal repression of economic science. Although the deficiencies of material balance planning and managerial behavior were likely known to the Soviet leadership, the Soviet economic system was declared infallibly directed by the planning principle. Criticism of the system became dangerous, and economic failures were attributed to individual mistakes and willful sabotage, not to the system itself. The "law of value"—supply and demand—was declared by Stalin not to operate in a socialist economy. Instead, a new economic regulator, the planning principle, had replaced the capitalist laws of supply and demand, and the tools developed by bourgeois economists to analyze capitalist economies were seen as unnecessary constraints no longer relevant to a socialist society. Such a socialist economy could be scientifically directed by technicians and engineers without observing "economic laws." This view came to be more firmly entrenched and is reflected in the growing disregard for market forces displayed by economic planners in the late 1920s.[12]

By the 1930s, it had become dangerous to argue for either the positive role of market forces or the existence of economic laws in a planned socialist economy. Increasingly, planners shied away from concepts such as "equilibrium" and "balanced growth" as unnecessary constraints on their freedom of action, and most economic theorizing ground to a halt.[13]

Soviet economic science entered into a dark age during the Stalin dictatorship. The economic system that emerged under Stalin was an ad hoc response to practical problems and crises, and it evolved without the benefit of a calculated blueprint. But it was the product of the party (Stalin) and as such could not be criticized. It is no wonder that serious work on defining an optimal planning system or improving the existing system was discouraged, and theorists on economic reform and mathematical planning went underground, only to reemerge after Stalin's death. The two attempts by high officials to initiate reform (in 1933 and 1947) led to the execution of the ill-fated reformers.[14]

The death of Stalin in 1953 unleashed pent-up pressure to enact economic reform. To a great extent, Khrushchev was the embodiment of the reform ethos, and his overthrow in 1964 signaled the return to a more conservative approach to reform. The resurgence of interest in economic reform assumed several forms in the 1950s. First, there was a slight shift from blaming all economic problems on human shortcomings to a willingness to experiment with organizational changes. Although the inclination to deal with problems via organizational reorganization continues to the present day, it probably reached its peak in 1957 with Khrushchev's attempted shift from a ministerial to a regional system of economic management. Second, there was a resurgence of interest in mathematical planning techniques and theories of rational planning. Prominent Soviet pioneers in this area such as L. V. Kantorovich and V. V. Novozhilov suggested that resources could be utilized much more efficiently, without loss of central control, if optimal planning procedures were used.[15] In 1959, the book *The Use of Mathematics in Economics* was published under the editorship of V. S. Nemchinov. It contained the original papers of Kantorovich and Novozhilov, written during the repressive Stalin years. Since then, subsequent volumes in this series have been published, prestigious mathematical economics institutes of the Soviet Academy of Science have been established, and prominent Soviet mathematical economists have been awarded the coveted Lenin Prize. Kantorovich has even received the Nobel Prize in economics.

A sign of the growing official toleration of reform discussion was the publication in obscure technical journals of papers suggesting various means to reform and improve the existing planning system by some decentralization (devolution) of decision-making authority.[16]

The official start of serious reform discussion in the Soviet Union can be dated to September 9, 1962, with the publication of the article "Plan, Profits and Bonuses" in *Pravda* by the then obscure economist Evsei Liberman.[17] The publication of Liberman's paper signaled official endorsement of open discussion of reform and initiated an important debate among orthodox planners, mathematical economists, and those advocating greater decision-making authority at the micro level. We shall return to this discussion and its outcome shortly, but first we must look at the reasons behind the party decision to allow open reform discussion.

WHY THE ECONOMIC REFORM DISCUSSION?

To understand the factors behind the first party endorsement of reform discussion, one must return to the scenario of the late 1950s and early 1960s. The 1950s was a period of heady growth of both agriculture and industry, and the Soviet leadership was emboldened to make rash claims about overtaking the United States and creating full communism. This optimism was nurtured by the perceived economic weakness of the United States, which had suffered mild recessions and slow growth throughout the 1950s. The pattern of declining growth of output and productivity that began to be perceived in the Soviet Union in the late 1950s and early 1960s provided the major impetus for discussions of economic reform. We can say that concerns about economic performance initiated the early discussions and that disappointing economic performance has kept interest in economic reform or change alive in the Soviet Union.

The chapters on Soviet economic performance outlined the reasons why the Soviet leadership would be disappointed with Soviet performance over the past 25 years. First, the rate of economic growth of the Soviet economy has been declining since the late 1950s. Growth rates of gross national product were generally above 5 percent in the 1950s, but had fallen to below 3 percent by the latter part of the 1970s. Although the Soviet rate of economic growth over the last two decades is not low by international standards, the long downward trend must be viewed as unacceptable for a country whose economic superiority (by its own perception) is to be demonstrated by rapid economic growth. Although Soviet measurements of their own economic growth have tended to exceed Western estimates, especially for the early years of Soviet economic growth, even official Soviet figures show a slowdown of economic growth.* Soviet figures on

---

*These differences stem, in large part, from measurement problems, especially for the early years of Soviet growth. They are discussed in greater detail in chapter 11.

national income show an average annual rate of growth of just under 10 percent in the 1960s and an average annual rate of just under 4 percent for the period 1980 through 1983.[18]

Second, there is increasing recognition that the Soviet years of "easy" or extensive growth are over. In the past, much of the Soviet growth achievement has come from expanding labor and capital inputs. From the late 1920s to the present, the capital stock has grown at very rapid rates, the labor force participation rate has been increased to one of the highest in the world, and land inputs to agriculture were expanded rapidly (especially in the 1950s) to act as a major source of increased production. Historical experience tells us that as a country becomes more mature, it must increasingly look to the better use of inputs— productivity growth—to generate overall economic growth. It cannot continue indefinitely to rely on rapid growth of labor, land, or capital inputs. A sagging growth rate cannot be revived in a mature economy by accelerating the growth of factor inputs.

Third, both Western and Soviet estimates of factor productivity find that there has been a significant slowing down in the rate of growth of factor productivity since the late 1950s.[19] Factor productivity growth has slowed more dramatically than factor input growth, so that declining factor productivity appears to be the main culprit behind the growth slowdown. To the extent that the marginal products of both capital and labor are declining, the rates of economic growth must also decline unless the slackening of productivity can be offset by expansion of inputs to the system. This latter option is not possible in an economy with already very high investment and labor participation ratios.

Fourth, there is no doubt that rising consumer pressure for more and better goods and services has been an issue of concern to the Soviet leadership. To the extent that monetary incentives are required to stimulate labor productivity, difficulties arise when there is persistent excess demand in some markets and unsold inventories in others. Since the 1950s, Soviet per capita consumption has grown at a quite respectable average annual rate of 3 percent.[20] The question is not whether the living standards of Soviet consumers are rising, since this is clearly the case. The important question is what rates of increase in terms of quantity and quality are necessary to bring forth desired work effort. In the early 1970s, the 3 percent growth rate of the 1950s dropped to 2.6 percent per annum, while for the late 1970s and early 1980s, this figure declined to under 2 percent.[21] Declining economic growth has meant that the growth rate of consumption has had to decelerate. The growth rate of consumption, however, can provide a misleading picture of the growth of material living standards. If the economy fails to produce the goods and services desired by the population (and price them appropriately), the increased physical outputs of goods and services will not be transformed into higher levels of consumer satisfaction.

A fifth reason for interest in economic reform is the growing complexity of the Soviet economy. This complexity is evidenced by the growing number of interconnections among producers, consumers and suppliers, which increases the difficulty of planning. In 1983, there were 45,374 industrial enterprises in the Soviet Union.[22] If one adds wholesale and retail trade outlets and scientific and cultural organizations to this myriad of interenterprise organizations, the problem of coordinating Soviet economic activity is clearly awesome. As the Soviet economy has grown, the number of sectors has grown and the product range has broadened. The priority principle has become less and less useful. No longer can "steel blinders" be used.[23] Trucks, machines, missiles, and plants can be built with steel, plastics, or other products all of which can be effective substitutes under certain circumstances. It is no longer clear which of these materials is "more important" to fulfill the economic goals of the Soviet leadership. Moreover, a more complex economy may be more vulnerable to mistakes in planning both in the sense that planning mistakes are more likely to be made and that, when made, they will be more serious as they reverberate throughout the system. With growing concerns over economic incentives, the use of consumer goods as a buffer sector becomes increasingly unattractive as a means to handle these problems.

Finally, the resurgence of economic theorizing in the Soviet Union in the post-Stalin era has had an impact upon the party decision to allow reform discussion in the 1960s and thereafter. Soviet economists in general and mathematical economists in particular claim that their preferred methods can improve the achievement of party objectives while leaving the determination of these objectives to the party. As Aron Katsenelinboigen, a former professor of economics at Moscow State University and now an emigré, writes: "When there is an urgent practical need for some method . . . Soviet leaders are in fact willing to sacrifice ideology."[24] In effect, the reform economists have been holding up the prospect of substantial improvements in the Soviet economic system with relatively small ideological concessions. In effect, reform-minded Soviet economists offer methods that they claim will bring about more effective resource utilization through familiar techiniques such as the proper costing and pricing of inputs and outputs and more effective incentive mechanisms.

Our discussion makes clear why the Soviet leadership sanctioned reform discussion in the early 1960s and why reform discussion continues to be tolerated to the present day. The Soviet leadership is obviously concerned about the declining growth rates of output and factor productivity. They understand the incentive consequences of declining growth of per capita consumption and of an economy that is not sensitive to consumer demand. The Soviet leadership is, therefore, willing to listen to proposals that promise to exploit the "hidden reserves" of the economy by utilizing existing resources in more effective ways.

THE THEORY OF ECONOMIC REFORM

There is no clear-cut theory of economic reform of the planned socialist economic systems that can provide a blueprint for the Soviet leadership. Economic reform refers to a nontrivial change in the working arrangements of the economic system. The organization of the economic system and/or its subunits may be changed, in which case we describe the reform as organizational change. The system mechanisms (levers) which are used to motivate economic agents to carry out plan objectives may be changed quite apart from organizational change. In fact, Soviet economic reform has consisted of both types of change.

Western discussion of Soviet economic reform has centered on the possibility of changing the locus of decision-making. Our description of the Soviet planned economy showed that major resource allocation decisions tend to be made at levels above the enterprise—by Gosplan, the ministries, the party, and the state committees. Relatively few decisions are made, at least formally, by the microeconomic units. Most Western specialists on reform of the Soviet planned economy suggest that a real change in Soviet working arrangements would require a shifting of more decision-making authority to units lower in the economic hierarchy. This shifting of decision-making to lower levels is called decentralization.[25]

There is no single concept of decentralization. At the most obvious level, decentralization means the shifting of decision-making authority and responsibility down an established administrative hierarchy to lower levels in the hierarchy. Using this notion, decentralization occurs when a Soviet ministry makes decisions that were previously made by *Gosplan* or when an enterprise makes decisions that were previously made by the ministry. Because it covers such a broad range of activities, the hierarchical approach to understanding decentralization does not have much operational meaning.

Morris Bornstein draws a more useful distinction between "administrative decentralization" and "economic decentralization."[26] Administrative decentralization occurs when local units (enterprises) are given increased authority to make decisions (previously made by higher administrative units) within a framework of rules and parameters set by higher administrative authorities. For example, the local unit may be given more authority to make its own input decisions based on the rule that managers should combine inputs in a least-cost fashion. To encourage the local unit to make "rational" input decisions, higher administrative authorities may reward the local unit on the basis of achieved percentage cost reductions. The key feature of administrative decentralization is that higher authorities control the parameters that the local unit uses to make its decentralized decisions. Higher authorities set input prices and the parameters of the local unit's reward structure. Administrative decentralization relieves the higher authority of much decision-making authority by permitting more decisions to be made by lower units. The higher authority, however, does continue to exercise authority and control over local units by keeping a firm hand on the parameters that motivate decentralized decisions.

Economic decentralization also allows the local unit to make more decentralized decisions but with the higher administrative authority setting fewer parameters. For example, higher authorities may allow input prices to be established by the forces of supply and demand in markets. They may allow the local unit to operate according to very general rules of the game, such as acting to maximize the economic well-being of the unit. Economic decentralization means that higher administrative authorities have given up more real authority to local units than under administrative decentralization.

The choice of administrative versus economic decentralization underscores the Soviet reform dilemma. As long as higher administrative authorities control the parameters that guide local decision-making, they are in a better position to impose the state's will upon microparticipants in the economy. In the 1930s, for example, administrative control and monitoring of local decision-making may have been at their peak, and the Soviet economy was indeed transformed according to the preferences of the ruling elite. The micro units, who possessed local information as to how best combine resources, were not allowed to exercise decentralized authority. Accordingly, numerous resource allocation mistakes were made that could have been avoided by enlightened micro-decision-making. In a setting in which the economy has already been transformed to conform to the preferences of the ruling elite, the elimination of resource allocation mistakes becomes more important. As efficiency becomes of paramount importance, local decisions must be better decisions, that is, they must achieve central wishes with a minimal expenditure of resources. If local decisions cannot be focused by centrally set rules, then local decision-makers must be given a parametric framework in which their actions will be harmonized with central wishes.[27] It is here that a redefinition of managerial success indicators occurs.

The theory of reform of the Soviet planned economy states that Soviet authorities should seek out an optimal mix of administrative and economic decentralization. Under the most ideal of circumstances, a system would be put in place that encourages local units (utilizing the local information at their disposal) to combine resources in an efficient manner while, at the same time, encouraging local units to implement the stated plans of higher authorities. It remains to be seen, in both theory and practice, whether these two objectives are compatible. Is the loss of centralized direction over local units the price that higher authorities must pay for better local decision-making? Moreover, the adoption of the decentralized model may create macroeconomic side effects that the system's directors are unwilling to tolerate. For example, decentralized choice of inputs may cause enterprises to lay off redundant workers, thereby creating nationwide unemployment.[28]

Even if the theory of reform could specify the ideal economic system toward which the Soviet planned economy should strive, there remains the problem of moving from the prevailing system to that ideal system. No one will know for sure whether the proposed "ideal" system will work as the theory says it should; the system's managers know that they are taking risks when they move toward the new system. If the system's directors choose to move cautiously in a piecemeal fashion (as has been the choice in the USSR and Eastern Europe),[29] how will the system function during the transition?

It is difficult to understand how several firms will interact with each other when some are acting under the new set of rules while the remainder act under the old set of rules. If one firm is to be released from the plan when it comes to selling its products, then potential buyers must also be freed from the plan constraint of buying from a specified seller. The proper sequencing of economic reform is as difficult a theoretical issue as is the identification of the economic system the reform process is supposed to install.

The remainder of this chapter concentrates upon *actual* rather than proposed economic reforms in the Soviet Union. The major exception to this is our discussion of the Liberman proposals, which remain largely unimplemented and were superseded by the 1965 reform. It is important to distinguish between proposed reforms and actual reforms in the Soviet context—a distinction often missed in popular writings. In the view of most experts, actual economic reform in the USSR has been quite modest, whereas some proposed economic reforms are quite radical and far-reaching.[30]

The Liberman Proposals

The proposals of Evsei Liberman, a professor of engineering economics at Kharkov University, much discussed in the West largely due to their emphasis on profits, are a convenient focus for the beginning of our reform discussion. Although Liberman had been writing about enterprise performance and arguing for a reduction in the tutelage over managers since the 1920s, his ongoing research was first brought to the level of public discussion in 1962 with the publication of his article "The Plan, Profits and Bonuses" in *Pravda.*[31] Most importantly, its publication in the official party newspaper signaled an official sanctioning by the Soviet leadership of reform discussion.

Several facets of this early reform era deserve comment. First, Liberman gained prominence well out of proportion to the importance of his proposals.[32] In fact, Liberman served to some extent as the figurehead of the liberal "profit group," which included the eminent mathematical economist V. S. Nemchinov.[33] To this day, his proposals remain largely unimplemented, and his renewed emphasis on profits—the aspect of his proposals that attracted most attention in the West—was most limited. Liberman was quite clear in pointing out that the central planning of output would be maintained in full vigor and that profits would serve as a basis for managerial rewards only after the output targets for quantity and assortment had been met. If enterprises failed to meet their output targets, they would be "deprived of the right to bonuses."[34] Thus, Liberman did not propose that profits act as the fundamental guide for economic activity but rather that profits were to have a more important role along with other success criteria and would be the source of bonus payments (if any were forthcoming). This major concession was a response to the critics of the "profit school," who argued that enterprises would cease production of important yet low-profit goods.

Turning to the details of Liberman's proposals,[35] we note that Liberman suggested that bonus payments (after fulfillment of the planned output target) should be an increasing function of the profit/capital ratio, thus encouraging the expansion of profits but the reduction of capital usage. Profitability norms established for each industry would serve as the basis for evaluating managerial performance. To encourage enterprise managers to set ambitious targets for themselves, rewards would be higher for successful fulfillment—or perhaps even underfulfillment—of an ambitious profitability plan than for the overfulfillment of an "easy" target.

The number of centrally planned enterprise directives would be limited to the quantity and assortment of output and its delivery. The enterprise itself would plan its own material, labor inputs, and new technology. This would prove possible under the new system, according to Liberman, because the new emphasis on profits would encourage managers to seek out cost economies and new reserves rather than build up excess stocks.

On the crucial issue of centralization versus decentralization of decision-making, Liberman remained ambiguous. All the basic instruments of central planning—price setting, the state budget, ruble control, state control of large investments—would be maintained, along with the centralized planning of material supply.[36] How this system could be made compatible with enterprises planning their own inputs was not spelled out in detail by Liberman other than by his assertion ("with reasonable confidence") that the two would prove compatible.[37] Liberman's conservatism on the issue of supply was in marked contrast to "marketeers" such as Nemchinov and A. Birman, who advocated free trade in producer goods.[38] On the crucial issue of the price system, Liberman also equivocated,[39] although he did suggest that the current Soviet price system would act as a serious impediment to the actual implementation of his proposals by giving unfair profitability advantages to some producers while discriminating against others. Nevertheless, he believed that his system would force managers to press for more rational prices.[40]

The publication of the original Liberman proposals in 1962 sparked considerable controversy and a period of open discussion in the Soviet press and academic journals between 1962 and 1965.[41] During this period, the various factions —ranging from the conservative antireformers to the Liberman supporters and the more radical reformers, especially the mathematical school—were given the opportunity to state their positions. Delayed by a politically conservative leadership, considerable criticism over the issue of profit and its meaning in a socialist economy, and, in particular, a lack of willingness to let important decisions be made by the "anarchy" of the market, the official decision came at the party plenum in September of 1965. Prior to the party decision, a series of experiments was undertaken to test various reform ideas on a partial basis.

Reform Experiments

Acting out of a sense of caution, the Soviet leadership authorized a series of experiments to test different reform ideas between 1962 and 1965. These experiments—the NVP experiment, the light industry reform, and the transportation experiment—were carried out between 1962 and 1965, testing the ideas of the profit group and the advocates of more conservative economic reform.[42]

The conservative NVP ("normative value of processing") experiment was initiated in the Tartar Republic in 1962 and then was broadened to selected consumer goods industries in other regions. The basic notion of the NVP experiment was to improve the efficiency of enterprise operation by replacing the much maligned gross output index by the new NVP index. The reader will recall that the use of gross output as the prime enterprise success criterion encouraged enterprise managers to meet their gross output targets by increasing their use of expensive materials. Under the NVP index, enterprise performance was to be judged on the basis of planned labor costs, fuel costs, and some overhead expenses, thus removing the incentive to overemploy expensive intermediate materials. Profit performance would not be included in the NVP index, to eliminate the conservatives' reservation that enterprises would only produce high-profit items. Stated in terms more familiar to Western economists, the NVP reform simply called for the substitution of enterprise value added (net output) for gross value of output. Its advocates argued that the NVP index provided a more reasonable measure of output performance. The NVP opponents argued that it was a mere palliative and did not deal with the fundamental issues of appropriate incentives, the encouragement of quality production, and the matching of consumer demands and supplies. The profit group was given its opportunity with the light-industry experiments initiated in 1964.

One of the major criticisms of the Soviet planning system has been the lack of a feedback mechanism between the consumer and producer—a phenomenon especially prominent in the clothing industry, where an accumulation of unsalable inventories had resulted. In a step to resolve this problem, an experimental program sanctioned by the Central Committee was begun in 1964.[43] The Bolshevichka factory in Moscow and the Maiak factory in Gorky were allowed to receive their production orders directly from a selected group of retail outlets rather than being assigned quantitative output targets. Unsold stocks or returned output would detract from plan fulfillment. In particular, attention was to be paid to consumer demand as a determinant of production, with bonuses (set between 40 and 50 percent of basic pay) dependent upon fulfillment of delivery and profit plans, not output plans.

Although these experimental enterprises remained under a considerable degree of constraint from above—in particular, in the centralized control of their material supplies—their performance in this program was considered a success; and in subsequent years the program was expanded, even to heavy industry. By 1965, this reform had been extended to 25 percent of the garment factories, 28 percent of the footwear factories, 18 percent of the textile mills, and 30 percent of the leather factories.[44]

The extent to which this reform, also dubbed the "direct links" reform, was continued after 1965 is not known. In fact, these changes were subsumed by the official general (and more conservative) reform of September 1965, and thus this direction of change seems to have been blunted. Apparently, there remained a general lack of willingness to free these experimental enterprises from administrative controls, and hence many of the supply, incentive, and other problems of Soviet industry continued to plague these enterprises. When this experiment was applied more broadly, the inability of the trade network to anticipate consumer demand and to coordinate orders with shifting consumer tastes became more apparent.

A third experimental program, begun in 1965, deserves brief mention. Several trucking enterprises were given the authority to seek out their own customers (especially on return hauls), to acquire trucks on their own initiative, and to pay drivers bonuses for picking up extra shipments and were encouraged to lay off unneeded workers. The thrust of this program was to interest these trucking enterprises in maximizing profits. The initial successes of this experiment caused it to be extended to other trucking firms.

THE OFFICIAL REFORM OF 1965

The most important—though most modest—economic reform in the Soviet Union was announced by Premier Alexei Kosygin in September of 1965 as a general reform to be gradually implemented over the next five years.[45] In light of the high expectations for significant change raised by the debates and experiments of the preceding years, the official response must have been disappointing to the proponents of decentralization of economic authority. However, the conservatism and caution of the party leadership should have been anticipated, given the power of the forces in support of the status quo. First, we consider the substance of the 1965 reform proposal, after which we evaluate its implementation in the period 1965 through 1971 and its modification thereafter.

Enterprise Planning and Management

The basic thrust of the 1965 reform was a reduction in the number of enterprise targets to be set from above, and most important, replacement of gross output by "realized output" (sales) as the primary indicator of success for an enterprise. In addition, the number of indicators for labor planning—previously four—was to be reduced to a single indicator: the magnitude of the wage fund. Thus, an enterprise manager was now to face the following eight targets established within the central plan, compared to the earlier system of 20 to 30 targets:

1. Value of goods to be sold
2. Main assortment
3. The wage fund
4. Amount of profit and the level of profitability
5. Payments to and allocations from the state budget
6. The volume of investment and the exploitation of fixed assets
7. Main assignments for the introduction of new technology
8. Material and technical supplies

Turning to the financial aspects of planning, several changes were decreed. An interest charge on fixed and working capital was proposed, to be implemented at a 6 percent rate effective in 1966.[46] In addition to this new capital charge, provisions were made for an enhanced role to be played by *Gosbank*. This new role centered upon a reduction in the importance of the state budget and, in its place, the utilization of *Gosbank* facilities for the financing of enterprise investment.

Thus, a new expanded role was envisaged for *Gosbank*, especially in the provision of investment funds at differentiated charges depending upon usage. Also, *Gosbank* was to facilitate the clearance of debts among enterprises and between enterprises and their customers in the trade network.

The 1965 reform also placed new emphasis upon the importance of accounting. Ties to the budget as a source of investment finance and subsidies were to be reduced and a production development fund was to be established. This fund was to be fed from three main sources: profits, amortization of equipment, and sales of unneeded equipment.

Profits and Incentives

The changing role of profits called for in the September 1965 reform was relatively modest. Prices were to be reformed to allow enterprises to be profitable under normal conditions of operation in order to end one of the long-standing results of average branch cost pricing, namely, that a good many enterprises continually suffered losses. In addition, the role of profit was to change in two respects. First, although profit was always a part of the Soviet managerial *(khozraschet)* system in the Soviet Union, it was given a position of greater importance, along with the now more limited number (eight) of indicators of managerial success.

Second, profits were to be an important source of funds for decentralized investment by enterprise managers (a 20 percent share for decentralized investment was projected[47]) and were to be used as a source of funds for bonus payments to workers. The former would be channeled through two funds—the production development fund and the fund for social welfare and housing (to build factory-owned apartments)—while the latter would be channeled through a new material incentive fund. These three funds were to replace the old enterprise fund and were designed to enhance the importance of profits for enterprise activity in addition to giving enterprise managers greater freedom of decision-making.

Prior to the 1965 reform, worker bonus schemes had been subject to criticism not only because of the meager amounts involved but also because the funding was typically from the wages fund rather than from profits. The 1965 rules for the utilization of the new material incentive fund were complex.[48] Briefly, however, this fund was to be placed largely under the control of the enterprise itself and was to provide material incentive payments above and beyond those normally provided by the wages fund.

Two observations should be made concerning the role of profits in the 1965 reform. First, it was apparent that in terms of increasing the importance of profits as a success indicator for management, little change was envisioned. Output (now in the form of sales) remained the all-powerful indicator, and profits remained a secondary indicator of enterprise success, along with seven other targets. In addition, where managers might enjoy a measure of freedom in the utilization of profits, for example, in the case of decentralized investment or worker bonuses, in many instances other constraints were erected, such as prohibiting management to contract for material supplies or tightening centralized regulations over bonuses.

Second, the behavior of profits in the immediate aftermath of the reform serves as a partial indicator of the importance of profits. For the first three years of the reform, profits in enterprises operating under the reform grew at a more rapid pace (about 50 percent faster between 1965 and 1968) than those in the nonconverted enterprises. Decentralized investment also increased, though at a rate substantially less than that envisaged in the original reform blueprint.[49] These figures suggest increased managerial interest in profitability in the years immediately following the 1965 reform.

Recentralization

One of the overlooked features of the official reforms was the recentralization of the Soviet economic bureaucracy. Power was returned to the ministries, and the regional economic councils (the *Sovnarkhozy*) put in place by Khrushchev in 1957 were abolished. Decision-making authority shifted from regional authorities to national authorities.

The 1965 reforms called for a variety of organizational changes in the economic management and planning system.[50] Key functions were centralized in three powerful new state committees: the State Committee for Material-Technical Supply *(Gossnab),* the State Committee for Prices *(Gostsen),* and the State Committee for Science and Technology *(Gostekhnika).* Industrial enterprises were to be combined into large associations, called "production associations," and research enterprises and institutes were to be grouped into "science-production associations." The rationale given for these associations was that they would yield economies of scale, reduce the bureaucracy, and assist in the planning process. *Gossnab* was given the primary responsibility for allocating producer goods, and the ministerial supply organizations that had dominated the rationing of funded goods were largely to disappear. *Gossnab* was to apply itself to the creation of a wholesale trade system based on direct contracting arrangements among suppliers and buyers. Changes in the planning process were also proposed: there was to be an increased emphasis on long-term plans; the "scientific basis" of planning was to be upgraded through the use of computers, mathematical programming, and the like; and "complex planning" (the planning of regional complexes) was to be emphasized.

Implementation of the 1965 Economic Reform

The manner in which the 1965 reform was implemented is a valuable case study of the barriers that stand in the way of economic reform in the Soviet case. It reveals those areas of the Soviet economic system most resistant to change. Initially, two phases of implementation of the reform were anticipated. The first, or "extensive," phase was to be the phased conversion of nonagricultural enterprises to the new system. The second, or "intensive," phase, scheduled to begin in 1970, would be the one in which the true potential of the reform would be realized.[51] In terms of the original format, all industrial enterprises were to be converted to the new system by the end of 1968 and the remainder of the economy by the end of 1970. The exception was agriculture, where the introduction of full *khozraschet* into *sovkhozy* was to take place at a somewhat slower pace. The progress of the reform is summarized in Table 51. Three general comments are in order.

First, although the original timetable was not met, in a formal sense, the major proportion of industrial enterprises were, in fact, converted to the new system. Until 1972, little progress was made in the direction of merging converted enterprises into production associations.

Second, the reform was not implemented in some important sectors of the economy, notably in the construction industry and also in the material-technical supply system. As of 1971, only 10 percent of both construction and repair organizations and material-technical supply organizations were operating under the new system.[52] These patterns indicate some resistance to the general reform movement. Finally, it is well to remember that these figures on reform implementation are formal, and, above all, they do not mean that where "implemented" the reform system actually operated according to the original conception outlined above.

Table 51 CONVERSION OF INDUSTRIAL ENTERPRISES TO NEW ECONOMIC SYSTEM, 1966–1970 (AS PERCENTAGES OF ALL INDUSTRY)

At end of:	Number of enterprises converted	Percentage of all enterprises converted	Percentage of total output	Percentage by number of staff	Percentage of total profit
1966	704	1.5	8	8	16
1967	7,248	15.0	37	32	50
1968	26,850	54.0	72	71	81
1969	36,049	72.0	84	81	91
1970	41,014	83.0	92	92	95

Source: K. Bush, "The Soviet Reform After Five Years," Radio Liberty Research Report, CRD 258/71, August 1971, p. 2; N. Fedoryenko et al., *Soviet Economic Reform: Progress and Problems,* translated from the Russian (Moscow: Progress Publishers, 1972), p. 202.

Reform Implementation—Financial Aspects

One of the seemingly significant aspects of the September 1965 reform blueprint was the emphasis on decentralized investment (at the enterprise level) through the newly formed production development fund and the utilization of bank credits, which had until then accounted for only a very small portion of investment in fixed capital.

The volume of decentralized investment derived from the production development fund did expand in the converted enterprises. In 1965, the share of decentralized investment was 12 percent, rising to the targeted 20 percent in 1972. Subsequently, the share of decentralized investment declined to about 12 percent in 1976.[53] More importantly, the distinction between decentralized and centralized investment quickly lost its meaning. The problem of appropriately marrying a centralized system with decentralized elements of resource allocation—particularly in the crucial area of investment—was especially acute in the case of the 1965 reform. On the one hand, managers were encouraged to invest on a decentralized basis, while, on the other hand, they were unable to purchase investment goods through the material supply network. These supply problems are familiar to any student of the Soviet system, and continued to exist in spite of a system of fines for nondelivery and various attempts to develop the concept of "free sales."[54] The supply system remained largely centralized and out of reach of the typical enterprise manager. A further factor limiting the manager's control over decentralized investment was the growing centralized regulation of the size and distribution of the production development fund.

The envisioned expansion of the banking system as a supplier of credit did not materialize. Credits, though available, were utilized less in the converted than in the nonconverted enterprises basically because it was the profitable enterprises that invested, and they had sufficient internal reserves. It should also be noted that those enterprises converted had surplus working capital resulting from the inability to spend production development and sociocultural and housing funds simply due to the absence of a mechanism for decentralized investment. Bank financing of state centralized investment grew slowly, accounting for only 2.3 percent of all investment in 1973.[55]

Labor Allocation Under the Reform and Shchekino

Clearly, any economic reform that attempts to decentralize decision-making must focus upon the enterprise management's ability to control labor inputs. The question of labor allocation is a crucial issue of economic reform, for if a cost-profit calculus is to have real meaning, substitution of inputs becomes a prime sphere of managerial decision-making and may well imply the dismissal of labor by enterprises.

Nominally, the 1965 reform enhanced the manager's freedom to allocate labor by retaining only one central constraint—the wage bill—over labor staffing, as opposed to the earlier system of detailed specifications. Of course, the wage tariff was still centrally determined. Because the original reform statement in 1965 placed considerable emphasis upon the reduction of the number of indicators governing the enterprise labor force, this was originally seen by some Western observers as the main decentralizing factor of the entire reform.[56] In fact, the significance of such changes was reduced for two reasons. For those enterprises not covered, obviously the change was of little importance, and that applied to all changes, of course, not just labor allocation. Second, and more crucial, the substance rather than the number of indicators was the important matter to the enterprise manager. Indeed, central control over both the wages fund and the utilization of this fund persisted after 1965, although new freedom was supposed to exist in the latter area.[57] This result, along with trade union pressure against the right of enterprises to dismiss workers, left enterprise managers' decision-making power virtually unchanged from the prereform era.

However, there were changes to come, in large part as an outgrowth of the much publicized Shchekino experiment. Begun in 1967, this experiment was so named because it was introduced at the Shchekino chemical factory near Moscow. The basic idea behind this reform was simple: the wage fund would be fixed, enterprises would have the right to reduce the labor force by the removal of unneeded workers, and the remaining workers and the enterprise in general would benefit from the paring of unnecessary labor.[58]

Understandably, there were difficulties with this concept. Soviet authors pointed out that the staffing freedom allowed by the Shchekino experiment could disrupt prevailing norms, break the normal relationship between productivity gains and wages, and create problems of regulating bonus funds. There probably was some lessening of interest in the Shchekino experiment in the 1970s, and thus the Western view of the program has generally been skeptical. This skepticism has been based upon the apparent lack of widespread application of the program, a number of post-1967 regulations intended to alter the original concept, and, most important, the perception that such a program could not be implemented on a widespread scale because it would introduce unemployment into the Soviet economy.

Recent evidence supports a more positive view of this program. In a major study of the original program, its changes, and its implementation, Peter Rutland finds surprising vitality. In 1982, 3,300 enterprises were operating fully on the Shchekino method, with 21 million employed and 11,710 enterprises partially on the program.[59] He further reports that the Shchekino approach has "saved" 968,000 jobs in the tenth Five Year Plan, not to mention a significant increase in labor productivity in those enterprises using this approach.

Rutland argues that Shchekino is now most appropriately considered as an approach, or method, rather than a narrow experiment.[60] This importance stems not only from the number of specific applications noted above but notably from the fact that a number of elements of the method have, in fact, meshed with ongoing decision-making arrangements. Moreover, Rutland notes that while central rules under the general rubric of the Shchekino method are complex, in fact, there have been many local variations facilitating implementation.

To understand the changes of the 1970s and especially those that would be introduced in 1979 and thereafter, it is useful to note briefly the specific areas in which elements of the Shchekino approach have meshed with ongoing arrangements.

As Rutland has noted, Soviet authorities have long been concerned with improvement in the organization and utilization of labor.[61] Much of this discussion, especially in the 1960s and thereafter, comes under the rubric of introducing NOT *(nauchnaia organizatsia truda),* or the scientific organization of labor. Two elements of this discussion, closely related to each other and also to the Shchekino approach, are the issues of establishing labor norms and setting the wage fund. In fact, during the 1970s, there were problems with the wage fund system, the most important being the setting of the wage fund and its distribution to workers based on a myriad of confusing indicators. Although the original 1965 reform was intended to simplify targets, there was much local variation. Moreover, there was great emphasis on the need to redefine labor norms, in effect, to move from the traditional coefficients to what is described as "normative" planning, or the setting of labor norms based on labor requirements per ruble of output. This issue would remain the subject of discussion throughout the 1970s and 1980s.

What, then, of the original Shchekino experiment? It would seem that the thinking of this approach has had an impact, indeed an impact that continues under constantly changing circumstances. Although the final chapter is yet to be written, Rutland argues that "there is no evidence that unemployment was a serious issue in the Shchekino method."[62]

MOVING AWAY FROM REFORM

As we have emphasized, the basic thrust of the 1965 reform program[63] was a reduction in the tutelage of the enterprise manager by higher planning organs. Was this goal achieved in any degree? Initially, the idea was to create a system whereby managers would be encouraged to respond spontaneously to various economic "levers"—profits, bonuses, increased authority over investment, and so on—so as to make the Soviet enterprise more efficient and release "hidden reserves." For these reasons, the number of plan targets was to be reduced, reliance was to be placed on more rational success indicators such as sales and profitability, managers and workers were to become materially interested in the outcome of enterprise performance by tying bonus funds to enterprise activity, and so on.

Initially, there was a tendency to view this reform as a major attempt to decentralize decision-making, that is, to shift decision-making authority and responsibility to lower levels in the hierarchy, notably to the enterprise level. In retrospect, it may be more useful to interpret this reform not so much as decentralization but rather as an attempt to change the framework in which enterprise managers would make particular decisions. In any event, the 1970s and 1980s brought continuing change that tended to move the Soviet system away from the ideas of the 1965 reform.

Between 1965 and 1971, there was evidence of greater managerial spontaneity in response to these economic levers, especially as regards the disposition of bonus funds. As managers began to exercise their newfound authority, planners and bureaucrats began to react against "undesirable" spontaneous enterprise actions and to press for amendments to the 1965 rules. During the very period when the reform was scheduled to move into its "intensive" phase, amendments and modifications were introduced that significantly altered the content of the original reform. The particular shortcomings that these amendments sought to correct were the unduly large shares of new bonus funds received by managerial personnel, the lack of attention to labor productivity and quality improvement, the unwillingness of managers to request taut production targets or to economize costs, and so on—many of the very shortcomings that the 1965 reform had sought to eliminate in the first place.

Between June 1971 and January 1978, a number of changes were introduced that significantly modified the spirit of the original reform proposal. First, rigid regulations governing the size of enterprise-incentive funds replaced the original more flexible system. Now the ministry, based upon limits determined by *Gosplan,* was to determine the size of enterprise-incentive funds by fixing planned incentive fund targets. The size of the various incentive funds was thus to depend upon enterprise performance vis-à-vis planned indicators, basically upon the fulfillment of output, profitability, and labor productivity targets. Incentive funds were also to depend upon three additional targets: the plan for key products in physical units, the plan for consumer goods, and the plans for changes in product quality and new products. Furthermore, the size of the incentive fund was tied to the tautness of the enterprise plan: the higher the output, profitability, and labor productivity targets, the larger the potential incentive funds. The more recent restrictions on enterprise funds restore most authority to the ministries. The ministry again has the authority to determine the conditions under which incentive funds will be accumulated and disbursed. Enterprises can be punished by fund reductions for failing to meet specific targets set by the ministries.

Second, strict controls over the distribution of enterprise-incentive funds were introduced. In the new regulations, limits were placed on the rate of growth of managerial bonuses, average wages were not allowed to increase faster than labor productivity, and regulations were established to reduce bonus differentials among branches. Significantly, managerial bonuses were tied to fulfillment of sales and profitability plans *plus* the fulfillment of the physical assortment plan, and the ministries were allowed to add additional conditions if they so desired. Ministries were to set the requirements for incentive funds, limiting income growth to targeted rates. Ceilings were set on managerial bonuses as a proportion of base salary, and the ministry could deny bonuses if delivery plans are not met.

Third, the manager's control over the production development fund (for investment) was circumscribed. Under the modified rules, the proportion of enterprise profits to be allocated to this fund was to be set by the ministry in accordance with bank credits planned for decentralized investments. The incentive effects of the enterprise investment fund were nullified. The concept of decentralized investment has been abolished by treating expenditures from the fund like all other investments.

Finally, and perhaps most important, the number of enterprise targets was expanded. New targets were reinstated since 1970: labor productivity, gross output, consumer goods assignments in heavy industry, quality targets, material and fuel economy targets, delivery obligations, new products, and the size of basic incentive funds.

Many of the administrative changes proposed by the 1965 reform were not implemented as initially planned. During the early years of the reform, enterprises did not amalgamate into productive associations; but after a party-government decree in April 1973, the formation of production associations proceeded at a rapid pace. In the 1980s, production associations account for some three-quarters of industrial output. The purposes of the production association were to gain the advantages of economies of scale in management through the amalgamation of firms involved in similar lines of business and to economize on administrative personnel. In practice, the formation of industrial associations meant little more than "changing the names on doors" in Moscow; supervisory power continued to remain in the hands of the chief administrations of the ministries, and there was a 60 percent expansion in the bureaucracy between 1966 and 1977.[64] The ministries continued to be the centers of economic power, allocating materials and equipment, dictating the incentive systems of enterprises and industrial associations, and controlling investment. *Gossnab* was supposed to replace the ministerial supply organs, but in 1978, *Gossnab* handled only one-half the value of rationed producer goods. The market for producer goods failed to emerge, and the traditional system of material supplies and central balances continued to function. The role of bank credits in regulating economic activity did not increase at the rate proposed in the 1965 reform, and most investment continued to be financed directly from the state budget rather than through bank credit. Capital was no longer granted to enterprises free of charge, but it was agreed that the low 6 percent interest charge did not promote the efficient utilization of investment resources.

The 1965 reform called for an enhanced role for long-term planning, seeking to establish the Five Year Plan as the basic operating plan of the national economy. Yet after 15 years' experience, the annual economic plan remains operative. One new feature of Soviet planning, "counterplanning," called for rewards to enterprises that adopt counterplans. If an enterprise voluntarily adopts more demanding targets than established in the Five Year Plan, its opportunities for bonuses are enhanced. Despite campaigns to promote counterplans, only 13,000 industrial enterprises were engaged in counterplanning in 1977. As late as 1981, only 6.6 percent of the industrial enterprises adopted counterplans. Moreover, managers appear to propose cosmetic counterplans that do not alter the substance of planned targets.[65]

What, then, is the status of the 1965 reform? As we noted at the outset, this is a difficult question to answer with any precision; indeed, it may be the wrong question. It is evident that since the introduction of the original reform program in 1965, there have been a myriad of changes derived from and affecting all levels of the Soviet economic hierarchy. Although many would argue that the reform has not been implemented, most would probably agree that things were being done differently in the late 1970s from the way they were done in the mid-1960s. But what can be said about these changes in terms of our original characterization of economic reform?

The thrust of the 1970s seems to have been toward the improvement of planning methods, for example, the greater emphasis on long-term plans, better norming, increased use of automated methods and computerization, and the like. Decentralization does not seem to be an appropriate characterization, yet the issue of changing the levers or mechanisms through which the economy is manipulated is relevant. Did the economic content of the levers change? One Western critic of the reform could write in 1973 that "after seven years of the reform, economic methods, or 'levers,' have been effectively converted into administrative 'levers' . . . as a consequence, centralized planning and administration are even more entrenched . . ."[66]

The issue of change, however, does not end with the 1965 reforms and the alterations of the 1970s. In 1979, a major new initiative developed, providing us, in effect, with the opportunity to assess the thrust of reform in the 1980s. We turn to an examination of this program.

REFORM AND CHANGE IN THE 1980S: THE JULY 1979 DECREE

In July of 1979, a major decree was introduced entitled "On Improving Planning and Strengthening the Economic Mechanism's Influence on Raising the Effectiveness of Production and the Quality of Work." This decree, usually cited in the literature as PIEM, or Program to Improve the Economic Mechanism, is not generally treated as an economic reform in the sense of being a systematic program to change the economic system. Thus, Morris Bornstein, in a major study of this effort, suggests that PIEM should be discussed on its own terms, that is, "as an attempt within the framework of a 'traditional' ('Soviet-type') socialist centrally planned economy to improve economic performance through changes in the arrangements for the choice of output, the allocation of resources to produce it, and the distribution of the associated personal income."[67] Thus, we discuss PIEM in this chapter not so much as a formal reform program but rather as the latest integrated effort to change Soviet economic decision-making procedures. What is the nature of PIEM, and to what degree does it continue trends evident in the 1970s?

The Content of PIEM[68]

In his concluding comments to a recent study of PIEM, Morris Bornstein summarizes the aims and means of this program as follows: ". . . to increase output; to reduce its cost, and particularly the use of materials and fuels; to improve quality, through the introduction of new products; to secure the timely delivery of output, according to the contracted product-mix; and to cut construction time and costs."[69] He further notes that these objectives will be pursued through "a variety of measures affecting planning, performance indicators, incentives, and finance."[69]

The improvement of planning is to be developed in five general areas.[69] First, enterprise (or production unit) capacity is to be better known through what is described as the "passport" system—a systematic effort to know more about production capability in each producing unit by requiring more information and on a regular basis.

Second, the norming process is to be improved and is to replace "directive indicators" so that the planning process can be simplified and differing local conditions accounted for. Thus, instead of an enterprise being specifically told how much labor can be used for a particular task, a predetermined norm will cover the particular application, and enterprise performance will, in part, be judged by the achievement of the norm.

Third, the issue of plan "tautness" is once again to receive attention. Specifically, enterprises will be encouraged to operate under taut plans, a concept that will be measured by such indicators as the percentage use of capacity. Rewards will follow and will be provided for the enterprise adoption of "counterplans" or plans that require more than the official plans.

Fourth, the emphasis is again on long-term planning, but now with greater emphasis on plan coordination. This emphasis on coordination relates to the One Year and Five Year Plans and also to the regional plans. Overall, the emphasis is again on the formulation of accurate but firm plan tasks, long an issue of contention in Soviet planning.

Finally, the material supply system is to be improved largely through the expanded use of contracting. Thus, enterprises will be encouraged to establish supply contracts with user enterprises that fulfill the contract terms not only by shipment of the basic product but also by meeting other requirements such as timeliness, quality, assortment, and the like.

How are these objectives to be met? As we have noted, the emphasis is on changed performance indicators, incentives, and investment arrangements.

A crucial part of the 1979 decree relates to performance indicators. Specifically, the decree addresses three traditional problem areas of Soviet enterprise performance, namely, the overutilization of material inputs, the lack of enterprise interest in quality, and, finally, neglect of product mix.

The emphasis on gross output as an enterprise success indicator has always led to the overutilization of material inputs. Under the new rules, labor productivity is to become a key indicator of enterprise performance, and it is to be measured as net output per worker, normed in accordance with the procedures outlined above. An additional word is in order, given the importance of this concept.

Normative output is the product of the physical output and the "net output normative." The net output normative is described as "a type of 'net' price established by the State Committee for Prices" and as a "planned branch average wage and social insurance cost plus profit."[70] This indicator is designed to discourage overuse of material inputs, a practice that will not contribute to net output.

Quality is to be emphasized under the new enterprise rules simply by making it an important indicator of enterprise performance, related to bonus payments. A commission will categorize products according to quality, and enterprises will be rewarded according to the share of better quality products in their output.

The assortment problem is to be attacked by better specification of output in the plan and by tying rewards to the completion of delivery contracts that include assortment. Efforts will be made to make the output specification more detailed so that deviations from plan can be spotted more readily.

Most of these changes will have a familiar ring to the reader—either they have arisen in previous decrees and/or they relate to problems familiar to any observer of the Soviet economy. How will they be enforced?

Changes are to be made in two main areas—incentive arrangements and investment procedures—plus a myriad of changes relating to specific problem areas in the economy. Let us consider the two main areas of emphasis.

PIEM will impose important changes in bonus arrangements. Although enterprise profit is to remain as the main source of bonus funds, the rules for forming and disbursing bonus funds will change and, indeed, will become more complex. Most important, the bonus system will be much more closely tied to labor productivity (as mentioned earlier) and the quality share indicator. Moreover, the basic work unit is increasingly to become the brigade, and brigades are to be on the *khozraschet* system.

Finally, important changes have been made in the area of investment planning. The emphasis here is self-financing, especially at the ministerial level. Ministries are to be on *khozraschet* and increasingly are to be accountable for their plan fulfillment. Ministries will have profit plans; and after various payments to the state budget, retained profits are to be used for investment purposes.

Implementation of the July 1979 Decree

It is evident, even from this very simplified discussion, that the 1979 program focuses on a number of crucial areas of Soviet planning and does so by adding substantial complexity. Although it is too early to assess the extent to which these changes are, in fact, implemented, some observations can be made.

Morris Bornstein, in the concluding section of his recent study of the reform, argues that the implementation has been modest in every respect, and that there are numerous obstacles to further implementation.[71] In another study of the reform, Gertrude Schroeder puts it this way: "Planning is more centralized, rigid, and detailed than ever; the scope for initiative of the producing units is more circumscribed; producer goods are more tightly rationed; administratively set, inflexible, average cost-based prices are retained; and intricate incentive systems are tied to meeting plans for many potentially conflicting variables, with priority given to production plans expressed in physical units."[72]

It is interesting to note that these changes both reinforce and contradict earlier reform emphasis. For example, the emphasis on long-term planning, especially the stability of plans, is a theme of long standing. Counterplans were a part of earlier discussion, but they were implemented to only a modest degree. Yet a major emphasis of the 1965 reform, namely, reduction in the performance indicators, seems to have been reversed.

Thus far, we have focused on major initiatives attempting to change decision-making procedures in the Soviet economy. Our emphasis has been the reform program of 1965 and the PIEM decree of 1979. Both were directed at similar issues, both have had only modest success, and yet both have probably changed the ways in which decisions are, in fact, made, though with great variation from one case to another.

INDUSTRIAL PRICE REFORM

An implicit factor in the Soviet reform discussion was the issue of industrial prices. As was pointed out in Chapter 8, industrial prices have been set to equal average branch cost of production (capital and rental charges omitted) plus a planned profit margin without reference to demand. Such prices are not scarcity prices, in the sense that they do not equate supply and demand, nor do they reflect full marginal cost. In fact, more often than not, industrial prices have been allowed to diverge from costs owing to the administrative complexity of price reform, thus necessitating state subsidies for enterprises that sustain losses.

Against this background, one can understand the complexities of the decentralization issue, that is, the extent to which crucial economic decisions can be left up to enterprise managers without first having the primary information mechanism upon which such decisions are to be based—a "rational" price system. In this context, one can perhaps understand the relative willingness of Soviet authorities to give managers more discretion in the area of labor staffing, where prices tend to be based more on scarcity.

Such considerations culminated in the general reform of industrial prices during 1966–1967. Did this reform transform the Soviet price system into a more useful information mechanism for decentralization? The answer is quite simple: it did not.

The 1966–1967 price reform was conducted separately from the official reform of 1965, and, as we already noted, was not a major consideration in the earlier Liberman discussions. The goals of the 1966–1967 industrial price reform were quite modest. In view of the enhanced role of profits and monetary incentives envisioned in the 1965 reform, it was deemed essential to set industrial prices at average cost plus a profit margin sufficient to eliminate the pattern of subsidization of unprofitable enterprises. Thus, price revision did become an important vehicle for implementation of the reform. No attempt was made to set prices to equate supply and demand—if this is possible at all in a planned economy. The more radical views—especially those of the mathematical school, advocating the generation of scarcity prices through linear programming models or through an auctioning process—were rejected. Prices were raised in 1966 and 1967, though still on the basis of average costs, and they notably reduced the number of planned loss enterprises and to some degree the profitability differentials among branches of industry.[73] In addition, a new centralized organ, the State Committee for Prices *(Gostsen)* had been established, with rather broad powers, to administer the price system.

The reform of prices would be crucial to any attempt to enhance the role of profits (which, as we have seen, was not a major goal of the 1965 reform) and to resolve the problem of low-quality consumer goods (which was a major goal of the reform). The price reforms of 1966–1967 and thereafter failed to confront the basic issue with regards to profitability, namely, to set prices in such a manner that enterprise profitability would reflect managerial performance. If prices fail to include all legitimate factor payments (such as for superior equipment, locational advantages, favorable raw materials, etc.), then it is unclear whether high profits are the consequence of pricing foibles or of effective management. The 1966–1967 price reform did not come to grips with these issues and continued to use the traditional formulas for setting prices. Ministries continued to redistribute profits from profitable to unprofitable enterprises. Some branches (food processing, for example) have prices that generally fail to cover average branch costs and require large subsidies. Thus, the failure to effect significant changes in the manner of price formation has meant that profit-oriented reforms could not be put into practice even if the leadership were willing.

A whole series of measures was adopted after 1967 to encourage technological progress, the production of high-quality consumer and producer goods, and realistic regional price differentials. The procedures for setting "limit prices," "sliding prices," and quality differentials are complex and require lengthy explanations. It is sufficient to say that such measures have not brought about significant change in the Soviet price system.

The major price revision announced in 1967 is not the end of the story. A major revision of wholesale prices took place in January of 1982. However, the basis of price formation remained unchanged. As Gertrude Schroeder has noted, "the new prices, like those they replace, are calculated on the basis of average unit labor, material, and depreciation costs plus an average percentage profit markup over cost."[74] This adjustment was designed simply to bring prices into line with new evidence. Thus, while the changes were obviously important, the basic formula for price computation did not change, with the exception of some resource prices, where pricing at the margin is used. As before, these price adjustments were designed to raise prices to a point where enterprises could be profitable. The most substantial price increases were granted for fuels and energy.[75]

AN OVERVIEW OF SOVIET ECONOMIC REFORM AND CHANGE

Reform and change of the planned socialist systems of the Soviet Union and Eastern Europe both have taken place on a continuing basis throughout the postwar years. Although there have been important differences, all have been aimed at improving the prevailing economic system. Much of the reform effort has been directed toward the improvement of decision-making arrangements to make these economic systems more efficient in operation. The term "reform" is commonly used to denote a significant change in working arrangements. Used in this sense, the Soviet economy has not had an economic reform. Instead, Soviet authorities have focused on organizational changes, partial experiments, and changes in the weights and numbers of performance indicators.

The most striking feature of Soviet economic reform is its conservative nature. None of the Soviet economic reforms discussed in this chapter has aimed to alter in a fundamental way the basic working arrangements of the economy. Moreover, proponents of the status quo have often succeeded in limiting the degree of implementation of reforms. The conservative nature of the Soviet reform experience is generally interpreted as meaning that change, in general, has been directed toward making the existing system work more effectively, not in changing the system. Why such a conservative stance by Soviet leaders? There are a number of possible reasons.

First, the Soviet political structure is not monolithic. Those in power do not exercise unconstrained power. They are not capable of instigating and implementing whatever change might be deemed appropriate. In fact, a careful reading of the various reform discussions makes it clear that there have been a wide range of voices and opposing forces discussing the subject. The history of Soviet reform reveals that those forces advocating little change have been in command.

Second, from the perspective of many in the Soviet Union, the existing system has been functioning reasonably well for many years. There is substantial pride in the view that this system has been the key to rapid economic growth and development. While leaders of the recent past are not ignorant of contemporary economic problems, neither are they willing to abandon this legacy.

Third, the development of reform blueprints is a much easier task than the implementation of those blueprints. Difficult questions must be answered. For example, if limited market elements are desired, can they be introduced in isolation from changes in other facets of the economic system? If such changes are made, what is the appropriate time sequence for implementation? Advocates of the status quo can argue convincingly that the known is better than the unknown and that current problems will eventually pass.

Fourth, there is the question of whether economic reform can be introduced into the Soviet system within the context of existing objectives. Consider unemployment and inflation, well known in the West but officially banished from the Soviet system. If significant changes in Soviet working arrangements were made such as giving managers discretion over firing and hiring or allowing prices to be determined in markets, the consequences might be more inflation and unemployment than the authorities are prepared to tolerate. Most would probably agree that the Eastern European experience indicates that even limited introduction of market methods results in some sacrifice of these objectives. Unless a new and acceptable socialist term for "unemployment" can be invented, the unemployment outcome would be especially unacceptable to Soviet leaders.

Finally, Soviet bureaucrats are no different from bureaucrats elsewhere; they don't like change. Whether it be the ministries, the provincial party organizations, the local governments, or the enterprises, Soviet discussion of their reform programs reveals significant resistance to change at different levels where vested interests are threatened by reform.

Does all of this mean that reform and change are dead issues? The answer is in the negative, though one might suggest a trend away from reform in the sense of major formal programs and toward change in the sense of continuous piecemeal adjustments. There are few signs of interest in changes in fundamental working arrangements. Instead, attention is focused on existing arrangements with an aim toward making them work better. Analysis of the evidence suggests such a commitment. In 1984, there was a reaffirmation of the need to continue pursuing the 1979 program. While in a formal sense much of the 1979 program has not been implemented, in an informal sense there has been considerable change with individual subunits in the system by adopting some parts of the intended change and modifying or ignoring other parts. The result is a substantial degree of diversification of prevailing decision-making arrangements. There is little evidence that such changes will be less popular in future years.

REFERENCES

1. V. S. Nemchinov, ed., *The Use of Mathematics in Economics* (Cambridge, Mass.: MIT Press, 1964), p. ix. Nove is the editor of this English translation, and this statement is from Nove's introduction.
2. A. Anchishkin, ed., *National Economic Planning* (Moscow: Progress Publishers, 1980), p. 27.
3. For a discussion of system classification, see P. R. Gregory and R. C. Stuart, *Comparative Economic Systems,* 2nd ed. (Boston: Houghton Mifflin, 1985), chaps. 1 and 2.
4. Anchishkin, ed., *National Economic Planning,* p. 26.
5. E. Zaleski, *Stalinist Planning for Economic Growth, 1933–1952* (Chapel Hill: University of North Carolina Press, 1980).
6. Zaleski, *Stalinist Planning,* pp. xxvii–xxviii.
7. See, for example, J. H. Wilhelm, "The Soviet Union has an Administered, not a Planned Economy," *Soviet Studies,* vol. 37, no. 1 (January 1985), 118–130.
8. For a discussion of the reform concept, see, for example, M. Bornstein, "Economic Reform in Eastern Europe," in U.S. Congress, Joint Economic Committee, *East European Economies Post-Helsinki* (Washington, D.C.: U.S. Government Printing Office, 1977), pp. 102–134; M. Bornstein, "Improving the Soviet Economic Mechanism," *Soviet Studies,* vol. 37, no. 1 (January 1985), 1–30; P. Hanson, "Success Indications Revisited: The July 1979 Decree in Planning and Management," *Soviet Studies,* vol. 35, no. 1 (January 1983).
9. For a discussion of alternative perceptions of decentralization, see M. Bornstein, "Economic Reform in Eastern Europe."
10. S. F. Cohen, "The Friends and Foes of Change: Reformism and Conservatism in the Soviet Union," *Slavic Review,* vol. 38, no. 2 (June 1979), 195.
11. On this, see V. S. Nemchinov's comments on the 1923–1924 balance in *The Use of Mathematics in Economics,* pp. 2–10. Popov's original presentation of the 1923–1924 balance is translated in N. Spulber, ed., *Foundations of Soviet Strategy for Economic Growth* (Bloomington: Indiana University Press, 1964), pp. 5–19. For a discussion of the early Soviet mathematical economics school, see L. Smolinski, "The Origins of

Soviet Mathematical Economics," in H. Raupach et al., eds., *Yearbook of East-European Economics,* vol. 2 (Munich: Günter Olzog Verlag, 1971), pp. 137–154.

12. E. H. Carr and R. W. Davies, *Foundations of a Planned Economy, 1926–1929,* vol. 1, part 2 (London: MacMillan, 1969), pp. 787–801.

13. Spulber, *Soviet Strategy for Economic Growth,* chap. 2; G. Grossman, "Scarce Capital and Soviet Doctrine," *Quarterly Journal of Economics,* vol. 67, no. 3 (August 1953), 311–315; R. Dunayevskaya, "A New Revision of Marxian Economics," *American Economic Review,* vol. 34, no. 3 (September 1944), 531–537; Smolinski, "The Origins of Soviet Mathematical Economics," pp. 150–151.

14. Cohen, "The Friends and Foes of Change," p. 196.

15. For a review of Kantorovich's and Novozhilov's contribution, see R. W. Campbell, "Marx, Kantorovich and Novozhilov: Stoimost' Versus Reality," *Slavic Review,* vol. 20, no. 3 (October 1961), 402–418. For a general survey, see M. Ellman, *Soviet Planning Today: Proposals for an Optimally Functioning Economic System* (Cambridge: Cambridge University Press, 1971); A. Zauberman, *The Mathematical Revolution in Soviet Planning* (Oxford: Oxford University Press, 1975). For an insider's view, see Aron Katsenelinboigen, *Studies in Soviet Economic Planning* (White Plains, N.Y.: M. E. Sharpe, 1978), chap. 3. Also see L. Smolinski, ed., *L. V. Kantorovich: Essays in Optimal Planning* (White Plains, N.Y.: International Arts and Sciences Press, 1976).

16. Evsei Liberman's reform proposals had been made in the journal *Voprosy ekonomiki* [Problems of economics] as early as 1955.

17. The original Liberman paper and the debate it generated are given in M. E. Sharpe, ed., *Planning, Profit and Incentives in the USSR,* vols. 1 and 2 (White Plains, N.Y.: International Arts and Sciences Press, 1966).

18. Computed from *Narodnoe khoziaistvo SSSR v 1983 g.* [The national economy of the USSR in 1983] (Moscow: Finansy i statistika, 1984), p. 36.

19. See, for example, A. Bergson, "Technological Progress," in A. Bergson and H. S. Levine, eds., *The Soviet Economy: Towards the Year 2000* (London: Allen & Unwin, 1983), pp. 34–78.

20. U.S. Congress, Joint Economic Committee, *USSR: Measures of Economic Growth and Development, 1950–80* (Washington, D.C.: U.S. Government Printing Office, 1982), 22.

21. *Ibid.*

22. *Narodnoe khoziaistvo SSSR v 1983,* p. 118.

23. This was Khrushchev's often quoted criticism of planning during the Stalin years. See M. Goldman, "Economic Growth and Institutional Change in the Soviet Union," in P. Juliver and H. Morton, eds., *Soviet Policy-Making: Studies of Communism in Transition* (New York: Praeger, 1967), pp. 63–80, reprinted in M. Bornstein and D. Fusfeld, eds., *The Soviet Economy: A Book of Readings,* 3rd ed. (Homewood, Ill.: Irwin, 1970), p. 350.

24. A. Katsenelinboigen, *Studies in Soviet Economic Planning* (White Plains, N.Y.: M. E. Sharpe, 1978), p. 79.

25. See, for example, L. Hurwicz, "Centralization and Decentralization in Economic Process," in A. Eckstein, ed., *Comparison of Economic Systems* (Berkeley and Los Angeles: University of California Press, 1971), pp. 79–102; L. Hurwicz, "Conditions for Economic Efficiency of Centralized and Decentralized Structures," in G. Grossman, ed., *Value and Plan* (Berkeley and Los Angeles: University of California Press, 1960), pp. 162–183; L. Hurwicz, "On the Concept and Possibility of Informational Decentralization," *American Economic Review, Papers and Proceedings,* vol. 59, no.

2 (May 1969), 513–524; T. Marschak, "The Comparison of Centralized and Decentralized Economies," *American Economic Review, Papers and Proceedings,* vol. 59, no. 2 (May 1969), 525–532.

26. Bornstein, "Economic Reform in Eastern Europe," pp. 109–110.

27. For example, a system that functions through imposed rules is the classic Weberian bureaucratic model. This model and its application to the Soviet case is discussed in D. Granick, *Management of the Industrial Firm in The USSR* (New York: Columbia University Press, 1954). The concept of a parametric framework implies rules, but not rules for each decision that has to be made. Rather, managers are given the authority and the responsibility to use locally available information to make decisions leading to some overall objective, for example, cost minimization. Such a framework generally implies the use of value parameters and hence gives great importance to the process of valuation.

28. This point is made by F. I. Kushnirsky, *Soviet Economic Planning 1965–1980* (Boulder, Colo.: Westview Press, 1982), pp. 41–42.

29. On this general issue, see Bornstein, "Economic Reform In Eastern Europe," p. 110.

30. Examples of this approach are: A. Bergson, "Planning and the Market in the USSR: the Current Soviet Planning Reforms," in A. Balinky et al., *Planning and the Market in the USSR: The 1960s* (New Brunswick, N.J.: Rutgers University Press, 1967), pp. 43–64; G. E. Schroeder, "The 'Reform' of the Supply system in Soviet Industry," *Soviet Studies,* vol. 24, no. 1 (July 1972), 97–119; G. E. Schroeder, "The Soviet Economy on a Treadmill of 'Reforms,' " in U.S. Congress, Joint Economic Committee, *Soviet Economy in a Time of Change* (Washington, D.C.: U.S. Government Printing Office, 1979), vol. 1, pp. 312–340; G. E. Schroeder, "Soviet Economic 'Reform' Decrees: More Steps on The Treadmill," in U.S. Congress, Joint Economic Committee, *Soviet Economy In The 1980s: Problems and Prospects,* part I (Washington, D.C.: U.S. Government Printing Office, 1982), pp. 65–88; A. Nove, *The Soviet Economic System* (London: G. Allen & Unwin, 1977), chap. 11.

31. Translated in M. Bornstein and D. Fusfeld, eds., *The Soviet Economy: A Book of Readings,* 3rd ed. (Homewood, Ill.: Irwin, 1970), pp. 360–366. Translations and analysis of Liberman's other writings are in Sharpe, *Planning, Profit and Incentives,* vols. 1 and 2.

32. For a discussion of Liberman's career, see R. C. Stuart, "Evsei Grigorevich Liberman," in G. W. Simmons, ed., *Soviet Leaders* (New York: Crowell, 1967), pp. 193–200.

33. Felker, *Soviet Economic Controversies,* pp. 58–67.

34. Liberman, in Bornstein and Fusfeld, *The Soviet Economy,* p. 361. Also see E. G. Liberman, *Economic Methods and Effectiveness of Production* (White Plains, N.Y.: International Arts and Sciences Press, 1971).

35. For succinct statements of the Liberman proposal and its relation to a cost-profit calculus, see A. Zauberman, "Liberman's Rules of the Game for Soviet Industry," *Slavic Review,* vol. 22, no. 4 (December 1963), 734–744; Felker, *Soviet Economic Controversies,* pp. 58–62; G. R. Feiwel, *The Soviet Quest for Economic Efficiency* (New York: Praeger, 1972), chap. 5; Sharpe, *Planning, Profit and Incentives,* vol. 1, introduction.

36. Liberman, in Bornstein and Fusfeld, *The Soviet Economy,* pp. 362–363.

37. *Ibid.,* p. 363.

38. Nove, *The Soviet Economic System,* pp. 309–310.

39. According to Nove, *The Soviet Economic System,* p. 309, Liberman never developed a coherent pricing model. Prices, in Liberman's own words, were to be "fixed and flexible."

40. M. Kaser, "Kosygin, Liberman, and the Pace of Soviet Industrial Reform," in G. R. Feiwel, ed., *New Currents in Soviet-Type Economies: A Reader* (Scranton, Pa.: International Textbook, 1968), p. 334.

41. For further English translations of the major contributions to the debate, see M. E. Sharpe, ed., *The Liberman Discussion: A New Phase in Soviet Economic Thought* (White Plains, N.Y.: International Arts and Sciences Press, 1965). For chronological accounts of the 1962 to 1965 debate, see Kaser, "Kosygin, Liberman," pp. 330–343; and Felker, *Soviet Economic Controversies,* chaps. 3 and 4.

42. These experimental programs are discussed in Felker, *Soviet Economic Controversies,* chaps. 4 and 5; and Feiwel, *The Soviet Quest for Economic Efficiency,* chap. 5. References to the light industry experiment are supplied separately.

43. For a discussion of this experiment, see Goldman, "Economic Growth and Institutional Change," p. 322; Kaser, "Kosygin, Liberman," pp. 337–338; E. Zaleski, *Planning Reforms in the Soviet Union, 1962–1966* (Chapel Hill: University of North Carolina Press, 1967), pp. 122–140.

44. Goldman, "Economic Growth and Institutional Change," p. 357; Feiwel, *The Soviet Quest for Economic Efficiency,* pp. 242–250.

45. See A. Kosygin, "On Improving Management of Industry, Perfecting Planning, and Enhancing Economic Incentives in Industrial Production," in Bornstein and Fusfeld, eds., *The Soviet Economy: A Book of Readings,* pp. 387–396.

46. This rate could be lower for unprofitable enterprises. See Zaleski, *Planning Reforms,* p. 143.

47. K. Bush, "The Implementation of the Soviet Economic Reform," *Osteuropa Wirtschaft,* no. 2 (1970), 67–90; and no. 3 (1970), 190–198.

48. L. J. Kirsch, *Soviet Wages: Changes in Structure and Administration Since 1956* (Cambridge, Mass.: MIT Press, 1972), chap. 7.

49. K. Bush, "The Soviet Economic Reform After Six Years," *Radio Liberty Report,* CRD 258/71, August 1971, p. 6; and Bush, "The Implementation of the Soviet Economic Reform."

50. For discussions of the organizational aspects of the 1965 reform, see Kushnirsky, *Soviet Economic Planning;* and National Foreign Assessment Center, *Organization and Management in the Soviet Economy: The Ceaseless Search for Panaceas,* ER77-10769, Washington, D.C., December 1977.

51. G. E. Schroeder, "Recent Developments in Soviet Planning and Managerial Incentives," in U.S. Congress, Joint Economic Committee, *Soviet Economic Prospects for the Seventies* (Washington, D.C.: U.S. Government Printing Office, 1973), p. 12.

52. *Planovoe khoziaistvo* [The planned economy], no. 5 (1971), as summarized by *AB-SEES: Soviet and East European Abstract Series,* vol. 2, no. 2 (October 1971), p. 99. See also Fedoryenko et al., *Soviet Economic Reform,* pp. 199–202.

53. National Foreign Assessment Center, *Organization and Management in the Soviet Economy,* p. 15.

54. Goldman, "Economic Growth and Institutional Change," p. 323; Schroeder, "Recent Developments in Soviet Planning," pp. 107–111. On the lack of material supplies as a brake upon decentralized enterprise investment, see, for example, D. Allakhverdian, "O finansovykh problemakh khoziaistvennoi reformy" [About the financial problems of economic reform], *Voprosy ekonomiki* [Problems of economics], no. 11 (1970), 63–74.

55. National Foreign Assessment Center, *Organization and Management in the Soviet Economy,* p. 15.

56. For example, Abram Bergson argued in a 1967 article that the Soviets chose to decentralize decision-making in the area of labor staffing because wage rates happen

to be the most rational—in the sense of equating supply and demand—of all Soviet prices. Thus, managers could be trusted to make correct decisions. See A. Bergson, "Planning and the Market in the USSR," in G. Feiwel, ed., *New Currents in Soviet-Type Economics: A Reader* (Scranton, Pa.: International Textbook, 1968), p. 345.

57. According to the reform plan, the wages fund was to remain centrally planned, while enterprises were to have freedom in distributing the fund to various classes of personnel. This freedom was in reality very limited, and thus, in essence, Soviet wage determination procedures remained substantially unaffected by the 1965 reform. See Kirsch, *Soviet Wages,* chap. 7.

58. Recently, there has been increased interest in Shchekino. For an excellent analysis of the approach and its implementation, see P. Rutland, "The Shchekino Method and the Struggle to Raise Labour Productivity in Soviet Industry," *Soviet Studies,* vol. 36, no. 3 (July 1984), 345–365; for a generally critical view in an ideological framework, see B. Arnot, "Soviet Labor Productivity and the Failure of the Shchekino Experiment," *Critique,* vol. 15 (1981), 31–56.

59. Rutland, "The Shchekino Method," 348.

60. *Ibid.,* 345.

61. *Ibid.,* 353–357.

62. *Ibid.,* 360.

63. This discussion is based on M. Bornstein, "Improving the Soviet Economic Mechanism," *Soviet Studies,* vol. 37, no. 1 (January 1985), 1–30; Schroeder, "Soviet Economic 'Reform' Decrees"; Schroeder, "Recent Developments in Soviet Planning and Incentives," pp. 11–38; Schroeder, "The Soviet Economy on a Treadmill of 'Reforms,' " pp. 312–340; G. E. Schroeder, "Post-Khrushchev Reforms and Public Financial Goals," in Z. M. Fallenbuch, ed., *Economic Development in the Soviet Union and Eastern Europe* (New York: Praeger, 1976), pp. 348–367; National Foreign Assessment Center, *Organization and Management in the Soviet Economy,* pp. 1–22; A. C. Gorlin, "Industrial Reorganization: The Associations," in U.S. Congress, Joint Economic Committee, *Soviet Economy in a New Perspective* (Washington, D.C.: U.S. Government Printing Office, 1976), pp. 162–188; Kushnirsky, *Soviet Economic Planning, 1965–1980.*

64. Schroeder, "The Soviet Economy on a Treadmill of 'Reforms,' " p. 314.

65. S. Linz, "The Negotiated Soviet Economy," *Soviet Interview Project Working Paper* December, 1985.

66. P. K. Cook, "The Political Setting," in U.S. Congress, Joint Economic Committee, *Soviet Economic Prospects for the Seventies* (Washington, D.C.: U.S. Government Printing Office, 1973).

67. Bornstein, "Improving the Soviet Economic Mechanism," p. 2.

68. This section is based on Bornstein, "Improving the Soviet Economic Mechanism;" Schroeder, "Soviet Economic 'Reform' Decrees;" P. Hanson, "Success Indicators Revisited: The July 1979 Soviet Decree on Planning and Management," *Soviet Studies,* vol. 35, no. 1 (January 1983), 1–13; N. Nimitz, "Reform and Technological Innovation in the 11th Five Year Plan," in S. Bialer and T. Gustafson, eds., *Russia at the Crossroads* (London: Allen & Unwin, 1982), chap. 7.

69. Bornstein, "Improving the Soviet Economic Mechanism," p. 23.

70. For a detailed discussion, see Bornstein, "Improving the Soviet Economic Mechanism."

71. Bornstein, "Improving the Soviet Economic Mechanism," pp. 23–25.

72. Schroeder, "Soviet Economic 'Reform' Decrees," p. 82.

73. G. E. Schroeder, "The 1966–67 Soviet Industrial Price Reform: A Study in Complica-

tions," *Soviet Studies,* vol. 20, no. 4 (April 1969), 464 ff.; M. Bornstein, "Soviet Price Policy in the 1970s," in U.S. Congress, Joint Economic Committee, *Soviet Economy in a New Perspective* (Washington, D.C.: U.S. Government Printing Office, 1976), pp. 17–67; J. S. Berliner, "Flexible Pricing and New Products in the USSR," *Soviet Studies,* vol. 27, no. 4 (October 1975), 525–544.
74. Schroeder, "Soviet Economic 'Reform' Decrees," p. 76.
75. Hanson, "Success Indicators Revisited," p. 2.

SELECTED BIBLIOGRAPHY

A. Balinky et al., *Planning and the Market in the USSR: The 1960s* (New Brunswick, N.J.: Rutgers University Press, 1967).
J. S. Berliner, *The Innovation Decision in Soviet Industry* (Cambridge, Mass.: MIT Press, 1976).
———, "Planning and Management" in A. Bergson and H. S. Levine, eds., *The Soviet Economy: Towards the Year 2000* (London: Allen & Unwin, 1983), pp. 350–359.
M. Bornstein, "Improving The Soviet Economic Mechanism," *Soviet Studies,* vol. 37, no. 1 (January 1985), 1–30.
K. Bush, "The Implementation of the Soviet Economic Reform," *Osteuropa Wirtschaft,* nos. 2 and 3 (1970).
S. F. Cohen, "The Friends and Foes of Change: Reformism and Conservatism in the Soviet Union," *Slavic Review,* vol. 38, no. 2 (June 1979), 187–202.
N. Fedoryenko et al., *Soviet Economic Reform: Progress and Problems,* translated from the Russian (Moscow: Progress Publishers, 1972).
G. R. Feiwel, *The Soviet Quest for Economic Efficiency* (New York: Praeger, 1972).
J. L. Felker, *Soviet Economic Controversies* (Cambridge, Mass.: MIT Press, 1966).
A. C. Gorlin, "Industrial Reorganization: The Associations," in Joint Economic Committee, *Soviet Economy in a New Perspective* (Washington, D.C.: U.S. Government Printing Office, 1976), pp. 162–188.
P. Hanson, "Success Indicators Revisited: The July 1979 Decree on Planning and Management," *Soviet Studies,* vol. 35, no. 1 (January 1983).
A. Katsenelinboigen, *Studies in Soviet Economic Planning* (White Plains, N.Y.: M. E. Sharpe, 1978).
W. Keizer, *The Soviet Quest for Economic Rationality* (Rotterdam: Rotterdam University Press, 1971).
A. Kosygin, "On Improving Management of Industry, Perfecting Planning, and Enhancing Economic Incentives in Industrial Production," in M. Bornstein and D. Fusfeld, eds., *The Soviet Economy,* 3rd ed. (Homewood, Ill.: Irwin, 1970), pp. 387–396.
E. G. Liberman, *Economic Methods and the Effectiveness of Production* (White Plains, N.Y.: International Arts and Sciences Press, 1971).
National Foreign Assessment Center, *Organization and Management in the Soviet Economy: The Ceaseless Search for Panaceas,* ER77–10769, Washington, D.C., December 1977.
A. Nove, *The Soviet Economic System* (London: Allen & Unwin, 1977), chap. 11.
P. Rutland, "The Shchekino Method and the Struggle to Raise Labour Productivity in Soviet Industry," *Soviet Studies,* vol. 36, no. 3 (July 1984), 345–365.
K. W. Ryavec, "Soviet Industrial Management: Challenge and Response, 1965–1970," *Canadian Slavic Studies,* vol. 2 (Summer 1972), 151–177.
———, "Soviet Industrial Managers, Their Superiors and the Economic Reform: A Study

of an Attempt at Planned Behavioral Change," *Soviet Studies,* vol. 21, no. 2 (October 1969), 208–229.

G. E. Schroeder, "The 1966–67 Soviet Industrial Price Reform: A Study in Complications," *Soviet Studies,* vol. 20, no. 4 (April 1969), 462–477.

————, "Recent Developments in Soviet Planning and Incentives," in U.S. Congress, Joint Economic Committee, *Soviet Economic Prospects for the Seventies* (Washington, D.C.: U.S. Government Printing Office, 1973), pp. 11–38.

————, "Soviet Economic 'Reform' Decrees: More Steps on the Treadmill," in U.S. Congress, Joint Economic Committee, *Soviet Economy In the 1980s: Problems and Prospects,* part 1 (Washington, D.C.: U.S. Government Printing Office, 1982), pp. 65–88.

————, "The 'Reform' of the Supply System in Soviet Industry," *Soviet Studies,* vol. 24, no. 1 (July 1972), 97–119.

————, "The Soviet Economy on a Treadmill of 'Reforms,'" in U.S. Congress, Joint Economic Committee, *Soviet Economy in a Time of Change* (Washington, D.C.: U.S. Government Printing Office, 1979), vol. 1, pp. 312–340.

M. E. Sharpe, ed., *Planning, Profit and Incentives in the USSR,* vols. 1 and 2 (White Plains, N.Y.: International Arts and Sciences Press, 1966).

L. Smolinski, ed., *L. V. Kantorovich: Essays in Optimal Planning* (White Plains, N.Y.: International Arts and Sciences Press, 1976).

E. Zaleski, *Planning Reforms in the Soviet Union, 1962–1966* (Chapel Hill: University of North Carolina Press, 1967).

A. Zauberman, "Liberman's Rules of the Game for Soviet Industry," *Slavic Review,* vol. 22, no. 4 (December 1963), 734–744.

————, *The Mathematical Revolution in Soviet Planning* (Oxford: Oxford University Press, 1975).

chapter *14*

Conclusions and Prospects

Few would disagree with the observation that as we move toward the end of the 1980s, more than half a century after the introduction of socialist economic planning in the Soviet Union, the Soviet economy presents a mixed picture of both substantial achievement and significant shortfall. Throughout this book, we have emphasized discussion of how the Soviet economic system allocates resources, the extent to which this allocation process differs from that generally found in market systems, and, finally, with what result. As we attempt to summarize our main findings, we shall focus on both the achievements and the failures of the Soviet system. Moreover, for an economic system that is generally viewed as facing important problems yet implementing only limited reform, it is important that we consider alternative future paths for the Soviet economy.

ACHIEVEMENTS[1]

The Soviet Union enters the 1980s, more than a half-century after the first Five Year Plan, with some impressive achievements. The Soviet economy's position vis-à-vis the industrialized West has improved substantially. In 1928, Soviet GNP was roughly one-quarter that of the United States; by 1980, the ratio had risen to three-quarters (both ratios measured in U.S. prices). This improvement in relative position was the result of a more rapid growth than in the industrialized West, where only Japan has rivaled the Soviet long-run growth record. For example, an annual growth rate differential of 1.5 percentage points compounded over 50 years will cause an improvement in relative GNP by a factor of more than 2. Soviet achievements in the military area need not be repeated beyond noting

421

that Soviet military power is now rivaled only by that of the United States, a country whose GNP well surpasses that of the USSR. The advent of centralized planning appears to have accelerated both the growth rates of output and of military power, as dictated by a succession of leaders. The historical rate of growth of the tsarist economy during its industrialization era (1885–1913) was slightly in excess of 3 percent per annum. From the first Five Year Plan to 1980, the Soviet growth rate has averaged 5 percent, if the war years are ignored. We cannot rule out the possibility that a capitalist Russia would also have experienced a rapid increase in its relative economic position after 1917, as did the United States in the nineteenth century and Japan in the twentieth century, but such cases are rare in world economic history.

We believe it fair to conclude, therefore, that the introduction of the Soviet system of central planning and management did, indeed, cause an acceleration of the growth rate and that without the change in the economic system, the relative position of the Soviet Union would not have improved as dramatically as it did. The structural changes desired by the Soviet leadership (the rise in heavy industry, the destruction of private economic activity, the reduced dependence on foreign trade) were implemented at an unprecedented pace by the Soviet economic system. The structural changes that occurred in the USSR between 1928 and 1940 typically required 50 years or more in the industrialized West.

What features of the Soviet economic system were responsible for Soviet growth achievements? Simply stated, Soviet planners were able to accelerate growth by allocating resources in such a manner as to maximize the growth of labor and capital inputs. If factor inputs had continued to grow at the rates of the late tsarist era, it is unlikely that any acceleration would have taken place. The mechanisms for maximizing the growth of factor inputs have been described in earlier chapters: administrative allocation to favor producer goods at the expense of consumer goods, the use of administrative and market mechanisms to raise labor force participation rates and to encourage the flow of labor out of agriculture and handicrafts into priority branches, the reliance on turnover taxes to create funds for investment, the use of the collective farm to ensure deliveries and to depress rural living standards, and so on.

In sum, the Soviet economic experience is unique in the sense that the state, through the planning mechanism, took control of available resources and harnessed them to achieve state objectives. Most notable of these objectives has been rapid economic growth and structural change beyond what would likely have been achieved in a market context. The achievements were purchased at a cost, however, an issue to which we now turn.

THE COSTS OF SOVIET ECONOMIC DEVELOPMENT

Economic growth and development are never without cost. The important question is the magnitude of the costs relative to benefits, and the distribution of the burden among participants and over time.

The rapid expansion of Soviet economic and military power was purchased at considerable expense to the Soviet Union. The growth of living standards was virtually halted during the 1930s and remained depressed after the death of Stalin. It can safely be said that the Soviet consumer, both in the city and the countryside, bore the burden of rapid industrialization. The relation between the Soviet economic system and Soviet productivity performance remains poorly understood, but a couple of points need to be repeated. The Soviet Union began the era of central planning with a large technology gap relative to the industrialized West. Yet since 1928, the growth rate of factor productivity has been at best average relative to these countries; there is no evidence that the USSR has succeeded in closing the technology gap it inherited from its tsarist predecessors. The sole exception to this judgment is military technology, an area where the technology gap has indeed been narrowed (or even eliminated). Expert studies of Soviet technology cited in this book conclude that the past two decades have not witnessed a noticeable reduction in the USSR's technological backwardness.

The most serious disappointment of the Soviet economy has been its inability to create intensive economic growth, that is, growth based upon increases in efficiency rather than upon the growth of factor inputs. In the industrialized West, at least two-thirds of economic growth is typically accounted for by the growth of efficiency. In the Soviet case, the ratio is one-third. This means that Soviet economic growth has been of a high-cost variety, for growth that depends upon the expansion of factor inputs calls for sacrifices of consumption and leisure. The relationship between the supply of consumer goods and productivity is a cloudy one, but it is likely that the deprivation experienced by Soviet consumers has impacted negatively over the years upon their performance as workers.

The probable causes of the Soviet technology gap have been duly noted. The existing system appears to discourage innovation and new ways of doing things because the reward structure fails to compensate Soviet managers for the risks of innovative activity. The pervasive emphasis on short-term performance, particularly output goals, has created an environment that does not encourage the efficient combination of resources to produce output. A side effect of the emphasis on the short run has been the failure to discourage environmental disruption, much like such activities are not penalized in the West.

It is not particularly novel to point out that the Soviet economic experience has been one of both costs and benefits. As we have already emphasized, of greater interest is an assessment of the costs relative to the benefits and an assessment of the Soviet experience in this respect vis-à-vis other systems. Possibly of special interest in this concluding chapter is our assessment of whether some costs, for example, the technology problem, threaten continuing rapid Soviet growth and development. To provide some perspective on this issue, we turn to a discussion of contemporary Soviet economic difficulties and possible solutions to these difficulties.

THE SOVIET ECONOMY: PROBLEMS OF THE 1980s

The Soviet economy entered the 1980s after a troubled decade. The industrialized West had its share of economic troubles as well—the energy crisis, rising inflation rates, the need to establish a new world monetary system—but this fact provides small consolation to the troubled Soviet economic system. This system saw its growth rate fall from 6 percent per annum in the 1950s to less than 4 percent in the 1970s. At the end of the decade, the growth rate had declined to 3 percent, the same growth rate as the tsarist economy.[2] During 1981–1984, the growth rate of GNP slowed further to a rate somewhere between 2 and 3 percent.

For the years 1971–1975, the average annual percentage change of factor productivity was −0.5, while for the years 1976–1980 and 1981–1982, the changes were −0.8 and −1.0, respectively.[4] The falling productivity of the Soviet economy was especially alarming. After 1973, the growth rate of factor productivity was negative in most years, and capital productivity (after growing at negative rates after 1960) declined to even lower rates. Even in industry, the priority interest of Soviet planners, factor productivity became negative after 1975.[5] The declining rates of growth of output and productivity emphasized that unless the Soviet leadership were to impose enormous additional burdens on a population that had become accustomed to a rising living standard, a new Soviet model of intensive growth would be required to restore the rate of growth to an acceptable level.

In the 1970s, the Soviet economy turned increasingly outward to meet its needs for grain and advanced technology. The proportion of imports to GNP rose substantially, and these imports were financed in large part by Western credits. Soviet indebtedness to Western countries increased but remained within manageable proportions. Hard-currency earnings were based principally on exports of petroleum products and raw materials, the supplies of which grew increasingly tight in the Soviet domestic economy. Although the declining ability to rely on petroleum exports could be countered initially by tightening up exports to COMECON nations, Soviet authorities began to realize that their imports from the West must remain limited. Moreover, the failure to gain trade and credit concessions from the United States during the 1970s worsened the Soviets' prospects of competing effectively in Western markets.

The 1970s also brought home the fact that economic reform, in the modest form tolerated by Soviet officialdom, would not release large volumes of "hidden reserves" as had been hoped. When faced with the choice of significant decentralization of economic authority or a return to the problems of the traditional planning system, the leadership chose the latter. Projections for the 1980s offer little prospect of quick solution to the problems of the 1970s. For two decades, Soviet birthrates have been declining (more so in the Slavic republics than in the Asian republics), and this means that the working-age population will necessarily grow at very slow rates in the 1980s. The prime working-age population is scheduled to grow only 5 percent (0.5 percent annually) in the 1980s.[6] The slow growth of the working-age population will be particularly apparent in the younger age groups, which will actually decline in absolute terms in the 1980s. Any growth that does occur will be in the non-Slavic republics, where the bulk of industry is not located. Moreover, the willingness of the non-Slavic nationalities to migrate to labor deficit areas is in doubt.[7] Thus, the Soviet leadership must increasingly channel resources into republics that have traditionally had lower productivity, possibly complicating the productivity problem. One option to counter the quantitative decline in the growth rate of labor is to increase its quality. This option has not been exhausted, and the median years of schooling of the working age population is forecast to increase at an annual rate of 1 percent in the 1980s. This projection may be overly optimistic, insofar as students will be under increasing pressure to enter the labor force and as an increasing portion of the labor force will be drawn from the Asian republics, where mean education is lower. Under most scenarios, the impact of rising education will have only a small compensating effect on the growing scarcity of labor.[8]

The Soviet Union ended the 1970s with a gross investment share of over 30 percent and a ratio of defense expenditures to GNP of 13 percent. Thus, less than 57 percent of GNP is left to meet consumption, public services, and administration requirements.[9] These figures fairly well rule out the possibility of a significant expansion in the share of resources devoted to investment without a drastic reallocation of priorities away from either defense or the consumer. If output grows at a slow pace, rates of growth of investment well above the output rate will be difficult to maintain. In the late 1970s, Soviet capital stock was growing at an annual rate in excess of 7 percent.[10] If the growth rate of output continues to slow, it will be difficult to maintain this growth rate without imposing hardships on the consumer. Even if the Soviets are able to maintain a rapid rate of growth of capital stock, there are serious questions about the continuing effectiveness of this strategy. In the 1960s and 1970s, increasing difficulties in substituting capital for labor were encountered, and with the expected decline in the growth rate of labor, one would expect such substitution difficulties to multiply.

In sum, Western economists have devoted a good deal of attention to analysis of the contemporary Soviet economy. A dominant theme of this analysis is the inability, thus far, of the Soviet economic system to move from an extensive to an intensive phase of development. This is not to say that the Soviet economy has not changed, for it clearly has. But it remains fundamentally an inefficient system attempting to meet the consumer goods demands of the population with largely (at this stage) inappropriate methods, namely, more inputs rather than better use of existing inputs.

Soviet leaders are not unaware of these economic problems. In some cases, possible solutions are not readily available; in other cases, they conflict with long-standing state and party objectives. What are the alternatives available to Soviet leaders?

THE SOVIET ECONOMIC SYSTEM: REFORM ALTERNATIVES

A number of Western writers have investigated the menu of possible reforms available to Soviet leaders.[11] Broadly speaking, Soviet leaders may choose to do nothing, or they may choose to implement some degree of reform and change. Should the latter posture be adopted, there are three broad possibilities: (1) limited reform to modify the price system, alter allocation arrangements among enterprises, or, to use the East European jargon, change or modify the "economic levers" with which the existing system is controlled; (2) medium reform to retain the socialist planned system, but with modifications such as decentralization of authority over some consumer goods, for example, possibly with some measure of private enterprise such as might be envisioned in a "two level" type of system; (3) major reform, for example, to decentralize decision-making in a major way, possibly through the market mechanism or some combination of market and plan.

The posture of doing nothing is not very attractive. The implications of such a strategy are that Soviet leaders are quite willing to accept low growth rates (by international standards) and believe that the Stalinist strategy of extensive growth can be restored. As we have seen, neither implication is very plausible. On the other extreme, most Western observers would probably agree that among the planned socialist systems, the Soviet Union is very conservative both in terms of the changes that have been made and the prospects for Soviet leaders to implement additional reforms. In this respect, few would see a major reform, or possibly even a medium reform, as likely.

It seems likely, therefore, that the Soviet Union will continue limited reform of the sort that has been pursued in the past, attempting to modify and to improve the system of "economic levers" but fully within the planned socialist system. Indeed, part of such a program has continued and will continue to include improvement of the planning mechanism itself, for example, through computerized modeling of the system. Within the context of limited reform, what options are available and what constraints exist?

Although we have emphasized the relatively conservative nature of the Soviet leadership in the sphere of economic reform, it is true that there has been reform and change. As noted, much of this change has been modification of the economic levers and/or changes in the organizational structure. Doubtless, more of this type of modification will take place.

While greater authority and responsibility will be given to intermediate authorities in both industrial and agricultural sectors, the rules of enterprise guidance will be modified to place greater emphasis on cost reduction and efficiency along with the introduction of new technology. The pecuniary side of the system will play a greater though still limited role in the spheres of prices, interest rates, credit, and the like. All will, however, fall within the purview of the plan, with the major directions of change dictated by the central authorities. Put another way, much of the reform activity of the past decade seems to suggest that Soviet leaders have chosen a path that will attempt to make the *existing system* work better—in short, better planning. If such a scenario prevails, Soviet leaders will be concerned with how best to handle information, at both the macro and micro levels. Many in the Soviet Union see the planned socialist system as ideally suited for meeting this task.

To the extent that Soviet leaders are committed to improving the effectiveness of their system even within its own confines, they may well look to sources other than specific reform programs for ideas. Of special interest in this context is the Soviet attitude toward and management of the scientific technical revolution (STR).[12]

Soviet writers devote a great deal of attention to STR. Obviously, this attention is cast in the progressive nature of the STR in a socialist society and its potentially widespread impact. Within the context of the economic system, however, there are two areas of special interest to Western observers. First, Soviet leaders have shown increasing faith in the ability of computers to solve problems of the planned economy, most notably the handling of information and the utilization of this information at all levels in the system from the central planners to the local decision makers. Thinking in this area is closely tied to the organizational structure of the economy. Although not a reform in any formal sense, computerization of the Soviet economy deserves our attention.

Second, a major and critical aspect of STR must be the manner in which the enterprise management system will be changed and integrated into the overall planning system.

HANDLING INFORMATION: COMPUTERS AND AUTOMATION

The past 25 years have witnessed major changes in the Soviet attitude toward and encouragement of the development and utilization of what are generally termed automated management systems. Since Western observers have often viewed the development of the computer as a major achievement for the development and implementation of economic plans, what are the prospects in the Soviet case?

Since the 1950s, a number of important developments in the Soviet Union have facilitated the development of a new and generally progressive attitude.

First, as Western observers have noted, the hostile attitude of the Stalin years, the ultimate expression of which was the total derision of cybernetics in the 1950s, came to an end. Cybernetics was no longer considered just a tool of the ruling classes in capitalist countries used for the purposes of exploitation. Indeed, cybernetics could serve socialist society.

Second, while early applications of computers in the Soviet economy were primarily for the purposes of automating processes in enterprises, the possibilities of their use for information processing was quickly becoming apparent.

Finally, the application of mathematical methods to economics, more specifically to modeling, enjoyed new status in the Soviet Union in the early 1960s, an important development after the darkness of the Stalin years. Evidence of this was the rising prominence of economists of the mathematical school, for example Nemchinov, Novozhilov, and Kantorovich. Formal recognition of the importance of this approach came in 1963 with the creation of TSEMI, the Central Economics and Mathematics Institute. This institute would be concerned with, among other tasks, the modeling of the national economy.

Although there was no clear path evolving in the 1960s, it was evident that growing attention was being paid to the development of a net of computer centers, ultimately to be unified as an automated planning and management system.[13] Interestingly enough, there was considerable effort expended by many organizations, including TSEMI, the Central Statistical Administration, and *Gosplan,* to be involved in this development. In the late 1960s and early 1970s, the party became involved. The result was the creation, in 1971, of OGAS, this being "the statewide automated system for collection, storage, and processing of data for national economic planning, management, and accounting."

The development of OGAS, in particular, the issue of departmental versus regional orientation, would be the subject of much discussion in the 1970s. The original design of OGAS touched all aspects of planning and automation, from the planning of technological change to the processing of statistics. A subdepartment was set up in *Gosplan* to oversee automated planning. Coordination was to be under a new institute, "the All-Union Scientific Research Institute on Problems of Organization and Management."

These developments were important in other dimensions. First, during the 1970s, there was a move to develop regional computer centers. These centers seemed to be more for developing local access to computer capacity than the basis of any integrated system. By the late 1970s, the branch concept for the development of computer capacity at the local level seems to have superseded the regional principle, the main argument for the former being conformity to systems that have been developed at upper levels.

Second, by 1980, and after much discussion, a set of uniform plan indicators was developed. These indicators would be used by local units for the purpose of providing information (with a degree of uniformity) to upper-level bodies.

Finally, and possibly most important from our perspective, the development of an automated management system was closely connected with the 1973 introduction of industrial associations *(ob'edinenie)*. These associations were now faced with the task of changing a management system that was useful only for a single producing unit. The basic idea of the associations was to have several producing units under a single association, though lack of homogeneity of the individual units would create problems for the development of a single management system. In addition, pressure increased to bring the ministries into the *khozraschet* system. Again, uniformity of rules and profitability would be important. Needless to say, there was resistance from the ministries such that only limited achievement was made in this area during the 1970s.

The development of a large-scale information processing system in pursuit of better planning implies that the enterprise management system will be modified for incorporation into such a system. While many changes have already been made in the system of enterprise management, we have noted that, on balance, they have left the basic administrative-type system largely intact. The implication here is that changes of a much more fundamental change might be implemented, a matter deserving additional attention.

The major issue facing Soviet leaders is what one Western specialist on Soviet management has described as the *modernization* of Soviet management.[14] Although a matter of substantial complexity, modernization generally refers to a gradual replacement of the traditional or administrative model of Soviet management with a new "automated" system based on contemporary cybernetic theory. In this context, future changes in the Soviet management system, whether gradual or in the form of a "reform" program, bear watching, for a number of reasons.

First, the Soviet Union has, in recent years, borrowed heavily from Western management thinking. For the Soviet Union, however, this is a mixed blessing. Western management theory is by no means a unified body of thinking. Moreover, within the Soviet Union, there has been substantial controversy over the proper role for cybernetics and, more generally, systems theory. The focus of discussion is, understandably, the extent to which such approaches can be harmonized with Marxian precepts.

Second, it would seem that in recent years, such management reform as has been implemented has been done on a rather piecemeal basis. In this sense, the era of reform per se may be over. More important for the analyst of the Soviet economy, this approach means that there may not be any uniformly implemented system, but rather general principles with significant local variations.

Third, a major problem associated with any change in the management system is change in the organizational arrangements, specifically the industrial associations and the ministerial system. Clearly, improvement of the Soviet planning system through "automation" at all levels is a program that appeals to Soviet leaders. At the same time, there are many reasons for expecting change in the Soviet system to be slow and difficult.

Several forces have and will continue to inhibit the effectiveness of reform. Three main factors stand out and bear repetition in this conclucing chapter. First, it is always difficult to introduce reform on a piecemeal basis. Thus, enterprise managers may be encouraged to invest from internal (to the firm) funds; but in the absence of a decentralized source of investment goods, managerial freedom and initiative are severely limited.

Second, desired reforms may conflict with long-standing objectives. For example, the official Soviet position that the socialist system has permanently eliminated unemployment makes it very difficult to introduce any degree of flexibility in labor markets, where a degree of unemployment is almost inevitable.

Third, we must emphasize again that in the planned socialist systems, as elsewhere, there are strong vested interests arguing against change. For example, those officials at the ministerial level who have benefited from the existing arrangements at the enterprise level naturally feel threatened by the prospect of a new arrangement.

Finally, it is important to note that while problem areas of the planned socialist systems may sometimes be relatively easy to pinpoint, solutions that are both theoretically sound and workable in practice may be difficult to discover. Most would agree that these systems have not done well in the diffusion of new technology, but ways to change this state of affairs are not quickly and easily at hand.

PROSPECTS FOR THE STATUS QUO

The case for major change in the Soviet economic system rests upon at least three major premises. First, an ample supply of statistics suggests that Soviet economic performance is not very good, at least not as good as it used to be and not as good as Soviet leaders would like it to be. Second, the notion prevails that there is substantial internal pressure, especially from consumers, to improve the rate of growth of the Soviet standard of living.

Moreover, the Soviet system is, after all, a revolutionary society capable of change and, above all, capable of knowing what change is appropriate from its theoretical (Marxian) underpinnings. Finally, the Soviet economy, long isolated from world market influences and directed by plan preferences, has a structure substantially unlike that of developed market systems. Thus, whether by direction or by convergence, one can make the case for the Soviet industrial structure becoming more like other world systems. Cast in terms of these four basic considerations, how strong is the case for change?

Is the Soviet economic system of 1985 the same as that which evolved in the 1930s, or has the Soviet system "converged" toward that of capitalism? Convergence could be noted either as a convergence of Soviet resource allocation patterns toward patterns prevailing in the West, as a change in Soviet economic institutions to resemble more closely those of capitalist countries, or as a growing homogeneity of all industrial societies.[15] The postwar era has indeed witnessed some change in the pattern of Soviet resource allocation, namely, the increasing share of resources devoted to agriculture and rising foreign trade proportions. But the central features of the Soviet allocational model—the priority of heavy industry, a high investment rate for the level of economic development, the relative neglect of services, a consumption gap—have persisted to the 1980s. Clearly, these structural differences could persist over a long period of time into the future. Even if they do lessen, the change could be very slow.

Institutional convergence, which is difficult to isolate and measure, depends on the extent of organizational reform in the Soviet system. As we have noted above, most observers of the Soviet system believe that such reform has been, and will continue to be, modest. The Marxian underpinnings of Soviet society and economy provide very little from which to develop a program of reform and change. Moreover, the revolutionary nature of Soviet society is rhetoric rather than reality.

How bad are the statistics, and how great is the pressure for change? Soviet performance leaves much to be desired, but the bottom line is the extent to which Soviet consumers can be satisfied by *some* increase in the standard of living. Soviet consumers, just like their counterparts elsewhere, complain; but why will this form the basis of meaningful pressure when there *is* improvement and the vast bulk of the population has a strong, basic admiration for the system?

Put another way, one can make a strong case for the status quo. Thus, within the context of continual reform announcements and relatively modest actual change, Soviet leaders will tolerate modest improvements in economic performance, shielded by their continuing isolation from political criticism from abroad.

THE SOVIET ECONOMY: LOOKING AHEAD

Looking ahead to the year 2000, what are the trends and prospects for the Soviet economy and for Soviet society in general? Long-range projections are difficult to make. Some trends can be projected well into the future (such as trends in the able-bodied population); other phenomena are much less certain (such as changes in the political leadership).

What things are known? What things are unknown concerning the next two decades? On the side of the "knowns" is the fact that labor will become an increasingly scarce factor of production. The growth rate of the able-bodied population (from which the working population is drawn) will be very slow over the next two decades; so the Soviet economy must learn how to adjust to a labor force that is scarcely expanding. Other economies have successfully bridged the transition from a fast- to a slow-growing labor force; whether the Soviet economy can do so will be a crucial determinant of future economic performance. Basic demographic trends also show that the regional allocation of Soviet population will be unfavorable, for population will continue to expand most rapidly in those republics where labor is in most abundant supply. The success of Soviet planners in adjusting the regional labor imbalance will be as critical as their response to the slowdown in labor force growth.

The prospect for a return to rapid rates of growth of investment and capital stock to compensate for the declining growth of labor appears to be dim. First, the Soviet consumer can no longer be treated as a residual claimant to resources (as the 1980 overthrow of a communist government in Poland once again demonstrated); the claims of the Soviet defense establishment also will remain strong. As a consequence, there is little "give" in the system for large reallocations to investment. Second, there is the question of the wisdom of allowing investment to grow at a rate disproportionately higher than that of GNP. With high rates of growth of capital and low rates of growth of labor, it has become increasingly difficult to effectively substitute capital for labor. The payoff of accelerated investment growth may therefore be meager and its costs high. Moreover, the Soviet leadership must be concerned about an incentive "threshold" if investment is favored at the expense of consumption. The loss of output due to declining incentives may offset the gains of greater investment.

The great unknown in projecting Soviet economic performance to the year 2000 is productivity performance. Will the Soviet economy learn how to grow rapidly with slowly growing inputs? It would appear that the potential for efficiency gains is great. The Soviet Union has yet to undertake the substitutions for petroleum forced upon Western countries by the rising relative price of energy. Therefore, the extent to which the Soviet economy will be able to economize on scarce energy inputs remains a real question mark. This is a vital question of wide-ranging economic and political significance, for it will affect Soviet relations with Eastern Europe, Soviet hard-currency earnings, and East-West competition for imported oil.

The available evidence also suggests that substantial efficiency gains in the use of labor are also possible. Over-full employment planning still prevails in the Soviet Union; much labor is redundant and could be used more effectively if transferred to other jobs. Yet better utilization of manpower resources would require significant changes in the Soviet system—the reduction of job security, greater pay differentiation among workers, greater freedom for managers to hire and fire workers, and the revision of managerial incentives to encourage the better use of labor.

There is little evidence that the Soviets are moving in these directions. The late 1970s witnessed the movement toward more (not less) equality among industrial wage earners and the abandonment of partial reforms to improve managerial incentives and grant more managerial flexibility.

One means of achieving efficiency gains over the next two decades is greater integration of the Soviet economy into the world economy. In this way, the Soviets could acquire advanced technology, become more intimately acquainted with Western business practices, and subject their own industries to outside competition. The 1970s did indeed witness a dramatic increase in Soviet participation in international trade. Much of this, however, may have been a matter of luck, such as the rise in gold, oil, and raw material prices that improved the Soviet terms of trade with the West. It is questionable whether such good fortune will continue into the 1980s and 1990s. If it does not, then the Soviets' ability to import from the West will depend more and more on the vitality of the domestic USSR economy. Can the planning system be restructured to improve the product quality of Soviet exports? Can the Soviets compete effectively in Western markets for manufactures? Can the Soviets make do with less oil and free this oil for exports? Moreover, can the Soviet economy assimilate imported Western technology effectively? Increased reliance on foreign markets does not represent a "quick fix" for accumulated problems. The effective utilization of foreign trade may ultimately depend upon the improved performance of the domestic Soviet economy.

Informed observers agree that the Soviet leadership must accept a rate of GNP growth that is low by Soviet historical standards. The growth rate of GNP to the year 2000 will likely be in the 2 to 3 percent per annum range, and the rate of growth of per capita consumption will be even lower than this rate. The ongoing decline in the rate of growth of factor productivity may be halted, but there is little prospect of raising this rate to above 1 percent per annum. In fact, rates of factor productivity growth below 1 percent would not be surprising because of the disincentive effects caused by slow consumption growth.

Soviet agriculture will continue to be a troubled sector. In the last decade, productivity growth has virtually disappeared and the annual growth rate of agricultural output has fallen below 2 percent per annum despite massive infusions of investment and subsidies into agriculture. The USSR will, therefore, continue to depend on foreign suppliers of grain, and a continuation of growth rates of the last decade means that the average Soviet family's diet will not equal that of the average 1978 Polish family until the year 2000.

Are there any bright spots for the Soviet leadership in these otherwise gloomy projections? The most important is the fact that the Western world enters the 1980s with significant troubles of its own. Productivity growth is a problem, high rates of inflation coexist with high rates of unemployment, and real wages are actually declining in some countries. The Soviet Union has no monopoly on economic problems. Moreover, the Soviet population may have adjusted its expectations downward, so that slower rates of growth of consumption may be tolerated without open political strife. Finally, the Soviet economy continues to supply the Soviet leadership with military power that is more or less equal to that of its major competitor, the United States.

REFERENCES

1. This section is drawn from P. R. Gregory, "Economic Growth and Structural Change in Tsarist Russia and the Soviet Union: A Long-Term Comparison," in S. Rosefielde, ed., *Economic Welfare and the Economics of Soviet Socialism* (Cambridge: Cambridge University Press, 1981).
2. H. Block, "Soviet Economic Performance in a Global Context," in U.S. Congress, Joint Economic Committee, *Soviet Economy in a Time of Change* (Washington, D.C.: U.S. Government Printing Office, 1979), vol. 1, pp. 110–141. These figures have been updated from press accounts of Soviet economic growth in 1979 and 1980; Gregory, "Economic Growth and Structural Change."
3. U.S. Congress, Joint Economic Committee, *Allocation of Resources in The Soviet Union and China—1983* (Washington, D.C.: U.S. Government Printing Office, 1984), pp. 296–297.
4. U.S. Congress, Joint Economic Committee, *Allocation of Resources in the Soviet Union and China—1983,* p. 336.
5. G. Baldwin, *Population Projections by Age and Sex: For the Republics and Major Economic Regions of the USSR, 1970 to 2000,* International Population Reports, Series P-91, No. 26, September 1979, Table 3.
6. M. Feshbach, "Prospects for Outmigration from Central Asia and Kazakstan in the Next Decade," in U.S. Congress, Joint Economic Committee, *Soviet Economy in a Time of Change* (Washington, D.C.: U.S. Government Printing Office, 1979), vol. 1, pp. 656–709.
7. M. Spechler, "Regional Developments in the USSR, 1958–1978," in U.S. Congress, Joint Economic Committee, *Soviet Economy in a Time of Change* (Washington, D.C.: U.S. Government Printing Office, 1979), vol. 1, pp. 141–164; NATO Economics Directorate, *Regional Development in the USSR: Trends and Prospects* (Newtonville, Mass.: Oriental Research Partners, 1979).
8. National Foreign Assessment Center, *USSR: Trends and Prospects in Educational Attainment, 1959–85,* ER79–10344, Washington, D.C., June 1979.
9. National Foreign Assessment Center, *Handbook of Economic Statistics 1979,* p. 29.
10. *Ibid.,* p. 65.
11. For a discussion of alternatives, see J. S. Berliner, "Planning and Management," in A. Bergson and H. S. Levine, eds., *The Soviet Economy: Toward the Year 2000* (London: Allen & Unwin, 1983), chap. 11.
12. For a discussion of STR and economic modernization, see, for example, P. B. Maggs, G. B. Smith, and G. Ginsburgs, eds., *Law and Economic Development in the Soviet Union* (Boulder, Colo.: Westview Press, 1982).
13. For a discussion of the role of computers in Soviet planning, see M. Cave, *Computers and Economic Planning: The Soviet Experience* (New York: Cambridge University Press, 1980).
14. For an in-depth discussion, see W. J. Conyngham, *The Modernization of Soviet Industrial Management* (New York: Cambridge University Press, 1982).
15. For discussions of the convergence hypothesis, see J. Tinbergen, "Do Communist and Free Economies Show a Converging Pattern?" *Soviet Studies,* vol. 12, no. 4 (April 1961), 331–341; P. J. D. Wiles, "Will Capitalism and Communism Spontaneously Converge?" *Encounter,* vol. 20, no. 6 (June 1963), 84–90. For a summary of general arguments, see H. Linnemann, J. P. Pronk, and J. Tinbergen, "Convergence of Economic Systems in East and West," in E. Benoit, ed., *Disarmament and World Eco-*

nomic Interdependence (New York: Columbia University Press, 1967), pp. 246–260. For more critical views, see L. Leontiev, "Myth About Rapprochement of the Two Systems," in J. S. Prybyla, ed., *Comparative Economic Systems* (New York: Appleton-Century-Crofts, 1969), pp. 477–483; J. R. Millar, "On the Merits of the Convergence Hypothesis," *Journal of Economic Issues,* vol. 2, no. 1 (March 1969), 60–68; J. S. Prybyla, "The Convergence of Market-Oriented and Command-Oriented Systems: A Critical Estimate," in J. S. Prybyla, *Comparative Economic Systems* (New York: Appleton-Century-Crofts, 1969), pp. 467–476; R. C. Stuart and P. R. Gregory, "The Convergence of Economic Systems: An Analysis of Structural and Institutional Characteristics," *Jahrbuch der Wirtschaft Osteuropas* [Yearbook of East-European economies], Band 2 (Munich: Günter Olzog Verlag, 1971), pp. 425–442.

SELECTED BIBLIOGRAPHY

A. Bergson and H. S. Levine, eds., *The Soviet Economy Towards the Year 2000* (Boston: Allen & Unwin, 1983).

J. S. Berliner, "Managing The USSR Economy: Alternative Models," *Problems of Communism,* vol. 32, no. 1 (January/February 1983), 40–56.

M. Cave, *Computers and Economic Planning: The Soviet Experience* (Cambridge: Cambridge University Press, 1980).

M. I. Goldman, *USSR in Crisis* (New York: W.W. Norton & Company, 1983).

———, "The Future of Soviet Leadership," *Challenge,* vol. 27, no. 2 (May/June, 1984), 4–10.

C. Kerr, *The Future of Industrial Societies* (Cambridge, Mass.: Harvard University Press, 1983).

D. K. Shipler, *Russia: Broken Idols, Solemn Dreams* (New York: Penguin Books, 1984).

H. Smith, *The Russians* (New York: Ballantine Books, 1976).

U.S. Congress, Joint Economic Committee, *Soviet Economy in The 1980s: Problems and Prospects* parts 1 and 2 (Washington, D.C.: U.S. Government Printing Office, 1982).

U.S. Congress, Joint Economic Committee, *USSR: Measures of Economic Growth and Development, 1950–80* (Washington, D.C.: U.S. Government Printing Office, 1982).

Index